D0504291

Restoration

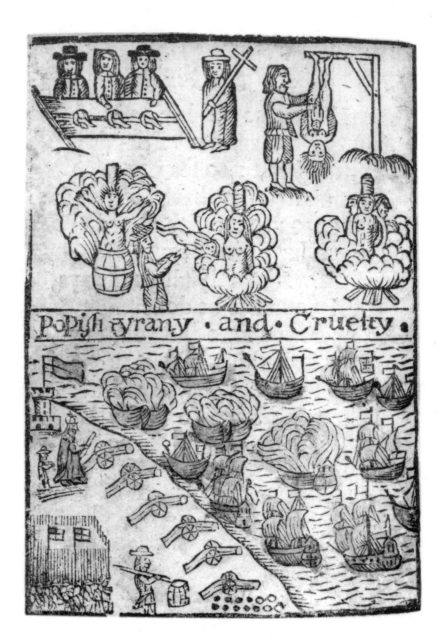

Popish Tyrany · and · Cruelty ·

TIM HARRIS

Restoration

Charles II and his Kingdoms,
1660–1685

ALLEN LANE
an imprint of
PENGUIN BOOKS

ALLEN LANE

Published by the Penguin Group
Penguin Books Ltd, 80 Strand, London WC2R ORL, England
Penguin Group (USA) Inc., 375 Hudson Street, New York, New York 10014, USA
Penguin Books Australia Ltd, 250 Camberwell Road, Camberwell, Victoria 3124, Australia
Penguin Books Canada Ltd, 10 Alcorn Avenue, Toronto, Ontario, Canada M4V 3B2
Penguin Books India (P) Ltd, 11 Community Centre, Panchsheel Park, New Delhi – 110 017, India
Penguin Group (NZ), Cnr Airborne and Rosedale Roads, Albany, Auckland 1310, New Zealand
Penguin Books (South Africa) (Pty) Ltd, 24 Sturdee Avenue, Rosebank 2196, South Africa

Penguin Books Ltd, Registered Offices: 80 Strand, London WC2R ORL, England

www.penguin.com

First published 2005
1

Set in 10.5/14pt Linotype Sabon by Palimpsest Book Production Limited, Polmont, Stirlingshire
Printed in England by Clays Ltd, St Ives plc

ISBN 0–713–99191–7

Frontispiece *Popish Tyranny and Cruelty*: Whig woodcut depicting alleged acts of Catholic cruelty against Protestants, and the Spanish Armada.

For Mark Goldie

Contents

PART I

From Restoration to Crisis, *c.* 1660–1681

PART II

The Royalist Reaction, *c.* 1679–1685

tremendous amount of constructive critical feedback. The project has taken a shape that it would not otherwise have done without Simon's influence. I would also like to thank Helen Dewen, who read the penultimate draft and gave me a valuable independent critical perspective while also encouraging me to believe that what I had to say was worthwhile; Alison Hennessy for help with the illustrations; and Caroline Wilding for compiling the index. I am extremely fortunate to have worked with a very thorough and highly efficient copy-editor, Bob Davenport, who did his best to rescue me from stylistic infelicities, grammatical mistakes, internal inconsistencies, and various other errors. It goes without saying that any mistakes that remain are mine. Special thanks must also go to my agent, Clare Alexander, whom I initially approached with the idea of her helping me place my next project, but who proved of immeasurable assistance once it became apparent that the present one would need to be split into two.

Neither my wife (Beth) nor my children (Victoria and James) read any of this book in draft, but they supported me in innumerable ways during the lengthy time it took to complete it, helping to sustain my sanity in the process. Words cannot convey how much I owe to them – for their forbearance and for their love. For a British historian based in the States, relatives and friends who are prepared to host one's trips to the archives are an invaluable resource. My parents, Audrey and Ron, whose home is conveniently located just off the M25 somewhere between Heathrow and Gatwick airports, made possible much of the research for this book by providing me with a home away from home when I needed to visit the English archives. My brother and his wife, Kevin and Tina, housed me when I undertook research in the Leicestershire Record Office, as did my parents-in-law, John and Grace, when I did research in the West Country, while my sister and her husband, Sarah and Matt, also provided support on my trips to England. Christine Macleod let me and my family stay in her flat overlooking Arthur's Seat in Edinburgh, while Adam Fox and his wife, Carolyn, hosted me on another trip to the Scottish capital. I am indebted to them all, and I hope I never outstayed my welcome.

Research for this project would not have been possible without the financial support of a number of institutions. In particular, I would like to record my gratitude for the receipt of fellowships from the later. It was an invitation from Mark Goldie to become involved in editing the Roger Morrice Ent'ring Book, a political journal covering the years 1677–91, which confirmed me in my idea that the project was worthwhile, especially when it became apparent that Morrice, like myself, thought in three-kingdoms terms. Mark Kishlansky and David Underdown contributed more to the conceptualization of this project than they perhaps realize, not least through various critical remarks the two of them made to me about the value of British history. The end result might not convince them, but their observations certainly made this a better piece of scholarship than it would otherwise have been. It seemed too much of an imposition to burden friends and colleagues with endless drafts of what seemed to be an endlessly growing manuscript; rather, I sought the necessary critical feedback by delivering discrete sections of what I was working on at conferences, lectures and colloquia across Britain and North America over the last decade or so. For their invaluable input, I would like to thank everyone who has attended whatever presentations I have given about different aspects of this work; they have had a much greater influence on shaping the final outcome than they would ever have realized. Certain individuals who have offered constructive advice, criticism, support and guidance over the years, in addition to those mentioned above, include Charles Carlton, Tom Cogswell, Brian Cowan, Adam Fox, Peter Lake, Allan Macinnes, Steve Pincus, Bill Speck, Stephen Taylor and the participants in a seminar I taught at the Folger Shakespeare Library in the autumn of 2003: Bill Carpenter, D'Maris Coffman, John Cramsie, Erin Kidwell and Joanne Tetlow. As ever, my students at Brown, many of whom have taken classes which in various ways have explored many of the themes explored here, have been a constant source of inspiration. One particular Brown student, Victoria Harris, a budding historian in her own right, conducted research for me on the loyal addresses of 1683, in the process learning the true meaning of the old methodological adage *il faut compter*. Above all, I have to express my immense debt to Simon Winder, who encouraged this project from the beginning, who patiently awaited the fruits of my labour amid my repeated complaints of disc problems (of the spinal rather than the computer kind), and who read everything in draft and offered a

List of Illustrations

Frontispiece: Whig woodcut depicting alleged acts of Catholic cruelty against Protestants, and the Spanish Armada of 1588, from *The Protestant Tutor*, 1679 (British Library)

Introduction (pp. 2–3): Tory print representing the tyranny of republican rule in the 1650s (British Museum)

Part One (pp. 40–41): Whig print from the Exclusion Crisis, 1681 (British Museum)

Part Two (pp. 208–9): Woodcut illustrating punishments meted out to Presbyterian dissidents in Scotland during the reign of Charles II. From Alexander Shields' *A Hind Let Loose*, 1687 (British Library)

Plate Section

1 Charles I and James, Duke of York, by Sir Peter Lely, 1647 (Bridgeman Art Library/Syon House, Middlesex)

2 Drawing of James II, by Robert White, pencil on vellum (Bridgeman Art Library)

3 Louise de Kerouaille, The Duchess of Portsmouth, by the studio of Sir Peter Lely (Bridgeman Art Library/Royal Hospital Chelsea)

4 Dutch attack on the River Medway, June 1667, engraving after Romeyn de Hooghe (Bridgeman Art Library)

5 The Great Fire of London, in a seventeenth-century print by Lieve Verschuier (Bridgeman Art Library)

6 James Butler, First Duke of Ormonde, by Sir Peter Lely, *c.* 1665 (by courtesy of the National Portrait Gallery)

7 The Duke and Duchess of Lauderdale, by Sir Peter Lely, *c.* 1670s (National Trust)

Berwick-upon-Tweed

NORTHUMB
Newcastle-upon-Tyne

CUMB
DURHAM
• Durham

WESTMLD
• Richmond

YORKSHIRE
• York

IRISH SEA

LANCS
Manchester •
• Sheffield

ANGLESEY

CHESHIRE
FLINT
• Chester
• Chesterfield
LINCS
• Lincoln

CAERN
DENB
DERBYS
NOTTS
Derby •
• Nottingham

MERION
STAFFS
Stafford •
King's Lynn
Great Yarmouth
NORFOLK
• Norwich

MONT
SALOP
LEICS
Leicester •
RUT-
LAND
• Oundle
Thetford •
• Barsham

CARD
RADNOR
Leominster •
WARKS
• Coventry
NORTHANTS
HUNTS
CAMBS
Newmarket
SUFFOLK

HEREFS
WORCS
• Worcester
Cambridge •
Woodbridge •

PEMB
CARM
BRECON
Hereford •
BEDS
Thetford •
• Newport

GLOUCS
Abergavenny
OXON
BUCKS
Buckingham •
HERTS
• Colchester
ESSEX

GLAM
MON
Gloucester •
Oxford •
Aylesbury •
London

• Bristol
• Abingdon
MDX
• Rochester
Bath •
WILTS
BERKS
• Windsor
Southwark •
Chatham
• Canterbury
KENT

• Wells
• Warminster
SURREY
Haslemere •
• Dover

SOM
Taunton •
HANTS
• Winchester
SUSSEX

DEVON
Crewkerne •
Salisbury •
Shaftesbury
• Lewes
Rye

Exeter •
Lyme
Regis
DORSET
• Dorchester
• Chichester
Portsmouth

CORNWALL
Saltash •
• Plymouth
Weymouth

ENGLISH CHANNEL

NORTH SEA

N

0   50   100 miles

0   50   100   150 km

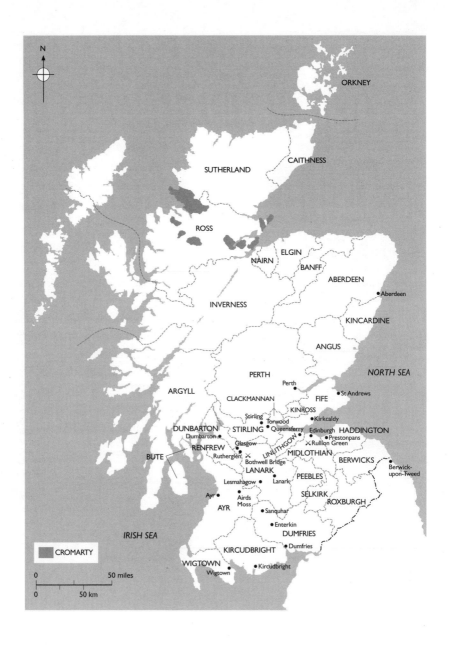

N

ORKNEY

SUTHERLAND

CAITHNESS

ROSS

NAIRN

ELGIN

BANFF

ABERDEEN

• Aberdeen

INVERNESS

KINCARDINE

ANGUS

NORTH SEA

PERTH

• Perth

ARGYLL

CLACKMANNAN

FIFE

• St Andrews

KINROSS

Stirling •

Kirkcaldy •

DUNBARTON

STIRLING

Torwood

Queensferry

Edinburgh

HADDINGTON

Dumbarton •

Glasgow •

LINLITHGOW

• Prestonpans

RENFREW

× Rullion Green

BUTE

Rutherglen •

MIDLOTHIAN

Bothwell Bridge

BERWICKS

LANARK

Berwick-

upon-Tweed •

Lesmahagow •

• Lanark

PEEBLES

Ayr •

Airds

SELKIRK

Moss

ROXBURGH

AYR

• Sanquhar

• Enterkin

DUMFRIES

IRISH SEA

KIRCUDBRIGHT

• Dumfries

WIGTOWN

• Kircudbright

Wigtown •

CROMARTY

0   50 miles

0   50 km

besides, how does one make an adjective from that term? Unnecessary because this study is about revolutions that affected three kingdoms which, whatever the complexion of their indigenous populations, were controlled and run by people who came from Britain. The monarchy itself was genuinely British: the Stewarts were originally a Scottish dynasty who inherited the English (and hence also Irish) crown in 1603 and subsequently anglicized their name. Those in positions of power under the British monarchy were invariably of British – English or Scottish – extraction themselves. Although there was a significant Gaelic culture in Scotland, it was the Lowland Scots, of Anglo-Saxon extraction themselves, who dominated the government of the country, whether under Charles II or James VII (as James II was styled in Scotland) or in the post-revolutionary regimes. Similarly, despite its sizeable Gaelic population, Ireland was under the suzerainty of a British monarch and was ruled at home by people who hailed (either immediately or ultimately) from the British mainland, and one can legitimately talk of it as being a British state at this time in the sense that it was ruled by people of British extraction – primarily English. Even the attempted Catholic revolution in Ireland under James II would have resulted in power being kept largely within the hands of the British, albeit Catholics of Old English (or Anglo-Norman) extraction. Moreover, Irish Catholics at the time used the term 'the British Monarchy' to describe the lands (including Ireland) over which the Stuarts ruled. This study, in other words, is a British history in the sense that it offers an examination of the fortunes of British rule across the three kingdoms that comprised the North Atlantic archipelago of Britain and Ireland. Having said that, this work makes every effort to do justice to the struggles, concerns and experiences of the non-British peoples who inhabited this Britannic archipelago, and to avoid terminology that might seem either misleading or unduly imperialistic.

In a project of this size, one inevitably accumulates numerous debts over the years. It was John Morrill who first encouraged me in my plans to write a book on the 1680s and suggested that I should also look at Scotland and Ireland; once I started to look at Scotland and Ireland, however, I realized that the book could not be just about the 1680s, but would have to start much earlier and finish much traced in book two. I began writing this book from 1685 onward; only when I had finished the chapters on the Revolutions did I go back and draft the chapters for the years 1660–85, with the aim of setting the context for what was to come thereafter. Nevertheless, in splitting the project into two I have made every effort to produce two stand-alone books – ones which are self-sufficient in the sense that each can be read on its own and does not require familiarity with its companion volume to be intelligible.

Many will no doubt see this study as an exercise in the new British history. Problems nevertheless remain over the use of the adjective 'British' to describe an integrated history of the three constituent kingdoms of the Stuart monarchy. Ireland was not part of Britain, in the literal geographical sense, since Britain was the island which comprised England, Scotland and Wales. It is true that Ireland was occasionally called West Britain or Lesser Britain, but that in itself was an imperialist usage, a view from the British mainland rather than an accurate geographical designation or a term used by the inhabitants of Ireland themselves. Politically, the island of Ireland as a whole was to be part of the British state for only a little over a century, between 1801 and 1922. Ethnically, the indigenous Irish population were Gaelic rather than British, although there were also many British peoples (English, Welsh and Scots) living in Ireland. On the other hand, there were also many non-British peoples living in Scotland and Wales. Strictly speaking, this study deals not with Britain nor with the British (exclusively), but with the various peoples who inhabited the Britannic archipelago in the North Atlantic off the coast of north-west Europe and who happened to be ruled over by the same monarch. Indeed, the style 'his Britannick majesty' was frequently used by contemporaries to refer to either Charles II or James II in his capacity as king of England, Scotland and Ireland.

Care is clearly needed over terminology. However, it seems both undesirable and unnecessary to outlaw the term 'British' in the context of this particular study. Undesirable because we would be forced to employ some rather cumbersome language if we were determined to avoid it; my editor cringed at my references to 'the Britannic archipelago', which he asked me to excise from the final version – and, which those below the level of the elite made to the political history of this period, through either their sufferings or their activism. However, the study became international rather than national, as it soon became apparent that the story of Scotland and Ireland would need to be told as well. It therefore also grew in scope – considerably so, as it turned out, since I was determined to do justice to the Scottish and Irish pasts for their own sakes, and not just bring them in for cameo appearances to help flesh out an Anglocentric narrative. In the process, the chronological boundaries of the book grew, to cover the years from 1660 to 1720, although with the focus remaining firmly on the 1680s.

It is important to be aware that the project has been conceived all along as an integrated whole. This influenced its organizational logic. The basic questions I sought to address were: how did a regime that had been so popular when it was restored in 1660 fall into crisis by 1680? how did it manage to recover from that crisis by 1685? and how did it sink back so dramatically into crisis by 1688 so that a reigning monarch could be toppled from his throne in England (Scotland and Ireland were very different stories) without being able to offer any significant resistance? The book, as originally conceived, was therefore divided into four parts: from Restoration to crisis, c. 1660–81; royal recovery under Charles II, c. 1681–85; the reign of James II, 1685–8; and the Revolutions and their outcomes, c. 1688–1720. Only after my editor at Penguin, Simon Winder, had read a complete draft of the whole was the decision taken to make it two books – with the first two parts (on the reign of Charles II) forming book one, and the last two book two. I might have thought about the structure somewhat differently had I started with the intention of writing two separate books. There is not a great deal, for example, on Restoration politics in England, in part because this is a story that has been told by others already, and in part because, given the conception of the project as a whole, an analytical discussion of the problems facing the Restoration polity in England seemed a more compelling way of guiding the reader about what was going wrong at this time and why the regime was to fall into crisis by the late 1670s. Moreover, there are certainly things that are explained at length in this first book because they provide a vital context for understanding developments

Preface

This book has been a long time in the making. I was advised several years ago by my colleague Gordon Wood that I should take my time and write a big book. I took him at his word, and ended up producing something that was too big to be published as one, and so it has now become two (still quite big) books. What is on offer here is the first.

My original aim had been to write a book which picked up where my study of *London Crowds in the Reign of Charles II* (Cambridge, 1987) had left off (roughly towards the end of 1682) and carry the story through to the Glorious Revolution, but to make my account a national one rather than focused on just the capital. This would therefore have been a study of the Tory Reaction, the reign of James II and the Revolution of 1688–9, and would have combined high politics with low politics and attempted to answer the call I had made in the introduction to my *Politics of Religion in Restoration England* (Oxford, 1990 – co-edited with Paul Seaward and Mark Goldie) for a social history of politics for this period. My project, I believed, would cause us fundamentally to rethink the 1680s and the nature of the Glorious Revolution – an event which I felt had been mischaracterized as a mere dynastic coup imposed from above and outside, but which to me seemed more like a genuine revolution and one brought about from below. Several years ago one of my students at Brown, after recognizing the elitist bias in traditional secondary accounts of 1688–9, had poignantly raised the question in class: 'Where was the crowd?' My desire was to write an account which would put the crowd back in, which would be people-focused as much as it was politician-focused, and which would recognize the vital contribution

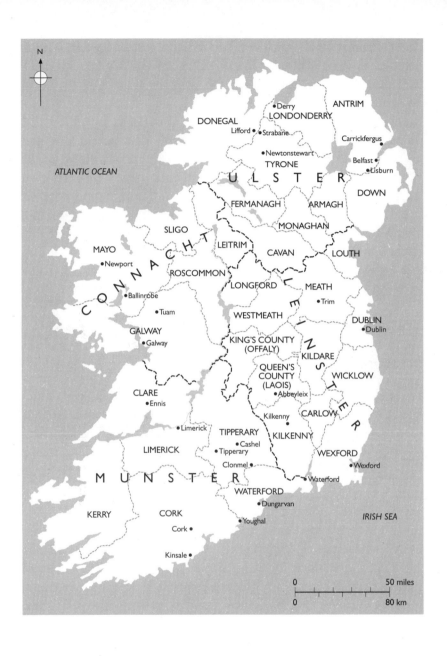

N

ATLANTIC OCEAN

DONEGAL
Lifford ● ● Strabane
• Derry
LONDONDERRY
ANTRIM
Carrickfergus ●
● Newtonstewart
TYRONE
Belfast ●
● Lisburn
U L S T E R
DOWN

FERMANAGH   ARMAGH
MONAGHAN

SLIGO
MAYO
● Newport
C O N N A C H T
LEITRIM
ROSCOMMON
CAVAN
LONGFORD
LOUTH
● Ballinrobe
● Tuam
WESTMEATH
MEATH
● Trim
GALWAY
● Galway
KING'S COUNTY
(OFFALY)
DUBLIN
● Dublin
L E I N S T E R
KILDARE
QUEEN'S
COUNTY
(LAOIS)
● Abbeyleix
WICKLOW
CLARE
● Ennis
KILKENNY
CARLOW
● Limerick
TIPPERARY
● Cashel
● Tipperary
KILKENNY
WEXFORD
LIMERICK
Clonmel ●
● Wexford
M U N S T E R
● Waterford
WATERFORD
IRISH SEA
KERRY
CORK
● Dungarvan
● Youghal
Cork ●
Kinsale ●

0   50 miles
0   80 km

National Endowment of the Humanities, the Huntington Library, and the John Simon Guggenheim Memorial Foundation, as well as research support and leave time from Brown University.

This book is dedicated to Mark Goldie, who first taught me in the late 1970s, who inspired me to become a later-Stuart historian and nurtured whatever talent he saw in me as an undergraduate and graduate student, and who has been a valued mentor, collaborator and friend for many years. I promised him this book a long time ago. Now it has finally arrived, I hope it does not disappoint.

In quoting from original sources, I have extended contemporary contractions but have otherwise adhered to the original spelling and capitalization, though I have very occasionally provided modern punctuation to assist in readability. Dates are in old style, although with the new year taken as having started on 1 January (rather than 25 March, as at the time).

Introduction

On 29 May 1660 Charles II made his triumphant royal entry into London to reclaim the thrones of his three kingdoms of England, Scotland and Ireland after more than eleven years of republican experimentation in government. The specially called Convention Parliament had voted to restore the Stuart monarchy on 1 May, and Charles was solemnly proclaimed king in London and the suburbs on the 8th. He actually arrived in England on the 25th, landing at Dover at about 1 p.m. Even given the condition of seventeenth-century roads, it would not normally have taken four days to make the journey of some 70 miles from the south-Kent coast to the nation's capital. The slowness of the pace was deliberate, however, so that Charles's entry and Restoration day would coincide with his thirtieth birthday.

The mood was certainly festive. According to contemporary accounts, great concourses of people gathered in all the towns through which the King passed as he made his way from Dover. When he reached Blackheath, just outside the capital, on the morning of the 29th, there were some 120,000 men, women and children who had assembled from 30 miles around 'to see his Majestie's princely march towards London'. The King's party comprised above 20,000 men on horse and foot, 'brandishing their swords and shouting with inexpressible joy' as they progressed the final few miles into the metropolis. The streets all along the way were 'straw'd with flowers' and hung with tapestries, the parish church bells rang, and the fountains ran with wine. The Lord Mayor and aldermen came out to meet the restored monarch on his entrance into London and, after performing 'those obedient ceremonies due in such cases', rode bareheaded before Charles and his two brothers, the dukes of York and Gloucester, escorting the royals 'all along the City'

The Common wealth ruleing with a Standing Army: Tory print representing
the tyranny of republican rule in the 1650s. The republic is represented as a
dragon which has swallowed parliament and is covered with armed troops;
it feeds on monarchy, episcopacy, nobility and the laws of the land, and
excretes taxes, excises and religious oaths and covenants.

Standing Army

A blessed Reformation

Laws Cuſtims

Statutes.

Episcopy

Monarchey

Magna Charta.
prerogative
priviledges
Liberties.

Church Land & tytlis

nobility
& House
of peers

gaine.

Food for a Com=
=mon wealth. ~

and through to Whitehall. The liverymen of the City companies together with numerous lords and nobles were there in their splendid ceremonial attire, and huge throngs of people lined the streets as far back as Rochester, 25 miles to the south-east. The noise was tremendous: trumpets sounded from the windows and balconies and, according to one observer, there was 'such shouting as the oldest man alive never heard the like'. Indeed, so large were the crowds that it took seven hours for the royal entourage to pass through the City – from two o'clock in the afternoon until nine at night. The day concluded with bonfires at almost every house, and a spectacular one at Westminster which saw the burning of effigies of Oliver Cromwell and his wife.[1]

Less than three decades later, in the second week of December 1688, Charles II's younger brother, the Duke of York, made a journey in the opposite direction, under somewhat less auspicious circumstances. York was a Catholic convert who had come to the throne in February 1685 as James II (James VII in Scotland), but his desire as king to promote the civil and religious interests of his co-religionists had proven controversial, to say the least, and by the autumn of 1688 he faced an invasion from Holland by his son-in-law and nephew, William of Orange, purportedly to rescue Protestant liberties across England, Scotland and Ireland from Catholic tyranny. Uncertain of the loyalty of his army, James panicked, dispatched his wife and newborn son to France, and planned to follow them himself. He left the capital in the early hours of 11 December, making his way through the back roads of Kent towards the Isle of Sheppey, where a small custom-house boat was taking on ballast ready for the Channel crossing. At about eleven o'clock that night a group of seamen from Faversham on the search for Catholic fugitives arrived and detained the party. James was with two fellow Catholics, Ralph Sheldon and Sir Edward Hales, but, although the seamen recognized Hales, who was a local man, they failed to recognize the King, who was sporting a short black wig and a patch on his upper lip as a disguise. Taking James to be Hales's Jesuit confessor, they began hurling insults, calling him 'old Rogue, ugly, lean-jawed hatchet faced Jesuite, popish dog etc.'. If the King had been prepared to reveal himself immediately, he undoubtedly would have saved himself the indignities that followed,

4

for, without knowing whom exactly they had on their hands, the sea-men decided to seize all the valuables from their detainees, taking nearly £200 in gold (most of which was on the King himself), before undertaking a strip-search of the man they took to be the Jesuit – that is, they undid his 'very breeches . . . and examined for secret treasure, so indecently, as even to the discovery of his nudities', as our contemporary account delicately phrases it. It was not until the King was eventually brought to the Queen's Arms in Faversham several hours later that his true identity was discovered.[2] On this occasion James was to be brought back to London, but William of Orange had no desire to allow his father-in-law/uncle to remain in the country, and encouraged him to flee once again for France, which James this time successfully did on the 23rd. In February 1689 another specially called Convention Parliament was to declare William and his wife, Mary (James II's daughter), king and queen of England and Ireland in James's stead, and a Scottish Convention was to confer the Scottish crown upon them shortly thereafter.

The troubles of the mid seventeenth century had seen England, Scotland and Ireland torn apart by civil war; had led to the overthrow of the existing order in Church and state and the execution of the king, Charles I, outside his own Banqueting House on 30 January 1649; and had culminated in a series of unsuccessful experiments with various non-monarchical forms of government in a desperate but elusive quest for stability until everything began to fall apart following the death of Lord Protector Oliver Cromwell in September 1658. By the winter of 1659–60 the return of the Stuarts, and with them the old order, seemed the only viable solution, and was much longed for by a population who had never really warmed to republicanism. It was a solution that within less than three decades had proved not to be viable. This time, however, the offending Stuart monarch was not to be hauled before a revolutionary court of justice and condemned to death for committing treason against his own people, but was allowed to slip away quietly in the dead of night in a political coup that has come to be known ever since as England's 'Glorious' Revolution – even as the 'Bloodless' Revolution. William and Mary became joint monarchs (though with the exercise of regal power vested in William alone) in a dynastic settlement that was accompanied by a Declaration of Rights (later enacted as the Bill of Rights) in England and a Claim of Right in Scotland, both of which were intended to vindicate and assert ancient rights and liberties. Affairs in Scotland were to be far from bloodless, however, while the Irish were to lose out in a bloody war of conquest. This was to be the last political revolution in English and Scottish history; moreover, in contrast to the upheavals of the middle of the century, it was actually styled a revolution by those who lived through it.

With the vantage of hindsight, we can see that the Restoration period was the last gasp for the Stuart monarchy. It would not have appeared that way to people at the time. There was a widespread belief after 1660 that the old order could be successfully restored – witness gestures such as tearing the pages out of council minute books for the intervening period, as if destroying the record of the past would be enough to effectively eradicate it. The restored regime certainly did not have things easy, but was it necessarily doomed to fail?

It cannot be denied that the Restoration regime faced serious difficulties. Indeed, by the late 1670s these had grown so severe that many contemporaries – including the King himself – genuinely came to fear the possibility of renewed civil war. Healing the divisions that had caused the outbreak of civil war in 1642, and which in turn had been exacerbated by the political experiences of the 1640s and '50s, proved no easy task, and political tensions soon began to reappear. In addition, new problems arose – not helped by Charles II's own political failings and by a crisis over the succession which developed once the Duke of York's conversion to Catholicism became publicly acknowledged in 1673. York stood as next in line to the throne, owing to Charles's inability to father any legitimate offspring, and his conversion gave rise to fears that the three kingdoms were drifting back along the path towards popery and arbitrary government. This combination of revived tensions and new anxieties caused the growth of considerable disaffection, both inside parliament and 'out-of-doors'. All that was needed was some form of trigger, a spark to ignite the wealth of combustible material that already existed, and this was provided by the revelations in the summer of 1678 of a supposed Popish Plot to murder Charles II and massacre English Protestants. With the heir to the throne an acknowledged Catholic, the situation seemed alarming, especially to those who already felt unhappy with the restored Stuart regime. By 1679–81 the restored monarchy had been plunged into renewed crisis, as an organized parliamentary opposition with seemingly considerable support among the mass of the population came to demand the exclusion of the Catholic heir from the succession and pressed for further reforms in Church and state. To many political observers the tactics of the Whigs, as this political opposition soon came to be known, appeared very similar to the those pursued by the parliamentary opposition to Charles I on the eve of the Civil War. It seemed as if '41 was come again, and thus that it was all but inevitable that '42 would follow.

Yet the monarchy managed to extricate itself from this crisis. Charles II not only survived the threat but was even able to rebuild the authority and prestige of the crown, so much so that in the final four years of his reign England appeared to be moving towards a style of monarchical absolutism similar to that which had developed on the Continent, especially in France. Indeed, France itself had successfully escaped from its own mid-century crisis, the 'Fronde', to emerge as the world's major superpower under *le roi soleil*, Louis XIV; perhaps England was destined to go the same way. Moreover, by the mid-1680s the Stuart monarchy had managed to consolidate its authority over Scotland, while Ireland seemed to be more prosperous and stable than it had been for a long time. Such was the nature of the royal recovery in the final years of Charles II's reign that when James II came to the throne, in 1685, he enjoyed the strongest position of any English monarch certainly since the accession of the Stuarts in 1603 and arguably since the accession of Henry VIII in 1509. Furthermore, he was not only powerful, but also popular, since Charles II and his Tory allies (as the opponents of the Whigs were called) had done a magnificent job in rallying public opinion behind the Stuart monarchy and the hereditary succession in opposition to the Whig challenge in the years after 1681.

However, everything was to fall apart dramatically within less than four years. It has been said of Charles I that he was an incompetent ruler, 'but not quite incompetent enough to leave the kingdom free from civil war'; he was, at least, able to muster a royalist party that would enable him to try to defend his cause by force of arms.[3] Yet, unlike his ill-fated father in 1642, by late 1688 James II was not even in a position to fight those who sought to bring him down, such had been the nature of his political collapse, with the result that flight – in the hope of enlisting the military support of Louis XIV to recapture his crowns – became his only realistic option. With the collapse of James's regime went the old political system. England and its dependent monarchies of Scotland and Ireland were to develop in very different ways after 1688–9 – different, that is, from how they would have developed otherwise, and different also from the way most of the Continent was to go. England was to get a Bill of Rights and begin the slow evolution towards its modern system of parliamentary monarchy; the Continent was to see the consolidation and enhancement of monarchical absolutism which it would take the bloody revolutions of the late eighteenth and the nineteenth centuries to overthrow.

On the face of it, then, the Glorious Revolution might seem to deserve a significant place in the nation's historical consciousness, akin perhaps to that enjoyed by the American Revolution, the French Revolution or the European revolutions of the nineteenth century in their respective national historiographies. After all, was not the Glorious Revolution the last major political landmark event before England's emergence as a modern political nation – an event which, to quote one modern-day scholar, made 'possible the emergence of England, and eventually Britain, as a great power'?[4] Indeed, was it not the Glorious Revolution, as Lord Hailsham claimed in the House of Lords in March 1986, which laid the 'foundations from which evolved, peacefully, the system of parliamentary democracy under a constitutional monarch which we enjoy today'?[5] Certainly the implications of the revolutionary settlements in Scotland and Ireland have remained with us until the present day – although it has proved much more difficult to put a positive gloss on these. The Revolution was ultimately to cost the Scots their political independence; when they threatened not to follow the English in settling the succession on the electors of Hanover once it became apparent that the Protestant Stuart line brought to power by the dynastic coup of 1688–9 would die out, they had to be brought into line by an incorporating union of 1707 which created the state of Great Britain and under the terms of which the Scots were granted limited representation in what hitherto had been the English parliament at Westminster. It was not until devolution in 1999 that Scotland was to regain a parliament of its own. Few readers will need to be reminded that the seemingly intractable troubles in Northern Ireland have in large part fed off the historical memory of events that happened in Ireland in the Jacobite war of 1689–91, such as the siege of Derry of 1689 or the Battle of Boyne of 1690. It might seem, then, that without a proper understanding of the so-called Glorious Revolution the inhabitants of the British Isles have no chance of fully understanding their own modern world.

Nevertheless, the Glorious Revolution has occupied a somewhat ambiguous place within the British historical imagination. It has proved difficult to know how to relate to it, as the tercentenary commemorations of 1988–9 testified. What exactly was there to commemorate? To those on the left it seemed nowhere near revolutionary enough; to most liberal-minded people it appeared to be an episode fuelled by anti-Catholic religious bigotry (hardly to be lauded in the multicultural Britain of the late twentieth century); while to ultra-conservatives clinging to a sentimental Jacobitism it had merely served to overthrow Britain's legitimate dynasty by an act of infamous treachery. Moreover, how could one commemorate the event without offering an affront to Scottish and Irish sensibilities?[6] Furthermore, however it might have been seen in the past, modern-day scholars have had the discomforting habit of reminding us that the so-called Revolution of 1688 was, in fact, essentially a successful invasion of England by a foreign power – by the Dutch, of all people, a nation with whom England had fought three exhausting wars in the 1650s, '60s and '70s. Indeed, 1688 was the last time that England was successfully conquered! William of Orange did not arrive with a team of diplomats and skilled negotiators in his attempt to rescue Protestant liberties in his father-in-law's kingdoms; he landed at Torbay on 5 November 1688 with a professional army of some 15,000 men. James's flight may have meant that William did not need to engage the King's army in major battle, but that does not detract from the fact that what happened was a foreign conquest. And, although civil war was avoided in England, this was not the case in Scotland, where several thousands died in the ensuing Highland War, while Ireland fell victim to a brutal war between the two kings, James and William, in which nearly 25,000 men died in conflict and thousands more of disease.[7]

If one focused less on the invasion aspect of 1688 and paid more attention to the settlement that was achieved in 1689, then it became much easier to cast the Revolution as an episode in which the English, at least, might deserve to take some pride. The great Whig historians of the past – from the late eighteenth century through to the eve of the Second World War – certainly believed that the Revolution merited a glorious place in the national (English) historical narrative. They nevertheless tended to see it in conservative terms, as a sanitized revolution which exemplified the moderate English way of doing things, in contrast to the excesses of the European revolutions of the late eighteenth and the nineteenth centuries. Thus Edmund Burke, speaking and writing at the time of the French Revolution, saw the Glorious Revolution as 'a revolution, not made, but prevented'; its intent had been 'to preserve our ancient and indisputable laws and liberties' against 'the fundamental subversion of the antient constitution' attempted by James II.[8] For the great Whig historian of the mid nineteenth century, Thomas Babington Macaulay, 1688–9 was 'a revolution strictly defensive', 'a vindication of ancient rights', 'of all revolutions the least violent'. Indeed, Macaulay believed that 'the highest eulogy' that could be pronounced on the Glorious Revolution was 'that it was our last revolution . . . It was because we had a preserving revolution in the seventeenth century that we have not had a destroying revolution in the nineteenth.'[9] For G. M. Trevelyan in 1938, although the expulsion of James II may have been 'a revolutionary act . . . the spirit of this strange Revolution was the opposite of revolutionary. It came not to overthrow the law but to confirm it against a law-breaking king.' Indeed, Trevelyan thought it might more aptly be styled 'The Sensible Revolution', which would distinguish it 'more clearly as among other revolutions'. It is a view that has continued to be endorsed by historians up to the present day.[10]

The result of such characterizations was to lead twentieth-century scholars to grow more interested in the mid-century crisis in England, attracted by the lure of what seemed much more like a genuine

revolution, albeit a failed one. Thus Christopher Hill, a towering figure in seventeenth-century English historiography from 1940 through
to the end of the twentieth century, saw the English Civil War as the
first of the modern revolutions.[11] Similarly Lawrence Stone was convinced that the upheavals of the 1640s and '50s constituted 'the first
"Great Revolution" in the history of the world' – indeed 'England's
only "Great Revolution"' – and 'an event of fundamental importance
in the evolution of Western civilization'.[12] Even revisionist historians,
who believe that there was no high road to civil war and that early
Stuart England was a most unrevolutionary place, seem to agree that
what eventually came to pass in the 1640s and '50s was not only a
revolution but also '*the* Revolution' (albeit 'the product of the trau-
mas of civil war'), which had 'profound effects on the subsequent history of the British Isles'.[13] As one influential recent textbook has put
it, summarizing conventional wisdom, 1648–9 was 'the only revolution in English history'.[14] The events of 1688–9 have been seen, by
most, as either a postscript or a tidying-up operation – an after-
tremor, not the 'major earthquake itself'[15] – or even as something that
was essentially conservative and backward-looking.[16] Though there
have been some attempts, of late, to reinvest the Glorious Revolution
in England with more radical credentials, these accounts still leave us
with the impression of an episode that was much less revolutionary
than what transpired in the 1640s and '50s.[17]

Such ways of thinking have affected the way historians have tended
to study the Glorious Revolution. If it was primarily a defensive revolution, against the innovations of James II, then no long-term causes
need to be sought. Our accounts can start with the accession of
James II in 1685; at most, perhaps, they need to go back to the final
years of Charles II's reign and the so-called Tory Reaction which set in
following the defeat of the parliamentary campaign for Exclusion in
1681. Many works, indeed, have concentrated on just the year of revolution itself. This short-term approach has caused a certain myopia,
an inability to perceive the underlying problems which undermined
the stability of the restored Stuart regime. The oft-repeated assertion
that the Glorious Revolution was bloodless and largely non-violent
has tended to deflect attention from the bloodiness and violence that
did occur, even in England. Whether this was really as sanitized a

revolution as is often implied is clearly open to question. And the illusion that it was has been sustained only by ignoring Scotland and Ireland, whose revolutions were both violent and bloody. Finally, the marginalization of the Glorious Revolution vis-à-vis its supposedly more important elder brother of the mid seventeenth century has served to perpetuate further the view that 1688–9 was not much of a revolutionary moment at all. Yet why should a revolt that failed be thought to have had a greater impact on Britain's subsequent historical evolution than one which succeeded?

This study aims to invite a fundamental rethinking of the way we approach the study of the Glorious Revolution and the significance we attach to its outcome. It is concerned, at a basic level, with the origins, nature and outcome of the Glorious Revolution in all three of the kingdoms over which the Stuarts ruled. But its objectives go much further. More generally, it seeks to explore the nature and reality of political power in Restoration England, Scotland and Ireland – how royal authority was made effective, and how it could be undermined. It investigates the root causes of instability in the Restoration period, and why, when monarchy had been so enthusiastically welcomed back in 1660, the restored regime seemed on the verge of collapse less than two decades later. It examines how this regime then managed to extricate itself from this crisis and rebuild the powers of the monarchy in the first half of the 1680s. Finally, it considers why the Stuart regime collapsed so precipitously under James II, how that collapse was brought about, the nature of the solutions devised in 1689, and the longer-term significance of those solutions. A major sub-theme is a consideration of whether there truly was a potential for monarchical absolutism in the Stuart kingdoms in the 1680s and, if so, how and why Britain and Ireland's absolutist turn during this decade was eventually defeated. Broadly speaking, this study is a work of political history. Yet it is also a work of legal–constitutional history and of intellectual history; a study of propaganda, public opinion and popular politics; a work that deals with the localities as well as the centre, and with the concerns of ordinary men and women as well as those of the great and powerful.

This project has been shaped by a belief that the period from the Restoration through to the Glorious Revolution and its aftermath needs to be treated as a whole. However, it grew so large that it became necessary to split it into two volumes. The present book deals with the monarchy under Charles II, from the joyful enthusiasm with which Charles was welcomed back in 1660, through to the crisis the restored regime faced by 1679–81, and on to the rebuilding of the monarchy during the years of the Tory Reaction from 1681 to 1685. A sequel deals with the Revolutions of 1688–9 and their aftermaths, tracing the story from the accession of James II in 1685 through to the early eighteenth century. Both volumes are intended to stand alone and thus to be self-contained. Nevertheless, the study has been conceived as a whole, and together the two books do tell a larger story.

There are a number of deficiencies within the existing corpus of scholarship on the Glorious Revolution, of both a conceptual and an empirical nature, which this study seeks to address. First, most works on the Glorious Revolution have focused on the political elite, concentrating either on events at court or at Westminster, the machinations of the key actors involved in the resistance to James, and the framing of the eventual Revolution settlement, or else on those political ideologues who published treatises and pamphlets seeking to offer intellectual justifications (or alternatively condemnations) of the dynastic shift and the accompanying reforms in Church and state. Less attention has been paid to the role of the middling and lower sorts, or those out-of-doors. Historians have, of course, always been aware that there was a certain amount of crowd unrest at the time of the Glorious Revolution; nevertheless, they have seemed unsure about how to integrate high and low politics in their analyses. The result has been that the crowd has tended to get pushed to one side, or even left out of the picture altogether.[18] The frequently encountered characterizations of the Glorious Revolution in England as a mere palace coup or a dynastic revolution highlight the extent to which those out-of-doors have been marginalized within the dominant interpretative paradigm. This seems at odds, however, with recent scholarship on the Restoration, which has emphasized the vitality of politics out-of-doors during the reign of Charles II, the importance of crowd agitation and public demonstrations (not just in London, but also in the provinces) and the vital role of mass petitioning campaigns. Indeed, Restoration scholarship has pointed to the need for a social history of politics: one that does justice to high politics, at the centre, but also sets the operation of politics in its appropriate social context, examining the impact the policies of the rulers had on those they ruled, and considering the extent to which those out-of-doors may have been involved in the political process and actively pursued political agendas of their own.[19] In short, the new approaches that have been developed for the Restoration period suggest the need to rethink our approach to the Glorious Revolution; we need an account of the period as a whole that can show the ways in which our understanding of the dynamics of politics out-of-doors for the reign of Charles II can in turn shape our perspective on the reign of James II and the revolution which brought about his downfall.

Second, we have no major modern study of the Glorious Revolution – nor, indeed, of the later Stuart period as a whole – that provides an integrated analysis of developments in all three Stuart kingdoms. Scotland, Ireland and England have typically been treated in isolation, even though the overthrow of James II (or James VII as he was in Scotland) and his replacement by William III (William II in Scotland) had ramifications throughout all three kingdoms of the Stuart composite monarchy. Three kingdoms lost their reigning monarch in 1688–9 as a result of the Dutch intervention in England. Not only did each of three kingdoms experience the Revolution, but there were also three very different revolutions in the respective kingdoms, albeit that they ultimately had the same trigger. Indeed, there seem to be compelling reasons for examining the entire period from the Restoration to the Glorious Revolution in a three-kingdoms context.[20] The restoration of monarchy was, in itself, a quintessentially three-kingdoms event, even if each individual kingdom was then to have its own respective Restoration settlement. When Charles II was restored in the spring of 1660, he was restored as king of all three of his kingdoms, and all three kingdoms had played a crucial role in helping to bring about the return of the Stuart monarchy. Ireland was the first to act, when conservatives in the army seized control of Dublin Castle in December 1659 and paved the way for the meeting of the Irish Convention which would ultimately declare for Charles II. It was the intervention in English affairs by the Scottish army under General George Monck from January 1660 that secured the final demise of the Rump Parliament (the rump of the Long Parliament which had declared war on Charles I in 1642, been purged by Colonel Thomas Pride in December 1648, dismissed by Oliver Cromwell in 1653, and recalled to power in 1659) and the calling of the English Convention which would formally restore Charles Stuart. Similarly, the Exclusion Crisis of 1679–81 was not an episode solely in English history, since the attempt in England to exclude the Catholic heir from the succession inevitably had repercussions for Scotland and Ireland, where the same man was also heir to the throne. However, for Scotland and Ireland the period from the Restoration to the Glorious Revolution remains seriously understudied, and is in desperate need of new research if we are to develop a full appreciation of the nature of Stuart rule in these two kingdoms, of the problems it created, and of the true significance of the respective revolutions in each.[21] This study therefore aims to fill a major gap by providing the type of contextualized study of the Glorious Revolution in both Scotland or Ireland that was previously lacking, hoping to generate new insights into the Scottish and Irish pasts in the process, while at the same time providing a fresh conceptual framework from which to re-evaluate the nature and significance of the developments within England itself as well as within the Stuart multiple-kingdom inheritance as a whole.

Third, the scholarly community has, on the whole, failed to appreciate the revolutionary significance of 1688–91. It is the contention of this two-volume study that it is in the later Stuart period that the true revolutions of the seventeenth century were located – revolutions, that is, both as contemporaries would have understood the term and also in the modern meaning of the word – involving fundamental and irreversible changes that transformed the way the world was for the inhabitants of England, Scotland and Ireland. The modern British state, and even many of the problems that bedevil the relationships between England, Scotland and Ireland today, is much more a product of the 'successful' revolutions that followed in the wake of the dynastic coup of 1688–9 than of the failed (or successfully undone) revolutions of the middle decades of the seventeenth century. Again, this is a point that can be fully grasped only by studying the period from the Restoration to the Glorious Revolution as a whole: we can appreciate how much was changed after 1688 only by understanding exactly what was restored in 1660. These are bold claims. Before we proceed any further, then, more needs to be said about the particular conceptual framework in which this study will be set.

A SOCIAL HISTORY OF POLITICS

A major theme of this study will be that the fortunes of the crown in the years between 1660 and 1688 were intimately linked to the climate of public opinion. Charles II got into trouble by the late 1670s because too many people had become alienated from his regime. Royal recovery in the early 1680s, by contrast, was related in crucial ways to the crown's ability to win back public opinion, while royal collapse under James II was tied up with the crown's failure to carry public opinion behind its ambitious and controversial policies. The emphasis offered here on the importance of public opinion will bear significant implications for our understanding of the Revolution itself, and whether it should be seen merely as a dynastic coup imposed from above (and even outside) or as a revolution wrought from below. It also necessitates setting politics in a broader social context. If this is to be done, however, we need to reflect at the outset on how politicized those below the level of the elite might have been. Did the people have any politics worth talking about? If so, how did they obtain a political education?[22]

One way, obviously, was through the media. There was a dramatic expansion of the output of the printed press in the seventeenth century, starting with the breakdown in censorship on the eve of the Civil War. Although restrictions were reimposed in the 1650s and at the Restoration, they were never fully effective, and broke down again with the temporary lapsing of the Licensing Act in 1679. During the Exclusion Crisis, and again at the time of the Glorious Revolution, members of the political elite (of all political persuasions) certainly made every effort to exploit the medium of print in order to woo public opinion.[23] Printed materials, especially the shorter pamphlets, news-sheets and broadsides, enjoyed a wide circulation, often being deposited in coffee houses and other public places so that they could be read by those who could not afford to buy their own copy. There may have been as many as 2,000 coffee houses in the greater London area alone by the end of the century, although they were far from being a metropolitan phenomenon, since coffee houses could be found throughout the country, in smaller towns as well as in larger urban areas, and also in Scotland and Ireland.[24] Though printed media were available, many people continued to learn their news from traditional scribal forms of publication, such as manuscript newsletters, and, while it could be expensive to subscribe to a newsletter service, newsletters were likewise frequently deposited at coffee houses and alehouses for more general consumption. Indeed, it was claimed that in Restoration England newsletters were to be found in every village inn, with the local squire often expounding upon their contents 'like a little newsmonger'; they were even on occasion posted up in the streets for public perusal, and there they could not only be read but also be recopied for further distribution.[25] In Scotland in the late 1670s and early 1680s the minister of Hamilton (on the outskirts of Glasgow) was receiving regular newsletters from a correspondent in Edinburgh, who reported not just Scottish news but also English news which he had presumably picked up from newsletters circulating in the Scottish capital.[26] In Ireland, newsletters were reaching not just the capital, Dublin, but also provincial towns, such as Kinsale and Youghall.[27]

But what impact would printed or written media probably have had on the people at large? After all, was not this a society with relatively low levels of literacy? There are, in fact, compelling reasons why we should not have too pessimistic a view of the political awareness of the mass of the population. In the first place, literacy levels were not as low as we were once led to believe. One important modern study has calculated that only 30 per cent of English men and 10 per cent of English women were literate in the early 1640s (as measured by the ability to sign one's name) – fairly low figures, one might think, though these had risen to 45 per cent and 25 per cent respectively by the accession of George I in 1714. These percentages are somewhat deceptive, however. National averages are not particularly meaningful, because there were marked regional and occupational variations in literacy profiles. The sample from which these totals were derived was biased towards rural communities, but town-dwellers tended to be more literate than those who lived in the countryside. Literacy rates were highest in London, where by 1641–4 nearly 80 per cent of the adult male population could sign their names. Furthermore, the middling sorts tended to be more literate than the lower orders: yeomen, craftsmen and apprentices were much more likely to be able to sign their names than were husbandmen, labourers and servants. Moreover, the signature test clearly underestimates literacy levels for early modern England, for the simple reason that reading was taught before writing: there were many more people who could read than had learned to sign their name – perhaps as much as half as many again. And, since females tended to be educated up until the point when they could read, but to leave school before they learned to write, there are reasons for suspecting that women were just as likely to be able to read as men.[28] Research on Scotland has shown that in the 1670s and '80s about two-thirds of Scottish males were literate, though here the sample was biased towards urban centres and the Lowlands, where literacy was more widespread. In fact Scotland evinced the same marked occupational and regional variations as England, with 82 per cent of labourers illiterate in the period 1640–99 and illiteracy rates much higher in rural areas and in the Highlands.[29] So, too, did Ireland, where literacy was again highest among the middle and upper classes and in the towns. One study of debt cases in Dublin for 1651–2, for example, has shown that 66 per cent of sureties could sign their names; by the 1690s the corresponding figure was nearly 80 per cent. All the obvious members of the local Dublin elite were literate, while between 70 and 80 per cent of craftsmen and those involved in the drink trades were too. Butchers and bakers, by contrast, were predominantly illiterate. The more prosperous tenant farmers could read: over 73 per cent of those who signed leases on the Herbert estate at Castleisland in Kerry between 1653 and 1687 could sign their names (66 per cent of the native Irish, 83 per cent of the settlers), as could 85 per cent on the Hill estate in County Down, though here we are dealing with people mainly from the middle ranks of society. In general, literacy was less needed, and also less likely to be obtained, if one were engaged in farming. Thus on the Adair estates around Ballymena, County Antrim, in the later seventeenth century, only 33 per cent of farmers and yeomen could sign their names, whereas 94 per cent of those engaged in trade could.[30]

In short, literacy was more widespread than once thought. Yet, even if one were illiterate, this was not necessarily a bar to gaining a political education. People did not have to be told what the government was up to by the press; they lived under government, and therefore experienced the implications of government policy directly themselves. Economic regulation, the imposition of taxes, the policing of religious conformity, and the ways in which law and order were enforced all helped shape people's attitudes towards those who held the reins of power. These attitudes, it is true, would be refined, modified, reshaped or even redirected by exposure to the media. And, when we talk about the media, we should not think just about the printed press. Traditional forms of oral communication remained vitally important. One of the most powerful tools for the dissemination of political information and ideas was the sermon, which is why both Charles II and James II sought to clamp down on the expression of hostile political opinions from the pulpit while doing their best to encourage clergy to propagate views favourable to the monarchy. Even when we are dealing with written materials, we have to recognize that often their content came to be transmitted orally. Inability to read did not necessarily prevent people from gaining access to political news conveyed in print or writing, since those who could not read could gather around someone who could and hear extracts of the latest political squibs read aloud. We can even find examples of party activists in the provinces reading pamphlets out for the edification of passers-by, or going into pubs and 'holding forth to a parcel of apron men' about the due bounds of political authority.[31] Word of mouth remained an essential way of spreading the latest news and gossip. People would typically greet travellers or those who had returned from a journey (particularly those who had come from the capital) with the question 'What news?', and the news obtained quickly spread through traditional local communication networks – whether the church, the market, the alehouse or the coffee house. People reacted as much to what they heard as to what they read, and this provided a fertile environment for the spreading of rumours;[32] indeed, time and again rumour was to play a crucial role in helping to destabilize the Restoration polity.

Public demonstrations were another form of political communication. An eyewitness could 'read' public rituals, such as the elaborate pope-burning processions staged by the supporters of Exclusion in London during the height of the Exclusion Crisis, rather as one could read a Whig anti-Catholic broadside. Here was another medium (like rumour) that the masses could exploit for themselves. And if processions could be read like pamphlets, people could in a sense write their own pamphlets by staging a dramatic ritual which observers could witness, and which the writers of news or political commentary could then carry accounts of in their manuscript newsletters or printed broadsides.

What we have, then, is a more complicated picture than that of the elite simply reaching out to the people and trying to politicize them through printed media – with those who were unable to read (or to read well enough) being left behind in some sort of apolitical void. People were politicized in a variety of other ways as well, particularly by how they came to experience the effects of government policy, and they had their knowledge, expectations, identities, ideals, perspectives and attitudes organized, shaped and mobilized not just by what they read in pamphlets or news periodicals, but also by what they heard in sermons or saw in public demonstrations, what was spread by word of mouth, and what they had been led to believe was true by rumours that were circulating at the time.

THE THREE-KINGDOMS APPROACH

We have suggested that our understanding of the Revolutions of the later seventeenth century would be enhanced by taking a three-kingdoms approach. Some of the reasons have been alluded to already. At the very basic level, given that the Stuart monarchs ruled Scotland and Ireland as well as England, any event or crisis that had implications for the succession of the crown had implications for all three kingdoms. This was true of the Restoration of 1660 itself, as well as of the Exclusion Crisis of 1679–81 and the Glorious Revolution of 1688–9. Further than this, many of the problems that beset the Restoration polity were related to difficulties in managing the multiple-kingdom inheritance and the different legacies bequeathed by the upheavals of the 1640s and 1650s in England, Scotland and Ireland. Thus what

Charles II tried to do to stabilize royal authority in one kingdom often had the effect of destabilizing politics in one of his other kingdoms. Contemporaries recognized that there were certain problems or issues facing them that operated on a three-kingdoms level, and not on separate national levels. The concern expressed by the Whigs in England in the late 1670s and early 1680s about the threat of popery and arbitrary government, for example, reflected not just a fear of what might happen, in the future, should the Catholic heir succeed to the English throne; it was also a reaction, in part, against what was going on in the present under Charles II, in Ireland and Scotland. Likewise, Tory fears about the threat posed by the English Whigs and their nonconformist allies were in part conditioned by the Tories' reaction to the subversive challenge offered by the radical Presbyterians north of the border. The extent to which contemporaries thought of the emerging crisis in a three-kingdoms context is evident from the very terms adopted to designate the competing factions or parties: the term 'Whig' referred originally to a radical Scottish Presbyterian; 'Tory', to an Irish-Catholic cattle thief. Both Charles II and James II frequently sought to play the three-kingdoms card, pursuing particular strategies in one kingdom in order to make political points to another: Charles did this with considerable success in his final years; James's efforts served only to provoke further alarm among his Protestant subjects in all three kingdoms. Indeed, it has long been recognized by Scottish and Irish historians that James would not have fallen in Scotland and Ireland had he not fallen in England; it also needs to be recognized that what James did in Scotland and Ireland goes a long way towards explaining why he lost the support of both the political elite and the mass of the population in England, and thus why he succumbed to the invasion of William of Orange.

Yet, although some factors operated on a three-kingdoms level, others did not. The separate national histories of the three constituent kingdoms of the Stuart composite monarchy also need to be treated on their own terms. We must guard against an Anglocentric approach – one that draws on Scotland and Ireland merely to explain developments within England; three-kingdoms history must not become an excuse for marginalizing those aspects of the Scottish or Irish past which seem irrelevant from an Anglo-imperialist perspective. Hence, in addition to exploring the interplay of events in England, Scotland and Ireland at this time, this book and its sequel devote separate chapters to analysing developments in each of the constituent kingdoms individually. Such a strategy also helps highlight another advantage of pursuing a three-kingdoms approach, namely the comparative perspective it can offer. What it was possible to achieve in one of the three kingdoms can set in sharp relief the significance of what transpired in the others.[33]

This is not intended to marginalize the Welsh. Scotland and Ireland need to be treated independently for analytical purposes in order to explore the interaction between separate kingdoms that happened to share the same king. The principality of Wales, by contrast, had been incorporated into the English state with Henry VIII's acts of union of 1536 and 1543, and, although political and religious developments could take on distinctive Welsh hues, administratively Wales was part of England. For that reason, developments in the principality will be treated in those chapters that deal with England.

It will be helpful here to say something more about the nature of the political relationship between the three constituent kingdoms of the Stuart monarchy. Scotland and England were two independent kingdoms; James VI of Scotland had simply inherited the English crown back in 1603, but his attempts as James I of England to bring a closer union of the two countries had foundered. Although Oliver Cromwell's conquests of Scotland and Ireland had brought about a temporary political union in the 1650s, this was dissolved at the Restoration. Scotland and England had separate constitutions, separate legal systems and laws, separate administrative and ecclesiastical structures.[34]

Each kingdom had its own parliament, but the bodies were very different in nature. The English parliament was bicameral, comprising an upper house of lay and ecclesiastical lords and an elected House of Commons. Following the passage of the second Test Act in 1678, which excluded Catholics from sitting in the Lords, there were 147 peers eligible to sit in the upper house (including 24 bishops and 2 archbishops); on average, however, only about half this number were ever in attendance. After the enfranchisement of the county and city of Durham and of Newark (Nottinghamshire) in 1673, the

Commons comprised 513 members, the elected representatives of 52 counties and 217 boroughs across England and Wales. Most constituencies returned two members; London was unique in returning four; the Welsh constituencies and five English boroughs returned just one. In some areas the franchise was quite broad. Given inflation, the 40-shilling-freehold requirement was no longer particularly restrictive by the later seventeenth century; in Yorkshire, for example, some 8,000 could vote. The franchises in the boroughs varied considerably, and although some were quite restrictive – in Buckingham, for example, only the thirteen town councillors could vote – others were extremely broad: in the populous borough of Westminster, where the franchise was invested in the inhabitant householders, the electorate numbered some 25,000 in 1679.[35] Indeed, it has been estimated that perhaps as many as one in four of the adult male population had the right to vote in parliamentary elections in the later Stuart period.[36] The precise position of parliament within the constitution was vague. Whigs tended to see parliament as a coordinate power, which shared in the king's sovereignty. Tories denied this, and emphasized parliament's subordination to the sovereign monarch. Certainly the king determined when parliament should meet; parliament was not an independent body in that sense. However, the king could neither collect taxes nor enact legislation without parliamentary consent.

The Scottish parliament, by contrast, was a unicameral body, where the three estates of clergy, tenants-in-chief (comprising both hereditary lords and elected shire representatives) and burgesses sat together. The shires had the right to return two commissioners to parliament, with the exception of Clackmannan and Kinross, which could send just one. The royal burghs sent just one commissioner, though the capital, Edinburgh, sent two. The electorate was small. In the shires the right to vote was restricted to the tenants-in-chief who held lands with an annual value of 40 shillings, although acts of 1661 and 1681 subsequently extended this to include some of the wealthier feuars or feuholders (those who held their land in perpetuity on condition of a substantial yearly payment to the crown). One historian has calculated that the average number of voters in shire elections in the Restoration period was 16. In the burghs the electorate was typically the members of the town council. There was some fluctuation in the composition of the representative element. The number of shires with the right to return commissioners did not become fixed at 33 until 1681, and even then they did not always return their full quota; the number of parliamentary burghs fluctuated between 58 and 68 over the course of the seventeenth century. The 1681 parliament comprised a total of 195 members: 2 archbishops and 10 bishops; 62 lay peers, together with 4 officers of state; 57 shire commissioners representing 33 shires; and 60 burgh commissioners for 59 burghs.[37]

In Scotland, parliament had to be called if the king wanted to enact legislation; if he sought only money, however, he could call a convention of estates. This meant that, unlike in England, the issue of supply could be kept divorced from the redress of grievances. Moreover, legislative initiatives in the Scottish parliament were managed by a select steering committee known as the Lords of the Articles, comprising eight bishops, eight nobles, eight shire and eight burgh commissioners, and eight officers of state. The original logic behind the Lords of the Articles had been to address some of the problems inherent in having a unicameral parliament. In the first place, the committee was designed to ensure that the different estates had equal representation 'in the Projecting, and Framing of the Laws'; otherwise, in an open vote in the house, 'the Estates not being equal in number, a greater State Combining, might overthrow the Interest of another.' (In England, where both houses had a negative voice, this situation could not arise.) Moreover, since the king could increase the number of nobles and royal burghs at pleasure, he could easily pack the parliament to the disadvantage of the shires, should he so desire. In the second place, it was intended to guarantee that due deliberation took place before any legislation was placed, for in Scotland, where 'the Procedure [was] quick, and the Forms of Parliament . . . Expedit and Summar', a sudden vote in favour of a piece of legislation could put the king into a quandary as to whether or not to assent to the bill, since he might still be ignorant of the design of the law framed; the fact that in England legislation had to go through both houses meant that the crown had more time to evaluate it. However, since 1633 the bishops had chosen the eight noblemen to serve on the Articles, and these eight noblemen had in turn chosen the eight bishops, with the sixteen nobles and bishops then choosing the shire and burgh representatives. Given that the king appointed the bishops (as well as the officers of state), this meant that the crown could effectively determine the complexion of the Articles. And, instead of the Articles being merely a preparatory committee, as originally intended, it came to be established practice that any proposals for legislation which the Articles rejected could not be brought before parliament. Scottish parliaments were thus relatively weak institutions, unable to offer the same sort of counterbalance to the political authority of the crown as their English counterparts.[38]

The nature of the relationship between Ireland and England was rather different. The English claim to suzerainty over Ireland dated back to the second half of the twelfth century, and stemmed from a papal grant of 1155 by Pope Adrian IV to allow Henry II 'to enter into the island' for the purpose of extending the boundaries of the Church, restraining vice, implanting virtues, promoting the growth of the Christian religion, and subjecting the native population to the rule of law. Whether the pope had had the right to give Ireland away in this manner was questionable. The papacy's original claim to the island rested on the Donation of Constantine – whereby in 337 the emperor Constantine had supposedly granted Rome and all the western regions to the pope following his decision to administer his empire from Byzantium – but this had long since been proved a forgery dating from the eighth century. Besides, seventeenth-century English Protestants would have been quick to deny that the popes had ever enjoyed any right to temporal jurisdiction.[39] The English therefore chose to base their claim to Ireland ultimately on the right of conquest, which had begun with the Anglo-Norman invasion of 1169 – although it was not to be until 1603 that effective English rule was extended over the whole isle. Henry II had set himself up as feudal overlord of the isle; it was only in Henry VIII's reign that the English king also took on the title of king of Ireland. By an act of 1541 the Irish crown was established as an 'imperial crown', possessing 'all maner honours, prerogatives, dignities and other things whatsoever' belonging 'to the estate and majestie of a King imperiall', but one which was nevertheless 'united and knit to the imperial crown of England'. It was, in other words, an independent crown that went with the job of being king of England.[40]

The act of 1541 embodied the crucial ambiguity that underlay the nature of the relationship between England and Ireland throughout the early modern period: were they two independent kingdoms, or was Ireland merely a colonial dependency of England, rather like Virginia? At first glance, the colonial analogy seems to fit well: Ireland was settled by people from the English mainland who expropriated the land from the natives, and it was ruled by the English in the interests of England, who treated Ireland in much the same way as they treated the American colonies. Yet Ireland was not strictly speaking a colony. The native Irish, unlike their American counterparts, were full subjects of the crown, and were even given feudal titles.[41] Moreover, Ireland possessed its own government and had its own parliament, though Poynings' Law of 1494, most famously, had established that the Irish parliament could not enact legislation unless this had been first approved by the English king and council.[42]

The Irish parliament itself was modelled on the English one: it was bicameral, with a House of Lords (lay and ecclesiastical) and a House of Commons elected by the counties and boroughs, which returned two members each. There were 22 lords spiritual (18 bishops and 4 archbishops), and in 1681 some 119 Irish temporal peers. There were 32 counties, but the crown increased the number of borough seats dramatically over the course of the seventeenth century, in order to assure a Protestant ascendancy in the Commons. Thus the Commons grew in size from 76 in 1560 (when only 10 of the then 20 counties received writs of election), to 232 by 1613, to 276 by 1666 and to 300 after the Glorious Revolution.[43] Like England, Ireland had a 40-shilling-freeholder franchise in the counties and a variety of franchises in the boroughs. By 1692 there were 117 borough constituencies; in 55 of these the right to return MPs lay with members of the corporation; in 36 with the freemen; while there were 12 potwalloper boroughs (a potwalloper being anyone not in receipt of arms or charity), 8 county boroughs and 6 manor boroughs. Trinity College, Dublin, also returned two MPs, elected by the fellows and scholars.[44]

Some ambiguity existed over the extent to which legislation enacted by the English parliament was binding in Ireland. The English parliament had typically claimed that it was; those in Ireland tended to take the line that this was the case only if such legislation was sub-

sequently allowed and published by the parliament in Ireland. In
1441–2 the English judicial bench had resolved that the English parliament did not have the right to tax Ireland – that much, at least,
seemed clear. However, in Calvin's Case (1608) Sir Edward Coke had
affirmed, though in mere *obiter dicta* rather than a judicial ruling,
that 'albeit Ireland was a distinct dominion, yet the title thereof being
by conquest, Ireland might by express words be bound by the Acts of
the Parliament of England.' By contrast, however, in 1641 the Irish
House of Commons passed a resolution that 'the subjects of His
Majesty's Kingdom of Ireland' were 'a free people, and to be governed
only according to the Common Law of England and Statutes made
and established by Parliaments in Ireland'. It was an issue that
remained unresolved during the Restoration. In 1685 Lord Guilford,
the Lord Keeper, advised the new Lord Lieutenant of Ireland, the second Earl of Clarendon, that Ireland was 'a kingdom subordinate to
England in so absolute a manner, that the King in his Parliament of
England, may make laws that shall be binding in Ireland'. This ability,
Guilford asserted, was inherent in the king as conqueror of Ireland.
Having made a seemingly unambiguous statement, however, he
clouded the issue by conceding that, because the people of Ireland did
not have 'representatives in the Parliament of England', it was unreasonable for the parliament of England to 'give away their money, or
make any laws to change property'.[45]

The attitude of the native Irish to the English crown was likewise
ambivalent. Many undoubtedly resented the English presence within
their own country; indeed, in Tudor times there had been a number of
rebellions against English rule. Following the failed Reformation in
Ireland of the sixteenth century, and the subsequent supplanting of
the Catholic Old English ruling elite with a new Protestant interest
from England, many of the Old English came to share the same
resentment, and even began to think of themselves as Irish, having the
same interests and concerns as their fellow Catholics among the
Gaelic Irish. Lord Guilford told Clarendon in 1685 that 'Ireland being
thus in subjection, not only to the King, but to the crown of England',
it was 'natural and necessary to believe, that the Irish' – by whom he
meant the Catholics of Ireland – 'will have an aversion to the English,
and their government; and if ever they can have it in their power, they

will shake it off'.[46] Yet with the accession of the Scottish house of Stuart to the English throne, in 1603, the Gaelic Irish came to feel that they at last had 'a monarch of their own race and blood', since the kings of Scotland were supposedly descended from the ancient kings of Ireland; according to this myth-history, James I was 'a Prince not only of Irish extraction', but also 'of the Royal Line', who, 'even, by the Irish Law, ought to be King of that Island'.[47] For most of the seventeenth century the majority of Irish Catholics (both Gaelic Irish and Old English) professed loyalty to the English king, and even, with some justice, claimed to be more loyal than the English themselves.[48]

Of the three Stuart kingdoms, England was both the largest – with a population of about 5.47 million in 1656 (though the second half of the seventeenth century saw demographic stagnation and even a slight decline)[49] – and ethnically and culturally the most homogenous. Although regional accents were marked, and many people in the localities would have felt a powerful sense of attachment to their county, region or town, most also had a strong sense of being English – an identity that was reinforced by the English common-law system, which applied uniformly throughout the realm – and of possessing certain rights and liberties as Englishmen. Wales, with its population of about 371,000, complicates the picture. Welshmen were guaranteed the same rights as Englishmen under English common law, yet three-quarters of them spoke Welsh as their language of choice.[50]

Both England and Wales were divided along religious lines, between members of the Established Church, various types of Protestant nonconformists (Presbyterians, Independents, Baptists and Quakers) and Roman Catholics. Catholics were the smallest religious minority, comprising only 1.2 per cent of the population. They were strongest in the north-west (Lancashire and Cheshire), in parts of the West Midlands and in the Welsh borderlands (notably Herefordshire and Monmouthshire), and there was also a sizeable Catholic population in certain areas of the London metropolis (particularly the western suburbs and the city of Westminster).[51] A religious census carried out by Bishop Henry Compton of London in 1676 found that Protestant nonconformists numbered just under 5 per cent of the population, although this is now accepted to be a serious underestimate, since the census in the main enumerated only those who had separated completely from the Church of England (such as the Baptists and Quakers), ignoring occasional conformists, partial conformists and occasional nonconformists, who divided their time between conventicles and the Established Church. Recent research has shown that nonconformity was geographically and sociologically widespread: it could be found in both town and countryside, in the north, south, east and west, and among all classes of people (from the landed elite, through to the professional and mercantile middle classes, down to the trading, manufacturing and labouring lower orders), and most conformist Protestants, regardless of where they lived, would have known dissenters. Having said that, there were some areas with particularly heavy concentrations: between 25 and 40 per cent of the population of Coventry (in the West Midlands) were nonconformists, as were over 33 per cent of the inhabitants of Lewes (Sussex), and somewhere in the region of 15–20 per cent of those who lived in London. Dissent may have tended to flourish more in urban environments – there was a significant dissenting presence in England's second and third cities, Norwich and Bristol, as well as in many other corporations, while in the countryside we often find that dissent was strong in areas of rural industry (such as the cloth-producing region of Wiltshire) – though local historians have warned against too reductionist an association of dissent with trade.[52]

Scotland had a population of about 1.23 million in 1691.[53] Linguistically and culturally, it was divided between the Gaelic-speaking peoples of the Highlands and the English-speaking Lowlanders. The Highlanders were an outgroup in this society, regarded as violent, uncivilized and prone to crime by the Lowlanders, who felt a stronger sense of identity with their English neighbours south of the border.[54] The Earl of Cassillis, a Lowland gentleman from Ayrshire, described the Highlanders in early 1678 as people who had 'nothing to shew they are Men, but the external Figure', since they differed 'in Habit, Language, and Manners, from all Mankind'.[55] There was a small Catholic minority in Scotland, with professed Catholics constituting less than 2 per cent of the total population in 1681 and concentrated overwhelmingly in the Highlands and Islands.[56] The Protestant majority, however, was split between Presbyterians, who were strongest in the south and west, and episcopalians, who predominated in the area north of the Tay.[57]

In Ireland we can identify at least eight distinct though overlapping interests in the later seventeenth century: the native or Gaelic Irish; the Old English, the descendants of the original Anglo-Norman settlers, the vast majority of whom remained attached to the pre-Reformation Church; the New English, who had come in various waves since the Reformation; the Scottish settlers, based predominantly in Ulster; the Catholic Church; the established Protestant Church; Protestant nonconformists; and the crown itself.[58] Even this typology does not do justice to the complexity of the situation. There were different types of New English interest, for example: the parliamentarian and Cromwellian soldiers and adventurers of the 1640s and 1650s had often acquired land at the expense of earlier Elizabethan and Jacobean Protestant settlers. The Catholics were divided between those who were willing to accept the supremacy of the English king and those who were not; the Protestant nonconformists comprised Scottish Presbyterians, English Presbyterians, Independents, Quakers, and Huguenot refugees from France. The native Irish and the Old English tended to be Catholic, and the New English and Scots to be Protestant – though some Old English and even some native Irish did convert to Protestantism, and some newcomers became Roman Catholics.[59] The total population of Ireland was about 1.7 million in 1672 (a decline from 2.1 million in 1641), rising to 2.2 million by 1687; roughly speaking, about three-quarters of these were Catholics, while the remainder were divided fairly evenly between Protestants of the Established Church, Scottish Presbyterians, and other Protestant dissenters (although the proportion of Scottish Presbyterians did rise during the 1670s and 1680s, owing to the influx of covenanters fleeing persecution in their homeland).[60] The precise balance, however, varied considerably from region to region. The vast majority of the Scottish Presbyterians, for example, were concentrated in Ulster, making them a very significant presence in this province; it has been estimated that between 43 and 45 per cent of the populations of the counties of Antrim, Londonderry and Down were Presbyterians.[61]

Earlier Anglo-Norman and English settlers may have regarded the Gaelic Irish as a race apart – and racially inferior[62] – but later-seventeenth-century English commentators appear not to have done.

The English certainly thought the Irish were backward and intellectu-
ally inferior. Discussing the Irish Cattle Bill in the English House of
Lords in 1666, the Duke of Buckingham asserted that he thought its
merits so transparent that any who opposed it must have either 'Irish
estates or Irish understandings', while one English writer, poking fun
at what he saw as the self-contradictory arguments of a pamphlet
written in defence of the Catholic Earl of Tyrconnell's government of
Ireland under James II, referred to his antagonist's 'Excellent Irish
Logick' before condemning 'The Irish' as 'a slothful and Idle people'.[63]
The second Earl of Clarendon, when he conducted a tour of the countryside surrounding Dublin in May 1686, found the natives to be lazy
and immoral, to live in houses no better than pigsties, and to 'work
never but when they are ready to starve'.[64] Yet the difference was coming to be seen as cultural and religious, rather than racial. Sir Richard
Cox, the Anglo-Protestant recorder of Cork, in his history of Ireland
written at the time of the Glorious Revolution, denied that the Irish
were 'a pure and ancient Nation' but instead concluded that they were
'a mingled People of Britons, Gauls, Spaniards and Easterlings', with
'most of the Original Inhabitants of Ireland' coming 'out of Britain'. In
short, the Irish were no other than 'Ancient Inhabitants of England'.
Many of the earlier generations of English settlers, moreover, had
intermarried with the native Irish, adopting their customs and manners and even their names. There was 'hardly a Gentleman among
them', Cox believed, who had not 'English Blood in his Veins'. Cox
attributed 'the Ignorance and Barbarity of the Irish meerly to their evil
Customs', among which he included their religion, which was 'no
more than Ignorant Superstition' – a statement which likewise condemned those of Anglo-Norman or Old English descent who had
become assimilated to Irish ways and continued to adhere to the old
faith.[65] Cox was writing propaganda at the time of the Williamite war
for the reconquest of Ireland, and wanted to tar all the Roman
Catholic supporters of James II with one brush. He did, moreover,
concede that, while the Old English endeavoured to bury the differences between themselves and the natives, the native Irish tried to keep
them up. Yet even the Gaelic Irish were coming to recognize that the
distinctions had become blurred. Thus Charles O'Kelly, a Gaelic land-
owner writing after the Revolution, talked about how, as a result of

intermarriage and a common commitment to the defence of the Catholic faith, the Old English and the native Irish 'blended together, and became an united nation', cemented by 'community of blood and interest'. O'Kelly still exhibited a tendency to talk about '*both* races of the Irish, or those of aboriginal and colonial descent'; what is significant is that he regarded both as Irish.[66] Similarly, another Jacobite historian, though one writing from the perspective of the Old English interest in Ireland, explained that by the term 'the nation of Ireland' he understood the 'Irish Catholics'.[67]

REVOLUTIONS

To what extent is it legitimate to describe the upheavals which occurred in the three Stuart kingdoms in the later seventeenth century as revolutions? In the first place, it needs to be pointed out that contemporaries described them as such. On 2 November 1688, before William's landing at Torbay, John Evelyn could write to Samuel Pepys about 'the impendent Revolution', which he thought could not 'but produce great Alterations and Changes amongst us'; in a subsequent letter to Pepys of 12 December 1688, 'Upon the great convulsion of State upon the King's withdrawing', Evelyn could speak of 'this prodigious Revolution'.[68] For Narcissus Luttrell, writing in 1689, it was 'this great revolution'.[69] A poem of 1689, set as a dialogue between the ghosts of William Lord Russell and Algernon Sidney (two Whig radicals executed for treason in 1683), has Russell ask Sidney, 'What thinkst thou of the Earth / And the Great Revolution that lately gave Birth?'[70] The author of a 1690 history of 'the Late Great Revolution in England and Scotland' described it as 'the Greatest Revolution in the World'.[71]

The term 'revolution' possessed a number of different resonances in the later seventeenth century. One meaning derived from astronomy, as in the revolutions of the planets, and therefore carried the implication of coming full cycle or returning to the *status quo ante*. The Restoration of 1660 was thus sometimes styled a revolution by contemporaries precisely because it marked an attempt to restore the pre-Civil War order. For example, in 1684 the high-Anglican cleric

George Hickes referred to the Restoration as 'the wonderful Revolution from our Slavery and Captivity'. Sir Richard Cox, writing in 1692 about the events of 1659–60 in Ireland, observed how 'the People being weary of so many Alterations and Changes . . . were generally inclined to the King's Restauration,' an occurrence he styled a 'great Revolution'.[72] It was in this sense, it has been suggested, that the events of 1688–9 were regarded by contemporaries as constituting a revolution: a vindication of ancient rights and liberties after the illegal innovations of James II.[73] Yet it is by no means clear that all contemporaries would have understood a revolution as being a restoration. Sir Richard Temple, in an unpublished work written in defence of mixed monarchy dating from the later Stuart period, seemed to draw an explicit distinction between a revolution and a return to the *status quo ante*. Thus he postulated that 'where the Government gives contentment to al [*sic*] estates, though if one or two of the Estates may sometimes attempt upon the other, and so produce great revolutions, yet will the Government return to its Old Course, as the experience which wee have had since the Conquest doeth abundantly shew.'[74] John Locke, discussing people's general aversion to change in his *Second Treatise of Government* (published after the Glorious Revolution, though written before), observed how in 'the many Revolutions which have been seen in this Kingdom, in this and former Ages', 'after some interval of fruitless attempts' we went 'back again to our old legislature of King, Lords and Commons'; it is clear from the context that for Locke revolution was associated with change, not reverting to the old order.[75]

In fact in the later seventeenth century 'revolution' was most commonly used in the looser sense of dramatic turnaround, change or upheaval – an overturning of the way things had been previously – without any clear implication of the direction of the change. It was in this sense that contemporaries most commonly referred to the Restoration as a revolution. Thus the Scottish Lord Advocate Sir George Mackenzie of Rosehaugh, in his *Memoirs,* could refer both to 1660 and to the ministerial changes wrought by Charles II and the Earl (later Duke) of Lauderdale in Scotland in 1663 as a 'revolution'.[76] Contemporaries often expected that revolution would involve violent upheaval. For example, the Scottish minister Robert

Lawrie, preaching in Edinburgh in June 1660, was amazed by 'how sweetly' the King was brought back, since 'No man lost his goods, no man lost his life in this late revolution,' implying that one would normally have expected this to have happened.[77] Revolutions might restore an older world. Thus the contemporary Whig historian Gilbert Burnet, writing in his *History of His Own Time* about the attempt to persuade Cromwell to take the crown in the 1650s, recalled how the kingship party had insisted that 'no new government could be settled legally but by a king,' and that until they had one 'all they did was like building upon sand,' leaving them 'in danger of a revolution: and in that case all that had been done would be void of itself, as contrary to a law yet in being and not repealed'.[78] Yet revolutions could equally well push forward in new directions, or just turn things around, leaving people with no clear sense of where things were going. On hearing the news of the death of Charles II in early February 1685, one London-based correspondent wrote, 'What changes in places and offices will attend this revolution I cannot as yet see into'; he clearly did not intend to convey the impression that he thought things would come full cycle and that James would restore all those who had lost place and office under his brother.[79] Similarly, the royalist journalist Sir Roger L'Estrange, writing in 1687, described the accession in 1685 of a prince in communion with the Church of Rome as 'that Great Revolution'.[80] In June 1686 a newsletter writer, anticipating the further reforms that Tyrconnell, as lieutenant-general of the Irish army, might introduce in favour of the Catholics of Ireland, commented on how people expected 'mighty revolutions in that kingdom'.[81]

Contemporaries often referred to the upheavals of the 1640s and '50s as revolutions, and even as a revolution (in the singular). John Paterson, preaching a thanksgiving sermon in Scotland for the restoration of monarchy in 1660, condemned the types of argument that had been 'most sinfully and factiously made use of' to justify the usurpation of royal authority 'in these late Troubles and Revolutions'.[82] A loyal address from the corporation of Ripon in April 1682 proclaimed how the authors had in their thoughts 'the Miseries, Calamities and direful Revolutions of the late Times, occasioned by the Hellish and Traiterous Practices of evil Men' who overthrew the

Church of England and usurped the royal authority.[83] Lord Guilford, in warning Clarendon in 1685 of the aversion of the Irish towards the English, could affirm that this aversion was all the stronger 'because by the late Revolutions many of the Irish lost their estates'.[84] Writing in September 1686 of the 'impossibility of Pleasing the People', L'Estrange insisted that this had been discovered 'most Eminently, and Experimentally, from Forty to Sixty, through the Whole Series of That Revolution: Where Every Succeeding Usurper was Destroy'd, by Those very Arguments, Practices, Instruments, Ways, and Principles, that the Faction had Joyntly made use of, for the Common Destruction both of Church and State'.[85] James II, in later life, recalled how the revelations of the supposed Popish Plot of 1678 'had so perfect an air of the fabulous reports which proceeded the late Revolution, that those who remember'd it, thought themselves gon back to forty one'.[86]

The overlapping but discrete resonances of the term are well illustrated in a contemporary history of the Society People, the radical covenanting faction of the Presbyterians in Scotland, written by Alexander Shields shortly after the Glorious Revolution. At the beginning of his work Shields complained of the 'dreadfull and almost universall Apostacy since the last featall revolution', a reference to the restoration of monarchy and episcopacy after 1660. Writing of the autumn of 1688, when news had reached Scotland of an imminent landing of the Dutch, he observed how 'All this time the Country was full of Commotions, talkings and Rumours of Wars, Every one looking for changes and Revolutions, some hopeing for and others fearing the same,' though many of those who welcomed the Dutch, he said, 'knew not wherefor they desired them'. As he moved in transition to a discussion of events in Scotland following the landing of the Dutch, he wrote, 'In Scotland the Revolutions and changes were neither small nor few.'[87]

It was in these senses of great upheavals, or reversal of political fortunes, that the events of 1688–9 (or more properly 1688–91 once Ireland is included) were regarded as revolutions. On 18 December 1688 one correspondent of the Earl of Huntingdon's could report how over the last few weeks there had been 'such strange revolutions and changes as are to be met with in history'. '40 dayes agoe', he went on, 'The King had 3 Kingdomes in peace under his command, A Great Armie of excellent Horse and foot, A great Fleet well Manned and provided of all things necessary for his Defence' and 'many strong Forts and Port-Townes'. Yet now 'the Armies, the Fleet, the strong fortified places, all or almost all the Lords about the Town, also most of the Lords in the North and Westward' had 'declared for the Prince of Orange'; the Queen and the Prince of Wales had gone away; the King had withdrawn himself; the Lord Chancellor had been imprisoned in the Tower; and all the papists had laid down their arms and quit their commands.[88] Protestants described the attempt by the Catholics of Ireland to seize control of that kingdom over the winter of 1688–9 as a revolution – albeit a deplorable one for British Protestants – and even as a 'National Revolution'.[89] Sir Richard Cox, after the overthrow of James II in England but before the English victory at the Boyne in July 1690, could write of 'the present stupendious Revolution', before he knew even 'where these Windings and Revolutions' would end.[90]

Contemporaries clearly had the concept of a revolution that could involve a fundamental break from the past, or the traditional order of things – even a turning of the world upside down. In 1689 an English Jacobite, referring to England, complained how 'this Revolution' had established a 'New Fabric', 'breaking the very Constitution' by making 'Our Monarchs [who] were ever Sovereign and Imperial' little more than 'Dukes of Venice; the meer Puppets of the People', and forcing us 'to Dance after the Pipe of a Common-wealth'.[91] A satirical tract of that year recalled how, when he asked a dissenter his opinion of the times, an Anglican clergyman was regaled with a story about a gentlemen who, on the verge of death, instructed his relations to bury him face downward, saying 'That in a short time the World would be turned upside down, and then he should be the only Person who lay decently in his Grave'; the Anglican cleric could only retort, 'Why, I must confess there has been a considerable Revolution.'[92] In July 1693 the Scottish parliament, the body that had introduced far-reaching reforming legislation since 1689, drew up a loyal address to William III praising him 'for his Care of their Concernes in the carieing on of the Late happy revolutione'.[93]

This study, then, is about what contemporaries regarded as the revolutions of the later seventeenth century. It deals with the implications of that 'fatal revolution' of 1660, and the problems bequeathed to the Restoration polity by the Restoration settlement itself. It examines swings and reversals in the crown's political fortunes across the 1660s, '70s and '80s. It also investigates the origins and nature of the revolutions which befell King James in all three of his kingdoms in 1688–91. The seventeenth century, it is true, lacked our modern concept of revolution, which dates from the French Revolution. Nevertheless, contemporaries certainly understood revolutions as potentially involving changes that were 'neither small nor few', and perhaps even involving the establishment of an entirely 'New Fabric'.

This study will go further and argue that it is to the later seventeenth century that we need to look in order to discover the revolution – in the modern sense of the word – that truly transformed the early modern British polity. Although there remains considerable disagreement among historians of the early Stuart period over just how revolutionary the events of the 1640s and '50s were, one thing that has come to be realized in recent years is how successfully the old order was restored in 1660 – even to the point, as one historian has quipped, of restoring all the old problems.[94] It would be foolish to deny that the 1640s and '50s had any long-standing significance at all – the first two chapters of this book will examine in depth the nature of the legacy of the upheavals of mid-century and exactly what was restored in 1660. Yet the work of Stuart historians increasingly seems to indicate that the mid-century crisis did little to deflect the course of historical development of the Stuart monarchy or to redress or resolve some of the basic problems that had bedevilled the Stuart polity.[95] Charles II and James II, like James I and Charles I before them, suffered from inadequate finances, an ill-defined constitutional relationship with parliament, a contentious domestic religious situation and an unstable multiple-kingdom inheritance. A solution to all these problems was found – for better or for worse – as a result of the revolutions of 1688–91. To put it another way, if we look at England, Ireland and Scotland in the reign of Charles II and make comparisons with the situation on the eve of the Civil War, it would not immediately be apparent that a revolution had occurred in the intervening period. Yet if one were to compare the situation in all three kingdoms in 1720 with that in the 1680s it would at once be obvious that things had become radically transformed. The fact that this transformation had taken place was due in no small part to the revolutions of 1688–91.

PART ONE

From Restoration to Crisis, *c.* 1660–1681

Though Hell, Rome, and France: have United their Powers: We Defye them all Three (Sir)

Necks or Nothing I love not Crippells

A Pen for Touzer

Protest House

They must goe the Devill Drives: Tanting: Tanting: Tanting

Roome for the Church for Rome Boyes

well; well

Presbiter: the Plover: Brow

O Rare Dogg: Ha-loo Touzer.

Touzer all Bum-dogg: of the Popes: But Mastiffs Elfic'd Rare Hound: Wylie Backs & Fiddle-Strings &c

Conformitie are Reformable

A Right Roman Crucifix

Out Fanaticks in Popery

Discoveries Masquerade

PARLIAMENT'S Ours: March the 41th 1680

(preceding pages) *Prospect of a Popish Successor*: Whig print from the Exclusion Crisis which brilliantly encapsulates the central themes of Whig propaganda. The Janus-faced figure 'Mack' (i.e. Irish Catholic) is half Duke of York, half Devil, and is burning Protestants at the stake and setting fire to the City of London. To his right is a figure who is half Anglican bishop, half Pope, who is driving Protestant nonconformists out of the Church of England. Sitting astride the roof of the church is a group of Anglican clergymen riding 'Tantivy' towards the Devil – hence the origin of the nickname 'Tantivy' for a Tory clergyman. The dog to the right with a broom tied to his tail and fawning at a Jesuit represents the Tory propagandist Roger L'Estrange, whose publisher was Henry Brome.

I

The Nation Would Not Stand Long

Weaknesses of the Restoration
Monarchy in England

*I ever thought that the Methods us'd in King Charles's Reign,
to introduce Popery and Slavery, were a thousand times better
laid, and more natural to effectuate the Design, than those
afterwards made use of by King James. The one was too bare
fac'd, and obvious to every Bodies Reason; but the other was
of a finer Texture, and not so easily discerned, though far
more dangerous.*[1]

The Restoration of monarchy in the spring of 1660, contemporaries
and modern historians alike agree, was popular. Republicanism had
had shallow roots in England, and, although Oliver Cromwell managed to hold things together reasonably well until his death in
September 1658, it proved impossible to establish a credible regime
following the fall of the Protectorate with the resignation of Oliver's
son Richard in May 1659. First the Rump Parliament was recalled
(May), next the republican army seized power (October), then the
Rump was restored again (December), and by the end of the year
England seemed to be drifting into anarchy. In the autumn and winter of 1659–60 there was considerable agitation out-of-doors – in the
form of demonstrations, riots and petitions – against rule by the
army and the Rump as people campaigned for a full and free parliament and a return to constitutional propriety. The English were
finally put out of their misery by General Monck, commander of the
forces in Scotland, who marched into England on 1 January and
headed for London, where he forced the Rump to readmit the
secluded members (February) and then vote for its own dissolution

(March), thereby paving the way for the calling of the Convention (April) which everyone knew would call back the King. Yet in carrying out these actions Monck was as much responding to popular pressure as pursuing any clear agenda of his own; in that sense the Restoration happened because people wanted it to, and most were glad to see the final demise of the republic. When Charles II was solemnly proclaimed king in Boston, Lincolnshire, in the second week of May, the 'yonge men' of the town took down 'the States armes' and proceeded to drag them up and down the streets, first having the beadles whip them, before they in turn 'pissed and sh[itted] on [them]', 'such was there malice to the States armes in that towne'; only then was the sordid debris thrown on to the bonfires which the locals had made 'for joy' at the recalling of the King.[2] Charles's eventual return to England at the end of the month prompted enthusiastic rejoicing throughout the realm; the Kentish gentleman Sir Edward Dering recorded in his diary that he believed 'there never was in any nation so much joy both inwardly felt and outwardly expresst, as was in this Kingdom from the day of His Majestie landing at Dover' on 25 May 'to his coming to London' on the 29th.[3] There were similar scenes throughout the three kingdoms. According to an account written by an Irish Jacobite of Old English stock in the early eighteenth century, there was 'nothing now to be seen or heard but joys and jubilees throughout the British empire, for the royal physician [was] come to heal the three bleeding nations, and to give them the life of freeborn subjects'.[4]

Charles II had tried to cement his popularity by appearing to be all things to all men. Thus in a declaration issued from Breda in the Low Countries on 4 April 1660, just before his restoration, he had promised to heal the wounds which had been kept bleeding for so long by offering 'a free and general Pardon' to all supporters of the republic (save those who might subsequently be excepted by parliament) and 'a Liberty to tender Consciences'.[5] The trouble was, the royal physician was unable to effect a cure – a failure that was all too apparent by the late 1670s. In June 1677 the radical prophetess Anne Wentworth heard 'a most dreadfull and terrible voyce' warning that there would soon be 'an overturning . . . in this Nation', which would not 'stand long as it is'.[6] Over the next several months she received several revelations concerning the imminent day of judgement, which would affect not just England, but 'all Europe', including also Scotland and Ireland. Thus on 8 October 1678 she foretold how 'In Scotland Judgments first there begun, / But upon England greater now will come,' and how 'Ireland surely will also deeply suffer then,' as likewise Holland, France, Italy, and Spain, none of which would be able to gain 'by all our loss'.[7] Wentworth believed that God's wrath was about to fall upon these nations for their ungodliness, and that Jesus Christ would come to the rescue of the oppressed minority who were the true believers. To us she might seem like a crank; most of her contemporaries condemned her as 'a Proud, Passionate, Revengeful, Discontented, and Mad Woman'.[8] Yet in crucial respects she was to be proved correct, if not quite in the way she predicted. By 1677–8 the Restoration regime did appear to be slipping into crisis, and there were many who were coming to feel that the nation could not 'stand long as it is'. There were to be great overturnings, not just in England, but also in Scotland and Ireland, over the next dozen or so years – 'mighty Revolutions', as contemporaries observed;[9] yet, despite this, none of the great powers of Europe was to profit at England's expense.

The purpose of this and the next chapter is to explore how 1660 became 1677–8: that is, to investigate how it was that a regime that had seemed overwhelmingly popular at the time of the Restoration could seem on the verge of falling apart by the eve of the Exclusion Crisis. What, exactly, had gone wrong? The present chapter will focus on the problems facing the restored monarchy in England. Three main factors, it will be suggested, contributed to the weakness of the restored monarchy in England: a legacy of political and religious division, a lack of effective royal power, and a loss of prestige. The following chapter will deal with Scotland and Ireland, in order to highlight the different sorts of problem that the restored monarch faced in his other kingdoms, as well as the ways in which the difficulties bequeathed by Charles's multiple-kingdom inheritance created problems that were of a genuinely British nature.

THE POLITICAL AND RELIGIOUS LEGACY OF THE CIVIL WAR AND INTERREGNUM

Restoration England was a society that desperately wanted to be able to forget its past, but which forever remained haunted by it. Most will have an image of an England after 1660 reacting against the austerities of Puritan rule, presided over by a 'merry monarch' (albeit one leaning towards the debauched) determined never to go on his travels again but who at the same time was going to enjoy himself after his years in exile. Things that had been out of fashion or proscribed for so long were immediately brought back – such as Christmas, maypoles and the theatre (now with actual women playing the female parts). In short, people were allowed to have fun again – and more. Indeed, in this respect, the Restoration did not so much restore an old cultural world as usher in a new era whose hedonism far exceeded anything that had been seen before the outbreak of the Civil War. At the centre of this world was a libertine court – a society of Restoration rakes given more to drinking, gambling, swearing and whoring than to godliness – presided over by the King himself and his equally rakish brother, James, Duke of York.

The contemporary Whig historian Gilbert Burnet – one of William III's propaganda geniuses, who was to become Bishop of Salisbury after the Glorious Revolution but who had briefly served as a royal chaplain under Charles II – later wrote that 'the ruin of [Charles's] reign, and of all his affairs, was occasioned chiefly by his delivering himself up at his first coming over to a mad range of pleasure.' Nevertheless, Burnet was balanced enough to recognize that Charles possessed a number of positive attributes. It was true the King had 'no sense of religion' – although Charles 'was no atheist', Burnet wrote, 'he could not think God would make a man miserable, only for taking a little pleasure out of the way.' However, he 'had a very good understanding', and 'knew well the state of affairs both at home and abroad', while 'his apprehension was quick, and his memory good'. He also 'had a softness of temper that charmed all who came near him', and 'was affable and easy'.[10] Charles II was clearly possessed of certain personality traits – intelligence, quick-wittedness and flexibility – that his father had lacked;

although Charles II may have been less fit than Charles I morally speaking, he was arguably more fit to be a king.[11] Whatever the personal attributes of the man at the helm, however, he was always going to face difficulties because of the troubled legacy bequeathed by the experiences of the 1640s and '50s. Could a way be found of, if not forgetting the past, then at least living with it?

Politically, the Restoration was a self-conscious attempt to put the clock back. Charles II's rule was dated as having begun immediately upon the demise of his father in January 1649; for the legal record, 1660 became the twelfth year of the new king's reign. Likewise, the English Convention which recalled Charles II did not impose any conditions on the restored monarch; it simply sought to return to the position on the eve of the Civil War – the last time a valid constitutional framework could be said to have existed – and start all over again. Thus all innovations that had been introduced without the King's free consent were deemed null and void; constitutionally, it was as if the last nineteen years had never happened. However, this did mean that the reforming legislation passed during the early months of the Long Parliament back in 1641 remained on the books. This left the crown shorn of prerogative courts such as Star Chamber and High Commission, and also of the ability to raise extra-parliamentary levies (such as ship money) during times of emergency. The desire to return to constitutional propriety helps explains why, in the end, the Convention chose not to exact any concessions from Charles as the price of his restoration. Since it had not been called by the King, the Convention was not a legal parliament; any measures it passed might therefore be deemed null and void once the King was restored. By a similar logic, it had no power to undo the reforms of 1641. The working-out of the political and religious settlement, and any further reforms or additional legislation that might be needed, would have to wait until monarchy had been restored and a legal parliament had been brought into being. The Convention made a start once the royal assent had been received to a bill declaring it to be a full and legal parliament in June.[12] Its most noteworthy achievement was the passage of a generous Act of Indemnity and Oblivion in August, offering pardon for crimes committed against the monarchy over the past two decades. The act exempted a mere thirty-three individuals from the pardon, of whom only a third were executed;[13] this did enough to satisfy the nation's thirst for revenge without instigating the type of bloodbath that might have been counterproductive. One of the last acts of the Convention was to order the exhumation of the bodies of Oliver Cromwell, Henry Ireton, Thomas Pride and John Bradshaw, so that they could be duly hanged and decapitated for their role in the regicide – a sentence which was carried out on 30 January 1661.[14] The main task of sorting out the details of the Restoration settlement in Church and state, however, was left to the Cavalier Parliament, which sat from May 1661 – a proper parliament, called in constitutionally correct circumstances, that could choose to usher in a new beginning or to restore more of the past, depending upon what the King, Lords and Commons saw fit.[15]

Although rejoicing at the return of the monarchy was widespread, it was not universal. In Lincolnshire, as most locals celebrated following the official proclaiming of Charles II in the second week of May, Mr Vincent, the minister of Cawthorpe and Covenham, tried to extinguish his neighbourhood bonfire, kicking the fire about with his feet and proclaiming, 'Stay! The rogue is not yet come over.'[16] In Herefordshire, Thomas Baskerville of Eardisley, a Commonwealth JP, took a list of the names of those who made bonfires on the news of the King's arrival in England and threatened them with punishment.[17] On hearing of the King's return, Cuthbert Studholme of Carlisle decided to make haste for London, laying his hand on his sword and announcing before he left, 'This is the sword shall run Charles Stuart through the heart blood.' It was a threat the government took seriously enough to issue orders that Studholme should be immediately seized and allowed nowhere near the King.[18] Local court records provide numerous examples of individuals accused of speaking out against the restoration of monarchy. On 22 May 1660 Edward and Alice Jones, a shoemaker and his wife from Westminster, acknowledged 'it was the King's time now to raigne,' but believed 'it was upon sufferance for a little time, and it would be theirs agine before itt be long.' Others from the greater London area – presumably former Cromwellian soldiers – threatened that, given the opportunity, they would run the King through with their rusty old weapons.[19] In the north of England an indictment was pressed against Margaret Dixon of Newcastle upon

Tyne for allegedly saying on 13 May 1660, 'What! can they finde noe other man to bring in then a Scotsman. What! is there not some Englishman more fit to make a King then a Scott?' She clearly did not have a very high opinion of Charles Stuart: 'There is none that loves him but drunk whores and whoremongers,' she averred. 'I hope he will never come into England, for that hee will sett on fire the three kingdoms as his father before him has done. God's curse light on him. I hope to see his bones hanged at a horse tayle, and the dogs runn through his puddins.' One Richard Abbott appeared before the northern assize circuit for saying on 20 May, 'If I had but one batt in my belly, I would give it to keep the King out, for Cromwell ruled better than ever the King will.' Puritan divine John Botts predicted in a sermon delivered at Darfield church in Yorkshire on 13 May that 'the man . . . the Parliament were about to bring in, would bring in superstition and Popery' and urged his congregation to 'feare the King of heaven and worship Him, and bee not so desirous of an earthly King, which will tend to the imbroileing of us againe in blood.'[20] Similar sentiments can be detected in most parts of the country – from the south-east to the West Country, through the Midlands to the far north – though the survival of the relevant court records is too patchy to allow any systematic analysis.[21]

The government received numerous reports of alleged plots against the monarchy by disaffected radicals across the country in the early years of the Restoration. However, it is difficult to know how widespread popular disaffection was. Some of those accused of seditious activity were victims of malicious prosecution, while a number of the rumoured plots were no more than fabrications by unscrupulous paid informers trying to feed off the government's own insecurities in an attempt to make money. There were, of course, some genuine conspiracies, but they were hardly of a scale to cause serious trouble to the security of the new regime. Thus there was a small uprising of perhaps some fifty Fifth Monarchists in London in January 1661, and a somewhat larger, though equally ineffective, rising in Yorkshire in 1663. But most historians remain sceptical about the extent of the survival of republican sentiment after 1660.[22]

Two points need to be made, however. The first is that, although those who were never able to accept the return of monarchy probably never posed much of a real threat to the security of the restored regime, they did succeed in frightening the government. The Restoration monarchy lived in continual fear that erstwhile supporters or clients of the old republican or Cromwellian regimes might rise in arms against it, and was particularly worried about the possibility that discontented elements in England might combine with the disaffected in Scotland and Ireland to mount a more significant challenge. This conditioned the Restoration regime's attitude towards questions of security, and helps explain why there was a desire to have a reliable, professional army in all three kingdoms to prevent any possible rumblings, why the authorities were so concerned about the problem of dissent (since most of the radicals were dissenters), and why there was a tendency to take an unduly harsh approach to the suppression of crowd unrest if there was ever the slightest suspicion that republican elements might be involved.[23] The second point is to warn against any desire to label critics of royal government according to a professed preference for a specific type of political arrangement in the state, such as a monarchy or a republic, and from that to assume that if fewer people seemed to be advocating a republic after 1660 then the platform of the so-called republicans of the 1650s must have been becoming less popular. Instead, we need to deconstruct what the political and religious opponents of the Stuart monarchy stood for, and recognize that they might endorse different political solutions, at different junctures, in order to achieve the same goals. In the context of the late 1640s and the 1650s, a settlement in which there was no hereditary monarch seemed to many radicals the best strategy to pursue – and it became a viable option after Colonel Pride's purge of the Long Parliament in December 1648. In the changed context of the Restoration, seeking the abolition of monarchy made little practical sense. Yet there were still many who continued to promote the cause of greater political, religious and economic liberty and justice, and who challenged the authority structures in both Church and state, even if they accommodated themselves to working within a monarchical framework. In other words, the champions of the 'Good Old Cause' might have come to favour a republic in the 1650s, whereas after 1660 support for a republic might have all but disappeared, but this should not lead us to conclude that support for the 'Good Old Cause' had necessarily all but disappeared.[24]

Even though the out-and-out republicans were a small minority, it should not be assumed that the desire to bring back the monarchy reflected the existence of a political consensus. There were some – mainly Presbyterians and old Puritans – who would have liked to have seen the monarchy reconstructed and stripped of many of its prerogatives, along the lines of the Treaty of Newport of 1648, which had proposed giving parliament control over the militia and the right of appointment to all offices of state. In this camp were influential Presbyterian peers such as the earls of Manchester, Bedford, Anglesey and Northampton, as well as commoners like Sir Gilbert Gerard, Sir Harbottle Grimston, Sir Denzil Holles and Sir Anthony Ashley Cooper (the future Earl of Shaftesbury). Then there were ultra-royalists – men like the Earl of Peterborough, Charles Berkeley and Henry Bennet (later Earl of Arlington) – who wanted to reinvest the crown with all the powers it had enjoyed in the 1630s, undoing the reforms of 1641. Proposals made in the early 1660s that Star Chamber should be revived came to nothing, though in 1664 the Triennial Act of 1641, which had compelled the king to call parliament every three years (and required the sheriffs to issue election writs if the king failed to do so) was repealed, and replaced by a measure which, while still stipulating that parliaments should be called at least once every three years, removed the machinery whereby this could be enforced. Tensions survived in the Restoration era, therefore, between those who believed that the authority of the crown should be limited and those who wanted to see it strengthened. Moreover, the nature of the relationship between the crown and parliament remained ambiguous as a result of differing interpretations as to what had actually happened when the monarchy was restored. To some it seemed obvious that the Convention had called back the King, with the implication that parliament, ultimately, was supreme. Anglican-royalists, however, tended to the view that the King had been restored by divine providence, and that the Convention had simply acknowledged Charles's rightful position as king, which he had technically been since the execution of his father on 30 January 1649.[25] Indeed, an act of August 1660, ordaining that 29 May (Charles's birthday and day of restoration) be kept as 'a Perpetual Anniversary Thanksgiving', declared that it was 'Almighty God' who 'by his all-swaying providence and power' had brought about 'his Majesty's late most wonderful, glorious, peaceable and joyful restoration'.[26]

The biggest source of contention was religion. The Restoration occurred in a climate of intense reaction against the sects, as reflected by many of the petitions of late 1659 and early 1660 against the army and the Rump, and also a number of crowd attacks on Baptist and Quaker meetings at this time.[27] Yet, beyond the desire to be rid of the sects, there was consensus on little else. Anglicans wanted the restoration of the old Church of the bishops and the Prayer Book. Indeed, without waiting to see what the settlement in the Church would be, episcopalians began to revive the Book of Common Prayer service, even before the King's return, and Anglican ministers took repossession of the livings they felt had been illegally taken from them during the Interregnum. The lead may have been taken by the Anglican gentry and the clergy, but there is plenty of evidence of grass-roots Anglicanism, as people welcomed back their old ministers, pranced around maypoles as a way of taunting the Presbyterians and Independents, rejoiced as local communities burned copies of the Solemn League and Covenant in accordance with a parliamentary proclamation of May 1661, and even enthusiastically cheered their bishops when they ventured back into their dioceses.[28] The Presbyterians, by contrast, although they recognized that the bishops would return, argued for limited episcopacy and some concessions to the Puritan reformist agenda, in the hope of comprehending as many as possible within the Church establishment. Indeed, some of the petitions against army rule of late 1659 seemed to intimate a Presbyterian reform agenda: that from the London apprentices of 15 November, for example, called for the restoration of the religion established by 'our three last Princes, with some amendment in Discipline'.[29] Yet, although the Presbyterians wanted comprehension, they did not, any more than the Anglicans, think it appropriate to tolerate those who worshipped outside the Church. Separatists, quite naturally, hoped at least to be allowed to worship freely, according to the dictates of their conscience. They thus put their faith in the promise which Charles had made in his declaration from Breda of April 1660 to grant 'a Liberty to tender Consciences'.

In the end, the Anglican vision won out. A narrow and intolerant episcopalian Church was re-established, backed up by a severe penal code – known to history, somewhat misleadingly, as the Clarendon Code, after Charles's leading minister of the period 1660–67, the first Earl of Clarendon – designed to guarantee an Anglican monopoly of office-holding, worship and education. The first measure came in December 1661, when parliament passed a Corporation Act stipulating that all municipal office-holders take the Anglican sacrament and renounce the Presbyterian Covenant. This was followed in May 1662 by the Act of Uniformity, which required all clergymen and teachers (from the masters and fellows of Oxbridge colleges down to village schoolmasters and private instructors and tutors) to conform to the liturgy of the Church of England, as prescribed by the Book of Common Prayer, and to renounce the Presbyterian Covenant, setting a deadline for compliance of 24 August (St Bartholomew's Day). Nearly 1,000 ministers – roughly 10 per cent of the clergy – found themselves unable to comply and were forced to give up their livings, among them many Presbyterians and moderate Puritans who would have preferred to remain part of the national Church. Separatist religious meetings were outlawed first by the Quaker Act of 1662, followed two years later by a somewhat broader Conventicle Act, which was to last for three years after the end of the parliamentary session in which it was passed and which provided for a series of escalating fines for any who attended nonconformist religious meetings – £5 (or three months' imprisonment) for the first offence, £10 (or six months' imprisonment) for the second, and £100 (or transportation) for the third. A second Conventicle Act, passed in 1670, reduced the fines for those who merely attended nonconformist conventicles (to 5 shillings for the first offence, 10 shillings thereafter), but laid down stiff penalties (£20 for the first offence, £40 thereafter) for those who preached at nonconformist meetings or allowed such meetings to be held in their houses. To stop ejected ministers from continuing to serve their old flocks or else establishing new congregations in major population centres, the Five Mile Act of 1665 forbade them from residing within 5 miles of their old parish or any corporate town.[30]

In addition to the new legislation, the pre-Civil War laws against recusants and separatists remained on the statute book. Most of these had been aimed against Roman Catholics, but there was also scope for their employment against Protestant nonconformists. The most hated of such measures was an act of 1593 (35 Elizabeth) stipulating that those convicted of not coming to church or of holding separatist religious meetings had either to conform within three months or abjure the realm, forfeiting their lands and goods to the crown, with failure to abjure being a capital offence.[31] As concerns grew about the threat of popery in the 1670s, parliament decided to introduce a religious test for office to protect the political establishment from subversion by Catholics, though in the process it imposed further disabilities on Protestant dissenters as well. Thus the Test Act of 1673 required all office-holders under the crown to take the Anglican sacrament and make a declaration against transubstantiation. A further Test Act of 1678 disabled all Roman Catholics from sitting in either house of parliament, although the King's brother and heir to the throne, the Duke of York, was excluded from its provisions.[32]

The Restoration settlement in the Church, it has been argued, was a victory for the Anglican squirearchy that dominated the Cavalier Parliament elected in 1661.[33] Yet, although there was considerable agreement in this parliament concerning the need for harsh measures against separatists, legislation aimed at moderate dissenters proved more controversial and was passed only after close divisions.[34] The divide that emerged in Restoration politics, in other words, was not a simple one between Anglicans and dissenters, but depended upon where one stood on the issue of dissent. Some Anglicans were sympathetic to the plight of dissenters, and favoured a relaxation of the penal laws against fellow Protestants; others were fiercely intolerant, and believed in the need for a strict enforcement of all laws against all forms of religious nonconformity. Nor was the dividing line between these two types absolute; attitudes towards dissent shifted over time, according to political contingency – normally dependent upon whether the greatest threat to the Established Church at any given time was perceived as coming from Catholics or from Protestant nonconformists. Such considerations explain why it is so difficult to calculate the size of the dissenting interest in Restoration England. Out-and-out separatists may well have been a small minority, as the Compton Census of 1676 alleged. When we include those who identified with the dissenters or sympathized with their plight – because they were old Puritans themselves, were partial conformists or occasional nonconformists, had nonconformist relatives or friends (or even business associates) or had come to believe (in a given political context) that the persecution of dissenters was undesirable – then the proportion becomes much larger.[35] The important point to understand is that the relative size of this group was never stable. Indeed, mobilizing the population at large either to be in sympathy with or to feel hostile towards the dissenters was to become one of the major political and ideological battlegrounds of the Restoration era, as will become apparent later in this book.

The argument for intolerance, furthermore, was political, not religious. Protestants did not believe in persecuting people for their religious opinions; that was a popish principle. Nonconformist conventicles were hunted down because they were regarded as nests of sedition – places where 'Seditious Sectaries and other disloyall Persons' met 'under pretence of tender Consciences' to 'contrive Insurrections', as the 1670 Conventicle Act put it.[36] The reality, however, was that most English nonconformists were not political subversives. The biggest group by far, the Presbyterians, had opposed the regicide and actively welcomed the restoration of monarchy, and most Independents, Baptists and Quakers were prepared to make their peace with the restored monarchy and merely wanted to be allowed the liberty of conscience they had been promised in Charles's Declaration of Breda. The trouble was, pursuing a policy of religious intolerance out of a fear of political subversives ran the risk of making the potentially loyal disloyal and creating the very problem that such a policy was designed to prevent.

A major problem facing Charles II in England, therefore, was that he had to rule over a divided people. Even in 1660 there was no true consensus beyond the desire to bring back the monarchy, and handling the legacy of political and religious tensions bequeathed by the Civil War would have been no easy task for any government. Things were made worse by the fact that the particular settlement reached in the Church was something that Charles himself did not want. Although personally he had little time for the Presbyterians, whom he held responsible for the outbreak of the Civil War in 1642 and hence ultimately for the death of his father, he would have preferred a more eirenic solution, so as not to unnecessarily alienate significant sections of the population right from the start. Instead, he got trapped into a partisan settlement – one that seemed to make him king not of all his subjects but only of those who conformed to the re-established Church. The issue of dissent was to prove a major source of political discord throughout his reign. The problem was that the King was in a no-win situation: a strict enforcement of the penal laws ran the risk of alienating substantial sections of the population (not just the non-conformists themselves, who might, it was feared, be pushed into rebellion, but also moderate Anglicans who felt that the measures against dissent were unduly harsh), while any moves to help the dissenters would provoke the opposition of the Anglican hardliners, whose support no restoration monarch could afford to lose.

CONSTRAINTS ON ROYAL POWER

Let us now move to a consideration of the nature and extent of royal power in Restoration England. Many contemporaries criticized Charles for his pretensions to absolutism, or for governing in an arbitrary way. One MP suspected as early as 1663 that there was an intention 'to change the constitution of the government of this kingdom and to reduce us to the model of France [where] they have lost all their liberties, and [are] governed by an arbitrary and military power'.[37] In 1675 the Earl of Shaftesbury, who had recently fallen from grace and moved into opposition, complained of a long-standing design to make the government 'absolute and Arbitrary' and to establish rule by a standing army, while in 1677 Andrew Marvell produced his famous *Account of the Growth of Popery*, bemoaning what he saw as a drift towards popery and arbitrary government under Charles II.[38] In theory, the powers of the restored monarch appear to have been considerable. In reality, however, there remained severe constraints on what he could do in practice, especially during the 1660s and '70s, which left Charles II vulnerable to the criticisms of the competing political and religious interests identified above, and made it difficult for him to assert his own will in government and to pursue policies he saw as in the best interests of the monarchy in England.

Before proceeding, we need to say something about what contemporaries understood by the words 'arbitrary' and 'absolute'.[39] Both terms possessed a variety of resonances, from the neutral to the derogatory. An 'arbitrary' power was one that was unbounded by law. Most seventeenth-century legal theorists believed that there was some degree of arbitrary or discretionary power vested in the monarch, by dint of his prerogative, normally to be used only in emergencies. Thus Sir Philip Warwick, writing in 1678, spoke of 'the usefulness and unavoidableness of arbitrary prerogative' to deal with cases 'that cannot be foreseen, or that come seldom, and clothed with divers circumstances, or fall under no certain rule, or are of great import or danger, and can stay for no formal council'. Such a power was arbitrary because it was not 'limited under strict forms or process of Law'. But it would be 'a piece of ignorance', he continued, 'to think, because a decision is arbitrary, therefore it is unjust'. The whole point of the king having an 'arbitrary prerogative' was so that he could promote justice or else preserve the interests of the state without causing injustice. 'No arbitrary power, or decision, or reason of state', Warwick insisted, 'must want justice, for the standing laws, and the arbitrary determinations of Sovereignty must both be reasonable and just.'[40] However, if the king repeatedly showed little respect for the rule of law or flouted existing constitutional conventions, this was arbitrary government, and no better than tyranny.

To say that the king was 'absolute', by contrast, meant that he was accountable to no human power. He was *ab legibus solutus* – exempt from the laws. This did not mean he could ignore the laws at will; he was supposed to rule according to law, and would be held accountable by God if he did not. But he could not be resisted by his subjects if he failed to observe the law, and he could not be tried in a court of law. The king was in that sense the supreme power within the state; he was sovereign. 'Absolute' also carried the meaning of 'complete': an absolute ruler had complete power, in the sense that he did not share it with anyone else. He did not share sovereignty with parliament, for example. Many people could champion the Restoration monarchy as absolute and mean it positively, without any negative connotations; they certainly did not believe that an absolute monarch should rule arbitrarily. Hence Warwick could acknowledge that the king was absolute and possessed certain arbitrary powers, but remain adamant that he was 'not an arbitrary Monarch'.[41] Marchamont Needham, writing propaganda for the royal administration in the mid-1670s in an attempt to discredit the position of Shaftesbury and his adherents, insisted that divine-right absolute monarchy did not exclude all limitations by human laws or mean that the king was under no obligation to his people. 'A Father hath a Divine Right to Rule his Son, and a Master his Servant,' Needham explained, 'else the Scripture had never made Divine Injunctions, investing them with Rights of absolute power over them; and yet the same Scripture also signifies . . . there are Obligations also upon the Father and Master, to the Son and Servant.' It was 'such a Personal, absolute Divine Right', Needham asserted, 'that the Kings of England have claimed and exercised over their Subjects, as that in all times . . . the Laws have generally run in course, for preservation of all the Rights and Liberties of the People, as well as those of the Crown'.[42]

Yet the dividing line between absolute and arbitrary was becoming blurred, especially in the minds of those people – such as Shaftesbury and the other members of the 'country' opposition of the mid-1670s – who did not believe that the king was absolute. If the king could not be held accountable, then not only was his power absolute but he could rule in an arbitrary way. Moreover, the meaning of 'absolute' as 'complete' carried with it the connotation that an absolute sovereign had total control over the government and could rule his kingdom according to his own whim. Thus in April 1678 the French ambassador, Paul Barillon, wrote to Louis XIV expressing his view that it was not in the interest of France 'that a King of England should be absolute master, and be able to dispose according to his will of all the power of the nation'. Revealingly, Barillon recognized there were different degrees of absoluteness; a week later he wrote to Louis saying that he did not believe Charles II cared much 'for being more absolute than he is'.[43]

At first glance, the powers of the restored monarch appear to have been fairly extensive. The return to the position of 1641 meant that the king was re-established as the chief executive, with control over the appointment of all officers of state and the right to determine all questions of policy (both foreign and domestic). The king could not tax or enact legislation without parliament, but he had the power of veto over parliamentary legislation, and he alone determined when to call, prorogue or dismiss parliament. He was also supreme governor of the Church, by dint of the powers vested in him by the Elizabethan Act of Supremacy of 1559. Additional legislation enacted by parliament in the early years of the Restoration sought to shore up the powers of the monarchy even further. Two Militia Acts, of 1661 and 1662, gave the king sole command of all armed forces within the country.[44] The Corporation Act and the Act of Uniformity reinforced the doctrine of non-resistance by requiring that municipal office-holders, clergy and teachers take an oath declaring it was 'not lawful upon any pretence whatsoever to take arms against the King'.[45]

The government also made efforts to restrict both public involvement in and discussion of politics. An Act against Tumultuous Petitioning of 1661, which blamed such activity for 'the late unhappy wars, confusions and calamities in this nation', made it illegal to solicit the hands or consent of persons 'above the number of twenty or more to any petition' to the king or parliament 'for alteration of matters established by law in Church or State', unless the petition had first been approved and ordered by three or more JPs from the area, or the greater part of the grand jury, or, in the case of London, by the Lord Mayor, aldermen and common council. The act also stipulated that no more than ten people were allowed to present a petition.[46] The Licensing Act of 1662 made it illegal to print anything heretical, seditious or schismatical, or any doctrine or opinion contrary to the Christian faith or the doctrine and discipline of the Church of England, and required all books to be licensed by the Stationers' Company of London, by one of the archbishops or the bishop of London, or by one of the chancellors or vice-chancellors of the universities.[47]

It was possible, within this legal framework, to take a very exalted view of monarchy. Many Anglican divines, in their sermons, preached up the divine-right nature of monarchy, insisting that kings were 'God's vice-gerents' and thus 'accountable to none but God'.[48] Most royalist writers vehemently condemned the theory of coordination, or mixed monarchy – the notion that the king was but a coordinate power who shared his sovereignty with the Lords and Commons. As the Lord Chief Baron Sir Orlando Bridgeman put it, at the trial of the regicides in October 1660, the king was 'not only Caput Populi, the head of the people; but Caput Republicae, the head of the Commonwealth, The Three Estates'. 'All must know,' Lord Chief Justice Sir Robert Hyde concurred, 'that the king is above the two houses.'[49]

However, the Restoration monarchy was nowhere near as strong as such rhetorical flourishes were intended to imply. A major cause of weakness was lack of money. The crown suffered from an inadequate system of finance. In 1660 the Convention had worked out a seemingly generous financial settlement whereby the crown was to receive £1.2 million per year in the form of receipts from customs and excise; this was double what Charles I's ordinary revenues had been in the late 1620s and early 1630s. But the Convention had miscalculated; the yield fell short by almost a third, and an additional tax on fire hearths imposed in 1662 made up only half the difference. It proved impossible for the crown to make ends meet, while wars with the Dutch of 1664–7 and 1672–4, coupled with Charles II keeping larger military and naval establishments than his father, pushed the monarchy further and further into debt. Indeed, in January 1672, when Lord Ashley (the future Earl of Shaftesbury) was Chancellor of the Exchequer, the government had to order a Stop of the Exchequer, unilaterally cancelling payment to government creditors in order to release funds for the third Anglo-Dutch War. Shortage of funds left the crown dependent upon parliament for grants of extraordinary supply. Although parliamentary sessions remained irregular, Charles II found himself having to meet with parliament virtually every year between 1660 and 1681 (the exceptions being 1671 and 1676). Moreover, unlike their early Stuart counterparts, Restoration parliaments were not coy about using the power of the purse to bring pressure on the crown to change its policies. On a number of occasions in the 1660s and 1670s parliament either threatened to or actually did withhold supply to try to force a change in royal policy.[50]

To free himself from dependence upon parliament, Charles II would have to make the crown financially independent; this was something he was not able to do until after 1681. The only other option was to try to control or manage parliament in such a way as to ensure its compliance with the crown's interests. This was difficult for a number of reasons. The legacy of ideological division bequeathed by the upheavals of the 1640s and '50s meant that contests at parliamentary elections became more frequent (replacing the older system whereby the local elite had reached a consensus over who should be 'selected'),[51] and the large electorates of the shire constituencies and the open boroughs' electorates were not easily susceptible to management from above. This is why Charles, having been presented with the return of a predominantly Cavalier-Anglican parliament in 1661, decided to keep it in existence for so long (it was eventually dissolved in January 1679), even though the large numbers of by-elections needed to replace MPs who had either died or been promoted to the upper house meant that it was becoming a body increasingly less sympathetic to the crown as time went on. In the mid-1670s the King's then chief minister, the Earl of Danby, tried to build up a loyal following in the Commons by doling out pensions and offices to potential supporters or those he wanted to buy off. Although Danby was heavily criticized by opposition peers and members for subverting the independence of parliament, the element of bribery should not be exaggerated. In days when MPs were unpaid, gifts or offices were regarded as fair compensation for past services rendered; they would not necessarily buy someone's support in the future. Danby was successful in building up a court interest or 'party' in the Commons because he pursued policies – a defence of the Church, the eradication of dissent, an aggressive stance against France – that were supported by the Cavalier-Anglican gentry who dominated the Cavalier Parliament.

Charles found it easier to control the House of Lords than he did the Commons. The bishops were restored to the upper house by an act of 1661;[52] there were twenty-six of them when all the seats were filled, and they were all royal appointees. Furthermore, the crown could always seek to extend its interest among the lay lords through new creations; Charles II in fact created a total of sixty-four peers between 1649 and 1685 – more than either his father or his grandfather.[53] Once appointed, however, the bishops enjoyed tenure for life, while it was virtually impossible to remove existing lay peers, short of a successful conviction for treason (though Catholic peers, as we have seen, were barred from sitting in the Lords by the Test Act of 1678). When the mood of the electorate led to the return of a Cavalier-Anglican House of Commons in 1661, the House of Lords still contained a number of Presbyterian peers, or peers with moderate Puritan sympathies, such as the earls of Devonshire, Manchester and Northumberland. Indeed, Charles promoted several former parliamentarians, and even erstwhile servants to the Protectorate, to the peerage as a reward for their services in helping to bring about the restoration of the monarchy – the most famous example being Sir Anthony Ashley Cooper (the Earl of Shaftesbury from April 1672), who first took his seat in the Lords as Baron Ashley in May 1661. Although careful management meant that Charles could typically rely on support from the upper house, and even use it to suppress or modify legislation initiated in the Commons of which he disapproved, the Lords were never mere pawns, and at times could mount a significant challenge to the royal will.[54]

The Restoration, for most people – former parliamentarians and Cavalier Anglicans alike – meant not just the return of the King, but also the restoration of parliaments and the rule of law. As the first Earl of Clarendon put it in the Lords in May 1661, 'We have our King again, and our Laws again, and Parliaments again.'[55] It was, nevertheless, the king's law: the Commons proposed, but it was the king who enacted legislation. Moreover, the men who interpreted the law, the judges, were all royal appointees. One of the sources of conflict between Charles I and his Long Parliament had been over whether judges should hold their office at royal pleasure (*durante bene placito*) or at good behaviour (*quamdiu se bene gesserint*), which made their tenure more independent. Although at first Charles reverted to his father's practice of 1641 of appointing judges at good behaviour, from about 1668 onward he made appointments at royal pleasure, enabling him later to dismiss or suspend judges at will.[56] The independence of juries from judicial interference, however, was established by Bushell's Case of 1671, which ruled that a judge's decision to imprison a jury for finding against the evidence in the prosecution of the Quaker William Penn in 1670 was illegal.[57]

The king, most agreed, possessed the power, under certain circumstances, to dispense individuals from the penalties of the law, if a greater injustice would follow if the law were strictly enforced. There were certain restrictions, however, on the scope of the dispensing power. The king could not dispense with a matter that was *malum in se*, that is, inherently wrong, and against the law of God or nature (such as murder); he could dispense only with something that was *malum prohibitum*, that is, which had been made criminal by statute. Even then, the king could not issue dispensations that aimed to destroy the intent or spirit of the original statute, or which would prejudice the interests or property of his subjects; for example, he could not dispense an individual from a law that allowed a third party to collect a fine by way of compensation.[58]

Whether the king could suspend the operation of a statute completely was another matter. Charles and some of his advisers appear to have believed that the royal supremacy, as confirmed by the act of 1559, implied a royal power to suspend penal statutes 'in matters ecclesiastical', though this was something Charles never managed to get recognized.[59] His attempt in December 1662 to issue a Declaration of Indulgence suspending the operation of the penal laws against nonconformists and Catholics provoked a storm of opposition when parliament reassembled the following February, the Commons complaining that it was 'a thing altogether without precedent' and 'inconsistent with the methods and proceedings of the laws of England', and he was forced to back down.[60] The same thing happened when he issued a second Declaration of Indulgence in March 1672. When parliament reconvened in February 1673 it withheld supply until Charles agreed to withdraw the Indulgence.

The precise legal situation is worth clarifying, since the royal pretence to a suspending power was to emerge as a major issue in the Revolution of 1688–9. Historians have typically argued that technically the king did possess the power to suspend ecclesiastical laws, under the terms of the royal supremacy. This was the view taken in 1673 by Shaftesbury, by now Charles's Lord Chancellor, who backed the Indulgence because he believed that the king's supremacy in ecclesiasticals 'was of another nature then that he had in Civills, and had been exercised without exception' by Charles I, James I and Queen Elizabeth.[61] The Commons, however, concluded by a vote of 168 to 116 that the suspending power was illegal.[62] Resolutions of the

Commons, of course, do not make law; the House might be able to force the King to back down, but they could not denude him of a power which he legally possessed. Yet, in taking their stand against the suspending power, the Commons did not think they were declaring something to be illegal that had formerly been recognized as legal; rather, in forcing the King to withdraw his Indulgence they believed they were getting him to acknowledge that this was a power which no king had ever legally enjoyed. On 14 February 1673 the Commons petitioned the King, informing him that 'Penal Statutes in Matters Ecclesiasticall' could not be suspended but by act of parliament. When Charles angrily replied that this suspending power in ecclesiastical matters had never been questioned 'in the Reigns of any of His Ancestors', they quickly sought to disabuse him of this notion. No such power had ever been claimed by his predecessors, they insisted, 'and if it should be admitted, might tend to the Interruption of the free Course of the Laws, and altering the Legislative Power, which hath allwayes been acknowledged to lodge in Your Majesty and the Two Houses of Parliament'. Charles at last gave way, withdrew his Indulgence, and promised 'that what hath been done . . . concerning the Suspension of Penal Laws' would 'not for the future be drawn into Consequence or Example'.[63]

Another major limitation on the power of the crown concerned its ability to police its subjects effectively and to protect itself against the possible threat of subversion at home. Although the Militia Acts had restored crown control over all armed forces within the kingdom, these acts dealt primarily with the militia, an amateur body of part-timers which when put to the test often proved to be far from an effective fighting force. Parliament tended to the view that if the militia could be reformed – kept better supplied with weapons, and with its members better trained – this would be adequate for domestic security; the Civil War and republican experiments had, besides, engendered a deep-seated antipathy towards standing armies among most English people. Charles II, however, as newly restored monarch of a kingdom that over the previous two decades had not shown itself the greatest friend of monarchy, saw the need to have well-trained, professional troops at his disposal. There was no technical reason at law why the king should not keep his own standing forces, if he could afford to pay for them. If he could not, however, he would need to get parliament to vote taxes to support them. Furthermore, the Petition of Right of 1628 had established that both the quartering of troops on private householders and the imposition of martial law in time of peace were illegal. In practice, these proved quite significant constraints. In 1660 the Convention voted a considerable sum for the disbanding of the Cromwellian army; however, it gave nothing specifically to pay for anything to put in that army's place. Charles managed to keep a force of about 3,000 to 4,000, paid out of his ordinary revenue, who were referred to as 'guards' rather than by the more opprobrious term 'army'. This was tiny: the Interregnum military establishment had peaked at 60,000, while by 1675 Louis XIV in France had an army of about 100,000. Whenever Charles sought to expand his armed forces, as he did in 1666 (in anticipation of a Dutch invasion), in 1672 (on the outbreak of the third Anglo-Dutch War) and again in 1678 (supposedly in readiness for war with France), suspicions immediately arose that he intended to rule through a standing army. Moreover, it proved impossible to house all of the expanded forces in garrisons, and so soldiers came to be quartered not just in public houses, but also on private householders, in violation of the Petition of Right. Parliament naturally proved reluctant to approve taxes to support such additional forces, unless they were needed for war. On 7 February 1674 the Commons resolved 'That the continuing of any Standing Forces in this nation other than the Militia, is a great Grievance and vexation to the people', and petitioned the King to disband all those troops raised since January 1663.[64] Parliament was to push again for the disbandment of the standing army in 1678–9.[65]

The King's guards were sometimes used to perform basic policing functions. In 1663 the royal horse guards were sent to disperse conventiclers in York, while in 1670 the life guards were used to break up various nonconformist meetings in London in the aftermath of the passage of the second Conventicle Act.[66] The government was particularly worried about the threat of possible disorder in the capital – now a large, sprawling metropolis of some half a million people. On the eve of the Civil War, in early 1642, crowd unrest had forced Charles I to abandon London, whose streets he could no longer police, and Charles II was determined not to succumb to the same problem. When thousands of (mainly young) people, armed with iron bars, pole-axes and other weapons, rioted against bawdy houses in the London area in Easter week of 1668, chanting 'Reformation and reducement' and threatening to pull down Whitehall if the King did not give them liberty of conscience, the government (fearing the riots had been instigated by former Cromwellian soldiers) immediately dispatched the life guards to restore order.[67] The problem with relying on parish constables, or even the local militia, was that they often did not have the requisite muscle to deal with larger-scale disturbances – and, besides, they had the infuriating habit of taking the rioters' side when their grievances seemed just. When thousands of weavers rioted in London in August 1675, to protest against the use of mechanized looms, the local peace-keeping forces simply refused to act. In the end, troops under the command of the Duke of Monmouth had to be called upon to suppress the riots.[68]

What happened in 1675 highlights another major structural weakness of the restored monarchy, namely the limitations to the effective coercive power of the state. Seventeenth-century England did not possess a professional civil service or police force, and for the implementation of government policy and the enforcement of law and order the crown was heavily dependent upon the cooperation of unpaid, part-time officials in the localities: from the Lord Lieutenants and their deputies who ran the local militias, the JPs and magistrates of the counties and boroughs who presided over the quarter sessions, down to the humble parish constables, beadles and nightwatchmen who were responsible for basic police work. Appointments to the lieutenancy and to the magisterial bench were in the gift of the crown, and undesirable types could be removed and replaced by men deemed more trustworthy. Thus the restored Lord Lieutenants appointed in 1660 were chosen for their known loyalty to the crown, the vast majority being staunch Anglican-royalists; their deputies, admittedly, came from a slightly more mixed political background – but only slightly.[69] The county JPs were a more varied group, however. A systematic purge of the magisterial bench in 1660 sought to restore control of the counties to their 'natural leaders' – namely the greater gentry – though in the interests of rapprochement a significant number of parliamentarians and former Cromwellians were retained alongside the Anglican-royalists who were brought in, and not all of these could be totally relied upon to carry out the crown's will. There was a series of minor purges in the 1670s aimed at ousting some of the politically less reliable types – that of 1670, for example, was carried out with an eye to remove those reluctant to enforce the second Conventicle Act – but it was not until 1680 that the crown attempted another systematic reconstruction.[70] It was more difficult to control the corporations, which enjoyed considerable rights of self-government protected by royal charter. A commission set up to enforce the Corporation Act in 1662–3 led to the expulsion from town governments of those who would not take the Anglican sacrament, renounce the Covenant, or swear the oaths of allegiance and supremacy (acknowledging the reigning monarch as supreme in both spirituals and temporals, and promising to bear allegiance to the King and his heirs and successors); yet the purge failed to remove all who sympathized with dissent, while others who technically failed to qualify themselves under the terms of the Corporation Act nevertheless managed to intrude themselves back into office thanks to a combination of connivance and a loose interpretation of the law. As a result, by the 1670s many corporations were to become hotbeds of partisan strife, often opposing intolerant Anglican zealots against those who saw little need to enforce the penal laws against Protestant nonconformists.[71] With town and even county magistrates not always trustworthy, it is hardly surprising that the humble parish constable might sometimes drag his feet when asked to enforce laws of which he disapproved. In particular, complaints were frequently made about the reluctance of constables to enforce the laws against nonconformist conventicles. Indeed, the government itself recognized this as a problem: hence its introducing a scheme of financial incentives to informers under the terms of the 1670 Conventicle Act – informers were to receive one-third of the fine that resulted from a successful prosecution – in an attempt to remedy this.

THE LOSS OF PRESTIGE

Failing institutional innovation, the only way to make the central government more powerful was to secure the support and cooperation of these unpaid brokers of central authority in the localities.[72] Purging local government of those suspected of disaffection and trying to compel local officials to perform their duties were part of the solution, but the crown also needed to ensure that those men it did have in place were convinced of the merits of government policy if it wanted them to carry it out. In short, the central government had to sell itself to the people. The king had to convince his subjects that it was in their best interests to see his policies enforced, but this also meant that, to a degree at least, the king had to pursue policies that his subjects wanted him to pursue. In short, he needed both to persuade and to satisfy. He could hope to do this successfully only if he could control the media through which royal policy came to be represented.

The traditional way in which monarchs had tried to sell themselves to their subjects was through an appropriate display of pomp and ceremony. On the eve of the Restoration, the Duke of Newcastle had advised Charles that he should show himself 'Gloryously' to his people, 'Like a God', since then the people would pray for him 'with trembling Feare, and Love, as they did to Queen Elizabeth', for 'nothing Keepes upp a King', Newcastle continued, 'more than seremoney, and order, which makes Distance, and this brings respecte and Duty.'[73] Charles appeared keen to follow Newcastle's advice. He did his best to tap into the popular enthusiasm for the return of monarchy in the spring of 1660 and promote an appropriate image of royal splendour and majesty. Hence the drawn-out nature of his triumphant return to his kingdom in May 1660, from his first landing at Dover on the 25th to his eventual entry into his capital on his birthday on the 29th.[74] Later that year the Convention established Restoration Day as an annual day of thanksgiving, and in the early years of the reign 29 May became the occasion for bonfire celebrations in a number of communities throughout the land. On 29 May 1661, for example, there were reportedly 'many thousand Bonfires in London, Westminster, and places adjacent (and proportionately all over the kingdom)', where crowds burned copies of the Solemn League and Covenant and, at some locations, images of Oliver Cromwell.[75] Charles II's coronation, in the spring of 1661, was an elaborate and meticulously planned three-day celebration, designed to revive the cult of monarchy after over a decade of republican government: there was a royal progress from the Tower to Whitehall on 22 April, the coronation itself on the 23rd (St George's Day), and a fireworks display the day after, and according to one contemporary 'the sumptuousness of it' exceeded 'the glory of what hath passed of the like kind in France'.[76] Charles also revived the practice of touching for the King's Evil – the royal touch supposedly being enough by itself to effect a cure for scrofula – in order to confirm the legitimacy of his rule in the eyes of his people. From April 1669, when records become complete, until the end of 1684, Charles touched a total of 28,983 persons, or an average of some 1,800 per year.[77]

At the same time, the Restoration regime did its best to ensure that it had control over the interpretation of political news. Thus the government had its own newspaper, the *London Gazette*, from 1666, and also engaged in a certain amount of pamphleteering – notably under Danby in the mid-1670s – to explain and justify its policies. In addition, it sought to silence critical voices by clamping down on illicit preaching, seditious publications, and collective agitation out-of-doors (in the form of petitions and demonstrations). However, it found it impossible to establish a monopoly over the interpretation of the news. Nonconformist preachers could not be silenced, and, although many no doubt simply ministered to their flocks peacefully, some undoubtedly did use their conventicles as opportunities to launch a critique of government policy and even to urge resistance in the face of oppression.[78] Nor could ministers of the Established Church always be relied upon to adopt a position in support of the government. When Charles issued his 1672 Declaration of Indulgence – a measure designed to relieve Catholics as much as Protestant nonconformists – the bishops responded by instructing their clergy to preach against popery. Charles complained to his archbishop of Canterbury, Gilbert Sheldon, that 'this preaching on controversy' was 'done on purpose to inflame the people, to alienate them from him and his government'; Sheldon, after consultation with some of the clergy, was ready to stand firm and tell the King that it would be unprecedented for him to 'forbid his clergy to preach in defence of a religion which they believed' while the King himself 'said he was of it', though Charles, in the end, decided not to force the issue and backed down.[79] The only way to prevent the clergy from broaching controversial topics and thereby possibly inflaming the people against the King and his government – the lesson appeared to be – was for the King not to pursue policies they would find controversial.

The Licensing Act did limit the output of the printed press. Whereas some 2,730 titles appeared in 1660 and 1,584 in 1661, by 1663 this figure had fallen to 1,035 and by 1666 to a mere 633 (though the Great Fire of London bore some responsibility here). There was then a small recovery, and output was hovering at around 1,000 to 1,200 titles per year by the 1670s. But it was not until 1679 – the year the Licensing Act lapsed, when there were 1,730 titles published – that the figure for 1661 was exceeded.[80] Nevertheless, manuscript newsletters, pamphlets and political poetry circulated through the coffee houses, disseminating what were sometimes heavily critical views of Charles II, his court or royal policy.[81] To meet this threat, on 29 December 1675 Charles took the dramatic step of issuing a proclamation ordering the closure of all coffee houses. Ten days later he announced that in future such establishments would be allowed to operate only under government licence, with all coffee-house owners being required to take the oaths of allegiance and supremacy and to take out bonds not to allow on their premises any scandalous papers or libels or to permit the uttering of any scandalous reports concerning the government or the ministers of state.[82] The initiative appears to have been of limited practical effect.

A major reason for Charles's inability to persuade and satisfy was that the policies he pursued, or the things he did or accomplished, were hardly persuasive or satisfying. As a result, over the period 1660–78 the crown experienced a considerable loss of prestige. What, then, lent a monarchy prestige at this time? At the basic level, majesty was supposed to be majestic. More particularly, a king was expected to achieve glory for his nation (normally this would be achieved in foreign policy), to defend the true religion (which, in the English context, of course, was the Protestant faith), and to protect and promote the secular well-being of his subjects (that is, guarantee them what they regarded as their due at law, which by the later seventeenth century was coming to be defined in terms of the trilogy of life, liberty and property). In all these respects the Restoration regime proved a bitter disappointment.

Charles's foreign policy was most inglorious – by any standard – and certainly appeared disastrous compared to what had been achieved under Cromwell in the 1650s. The war of 1664–7 against the Dutch (and also, from 1666, the French) went humiliatingly badly: much of the English fleet was destroyed, and colonial possessions were lost, while in June 1667 came the ultimate disgrace when the Dutch fleet managed to sail up the Medway to Chatham and destroy four of the English navy's biggest vessels and capture the flagship, the *Royal Charles*. In the ensuing peace, England ceded Surinam, on the north-east coast of South America, to the Dutch, and had to acknowledge Dutch claims in West Africa and the East Indies. The fact that England managed to keep the New Netherlands (modern-day New York) – seized from the Dutch by the English government in August 1664 – hardly seemed much of a consolation at the time. England also had to give up Nova Scotia to the French – though England did regain possessions lost to the French in the West Indies.[83]

From the late 1660s, following Clarendon's fall from grace in 1667 and during the administration of the Cabal (1668–73) – so-called after the initial letters of the leading ministers of the time: Thomas Clifford, Arlington, Buckingham, Ashley Cooper and Lauderdale – Charles moved into an alliance with the French. At Dover in 1670 he made a private treaty with Louis XIV whereby he promised, in return for French subsidies, not only to join France in declaring war on the Dutch, but also to announce his own conversion to Catholicism. (Only Clifford and Arlington of the Cabal were privy to the secret treaty; a fake treaty had to be concluded for the benefit of the rest of his ministers and his English subjects, concealing the religious clause.) The ensuing Dutch War of 1672–4 achieved no positive gains for the English, though by its end – thanks in part to a highly successful propaganda campaign by the Dutch themselves – most people in England had come to believe that fighting the Protestant Dutch was against the national interest, and that the much greater threat was posed by

Catholic France. Louis XIV's expansionist ambitions had become all too apparent during the late 1660s and early 1670s, and it was coming to be feared that he had pretensions to universal monarchy.[84] By the mid-1670s, parliament was clamouring for a more aggressive stance to be taken against France. Indeed, Danby, Charles's chief minister from 1674, did his best to take England out of the French orbit, and by 1678 was on the verge of declaring war on France in alliance with the Dutch. Charles remained reluctant, and continued to take bribes from Louis XIV behind his first minister's back. Yet Charles was not the only one playing a duplicitous game; so too was Louis XIV, who kept a number of opposition MPs in his pay, so that he could put the screws on the English king whenever it proved to his advantage. England had become little more than a client of the French king. What was worse was that most people knew it.

The government had also fallen down on its duty to defend the true religion. Charles's own sympathies for Roman Catholicism had become readily apparent, not only as a result of his foreign-policy alliance with Catholic France, but also through his attempts to relieve the plight of Catholics through the use of the royal suspending power. There also seemed to be an alarming number of Catholics at court, and these were feared to have an undue influence on royal policy. During the early 1660s the most prominent Catholic at court was the erratic Earl of Bristol, part of the Queen Mother's circle, although he never gained the influence he craved. More worryingly, during the administration of the Cabal, a time when the government seemed bent on pursuing policies at home and abroad designed to promote the interest of Catholics (notably the Indulgence of 1672 and the war with France against the Dutch), one of the King's leading ministers (Clifford) was a Catholic and another (Arlington) was a Catholic-sympathizer.

Of equal concern, however, were the royal mistresses. As that most notorious of Restoration rakes, the Earl of Rochester, John Wilmot, put it with his typical indelicacy, Charles's 'sceptre and his prick are of a length, / But she who plays with one may sway the other'.[85] The problem was that those women who had most intimate access to the King's person were Catholics. Charles's leading mistress from 1660 to 1668 was the Catholic Barbara Villiers, Countess of Castlemaine (later the Duchess of Cleveland), five of whose children Charles acknowledged as his own. From about 1663 Charles also developed a passion for Frances Stuart, the daughter of a Scottish Catholic royalist, described by Charles's sister the Duchess of Orléans as 'the prettiest girl in the world, and the best fitted to adorn any court'. Although it is unclear whether they ever actually became lovers, there was talk at one time of Charles divorcing his wife and marrying Frances, until she eloped in the spring of 1667 with the King's relative the Duke of Richmond.[86] From the early 1670s the King's most influential mistress was the French Catholic Louise de Kéroualle (typically Anglicized as 'Carwell' by contemporaries), created Duchess of Portsmouth; she was actually 'married' to Charles in a mock ceremony in 1671, and was to bear him a son – Charles Lennox, Duke of Richmond and Lennox – in July 1672.[87] The orange-girl and actress Nell Gwyn, who became Charles's mistress in the late 1660s, was conspicuous for being 'the Protestant whore', as she herself famously quipped.[88] All told, Charles had fourteen natural children by various mistresses during his lifetime.

Charles's sexual exploits became the subject of much scurrilous verse, which typically circulated in manuscript. Some of this, to be sure, was written by fellow rakes who were as much celebrating as condemning the activities they were describing. Some of it, however, carried a biting, critical edge, and all of it served to help degrade the monarchy in the public eye and to encourage the perception that the political failings of the regime were linked to the moral failings of the court. Rochester was partly rejoicing when he recalled how 'the Isle of Britain' was 'long since famous grown / For breeding the best cunts in Christendom', and perhaps even when he described Charles as 'the sauciest one that e'er did swive, / The proudest, preremptoriest prick alive'. But he overstepped the mark when he referred to his 'merry Monarch' as someone 'scandalous and poor', who rolled 'about from whore to whore', and concluded with the lines 'I hate all monarchs with the thrones they sit on, / From the hector of France to the cully of Britain'; this earned him a banishment from court for his pains.[89] Many rhymesters pointed out how Charles's whoring was ruining the country. Charles's mistresses, after all, cost a lot of money: during the 1670s Cleveland and Portsmouth and their children were in receipt of permanent grants worth more than £45,000 per year.[90] One anonymous rhymester had 'Old Rowley the King' saying, 'The making my Bastards so great / And Dutchessing every Whore / The surplus and treasury cheat / Has made me so wonderfull poor.'[91] Another asked, 'Why art thou poore O King?' and concluded, '. . . imbezzling C—t, / That wide moth'd, greedy Monster that has don't.'[92]

England's foreign-policy disasters seemed naturally linked to the degeneracy of the court. One poet, writing about the Medway disaster, rhymed:

> So our great prince, when the Dutch fleet arriv'd,
> Saw his ships burn and, as they burn'd, he swiv'd.
> So kind was he in our extremest need,
> He would those flames extinguish with his seed.[93]

In *c.* 1673, at the time of the third Anglo-Dutch War, a mock advertisement which circulated for a public sale at the Royal Coffee House near Charing Cross proclaimed that the following items were for sale:

One whole peece of the Duchess of Cleveland's honesty . . . Two Ells of Nell Gwin's Virginity . . . Two whole peeces of new fashioned paradoxes, the one to suppress popery by the Suppression of the Protestant interest abroad, the other to maintain libertie by the raiseing of a standing Army at home . . . Two dozen of French wenches, the one half paid by his Majesty to keep him right to the Protestant religion, the other to incline him to the Catholicks.[94]

There was thus no underlying mirth when the republican poet and future Whig conspirator John Ayloffe bemoaned in *c.* 1674–5 how 'A colony of French possess the court' and Charles's 'fair soul, transform'd by that French dame [i.e. Portsmouth], / Had lost all sense of honor, justice, fame' so that the King sat 'Besieg'd by whores, buffoons, and bastard chits'.[95]

The prominence of Catholics in high places and the pro-Catholic leanings of the court inevitably created the impression that popery was on the increase. In fact, it probably was not, but this did not stop parliament from introducing a series of measures during the 1660s and 1670s designed to check its growth, culminating in the Test Acts of 1673 and 1678 aimed at excluding Catholics first from office and then from parliament.[96] What made matters worse was that the heir to the throne was a Catholic. Despite all his swiving, Charles was unable to produce any legitimate offspring, since his wife, Catherine of Braganza, was barren. Thus the next in line remained his younger brother by three years, James, Duke of York, who sometime during the late 1660s or early 1670s became reconciled to Rome, his conversion finally being publicly acknowledged following his non-compliance with the Test Act in 1673.[97] In October of that year York married a young Catholic princess, Mary of Modena – a French client – his first wife, Anne Hyde, who had given him two Protestant daughters, having died two years earlier. The marriage not only seemed to tie the Stuart dynasty firmly to the French interest, but also raised the prospect of a never-ending succession of Catholic monarchs, should Mary be able to bear James a son.

Developments in 1673 placed the issue of the Catholic succession firmly on the political agenda. In midsummer, Charles told the French ambassador that he feared that when parliament next met it would introduce bills to send his brother into exile and exclude Catholics from the succession.[98] In October 1673, when parliament convened for the first time after the Modena match, the Speaker found a wooden shoe in his chair, with 'the arms of the king of France carved on one side and those of his Britannic Majesty on the other, with a crown and a crucifix'. Inside was a note with the words 'of one of the two'.[99] In early 1674 a group of opposition peers – spearheaded by Viscount Halifax and the earls of Salisbury and Carlisle, and backed all the way by Shaftesbury – tried to introduce legislation into parliament that would have provided for the education of the Duke of York's children as Protestants and prevented in future any king or prince of the blood from marrying a Catholic without parliamentary consent – with the penalty for non-compliance being exclusion from the succession. On this occasion, however, they backed down in face of stern opposition from the bishops, who would countenance no breach in the hereditary principle.[100] The prospect of a Catholic successor nevertheless continued to be a destabilizing factor in politics. Indeed, it was in large part to deal with this threat that in 1677 Danby arranged the marriage between York's eldest daughter, Mary (at the time second in line to the throne, after her father), to her cousin the staunchly Protestant and anti-French Dutch stadtholder William of Orange (who himself was fourth in line, by dint of being the son of Charles II's sister Mary). Danby even came up with a scheme himself that year for imposing limitations on a popish successor; this would have given the bishops control over all ecclesiastical appointments in the event of a Catholic coming to the throne (in effect, temporarily undoing the royal supremacy in the Church), but it was abandoned in the face of opposition from those who distrusted the Anglican bishops as much as they did the Catholic heir.[101]

Particularly galling was the fact that, while the government seemed to be making little serious effort to meet the Catholic threat, peaceable Protestant dissenters continued to be harassed for worshipping outside the Church of England. The penal laws against nonconformists were not consistently put into execution throughout this period; enforcement came in waves, with the first half of the 1660s, the year following the passage of the 1670 Conventicle Act, the mid-1670s, and then the years of the Tory Reaction in the 1680s seeing the heaviest persecution. Yet, when the laws were being enforced, the suffering could be immense. Nonconformists faced heavy fines, often imprisonment, and even death. In Huntingdonshire, in 1670, some eighty Quakers were fined a total of £254 5s. for violations against the Conventicle Act; their inability to pay meant that they had their goods distrained to cover the amounts owed (and often more) – 'Sheep, Cowes, Horses, Hoggs, Wool, Oatmeal, Carts, Pewter, Panns, and Potts, and other Goods'. One John Arthur had all his possessions taken away, leaving him with not 'so much as a Dish, or Spoon, nor the Dung in his Yard'.[102] These were arguably the luckier ones. Many were hauled off to prison in lieu of non-payment; there the cells could be so crowded after a round-up of conventiclers that there would be standing room only, with no space to lie down when someone needed to sleep. During one clampdown on Quakers in York, for example, the castle prison was so full that two of the Friends 'were forced to Lay in a great Oven which stood in the Castle yard wall'.[103] Persecution was thus a threat to both liberty and property. It could also be a threat to life. Indeed, under the provisions of the Act of 35 Elizabeth separatists could technically be sentenced to death. In fact no one did suffer the ultimate sanction during the Restoration, although there were some close calls. In 1664 twelve Baptists (two of them women) from Aylesbury, Buckinghamshire, were sentenced to death for refusing to conform or to abjure the realm, though when Charles learned of this he granted a reprieve. Likewise in 1682 a Quaker merchant from Bristol lay under sentence of death until William Penn used his influence at court to get the sentence quashed.[104] Nevertheless, several thousand nonconformists did die for their beliefs. A rare few were victims of murderous anti-sectarian bigotry. Thus the 'rude Company' which disturbed the Quaker meeting at the Bull and Mouth in Aldersgate Street, London, in October 1662, actually killed two of the worshippers, though the law obviously did not sanction such violence and the murderers were arrested and sent to prison.[105] The vast majority were the victims of incarceration at the hands of the state, the conditions in Restoration jails being so wretched that many never made it out alive. Others, though they did not forfeit their lives, nevertheless lost their livelihoods and thus the means of keeping body and soul together. One writer estimated that Quakers in Yorkshire suffered losses totalling some £2,381 0s. 3d. under the Conventicle Act, although this was nothing 'compared to the Loss of their Trades, many of them being Trades men, and Labouring Poor men, who have had their Looms, Leads, and Tenters taken away, which was the Upholders of their Families', while 'some poor Women had their Goods taken, who were hardly able to get Food and Necessaries.'[106] The New England Puritan divine Cotton Mather claimed that 'by a modest calculation' the persecution resulted in 'the untimely death of 3,000 Nonconformists, and the ruin of 60,000 families' within a twenty-five-year period.[107] Dissenters thus quite rightly came to complain that they were suffering in their lives, liberties and estates.[108]

It was not just their personal liberty but also their political liberties that were in jeopardy. Particularly resented in this respect was the 1670 Conventicle Act, which, although it reduced some of the penalties proscribed by the 1664 act, allowed conventiclers to be convicted by two JPs acting summarily, thereby denying nonconformists the right to a trial by jury as guaranteed by Magna Carta. One pamphleteer alleged that the act was 'directly against our Fundamental Laws, and our

English Rights' and was therefore 'Illegal'.[109] Rather than blame the King, who on a number of occasions showed himself sympathetic to liberty of conscience, nonconformists and their sympathizers tended to hold the high-Anglican interest in parliament, and especially the bishops, responsible for the intolerant attitude towards dissent. Increasingly, more moderate Anglicans began to doubt the wisdom of harassing Protestant dissenters when a more dangerous threat to the Protestant religion seemed to be posed by the international threat of popery.

In fact by the mid-1670s political liberty appeared under threat for a number of reasons – and not just to dissenters, but also to many mainstream Anglicans. Charles had demonstrated an open preference for the French style of government, he had attempted to set up a standing army, and he had tried to suspend parliamentary statutes. During the mid-1670s Danby had threatened to subvert the independence of parliament through a system of pensions and bribery, and he seemed intent on introducing measures that would have made legitimate political opposition almost impossible. Thus when, in 1675, Danby tried to introduce a Test Bill into the Lords, which would have required all office-holders and members of both houses to make a declaration against resistance (either to the king or to those commissioned by him) and swear never to endeavour to alter the government in Church and state, Shaftesbury, Halifax and other opposition peers vehemently attacked the measure, insisting that there might well be occasions when it could be legitimate to resist those commissioned by the king and that the non-alteration oath was against 'the very nature, being, and ends of Parliament', which was to make alterations.[110] In a pamphlet which appeared later that year, and rapidly became a best-seller, Shaftesbury charged the Danby administration with wanting to 'declare the Government absolute and Arbitrary, and allow Monarchy, as well as Episcopacy to be *Jure Divino*, and not to be bounded or limited by humane Laws', and represented this as part of a long-term design by 'the High Episcopal Man, and the Old Cavalier' dating back to the Restoration.[111]

In short, then, the honeymoon period for the Restoration monarchy did not last long. Things were already looking gloomy by the mid- to late 1660s, as the political and religious failings of the restored regime – the Medway disaster, the pro-Catholic leanings of the court, the persecution of Protestant nonconformists – led many of those who had initially rejoiced at the monarchy's return to realize that they had not got quite what they had hoped for. On top of this, a series of natural disasters began to make some wonder whether the Stuarts, who had seemingly been miraculously restored by God's providence, had already forfeited divine favour. In November 1663 the bubonic plague was reported in Great Yarmouth – introduced by ship from Holland – and in the following spring there were cases in London. The mass outbreak, however, occurred in London in 1665; by the end of the year perhaps as many as 100,000 of the city's inhabitants had died.[112] The London-based nonconformist divine Thomas Vincent wrote of death riding 'triumphantly on his pale Horse through our streets', breaking 'into every House almost, where any Inhabitants are to be found'; people were falling 'as thick as leaves from the Trees in Autumn', he observed, so that 'we could hardly go forth, but we should meet many Coffins, and see diseased persons with soares and limping in the streets.'[113] In September 1666 occurred the Great Fire of London, destroying most of the built-up area of the City proper and causing damage to property estimated at some £10 million. The fire started by accident in a baker's shop in Pudding Lane; the instinct, however, was to blame the catastrophe on the perceived enemies of the state. Thus there were rumours that the Fifth Monarchists or alternatively the Catholics had been responsible. Indeed, a French Catholic watchmaker named Robert Hubert confessed to having started the fire as part of a conspiracy hatched in Paris, and was hanged as a result, although he was almost certainly deranged.[114] Preachers, however, were quick to see both the plague and the Fire as God's judgement upon the nation's sins, stretching from sabbath-breaking, swearing, drunkenness, fornication, adultery and pride through to persecution. The Anglican divine Richard Kingston, preaching about the plague, blamed the sin of uncharitableness for provoking God's wrath: 'The Turk cannot hate a Christian with a more Vatinian hatred,' he proclaimed, 'then we persecute one another, though baptized into the same Faith, and equally Professors of the same Gospell'; we had affronted Christ's injunction which bid us 'love one another'.[115] Similarly the minister of St Lawrence

Pountney, Robert Elborough, preaching on the Fire, alleged that 'Times of oppression and cruelty' were occasions when God was likely to be more severe in his judgements: 'It's an hard thing for us to be hard-hearted', he warned, 'and God to be tender-hearted.'[116] Yet, predictably, it was the Puritan divines who went furthest in their criticisms. Gilbert Burnet commented on how nonconformist ministers had taken over the pulpits left empty by Anglican clerics who had fled the plague and had begun 'to preach openly . . . on the sins of the court, and on the ill usage that they themselves had met with'.[117] Thomas Vincent, himself an ejected Presbyterian minister, produced a lengthy tract arguing that the plague and the Fire were visitations from God for the slighting of the Gospel; he not only bemoaned the rise of sectarianism and the lukewarm formalism of the Established Church, but also decried the Bartholomew Day ejections of 1662, the driving of God's ministers from the towns by the Five Mile Act of 1665, and the persecution of the godly.[118]

By the mid-1670s, with the threat of popery and arbitrary government seemingly confirmed by the King's Declaration of Indulgence, the Anglo-Dutch war fought in alliance with the French, the prospect of a popish successor, and the blatant attempts by the court to build up a standing army and subvert the independence of parliament, things appeared to have gone from bad to worse. Serious political and religious tensions had re-emerged in England, and voices calling for a return to a republic began to be heard. One poem of 1674, which circulated in the coffee houses, claimed that the miracle of the King's restoration had now become England's 'curse and punishment', and expressed the hope that the English would send Charles back to Breda and re-establish a commonwealth.[119] In another poem from the same time, John Ayloffe pleaded for the erection of a Venetian-style republic: 'To the serene Venetian state I'll go,' he has Britannia proclaim, 'From her sage mouth fam'd principles to know.'[120] Significantly, the republican poetry of the mid-1670s evinced a marked anti-Scottish – in the sense of anti-Stewart – bias. Ayloffe refers to the present dynasty as 'this stinking Scottish brood' after Britannia bemoans how she has tried 'too long in vain' to divide 'the Stuart from the tyrant'.[121] Another poem from 1676 (possibly also by Ayloffe) alleged that tyranny would 'be our case / Under all that shall reign of the false

Scottish race', and boldly proclaimed that the author was 'for old Noll' (i.e. Cromwell), for, 'Though his government did a tyrant's resemble, / He made England great and its enemies tremble.'[122] 'The Isle was well reform'd, and gain'd renown,' another rhymester asserted, 'Whilst the brave Tudors wore th' Imperial Crown, / But since the race of Stewarts came / It has recoil'd to Popery and shame.' He therefore concluded, 'Let Cromwell's Ghost smile with Contempt to see / old England struggling under Slavery.'[123]

Perhaps more worrying than the disaffection of the radicals, however, was the growing alienation of moderate opinion in the nation at large. The government was losing its hold over the middle ground. Within parliament, a broad country coalition had begun to emerge, embracing Presbyterian politicians, disgruntled former courtiers and old Cavaliers, and a younger generation of political aspirants who were distrustful of Danby's political and religious agenda. Its members were united in their concerns about the security of the Protestant interest at home and abroad and the liberties of English people in the face of the government's foreign policy, attitude towards France, stance on dissent, and efforts to subvert the independence of parliament. Moreover, this opposition was beginning to organize, holding meetings in advance of and during parliamentary sessions to coordinate tactics and to plan the best ways to bring pressure to bear for a change of royal policy.[124]

The mid-1670s also saw a revival of popular political agitation out-of-doors, especially in the capital. For example, there were widespread anti-Catholic demonstrations in London on 5 November 1673, as crowds burned effigies of the pope and his cardinals to protest against the Duke of York's marriage and England's alliance with France; one observer counted 200 bonfires between Temple Bar and Aldgate alone.[125] There was another pope-burning in Southwark on 26 November, the day that York's new bride arrived in England.[126] To demonstrate their growing concern about the threat of popery, Londoners also revived the commemoration of Elizabeth's accession day, 17 November – associated in people's minds with the restoration of Protestantism to England following Mary I's attempted Counter-Reformation of 1553–8 – and there were pope-burnings on this day at Temple Bar in 1676 and 1677. There were also signs of growing links between the country opposition in parliament and discontented elements out-of-doors. Some of the pope-burnings may well have been organized at the Green Ribbon Club, a meeting place for country and, later, Whig politicians which was just up from Temple Bar in Chancery Lane, and seems to have been founded in about 1674.[127] The enigmatic Duke of Buckingham, Shaftesbury's ally in the Lords, had connections with the London radical underground, including erstwhile Levellers such as John Wildman. It was at Buckingham's instigation that Francis Jenks, a London linen-draper, gave a sensational speech at the annual election of sheriffs in June 1676, during the long prorogation of the Cavalier Parliament between November 1675 and February 1677. Jenks warned of a threat to London from arsonists, impending economic ruin at the hands of the French, and a 'danger to his majesty's person' and the Protestant religion; he closed by calling upon the Lord Mayor to petition the crown for a new parliament, citing statutes from Edward III's reign which required annual parliaments.[128] When, in February 1677, Shaftesbury and Buckingham pressed in the Lords that the Cavalier Parliament was *ipso facto* dissolved because it had been prorogued for more than one year, 'a prodigious rabble' of their supporters gathered outside the House, ready 'to proclaim through the city with triumphant shouts and huzza, that the Parliament was dissolv'd', should they have carried their point.[129]

CONCLUSION

There is no reason to doubt the genuineness of the enthusiasm with which people greeted the return of monarchy in 1660. Most welcomed the restoration of Charles II, firm in their belief that he would make their world a better place. Many – perhaps a large majority – did so from a conviction that monarchy was both the natural order and the best form of government, and that this was why things had never been right since the setting-up of a republic. Others may have done so out of desperation as things seemed to go from bad to worse following the fall of the Protectorate, believing that the return of the house of Stuart was the only viable alternative to the anarchy that threatened to grip the country by late 1659. There were, to be sure, some who never wanted monarchy back, but these were a minority (and a relatively small one at that). We should not downplay their significance, but we cannot explain why things began to go wrong for the Restoration monarchy simply in terms of the survival of an underground republican tradition in England after 1660.

Instead, this chapter has sought to emphasize various structural problems that bedevilled the Restoration regime. One was the legacy of political and religious division bequeathed by the Civil War. Charles II was popular on the eve of his return because he could appear to be all things to all people. Yet he could not *actually* be all things to all people, and the partisan nature of the Restoration settlement and the fact that there were many whose expectations of the Restoration came to be disappointed – and who came to experience persecution as the price for having lost out – go a long way towards explaining why disaffection soon re-emerged. A second problem was the practical restraints on royal power, which served to frustrate efforts to rebuild royal authority effectively after 1660. Charles's lack of fiscal independence made him vulnerable to criticism from parliament, while his lack of a professional police force or bureaucracy made him heavily reliant on the cooperation of unpaid agents of the executive (from the lofty Lord Lieutenants to the humble parish constables) to enforce the royal will in the localities. On top of all this were the problems created by the King's style of government and the policies he chose to pursue. The various efforts he made to try to confront the political weaknesses of the crown served only to make matters worse – such as his experiments with religious indulgence, his efforts to manage parliament, his attempts to build up a standing army, and his decision to ally with the strongest power in Europe, Catholic France. Nor was he helped by his own personal weaknesses, such as his penchant for ladies of pleasure who happened to be Catholic, or by accidental contingencies which could hardly be laid at his door – such as the plague and the Great Fire, and, most importantly, the barrenness of his queen, which left his younger brother (who for his own reasons had decided to convert to the Catholic faith) as next in line to the throne. By the mid-1670s, as a result, many English people had grown concerned about what they perceived to be a drift towards popery and arbitrary government manifested by a pro-French foreign policy; a desire to help Catholics at home; a Catholic heir; and various efforts to subvert cherished English liberties by issuing royal proclamations suspending certain laws, attempting to subvert the independence of parliament by bribing members with offices and pensions, and imposing an oath promising never to endeavour any alteration in Church or state. It was in this context that, in 1677, Andrew Marvell launched his scathing indictment of the record of Charles II's government, alleging that since the early years of the Restoration there had been a design carried on 'to change the Lawfull Government of England into an Absolute Tyranny, and to convert the established Protestant Religion into down-right Popery' – pointing to the pro-Catholic leanings of the court, the attempt to draw England into the French orbit, the threat posed by political management to the independence of parliament, and the efforts to establish a standing army.[130]

Developments in England seemed bad enough. Yet people did not judge the Restoration monarchy solely by its record there. For Charles II was also king of Scotland and Ireland, and when developments in these two kingdoms were added to the equation the situation – to large numbers of British Protestants – seemed highly alarming indeed.

2

Popery and Arbitrary Government

The Restoration in Ireland and Scotland and the
Makings of the British Problem

It cannot be denyed, but that the Roman Catholicks of Ireland
have infinitely suffered, during the late Usurped Governments;
But they have done it cheerfully . . . having had all that time,
as Companions in Suffering, not only some of the Nobility and
Gentry of England and Scotland, but the King himself, and all
the Royal Family . . . But now since His Majesties happy
Restauration, and during the universal Jubilee of Joy over all
the British Monarchy, that the Irish alone shou'd be . . . con-
demned to a perpetual Sufferance, far surpassing those they
formerly endured under the Government of Cromwel, is a
Calamity rather to be deplored than exprest.[1]

The Bishops of England were like the Kings of Judah, some
good, some bad; but the Prelates in Scotland were like the
Kings of Israel, not one of them good, but . . . who made Israel
to Sin.[2]

The Restoration in Ireland and Scotland – as in England – was welcome
to broad cross-sections of the population. Yet in both kingdoms the
eventual settlement in Church and state was highly partisan, and left
substantial numbers of those who had supported the return of monarchy dissatisfied. In Scotland the re-establishment of episcopacy, coupled
with the way the government chose to deal with the problem of
Presbyterian nonconformity, created severe political and religious tensions. In Ireland there were a cluster of political, economic and religious
grievances, though the most contentious issue by far proved to be the

land settlement, especially the extent to which those (mainly Catholic) who had been dispossessed during the 1640s and '50s should be restored to their estates. The purpose of this chapter is to explore not only how these issues and tensions created instability in Ireland and Scotland respectively, but also how they interacted with developments in England to generate problems of a British nature. This will in turn set the context for the crisis that was to befall the Stuart monarchy in the late 1670s. It is impossible to appreciate the depth of the fears that English Whigs came to hold during the Exclusion Crisis about the threat of popery and arbitrary government unless we recognize that the Whigs were reacting, in part, to the threat of popery (in Ireland) and arbitrary government (in Scotland) that they already thought existed within the Stuart kingdoms. This chapter will also establish the necessary background for understanding the revolutions that occurred in Scotland and Ireland in 1688–91 (to be explored in the sequel to this book), both of which were reactions not just to developments in the 1680s, or under James II, but to what had been going on since 1660.

IRELAND

Most of the inhabitants of Ireland welcomed the return of monarchy in 1660. The regime established in the wake of the execution of Charles I in 1649 and parliamentary victory in the wars of 1641–52 had rested on a very narrow support base. Most Protestants in Ireland had sided with the English parliament during the Civil War, in reaction against the Irish Rebellion of October 1641 – a rebellion of Gaelic Irish and Catholic Old English in which over 3,000 Protestant settlers were violently killed and thousands more left to die after they had been stripped of their clothes and possessions and driven from their homes in winter. However, from 1648 those in the south rallied behind the crown, and by early 1649 an alliance of Catholic and Protestant royalists under the leadership of the Earl of Ormonde was in control of most of the country outside Dublin. Cromwell had to reduce Ireland to subservience to the newly born English republic by a brutal military campaign, and then use a policy of expropriation and plantation to try to create a new, Protestant, ascendancy that would be loyal to his regime. By the terms of the Act of Settlement of 1652, all those who had taken an active role in the rebellion of 1641, had been responsible for killing Protestants, or were still in arms and failed to submit to the new regime were to have their lands confiscated; unless they had 'manifested their constant good affection to the commonwealth of England', all other landowners were to suffer partial forfeiture, proportionate to their supposed 'delinquency'. The execution of the act involved the transplantation of delinquents across the river Shannon to Connacht, regularized by the Act of Satisfaction of 1653. The confiscations hit Catholics and Protestants, native Irish and Old English, alike, although it was Catholics of Old English stock who had the most to lose. The result was that Catholics, who had held 60 per cent of the profitable land of Ireland in 1641, held only 8 or 9 per cent by 1660. The beneficiaries were the parliamentary adventurers (those who in the 1640s had invested in parliament's war effort in return for the promise of land once the reconquest of Ireland had been achieved) and those soldiers who had served in Ireland under Cromwell, although many of the latter – being either unwilling to settle in Ireland or unable to wait until the land they had been promised became available – sold their debentures to speculators.[3]

The Cromwellian conquest also resulted in the loss of Ireland's political independence, such as it was. Ireland (along with Scotland) was merged into one commonwealth with England and, instead of having its own parliament, was given the right to send thirty members to sit in the parliament in Westminster. On the religious front, the 1650s saw an attempt to export the English ecclesiastical settlement into Ireland: prelacy was suppressed and the Book of Common Prayer was prohibited, but a national Established Church was maintained (with allowance for worship outside this framework), and an attempt was made to provide a preaching ministry to encourage the spread of Protestantism. Cromwell evinced little of his noted belief in religious toleration when it came to dealing with the Irish Catholics, however. Although the Catholics were not forced to attend Protestant services, the Catholic clergy – generally excluded from any of the negotiated peace settlements – were hunted down and, if caught, were liable to imprisonment, exile or even execution. In 1656 parliament passed an act whereby people over the age of sixteen could be required to take an oath abjuring the papal supremacy on pain of losing two-thirds of their real or personal property. The hope was that, once the influence of the Catholic clergy over their flocks was destroyed, the mass of the population would have no choice but to listen to Puritan ministers and, with the threat of coercive measures hanging over their heads, might be induced to convert. It proved totally misguided. The Catholic clergy managed to cling on, and even began to increase in number as the 1650s progressed; few conversions materialized; and the result was merely to strengthen the belief of Catholics in Ireland that they could not be safe so long as Protestants remained in charge.

With the collapse of the Protectorate in 1659, the republican regime in Ireland quickly fell apart. Following the resignation of Henry Cromwell as Lord Lieutenant of Ireland in June, a power struggle emerged between different factions of the army, and, in the face of a rapid drift towards political instability and a radicalization of the army under Edmund Ludlow, Protestant landowners grew increasingly anxious about the security of their newly acquired estates. The dissolution of the Rump Parliament and the seizure of power by the army in England in October 1659 was the last straw. On 13 December a group of officers under Sir Theophilus Jones, backed by gentry of old Protestant stock, seized Dublin Castle and declared for parliament.[4] Shortly thereafter, Sir Charles Coote and Lord Broghill, two ex-royalists turned Cromwellian collaborators, secured the garrisons in Connacht and Munster. The instigators of the coup purged the army of radicals and called an Irish Convention, representing the pre-war constituencies (though with boroughs and cities, except for Dublin, limited to one member instead of two), to meet at Dublin on 27 February 1660. Although dominated by Cromwellian settlers and the army, the Convention's members were persuaded (largely through the skilful management of Broghill and Coote) that only a restoration of monarchy could secure their interests.[5] As the second Earl of Clarendon was later to recall, 'of all his Majesties Subjects' it was the English in Ireland who 'made the Earliest advances towards his Majesties Restoration when the 3 Kingdoms were Governed by Usurpers'.[6] Indeed, the future Earl of Shaftesbury claimed in his autobiography that General Monck, commander of the army in Scotland, would never have acted against the English army and forced the dissolution of the Rump without knowing that he had the support of Coote and the army in Ireland.[7] In that sense, the Restoration was made in Ireland.

Charles II was proclaimed king in Dublin on 14 May, amid widespread celebrating. One contemporary confessed he had never seen 'the like for rejoyceing': the nobility, gentry, citizens and army were out in all their splendour; 'the streets ran with Wine', paid for by the corporation, for the consumption of 'the multitude'; and the evening saw salutes from the great guns, fireworks, and 'almost a Bonfire at every house'. The city also staged a mock funeral of the Rump, represented 'by an ugly mishapen body without an Head' but with a huge belly and enormous backside, which was carried through the city on a hearse, preceded by a group of mourners dressed in white carrying banners bearing the motto 'Vive le Roy.' The procession ended at the mayor's house, where the mayor first gave the funeral guests cakes and ale before they proceeded to burn the Rump at a bonfire outside his door.[8]

Settlement and Sale – Leaving them 'cloakless and shirtless in poverty'

Constitutionally, the Restoration in Ireland – as in England – saw a return to the *status quo ante*. This meant that Ireland reacquired its status as a separate kingdom (albeit one belonging to the crown of England), with the right to hold its own parliament, though subject, of course, to the restrictions of Poynings' Law. What made the Restoration in Ireland crucially different, however, was that it was brought about by those who had benefited from the Cromwellian regime – a factor that was to shape decisively the nature of the settlement. Their main concern was to retain control of their land, and – initially, at least – they were in the driving seat. Those Irish Protestants who had suffered for their support of the Stuart cause, of course, likewise welcomed the return of monarchy, but naturally hoped for a return to political dominance and for the restoration of their estates. On the religious front, episcopalians, Presbyterians and Protestant nonconformists all hoped to secure their respective religious interests. The Irish Catholics, on the other hand, 'sat still' during the spring of 1660, 'and contributed nothing to this great Revolution', as one Protestant put it, though most undoubtedly welcomed the return of monarchy, expecting to be allowed the same degree of practical religious toleration they had enjoyed before 1641 and to be restored to their estates.[9] The promises Charles made in his Declaration of Breda of April 1660 encouraged all groups to believe that he would satisfy their desires. Thus, on the day that Charles was proclaimed, the corporation of Trim in County Meath rejoiced at God's providential restoration of the ancient government and proclaimed their joyful acceptance of everything contained in 'his Majesties favourable and merciful declaration [of Breda]'.[10] Only a handful of radical sectarians remained consistently opposed to monarchical government.

Those who sat in the Irish Convention agreed on the need for a state Church, though they differed over whether a Presbyterian or an episcopalian settlement was preferable. Their priority, however, remained land. Thus they instructed the commissioners sent to London in June to treat with the King – a combination of episcopalians and Presbyterians – to secure the estates of the parliamentary adventurers and Cromwellian settlers, but gave them no specific orders concerning the settlement in the Church. Once the King's own preference for episcopacy became apparent, the commissioners conceded that the Church in Ireland should be 'resettled in Doctrine, Discipline and Worship' according to the laws in force in Ireland in Charles I's time, though 'with such Liberty to tender Consciences' as Charles II had promised in his Declaration of Breda. The corporation of Dublin likewise petitioned the King in late May for the settlement of that 'forme of church government and divine worshipp' used under Charles I and James I 'and which is already established here by lawe'.[11]

Such cues were all that Charles needed. By the end of June 1660 he had made appointments to the vacant bishoprics, and, although several months elapsed before the consecrations could take place, by the beginning of the next year episcopalianism had been fully restored.[12] On 22 January 1661 the King issued a proclamation declaring all meetings by papists, Presbyterians, Independents and separatists illegal and prohibiting such people from appointing days of humiliation or thanksgiving and from making ordinations. Then in May the newly convened Irish parliament issued a proclamation requiring 'all persons whatsoever' to obey the laws establishing the government of the Church by bishops and to conform to the Prayer Book, and passed a declaration ordering all towns to burn the Solemn League and Covenant and requiring those clergy who had taken it to renounce it in public.[13] Although several English Presbyterian ministers in the area around Dublin conformed, most nonconformist ministers found themselves driven out. In the province of Ulster, with its nearly seventy Presbyterian ministers who had taken the Covenant 'with great solemnity', only a handful conformed – these changing from 'solid and gifted' men of God to 'loose, oppressive, proud' and even 'profane' creatures under the influence of episcopal government, according to the contemporary Ulster Presbyterian historian Patrick Adair.[14] The Irish Convocation, which sat between 1661 and 1663, established that preachers should pray for 'Christ's holy Catholick Church' – in other words, 'for the whole Congregation of Christian People dispersed throughout the whole world and especially for the Churches of England, Scotland and Ireland' – revealing their belief that there was one true Church and that therefore the religious settlements in the three kingdoms needed to be in conformity with each other. They further stipulated that preachers should pray for the king as 'Defender of the Faith and Supream Governour . . . over all Persons in all Causes as well Ecclesiasticall as Temporall'.[15] For the time being, however, the legal basis of the restored Church remained the old Elizabethan Act of Supremacy and Act of Uniformity of 1560, together with the articles and canons of 1634. It was not until 1666 that the Irish parliament passed an Act of Uniformity (based on the English act of 1662) prescribing a revised Book of Common Prayer, requiring episcopal ordination of all clergy, and stipulating that all clerics and teachers subscribe a declaration against the Solemn League and Covenant and renounce resistance to the king or anyone 'commissionated by him'. This non-resistance oath subsequently came to be imposed by many corporations as a test for membership.[16] The Restoration ecclesiastical establishment, like its English counterpart, was to be narrowly episcopalian and firmly committed to the principle of non-resistance.

Although the Restoration brought no formal toleration for Catholics, the dissolution of the Cromwellian union did mean an end to the harsh persecution of the 1650s, which had been based on the application of English anti-Catholic legislation to Ireland. Irish legislation which applied to Catholics was mild in comparison. The main disabilities were spelled out by the Irish Act of Supremacy (1560), which required all office-holders, ecclesiastical persons and those taking holy orders or university degrees to take the oaths of supremacy and allegiance, and by the Act of Uniformity (1560), which laid down fines of 1 shilling per Sunday for those who failed to come to church.[17] Yet for much of Charles II's reign the penal laws against Catholics were laxly enforced, resulting in a *de facto* toleration – though there were to be bouts of repression, typically when political exigencies in England led to pressure for stricter measures against papists in Ireland. The law did, at least in theory, guarantee the Protestant political and economic ascendancy in the towns. The requirement to take the oath of supremacy excluded Catholics from corporate office, while most corporations at the Restoration revived old by-laws excluding Catholics even from becoming freemen and thus engaging in trade, although even these stipulations (as we shall see) were not consistently or uniformly enforced.[18]

The most controversial issue in Ireland proved to be the land settlement. Catholics expected the restoration of their estates, which they regarded as having been illegally taken from them during the 1640s and '50s; indeed, some immediately tried to repossess their former lands, and Charles II had to issue a proclamation against this on 1 June 1660.[19] The current occupiers, by contrast, wanted to protect what they believed they had legally acquired. Broghill and Coote insisted that 'the English interest in Ireland' had to be preserved, and convinced Ormonde – now Lord Steward of the Household – that the Catholics in Ireland should be excluded from the English Act of Indemnity of August 1660, though the Catholics felt this was contrary to the Declaration of Breda. Their fate was to be determined by future legislation.[20] Charles realized that he would need to help those who had lost their estates in his father's cause, both Protestant and Catholic, while at the same time providing some form of compensation for the purchasers. In an impossible attempt to appease these competing interests, on 30 November 1660 he issued a declaration promising that Catholics innocent of involvement in the Irish Rebellion should recover their estates and that soldiers and adventurers should keep their acquisitions or be compensated ('reprised') for the land they had to restore to innocents, and offering land to Protestants who had served in the royal forces in Ireland before June 1649.[21] He appointed a body of commissioners – all Protestants, and many of them Cromwellian purchasers – to administer the redistribution of land, but the Irish courts refused to enforce their decisions, as lacking statutory authority. Charles was thus forced to defer the land question to parliament, which assembled in Dublin in May 1661.[22]

Catholics were not formally excluded from this parliament: there was no legal bar to their election, and a proposal that no one should be allowed to sit unless he took the oaths of supremacy and allegiance was rejected in England. Only one Catholic was returned, however, and his election was subsequently overturned on petition. A few Catholic peers sat in the Lords, but many Catholics were debarred as a result of outlawry proceedings following the rebellion of 1641. The parliament which made the land settlement was therefore scarcely representative 'of the people of Ireland', as one Irish Catholic later complained. On top of this, the operation of Poynings' Law meant that any legislation the Irish parliament agreed to would have to be approved by the privy council in England, thus guaranteeing that English interests would be put first.[23]

The resultant Act of Settlement of May 1662 gave statutory force to the royal declaration of November 1660.[24] The problem was, as contemporaries were well aware, that Ireland would need to be two or three times its size to satisfy all the competing interests.[25] A court of claims set up to administer the act's provisions heard some 800 cases, issuing 566 decrees of innocence to Catholics and 141 to Protestants, and declaring 113 Catholics 'nocent'; but when the time allowed for hearing cases expired, in August 1663, several thousand claims remained unheard. Protestants complained about the liberality to Catholics, especially since it was apparent that they themselves would not receive adequate land in compensation, and alleged that decrees of innocence had been obtained on false evidence. Many Catholics, on the other hand, felt they had been denied the chance to prove their innocence, while some of those restored found that they could not recover their estates because the present occupiers could not be settled elsewhere. In 1665 parliament passed an Act of Explanation in an attempt to clear up the mess: soldiers and adventurers were to hand over one-third of their land to meet the requirements of restoration and reprisal; existing decrees of innocence were confirmed; but no more claims were to be heard, the act instead naming certain individuals who were to have full or partial restoration of their estates. The end result was that Catholics were restored to the ownership of about 20 per cent of the profitable land of Ireland – a mere third of their holdings in 1641. Charles himself did not help matters by giving the land taken from the regicides, estimated at 169,431 acres, to his brother, the Duke of York, thus diminishing the stock available for reprisals. Other courtiers also benefited from royal largesse: Ormonde, who served two stints as Lord Lieutenant of Ireland (1662–8 and 1677–85), vastly increased the size of his estates, as did the Earl of Anglesey, while the English Secretary of State, Henry Arlington, was given a grant of estates in Queen's County and King's County (Laois and Offaly) as a 'sweetener' in order to ensure his support for the Act of Explanation.[26] To Irish Catholics the land settlement was 'the greatest injustice' ever seen, with 'an innocent nation' being 'excluded from their birth-rights' and 'condemned before they were heard'.[27] Nicholas French, the Catholic Bishop of Ferns, in a pamphlet of 1668 condemning the 'Settlement and Sale of Ireland', blamed the King's ministers, and particularly Clarendon, who, he alleged, aimed at 'the general extirpation of the whole Irish race'. Yet he also criticized the King himself for conferring lands taken from the regicides on his courtiers and favourites, and in particular on his brother, since these lands had been acquired illegally by the regicides in the first place and were not the King's to give away.[28] As the Gaelic Irish poet David Ó Bruadair bemoaned, the Irish nobility had remained loyal to Charles II and followed him into exile, 'Yet when home they returned they got nought of their old demesnes / But to gaze at their lands like a dog at a lump of beef.' The Act of Settlement, he concluded, 'hath broken their banks, / And left them all cloakless and shirtless in poverty'.[29]

As in England, there were attempts to encourage attachment to the restored monarch through the promotion of public celebrations and annual commemorations. On 23 April 1661 several towns celebrated Charles's coronation in England with civic displays, street parties and bonfires.[30] In 1662 parliament added 29 May to the calendar of annual celebrations.[31] Many corporations throughout Ireland enthusiastically commemorated the anniversaries of both the coronation and the Restoration each year, providing alcohol for the local inhabitants and encouraging the construction of bonfires.[32] More provocatively, in 1662 parliament passed an act establishing 23 October as a day of commemoration for deliverance from the Irish Rebellion. As a result, each year pulpits were to thunder with sermons recounting the alleged atrocities committed on the Protestant population by Irish Catholics, and any incumbent who chose not to give a sermon was nevertheless obliged to read the 1662 act aloud to his congregation, thus helping to forge and reinforce a Protestant memory of what supposedly had transpired in 1641. Protestant parishioners themselves often marked the occasion with anti-Catholic rituals, such as pope-burnings, which inevitably proved contentious in an overwhelmingly Catholic country. In 1666 parliament went further and added 5 November to the calendar of commemorations.[33]

The Sources of Discontent

Although most in Ireland had welcomed the return of monarchy, many felt some degree of dissatisfaction with the Restoration settlement. This was true, to varying degrees, of all the different interest groups within the kingdom. The Restoration benefited Protestants of the Established Church most. Nevertheless, some of these had to turn over land to Catholics, and, given that they made up less than 10 per cent of the population, they feared that any further concessions to Catholics or to Protestant nonconformists would make their position highly vulnerable. Moreover, although the English government guaranteed their ascendancy within Ireland, their interests were always subordinated to those of England whenever the two clashed. Thus the Restoration regime in England continued the long-established policy of making sure that the Irish economy could not threaten its own. The export of Irish wool to foreign countries had long been prohibited, and in 1662 the English parliament passed an act making it a felony.[34] Two acts of 1663 and 1667 put a stop to the rapidly expanding and highly prosperous Irish cattle trade, in order to protect the interests of English cattle-breeders.[35] Breeders in Ireland, who had suffered considerably as a result of the restrictions placed on the import of Irish cattle into England imposed in 1663, were outraged when it became apparent in late 1666 and early 1667 that the English government was planning a total prohibition. One Dublin Protestant predicted the new bill would 'certainly beggar us';[36] similarly, Sir Heneage Finch, speaking in the English parliament, reminded his fellow MPs that the Protestant adventurers had just been forced to give up two-thirds of their estates and claimed that the proposed bill would ruin them.[37] Yet it was not only Protestants in Ireland who would suffer; Catholic breeders also had much to lose. Revealingly, we find opponents of the Irish Cattle Bill prepared to embrace the argument that, by enacting a measure that would strike at the economic prosperity of the Catholic community, the English government would jeopardize the well-being of the English interest in Ireland. In February 1667, shortly after the passage of the second Irish Cattle Act, the earls of Anglesey and Burlington and Viscount Conway (all peers with substantial Irish landholdings) drew up a detailed memorandum to the King representing 'the growing evils that Act must inevitably bring', claiming that many Irish 'who cannot find a livelyhood by the breeding of Cattle' had 'already gone into actuall rebellion, burning and spoyling the English', and warning that 'the necessities and poverty of the Generality' not only would decrease the King's revenues but might even 'invite and facilitate forreigne invasion'. The solution, they suggested, was to lift the prohibition and allow free trade.[38] Protestant traders in Ireland received a further blow from the Navigation Act of 1671, which undermined Irish overseas trade by insisting that all imports from the colonies had to be landed first in England.[39] As a *Letter from a Gentleman in Ireland* put it in 1677, the jealous English 'interpret our industry as Theft': 'you prohibit our Cattel, you restrain our Wool; our Manufacture is intolerable; you forbid our Trading with any Forreign Commodities in your own Plantations . . . We are in all things, indeed, treated by you like, or worse than Aliens.'[40]

Protestant nonconformists, who in Ireland outnumbered members of the Established Church, and the Cromwellian settlers (most of whom were themselves nonconformists) were alike upset with both the settlement in the Church and the land settlement. A minority of extremists resorted to active conspiracy against the restored regime. In the spring of 1663 a group of discontented army officers, led by Lieutenant Thomas Blood and Colonel Alexander Jephson, together with a few nonconformist ministers, launched an unsuccessful plot to seize Dublin Castle and the strongholds of Cork, Limerick, Waterford and Clonmel, with the aim of overthrowing both the land and the ecclesiastical settlements. In their printed declaration, they proclaimed their intent to secure 'the English interest in the 3 Kingdoms', which they alleged was being ruined 'by countenance given to popery', and demanded that 'all the English' should be restored to the estates they possessed as of 7 May 1659 and 'That Religion should be setled according to the Solemne League and Covenant'. They did not call for the reinstitution of a republic, however, but intended to declare 'For the King, and English intrest'.[41] Rumours of republican conspiracy in England in the 1660s often contained an Irish dimension. Thus in 1664 there were reports of a plot linking England, Holland and 'the old army in Ireland', headed by the exiled republicans Algernon Sidney and Edmund Ludlow, while in August 1665 there surfaced rumours of a plot in the English West Country, which again involved a simultaneous conspiracy in Ireland.[42] Fears of a French or Dutch invasion of Ireland in 1666, at the time of the second Anglo-Dutch War, prompted the government to take heightened security measures as it feared for the loyalty of the more disaffected nonconformists of Ireland (especially in Ulster); the covenanter rebellion in the south-west of Scotland in November of that year had the same effect. The government was probably overreacting, as Ireland was to remain quiet, but it clearly felt that it was better to be safe than sorry.[43]

The extent of discontent among Cromwellian settlers and nonconformist elements in Ireland is difficult to gauge. In 1663 Jephson had alleged that the discontent among the English was 'so generall' following the proceedings of the court of claims that they would not 'long beare it', though his remarks undoubtedly betray the self-delusion of a desperate plotter.[44] Some of the revelations of supposed republican plots involving malcontents in England and Ireland were little more than the product of the fertile imaginations of unscrupulous informers seeking to feed off government paranoia. Nevertheless, the assize records for Clonmel, County Tipperary, which happen to survive, hint at pockets of disaffection in the Irish south. For example, one Charles Minchin was indicted at the April 1663 assizes for having said on several occasions over the past couple of years 'that if there were but three men [in Ireland] to oppose the King his comeing into his Kingdomes, he would be one', adding that he would readily engage against the government rather than hand over his estate. At the same assizes, one Henry Feltham was indicted for saying that he hoped the King 'were served as his father . . . was' and 'That it was like to goe hard with the English Enterest' that Ormonde 'did rather favour the Irish Entrest then the English Enterest', while one Daniell Quinlyn was indicted for saying he cared not 'for the King Queene or Duke of York' since he got more by Cromwell than by them. All three were found not guilty, it should be said, perhaps suggesting that the prosecutions were malicious. On the other hand, the Clonmel records abound with allegations of seditious talk in the early years of the Restoration, intimating at least that political tensions ran high in this area and that many were suspected of harbouring deep grievances against the new regime. They also point to tensions between the Gaelic Irish and the Cromwellian interlopers: one of Feltham's accusers was a man called Teige Magrath; at the April 1663 assizes Thomas O'Dwyer was indicted for refusing to help a constable pacify an affray and accusing the constable of being a rebel; while in October 1665 one David Davies was accused by one Mortagh O'Bryen of saying that he wished 'Oliver Cromwell were alive againe' and 'the King hanged'.[45]

When all is said and done, it appears that the great majority of Protestant dissenters in Ireland did become reconciled to the Restoration regime, which afforded them a good measure of *de facto* toleration. Ireland never saw the establishment of the same type of penal code as was to emerge in England; it thus had no Conventicle Act nor Test Act. One Dublin correspondent observed in late 1666 that local officials were prepared to 'winck at' nonconformist worship, 'It stomaching our Constables', he said, 'to secure such when they say they may not disturbe the Papists at their meeting'; even the bishops, aware that the Irish dissenters were not as 'troublesome nor quarrelsome as those of Scotland', seemed willing to connive at them.[46] In the late 1660s and early 1670s the royal administration in London moved towards a policy of informal indulgence, instructing successive Lord Lieutenants not to proceed against nonconformists without specific authorization from the King. By leaving alone those who accepted the Restoration settlement, the government thereby hoped to isolate the more militant types and thus concentrate its energies on those who posed a true threat. The biggest worry were the Scottish Presbyterians in the north, who were well organized with their own, independent, ecclesiastical structure. However, the tacit support of the vast majority of Presbyterians in Ireland was secured by the *regium donum* of 1672, a grant by the crown of £600 per year to ministers of the Presbyterian Church, which was graciously accepted, even in Ulster, as a gesture of the government's goodwill. Although tensions existed within the Presbyterian movement in Ireland, and itinerant preachers from Scotland did their best to keep the covenanting tradition alive among the rank and file in Ulster, most of the better-off Presbyterians and their ministers were reluctant to rock the boat by engaging in any intrigues with their covenanting brethren across the North Channel – not least, perhaps, because of their recognition that any threat to the existing Protestant ascendancy could only work to the advantage of Catholics. Nonconformists were also made freemen of some towns, meaning that economically they were not as marginalized as their counterparts in England. However, neither the government nor the Established Church wanted to see the spread of dissenting congregations, and both remained hostile to any efforts – particularly by the Ulster Presbyterians – to expand into new areas of Ireland. At best, an uneasy equilibrium prevailed.[47]

It was the Catholic majority who had most reason to feel aggrieved, suffering as they did from religious, economic and political disabilities. It is important, however, not to generalize about the Catholic interest in Ireland. Some Catholic landowners, mainly those of Old English stock, did recover their estates at the Restoration, and they were naturally less resentful towards the restored regime than those who did not. The Old English, of course, saw themselves as the heirs of the original English conquerors of Ireland, and thus have to be distinguished from the Gaelic Irish, very few of whom made any gains from the Restoration land settlement and who were most resentful of English rule (though, significantly, it was the Gaelic Irish who typically embraced the myth that the Stuart kings were originally descended from the ancient kings of Ireland and believed therefore that in Charles II they had a king who was theoretically one of their own). We also have to recognize that the concerns of the Catholic landowning classes were different from those of the Catholic tenantry or the Catholic merchants or working classes of the towns, as well as the existence of differences of interest between the laity in general and the clergy. Certainly, the vast majority of Catholics, whatever their background, hoped for some alleviation of their plight, though most, it is probably fair to say, wanted to show that they deserved better treatment because they were loyal subjects. Thus in December 1661 the Earl of Fingall and ninety-seven other Catholic peers, gentry and proprietors subscribed a remonstrance addressed to Charles II pledging their unqualified allegiance to the crown and renouncing all foreign power, 'be it either Papal, or Princely, Spiritual, or temporal', in return for religious toleration. More signatures were collected over the next few months, bringing the total number of subscribers to 164 of the 'chiefest' of the Catholic laity together with some 70 of their clergy; most of the clergy remained hostile, however, and after a prolonged controversy the subscription was eventually dropped.[48] Yet spokesmen for the dispossessed Catholics tended to insinuate that the natural desire of the Catholics to be loyal would evaporate if something were not done to ease their burden. Thus the Bishop of Ferns warned that if, out of despair, 'the destroyed Irish' chose 'to joyn with the Scots against the English that possess their Estates', 'the English Interest' would without a doubt 'be lost in Ireland'; it was thus in 'the true Interest of England' to raise 'the Irish as a Bulwark, or ballance, against our English and Scotch Presbyterians'. Favouring the Irish would also 'quash all the Designs against England, That France or any Foreigner may endeavour to ground upon the discontents of a destroyed, and desperate people'.[49]

The trouble for the crown, however, was that any concessions granted to Catholics in Ireland ran the risk not only of alienating the Protestant interest in Ireland, but also of stirring up political trouble in England, where suspicions were already emerging that the royal administration was soft on popery. During the administration of the Cabal, when Charles was experimenting with a policy of greater indulgence for Catholics and for Protestant nonconformists in England, moves were made to ease the plight of the Catholics in Ireland. Lord Berkeley, appointed Lord Lieutenant in 1670, not only showed considerable favour to the Catholic clergy, but also admitted some Catholics as JPs and to other minor offices, and in March 1672 he issued a general licence allowing Catholics to buy or lease property in corporate towns and to be admitted as freemen, as well as restoring them to 'all the privileges and freedoms' they or their ancestors had enjoyed during the reign of Charles I. In May 1672 Berkeley was replaced by the Earl of Essex, whose 'New Rules' for the corporations of Ireland in September 1672 allowed the head of the government in Ireland to dispense office-holders and freemen from the requirement to take the oaths of allegiance and supremacy. The primary aim was to enhance royal control over the corporations in Ireland – the new rules also provided that all new office-holders had to be approved by the Lord Lieutenant and the Irish privy council – but the effect was to raise a challenge to the Established Church's monopoly of office-holding. Thus over the next few months Essex issued a number of dispensations to both Catholics and Protestant nonconformists; in Dublin alone, some nine or ten Catholics took their seats on the common council, while Kinsale saw the intrusion of several new freemen with Irish names.[50] During this time the royal administration in England also showed itself willing to re-examine the land settlement. In January 1672, responding to a petition from Colonel Richard Talbot (the future Earl of Tyrconnell) on behalf of the 'distressed subjects of Ireland . . . outed of their estates' by the late usurped powers, Charles II set up a commission of inquiry to inspect the Act of Settlement and the Act of Explanation, their implementation and the disposing of forfeited lands.[51]

The new spirit of self-confidence that such concessions engendered among Catholics proved alarming to many Protestants. From Munster, the Earl of Orrery (the former Lord Broghill) reported how, following the council's decision of March 1672 to allow Catholics to become freemen, 'the old Rebellinge Irish Magistrates' of Cashel, in County Tipperary, 'Came in a body' and demanded that the present magistrates hand over power to them. The English, 'haveinge noe Garrison to Defend them', were terrified, but after stalling for time eventually secured a letter from the King explaining that the intent (at this time) was only to allow Catholic merchants to dwell in the towns, not admit them to the magistracy. Orrery also complained about the greater insolence of the Catholic clergy. In Limerick, one priest conducted a Catholic funeral in broad daylight in a Protestant churchyard 'almost under the Nose of the Bishop of Lymerick', without so much as asking leave. Although the Catholic clergy did seek Orrery's permission to hold masses publicly in the city, they had already signalled their intention to worship openly, having erected convents and mass houses 'in hundreds of Places', some in open view right by the highway, while one of their archbishops was reported to have boasted that shortly all Protestants 'should be Compeld to goe to Mass'. Indeed, in parts of the west Catholics were refusing to pay tithes to the parish minister, declaring that 'they would Pay them to the Romish Priest of the Parish'.[52]

News of such developments provoked a strong reaction in the English parliament. On 10 March 1671, in a petition to the King against the growth of popery, parliament complained of 'the great Insolencies of the Papists in Ireland', 'the open Exercise of Mass' and the activities of the titular archbishops and bishops.[53] Then in March 1673, with concerns about the growth of popery already heightened by the English Declaration of Indulgence of the previous year, the Commons called for the maintenance of the Acts of Settlement and Explanation, the recalling of the commission of inquiry, the removal of Catholic judges, JPs, sheriffs and magistrates, the banishment of all Roman Catholic clergy out of Ireland, and the exclusion of Catholics from the corporations.[54] A period of tightening-up followed. Several corporations, including those of Dublin, Waterford and Kinsale, passed by-laws stating that no one was to be admitted as a freeman unless he first took the oaths of allegiance and supremacy.[55] Nevertheless, the question of the land settlement remained on the agenda. Over the course of 1678 the Irish privy council considered various proposals for a bill to be brought before a forthcoming parliament in Ireland for the confirmation of estates and the remedy of defective titles; this caused considerable alarm to those Protestants who felt that the Catholics had already received more land than was their due while they themselves had remained inadequately compensated for land given up at the Restoration.[56] The outbreak of the Popish Plot in England in 1678, however, meant that no Irish parliament was called and thus no such bill was forthcoming.

Protestants in both Ireland and England perpetually worried that Irish Catholics were conspiring with the Catholic superpowers of Europe, especially France, to destroy the Protestant interest in Britain. During the war with France and the United Provinces in 1666–7, for example, there were repeated reports that 'the Irish were tampering with France' and that the French were going to send an invasion force to help the Irish rise up against Anglo-Protestant domination.[57] As fears of France intensified in the 1670s, such alarms became more common. In February 1674 Shaftesbury was set to introduce a petition into the Lords proclaiming that Ireland 'had been in danger of an invasion' during the third Anglo-Dutch War, of 1672–4, and that the 'French had intrigues everywhere' and would have descended upon Ireland 'if the last battle with the Dutch had been successful', though the petition was lost with the prorogation on the 24th.[58] In December 1676 it was reported that Dr Oliver Plunket, the titular Roman Catholic primate of Ireland, had been conspiring back in October 1672 to get the French king and some of the other 'Catholicke princes abroade' to send an army to Ireland to assist the Catholics there ('there beeing very many, whoe hee knew, thatt would take Arms withe them') and to 'propagat the faith to the Advantage off the Romishe Church'.[59]

There is no firm evidence that the Irish Catholics ever did contemplate treasonous activity against the crown. To many English Protestants, however, they could never be trusted; hence the need for stern measures. Yet stern measures were likely to provoke the Irish Catholics into desperate action against the English interest. It was a vicious circle. If the King and his ministers tried to alleviate the situation by making certain gestures, however small, towards the Catholic community, they were likely to run the risk of being accused back in England of being soft on popery. In this sense, the Irish problem was inevitably also an English problem, even if the Catholics in Ireland themselves were not actually causing any problems.

The tensions within Ireland were so deep, and so difficult to address without creating adverse knock-on consequences, that it might seem fair to conclude that the situation there was inherently unstable. Yet it would be wrong to paint too bleak a view. Indeed, for much of Charles II's reign a relative equilibrium established itself in Ireland. The Irish economy began to recover after the devastation caused by warfare in the 1640s, and many of those who lost out as a result of the Restoration settlement in Church and state, while far from happy, found that they were able to make their peace with a regime that was not too strict in enforcing the penal codes and managed to provide for some degree of economic prosperity. One Protestant pamphleteer, writing in 1689, looked back on the reign of Charles II and observed that

> though the Papists were too much countenanced and indulg'd; and many hardships placed on the Protestants, especially in relationship to the Act of Settlement, yet by the favour of Heaven . . . Ireland was under very auspicious circumstances: The church Flourished, Trade Increased, the Cities and Towns were every Year inlarged with new Additions, the Country Inriched and Beautified with Houses and Plantations, the Farms were loaden with Stock, and ready and quick Markets there were to vent them: The Laws had a free and uninterrupted course, and a standing Army was so far from being a Terrour, that they were the comfort and security of the people.[60]

The imperial Protestant bias as well as the retrospective nostalgia is transparent: for English Protestants in Ireland, almost any year would have been better than 1689, while the very qualifications the author himself introduces hint at the existence of deep-seated discontents brewing beneath the surface. At the same time, however, such observations contain an element of truth. Things were not *that* bad in Ireland, or, at least, they were not as bad as they might have been, or had been in the past, or were to be again in the future. In many respects, Ireland proved less troublesome for Charles II than did England. And the situation in Ireland was nowhere near as volatile as it was in Scotland.

SCOTLAND

It had been Scottish resistance to the imposition of the Laudian Prayer Book in 1637 which had triggered the crisis that had led ultimately to the overthrow of the Stuart monarchy. In the late 1630s and early 1640s the Scottish covenanters achieved a revolution in Church and state that resulted in the overthrow of episcopacy, the establishment of a Presbyterian system of church government, and the curtailment of certain royal prerogatives (such as the right of the Scottish king to choose his own ministers, to call parliament, or to control the armed forces). The Scots had no sympathy for a republic, however; their ideal was a covenanted king. They allied themselves with Charles I during the second civil war of 1648, on condition that he support

Presbyterianism, and, following the regicide in January 1649, they proclaimed his son king not just of Scotland, but also of England. Charles II was subsequently crowned at Scone in January 1651, though not until after he had been made to sign the National Covenant of 1638 and the Solemn League and Covenant of 1643. Scotland had to be conquered and occupied by the English to keep it subdued. It is true that a minority of hardline covenanters, or 'Protesters', distanced themselves from the explicit royalism of the moderate 'Resolutioners'; their goal was the extension of a Presbyterian theocracy over all of Great Britain. Yet the Protesters, as much as the Resolutioners, disliked the Erastianism and the religious tolerance of the republican regimes of the 1650s, and, although both ecclesiastical groups flirted with the Interregnum governments in an attempt to secure power and influence and promote their own religious agenda, the roots established by the republic north of the border were even shallower than they were in England or Ireland.[61]

The restoration of monarchy in the spring of 1660 – triggered, as it was, by the intervention in England by the army of Scotland under the command of General Monck – thus proved welcome to most Scots. According to the Earl of Balcarres, never did a king succeed 'to a Crown or Throne more with the Love and Esteem of his Subjects' than did Charles II 'generally to all Scotland, of all Professions'.[62] Edinburgh saw elaborate civic celebrations on 14 May, the day Charles was proclaimed king in the Scottish capital, followed in the evening by bells, fireworks and bonfires, as magistrates and citizens alike celebrated 'this great deliverance'. There were bonfires and bells in many places throughout the country on 19 June, the official day of thanksgiving in Scotland for the King's restoration; in Edinburgh, on this occasion, an effigy of Oliver Cromwell, with the Devil pursuing him, was 'blown up' on Castle Hill.[63] Preachers encouraged such celebrations, exhorting their flocks to rejoice at the providential return of a divinely ordained monarch (though warning them not to drink to excess); at Linlithgow, to the west of Edinburgh, James Ramsey delivered a fiery sermon in which he not only preached of the sinfulness of rebellion, but insisted that the king was *legibus solutus* (that is, absolute), irresistible and unaccountable (except to God alone), and possessed of the power to dispense with or even abrogate the laws in certain instances.[64]

The Resolutioners welcomed the Restoration in anticipation of a Presbyterian settlement; Charles II had, after all, signed the covenants. Charles in fact resented the way he had been treated by the Scots in 1650–51 and disliked Presbyterianism, but his first ministerial team, appointed in the summer of 1660, showed a willingness to compromise. Prominent positions went to the two leaders of the Scottish royalist uprising of 1653–4, the Earl of Middleton and the Earl of Glencairn – the former named commissioner to parliament, the latter chancellor. Yet the earls of Rothes, Cassillis and Crawford – three ex-covenanters – became Lord President of the Council, justice-general and Lord Treasurer respectively, while the crucial position of Secretary of State went to another ex-covenanter, the Earl (later Duke) of Lauderdale, a man of moderate Presbyterian sympathies but whose loyalty lay first and foremost with the crown. Only Protester opinion was not represented.[65]

Rendering the King Absolute

Charles certainly did not want clerics determining the nature of the Restoration settlement north of the border, however. He therefore decided that the general assembly of the Church should not be allowed to meet; as a result, the working-out of the Restoration settlement was left to the laity in parliament, which sat from 1 January 1661. Middleton secured the enactment of a legislative package that undid the Presbyterian constitutional and political reforms of the 1640s and returned the Scottish polity in Church and state to the position of 1633. He was helped by the decision to revive the Lords of the Articles, the select parliamentary steering committee used to manage the passage of legislation through parliament – an act of 1640, which had received the royal assent in 1641, had determined that parliament could choose or not choose a committee of Articles, as it thought expedient – although the committee was not, for the time being, the mere tool of the court that it had once been, since the peers, shire commissioners and burgh commissioners were allowed to choose their own representatives (there were as yet, of course, no bishops).[66] Middleton's programme did meet with a fair amount of opposition, but bribes and threats enabled the government to win over potential opponents, thereby leaving diehard critics isolated and in no position to mount an effective challenge. Yet Middleton was also able to tap into a marked royalist and anti-clerical reaction among the traditional ruling classes of Scotland, who were eager to diminish the influence of the clerical estate in policy formation and anxious to do what they could to please their restored monarch, in the hope of reviving their own political and economic fortunes, which had suffered a serious decline during the troubles of the 1640s and '50s.[67]

On the opening day of the session, parliament passed an act requiring all members to take an oath of allegiance recognizing Charles II as the 'only Supream Governour of this Kingdome over all persons and in all causes' and acknowledging that 'no forrane Prince, Power or State, nor persone civill or ecclesiastick' had 'any power or superiority' over him. The wording was vague, and some members cavilled at the oath – among them the Earl of Cassillis, who quit the parliament – because it seemed to imply that the King was also supreme in ecclesiastics, although the King's advocate hastily issued a reassurance that the supremacy applied only to civil matters.[68] Then parliament set about undoing the constitutional and religious revolution of the late 1630s and the 1640s. At first it proceeded piecemeal. On 11 January it passed two acts designed to undo the most important constitutional reforms of 1640–41. One affirmed that it was 'ane undoubted parte of the Royall Prerogative', by virtue of 'that Royall power' which kings 'hold from God Almichtie', to appoint officers of state, privy counsellors and Lords of Session, thus undoing a measure of 1641 requiring officers of state to be chosen with the advice of parliament or the privy council. The other confirmed that the power of calling, proroguing and dissolving parliament resided solely in the king, thereby rescinding the Triennial Act of 1640.[69] Five days later, parliament passed an act ratifying laws from James VI's reign making it illegal for subjects to assemble 'to treat, consult and determine in any matter of state civill or ecclesiastick' or to make leagues or bonds without the king's permission, together with a Militia Act asserting that it was the king's right alone to make war and peace and control the armed forces (though this did insist that his subjects should be 'frie of the provisions and mantenance' of such forces unless authorized by parliament or a

Convention of Estates).[70] On 22 January parliament declared all acts passed by the Convention of Estates of 1643 – the body that had issued the Solemn League and Covenant – null and void.[71]

On 28 March parliament took the more dramatic step of passing a sweeping Rescissory Act, rescinding all legislation passed by 'the pretendit Parliaments' of 1640, 1641, 1644, 1645, 1646, 1647 and 1648, thereby putting the constitutional clock back to 1633, the last time a valid parliament was deemed to have sat. In the process, the Rescissory Act undid all the laws establishing Presbyterianism, though it did not define the legal framework within which the Church was to operate. An Act concerning Religion and Church Government, passed that same day, allowed for the continuance of sessions, presbyteries and synods until a future settlement was reached, but declared that it was the King's resolution to maintain the doctrine and worship of the Protestant religion as established in Scotland during the reigns of Charles I and James VI, adding that the King would 'make it his care to satle and secure' a frame of Church government that was 'most agreeable to the word of God, most suteable to monarchicall Government, and most complying with the publict peace and quyet of the Kingdome'. In effect, it established that it was the king's right to settle the government of the Church.[72]

In England, the political settlement had involved a return to the constitutional position of 1641, keeping the reforming legislation that had been enacted in response to royal initiatives in the 1630s. Scotland, by contrast, returned to 1633. Given that the troubles in Scotland had started in 1637, undoing everything enacted since the parliament of 1633 might seem a logical way of returning to the *status quo ante*. According to George Mackenzie of Tarbat, 'a passionate cavalier', all the acts passed by parliament since 1640 'were but a series of rebellions'. Moreover, the acts of January–March 1661 restored prerogatives to the king in Scotland – such as the right to appoint officers of state, to determine the sitting of parliament, and to control the armed forces – that he was acknowledged to possess in England. However, there were some moderate Cavaliers who thought that the legislation of the 1641 parliament should not have been rescinded, since Charles I had sat in that parliament and it was 'dishonourable' to his memory as well as 'a dangerous preparative, to rescind all that had past in a time when the people were made to believe, that these Parliaments were warranted by his Majesty'.[73] Yet it was the Presbyterians who found most to object to about the constitutional settlement of 1661. Because the Reformation in Scotland (unlike that in England) had been carried out in resistance to the monarchy, the confirmation of the royal prerogatives and the attack on resistance in the legislation of 1661 embodied a condemnation (in Presbyterian eyes) of the principles upon which the Protestant state in Scotland had been founded. As the contemporary Presbyterian historian James Kirkton was later to complain, between them these measures condemned 'all the resistance that ever hade been made to any of the antient tyrants; and more especially all that the estates of Scotland had done in the late Reformation'. They therefore 'changed both the frame and principall of the people of Scotland'; in short, the Scottish parliament 'hade done what they could to render their King absolute'.[74] Other Presbyterian apologists agreed. For Alexander Shields, the Restoration political settlement was a conscious attempt 'to pervert and evert the well modelled and moderate Constitution of the State-Government . . . by introducing and advancing ane Arbitrary Tyranny'.[75]

There was no need for a coronation in Scotland, since the Scots had already crowned Charles II in 1651. They did nevertheless commemorate the English coronation of 23 April 1661: the Scottish capital saw a lavish civic feast, loyal toasts at the market cross, and a huge bonfire at Holyroodhouse, while there were similar celebrations in other large towns throughout the kingdom.[76] To help cement the loyalty of the Scottish people to the restored monarchy, parliament passed an act stipulating that 29 May should 'for ever be set apart as a holy day' to commemorate Charles's birthday and 'blessed restitution to his Government': all work was to stop; public prayers were to be said in church; and the rest of the day was to be spent in suitable 'lawfull diverteisments'. The act's preamble condemned what had happened over the previous twenty-three years (that is, since the National Covenant of 1638) as resulting in the 'ruine and destruction . . . of Religion, the Kings Maiestie and his Royall Government, the lawes, liberties and propertie of the people and all the publict and private interests of the Kingdome', and complained how when the King was driven out of his kingdoms not only were the foundations of Scotland's ancient constitution overturned but the Scots were also 'exposed to be Captives and slaves to Strangers' (an allusion to the Cromwellian conquest). There was no tradition of celebrating the king's birthday in Scotland, and 29 May had no special significance in the Scottish context, marking, as it did, Charles II's restitution to his government in London; yet, despite its being an English import, the Scots were being asked to celebrate Restoration Day as marking the return of Scottish liberties and Scottish independence. The Presbyterians would have nothing to do with it, being against all anniversary holy days in principle; they refused to keep Christmas or Easter, so they were hardly likely to 'doe that for Charles [which] they scrupled to doe for their Saviour'. Nevertheless, Presbyterian complaints that this was 'the most prophane day in the year', given over to 'riot, madness, swearing [and] . . . drunkenness', suggest that it was celebrated in style by many. There were grand festivities throughout much of the kingdom in 1661. Edinburgh saw sermons in all the churches in the morning, followed by a sumptuous feast prepared by the city authorities for the nobility and principal members of parliament, and bonfires throughout the town in the evening.[77]

At the Restoration the Scots also revived the commemoration of 5 August (for James VI's deliverance from the Gowrie Conspiracy of 1600) and 5 November (for James VI and I's deliverance from the Gunpowder Plot). The Scots had dared not commemorate either during the time of 'the late Usurpation', because both were celebrations of the Scottish monarchy; for the Scots, the Gunpowder Plot had been an attempt against the Scottish royal race 'by sume Englishche traitouris'. The days therefore took on nationalist overtones after 1660, their revival after years of subjection to English rule marking deliverance from 'thair bondage'.[78]

There was to be no general indemnity in Scotland as there was in England (where only thirty-three individuals were excluded from the Act of Indemnity and Oblivion of 1660), and Middleton and Glencairn showed a vindictive thirst for revenge. A number of prominent Protesters were pursued to death: the covenanter leader the eighth Earl of Argyll was executed in May 1661 for his alleged treasonable compliance with the Cromwellian regime; James Guthrie on 1 June for authoring his *Causes of the Lord's Wrath*; Samuel Rutherford died in prison in March of that year while awaiting trial for treason for his tract *Lex Rex*; and the Earl of Wariston, the author of the National Covenant, was executed in July 1663.[79] When parliament eventually did pass an Act of Indemnity, in September 1662, some 700 were excluded from the act's provisions and became liable to heavy fines ranging anywhere from £200 to £1,800 Scots, and totalling in excess of £1 million Scots (£83,333 sterling).[80]

As with England, it proved difficult to put the monarchy in Scotland on a sound financial footing. In 1661 parliament granted what it thought would prove a generous settlement of £40,000 sterling (£480,000 Scots) per year for life, to be raised from customs and excise, though the yield fell below that anticipated.[81] In 1663 parliament therefore granted the crown the right to impose customs and excise on foreign trade.[82] Nevertheless, Charles still found his income inadequate. The situation was not helped by weaknesses in the Scottish economy, in turn made worse by the policies pursued by the English government. The special trading privileges that the Scots had formerly enjoyed with France, which had been taken away during the period of Cromwellian rule, were not restored at the Restoration.[83] Furthermore, the English Navigation Act of 1660 excluded the Scots from colonial trade, and, although the measure was designed primarily to hit the Dutch, England seemed unconcerned by the fact that the Scots were a major trading partner of Holland.[84] The situation was exacerbated by the second Anglo-Dutch War, of 1664–7, which caused a further depression in the Scottish economy. By March 1665 it was being reported that trading and traffic by sea had 'ceased universallie . . . to the havy dampnage and wrak of the pepill', as international commerce became disrupted and all the seamen of Scotland were pressed into the King's service – to fight in a conflict from which the Scots themselves had nothing to gain.[85] Yet, since the depression hit Charles's Scottish revenues, he had no option but to ask parliament for additional money – a risky proposition during a time of recession. In 1665 parliament voted a land tax of £666,667 Scots (about £55,000 sterling), to be raised over five years, to meet the extraordinary expenses associated with the Dutch war. In 1667 it reintroduced the cess (a covenanting innovation of 1645, which taxed the valued rental income of land rather than its capital value), providing an additional supply of £72,000 Scots (£6,000 sterling) a month, for a period of a year.[86] This assessment was to provide the basis for all future parliamentary subsidies during the reign.

Shortage of money weakened the coercive power of the state in Scotland. The remains of Monck's Scottish army were disbanded by 1662, and all the King could afford to keep was a small contingent of foot and horse guards, totalling some 1,200 men.[87] For internal security, the crown was forced to rely on the militia. In September 1663 parliament – ostensibly concerned about the international situation, and especially the threat to western Christendom posed by the Turks, who had already overrun much of central Europe – passed a remarkable act which not only reaffirmed that the king possessed the 'sole power' to raise, arm and command his subjects, but also made an offer of 20,000 foot and 2,000 horse to be raised by the shires 'to be in readinesse', at the king's summons, 'to march to any parte of his dominions of Scotland, England or Ireland for suppressing of any forraigne invasion, intestine trouble or insurrection or for any other service whairin his Majesties honour Authority or greatness may be concerned'.[88] The government found law and order most difficult to establish in the Highlands, where clan chieftains such as the ninth Earl of Argyll and the earls of Atholl and Seaforth enjoyed a great deal of autonomy in their private fiefdoms. The military resources of the Highlands, however, were to be effectively harnessed by the Restoration regime on a number of occasions to deal with domestic discord in the Lowlands.[89]

It was the religious settlement that proved most controversial. As in England and Ireland, full diocesan episcopacy was restored. However, there had never been a particularly powerful episcopalian tradition in Scotland. Charles wanted to restore bishops in Scotland in part to keep the religious establishment there in conformity with his other kingdoms and in part because bishops, being royal appointees, afforded the crown greater control over the Church than was possible under Presbyterianism. Among Charles's chief Scottish advisers, Middleton, Glencairn and Rothes (despite his covenanting past) all supported an episcopalian solution; Crawford remained staunch in his defence of Presbytery; Lauderdale, caught between his instinctive (and self-interested) loyalty to his royal master and his sympathies for Presbyterianism, could only suggest deferring the matter to the churchmen. But the voice of the churchmen was not to be heard. Following the Rescissory Act, the synods of Glasgow and Ayr, Fife, Dumfries, and Galloway all drew up resolutions against episcopacy and in favour of Presbyterianism; all were forcibly dissolved to silence their opposition. The synod of Aberdeen was alone in expressing support for episcopacy. No wonder the King remained resolute in his determination not to allow a general assembly to meet.[90] On 14 August 1661 Charles II sent instructions to his Scottish privy council informing it that, in accordance with the power placed in his hands by the Act concerning Religion and Church Government of 28 March, it was his intention 'to interpose our royall authority for the restoring of that church to its right government by bishops, as it was by law before the late troubles', in order to promote 'its better harmony with the government of the churches of England and Ireland'; Presbyterianism he condemned as unsuitable 'to our monarchicall estate'. The privy council issued a proclamation to this effect on 6 September. In other words, bishops were restored to Scotland by royal fiat – 'the mere Effect of Royal Pleasure', as the historian of the Presbyterian sufferings Robert Wodrow put it.[91] The government hoped it would be able to persuade Resolutioner ministers to accept bishoprics under the restored Church; most refused, however, with the notable exception of James Sharp, who became archbishop of St Andrews. The result was an episcopate of largely second-rate men.[92]

A legislative package formally re-establishing episcopacy was enacted during the parliamentary session of 1662. On 8 May the bishops were restored to parliament and to the Lords of the Articles. (The following year the Lords of the Articles were restored to the 'forme and order' used before the beginning of the troubles, where the key role in determining the committee's complexion was assigned to the bishops.) On 27 May parliament passed an act 'for the restitution and reestablishment of the antient Government of the Church by Archbishops and Bishops', and on 11 June this was followed with a measure restoring lay patronage and depriving all ministers appointed since 1649, unless they had subsequently applied for and received presentations from the former patrons and collation from their local bishop. June 11 also saw the passage of an act threatening with deprivation those who refused to commemorate 29 May. An act of 24 June required all masters, regents and professors of the universities and all ministers to acknowledge and comply with the government of the Church under episcopacy and forbade all private meetings or house conventicles. Another measure passed that day condemned as 'rebellious and treasonable' entering into leagues or covenants, taking up arms against the king, and putting limits on obedience, and declared the covenants of 1638 and 1643 unlawful; any who acknowledged the covenants or defended such principles were debarred from holding office. This was reinforced on 5 September with an act requiring all office-holders to subscribe a declaration renouncing the National Covenant and the Solemn League and Covenant and affirming that they lay under 'no obligation . . . from the said oaths . . . to endeavour any change or alteration of the Government either in Church or State As it is now established by the lawes of the Kingdom'.[93]

As a result of this religious legislation, approximately one-third of the established ministry of about 952 were driven out of the Church. The western and south-western shires – the area south-west of a line from Glasgow, through Lanarkshire and Dumfriesshire to the border with England (typically referred to simply as 'the west' by contemporaries) – were the worst hit. The synod of Dumfries lost over half its ministers; that of Glasgow and Ayr two-thirds; while in the synod of Galloway (comprising the counties of Wigtown and Kirkcudbright) 34 ministers were deprived in a total of just 37 parishes. The proportions were lower in the east, though a third of the ministry was driven out in the synod of Merse and Teviotdale and in that of Lothian and Tweeddale (that is, the area from Edinburgh down to the border counties of Roxburgh and Berwick). The most highly respected ministers from the presbyteries of Edinburgh and St Andrews also refused to conform. In contrast, there were very few deprivations in the ecclesiastically conservative areas north of the Tay.[94]

The extent to which people were prepared to accept the changes in the Church also varied according to region. Episcopalians and Presbyterians agreed on doctrine and discipline (both were Calvinists), and forms of worship were very similar in church and conventicle; there were no ceremonies enjoined by the episcopalian Church, and no liturgy nor form of prayer, though the episcopalians tended to use the

Lord's Prayer and say Amen and thought it proper not to wear their hats during the service.[95] As one Church of Ireland Protestant put it, those that 'go under the name of Episcopall men' in Scotland 'would seem to us to bee rank fanaticks'.[96] In those parishes where ministers conformed, things must have appeared to continue much as always. In some areas, people were pleased to see the Presbyterian ministers go. Glencairn exaggerated when he claimed 'that the insolence of the Presbyterian had so far dissatisfied all loyal subjects and wise men, that six for one in Scotland long'd for Episcopacy'; yet even Presbyterian leaders acknowledged that there was a significant reaction 'agaynst the Covenant and work of reformation and Presbyterial government' after 1660.[97] In some places there was a deliberate attempt to whip up anti-Presbyterian sentiment. On Restoration Day 1662 the magistrates and minister of Linlithgow, with the backing of the Earl of Linlithgow, staged an extravagant anti-Presbyterian ritual in the market place, involving a specially constructed four-pillared arch, on one side of which was a statue of 'an old Hag' holding the Covenant with the superscription 'A Glorious Reformation', and on the other a statue of a Whig holding the radical Presbyterian Remonstrance of 1650 in his hand. In the middle of the arch hung a tablet with the litany

> From Covenants with uplifted Hands,
> From Remonstrators with associate Bands,
> From such Committees as govern'd this Nation,
> From Church Commissioners and their Protestation,
> Good Lord deliver us.

On the rear side was a Presbyterian cleric, brandishing Rutherford's *Lex Rex* and Guthrie's *Causes of the Lord's Wrath*, while round about lay 'Acts of Parliament, Acts of Committees of Estates, Acts of General Assemblies, and Commissions of Kirk, with their Protestations and Declarations' of the past twenty-two years. Above was written, 'Rebellion is as the Sin of Witchcraft.' After the minister had said a prayer, the whole contraption was set on fire, as the onlookers toasted the health of the King.[98]

Nevertheless, in many areas – especially the south-west – locals bitterly resented the purge of the Church, and often did what they could to prevent the new ministers taking up their cures. There are reports of parishioners stealing the tongue of the church's bell to stop the bell being pealed to summon people to church, or barricading the church door to prevent the new incumbent from getting in. At Irongray, in Dumfriesshire, the new incumbent met such opposition when he tried to enter the church that he had to return under the protection of a party of armed soldiers, who were then pelted with stones by the women of the parish; the privy council later sentenced the ringleader, Margaret Smith, to be banished to Barbados. The women of Kirkcudbright put up similar resistance, though again to little ultimate effect besides earning some of their number a stint in the pillory.[99] People's reactions were shaped not just by loyalty to the old ministers but also by hostility to the new recruits, mainly young men from the north, who were widely regarded as unsuitable candidates: not just 'ignorant', but even of dubious moral character – in short, 'the very Scorn of Reformation and Scandal of Religion'.[100] Even the episcopalian apologist John Sage acknowledged that there was a 'too hasty Planting of Churches in the West . . . by which many Young Men were preferr'd', some of whom were guilty of 'Imprudent Conduct'.[101] The result was widespread withdrawal from church throughout the southwest, as parishioners chose instead to attend the family worship and exercises of their outed ministers, or else those of Irish Presbyterian ministers who had fled to Scotland following the religious settlement in their own country. Often more people attended such meetings than could possibly fit into the minister's house, with the result that some of the deprived clergy had to preach outside or else hold their services in a field; hence the beginning of field conventicles.[102]

Cold Friends and Violent Enemies –
Lauderdale's Ascendancy

The settlement in the Church was accompanied by a change in the royal administration. Crawford resigned, rather than renounce the covenants; an attempt by Middleton in 1663 to exclude Lauderdale from the indemnity backfired and led to his own disgrace; while the ageing Glencairn died in 1664. From 1663 Lauderdale emerged with unrivalled control over affairs in Scotland – a position he was to enjoy until his fall in 1680. He was by all accounts a somewhat uncouth individual: 'very big', with his red hair 'hanging oddly about him'; 'His tongue was too big for his mouth,' Gilbert Burnet tells us, 'which made him bedew all that he talked to: and his whole manner was rough and boisterous.' 'Very learned' and blessed with 'an extraordinary memory', he nevertheless 'had a violence of passion that carried him often to fits like madness, in which he had no temper'. Burnet found him 'the coldest friend and the most violent enemy' he ever knew. Clarendon thought him proud, ambitious, insolent and imperious. The King liked him because of his political experience and because of his willingness to do everything that he thought would please the King. In large measure this meant vaunting the King's authority in Scotland and making sure that the Presbyterians posed no threat to the security of the restored regime.[103]

During the period of his ascendancy, Lauderdale's stance on dissent underwent a series of dramatic shifts. Initially, while still dependent on the support of the increasingly hawkish Rothes (now Lord Treasurer) and Archbishop Sharp, who were backed from 1664 by the aggressive hardliner Alexander Burnet, archbishop of Glasgow, Lauderdale was prepared to fall in with a policy of repression. On 10 July 1663 parliament passed a severe act which not only ratified the ecclesiastical legislation of the previous year, but also laid down stiff fines for those who withdrew from church: those with land were to be fined a quarter of their yearly rent; those without, a quarter of their movable goods (with burgesses in addition forfeiting the right to trade and other associated privileges).[104] In January 1664 the crown, by dint of its own prerogative, controversially decided to revive the High Commission, with powers to suspend and depose ministers and to fine or imprison transgressors without indictment, though arguably this was in direct contravention of an act of 1584 which discharged 'all New Courts not approven by Parliament'. Presbyterians thought the High Commission 'odious and tyrannical', because it used an 'Arbitrary form of Inquisition and summary procedour without any shadow of Legal Process' and on occasion resorted to savage punishments – such as scourging, branding and transportation – against the enemies of the episcopacy. The High Commission was dissolved after only two years. Not only had it proved ineffectual in dealing with dissent on the scale that existed in Scotland, but it had also served to make the episcopalian order even more unpopular than it had been before.[105]

Conventicling activity in the south-west reached such a height that the government decided upon military intervention. Starting in 1663, it dispatched troops under the command of Sir James Turner to the south-west to collect the fines from those who refused to come to church. There was a series of such expeditions over the next few years, the most repressive being in 1666, when the government was concerned that Scottish Presbyterians might cause trouble at home during the time of the Dutch War. The fines exacted were often in excess of the already high statutory limits, and refusers were subjected to free quarter and the distraint of goods. Many not only were reduced to poverty but also experienced physical abuse at the hands of the soldiery.[106] One Presbyterian author, writing after the Glorious Revolution, compared the policy to Louis XIV's dragonnades against the French Protestants in the early 1680s, stating that this was one instance, at least, where 'we were in fashion before France.'[107] To protect themselves, conventiclers started carrying weapons to their meetings, but this merely convinced the authorities that the Presbyterians were intent on armed insurrection and therefore of the need to step up repression.

It became a self-fulfilling prophecy. In 1665 the exiled minister John Brown produced a lengthy tract, which was smuggled into Scotland from Holland, documenting the sufferings of the covenanters, justifying the resistance to Charles I during the late wars, and insisting that every private man had the right to use force against magistrates turned tyrants.[108] Then, in November 1666, Presbyterian malcontents took Turner captive at Dumfries and proceeded to march on Edinburgh to demand concessions, their ranks swelling to about 1,500 to 2,000 men at their peak, before a combination of defections, disagreements and bad weather forced them to retreat. Government forces eventually put down the remaining insurgents (probably only 8–900) at Rullion Green in the Pentland Hills on 28 November, killing about 50 and capturing another 120. Those arrested were brought for examination to Edinburgh, where, according to the covenanter historian Alexander Shields, they were 'treated so treacherously and truculently, as Turks would have blushed to have seen the

like'. The council used torture – in this case the 'boot', a metal contraption affixed to the lower leg which could be gradually tightened
so as to crush the bones of the individual under examination, which
Rothes believed was 'the only torture used in this kingdome' – to try
to extract information from those who refused to tell what they knew
of the conspiracy.[109] At the same time it dispatched General Tom
Dalziel to the south-west with 3,000 foot and 8 troops of horse to
pacify the region.[110] The soldiers not only took free quarter but even
used torture in their examinations of suspected conspirators or
accomplices. One commander, Sir Mungo Murray, ordered two farmers to be tied to a tree by their thumbs and left hanging overnight, for
allegedly giving shelter to two rebels; they would almost certainly
have died had not some soldiers, out of compassion, cut them down.
When alleged Pentland rebel David McGill, from the parish of Dalry
in Ayrshire, managed to evade arrest by slipping away disguised in
women's clothing, the soldiers seized his wife, 'bound her, and put
lighted Matches 'twixt her Fingers for several Hours'; she lost one of
her hands, and died a few days later. One man, who had been in
Lanark on the day that the rebels had marched through that town,
was shot by soldiers when he said he could not name any of those
involved in the rebellion.[111]

However, such was the depth of support in the south-west for the
rebels that the authorities were able to apprehend very few of the ringleaders. In the end, the government decided to execute just thirty-six
of the rebels (although that total would undoubtedly have been higher
if more had been captured); others deemed guilty were banished to
Barbados or Virginia, while a further fifty-six were indicted for high
treason *in absentia* and declared fugitives. The whole effort was
designed to instil fear into the region, and it did achieve some results:
fines came in, and some nonconformists were induced to return to
church out of fear.[112] But the cost was tremendous. The economy of
the region – at a time when Scotland was experiencing an economic
recession brought on by a disruption to trade caused by the Anglo-
Dutch War – was devastated, and there was simmering discontent.[113]
Tracts urging resistance continued to appear, maintaining that the
kings of Scotland derived their authority from the consent of the
people and that the people had the right to call their rulers to account

if they exceeded their duty or failed to live up to their side of the contract (which was to preserve the people's rights from injury or oppression). More disturbingly, in July 1668 the Pentland rebel James Mitchell launched an unsuccessful attempt to assassinate Archbishop Sharp of St Andrews.[114]

Convinced that repression was not working, Lauderdale decided to shift to a policy of moderation. He sought to break free from dependence upon the episcopalian interest in Scotland, using the Pentland rising as a way of discrediting Rothes and Archbishop Sharp, and to tie Presbyterians to the interests of the crown by granting concessions based on the royal prerogative. On 7 June 1669 Charles II granted his first Scottish Indulgence, authorizing the Scottish privy council to reappoint outed ministers who had lived peaceably either to their former parish churches (if they were vacant) or to other vacant livings, though they were to receive their stipends only if they accepted collation from their bishop.[115] Under its provisions, a mere forty-two Presbyterian ministers were reinstated. The episcopalian interest was nevertheless deeply alarmed. Sharp thought the Indulgence violated the legislation of 1662 re-establishing episcopacy, and with Rothes's assistance he managed to keep indulged ministers out of his diocese. Alexander Burnet of Glasgow went so far as to get his clergy to frame a remonstrance against the Indulgence in September 1669. The council had the remonstrance suppressed, and in December Charles dismissed Burnet, replacing him by Robert Leighton, bishop of Dunblane, a supporter of concessions, who became first commendator of the see of Glasgow in 1670 and then, from 1672, archbishop.[116]

The Indulgence was followed in October 1669 by the Act of Supremacy, which confirmed that the King and his successors might 'setle, enact, and emit such constitutions, acts and orders, concerning the administration of the externall government of the Church, and the persones imployed in the same, and concerning all ecclesiasticall meitings and maters to be proposed and determined therin, as they . . . shall think fit', and rescinded all laws that were inconsistent with 'his Majesties supremacie'. The act was deeply resented by the Presbyterians, who thought it set up Charles II in Christ's stead. But it was also a substantial blow to the position and prestige of the Scottish episcopate, who felt that they should be consulted by the

King on matters of Church policy and alleged that it made the 'king our pope'. According to Lauderdale, not only was the King now 'Soveraigne in the Church', with the right to appoint all bishops and ministers, but he could also 'remove and transplant' clerics at will, a power he did not enjoy in England. On the same day, another Militia Act confirmed the King's ability to raise a force of 22,000 men to police not just Scotland, but also England and Ireland. In November 1669 Lauderdale confidently boasted to Charles II that 'never was [a] King soe absolute as you are in poor old Scotland'.[117]

Lauderdale's efforts to comprehend Presbyterian ministers within the Church establishment were accompanied by the pursuit of even tougher measures against those who remained active in their dissent. At the beginning of August 1669 the council issued a proclamation requiring heritors to report any who held conventicles on their land.[118] Reports of attacks on the houses of episcopalian ministers in the southwest (by Presbyterians, the government assumed, though the Presbyterians blamed highwaymen) led parliament in late November to pass an act making parishes liable for offences committed against incumbent ministers.[119] On 13 August 1670 parliament made assaults on ministers or attempts to rob their houses a capital offence.[120] That same day it also passed a savage Act against Conventicles. This stipulated that unlicensed outed ministers who held religious meetings were to be imprisoned until they either posted bonds for 5,000 Scots merks (£175 sterling) or else agreed to leave the kingdom and never return. Those who attended such conventicles were to be subject to a sliding scale of fines, dependent upon social status: heritors were to pay a quarter of their rent; tenant farmers £25 Scots; cottars £12 Scots; servants a quarter of their annual wage. The master or mistress of any house where such a conventicle was held were to be fined double these amounts, while magistrates of royal burghs where conventicles were kept were to be liable to such fines as the Scottish council thought fit to impose. Any unlicensed minister who preached at field conventicles, including conventicles held 'in any house wher ther be more persons' than the house could contain 'so as some of them be without Doors', was to 'be punished with death'. Anyone who helped arrest field conventiclers, on the other hand, was to get a reward of 500 merks for every person he seized and to be 'indemnified for any slaughter . . .

committed in the apprehension and secureing of them'. Presbyterians complained that the unscrupulous could simply post someone outside the door of a house conventicle, thereby converting it into a field conventicle; the act therefore exposed 'the Lives of them that so meet . . . to the mercy of their most malicious Enemies'. Those present at field conventicles were to be fined double the amount for house conventicles. To encourage local officials to be diligent in enforcing the law, they were to be allowed to keep all the fines levied on those under the degree of heritor. The act was set to last for only three years in the first instance, since it was hoped its severity would soon reduce people to obedience, though the King could extend its operation if he thought fit.[121] A few days later parliament passed another act against those who withdrew from church, slightly reducing the scale of fines laid out in the act of 1663, though, like the Conventicle Act, allowing local officials to collect the fines of those who were not heritors and also requiring long-term recusants to subscribe a bond renouncing resistance, on pain of banishment. It too was to last for only three years.[122]

Lauderdale agreed to such measures both to defuse criticism that he was being too soft on dissent and to encourage the process of accommodation by warning Presbyterians of the dire circumstances should they refuse to comply. He remained committed to the policy of accommodation. In September 1672 the King issued a second Indulgence for Scotland, increasing the scope of the first; it provided for the appointment of two outed ministers to those parishes still vacant, as well as an additional one to serve alongside those already indulged in 1669. As a result, a further eighty-nine Presbyterians were indulged, most of them in the west and south-west.[123] The second Indulgence, however, was accompanied by an act reviving for a further three years the legislation of 1670 against conventicles and withdrawing from church.[124]

Nevertheless it was becoming clear by now that Lauderdale's strategy was not working, and the political cost was proving high. Many Presbyterians disliked the Erastian implications of the Indulgences and continued to hold meetings outside the law, and even actively sought to discourage people from attending the services of those outed ministers who now seemed willing to make a compromise with episcopacy. Field conventicles increased as churches were deserted, while some ministers found themselves subjected to physical abuse: Archbishop Leighton learned that some of the incumbents he appointed to vacant parishes in the west were 'beaten and stoned away'.[125] On the episcopalian side, Rothes, Burnet and Sharp all condemned the Indulgences for undermining the position of the Established Church and threatening the security of the state. In 1674 the synod of Edinburgh drew up an address warning of the increase of schism and conventicling and the intrusion into parishes of 'irregular preachers' who offered the people 'what doctrines they please'.[126] Meanwhile, the political tide had turned in England, with parliament's successful attack on Charles's English Indulgence in 1673. Lauderdale was the only member of the Cabal to survive the crisis, but, on the defensive in England and facing increasing opposition in Scotland from those who not only disapproved of his policies but also resented his monopoly of power and patronage, he found it necessary to pursue measures that could gain him more political support. He therefore abandoned concessions and called for the strict enforcement of all laws against dissent. Leighton resigned as archbishop of Glasgow in August 1674, and Burnet was reinstalled.

The result was a progressive tightening of the screw. On 18 June 1674, in response to an order from the King, the Scottish council issued a proclamation requiring heritors to have their tenants subscribe a bond promising not to violate the 1670 Conventicle Act; if the tenants refused, the heritors were to eject them, or face punishment for the offence themselves. Masters were similarly held accountable for their servants, and burgh magistrates for burgesses and inhabitants.[127] Meanwhile, the fines laid out in the legislation of 1670 began to be imposed in full. In Renfrewshire alone in 1674–6, eleven landlords were fined a staggering £368,031 13s. 4d. Scots for conventicling and nonconformity.[128] In July and August 1675 the Scottish council decided upon the legally dubious policy of appointing garrisons in certain specified houses in the Presbyterian trouble spots for the purpose of suppressing conventicles, thereby effectively imposing military rule in time of peace.[129] Then, on 2 August 1677, the council reissued the bond, this time also holding masters and heritors accountable for their servants and tenants observing the laws against withdrawing from church and against illegal marriages and baptisms. The landowning elite bitterly resented being held liable for the behaviour of people over whom they felt they had little control.

The heritors of Lanarkshire, following the lead of the Duke of Hamilton, unanimously agreed to refuse the bond. Elsewhere, many decided not to comply. The gentry of Ayrshire and Renfrewshire suggested that a better way of keeping the country quiet would be to extend and enlarge the liberty allowed to Presbyterians.[130]

The government, however, alarmed by the growth of conventicling activity and reports of 'extraordinary Insolencies' perpetrated against the orthodox clergy (such as 'usurping their Pulpits' and verbal and physical threats), was in no mood to conciliate. Although Lauderdale favoured indulgence, he backed down in the face of opposition from the bishops. The King was also against concessions, refusing to sacrifice 'the Laws to the Humours and Fashions of private men'. The government therefore decided upon military intervention. Following a suggestion from the Scottish council, on 11 December 1677 Charles ordered the raising of a Highland Host, which was to be sent to reduce the Presbyterian heartlands 'to due Obedience . . . by taking free Quarter from those that are disaffected', disarming all suspected persons, and enforcing the bond. Wodrow had a sinister interpretation of the government's motives, believing that, with Charles II under pressure in England to disband his standing army, 'it was concerted in the Cabin-council, that all Measures should be taken to exasperate the Scots Phanaticks . . . to some Broil or other, that there might be a Pretence to keep up the Standing Forces', at least in Scotland. Not that we should accept Wodrow's charge at face value, since he was clearly imposing a restrospective Whig gloss; however, his remarks do shed some insight into the suspicions that many in England came to harbour about the King's intentions.[131]

A force of about 8,000 men assembled at Stirling on 24 January 1678 – some 5–6,000 Highlanders, the rest being regular soldiers or militiamen.[132] The mere threat of military intervention led the heritors of Fife to submit, while in Dumfriesshire all 'save some few pitifull persons signed'. Elsewhere, however, most held out. In Glasgow, only 153 took the bond; in Renfrewshire only 2 gentlemen and 3 burgesses subscribed; in Lanarkshire all but 19 of the 2,900 heritors and feuars refused.[133] The Highlanders were therefore dispatched to Glasgow and thence to Ayrshire, Dunbartonshire, Lanarkshire and Renfrewshire. Presbyterian apologists have painted a dismal picture of terrible atrocities allegedly committed by the Highland Host: murder, rape, torture, theft, illegal exactions of money, and physical abuse – even 'cutting off Fingers and Hands'. If much of this is apocryphal, as some modern historians have contended, plunder was certainly fairly extensive, with soldiers taking anything from money to possessions to livestock. Wodrow calculated that the heritors of Ayrshire suffered losses totalling well in excess of £200,000 Scots.[134] One local correspondent observed that all he could write was 'anent oppressions, robberys, exactions, and stresses of law';[135] another complained how 'the best part in the Kingdome' had been 'impoverished and almost laid waist by a Crue of Barbarous and Savage men of another language, custome and of no religion'.[136]

Such intimidation nevertheless proved largely ineffective, so in mid-February the council passed an act imposing lawburrows on those who still refused the bond. Lawburrows were essentially bonds to keep the peace: an individual in conflict with a neighbour could swear before the courts that he was in fear of bodily harm and have his neighbour find sureties not to cause him (or his family) any trouble or molestation. They were thus a not uncommon way of resolving disputes between private persons, and the sureties involved were normally quite trivial sums. For the king to demand lawburrows of his subjects, however, was more controversial, for it was tantamount to declaring that he was 'in Dread of them'. Moreover, the penalty demanded in this instance was enormous: those pressed with lawburrows would forfeit two years' valued rent if they attended a conventicle or otherwise failed to keep the peace.[137]

Critics of the government challenged the legality of the actions taken against the Presbyterians. On 28 March the Earl of Cassillis presented a detailed paper to the court in London, complaining about the Highland Host, the bond and lawburrows, which he had been assured, he said, 'were illegal, and not warrantable, either by the Statutes or Customs of the Kingdom of Scotland'. The taking of free quarters, he went on, was against the Militia Acts of 1661 and 1663, which had provided that the Scottish people were to be free from the provision and maintenance of any armies or garrisons, while he had refused the bond himself because he believed it 'was found on no Law'.[138] Several papers appeared alleging that the council had 'no

Power to press this Bond', and that no such bonds might be imposed without parliamentary warrant. John Blackadder, the deposed minister of Troqueer and now a leader of field conventicles, denied that a council edict was sufficient to make masters and heritors answerable beyond what any law had hitherto obliged them, or that it could make men's private rights of possession void for refusing to take a bond which no law required. Two leading lawyers, Sir John Cunningham and Sir George Lockhart, both of whom had actually subscribed the bond, told the government in London that they thought 'the imposing of it and the Lawborrows was contrary to Law'. Towards the end of May, Hamilton, together with Lord Cochrane, Sir John Cochrane and Lieutenant-General Sir William Drummond, met with the King to put their case against the bond, in which they insisted that 'Masters could not be obliged to turn their Tenants out of their Land' for attending a conventicle, since parliament had prescribed that the punishment for such an offence was to be a fine.[139]

The King withdrew the Highlanders at the end of February and the rest of the forces towards the end of April, when he also cancelled the bond and lawburrows. Pressure from within Scotland, however, had little influence on his decision; Charles was responding to developments within England, where parliament was criticizing Charles's build-up of troops and raising the spectre of rule by a standing army. The Committee of the West, which oversaw the operations of the militia, was told that the King fully approved its proceedings, but that 'Affairs in England, where the Militia made a mighty Noise, made a present disbanding of them necessary'.[140] Charles persistently stood by the actions he had taken in Scotland. He wrote to his Scottish council in March approving all it had done: the law regarded field conventicles as 'Rendezvous of Rebellion', and the refusal to suppress them 'did justly oblidge yow to look upon theire shyres as in a state of rebellion'.[141] He had no time for Hamilton's complaints of May, bidding him and his associates to 'returne to their country and live quiatly and peaceably under the government', and afterwards he wrote again to his Scottish council to confirm his approval of its proceedings and his dissatisfaction with those who had alleged they were illegal. 'Wee will upon all occasions', he insisted, 'proceed according to our laws against such as endeavour to lessen our prerogatives, oppose our laws or asperse our Privy Councill.'[142]

The privy council similarly denied that it had gone beyond the law. In answer to the Earl of Cassillis's complaint of 28 March, it insisted that the 1661 provision against free quarter applied only 'to regular times', but the western and south-western shires were 'in a state of rebellion', given the large number of armed men who assembled 'almost weekly' in field conventicles. Moreover, the 1663 Militia Act had provided for the militia to be used to suppress 'intestine trowble or insurrection'. Lawburrows were 'expresly warranted' by an act of 1429, and universal lawburrows by one of 1449. With regard to the question of the bond being pressed without law, the council insisted it was only 'offered' but not 'pressed', and further claimed that no express law was needed to authorize it, since the king and council might do whatever was necessary to secure the peace of the country, 'providing it be not against expresse laws'.[143] Lord Advocate Mackenzie, writing in 1679, claimed that making heritors responsible for their tenants was justified by an act of 1529 which recognized the obligation that lay upon 'all vassals by the feudall Law of entertaining non upon their superiour's lands who shall disobey him'. Anticipating the objection that this law was obsolete, Mackenzie insisted that, although laws whereby subjects were bound to one another might run into desuetude, 'Lawes wherby wee ar tyd to the King' could not; nor could 'publict Lawes relating to the Saftie of the Kingdom'.[144]

Field conventicles resumed as soon as the troops were removed, while some who had subscribed the bond publicly repented. Dragoons were once more dispatched to round up conventiclers. Those arrested were allowed their freedom on condition they subscribed the bond, but few did; many ended up being banished to the colonies.[145] At Whitekirk in Haddingtonshire, towards the end of May, a soldier was killed when the King's forces tried to disperse a meeting. The government therefore decided to make an example of the perpetrators and had two of the conventiclers, James Learmont and one Temple, indicted 'for being art and part' of the murder. Neither of them had killed the soldier, though Temple had been wearing a sword, while Learmont, though unarmed, had shouted instructions to those who were armed. At first the jury found the pair guilty simply of being at a field conventicle, and the court had to send the jurors back not once but twice to reconsider before they found them guilty of murder. Learmont was executed at the Grassmarket on 27 September; Temple was banished. Many legal experts were 'alarmed' at such 'a terrible stretch' of the law 'and a most arbitrary decision'.[146] Instead of serving as a deterrent, such vindictiveness simply induced conventiclers to make greater efforts to defend themselves. In August 1678 John Welsh and at least twelve other nonconformist ministers (one report said thirty-six) held a huge conventicle of some 10,000, lasting three days, at Maybole, near Ayr, where they 'preached up the Solemn League and Covenant and the lawfulness, conveniency and necessity of defensive arms'. Both before and after sermon they carried out various military drills and armed exercises, declaring they would 'defend themselves if opposed by his Majesty's forces'. One alarmed contemporary heard they were planning another such conventicle at Fenwick, a mere 34 miles from Edinburgh, and wondered where it would all end. 'What if they should beat his Majesty's forces, take possession of this principal city, fine, imprison and banish all that oppose them in the first place and in the next all that will not concur with them?' he pondered. 'A peaceable government' would be overturned, and 'his Majesty's power questioned and limited'. Was 'this to turn swords into ploughshares?' Was 'it not rather to make swords of pruning hooks, and instead of the turtle to set up the alarm of war in our land?'[147]

Particularly galling to the Presbyterians was that, while they were experiencing the full brunt of increasingly severe legislation, the Scottish prelates seemed largely unconcerned about the Catholics. An act of 1567 had outlawed the celebration of the mass, stipulating the punishments of banishment and death for the second and third offence, while an act of 1661 had confirmed the prohibition against the mass and ordered all mass priests to leave the country within one month, under pain of death.[148] Furthermore, the legislation of 1663 against withdrawing from church would also have applied to Catholics. However, the laws against popery were but sporadically enforced. Indeed, during the administration of the Cabal, Catholics in Scotland enjoyed what was in effect 'a Kind of Toleration'. In 1671, for example, while unlicensed Presbyterian conventicles were being harassed in the south-west, the Catholics in the north were busy setting up mass houses and worshipping in the open. Perhaps most insensitively, the council was even willing to employ Catholic noblemen in the drive against Presbyterian dissent. In February 1677, for example, it gave a commission to the Catholic Lord Maxwell to apprehend Presbyterian conventiclers and preachers in Dumfries, Wigtown and Kirkcudbright.[149]

Scottish Policy and the British Problem

The position of the restored monarch was both stronger and at the same time more vulnerable in his northern kingdom than it was in England. The crown's theoretical powers were certainly greater in Scotland, and parliament provided less of a check on the King's freedom of manoeuvre. There is a genuine sense in which the King in Scotland was absolute. On the other hand political and (particularly) religious tensions were more acute than they were in England (where they were hardly insignificant), and domestic peace seemed more fragile. The government was perhaps justified in fearing what might happen if satisfactory measures were not taken to deal with the problem of dissent. A warning had already come with the Pentland rebellion of 1666, and the fact that conventiclers continued to meet in large numbers – armed – and that some even published works advocating resistance, understandably caused alarm. Yet successive attempts to deal with the problem had failed and had probably only made matters worse. It is revealing that, despite the supposed absolutism of the monarchy in Scotland, Charles's chief minister, Lauderdale, often found his own freedom for manoeuvre quite restricted. The need to court the episcopalian interest forced him on more than one occasion to abandon his preferred policy of conciliation. Being driven into the hands of episcopalian hardliners, on the other hand, not only made him political enemies among the elite, but also risked provoking widespread disaffection in certain areas of the country. There were, in other words, fundamental structural problems facing the Scottish polity that made the kingdom difficult to rule and perhaps even inherently unstable.

Lauderdale's monopoly of power and patronage, coupled with the policies he chose to pursue, made him many political enemies in Scotland. By June 1678 it was being said that the kingdom was divided into 'three several interests': 'the Episcopal and Court interest', headed by Lauderdale, and 'the interest of religion and presbytery', at the two poles, and a third 'interest for liberty and privileges', headed by Hamilton.[150] Even the likes of Atholl and the Earl of Queensberry, who in the 1680s were firmly in the court and episcopal interest, had moved into opposition to Lauderdale, having broken with him over the bond and the Highland Host. Lauderdale also displayed a ruthless determination to enhance his own power and that of his royal master at the expense of other members of the Scottish ruling elite. For example in August 1677, when he learned that Chancellor Rothes held his office *ad vitam* (for life), and could not easily be removed, he got the King to write a letter to the Scottish council declaring that henceforth all officers of state should serve during royal pleasure, and inviting present state officials to renounce their rights for life. All complied, and signed a declaration to this effect on 4 September.[151]

Yet Scottish policy was not simply part of a Scottish problem; it also became part of a larger British problem. As people in England grew increasingly alarmed by the spectre of arbitrary government during the 1670s, what was going on in Scotland emerged as a growing source of concern. In April 1675 the English House of Commons petitioned Charles to dismiss Lauderdale from his counsels, accusing him of seeking to promote 'an arbitrary form of government over us', as evidenced by his supposed claim (in reference to the 1672 Declaration of Indulgence) that the King's edicts were 'equal with laws'. They were also worried that the Scottish Militia Acts gave him command of a force of 22,000 which could be marched 'into any part of this kingdom, for any service', and which they learned he had threatened could be used to tame the critics of royal policy in England. On this occasion Charles stood by his minister, and Lauderdale survived the attack.[152] However, Shaftesbury, a prominent spokesman for the country opposition and a future leading Whig, was monitoring the situation in Scotland closely. In his papers is a letter from Edinburgh, dated 10 September 1675, detailing the abuses and oppressions of Lauderdale north of the border and accusing him of threatening 'to overthrow all our [Scotland's] liberty'.[153] Shaftesbury would again raise the cry of the threat to liberty in Scotland during the Exclusion Crisis.

Throughout the Restoration period, the government remained haunted by the prospect that discontented elements in all three kingdoms might unite against the crown, with Scotland leading the way, as in the late 1630s and early 1640s. At the end of 1677 Sir Cyril Wyche, in the Dublin administration – bemoaning the perilous state of affairs in Scotland and complaining how 'discontented great men' in all three kingdoms had set up in alliance with disaffected Protestant nonconformists – proclaimed that he thought the situation was 'very like the case in the beginning of the late Revolutions'.[154] Within Scotland, the episcopalian interest, sensing the vulnerability of its position in the face of Presbyterian dissent, naturally looked to England for support.[155] The King himself was prepared to tap resources in Ireland and England to manage discontent in Scotland. Thus in 1674 and again in 1677, when faced with reports that the Scottish south-west was threatening once more to erupt in rebellion, Charles hastily mobilized troops in Ulster and at Berwick-upon-Tweed to be ready to move into Scotland at the slightest sign of trouble.[156] In short, the developments in Scotland also had implications for England and Ireland; the Scottish problem was, in other words, also a three-kingdoms problem.

Nevertheless, Scotland was coming to be appreciated as a potential source of strength for the crown, which might be used to buttress its position within Britain as a whole. We can see this reflected in the debates over a possible union with England in the late 1660s. Initially, in 1668, a commercial union was proposed, as a way of dealing with the recession that had hit Scotland as a result of the Dutch War and also of addressing Scots' complaints over their exclusion from trade under the English Navigation Act of 1660. The talks came to nothing, but in 1669–70 the emphasis shifted to political union, involving the merger of the two parliaments into one, with the Scots being promised the benefits of free trade in compensation for loss of sovereignty. The idea met with little support in either country: the Scottish ruling elite thought it would be political suicide, the English parliament proved decidedly unenthusiastic, while Charles himself does not appear to have been serious, using the talks simply as a subterfuge to distract attention from his own concurrent negotiations with Louis XIV.[157] Some feared that political union would enable Charles to increase his power over his parliament at Westminster by intruding a solid voting block of pliant Scots, thus rendering him 'as absolute in Brittain as the French king . . . was in France'.[158] Yet union was also opposed in Scotland by those who championed absolute monarchy. As Lord Advocate Mackenzie put it in his *Memoirs*, there were many in Scotland who thought union destructive to the King's interest, 'seeing whilst the Kingdoms stood divided, his Majesty had two Parliaments, wherof the one might always be exemplary to the other, and might, by loyal emulation, excite one another to an entire obedience; and, if either should invade the royal prerogative, or oppose unjustly their Prince's just commands, the one might prove a curb to the other's insolence'. It would be misguided for the King, they felt, to 'extinguish a Kingdom' which could prove 'so serviceable to him . . . a Kingdom wherein he might, by his prerogative, govern much more absolutely than in England', where his power over the Church 'was as absolute . . . as could be desir'd', and where he had 'more influence upon our Parliaments than in England'.[159] Charles was indeed to appreciate the value of being able to play Scotland off against England, using his parliament in his northern kingdom as 'a curb to the other's insolence' to great effect during the Exclusion Crisis, as we shall see later in this book.

CONCLUSION

We have seen how in England many people who initially welcomed the Restoration had their expectations disappointed; not only were there winners and losers, but many of those who lost out had to pay a huge price for having done so. Yet the sufferings in England seem mild in comparison with those in the Stuarts' other two kingdoms. In both Ireland and Scotland many people who by instinct would have identified themselves as loyal supporters of the Stuart monarchy came to feel that they were being denied basic rights or protection at law. In Ireland, huge numbers of Catholics were left dispossessed as a result of the working out of the Act of Settlement and the Act of Explanation, being denied the right even to prove themselves innocent of treason in a court of law so as to have a hope of reclaiming ancestral lands which had been taken from them in the 1640s and '50s. Catholics and Protestant nonconformists alike were treated as second-class citizens, facing restrictions on their ability to engage in trade, hold office under the crown, or even practise their faith – though in fact both groups were allowed a considerable degree of *de facto* religious tolerance, which meant that, ironically, in Ireland purely religious issues (as opposed to secular issues which tended to divide people along confessional lines) were never quite as explosive as in England or Scotland. In Scotland, a significant proportion of the population – the overwhelming majority in the south-west – became liable to prosecution under a spiteful penal code because of their adherence to Presbyterianism, and large numbers of people were brutalized at the hands of government troops or officers as the Restoration regime sought to eradicate what it took to be a subversive Presbyterian threat. As a result, the Presbyterians of the south-west responded in the way that we would expect people who had been brutalized to respond: they rose in rebellion, which of course merely confirmed the government's suspicions that the Presbyterians did pose a subversive threat. It became a vicious cycle. While those in England were worried about potential threats to cherished English liberties through the regime's fondness for France, its attempt to establish a standing army and subvert the independence of parliament, and the prospect of a popish successor, and while a minority of the population were genuinely suffering in their lives, liberties and estates during the periodic enforcement waves against Protestant dissent, in Ireland and Scotland the suffering was much greater and more widespread (in the sense that it touched a much higher percentage of the population).

The divisions and tensions that emerged in Restoration Ireland and Scotland were partly related to attempts by the restored monarchy to deal with problems that were of an intrinsically Irish or Scottish nature. But they were also part of a broader British problem. As we have seen, by far the greatest source of contention in Restoration Scotland related to the settlement in the Church. Yet episcopacy was restored north of the border after 1660 not just because it afforded the King greater control over the Church than did Presbyterianism, but also because Charles was determined to bring the Scottish ecclesiastical settlement into line with that achieved in both England and Ireland. In other words, it was a British agenda which forced the pace of the ecclesiastical settlement north of the border. Likewise the land settlement in Ireland was shaped partly by British considerations – a desire not just to keep the Protestant interest in both Ireland and England placated, but also to reward those loyal supporters of the crown within England when English sources of patronage proved insufficient. Time and time again we have seen how initiatives in one kingdom were dictated by developments in another. The periodic clampdowns against Catholics in Ireland, for example, were typically triggered by increasing anxieties in England about the threat of popery. Likewise, the attempts to bolster the authority of the crown in Scotland – we think here of the Militia Acts, the Supremacy Act and Lauderdale's boast about how absolute the King was in Scotland – were in part undertaken to compensate for the crown's awareness of its weakness (in practice) in England. Yet the government's attitude towards the problem of Presbyterian dissent in both the north of Ireland and the south-west of Scotland was tempered by a realization that, if unduly provoked, the two groups might unite in resistance to the restored regime, while the crown found it necessary to withdraw the Highland Host from the Scottish south-west in 1678 in part because of concerns about adverse political repercussions in England. Indeed, English people's growing fears about the alleged threat of popery and arbitrary government in the 1670s were shaped to a significant extent by anxieties about what seemed to be going on in Charles's other two kingdoms, where the threat of popery and arbitrary government seemed real enough.

Put like this, it might seem that the Restoration simply restored the old British problem which had bedevilled the Stuart monarchy in the first half of the seventeenth century. However, certain qualifications need to be made to this view. In the first place, although the Restoration settlements in all three kingdoms were backward-looking, they in fact restored each kingdom to a different phase of its historical development. In England the clock was put back to 1641;

in Scotland to 1633; in Ireland to an intermediary situation – pre-Civil War on the constitutional front but not on the landholding front, since a significant number of those who had benefited from the changes in landownership in the 1640s and '50s were able to hold on to their estates (or else were compensated for having to give them up). This asynchronous Restoration across England, Scotland and Ireland means that there was no simple return to the pre-Civil War order when viewed from a three-kingdoms perspective. The three kingdoms had never stood in the same sort of relationship to each other in the past as they were to by 1665–6, say, with the result that the nature of the British problem was different from what it had been before. We should also be wary of talking about the later-Stuart multiple-kingdom inheritance as if it was inevitably a problem. It could certainly create problems, as we have seen in this chapter and as we shall see again in the following chapter. Yet it could also work to the crown's advantage, if the King were shrewd enough to know how to play his separate kingdoms off against each other. We have already seen hints in this chapter that Charles II and his advisers recognized this – notably in the discussion over the proposed plans for union between Scotland and England in 1669–70. We shall see in subsequent chapters that knowing how to play the three-kingdoms card to the crown's advantage was to prove crucial to Charles's success in defeating the challenge of the Exclusionist movement.

3

Fearing for the Safety of the People

*The Popish Plot, Exclusion and the Nature of the
Whig Challenge, c. 1678–1681*

*[The Popish Plot] had so perfect an air of the fabulous reports
which preceeded the late Revolution, that those who remember'd it, thought themselves gon back to forty one . . . all
people's ears were fill'd with dismall rumours of a design to
kill the King, and subvert the Government to bring in Popery,
and Arbitrary Power.*[1]

Although the Restoration regime might appear, with hindsight, to have
been inherently unstable, it had yet to be radically destabilized. What
brought matters to a head were the revelations by Titus Oates, in the
late summer of 1678, of a Popish Plot against both the King and his
subjects. Oates – famously depicted in contemporary prints with his
excessively elongated chin – was by all accounts a most unsavoury
individual. His pastimes included lying, cheating, blasphemy and
sodomizing young boys. Forced to leave Cambridge in disgrace and
without a degree, he nevertheless contrived to enter Anglican orders,
only to be subsequently dismissed from his living for drunken blasphemy. After a brief spell as a navy chaplain (to be dismissed this time
for committing a homosexual act), he eventually decided to convert to
Roman Catholicism, studying at the English College at Valladolid in
Spain, which he was soon asked to leave, though before returning to
England he was to award himself a doctorate from the University of
Salamanca. His conversion was no doubt insincere, though it did,
Oates was later to claim, gain him admission to the secret cabals of the
Jesuits, which was how he supposedly came to be privy to the inter-
national conspiracy against the life of Charles II. It was all brilliant

Oatesian fantasy, but by now practice had made Oates a rather convincing liar – not least, perhaps, because he was to tell people what they wanted (or feared) to hear.[2]

The story Oates had to tell was a self-consciously British one. The Jesuits were first to send priests disguised as Presbyterian ministers into Scotland to stir up those suffering under 'Episcopal Tyranny' into rebellion, and then raise a Catholic uprising in Ireland. With these two kingdoms in revolt, they would proceed to assassinate Charles II and burn London to the ground, prompting Catholics to rise up and massacre thousands of Protestants, with the ultimate goal of restoring the Roman Catholic faith in England.[3] The narrative eerily mirrored the sequence of events of 1637–41 that had triggered the outbreak of civil war in England in 1642, and circumstantial evidence served to lend it credibility. For example, a Middlesex magistrate, Sir Edmundberry Godfrey, was mysteriously found dead (presumed murdered) in October 1678 after taking further depositions about the plot from Oates and his associate, Dr Israel Tonge.[4] Some incriminating letters concerning the enhancement of Catholic interests, dating back to the mid-1670s, were found in the possession of the Duke of York's former secretary Edward Coleman, a Roman Catholic convert and one of the leading conspirators named by Oates. Then, in May–June 1679, some 8,000 covenanters actually did rise in rebellion – starting at Rutherglen, on the outskirts of Glasgow, though establishing their main camp at nearby Bothwell Bridge – to protest against their sufferings under the episcopal regime in Scotland. Alarmingly, Oates's predictions seemed to becoming true. Moreover, further investigations into the plot over the next couple of years were to reveal a supposed Irish dimension to the conspiracy.

The revelations of the Popish Plot gave rise to what has come to be known as the Exclusion Crisis. Although initially Oates did not name the Duke of York as complicit in the plot, the fact was lost on no one that should Charles die he would be succeeded by his Catholic brother. And as a Catholic, it was feared, York would not only feel obliged to promote Roman Catholicism but also seek to enhance royal power and to rule in an arbitrary fashion like Louis XIV in France. In this context, an opposition grouping emerged – comprising peers, MPs and local politicians – intent on securing England against

the perceived threat of popery and arbitrary government. It was a battle they fought in parliament – three parliaments met in the years
1679–81, following the dissolution of the Cavalier Parliament in
January 1679 – as they tried to obtain the passage of measures
designed to protect the Protestant religion and secure the liberties of
English people. It was one they took to the hustings, as they sought to
persuade the electorate to vote for candidates who would support
their agenda. And it was one which they took out-of-doors, via the
press and through the encouragement of mass activism (in the form
of petitions and rallies), as they endeavoured to harness public opinion behind their cause. Most famously, they came to demand that the
Duke of York should be excluded from the succession, bringing three
Exclusion Bills before the three respective parliaments of 1679–81.
They also attacked ministers of the crown believed responsible for
this drift towards popery and arbitrary government (starting with
Danby himself, who was the chief minister when the crisis broke),
championed the sovereignty of parliament and the theory of the
mixed constitution against the proponents of divine-right royal absolutism, and demanded a number of reforms in Church and state that
would have given subjects greater legal securities and alleviated the
plight of Protestant nonconformists. Collectively, those who supported this agenda, together with their supporters out-of-doors, came to
be styled the Whigs. Their opponents – those who sought to preserve
the hereditary succession – were christened the Tories. As we have
seen, it was a nomenclature which reflected the perceived British
dimension to the crisis, a Whig originally being a radical Scottish
Presbyterian, and a Tory an Irish-Catholic cattle thief.

There has been considerable debate in recent years over how we
should understand the Exclusion Crisis. Some have even questioned
whether the term 'Exclusion Crisis' is really appropriate, either
because there was no real crisis,[5] or because the crisis was not just –
or even primarily – about Exclusion.[6] This chapter will therefore be
organized around two basic questions: what was the crisis about, and
did the situation ever become critical for the government? For a long
time, historians tended to see the Exclusion Crisis in somewhat one-
dimensional terms: it was in essence about an imagined fear of what
might happen in the future, should York become king, and the crisis

therefore centred around whether or not parliament could exclude the Catholic heir from the succession.[7] Representing the fear as imagined served to encourage the view that the response to the Popish Plot was hysterical; indeed, it has been described as 'one of the most remarkable outbreaks of mass hysteria in English history'.[8] This is clearly unsatisfactory. The Exclusion Crisis was not about one thing, but about several interrelated anxieties, all centring around the fear of popery and arbitrary government: about what would happen in England in the future under a popish successor; about the threat of popery, in the present, within England; about the current international situation, and especially about what was going on in France under Louis XIV; and about Charles II's style of government, not just in England but also in Scotland and Ireland. Although there were certainly imagined fears, and some people's imaginations (fuelled by Whig propaganda) perhaps had a tendency to run riot, there was also the perception of a very real threat in the present, belying any notion that the response was hysterical. The bulk of this chapter will therefore be dedicated to looking at what the fuss was all about: the nature of the Whig campaign; the concerns that the Whigs had (about both the future and the present, and about the domestic, the British and the international situations); and the remedies that they proposed. The final section will examine the extent to which the Whigs represented a significant challenge to the Restoration regime. The aim here will be to demonstrate the depth of the crisis into which Charles II's government had sunk by the late 1670s and from which it would need to extricate itself – a crisis which, we shall see, was not purely English in nature but genuinely British in the making.

THE WHIG CAMPAIGN

Restoration scholars have stressed the need to rid ourselves of any notion that the first Whigs were a monolithic party, united behind the leadership of one man – the Earl of Shaftesbury – in pursuit of a single goal – Exclusion. Instead, we have come to recognize that the first Whigs were a broad church, comprising different factions or interests. Thus we can perhaps speak of a Shaftesbury–Russell interest (William

Lord Russell being Shaftesbury's right-hand man in the Commons) committed to Exclusion and moderate constitutional reform; a more radical Sidney–Capel interest (the supporters of Algernon Sidney and the Earl of Essex, Arthur Capel), whose ideal would have been a republic; and a Monmouth interest, centring around the Protestant Duke of Monmouth and his personal followers such as Lord Colchester and Sir Thomas Armstrong, who wanted to switch the succession to the King's eldest illegitimate son – though even this is somewhat formulaic, since allegiances remained fluid as people pursued alternative strategies and alliances as they strove in their various ways to achieve their main concern: to rid England of the threat of popery and arbitrary government.[9] Although Shaftesbury played an important leadership role – he drew up lists predicting how politicians would act in parliament, was a leading ideological spokesman for the Whig cause in the House of Lords, and was active in promoting the Whig agenda out-of-doors – he was not *the* leader of the Whigs; indeed, he often found himself at odds with other leading figures in the Whig movement, and did not always find it easy to persuade others to follow his initiatives. Many Whigs were politically quite conservative, simply wishing to preserve strong monarchy in England though keeping it in the Protestant line by diverting the succession. Others were constitutional reformists, bent on curtailing the powers of the monarch and exalting the powers of parliament. A few even hoped to make the monarchy elective or else transform the English government into a virtual commonwealth where the head of state was king in name only, though these were a small minority. Nor did all Whigs believe that passing an Exclusion Bill was the only way to rescue the land from popery and arbitrary government. Alternative solutions that came to be endorsed at various times by different groups of Whigs included limiting the powers of a popish successor, so that he could not be a threat to the Protestant establishment; establishing a regency during the lifetime of a popish successor; persuading the King to remarry, so he could father a legitimate heir; and trying to get Charles to declare his eldest illegitimate son, the Duke of Monmouth, legitimate. It has also been pointed out that the parliaments of 1679–81 spent relatively little time discussing whether or not to exclude the Catholic heir, but instead busied themselves with other issues that members deemed important – such as investigating the plot, trying to provide for national security at a time of imminent danger, combating perceived abuses of power by the court and the court's servants, promoting the cause of Protestant unity, and trying to safeguard the liberties of parliament and the subject. Moreover, the general elections of 1679–81 were not fought predominantly over the issue of Exclusion; other factors, such as court–country tensions, the issue of religious dissent, and local concerns were more important – certainly in the two general elections of 1679, and arguably in that of 1681 – while a study of the pamphlet literature of this period reveals a preoccupation with a diversity of issues over and above Exclusion.[10]

Such revisionist perspectives are of undoubted importance, and have served to provide a fuller and more realistic appreciation of the politics of 1679–81. They should not mislead us, however, into thinking that the Whigs lacked organization or that Exclusion was not an issue. One of the main reasons why the Whigs represented such a challenge to the royal administration was because, for an age that did not accept the legitimacy of partisan politics or of organized opposition to the crown, they appeared disturbingly well organized. Politicians gathered in clubs held in London's numerous coffee houses and taverns to coordinate tactics for the parliamentary session. There were twenty-nine clubs in London alone – including Shaftesbury's club at the Swan in Fish Street, Buckingham's at the Salutation Tavern in Lombard Street, and the famous Green Ribbon Club, which met at the King's Head Tavern in Chancery Lane – as well as numerous provincial clubs, in places such as Bristol, Buckingham, Newport (Essex), Norwich, Oxford, Taunton and York.[11] Although it would be wrong to convey the impression that the Whigs fought centrally coordinated campaigns at the three general elections of 1679–81, electoral agents were employed to promote the interests of Whig candidates at the polls, while Whig magnates such as Shaftesbury, Buckingham and Lords Wharton and Grey used what resources they could muster to procure the return of sympathetic MPs.[12] The Whigs also launched a propaganda campaign designed to win over public opinion, and actively encouraged mass petitioning campaigns and public demonstrations in order to pressurize the government into acceding to their demands.

One of the most striking things about the Whig campaign is the extent of its reach. The Whigs made every effort to ensure that as many people as possible throughout the kingdom were apprised of the threat of popery and arbitrary government and educated about the things that might need to be done in order to avoid it. This was achieved through a brilliant exploitation of the media. The lapsing of the Licensing Act in 1679 led to the breakdown of pre-publication censorship, and as a result a host of printed artefacts began to pour forth from the presses. The number of books and pamphlets published annually shot up from about 1,081 in 1677 and 1,174 in 1678 to 1,730 in 1679, 2,145 in 1680, and 1,978 in 1681.[13] Taking into account contemporary print runs, somewhere between 5 and 10 million pamphlets must have been in circulation in the years 1679–81.[14] There were also several Whig political periodicals and bi-weekly newspapers – such as Henry Care's *Weekly Pacquet of Advice from Rome* (which ran from December 1678 to July 1683); Benjamin Harris's *Domestick Intelligence*, later retitled *The Protestant (Domestick) Intelligence* (July 1679 to April 1681); Langley Curtis's *True Protestant Mercury* (December 1680 to October 1682); Richard Janeway's *Impartial Protestant Mercury* (December 1680 to October 1682); and Francis Smith's *Protestant Intelligence* (February–April 1681) – intended to keep readers alert to the nature of the popish threat and abreast of the latest foreign news and domestic developments. In addition to printed artefacts, there were manuscript newsletters which remained much in demand because they provided more complete and reliable news than the published bi-weeklies.[15]

Not that the media became totally unregulated with the lapsing of the Licensing Act. The government could still invoke the law of seditious libel in an attempt to silence opposition publicists. In the first half of 1680 a vigorous campaign conducted by Lord Chief Justice Sir William Scroggs led to the successful prosecution of a number of Whig publicists, including Care, Jane Curtis (Langley Curtis's wife), Smith and Harris. The last, for example, was fined £500 and sentenced to stand in the pillory for publishing *An Appeal from the Country to the City*, a tract that vividly rehearsed the horrors that English people could expect from a popish ruler and advocated Monmouth as an alternative successor to York.[16] Regulating the press through the law of seditious libel proved of limited effectiveness, however. The courts could go after an author or publisher after a work had appeared in print, but by that time the damage had already been done, while taking legal action might only serve to give the work further publicity and provoke sympathy for the publicist who was being prosecuted. Harris, for example, was fêted by crowds when he stood in the pillory in the Old Exchange in London on 17 February 1680.[17] Moreover, it became virtually impossible to bring successful prosecutions against London-based publicists following the election of two Whig sheriffs, Slingsby Bethel and Henry Cornish, in the summer of 1680; because sheriffs were responsible for empanelling juries in London and Middlesex, they could ensure that only those sympathetic to the Whig cause were chosen to serve.

The reach of Whig propaganda was undoubtedly very wide – both sociologically and geographically. The lengthier pamphlets, to be sure, would have been quite expensive and necessitated an advanced level of literacy in their readers. Newspapers and broadsides, on the other hand, were relatively cheap – typically costing just a penny – and written in a popular idiom so that they could easily be understood by those with limited literacy skills. People could also find the latest publications in pubs or at that 'Great Pond or Puddle of News, the Coffee House';[18] indeed, the owners of such establishments found it necessary to provide the latest pamphlets for their customers in order to attract business. In other words, one did not need to be able to afford to buy news in order to be a consumer; often all that was needed was a thirst. Nor did one even need to be literate. The cheaper news-sheets and more down-market publications could easily be read aloud to those who could not read themselves. In addition, various propaganda devices were deployed that were not dependent upon literacy. There were visual materials such as satirical prints – both the more expensive copper-plate engravings and also the cheaper (and cruder) woodcuts – which might either stand alone or illustrate broadsides; some publishers even produced packs of playing cards illustrated with political prints. Then there was what one might call the performance media: both where the target audience was performed to and where they were involved in the actual performance. The clearest example of the former would be sermons – by nonconformist ministers in their conventicles;

by those few Whig-leaning clergymen who were prepared to raise the alarm about the threat of popery from the pulpit; even by Titus Oates himself, who gave a number of guest sermons in London at this time.[19] Whig playwrights used the London stage to convey pointed partisan messages to the theatre-going public, though there were also political plays put on at the London fairgrounds, such as the virulently anti-Catholic *Coronation of the Queen Elizabeth*, performed before the huge crowds that visited Bartholomew and Southwark fairs in 1680.[20] Then there were poems and ballads – large numbers of them – which might be performed by ballad singers or travelling musicians but which also could be learned by rote and recited by members of the public themselves. Last but not least we have the famous pope-burning processions staged in London on 17 November (the anniversary of Queen Elizabeth's accession) between 1679 and 1681; these involved elaborate anti-Catholic pageants, acted out by ordinary Londoners, processing through the streets of the capital, and a spectacular finale which witnessed the burning of the pope's effigy before thousands of spectators at Temple Bar (in 1679 and 1680) or Smithfield (in 1681).[21]

It would certainly be misleading to give the impression that all this output was controlled by some sort of central party headquarters. There were writers and publishers who worked independently and who just wanted to make a living, being prepared to produce anything that they thought would sell. Nevertheless, there was some orchestration from above. Although Shaftesbury did not have the sort of control over the opposition press that was ascribed to him by his political opponents, he clearly was behind some of the polemical work that came out during the Exclusion Crisis, and he appears to have employed a small group of stationers to produce and distribute tracts.[22] Some of the London clubs also played a role in coordinating the Whig propaganda efforts. The Green Ribbon Club, for example, sponsored the London pope-burnings of 17 November and other Whig demonstrations; the pageant of 1680 was said to have cost £2,500. It also gave a subsidy to Henry Care when he was temporarily imprisoned in October 1679 for his *Weekly Pacquet*.[23]

Much of this material emanated from London, and it is probably fair to assume that the metropolitan population possessed the most heightened degree of political awareness at this time. Nevertheless, the impact was not limited to the metropolis. Lord Keeper Sir Francis North may have exaggerated when he claimed that the Whigs, through their network of coffee houses 'where they vented news and libels . . . could entirely possess the city with what reports they pleased' within twenty-four hours and spread them 'all over the kingdom' in less than a week, but his picture of how political news and propaganda was disseminated was essentially correct.[24] In September 1681, for example, the government uncovered a network of newsletter writers in London who busied themselves 'composeing and writing . . . scandalous papers and letters' which were then sent to the chief post house in Lombard Street for distribution to different parts of the kingdom.[25] In Bristol the nonconformists used to gather at Kimbar's coffee house to learn the latest news, spreading what they learned either by word of mouth or by distributing 'Libells' up and down the streets.[26] In Gloucester a local clergyman called Vernon was active in spreading what news he had learned from the newsletters sent to local coffee houses, sometimes using his pulpit to reproach the government. The fact that he had recently moved to the city to take up a position as a curate paying a mere £10 p.a., when he had two good livings elsewhere worth £400 p.a. between them, raised the suspicion that he was a planted agent.[27] In Stafford in 1680–81 a local apothecary named Thomas Gyles took on the job of dispersing Whig tracts in his neighbourhood, among them a printed copy of one of Shaftesbury's speeches in the Lords, which came to him through the post.[28] From 1682 we have a report of William Lord Russell and a group of London citizens and nonconformist ministers spreading 'fears and jealousies of Popery and arbitrary government' in Tunbridge Wells, Kent, circulating the latest tracts out of London and even reading extracts out loud for the edification of passers-by.[29] Loyalists, too, helped ensure that Whig propaganda made it to the provinces, since they were eager to read what the Whigs had to say even if they did not agree with it. According to an account from late 1682, 'Factious Intelligences' were regularly sent to Chichester, in Sussex, though 'it was rather to admire at their Impudence, (and to see their folly), than to encourage such promoters of seditions'.[30] Whig materials also found their way into Scotland and Ireland, by a similar variety of means.[31] It was difficult, in other words, to be alive and conscious in 1679–81 without being aware that the Whigs had a view that they were trying to get across. One might not agree with it (a point to which we shall return in subsequent chapters), but one was unlikely to be completely ignorant about it.

IMAGINING THE FUTURE

Why all this effort? What were the Whigs so worried about? The brief answer would be the threat of popery and arbitrary government. As such, they were deeply concerned about the prospect of a Catholic successor, and keen to pursue whatever measures they thought would best protect the Protestant religion and safeguard the interests of the King's subjects. The simplest way out of the dilemma, and the solution that came to appear most attractive to the majority of Whigs, was to exclude the Duke of York from the succession.

Concern over the Catholic succession was nothing new. The idea of Exclusion had first been mooted in 1674, while in 1677 the Earl of Danby had put forward a scheme of limitations as a way of trying to safeguard the Protestant establishment should York one day come to the throne.[32] York suspected from the very start that the Popish Plot was a ploy to strike at him – an opinion the King himself seems to have shared.[33] And York was indeed soon to find himself under attack. In early November 1678 Shaftesbury moved in the Lords that York should be removed from all councils and public affairs, and a few days later the Commons considered addressing the King to remove the Duke from court. In a debate in the Commons on 4 November, William Sacheverell asked 'whether the King and the Parliament may not dispose of the Succession of the Crown? and whether it be not Praemunire to say the contrary?'[34] The King tried to make a pre-emptive strike by informing both houses on 9 November that he would give the royal assent to any bills that would make them 'safe in the reign of my successor, (so as they tend not to impeach the Right of Succession, nor the descent of the crown in the true line)'. It was reported in the streets, however, that Charles had declared in favour of choosing a Protestant successor or settling the succession on Monmouth, prompting bonfire celebrations throughout London as crowds gathered to drink Shaftesbury's and Monmouth's healths.[35]

Exclusion was already in the air, then, by November 1678. But Charles's speech may have temporarily deterred further immediate attacks on his brother, and in any case the King chose to prorogue the Cavalier Parliament in December and dissolve it in January. Although the new parliament, which met in March 1679, did not immediately taken up the issue of Exclusion, its further investigations into the Popish Plot soon led to suspicions of York's complicity. Thus on 27 April the Commons resolved that 'the Duke of Yorke's being a Papist, and the hopes of his coming to the Crown' had given 'the greatest Countenance and Encouragement to the present Conspiracy and Designes of the Papists against the King and Protestant Religion', and on 11 May they at last introduced a bill to exclude York from the succession – though Charles was to prorogue and then dissolve this parliament too before the bill could come to anything.[36] A second Exclusion Bill was introduced into the next parliament in October 1680, although this was to be defeated by a vote in the Lords on 15 November. A third one made it into the ill-fated Oxford Parliament of March 1681, which sat for just eight days. Other methods were also tried to strike at the Catholic heir. Towards the end of June 1680 Shaftesbury and some fellow MPs brought an indictment against York for recusancy before a Middlesex grand jury at Hicks Hall; on this occasion, Scroggs discharged the grand jury three days before the end of the term, to prevent it from considering the indictment. In late November, following the defeat of the Exclusion Bill in the Lords, the London magistrates at the Old Bailey decided to follow up on the matter, summoned the Middlesex grand jury to reappear before them, and proceeded to present York for recusancy; this time the indictment was removed by *certiorari* to the court of King's Bench and the case was never tried.[37]

Although it may be correct that parliament spent relatively little time discussing Exclusion, concern over the issue of the Catholic heir manifested itself in other debates, over seemingly unrelated issues. York himself – if the retrospective *Life of James II* is to be trusted – appears to have interpreted virtually everything these parliaments did as directed against him. Thus the *Life* notes how, following the failure of the second Exclusion Bill, the Commons began to 'fall upon those who had lately espous'd his interest', including Edward Seymour, one of York's staunchest defenders in the Commons, and the now Earl of Halifax, the man who had spoken most passionately against Exclusion in the debate in the Lords. Similarly, York saw the trial of the Catholic peer Lord Stafford in late 1680, for alleged complicity in the Popish Plot, and even the parliamentary debate over whether to vote funds for the garrison at Tangier, which some members castigated as 'a nursery' for papists, as but further attempts to damage his political interest and heighten public concerns about the prospect of a popish successor.[38] Contemporary accounts confirm that the main reason why the King and his parliaments remained at loggerheads in 1680–81 was because they differed 'about the point of Exclusion', as the latitudinarian clergyman John Tillotson reported to a friend in Paris in January 1681.[39]

It should also be pointed out that passing an Exclusion Bill was not the only way of excluding York from the succession. Trying to persuade Charles to remarry (so that he could beget a Protestant heir), or to declare Monmouth legitimate, was just as much an attempt to exclude the Catholic heir, as far as contemporaries were concerned, as a bill barring him from the succession, while the idea of imposing limitations on a popish successor was a way of trying to find a solution to the succession crisis which would not necessitate York's 'exclusion'. Thus there is no need, as some scholars have suggested, to rename the Exclusion Crisis; even if the crisis was 'more a controversy over the succession problem and the political and constitutional implications of all the various expedients offered to solve it', this is nevertheless just another way of saying that it was indeed about exclusion.[40] However, an Exclusion Bill came to be seen by most Whigs as the best solution for the simple reason that the alternatives were not viable. Charles was not going to divorce his wife, nor was he going to declare Monmouth legitimate. Schemes proposing some form of limitations on a popish successor, curtailing his powers so that it would be impossible for him to hurt the Protestant establishment, or even setting up a regency for the lifetime of a Catholic king, were taken more seriously, not least because Charles himself said he was prepared to entertain such solutions. Both Essex and Sidney backed limitations, for example, while the notion that it would not matter if England had a Catholic king if the powers of the monarchy were curtailed sufficiently to make the English king little more than a doge of Venice was touted by the classical republican theorist Henry Neville in his *Plato Redivivus* of 1681.[41] Limitations may have held a particular appeal for the republican Whigs (or commonwealthsmen, as they were known); Halifax, who himself preferred limitations to Exclusion, supposedly tried to convince his republican friends that such limitations 'brought us really into a commonwealth, as soon as we had a popish king over us'.[42] However – as most Whigs recognized – whatever the theoretical appeal, it was highly questionable whether any such limitations would be enforceable in practice, or whether York, once king, would not simply be able to ignore any constraints placed on his power which he had not agreed to. York himself opposed limitations, which he thought were 'worse then the bill of exclusion', as he told Clarendon in December 1680, because 'this absolutly destroys for ever the monarchy'.[43] Likewise the Prince of Orange, whose wife was second in line to the throne and who was himself fourth in line, was against limitations because he feared that if any prerogatives were taken away from the crown they would never be returned once England had a Protestant king. Besides, Charles himself seems not to have been serious about limitations, and secretly assured Orange that he would never consent to them.[44] Although a few Whigs, at various times between 1679 and 1681, flirted with the idea of limitations, most came to recognize that such schemes were 'only a snare', as Sir William Jones put it in the Oxford Parliament – a mere trick to try to secure the succession by dividing the Exclusionists among themselves.[45]

The concern over a popish successor certainly was based, in part, on an imagined fear about the future: what would happen if a Catholic – and this Catholic, in particular – became king? Would he seek to overturn the Reformation? Would Protestants be allowed to worship freely, or would they be condemned to die as heretics if they refused to convert back to Rome? What would happen to those former church lands sold off to the gentry following the dissolution of the monasteries? The reason why William Lord Russell, Whig MP for Bedfordshire, was such a staunch supporter of Exclusion was because most of his estate was from the lands of dissolved monastic institutions, such as the abbeys of Tavistock (Devon) and Woburn (Bedfordshire) and the monastery of Thorney (Cambridgeshire).[46] How would a Catholic king impose his will on a Protestant nation? It seemed unlikely that he would be able to work with parliament, so he would have to rule with a standing army. Gone, therefore, would be English political liberties.[47] Whig poet and playwright Elkanah Settle predicted that a popish king would 'find sufficient Assistance from the Pope, English Papists, and Foreign Princes' to enable him to rule without parliament and would also raise a standing army, 'ready to cut our Throats at home, if we do not submit, and give all that this King shall ask. And then', Settle continued, 'his Revenue may be as great as he and his Popish Counsellors shall think fit to make it.' In short, the people of England would face from a popish successor 'certain Prospect . . . of the ruine of their Estates, Lives, and Liberties'.[48]

The case against a popish successor was based in part on history. Pamphleteers repeatedly harped on the atrocities allegedly committed against Protestants under England's last Catholic monarch, Mary Tudor (r. 1553–8). One author recalled that 'the last time when Popery Reign'd amongst us' not only were 'many of our Laity . . . torn to pieces, and tied to a Stake in the midst of flames at Smithfield, and other places', but 'our Divines were butchered by the Name of Heretick Dogs, our Houses plundered, our Wives and Daughters ravished', and 'our Churches . . . converted into the Temples or Places of Idolatry and Superstition'.[49] MPs similarly appealed to the public memory of Mary's reign in parliamentary debate. It was essential to pass the Exclusion Bill, Hugh Boscawen argued in the Commons on 2 November 1680, to avoid being 'hauled to Smithfield'. In return for their support against Lady Jane Grey in 1553, Mary had promised the Protestants of East Anglia she would not alter religion, Colonel Silius Titus recalled, 'but when she came to the Crown, she burnt them . . . and for the Crown of England she gave them a Crown of Martyrdom.'[50] Then there were the subsequent attempts by the forces of international Catholicism to strike at the English monarchy and destroy the Protestant establishment in Church and state – most famously with the Spanish Armada of 1588 and the Gunpowder Plot of 1605. Finally, there was the Great Fire of London of September 1666, the blame for which had officially been laid at the Catholics' door; indeed, a French Catholic had confessed to having started the conflagration. In 1681 London Lord Mayor Sir Patience Ward had a plaque attached to the Monument constructed on the site where the fire had started explaining how 'the most Dreadful Burning of this Protestant City' had been 'Begun on by the Treachery and Malice of the Papists'.[51]

Whig polemicists also recalled events overseas, especially the terrible atrocities allegedly perpetrated against Protestants in Germany during the Thirty Years War (1618–48). One tract, ominously entitled *England's Calamity,* recollected how during the 1630s Catholics had roasted Protestants alive, mutilated and tortured them, devoured young infants, and deflowered virgins. It also contained two prints: one showing 'Protestants burning for the true Christian Religion', the other depicting Catholics inflicting various other 'devilish torments', such as raping wives and daughters, and smashing the heads of little children against walls.[52] Closer to home, there was the example of the Irish Rebellion of 1641. Sir John Temple's famous history of *The Irish Rebellion,* which had first appeared in 1646 and was republished in 1679, was not only highly readable but also carried considerable conviction, since the author provided abundant source citations to support his claims and made powerful use of testimonies given on oath before the commissioners set up to investigate the rebellion in the early 1640s. Containing gruesome accounts of the alleged atrocities perpetrated on Protestants by Catholics, it made the wildly exaggerated claim that some 300,000 Protestants had been either killed or driven from the kingdom as a result of the rebellion.[53] The same year saw the publication of the self-explanatory *A Collection of Certain Horrid Murthers in Several Counties of Ireland. Committed since the 23. of Octobr. 1641,* which alleged that some 150,000 Protestants had died at the hands of Catholic rebels,[54] while in 1680 Edmund Borlase published his own, fully documented *History,* taking the story up to the Act of Settlement of 1662 and outlining in an appendix the number of murders in the several counties of Ireland since 23 October 1641.[55] Such works were intended to instruct 'this present age in what they are to expect from Popery, by the sad experience of the last generation',[56] and the persevering reader would have come away with an image of the Irish, to quote from Borlase's

account, as 'wild Beasts of the Wilderness', bent on 'the utter extirpation of the English nation, and Protestant Religion' out of Ireland,
and guilty of 'execrable Cruelties . . . and cruel Deaths' by
'Strip[p]ing, Starving, Burning, Strangling, [and] Burying alive'.[57]
MPs naturally appealed to the example of the Irish Rebellion when
making the case for Exclusion. As Boscawen put it in the Commons
on 2 November 1680, it was impossible to think of the Catholics as
'disciples of Christ', when they had 'murdered so many good
Christians, and committed that Massacre in Ireland, where the
Government was Protestant' – though Boscawen was to exceed even
Temple in putting the number of Protestants killed at 'some four hundred thousands'.[58]

In addition to the lessons of history, there was the contemporary
example of France, the major Catholic power in Europe. Exclusionists insisted that English Protestants would be naive to expect they
could be safe under a popish successor – after all, Louis XIV showed
no desire to protect the civil and religious liberties guaranteed to his
Protestant subjects under the terms of the Edict of Nantes (1598).
Pamphlets and newspapers documented the plight of the Huguenots
for the benefit of the reading public, while Huguenot refugees fleeing
to England and Ireland in the face of persecution (there was already a
steady stream before the Revocation of the Edict of Nantes in 1685)
brought with them 'dismall storys of the inhumanitys excerysed upon
them'.[59] Persecution had started at the beginning of Louis XIV's personal rule in 1661, but had intensified from the late 1670s: Protestant
churches and schools were shut down; Huguenots were denied the
right to hold civil office, exercise certain professions, or even practise
their trades; they were subject to higher taxes; their children were
taken from them and placed in Catholic boarding schools; and
relapsed converts were to have their estates seized. Then from 1681
began the dragonnades, the practice of billeting troops on Huguenot
families, at free quarter, in the hope that a combination of economic
privation and physical intimidation might induce conversions.[60] Yet,
if Whig propaganda was to be believed, Louis XIV's Catholic subjects
were not much better off. One pamphlet, purporting to be a letter
written by an English gentleman in Paris, proclaimed that 'the
Government of France' was 'an Absolute Monarchy, imposed upon

the People by a standing, illegal and oppressive Army': 'the Nobility of all sorts' were 'very much Oppress'd'; 'the Clergy' were 'also over-awed'; the trading classes of the towns suffered from heavy imposi-tions; and the peasantry, 'out of that little which belonged to them . . . paid near two Thirds to the King'.[61] Another pamphleteer observed 'how the French King, a Popish King, levyes Arbitrary Taxes at his pleasure, and imposes several other Tyrannical Oppressions', and reminded his (English Protestant) readers that 'the Pope and Papists' were their 'mortal Enemies, and would fain Reign and Dominere over this Kingdom in the same nature as the French King doth in France'.[62]

That was why Whigs insisted that 'popery and slavery, like two sis-ters', went 'hand in hand', as Shaftesbury famously put it in a speech in the Lords in March 1679.[63] English Protestants were repeatedly reminded of the horrors that would befall them should a Catholic come to the throne. 'First, Imagine you see the whole Town in a flame, occasioned this second time, by the same Popish malice which set it on fire before,' Charles Blount warned in his influential *Appeal from the Country* of 1679. 'At the same instant fancy, that amongst the dis-tracted Crowd, you behold Troops of Papists, ravishing your Wives and Daughters, dashing your little Childrens brains out against the walls, plundering your Houses and cutting your own throats, by the Name of Heretic Dogs . . . Also, casting your eye towards Smithfield, imagine you see your Father, or your Mother, or some of your nearest and dearest Relations, tyed to a Stake in the midst of flames.'[64] If people did not get the message from reading the Whig press, they might from looking at a Whig print. Thus *A Prospect of a Popish Successor* (1681) showed a figure, 'Mack' (for Irish Catholic), who was half devil and half Duke of York, burning Protestants at the stake and firing the city of London. Or else they might hear it at the hus-tings. One of the candidates at the County Durham election for the second Exclusion Parliament told voters before the poll 'about the jails, Inquisition, and French mercenaries that a Catholic King would employ against Protestants'.[65] They might see it in a play, either in a theatre or at a fair, or hear it in a song. And they were regularly reminded of what Catholicism stood for in sermons delivered on the anniversary of the Gunpowder Plot and on other occasions, as they had long been. Thus in a sermon preached on 5 November 1673, though not published until 1679, Isaac Barrow (master of Trinity College, Cambridge, and a royal chaplain) called for Protestants to 'confide in God for his gracious preservation . . . from Romish Zeal and Bigotry', which Barrow saw as 'the mint of woful Factions and Combustions, of treasonable Conspiracies, of barbarous Massacres, of horrid Assassinations, of intestine Rebellions, of foreign Invasions, of savage Tortures and Butcheries'.[66] The gap between delivery and publication – Barrow himself had died in 1677 – hints at the time-lessness of the sentiment expressed; if anything, the message seemed more pertinent in the context of 1679. Preaching on the anniversary of the regicide in 1681, one cleric, after first reminding his auditors that on this day 'such a blot [was] cast on England, as she be glad it [be] forgot to posterity', then proceeded to forget the day himself and discuss 'our just, our great and scarce enough great detestation and abhorrency of Popery':

Popery, that silly, that foolish, that cruell Religion, a Religion which changes soe many of its professors into blood sucking leeches . . . a Religion that joys in murthers by retayle, but not satisfied without whole sale Massacres, a Religion that hopes at this day to turne the whole Christian world into an Aceldama, a field of blood, a Golgotha, a place of sculls etc. every where burying Protestants in heaps. If popery prevayle then stabbing, tearing out bowels will be every where practicd, then we shall be not only forsaken, turned out, but to be burnt, hangd, gibbets our portion, if popery prevayle the pavements sprinkled with children's blood, and walls besmeared with enfant's brains.

The prose is rough, because we are dependent upon sermon notes for our account; it nevertheless conveys well the frenetic nature of the clergyman's delivery. And he said all this, he claimed, not to make popery more bloody than it was, for 'who reads history of Waldenses, butchery of Paris, the cruelty of the Marion dayes, the bloodynesse of the Irish destruction, and the vaunts, threats, designes of these pres-ent plotters, will soon conclude worse cannot be sayd of them than they deserve.'[67]

It was one thing to warn of the dangers of a popish successor; it was quite another to demonstrate that anything could be done about it in an hereditary monarchy. Whigs deployed a wide range of arguments to try to justify parliament's right to alter the succession, some based on history, others on an appeal to natural law. In parliament itself, supporters of Exclusion sought to show that parliament had altered the succession on many occasions in the past, from Richard II's deposition in 1399 through to the reign of Henry VIII. Yet what appeared the most telling precedent was the Elizabethan statute of 1571, likewise enacted in a climate of concern about the possibility of a popish successor, which made it treason (during the queen's lifetime, and *praemunire* ever after) to deny 'That the Queen, by authority of Parliament', could 'limit and bound the Succession of the Crown'. This proved, as Paul Foley put it in the Commons on 11 May 1679, that king, Lords, and Commons could 'exclude any man from the Crown'.[68] Quoting the statute of 1571, Whig journalist Henry Care concluded in 1681 that parliament had the power 'to order the Right to the Crown' and 'had very frequently undertaken and actually Limited the same, Contrary to and different from the Common Line of Succession'.[69] The Whig lawyer John Somers sought to provide the scholarship to back up such claims in his *Brief History of the Succession* of 1680, where he showed that parliament had frequently meddled with the succession and concluded therefore that 'the Parliament of England had an unquestionable power to limit, restrain, and qualify the Succession as they pleased.'[70]

Yet, even if there were no precedents to support the case for the Exclusion Bill, the Whigs felt that 'the law of nature and self-preservation would afford us sufficient arguments,' as MP Hugh Boscawen typically put it in the debate on Exclusion in November 1680.[71] Monarchy was 'far from being de Jure Divino', one pamphleteer asserted, 'but ariseth by consent'; and the reason why people entered civil society was to secure 'the publick good'. It therefore followed 'that the succession is transferable, when the publick safety requires it'.[72] 'The King, Lords and Commons have a Power to dispose of the Succession as they shall judge most conducible to the Safety, Interest, and Happiness of the Kingdom,' another author insisted; 'and . . . he is His Majesties Heir and Successor, upon whom the whole Legislative Power shall think meet to settle the Inheritance of the Crown.'[73] The safety of the people demanded that in this instance the succession be breached. *Salus populi, suprema lex* ('The safety of the people is the

supreme law') became a key Whig catchphrase; it appeared promi-
nently on the title page of Blount's famous *Appeal from the Country*
of 1679, and was invoked time and time again by Whig pamphleteers.

Most Whigs explicitly championed the theory of coordination,
claiming that the king was but one of the three estates and shared his
sovereignty with the Lords and Commons. They also embraced the
myth of England's ancient constitution, alleging that the rights of parliament dated back to times immemorial.[74] Parliament's authority
was justified on the grounds that parliament was the representative of
the people. Ultimately, this placed sovereignty in the people themselves, and led to the view that government was based on consent.
'Every form of Government', Thomas Hunt wrote in 1680, 'is of our
Creation and not Gods, and must comply with the safety of the
people in all that it can.' In answer to the question 'whence the
Parliament derives their Power', Hunt boldly proclaimed, 'from the
same Original the King derives his', namely 'from the Consent of
the People in the first Constitution of the Government'. No government could be safe 'without a Power to exclude a Person inhabil in
Nature to support it, or of one Principled to destroy it' (i.e. a popish
successor), since it was impossible to 'imagine a Government which is
of Humane Contrivance, to be without a Power to Preserve itself'.
Hunt nevertheless insisted that this was an emergency power only,
and did not make England an elective monarchy and certainly not a
republic: 'our case will never be Cromwels'.[75] The author of a
Dialogue at Oxford encapsulated the typical Whig view when he
asserted that 'only Government in general is of Divine Right'; 'the
particular Forms and Limitations of it' were 'from humane Compact',
or contract (the author used both terms), which established that 'the
common Good of Humane Societies' was 'the First and Last End of
all Government'.[76] This was certainly a radical position, as contemporaries understood the term, since it placed power 'Radically and
Originally in the People', as the Tory press complained.[77]

Typically, those who defended Exclusion felt the need to insist that
they were not seeking constitutional innovation, claiming that they
did not want to change the nature of the monarchy, but only to keep
the succession in the Protestant line.[78] The Earl of Huntingdon might
not have been completely correct when he said in a debate in the

Lords on 15 November 1680 that there was 'not a man in this House' who supported the Exclusion Bill who was 'not most zealous for the support of this monarchy and the King in his royal prerogatives', but he was undoubtedly accurately representing the typical rhetorical posturing that Whig spokesmen found it wise to adopt at this time.[79] Nevertheless, two qualifications need to be made before we allow ourselves to take Whig self-professions of constitutional conservatism at face value. First, although the Whigs may have been careful about what they said or wrote in the present, they had fewer qualms about letting parliamentary spokesmen from the Civil War era make their case for them. Most significant in this respect was the republication in 1680 of Philip Hunton's *Treatise of Monarchy* of 1643, which set out to show that the English monarchy was limited, not absolute, based as it was on contract and the consent of the governed, and that the three estates of the realm had the right to resist a king who degenerated into tyranny.[80] Second, the way that the Whigs of the Exclusion Crisis came to articulate their case – however carefully they trod or circumscribed their claims – was nevertheless deeply subversive of the Cavalier-Anglican view of the constitution, involving, as it did, a denial of conventional notions of divine-right monarchy, and implying that the king was beneath the law, accountable to parliament, and that ultimately the people were sovereign. The king of England, the author of *Vox Populi; Or, the People's Claim* insisted, 'has no Prerogative, but what the Law gives him'; he is 'a king whilst he Rules well, but a Tyrant when he Oppresses'. As the famous medieval jurist Henry de Bracton had taught, 'The Common Law doth allow many Prerogatives to the King, yet it doth not allow any, that He shall wrong, or hurt any by His Prerogative.' Therefore kings, this same author continued, should use their power or prerogative only 'for the Preservation and Interest of the People. And not for the disappointing the Councils of a Parliament'; indeed, 'whenever it is applied to frustrate those ends, it is a Violation of Right, and Infringment of the King's Coronation Oath, who is obliged to Pass or Confirm those Laws His People shall chuse.'[81] Another author, likewise following Bracton, insisted that 'The Law bounds, and limits the King's Power,' and then, taking his cue from the late medieval constitutional theorist Sir John Fortescue, proclaimed that the king cannot 'Govern his

People by any other Power, than the Law'. To be sure, the king's ministers 'may act illegally', and if so 'they are Lyable to answer for it; but
he [the king] can do nothing but what the Law Directs and Justifies',
since not only is he bound by his coronation oath, 'but his own
Greatness, and his very Prerogative, as having their Foundations in
the Law, oblige him to it.' In short, this writer concluded, 'the fundamental constitution of the Land' as much 'limits the Prerogative of the
King' as it 'fixeth the Rights, Liberties, and Authority of Lords and
Commons'.[82] Responding to the court charge that the Whigs were
'lovers of Commonwealth Principles', Sir William Jones and Algernon
Sidney wrote that, if by this was meant 'men passionately devoted to
the Publick good, and to the common service of their Country, who
believe That Kings were instituted for the good of the People, and
Government ordained for the sake of those that are to be governed',
then 'every Wise and Honest Man will be proud to be ranked in that
number.' This did not mean, they continued, that they were for 'setting up a Democratical Government, in opposition to our legal
Monarchy', but the point was that the English monarchy was a legal
one. As Bracton had said, 'It is from the Law that he [the king] hath
his Power; it is by the Law that he is King, and for the good of the
people by whose consent it [the law] is made.' Indeed, 'all his
Commands that are contrary to Law, are void,' which was 'the true
Reason of that well known Maxim, that the King can do no wrong'.
For 'the essential principle of the English Monarchy', they averred,
was 'that well proportioned distribution of Powers, whereby the Law
doth at once provide for the greatness of the King, and the safety of
the People', adding that 'the Government can subsist no longer, than
whilst the Monarch enjoying the Power which the Law doth give him,
is enabled to perform the part it allows unto him and the People are
duly protected in their Rights and Liberties.'[83]

The implication was clear. If the king ceased to rule according to
law or to protect the rights and liberties of the people, he ceased to be
a lawful ruler and his subjects were no longer obliged to obedience.
Indeed, a number of authors explicitly challenged traditional Tory-
Anglican teachings on passive obedience, cautiously arguing a case
for the possibility of defensive resistance in the event of a popish successor. Clerical Whigs – that is, those in Anglican orders (there were

few of them, but they made a significant contribution to this debate) – felt obliged to uphold the Church's standard position that the king himself (even a Catholic one) was sacred and could not be harmed; nevertheless, they suggested that it would be legitimate to resist those who acted illegally in the name of the king. Thus Edmund Hickeringill, rector of All Saints, Colchester, maintained that, if a magistrate acted against the law, he acted not like a magistrate, but as a robber. Would the Tory clergy, he asked, 'perswade us to bind our own Hands 'till our Throats be cut, by Hectors and Tories, against Law, and that It is Divinity so to do'? He would 'rather dye than be a Rebel', Hickeringill protested, but then he did not think taking up arms to remove evil counsellors from the king was rebellion.[84] Similarly, Samuel Johnson, rector of Corringham in Essex and chaplain to the Whig leader William Lord Russell, wrote a stinging attack on the doctrine of passive obedience in his *Julian the Apostate* of 1682; that doctrine, he alleged, was 'calculated and fitted on purpose for the use of a Popish Successor, and to make us an easier Prey to the Bloody Papists'. Claiming that 'the Laws of a Man's Country' were 'the measures of all Civil Obedience', he insisted (following Bracton) that a king who failed to act 'according to Law' was no longer 'God's Vicegerent'. He had no gripe with Charles II, whose reign, he hoped, God would prolong, but he feared the worst under a popish successor, who (he predicted) would persecute Protestants unto death. However, we had 'our Religion nestled by such Laws as cannot be altered without our own consent', Johnson pointed out, and a popish successor had 'no Authority to exercise any illegal Cruelty upon Protestants': 'an Inauthoritative Act, which carries no Obligation at all', cannot, he proclaimed, 'oblige Men to Obedience'. It was true, Johnson conceded, that by the laws of England 'this Popish Prince, when he is lawfully possesst of the Crown', would be 'inviolable and unaccountable, as to his own Person, and ought by no means to have any violence offered to him'. Yet bad princes were rarely the executioners of their own cruelty, and it was possible to resist those who acted illegally in the king's name: 'We readily acknowledge, that no Inferior Magistrate is to be resisted in the exercise of his Office, so far as he is warranted by Law; but illegal Force may be repelled by Force.'[85]

Lay Whigs, however, were more willing to embrace the possibility that the Catholic monarch himself might be resisted. One author, writing in 1679 about whether people were obliged to be loyal to the Catholic successor, insisted that fidelity was 'due by nature to the Prince, so long as he lives and intends the publick good', but added, 'When he declines from that, Querie, for then I am bound patiently to let him Cut my Throat, if he will, which is repugnant to the Law of Nature, which Commands my preservation, which was perhaps the reason why the Barons in King Johns time took up Arms for their liberties.' The awkward syntax reveals the sensitivity of the subject – this was, after all, treasonous – and the author declined to discuss it further.[86] Elkanah Settle, in 1681, admitted that people were 'bound indeed by [their] Oaths of Allegiance, to a Constant Loyalty to the King and his lawful Successours', but were not bound to be 'his lawful Successour's . . . Loyal Slaves'. Besides, he asked:

how is an Arbitrary absolute Popish Tyrant any longer a lawful Successour to a Protestant establisht and bounded Government, when lawfully succeeding to this limited Monarchy, he afterwards violently, unlawfully, and tyrannically over-runs the due bounds of power, dissolves the whole Royal constitution of the Three Free-States of England, and the Subjects Petition of Right? Whilst wholly abandoning those Reins of Government which were his lawful birthright, and making new ones of his own illegal creation, he makes us neither those Free-born Subjects we were when we took that oath, nor himself that King we swore to be Loyal to.

Even 'the most vehement Disputants against the Peoples Right of defending themselves', Settle continued, 'must at least acknowledge thus much, that whenever a Popish King shall by Tyranny establish the Pope's Jurisdiction in England, undoubtedly in the Eye of God he is guilty of a greater Sin, than that people can be, that with open Arms oppose that Tyranny.' The conclusion was clear: 'The People of England, in taking Arms against that Tyranny, defend a just Right, viz. their Religion, Lives and Liberties.'[87]

It is easy to see how such arguments could be extended to apply not just to ministers of the crown or to a future Catholic monarch, but to the current Protestant one. Indeed, by late 1682 or early 1683 Johnson's patron, Lord Russell, was heavily involved in the radical

Whig intrigues against the government of Charles II and the Catholic succession known by the umbrella term the Rye House Plot. Moreover, it was at this time that John Locke wrote his famous *Two Treatises of Government*, the second treatise of which sought to establish that it was legitimate to resist the illegal government of Charles II and that this right to resist inhered in every single individual. Such a radical stance was forced on the Whigs by desperate circumstances – there was no alternative to resistance by 1682–3 – and even then only a minority of the more extreme Whigs were prepared to engage in active resistance to the present regime. The point is that the potential for such a radicalization was always implicit within the types of argument that the Whigs sought to deploy in order to justify their stance against a Catholic successor.

Exclusion would have favoured Princess Mary, James's eldest child and the wife of William of Orange (James's nephew), not Monmouth. The first Exclusion Bill stated that upon Charles II's death the crown should devolve upon that person who was the 'next Lawful Heir' and who had 'always been truly and professedly of the Protestant Religion now established by Law within this Kingdom, as if the said Duke of York were actually dead'.[88] Initially the second Exclusion Bill simply provided for the exclusion of James and remained silent about the succession – a form of wording favoured by Monmouth's friends, since it potentially left the way open for parliament to settle the throne on Monmouth at some future date – though it was modified in the committee stage to specify that the succession should descend to that person who would have inherited 'in case the Duke were dead', making it clear, once more, that Mary was parliament's preferred alternative. The third Exclusion Bill, introduced into the short-lived Oxford Parliament of 1681, returned to the ambiguous wording of the first draft of the second bill, though, since the bill never reached the committee stage, there is no telling whether this wording would have survived.[89]

Whig attitudes towards Monmouth were, in fact, ambivalent. For most, he was not the ideal alternative to York: he lacked political experience, was not particularly intelligent, and was too eager to retain the favour and affections of his father. In the early months of the Exclusion Crisis, Monmouth remained firmly identified with the court. In 1678 Shaftesbury had labelled him 'very very vile' when drawing up a list of the political sympathies of those who sat in the Cavalier Parliament; Monmouth sided with the court in opposing the attempted impeachment of Danby in December 1678; and Shaftesbury regarded those associates of Monmouth who were returned to sit in the first Exclusion Parliament as among his political opponents.[90] Yet Monmouth did not get along with his Catholic uncle, and the personal feud between the two men deepened as the Exclusion Crisis progressed. Moreover, 'the Protestant Duke', as Monmouth came to be styled, was extremely popular with the masses, as the demonstrations of November 1678 had already revealed – and this popularity was enhanced by the role he played in the investigations into the Popish Plot and by his soon being named as an intended victim of the plot himself. There had been talk in the past that Monmouth might be declared legitimate, and now stories began to circulate, with the help of the Whig press, that Charles had secretly married Monmouth's mother while in exile in the late 1640s and early 1650s and that the marriage certificate had been secreted in a 'black box' once belonging to the late Bishop of Durham, if only that could be found.[91] Charles was quick to deny all such rumours, but, concerned about Monmouth's growing popularity, he decided to send his son into temporary exile in Utrecht in September 1679. When Monmouth returned against his father's wishes towards the end of November, Charles had little option but to disgrace his son by stripping him of most of his offices. With the growing estrangement between Monmouth and his father from late 1679 onward, the Duke became increasingly identified with the opposition interest. Those who opposed York's succession needed to keep all their options open, and Monmouth did appear attractive for a number of reasons: as the King's son, he had a potential claim to the succession in his own right; he was popular, and might be a more acceptable king than Mary's husband, William of Orange; shifting the succession in his favour might provide the opportunity for introducing various constitutional reforms and establishing a more limited monarchy than if the succession had simply passed to William and Mary; and, finally, if parliamentary attempts at Exclusion were to fail, then Monmouth would be an ideal person – given his military experience and his following among the masses – to spearhead an armed resistance movement. Yet it would be misleading to imply that the Whigs started to promote him as their preferred successor; Shaftesbury himself always remained suspicious of Monmouth's intentions and trustworthiness, and Monmouth's main ambition at this time was probably to get his offices back and be restored to his father's favour.[92]

FEARING THE PRESENT

What we have been documenting so far is an imagined fear about a threat of popery and arbitrary government in the future, should York become king. It is important to recognize, however, that there was also a perceived threat of popery and arbitrary government in the present. Englishmen had cause to be concerned not just about what might come to pass, one day, but about what was actually going on right then.

The Catholic Menace

One concern was over what Catholics within England might be up to, particularly in those areas that had disproportionately large Catholic populations. In the provinces in late 1678 rumours circulated of stashes of arms found in papists' houses and of suspicious nocturnal gatherings by those of the Catholic faith.[93] Sometimes local Catholics made provocative gestures. At Snaith in the West Riding of Yorkshire in November 1678 two men (one a Catholic priest) and a woman, when visiting the local church, horrified the sexton by boasting that mass would be said there soon.[94] More generally, the revelations of the Popish Plot often served to bring a history of Protestant–Catholic antagonisms in certain communities to the fore, as they did, notably, in South Wales and the border counties of the Welsh marches.[95] There was a particularly acute sense of panic in London, which not only contained the largest concentration of Catholics in the country, but which also had been singled out by Oates as the prime target for Catholic incendiarists. In the third week of November 1678 a book-seller in St Paul's Churchyard found a letter addressed to the 'pitifull silly' Protestants of London, warning that before Christmas the Catholics would make their 'blood lye thick on the ground', and that perhaps they might have 'a hott day before Christmas in London' – one 'as hott as the third of September 1666' (the day of the Great Fire).[96] Any fire that chanced to break out in London over the next couple of years raised suspicions that the Catholics were to blame.[97] Londoners became so enraged 'against the Papists', the Puritan divine Richard Baxter recalled, that they began to keep 'private Watches in all streets . . . to save their houses from firing'.[98] Charles II tried to calm fears by issuing a series of proclamations ordering all the existing laws against Catholics to be enforced, calling for the removal of Catholics from within 10 miles of London, and requiring all recusants to be disarmed and to take out recognizances to keep the peace. Many communities across England ordered a strengthening of the night watch and began a stricter enforcement of the penal laws against the local Catholic population; conviction rates for recusancy shot up as a result, albeit temporarily. Yet, rather than calming local anxieties, such measures only added to the general sense of panic that was rapidly engulfing the nation.[99]

There was also an international threat in the present from Catholic powers, particularly France. As the London merchant William Lawrence noted in his diary in early 1679, what was feared, besides the papists, was 'the power of the French'.[100] And with good reason. To the English, Protestantism had appeared to be on the retreat throughout much of Europe in the late sixteenth and the seventeenth centuries, thanks to the successes of the Counter-Reformation powers in the wars of religion and the Thirty Years War. The last strongholds of Protestantism in north-west Europe were now the Stuart kingdoms of England and Scotland and the United Provinces, and they faced in France an aggressive neighbour with clear expansionist ambitions.[101] Not only had Charles done little to meet this threat, he actually appeared to be in league with Louis XIV. As Lawrence pointed out, 'by a great errour in our politicks' the French had been allowed 'to rival our naval Forces'. It was undeniable that the French kings had 'long gap't after the Universal Empire (at least of Europe)', and Louis XIV looked like acquiring it if England did not do something to 'retard his hasty motion'. Indeed, under the terms of the Treaty of

Nijmegen, agreed in July 1678, Louis not only had made peace with his continental European enemies but had gained considerable territories along his north-eastern frontiers, and it seemed logical to assume that England was next on his list. England therefore needed 'an early War with this mighty Monarck', Lawrence concluded, 'before he hath got more ports and encreas't his naval power', otherwise he would be able first 'to ruine the strength and Trade' of this island, then invade and subdue it.[102] Many English Protestants – especially those living near the south coast – became gripped with fear of an imminent French invasion. Sir Edward Dering, MP for Hythe (one of the Cinque Ports), recorded how in Kent 'all men' were 'affrighted' that 'a French armie would land' and cut 'their throats . . . in their beds'.[103] At the end of the first week of December a report began to circulate that 'great numbers of men' had landed in the Isle of Purbeck in Dorsetshire;[104] it proved a false alarm, but within a few days a letter had carried the news to London, affirming 'that 1000 or 1500 french were landed',[105] while those who lived in Somerset heard 'that an Army of 40,000 French' had landed at Weymouth.[106] 'Rumours and feares of a French Invasion' continued through the early months of 1679, and by the spring reports were rife that Louis XIV was assembling a huge invasion force in Brittany 'to be transported into England to assist the Catholicks'.[107] MPs likewise feared the possibility of a French invasion. Thus in the Commons on 14 April 1679 Sir William Coventry, noting that Louis XIV was not disbanding his troops, despite having recently made peace with Holland and Spain, predicted that he was intending to employ them 'upon us'.[108] English xenophobia tended not to be particularly discriminating, it should be pointed out; the public were also concerned about the French already in England, the vast majority of whom were Protestants (many having fled religious persecution), because it was feared they took jobs away from English workers. Thus in 1679 the author of *England's Alarm*, while calling for action against the French king lest he soon be crowned king in England, also urged Charles II 'to extirpate out of your Royal Territories, and this City of London, all those Amalekites that trouble Israel, (I mean the French) that devour and eat the bread out of your Subjects mouths'.[109]

Whether Charles could be trusted to pursue England's true

foreign-policy interests became a grave cause for concern. In late 1678, as inquiries into the Popish Plot got under way, the Commons learned the stunning news that the reason why Charles had been able to prorogue parliament so frequently in recent years was that he had been receiving a pension from the French king.[110] Rumours abounded that Charles was actually working in league with Louis XIV for the promotion of a shared agenda. In mid-January 1679 a paper was found in the Royal Exchange in London, purportedly written by a former Catholic who was privy to all the details of the Popish Plot, revealing that Charles had taken a £600,000 bribe from Louis XIV so that he could get rid of the Cavalier Parliament, 'and all this is to make our King absolute by bringing in Popery and arbitrary Government.'[111] In mid-November 1679 the Earl of Huntingdon wrote home from London of 'terrible newes of a league with France for five yeares, In which time', he feared, 'Wee shall see foreiners our Masters'.[112] At the end of December 1679 an anonymous letter addressed to the mayor of Bristol alleged 'that our popish And treacherous King hath sould the Kingdomes of England, Scotland, and Ireland, together with all his dominions To the King of France', and that 'we are all bought as slaves, and designed as innocent sheep for the slaughter, to be butchered and sacrificed to the fury of the papists.' (The author claimed he had learned the news whilst serving as a page in the household of the Duke of Orléans, Louis XIV's brother.)[113]

MPs and pamphleteers tended not to attack Charles directly, but rather to blame the neglect of English foreign-policy interests on the King's ministers. Parliament set about trying to remove those ministers who were believed to have given the crown bad advice, hence the parliamentary attack on Danby in the winter and spring of 1678–9 (to be discussed below). They were nevertheless deeply concerned about Charles's stance on France. As William Sacheverell put it in the Commons on 14 April 1679, it seemed 'strange' that England had for some years made it her business 'to greaten France'.[114] Even when Louis XIV began to threaten the Low Countries, Charles saw no apparent need to try to check the expansionist ambitions of the French king, despite the alarming implications for both Britain and the Protestant interest in northern Europe, as well as for the balance of power in Europe as a whole. In early 1681 Francis Smith published a copy of the Spanish ambassador's plea to Charles of the previous December to do something to 'restrain the Torrent of France' before the French overran the Low Countries. The Low Countries were 'the Master-key of the Universal Monarchy, and the first door' which Louis would 'open with it', the ambassador warned, would 'be that of England'.[115]

Whigs tended to see the cause of Exclusion and the international situation as inextricably linked. In the Commons debate on the Exclusion Bill on 11 May 1679, Hugh Boscawen warned fellow members that, if they did not seize this 'opportunity to secure the Protestant Religion', posterity would curse them in their graves: 'The whole Protestant Religion in Europe', he insisted, 'is struck at, in a Popish Succession in England. If the Protestant Religion keeps not up its head now, under a Protestant King, it must be drowned under a Popish.'[116] One Exclusionist tract, produced at the time of the elections to the Oxford Parliament, advised voters that 'Upon the Choice of this Parliament' depended 'the happiness or misery not only of his Majesties Dominions, but of the whole Protestant Religion, and of all the Reformed Churches in Christendom': a 'good Parliament' might be the means of saving Flanders, Holland, and the Holy Roman Empire 'from being reduced to the French Yoke; after which, the ruine of this Kingdom would be an unavoidable consequence'.[117] In mid-February 1681 Curtis's *True Protestant Mercury* printed letters from Holland and the distressed Protestants in Germany and France stating that they hoped Charles II would adhere to his parliament, 'for that the Protestant Interest in all Europe lies at stake, and the Welfare thereof depends upon the Conduct of Affairs in England'.[118]

The Scottish and Irish Dimensions

As these last examples make clear, people were worried not just about what the Catholic heir might do, or what Catholics at home and abroad might be up to; they were also concerned about what Charles II himself was up to. It is in this context that the multiple-kingdom dimension becomes important. We cannot understand the full intensity of people's concerns about popery and arbitrary government unless we recognize that their fears were shaped, in large part, by what had actually been going on, under the restored monarchy, in Scotland and Ireland.

When Shaftesbury warned his fellow peers in March 1679 that 'Popery and slavery' went 'hand in hand', he was thinking not in narrowly English terms but explicitly about the three Stuart kingdoms as a whole. 'In England', he said, 'popery was to have brought in slavery,' whereas 'in Scotland slavery went before, and popery was to follow.' The Scots were under 'the same prince, and the influence of the same favourites and councils', and when 'they are hardly dealt with', Shaftesbury asked, could 'we that are richer expect better usage?' Shaftesbury then attacked a number of initiatives that had happened in Scotland under Lauderdale – such as the increasing centralization of the government, the violation of basic legal rights, and the deployment of the Highland Host in the Presbyterian south-west – and alleged that 'Scotland hath outdone all the eastern and southern countries in having their lives, liberties and estates subjected to the arbitrary will and pleasure of those that govern.' 'Till the pressure be fully taken off from Scotland', he concluded, 'it is not possible . . . to believe that good is meant to us here,' especially when one considered that under the terms of the Scottish Militia Act the Scottish government had the power to raise 22,000 men 'to be ready to invade us upon all occasions'. Shaftesbury also expressed concern about the security of the Protestant establishment in Ireland, where 'the Papists [had had] their arms restored' and both the inland and coastal towns were 'full of Papists'; he predicted that the kingdom would not 'long continue in English hands, if some better care be not taken of it'.[119] Similarly, in the Commons debate on Exclusion of 26 October 1680, Sir Henry Capel (brother to the Earl of Essex, who had recently served as Lord Lieutenant in Ireland), after first rehearsing the threat of popery in England since the Restoration, went on to express his concerns about 'how things have been carried on in Scotland and Ireland'. Thus in Ireland the papists, who outnumbered the Protestants by at least five to one, 'and may probably derive from their cradle an inclination to massacre them again', were allowed to wear arms contrary to law and were living in corporations, and in Scotland the government was 'quite altered, the use of parliaments in a manner abolished', power lodged 'in a commissioner and council' and 'a standing army of 22,000 men settled' – all of which was done, Capel thought, 'to divide the Protestant Interest, and to encourage the Papists'.[120]

The English parliament could do little directly to influence policy in Scotland, since Scotland was an independent kingdom. It could, however, legitimately strike at the Duke of Lauderdale, who was also an earl in the English peerage and a member of the English privy council. On 6 May 1679 Sir Richard Graham moved that the Commons should address the King 'to remove the Duke of Lauderdale from his Presence and Councils'. Lauderdale, Graham charged, had been instrumental in breaking up the temporary alliance formed between the Protestant powers of England, Sweden and the Netherlands in 1678, and it was he who had advised issuing the Declaration of Indulgence of 1672, which gave religious freedom to Catholics, so that he could 'bring in Popery like a stream, and Tyranny like a torrent'. He had also 'brought in arbitrary Power' north of the Tweed. Colonel John Birch agreed that 'If there be any arbitrary power in the World, it is in Scotland,' adding that he feared 'this Duke may go through with it here.' Sir Francis Winnington similarly felt that 'Arbitrary power' was 'the more ready to be exercised here, for being begun in Scotland'; after all, Lauderdale had boasted that he had 'made the King absolute in Scotland'. He had brought 'his fellow-subjects into servitude and slavery', and his principles were inconsistent 'with the Protestant cause'; it was 'dangerous for him to be near the King'. Sacheverell pointed out that Lauderdale had used Scotland as a testing ground, beginning those 'arbitrary things in Scotland, which he afterwards did attempt in England', such as the Declaration of Indulgence.[121]

Although Graham's motion was carried, the dissolution at the end of the month saved Lauderdale from the English parliament. The Bothwell Bridge rebellion of May–June 1679, however, effectively spelled the end of Lauderdale's political career. In June 1679 Charles allowed a delegation of Scottish nobility, headed by Hamilton, Atholl, and Sir John Cochrane, to come to court to present a written testimony against Lauderdale. They started by castigating Lauderdale's policies towards the Presbyterians of the Scottish south-west, which had triggered the Bothwell Bridge uprising, accusing the Duke of deliberately misrepresenting this area as being in a state of rebellion so that he could raise an army against the King's peaceable subjects. This army had in turn taken free quarter in a time of peace, which was against the whole constitution; subjects had been forced to subscribe an exorbitant bond; the nobility and gentry of Ayrshire had been falsely indicted for treason; others had been declared incapable of public trust; subjects had been kept prisoner contrary to law; while the Scottish privy council had imposed unreasonable and arbitrary fines and seized gentlemen's dwellings and put garrisons in them, again contrary to law. They further alleged that Lauderdale had been engaged in a long-term 'Designe of Bringing in Popery and Arbitrary Government'. Thus in 1669, already aware that York had converted to Catholicism, Lauderdale had induced the Scottish parliament to pass an act asserting the king's supremacy in religious affairs, thus giving the king absolute power over the disposal of the external government of the Church. He had 'expressly Excepted' Catholics from the act of 1670 against withdrawers from public worship, which was aimed only at members of the reformed religion, and proceeded to give Catholics public employment in the service of the crown. He had also received a pension from the French king, kept up a correspondence with papists and Catholic priests, and done his best to suppress information reaching Scotland about the Popish Plot. Lauderdale's lust for arbitrary power, they claimed, was just as self-evident: note the legislation establishing a military force of 22,000 men that could be brought into England on any cause, and the fact that he had forced all officers of state to hold their commissions at royal pleasure. He had put members in and out of the Scottish council to suit his own designs, packed all judicatures so that 'Justice and Equity' were 'Administered according to his pleasure', and opposed the union of Scotland and England because he thought it would cost him 'that absolute Power he had in Scotland'. Such was his contempt of the House of Commons that he had been heard to say that 'if they would Address against him, he would fart against them, and . . . put a dog in his Arse and bark at them,' boasting that every time they had complained against him he had only risen higher. Magna Carta he called 'magna farta'.[122]

Charles by this time had clearly decided to let Lauderdale fall, albeit gently. His replacement, however, was hardly more comforting to the Whigs. Although in the immediate aftermath of Bothwell Bridge Monmouth, the man responsible for putting down the rebellion, emerged as the dominant voice in Scottish affairs, from the autumn of 1679 that role passed to the King's Catholic brother and heir. In March 1679 Charles had sent York into temporary exile in Brussels, to get him out of the way while the crisis over the succession unfolded in England. In October he decided to let him take up residence in Edinburgh. York went there via London, for a quick visit on the way. Essentially it was a continuation of his exile, yet during two stints in Scotland (the first from November 1679 to the end of February 1680; the second from October 1680 to March 1682) he took over the helm of government north of the border. The Duke's success in building up a loyalist interest there will be considered in Chapter 6. In England, however, York's presence at the head of the government in Scotland proved a cause of some concern. One man allegedly said in the autumn of 1680 that he thought 'it would not be long before the Duke came with an army out of Scotland to cut all the throats of the true Protestants and fire their houses and beat their children's brains out before their faces, which plot he was sure was now a-hatching in Scotland.'[123] That November Shaftesbury voiced his concern in the Lords that the Duke was now 'in Scotland raising of Forces upon the Terra firma, that can enter dry foot upon us, without hazard of Winds or Seas . . . to be ready when from hence he shall have notice'.[124] In a tract published in the spring of 1681, Jones and Sidney complained that Scotland had already been 'delivered into the hands of a Prince' who was 'the known head of the Papists in these Kingdomes, and the Occasion of all their Plots and Insolencies'.[125] York's style of government in Scotland, where he presided over an increasing clampdown on Presbyterian dissent and over legislative initiatives by the Scottish parliament in 1681 designed to enhance the authority and autonomy of the monarchy in Scotland, seemed to offer an ominous foretaste of what could be expected in England once he inherited the throne. As one manuscript satire of *c.* 1681 warned, 'In Scotland we a well-drawn Model see / Of what he proposes we [in England] once shall be.'[126]

English Protestants were also concerned about the state of affairs in Ireland. Following Shaftesbury's speech of March 1679, the Lords decided to initiate an immediate inquiry into what security measures had been taken in Ireland 'in this Time of Imminent Danger'.[127] They learned that the Lord Lieutenant, Ormonde, had ordered the arrest of the titular archbishop of Dublin, Peter Talbot, and his brother Richard, for alleged conspiracy in the Popish Plot (the former was to die in prison, the latter was allowed to go abroad for his health); had instructed the Catholic bishops and other dignitaries, together with the Jesuits and regular clergy, to leave the kingdom; and had forbidden Catholics from carrying firearms and from residing in any garrison towns – although apparently with limited success, since Ormonde was soon issuing further proclamations ordering those Catholic clergy who had not left the kingdom to be imprisoned, and castigating local magistrates for being remiss in searching for and seizing arms. The Irish privy council had rejected a proposal to remove Irish Catholics from the corporations, however, since the English needed them as 'Servants, Tenants, and Tradesmen', though Ormonde did revive the commission of array and raise the militia in all parts of the kingdom, doing what he could to supply the deficiency in arms and reinforcing the army with some 1,200 men from England.[128] Yet, despite being advised that 'all Things' in Ireland were 'in full Peace and Quietness', the Lords asked for a stricter enforcement of the laws against Catholics, and even suggested that legislation be prepared to prevent Catholics from being lawyers, clerks of the peace or undersheriffs, and from serving on juries, and requiring members of both houses of the Irish parliament and the inhabitants of all ports and forts in Ireland to take the oaths of allegiance and supremacy and any other tests designed to distinguish Protestants from papists. However, the English parliament was to be dissolved before further action on this front could be taken.[129]

Rumours about what allegedly was going on in Ireland served to heighten public anxiety in England about the threat of popery. For example, in October 1679 one London-based newsletter writer spoke of 'a Report about Towne of a discovery of a designed Massacre in Ireland' and the seizure of some '6000 Armes'.[130] Then in the spring of 1680 Shaftesbury revealed to the English privy council that he had learned that the Catholics in Ireland, with French assistance, were planning to rise in revolt and massacre Protestants.[131] There seems to have been no truth to this supposed Irish Plot – not that Shaftesbury fabricated it himself, though he showed little desire to question the credibility of the witnesses as he sought to exploit the plot for political advantage – but before it was discredited it was to claim the life of the unfortunate Oliver Plunket, titular archbishop of Armagh, executed in 1681 for alleged conspiracy with the French against the English government.[132] The Irish Plot and the Plunket affair served to highlight two deep-seated anxieties that many English people shared at this time: that Ireland might be used as a launching pad for an invasion of England by France, and that Ormonde was not doing enough to secure the Protestant interest. There had been recurrent reports in the 1660s and '70s that the Catholic powers of Europe, and especially the French, were preparing to make an attempt on Britain through the back door of Ireland,[133] and fears of a foreign Catholic invasion of Ireland persisted throughout the Exclusion Crisis.[134] Ormonde, who came from a Catholic family, was accused of shielding Catholics from the rigours of the penal laws, even allowing them to hold office under the crown, despite the anti-Catholic initiatives of the winter and spring of 1678–9.[135] He came under attack in the Commons debate on Exclusion on 26 October 1680, notably from Sir Henry Capel (whose remarks have been noted above).[136] In early January 1681 the Lords declared that they were 'fully satisfied' that 'for divers Years . . . there hath been a horrid and treasonable Plot and Conspiracy, contrived and carried on by those of the Popish Religion in Ireland, for massacring the English, and subverting the Protestant Religion, and the ancient established Government of that Kingdom.' In the Commons, Capel concurred, saying that, although some people 'smiled at' the Popish Plot in England, 'it is plain there was a Plot in Ireland', and 'the hopes of a Popish Successor' were 'the Grounds of all this'.[137]

Although the attack on Ormonde was to fail, the Whig media continued to fuel fears about the Irish situation. In early 1681 Curtis's *True Protestant Mercury* carried a number of reports of how the Protestants in Ireland lived in daily fear of an imminent French invasion.[138] When the second Exclusion Parliament was prorogued in January 1681, Curtis reported how the Papists in Dublin were so 'elevated at the News . . . that they Hector about the streets with

Swords and other Arms', leading the Protestants to fear 'they will execute some desperate Design upon them.'[139] An electioneering pamphlet for the Oxford Parliament predicted that 'A good Parliament' might 'retrieve the distressed Protestants in Ireland, from that second Popish Massacre which so daily threatens them'.[140] Likewise in 1681 a tract by Sir William Petty (though published anonymously) rehearsed the likelihood that the French might try to invade Ireland as a way of striking at England and, recalling that the Catholics in Ireland greatly outnumbered the Protestants, asked whether it was likely that the Irish would 'sooner joyn with the English, against whom they have a blind Antipathy . . . than with the French Romanists, whom they would welcome as Saviours and Restorers of their All'? Candidly reminding his readers that the Catholics of Ireland 'think they lost all by the English', he predicted that 'they'd venture all they have, viz. their Lives, for the French or other Foreigner.'[141]

Charles II's Style of Government in England

Public anxiety about the threat of popery and arbitrary government, then, was structured in significant ways by what was represented as the reality of the situation in Ireland and Scotland. The threat was already a real one, in the present, and could be seen in the two other kingdoms over which Charles II ruled. Swift action would need to be taken if England were to avoid falling victim. The problem was, however, that for many England already seemed to have become a victim. As we saw in Chapter 1, concerns about popery and arbitrary government in England had begun to be raised during the mid-1670s, during the time of Danby's ascendancy. They were to come to a head in the aftermath of the Popish Plot.

One cause for alarm was the army that Charles had begun to build up in the winter of 1677–8, supposedly for war with France. Once it became apparent that Charles was not going to go to war, the continuance of these forces seemed both unnecessary and potentially dangerous. Parliament had already voted money for the disbanding of the troops in June 1678, yet by the autumn some 25,000 troops were still in arms, and some members came to fear that Charles would use the excuse of the Popish Plot to keep the army in being. Parliament pushed ahead with a Militia Bill in an attempt to secure the disbanding of the troops, but Charles rejected this in November, on the grounds that it encroached upon his prerogative by temporarily removing the militia from his control.[142] In addition to the question of why the army was still in being, there were also concerns about the burdens being borne by those communities where the troops were stationed. The Petition of Right of 1628 had declared that it was illegal to compel inhabitants to receive soldiers and mariners into their houses against their will. This meant that troops could be billeted only in public houses, and had to pay for their board and lodging. Yet Charles II's army did not always pay its way; in March 1679, for instance, the Reading victuallers complained that if they were not reimbursed soon they would be unable to 'subsist any longer'.[143]

The campaign against the army was resumed in the first Exclusion Parliament. In a Commons debate on 29 March 1679, Sir Nicholas Carew demanded to know 'whether the Army has been upon free quarter, against the Petition of Right'. James Vernon (the Duke of Monmouth's secretary) insisted that it had not, but suggested that people had sometimes relieved soldiers out of compassion when they saw they had nothing to live on. As far as Sir Henry Capel was concerned, however, 'By the Petition of Right, they ought to be quartered in no man's house.'[144] When the debate resumed on 1 April, William Garraway declared 'that this Army' was 'kept up to the oppression of the people' and 'contrary to the Laws of the Nation'; Colonel Birch insisted that 'this Army was disbanded by Act' and should not be kept up; Sir Thomas Lee claimed that 'the Petition of Right [was] invaded'; while Sir William Coventry thought there was no doubt that 'the Law has been broken by keeping them up.' The Commons concluded by passing a resolution 'That the continuing of any standing Forces in this Nation, other than the Militia, is illegal, and a great grievance and vexation to the people.'[145] In May parliament passed another Disbanding Act, calling for the disbanding of the troops still in existence and confirming that it was illegal to force private householders to receive soldiers into their homes without their consent.[146]

The standing army was a factor in the fall of Danby. In December 1678 the Commons had tried to impeach Danby for high treasons, crimes and misdemeanours, charging him (among other things) with having attempted to subvert the ancient form of government by introducing an arbitrary and tyrannical form of government; raising a standing army and continuing it in being contrary to the statute disbanding it; encroaching upon the royal power by treating of war and peace with foreign princes without informing the Secretaries of State; negotiating a peace with France contrary to the King's interests; trying to hinder the meeting of parliament, taking a bribe from the French king, and paying unnecessary pensions; and being popishly affected and having endeavoured to suppress evidence relating to the Popish Plot.[147] The Lords refused to commit Danby, and Charles, to forestall the inevitable conflict between the two houses, decided first to prorogue and then to dissolve parliament. However, when a new parliament convened in March, the Commons immediately resumed the case against Danby. With a trial seeming inevitable, Charles dramatically announced on 22 March that he had granted the Earl a pardon under the Great Seal.[148] The Commons therefore decided to proceed against Danby by bill of attainder; the Lords tried to turn the bill into one for banishment; and Danby himself finally resolved the matter by surrendering to the Usher of the Black Rod on 15 April, whereupon he was committed to the Tower. When he stood before the bar of the Lords on 25 April to enter his plea against the articles of impeachment, he denied all charges and invoked his royal pardon. The Commons, however, insisted that the pardon was null and void and that the Lords should proceed to judgement, since invoking a pardon was tantamount to admitting guilt.[149]

The dispute over the validity of Danby's pardon is worth examining in detail, since it raised fundamental questions over the extent to which the king could shield individuals from prosecution under the law. Most accepted that the power to pardon was 'an essential prerogative' belonging to the king, 'Connate with his Kingshipp', the logic being that the prosecution of all crimes was in the king's name and therefore releasable by the warrant of his attorney-general. The chief limitation was that the king could not free a convicted individual from any claims that an injured third party might have on his estate; a royal pardon could not interfere with someone else's property rights. Yet medieval precedent (notably the cases of William Lord

Latimer and Richard Lyons in 1376) seemed to confirm that the king did have the power to pardon parliamentary impeachments.[150]

The Commons, however, challenged the legality of Danby's pardon. If nothing else, procedural irregularities (the pardon had not gone through all the appropriate offices) were enough to make it void.[151] Yet, more fundamentally, there was the issue of whether 'this Pardon can be just', as Edward Vaughan, MP for Cardiganshire, asked.[152] Serjeant Sir William Ellis argued in the Commons on 24 March that, although the king, as 'the fountain of Justice and Mercy', was allowed to 'pardon offenders', there were some things he could not pardon, even when the indictment was in the king's name, such as offences against the public good. This impeachment was 'at the suit of all the Commons of England', he continued, and neither the King nor the attorney-general was a party to it; it was 'in the nature of an Appeal of Rape, which the king cannot pardon'.[153] It was true that the crown had pardoned impeachments in the past, but never before judgement had been given in parliament. Besides, in the cases of Latimer and Lyons Richard II had pardoned only what belonged to him. Latimer, for instance, had confessed to having collected impositions in Brittany without telling the King, delivering up the fort of St Saviour, and releasing prisoners without the King's order; if the King decided to forgive Latimer the money that he was owed, that was up to him.[154] However, as the veteran lawyer Sir Harbottle Grimston pointed out, the charge against Danby was 'an universal Grievance', which it was not in the king's power to pardon.[155] Charles I had himself acknowledged, in his *Answer to the Nineteen Propositions* of 1642, Richard Hampden recalled, that a prince might not use his power of pardoning 'to the hurt of those for whose good he hath it', or 'make use of the name of public necessity, for the gain of his private favourites and followers, to the detriment of the people'.[156] Sir Francis Winnington, who had already questioned the legality of the pardon during the debate on 22 March, spelled out his argument more fully in a speech delivered on 5 May. 'In Appeals, etc. where the King has an interest and share in the Suit, there the King may bar an Indictment', or pardon his share of the forfeiture. Yet it was very different 'where the King has no share' and the prosecution is brought 'only by the Commons of England'. In such cases 'it is you that have the interest in the Suit, and all the Commons of England,' and 'if what is grievous to the people be pardoned, it is to no end that the Parliament should meet,' other 'than to give Money when it is asked'. In a dramatic climax, Winnington went on to suggest that 'if such a Pardon be allowed, the Government of England will be destroyed, and the Commons of England cannot be relieved from the exorbitances of great men.'[157] A Commons committee, set up to investigate the whole affair, concluded on 26 May that 'the setting up a Pardon to be a Bar of an Impeachment' defeated 'the whole Use and Effect of Impeachments', and if admitted would destroy 'the chief Institution for the Preservation of the Government', and 'consequently the Government itself'.[158]

The case against Danby was also carried out-of-doors. An account claiming to be a copy of Winnington's speech of 22 March, but which differs significantly from that transcribed by the parliamentary diarist, circulated in manuscript. In it, Winnington insists that the king cannot 'pardon treason against the government', otherwise the government will not 'be safe against evil ministers'. The prerogative is supposed to be used 'to abate rigorous Justice, not to destroy it'; if ministers can 'be pardoned at the prince's pleasure for all the wrongs they do the people', Winnington concludes, 'there is no security, and our pretended free and legall government is a meer cheat, and we arrant slaves.'[159] One pamphleteer, after an unconvincing attempt to exonerate the King from blame on the grounds that he could not have been properly acquainted with the true nature of Danby's crimes, stated that he was certain that the consequences of the pardon were 'evil, since if a Pardon stands good against such an Impeachment in parliament', a subject (notwithstanding Magna Carta) would have no redress 'against any Courtier, who when he hath ravish'd his Wife or murdered his Children, produces such a Pardon from his Master'. The argument was a *reductio ad absurdum*, but the point was clear enough: 'Is not the King in this case as absolute as the great Turk?'[160]

The Commons did not win their point of principle. Opinion in the Lords was divided over Danby, but he had a strong following in the upper house, not least among the bishops, whose votes seemed likely to tip the balance in his favour. Shaftesbury and other opposition peers, fearing defeat, tried to argue that bishops should not be allowed to exercise a judicial function in the Lords in capital cases, since under canon law they were prohibited from shedding blood and it was inevitable they would not convict – a position which came to be endorsed by the Commons. With the dispute still unresolved, Charles decided at the end of May to prorogue parliament; in July, he changed the prorogation into a dissolution. Nevertheless, Danby was left to stew in the Tower for another five years. He was eventually bailed in February 1684, on a personal recognizance of £10,000 and a further four sureties of £5,000 – a staggering £30,000 in total.[161]

The conflict over the impeachment of Danby, coming as it did early in the Exclusion Crisis, did not break down along Whig/Tory lines. Rather, it was driven by faction: the Earl had made many enemies both at court and in parliament, and there were many who were keen to see him fall who would later side with the Tories over the issue of the succession.[162] Yet Danby's policy towards the Church, and the particular brand of intolerant high Anglicanism he chose to promote, had also aroused the opposition of Shaftesbury and many country MPs who were later to become Whigs. Indeed, the Whigs were concerned not just about developments in the state under Charles II; they were also concerned about developments in the Church. Most Whigs sympathized with the plight of the Protestant nonconformists: many came from a Puritan or low-church background (as did Shaftesbury himself, who during the Restoration had emerged as a bitter critic of the pretensions of the high-church bishops), while not a few were only occasional conformists or even dissenters themselves. They were deeply alarmed that Protestants could still be persecuted for their religious beliefs when the very security of Protestantism in England seemed in danger. Unity in the face of the Catholic threat, and hence some form of religious toleration for Protestant nonconformists, therefore became a central plank of the Whig platform. One pamphleteer claimed that 'woful Experience' had shown the laws against Protestant dissenters to be 'not only useless, but inconvenient, both to the Protestant Religion, and the Safety of the Kingdom'.[163] Whigs thus supported measures for comprehension and toleration, and also sought the repeal of the act of 1593 against seditious sectaries (the infamous 35 Elizabeth), which allowed Protestants who did not come to church to be prosecuted as recusants and which carried with it the punishments of exile, forfeiture of goods, and potentially even death if those convicted refused to conform.[164]

Pleas for unity could not conceal that Whig grievances with the existing establishment in the Church ran deep. The Whigs were fiercely critical of the high-church clergy, and especially the bishops, whom they saw as champions of divine right, absolute monarchy and the indefeasibility of the hereditary succession. They thus condemned the Tory clergy (or Tantivees, as the Whigs called them) as church-papists, because they opposed Exclusion and the rights of parliament and backed the persecution of Protestant dissenters. The London merchant William Lawrence confided to his diary in the spring of 1679 that the clergy had already begun 'to adore the rising Sun, and to entertain very kind thoughts of a popish Successor', adding that he thought that, 'if the Church of England' should be 'so blind and mad as to oppose' Exclusion, she deserved 'to forfeit all her Goods as a Felo de se and as guilty of her owne Murder'.[165] One print from 1680 shows the pope holding out a cardinal's hat to a group of Anglican clerics, while an engraving from 1681 shows a Tory and a Tantivee galloping off towards the pope, who offers them protection.[166] The bishops were in truth 'Protestants in Masquerade', Whig polemicists claimed, and the clergy were debauched 'knaves' whose doctrines threatened to make us 'slaves'.[167] Benjamin Harris pondered whether the maxim 'No Bishop, No Pope; no Prelacy, no Popery, Be not more Infallible than that, no Bishop no King'.[168] A tract that circulated in 1679 (though which was a reprint of a 1667 work) blamed a whole series of civil grievances on the ecclesiastical hierarchy in England, including 'Impoverishing the Nation' and the 'Ruin of Trade' (which the author attributed to 'the Pomp, Pride, Luxury, Exaction and Oppressions of the Prelates'); it then asked why, when other reformed Churches had abolished the office of bishop as popish, England had kept it, pointing out that other reformed countries took the lordly revenues from the prelates and reserved them 'for publick use'.[169] Following the defeat of the second Exclusion Bill in the Lords in mid-November 1680, a ballad called 'The Magpye, Or the Song against the Bishops' appeared, accusing 'our Prelatick Pies' of preying 'on church and state . . . In the open face of day'. 'They say Protestants they are,' it ran, 'Yet they wish a

Popish Heire / And 'tis plaine they lye at lurch / To give up State and church.' Complaining how the bishops, 'without knowledge in our laws', taught 'obedience implicit' to the king, and used scripture ''Gainst Magna Carta', the rhymester concluded that for 'Jus divinum . . . wee care not a turd' and emplored:

> Send the magpies then to Rome
> From where they all did come
> There they do the Popes work
> And like Romens crye Yorke, Yorke.[170]

Because the bishops were associated with a championship of the crown, and vice versa, occasionally the condemnation of the former was linked with criticism of the latter. Thus one mock litany of 1681 prayed for deliverance 'From the Lawless Dominion of the Miter and Crowne / Whose Tyranny is so absolute growne'.[171]

Nor was this just propaganda; there is plenty of evidence of anti-episcopalian or anti-clerical sentiment among supporters of the Whigs at the grass-roots level. At the Exeter election of March 1679 the 'loyal party', spearheaded by the staunch churchman Sir Thomas Carew, was opposed by William Glyde, the former nonconformist mayor, and by the dissenting interest, whose supporters allegedly ran up and down the streets threatening their opponents and chanting 'Down with the Church.'[172] At Essex in August 1679 those who supported the Whig candidates came to the polls crying 'No popish Clergy' and 'No bishops,' in addition to 'No Courtier, no Pensioner.' Cries of 'No clergy, no bishops' greeted the return of the Whig candidates at the Oxford election of 1681.[173] In September 1680, when he was entertained at Oxford by Robert Pauling, Oxford's Presbyterian mayor, and several aldermen, Monmouth was welcomed with cries of 'God bless the Protestant Duke' and 'No York, no bishops, no university.'[174] At about Christmas that year one Francis Cary, a gentleman from Ilminster, Somerset, when out drinking with a group of friends, was overheard giving a toast 'to the Confusion of all the Clergy of England', whom he thought were 'Rogues', and especially his local Bishop of Bath and Wells and his adherents.[175] Edward Dering, son of Sir Edward and Whig MP for Kent during the Exclusion Crisis, was accused by his enemies of having drunk 'a healthe to the confusion of lawn sleeves' when campaigning at the polls – a charge which he later denied as he sought to reingratiate himself with the crown following the defeat of the parliamentary Exclusion movement, though he did admit that 'all the fanaticks' of the county backed him and that he thought there was 'more present danger to church and state from the papists then from dissenting protestants'.[176]

The way Charles chose to frustrate the Whigs' demands – through recourse to his prerogative power to prorogue and dissolve parliament – raised concerns about the security of parliamentary government in England. On 17 December 1680 the Commons resolved that a bill should be brought in to secure the meeting and sitting of frequent parliaments.[177] Ironically, it was an initiative that was lost because of the prorogation and subsequent dissolution of this parliament. When Charles announced the dissolution of the second Exclusion Parliament, in January 1681, the Commons responded with a resolution that whoever had advised the King to do this was a 'Betrayer of the king, the Protestant Religion, and the kingdom of England; a Promoter of the French Interest, and a Pensioner to France' – unless his motive had been to secure the meeting of another parliament which could then pass an act excluding the Duke of York.[178] The dissolution also saw the demise of a bill for repealing the Act of 35 Elizabeth; the bill had passed the two houses, but the clerk of the Lords failed to tender it to the King for the royal assent.[179]

Whigs responded to what they saw as a threat to parliamentary government by repeating claims first made by the country opposition in the mid-1670s: that legislation dating back to Edward III's reign required that there be annual sessions of parliament. This did not help, of course, if there were regular meetings of parliament but the King kept proroguing or dissolving them to frustrate their initiatives, and so the Whigs now began to insist that parliaments should be allowed to continue to sit until they had completed their business. In November 1680, during the long prorogation of the second Exclusion Parliament, the common council of London petitioned the King asking not only that he allow the parliament to sit but also that he continue its sitting until it had finished the matters before it. Charles's response was to tell the common council not to meddle with things that did not appertain to it.[180] Writing shortly after the dissolution of the Oxford Parliament, Jones and Sidney, while accepting that English kings had generally 'been Intrusted with the Power of calling and declaring the Dissolutions of Parliaments', nevertheless insisted that 'our Ancestors [had] provided, by divers Statutes, both for the holding Parliaments Annually, and that they should not be Prorogued or Dissolved till all Petitions and Bills before them were answered and Redressed.'[181] Similarly, the author of *Vox Populi; Or, the People's Claim* of 1681, after reviewing the relevant medieval legislation, concluded 'that Parliaments ought Annually to meet, to support the Government, and to redress the Grievances which may happen in the interval of Parliaments', so that 'For Parliaments to meet Annually, and not suffered to sit to Answer the Ends' for which they had been called, 'but to be Prorogued or Dissolved before they have finished their Work, would be nothing but a deluding the Law, and a striking at the foundations of the Government it self, and rend'ring Parliaments altogether Useless'.[182] Out-of-doors it was coming to be believed that Charles himself was the man who had betrayed the kingdom. For instance, in early February 1682 the mayor of Bristol received an anonymous letter from an unknown hand with instructions to 'send the enclosed to his Majesty'; inside were the words 'We, the people of England, finding our parliaments dissolved, demand of thee, Charles Stewart, *Quo Warranto* are thou King of England?'[183]

CRISIS? WHAT CRISIS?

The Whigs had extensive support for their position among the nation at large. Anti-court or pro-Exclusionist interests were dominant in the Commons in all three parliaments that sat between 1679 and 1681, by roughly a proportion of three to two. Dominance in the Commons meant superiority at the polls. In the three general elections between 1679 and 1681, the Whigs tended to do better in the more open constituencies with larger electorates, while Tory electoral success was as great as it was only because the government or government supporters were able to control a significant number of smaller borough constituencies. Although there were some exceptions to this pattern and the Tories did achieve success in a few open constituencies, the majority of the enfranchised classes were clearly behind the Whigs at this time. Indeed, the number of contested elections dropped steadily as the Exclusion Crisis progressed (there were 101 contests in the first general election of 1679, 77 in the second, and only 54 in that of 1681), as court supporters in several constituencies came to recognize they had no realistic chance of ousting the incumbent Whig members.[184]

Other evidence points to the strength of support for the Whigs out-of-doors. During the long intermission between the calling and the eventual meeting of the second Exclusion Parliament (it was supposed to meet on 17 October 1679, but did not actually do so until 21 October 1680), the Whigs launched a petitioning campaign calling upon the King to let parliament sit.[185] The way was led by sixteen Whig peers, who delivered a petition to Charles to this effect on 7 December 1679, although this soon met with a metropolitan and provincial response. There was certainly orchestration from the centre. Printed sheets containing an agreed wording were sent down from London to the provinces, where local agents would then busy themselves collecting signatories – although some areas seem to have modified the wording or adopted their own in order to reflect local concerns. The Green Ribbon Club may well have served as the organizational nerve-cell; Somerset certainly received the copy of its petition from club member Hugh Speke. The petitioning movement achieved greatest success in London; in January 1680 the City presented a monster petition signed by well over 16,000 people.[186] It is true that the provincial response was less encouraging than the Whigs might have hoped – the fact that on 12 December 1679 Charles issued a proclamation condemning the petitions undoubtedly served as a deterrent[187] – and in the end only five counties and one city presented petitions (Berkshire, Essex, Hertfordshire Somerset, Wiltshire and York).[188] In many areas there was also a certain amount of opposition to the Whig agenda, and some local grand juries drew up abhorrences of the petitions (discussed in Chapter 5). Nevertheless, the petitioning campaign seemed to point to the ability of the Whig central leadership to mobilize the masses, and the numbers of signatories that some of the Whig petitions could boast were alarming: 10,000 in Hertfordshire, 30,000 in Wiltshire, and allegedly over 40,000 in

Essex.[189] The circumstances surrounding the collection of signatures were also a source of concern. For telling signatories that they had 'but two ways of redress, by petition or rebellion', the Taunton assizes slapped a £500 fine on the man who promoted the Somerset petition, a Taunton goldsmith named Thomas Dare, bound him over for good behaviour for three years, and sent him to prison until the fine was paid. (Dare protested that he was advocating petitioning and had explicitly denounced rebellion, but was tricked into confessing by the presiding judge, Sir Thomas Jones, on the promise of lenient treatment.)[190]

Further petitions calling for parliament to sit came in the summer – with London once more leading the way – and again following the prorogation and then dissolution of the second Exclusion Parliament in January 1681. Within less than twelve hours of the announcement of the dissolution on 18 January, for example, 6,000 people had allegedly put their names to a petition circulating in Warwickshire calling for the sitting of a new parliament.[191] Several counties and towns throughout England sent addresses to their representatives, 'returning them their hearty thanks for their unwearied endeavours in preserving the king's person and the protestant religion'.[192] London's thanked the city's four Whig MPs for their efforts in searching into the Popish Plot, working towards the exclusion of all popish successors (and particularly James, Duke of York), repealing the Act of 35 Elizabeth, and trying to promote the unity of Protestants; it promised to stand by them in their future endeavours to secure the realm from popery and arbitrary government, and suggested that no taxes should be voted until that end had been achieved.[193] During the general election of February and March, several provincial constituencies built on London's example and drew up instructions to their newly elected members informing them how they expected them to behave in the forthcoming parliament. The freeholders of Yorkshire thanked their two MPs for their services in the previous two parliaments, in which they had endeavoured 'To preserve the Protestant religion, his Majestys person and the Kingdomes of England and Ireland from the many dangers which threaten'd them', 'Exclude a Popish Successor' and 'Unite all his Majestys Protestant Subjects', and urged them to pursue the same agenda in the upcoming parliament in order 'to secure us for the future against popery and arbitrary power'.[194] The

Northamptonshire addressers told their newly elected MPs that they wanted to 'be secured against a Popish successor' and a means to be 'found of uniting his Majesty's subjects against the common enemy'. By the latter, the addressers clearly had in mind some form of toleration for Protestant dissenters, although one paranoid commentator observed that by 'common enemy' could 'be intended the King and the Church', adding that, since the means were not specified, the MPs might seek to do this by a rebellion – 'seizing the militia, usurping the King's prerogative, entering into a conspiracy, [and] levying men, money and arms' as parliament had done back in 1642.[195]

Then we have the evidence of the huge crowds that attended Whig rallies or demonstrations. The famous London pope-burning processions of 17 November attracted thousands of spectators: one estimate put the number as high as 200,000 in 1679.[196] There were provincial counterparts. On 5 November 1679 Lewes in East Sussex was the site of an elaborate pope-burning procession in which 'several pictures' depicting members of the Catholic clergy 'were carried upon long poles' and 'an effigy of the Pope . . . [was] paraded around the town before being burnt at a bonfire'. At Abergavenny in Monmouthshire, that same day, the 'Ancient Gallant Brittains' held a similar display, in which individuals dressed as Catholic clerics processed through the town with banners bearing the words 'Gunpowder Treason', 'Murder of Sir Edmundberry Godfrey', 'Cruelty', 'Assassination', 'Burning of London', 'Rebellion', 'Superstition' and 'Idolatry'; behind them came an effigy of the pope, seated on his chair of state, which was made to bow its head at the house of every local Catholic, much to the amusement of the numerous onlookers. Eventually the effigy was brought 'to the fatal place of Execution' and mounted on top of a huge pile of faggots provided by the local bakers to meet its fiery end.[197] At Salisbury on 5 November 1681 an effigy of the pope, 'in his Chair of State, with a Triple Crown on his Head, a Cross in one hand, and a Scepter in the other', was carried through the streets 'with Thousands of People following it', before eventually being burned at nightfall at 'a great Bonfire' in the market place. The list could be extended. Many provincial towns commemorated Gunpowder Treason Day with similar displays – not just notoriously Whig locales such as Taunton, in Somerset, but even (in 1681) places such as Chatham, the home of the royal ship-yard (where the yard's carpenters prepared several carved images of the pope), and Oxford, Charles's preferred site for the meeting of parliament earlier that year because it was regarded as being one of his most loyal towns at the time.[198]

There were copy-cat rituals north of the border. Towards the end of 1680 a group of scholars at Edinburgh University happened to be at a tavern 'where there was hanging a Copper Plate, representing the Manner of burning the Pope at London'; this gave them the idea of staging a similar event in the Scottish capital. They fixed on Christmas Day for their pope-burning, since this was when the pope excommunicated Protestants, and entered into a combination to pursue their design, hiring a carver to construct a wooden effigy 'with Cloathes, Tripple Crown, Keys, and other necessary habilments'. The Scottish council got wind of the plan on Christmas Eve, and ordered the regents of the university to put a stop to it; the students protested that they could not understand why they could not 'do it here as well as it was done in London'. Although the authorities arrested several of the ringleaders in advance and stationed soldiers on guard the next day, the scholars went ahead with their procession, being joined by large numbers of apprentices and tradesmen, many of them wearing blue ribbons in their hats with the words 'No Pope', 'No Priest' and even 'No Bishop' and 'No Atheist' embroidered upon them. Giving the troops the slip by pronouncing that they were heading for the Grassmarket, the place where criminals were executed, they managed to proceed up the High Street before the soldiers eventually stopped their progress, whereupon the youths decided to blow up their effigy on the spot, with the help of some gunpowder, to the cries of 'Noe Pope, Noe Pope in Scotland, and noe Papist.' There were scuffles with troops, and several arrests were made. The authorities perhaps overreacted, though they were worried that the design was intended as a deliberate affront to the Duke of York, who was then present in the Scottish capital. They also suspected that English agitators had put the students up to it; indeed, two Englishmen were among those arrested as ringleaders. The fallout occurred on 11 January, when the official residence of the town provost was torched – the government thought in retaliation for his role in suppressing the demonstration,

RESTORATION

though the students were quick to deny any responsibility. The council responded by ordering the college temporarily to be shut and banishing the scholars 15 miles from the town, until their parents could find bonds for their good behaviour. If the original intention had been to nip things in the bud before they got out of hand, it had hardly worked. Indeed, according to the Whig press in London, the students of every other university in Scotland soon mimicked those of Edinburgh in carrying out their own mock execution of the pope. And all this from a students' night out drinking in a local pub.[199]

There were also a number of demonstrations in support of Monmouth. His return from exile in Holland towards the end of November 1679 prompted widespread bonfire celebrations through-out London, as hordes of well-wishers gathered to drink the Duke's health, and there was similar rejoicing in 'several county towns' throughout England.[200] In February 1680 he made a brief progress to Chichester, where the local gentry, civic authorities and townsfolk afforded him a warm reception.[201] At the end of June, when he went to dine with some sixty-five Whig nobles and gentry at the Sun Tavern behind the Exchange in London, 'a vast multitude of common people' showed up to wish the Duke and the Earl of Shaftesbury well.[202] Similarly, 'hundreds of Spectators crowded to see his Grace take Coach and loud acclamations sounded his welcome' when he went to dine with a number of Whig peers and MPs at the Crown Tavern in Fleet Street in January 1681.[203] Towards the end of July 1680 Monmouth set off on a tour of the West Country, which became a quasi-royal progress; wherever he went, the local gentry came out to greet him on horseback and accompany him to his host's residence, while a number of urban centres commemorated his visit with the inevitable bells, bonfires and toasts. At Crewkerne, in Somerset, Monmouth even touched for the King's Evil, thus making a powerful public statement about his belief in his own legitimacy. When he visited Oxford on his return to London in September 1680 crowds were out in force shouting, 'A Monmouth, no York, no Bishop, no Clergy, no University.'[204] In February 1681 Monmouth made another trip to Chichester, where he was greeted by over 400 gentry and the city's two MPs, and treated to dinner by the Whig peer Lord Grey of Warke, who lived near by; the local inhabitants celebrated with the inevitable bonfires.[205] When he returned to London on Saturday 26 February he was greeted by 'a great number of Gentlemen and Citizens', and when he went to church at St Martin-in-the-Fields the next day, we are told, 'the people expressed their joy to see him' by 'Crying out, God Bless the Protestant Duke'.[206]

At the same time, crowds were quick to show their resentment of the Whigs' enemies. Lord Chief Justice Scroggs, who had achieved notoriety in July 1679 for questioning the evidence of Oates in the trial of Sir George Wakeman (the Queen's physician accused of poisoning the King) and thereby helping induce the jury to return a verdict of not guilty, met with 'severall affronts' when he went on his assize-court circuit the following month, with crowds chanting 'A Wakeman, a Wakeman.' In one place 'they threw a dog half hanged into his coach.'[207] Not even York himself was immune. When, in January 1679, he tried to help extinguish a fire that had broken out at the Temple, he was jeered by crowds calling him a 'popish dog', while he had a similar experience the following October when he attended the Artillery Company's feast.[208]

Nevertheless, it has been suggested that the situation never really became critical for the royal government, since ultimately the crown held all the trump cards.[209] Charles repeatedly said that he was willing to agree to any measures that would guarantee the security of the Protestant religion under a popish successor, but that he would not agree to an Exclusion Bill. And, since the King alone determined when parliament could sit, he could always prorogue or dissolve parliament if it proved hostile (as he did to frustrate the efforts of the Exclusionists in all three parliaments between 1679 and 1681) or simply refuse to call it at all (as he did after 1681). Charles II was not in the same position as his father on the eve of the Civil War, when the King had become trapped by an act of 1641 prohibiting the dissolution of the Long Parliament without its own consent. Moreover, there was never any realistic chance of Exclusion passing the Lords, where the court interest enjoyed a clear majority; thus, when the second Exclusion Bill was brought before the Lords on 15 November 1680 it was defeated by a vote of 70 to 30.[210] The only way the Whigs could affect policy would be if they could win over the King; they appear to have hoped that in the face of concerted and demonstrable hostility to a popish successor in the nation at large Charles would back down and give them what they wanted. It was not an unreasonable belief, since Charles had been known to bow in the face of public pressure before, but on this occasion he chose to dig in his heels. Once this became apparent, people had the choice either to buckle under or to rebel, and very few had the stomach for another rebellion. Besides, the Whig crowds of the Exclusion Crisis on the surface appear to have been much less threatening than those on the eve of the Civil War. Thus, according to one modern scholar, the Whig demonstrations 'smacked more of theatre than riot', and, after they were over, the 'participants and spectators reeled tipsily and innocuously off to bed.'[211]

Despite a seeming logic to this argument, it is ultimately unconvincing. We have to ask whether Charles, York or many of the leading royal advisers would have seen things this way. The answer is surely 'no'. The crown was in deep trouble by 1679–80, and knew it only too well. The King might be able to frustrate the agenda of the Commons, but he could not pursue his own agenda. He found it difficult to establish an effective ministry. Following the revelations of the Popish Plot and the attack on Danby, Charles made a bold attempt to rebuild consensus by bringing key opposition spokesmen back within his administration. When Danby resigned his treasuryship on 26 March 1679, Charles put the treasury into commission, and made Essex its head. The following month he remodelled his privy council, reducing its size from 46 to 30 members and bringing in a number of critics of the court – including Shaftesbury, whom he appointed Lord President.[212] The tactic failed; the council came to be hopelessly racked by internal division, and the experiment was quickly abandoned. Without control over the Commons, Charles could not raise the revenue necessary to pursue an effective foreign policy; indeed, Whig MPs were adamant that no supply should be granted until the King had redressed their grievances.[213] Moreover, the French king, who had been providing subsidies to the crown on an intermittent basis in the 1670s, temporarily decided to withdraw his financial support and instead offer subsidies to the political opposition in England, believing that by keeping Charles embroiled in domestic intrigue at home he would be effectively neutralized on the international front. On the domestic front, the crown became so preoccupied with trying to deflect the attacks of the political opposition that it found itself unable to pursue any policy initiatives of its own.

Moreover, Charles was not particularly successful in protecting his political supporters. He pardoned Danby, but could not save him from the Tower. Likewise, he frustrated Exclusion, but had to send his brother into exile (first to the Low Countries, and later to Scotland). Those who were too vigorous in the pursuit of the crown's interests found themselves in a vulnerable situation – as did those who took a stance against the Whig petitioning campaign, for example. On 27 October 1680 the Commons resolved that it was 'the undoubted Right of the Subjects of England, to petition the King for the calling and sitting of Parliaments, and redressing of Grievances', and that to represent such petitioning 'as tumultuous and seditious' was 'to betray the Liberty of the Subject'.[214] They went on to demand the removal from office of Sir George Jeffreys, for 'maliciously' declaring petitioning to be 'tumultuous, seditious and illegal'; to impeach North, for his role in issuing the royal proclamation of December 1679 against petitions; and to launch an inquiry into the abhorrers, expelling Sir Francis Withens from the House for promoting an abhorrence from the Westminster grand jury, and sending another abhorrer, Sir Robert Cann of Bristol, to the Tower for having said back in his constituency on the eve of the sitting of parliament that he thought 'there was no Popish Plot, but a Presbyterian Plot.'[215] The Commons also set up a committee to investigate the Westminster judges, and voted to impeach Scroggs, Sir Thomas Jones and Richard Weston for various illegal acts committed in office, including discharging the Middlesex grand jury before the end of the term (in order to frustrate the attempt to indict York for recusancy); issuing an order prohibiting the future publication of Care's *Weekly Pacquet* (thereby usurping a legislative power); issuing illegal warrants against the authors, printers and publishers of seditious books, libels and pamphlets and for the seizure of such literature (illegal because the warrants did not name those who were to be arrested or the works that were to be seized); refusing bail to those whose offences were bailable (that is, to certain Whig printers and booksellers charged with publishing seditious libels); and imposing arbitrary and exorbitant fines (such as the £500 fines imposed on

Benjamin Harris, for publishing his *Appeal from the Country to the City*, and on the Somerset petitioner Thomas Dare).[216] The Whigs pointed to the abuse of power by the judges as a further argument for why limitations on a popish successor could not work. As Capel put it in the Commons on 11 November 1680, 'If Judges may do these things, neither the Laws we make, nor can make, will protect us.'[217] To ensure that judges would not be able to abuse their power in the future, the Commons resolved to introduce legislation to change the terms of judges' commissions from 'at royal pleasure' to 'at good behaviour' and also to prevent the imposition of excessive fines.[218] In addition, the Commons impeached Edward Seymour, York's most outspoken champion in the lower house, for misappropriating funds as treasurer of the navy, and addressed the King for the removal from the privy council of the Earl of Halifax, the man who had led the opposition to Exclusion in the Lords in mid-November 1680, for having advised the dissolution of the first Exclusion Parliament.[219] It is true that the dissolutions of the second and third Exclusion Parliaments saved Seymour and the other men impeached, whereas Charles simply refused to sack Halifax. Yet the fact was that a climate of intimidation had been created, in which doing the King's business or supporting him in public was clearly seen to be dangerous. Jeffreys, indeed, did resign his recordership of London out of fear.[220] Scroggs proved too controversial a figure to keep on, and in April 1681 he was dismissed from the bench.

The crown's grip on local government also seemed precarious. Attempts at the Restoration to secure a Cavalier-Anglican monopoly of local office-holding had not been that effective, and, as the 1660s and '70s progressed, a number of those friendly to dissent – or even outright nonconformists – managed to get back into power in many areas. For many local magistrates, in both town and countryside, by the late 1670s the threat of popery and the political and religious leanings of the court seemed more worrisome than the problems posed by dissent, with the result that the penal laws against Protestant nonconformists were now seldom enforced. Moreover, county JPs and civic leaders could often exercise considerable influence in parliamentary elections; the disappointing performance by candidates sympathetic to the court in the two general elections of 1679 told its own story.

The court recognized that it needed to act, and therefore set about trying to reassert its control over country government. Although the lieutenancy was already in reasonably safe hands, before the return of the second Exclusion Parliament the crown did purge the deputy lieutenancy of a few of the more prominent Whigs and replace them with known anti-Exclusionists. More worrying was the state of the county bench, and in late 1679 the government began a systematic review of the lists of JPs. By April 1680 every county in England and Wales had received a new commission of the peace, while further adjustments were to follow in June and July. In all, some 272 JPs (out of a total of 2,559) were removed. The political agenda was transparent. Between about 45 and 50 of those MPs who had voted for Exclusion in May 1679 were left out, as were a number of JPs who had been active in promoting Whig petitions or particularly zealous in their pursuit of Catholics. However, the purge was far from complete. More than 60 Exclusionist MPs, for example, retained their commissions. In general, the government lacked the nerve to attempt a removal of Whigs of high social standing. Rather than removing all those who appeared disaffected, it seemed better to try to readjust the political balance on the county benches by adding new men of known loyalty. Even so, the remodelling was at best only a partial success. The court interest was to fare no better in the general election of February and March 1681.[221]

It was the situation in the corporations that was most alarming. By the end of the second decade of Charles II's reign, opposition interests seemed firmly entrenched in power in a number of important cities and towns. London was the biggest worry. By the summer of 1680, the mayor was Whig, both the sheriffs (who were responsible for impanelling juries in London and Middlesex) were Whigs, and the Whigs had a majority on the common council, dominated many of the city companies, and enjoyed a numerical superiority among the liverymen (who elected the city's four MPs) and in common hall (the city electorate).[222] Norwich was described by the local bishop in 1673 as 'the worst corporation' he 'had met with', because nonconformists or nonconformist sympathizers had become so entrenched in office.[223] In Coventry – a notoriously fanatic town – some 37 per cent of those who held municipal office between 1660 and 1687 were dissenters or possible dissenters, and a staggering 48 per cent of the mayors.[224] Between 1671 and 1682 Dorchester, in the West Country, had seven mayors who were either nonconformists or only occasional conformists.[225] In Oxford – not normally thought of as being a major centre of dissent – two formerly purged men served as mayor during the Exclusion Crisis: Robert Pauling (elected in 1679) and John Bowell (elected the following year). On the day of Pauling's election, the council made a pointed political gesture by admitting Titus Oates and his brother to the freedom of the city, while the following year they granted freedom to Monmouth and to the Whig peer Lord Lovelace, celebrating their admission with the toast 'to the confusion of all Popish princes'.[226] A riotous mayoral election in the borough of Saltash in Cornwall in the autumn of 1679, at which 'great disturbances' were committed 'by a Rabble of unsworn Inhabitants of the said Burrough, having no Right of Election', resulted in the choice of one Mr Skelton, a nonconformist who had formerly been ejected from the aldermanic bench for not taking the oaths prescribed by the Corporation Act.[227]

The government did make some attempt to clean up the corporations. In the spring of 1680 it launched an inquiry into the extent to which boroughs had enforced the provisions in the Corporation Act concerning taking the oaths and the Anglican sacrament and subscribing the declaration against the Covenant. Some could honestly claim that they had; too many had to acknowledge that they had not kept particularly good records. In a few towns high-Anglican zealots used the opportunity to drive their political opponents out of office. Many towns simply admitted their shortcomings and promised to do better in the future, taking little if any action. Besides, the Corporation Act provided no weapons against occasional conformists. Thus some corporations dismissed those guilty of non-compliance only to reinstall them promptly once they had nominally conformed, leaving the situation exactly as it had been before.[228]

The loss of control over corporate government made it difficult to use the law as a weapon against the enemies of Church and state. There were so many nonconformists in Berwick-upon-Tweed, it was reported in August 1679, that no one was willing to inform.[229]

William Glyde, who served as mayor of Exeter in 1676–7 before going on to represent the city in parliament, sought to build up electoral support among the dissenters by allowing 'fifteen or sixteen Nonconformist ministers to resort thither and preach in their seditious conventicles without control', thereby – according to a hostile source – 'poisoning and depraving the people's loyalty and obedience to the government both of Church and State'.[230] At York both magistrates and those impanelled to serve as jurors were notoriously lax in dealing with conventicles; in April 1682 the circuit judge at the local assizes bemoaned the 'misgovernment' of the place and reckoned that no more than two of the aldermen were fit for office.[231] But again the situation was most worrisome in London, where in the late 1670s and early 1680s the government found it impossible to bring indictments not only against religious nonconformists but even against those accused of high treason. During the course of 1681, London juries threw out indictments for treason brought against a number of notorious Whig activists, including Stephen College, Sir John Rouse, and Shaftesbury.[232] As Secretary of State Sir Leoline Jenkins complained to Ormonde in October 1681, the composition of jury panels in London and Middlesex was such 'that the king cannot hope to have justice . . . in his own courts'.[233]

Local officials in town and countryside, such as the parish constables, beadles and nightwatchmen – being, as they were, unpaid members of the local community, typically of middling or even lower social status – often sympathized with those who worshipped in illegal conventicles (they were, after all, fellow Protestants) or who took to the streets in political demonstrations or riots, and were reluctant to make arrests.[234] Even when local magistrates or law-enforcement agencies identified with the court and would have willingly initiated a clampdown on dissident activity, they would refuse to act if they suspected that public sentiment was hostile to such an attempt. The problem is well illustrated by what happened in December 1682 when the King sent orders to the (by now) Tory Lord Mayor of London to suppress nonconformist meetings. In response, thousands of people flocked to the meeting houses, 'every man haveing a Lusty Kane in his hand' to protect the nonconformist ministers from arrest. The mayor therefore did nothing, protesting that he would gladly act upon the King's orders, 'But I clearly see mischiefe and ruine will follow it; you may read as much in the peopells faces.'[235]

It would be wrong to assume, then, that the alienation of public opinion mattered only in so far as it might potentially lead to a popular uprising. Widespread public dissatisfaction, electoral defeat at both the central and local level, and the reluctance of those in local-government service to act to defend the crown's interests against its open or perceived enemies meant that Charles experienced considerable difficulty in the basic task of ruling the country. To those at the centre of power, it seemed far from clear that the crown held all the trump cards.

On top of all this, however, there was indeed a genuine threat of rebellion. The Scots did rebel. The government's policy of intensified persecution had brought increasing conflict between conventiclers and authorities in 1678–9, and encouraged extremism. Then on 3 May 1679 a small band of covenanters, led by David Hackston of Rathillet, while apparently on the search for a local sheriff-depute who was a notorious persecutor, chanced to come across a coach carrying James Sharp, archbishop of St Andrews, at Magus Muir, just outside St Andrews. The group stopped the coach and brutally murdered the Archbishop in front of his own daughter and servants.[236] The assassins then fled to the south-west, where they joined with other militant covenanters to plan a general uprising. On 29 May a group of about sixty to eighty armed men rode into Rutherglen on the outskirts of Glasgow, where they posted a declaration at the market cross proclaiming they had risen in defence of the covenants and protesting against the royal supremacy, episcopacy, the Indulgence, the commemoration of 29 May, and the Rescissory Act, before proceeding to burn all the 'sinful and unlawful' acts of parliament (as they styled them) 'against our Covenanted Reformation'.[237] Over the next few weeks their numbers swelled, and at its peak the covenanter army may have numbered some 8,000 men. In June, at the market cross in Hamilton, they posted another declaration, in which they detailed the 'Cruelty, Injustice and Oppression' they had suffered under episcopacy since the Restoration, proclaimed their desire to secure 'the True Protestant Religion, and Presbyterian Government' against the royal supremacy, and demanded both a free parliament and a general assembly 'for preventing the Eminent Danger of Popery, and Extirpating of Prelacy from amongst Us'. They ended with a plea that 'all things' be restored to how the King 'found them, when God brought him home to His Crown and Kingdoms' in 1660.[238]

In the end, the rebellion was put down by government troops under the command of Monmouth, who easily overcame a woefully ill-equipped army of some 6,000 covenanters at Bothwell Bridge on 22 June. Nevertheless, the rebellion caused some nervous moments, not just for the authorities in Scotland, but also for those in England. In mid-June, for example, Secretary of State Henry Coventry received a letter from Bristol reporting how the numerous Scots in that city seemed 'to be revived at their rebellion' and warning that, if orders were not received from the central government 'to keep this Citty in peace', Bristol would soon 'be in a Sad Condition', since the city's conventicles consisted 'of many persons able in body but weak in apprehension' who might easily threaten 'the peace of the Kingdome'.[239] Some in England clearly sympathized with the Scots and hoped that their idol, Monmouth, would take the Scots' side. Thus William Mandeville, a gentleman from Rotherham in Yorkshire, was found guilty of having said on 17 June that the Scottish rebels would 'beat all England' and that, 'Though the Duke of Monmouth bee gone down to suppresse them, its thought hee is gone to take their and the Kirke's part.' He had then added that he hoped 'to see the Church downe and the priests buyred in their surplices; for I know noe good they do, but are a great charge to the parish in washing them'.[240] Although Monmouth remained true to his trust, his speedy suppression of the uprising coupled with his subsequent pleas for leniency in dealing with the rebels merely served to increase his popularity north of the border, which could only be a worrying development for the authorities in the south. It may be significant that the scholars who staged the pope-burning in Edinburgh on Christmas Day 1680 wore blue ribbons in their hats with the motto 'No Pope' printed upon them; in England blue ribbons were worn to designate support for Monmouth's claim to the throne.[241]

Following defeat at Bothwell Bridge, a group of militants under the leadership of Richard Cameron, an exiled minister who returned to

Scotland in October 1679, continued to meet in field conventicles, proclaiming their opposition to the Scottish establishment. At Queensferry (on the southern side of what is now the Forth Bridge) on 3 June 1680, following a failed attempt to seize Donald Cargill, one of the leading figures in the Cameronian movement and a Bothwell fugitive, authorities found a paper called a 'New-Covenant', wherein the Cameronians engaged to 'free the Church of God from the thraldom, tyranny, incroachment, and corruption of Prelacy . . . and Erastianism'. The Cameronians renounced the King and those who associated with him as their 'lawful Rulers', the 'New-Covenant' affirmed, 'because standing in the way of our Right, free and peaceable serving of God . . . according to our Covenant', and insisted that they would not 'yield any willing obedience to them' because they had 'altered and destroyed the Lord's establish'd Religion, overturned the fundamental and established Laws of the Kingdom, taken altogether away Christ's Church and Government, and changed the Civil Government of this Land (which was by King and free Parliaments) into Tyranny'. The paper added that they would 'no more commit the Government of our selves, and the making of Laws for us, to any one single Person, and lineal Successor . . . this kind of Government by a single Person, etc. being most liable to inconveniences, (as sad and long experience may now teach us,) and aptest to degenerate into Tyranny'. On 22 June 1680 Cameron and Cargill posted their radical manifesto 'The Declaration and Testimony of the True-Presbyterian, Anti-Praelatick, and Anti-Erastian, Persecuted-Party in Scotland' to the town cross at Sanquhar in Dumfriesshire. In it they condemned Charles II's 'Usurpation in Church matters and Tyranny in matters Civil', and proceeded to 'disown Charles Stuart', who had been 'Tyrannizing on the throne of Scotland' (alleging he had 'forfaulted' any right to the crown of Scotland 'several years since by his Perjury and breach of Covenant with God and His Church'), and to 'declare War against such a Tyrant and Usurper, and all the Men of his Practices'. They further stated that they disowned the Duke of York – 'a professt Papist' – and protested 'against his succeeding to the Crown'.[242] Then on 12 September, at a large, armed field conventicle at Torwood, south-east of Stirling, Cargill proceeded to pass sentence of excommunication on Charles II as a 'Tyrant, and Destroyer', charging him with perjury for having renounced the Covenant, with 'rescinding all Lawes for establishing the Reformation, and enacting Lawes contrarie thereunto', with having employed the army 'to destroy the Lords people', and with 'being an Enemy to true Protestants, and helper of the Papists, and hindering the execution of just Lawes against them'. He also excommunicated York, for idolatry, together with various other ministers of the crown (including Monmouth, for suppressing the Bothwell Bridge rebellion, and Lauderdale, for his apostasy from the Covenant and for persecuting the godly), and posted copies of the excommunication throughout Torwood.[243]

England may not have witnessed the same type of extremism as Scotland, but the situation south of the border nevertheless seemed potentially highly volatile. Opponents of Exclusion were quick to point out that the political opposition seemed to be engaged in exactly the same type of propaganda offensive that had been launched by John Pym and his associates on the eve of the English Civil War. Moreover, during the Exclusion Crisis – and unlike in the early 1640s – there was a viable pretender, Monmouth, who not only was a successful military commander but also had an extensive popular following. When York, then in exile in Brussels, learned of the passage of the first Exclusion Bill through the Commons in May 1679, he observed to his son-in-law, the Prince of Orange, how 'it was the presbyterians and the Duke of Monmouth's friends carried it,' and predicted that, if the King did not 'entirely submit to them, and become less than a Duke of Venice', they would 'fly out into an open rebellion'.[244] Such fears were not totally unfounded. Many Whigs openly admitted that they would take whatever measures might be necessary to protect their lives, liberties and estates in the event of a Catholic becoming king, even if this meant having recourse to armed resistance. In the Commons debate on Exclusion of 27 April 1679, Sir Thomas Player urged the need 'to alter the oath in the Militia Act, about taking up arms against such as are commissioned by the King'; at the moment, he said, Protestants were under no 'temptation to break that oath', but 'A Popish Successor' might 'send Popish Guards' to cut their throats like dogs, yet under the terms of this oath 'I must not take up arms to defend myself against such rogues.'[245] Following the failure of the second Exclusion Bill in the Lords in November 1680, the Whigs proposed a Bill of Association, along the lines of that passed under Elizabeth in 1585, whereby Protestants would rise up to defend the Protestant realm should the Catholics murder the King and attempt to install his brother on the throne.[246] On 30 December 1680 the Commons agreed to an address to the King begging him to exclude the Catholic heir and warning him that, if the crown 'should descend to the duke of York, the opposition which may possibly be made to his possessing it' might 'not only endanger the further descent in the royal line, but even monarchy itself'. This, the Scottish lawyer Sir John Lauder of Fountainhall observed, was tantamount to the Commons boasting 'that they will erect themselves in a commonwealth'.[247]

The more extreme Whigs did contemplate rebellion. The possibility may have been first mooted at the time of the Oxford Parliament of March 1681, with some Whig peers allegedly talking about staying behind in London ready to raise the City should Exclusion fail yet again. Indeed, in the summer of 1681 a document was found in Shaftesbury's closet calling for an 'Association' of 'all true Protestants' to oppose York 'by all lawful means, and by force of arms if need so required', if he ever sought to set himself up as king, although the indictment against Shaftesbury on treason charges was thrown out by a Whig jury that November.[248] By late 1682 and early 1683, however, plans were certainly being discussed for coordinated uprisings in various parts of England and Scotland, and many of the conspirators who survived the revelations of the so-called Rye House Plot in the summer of 1683 did end up joining with the Monmouth and Argyll rebellions of 1685.

Some of the talk that could be heard in the streets or alehouses across the land was giving serious cause for concern. We cannot take all accusations of seditious words at face value, of course. Some suits were undoubtedly vexatious. There were more cases after 1681, during the years of the Tory Reaction, when there was heightened government concern about the possibility of conspiratorial activity by disaffected Whigs, than during the years of the Exclusion Crisis, when the domination of local government by the Whigs made successful prosecution of Whig sympathizers more difficult. Some charges brought after 1682 referred to words allegedly spoken much earlier; what is impossible to tell is whether it was only as the Tories strengthened their hold on the machinery of law enforcement that it became possible to bring such prosecutions, or whether the time that had lapsed since the date of the alleged offence suggests that people were taking advantage of government phobias to use the law to strike out at their local enemies. Nor does the knowledge of whether the prosecution was successful or not necessarily help, because of the blatantly partisan decisions of packed juries: Whig jurors of 1679–81 were typically highly reluctant to convict their political fellow-travellers, no matter how convincing the evidence against them, while Tory jurors during the years of the Tory Reaction were often all too credulous when it came to convicting their political opponents.

Despite all these caveats, however, cases of sedition can nevertheless still be revealing; the words charged were often so specific that they suggest some basis in reality and probably reflect the sorts of concern that were being articulated at the local level. And they suggest that for some people, at least, disaffection ran so deep that they were eager to see a regime change. In March 1679 one Leicester man was accused of saying 'That King Charles the First was a papist which brought him to the Block, and his hand and Seale was at the Rebellion in Ireland And that his death was Just'.[249] A couple of months later a Yorkshire Quaker was alleged to have forecast that 'The Parliament will downe with the Lords and Bishopps, and will doe with this King as they did with last.'[250] Shortly after the dissolution of the Oxford Parliament, a London tailor was accused of having said that 'the King was as great a Papist as the Duke of York' and that he wondered why 'the Parliament doth not chop off his head';[251] a Northamptonshire knight was supposedly holding forth to the 'substantial freeholders and considerable men' in the county 'that they must stand up for their liberties and properties, which were like to be invaded by arbitrary government, and their religion, by Popery', magnifying 'the power of parliaments and great privileges of the people';[252] while a Yorkshire correspondent could report that 'many' in the Peniston area spoke 'treason' and were in favour of 'a commonwealth'.[253] In late July 1681 a bookseller from near the Old Exchange in London was committed for having said that 'he knew of engines at work to depose the

King, and that he hoped to see a Commonwealth again in England.'[254] In the autumn of 1682 informations were brought against one Ferdinando Gorges for various seditious speeches allegedly uttered some two years earlier, in which he had (among other things) condemned the King for being a papist and a whore-monger who must not be allowed to 'fright honest men out of their rights and privileges', since 'a King was no more than a private man to the laws of the land and must be subject to them', adding that 'the Parliament and the rest of the good subjects were fools, if they did not compel him to it, as they did his father.'[255] Similarly, Edward Whitaker was convicted in October 1682 for supposedly saying at Bath towards the end of July 1680 'that the late King was putt to death by a judiciall processe, and not murder'd', and that the people had a right 'to call a parliament every year, and they ought to sitt, whither called or not'.[256] In November 1684 a prosecution was brought against Yorkshireman James Appleby for words spoken back in 1679 when he tried to confiscate a gun from a local Catholic, William Orfeur. When Orfeur asked whether Appleby had the King's commission to act, Appleby replied that 'he had better warrant' than that, namely 'the fundamentall laws of the kingdom', adding that 'he hop'd in a few days now that the Commonwealth of England should be once up againe', so that they could be rid of both the King and the papists. 'The law hath as good right to try a king as a subject,' he proclaimed – witness 'the fair tryall of the last King Charles the First. And the same law hath the same power over this Charles the Second,' which he would see 'before he be a yeare elder'. Appleby's kinsman Edward was also charged at the same time with having 'made use of strong sophisticall arguments to the disparagement of monarchicall government in England' back in the spring of 1678, when he had supposedly claimed that Charles I had deserved to be executed for attempting to introduce popery and 'murdering his subjects in Ireland', which was 'worse then the massacres of France', warning that 'Charles the Second was going the same rode, and had made further progress in the same . . . and consequently better deserved to undergoe the same punishment then his father.'[257]

Conclusion to Part I

By 1679–81 the situation had indeed become critical for the government. The restored monarchy, brought back a mere twenty years earlier amid popular rejoicing in all three kingdoms, was in serious trouble. Charles II was in practice finding it difficult to rule his country. Opposition to a popish successor and fears of popery and arbitrary government had so gripped the nation that the King not only had lost control over parliament (or more particularly the House of Commons), but also had lost the support of many of those who were responsible for enforcing royal policy in the localities, from county JPs to borough magistrates down to local jurors and parish constables. Furthermore, the crisis was not just an English one: it was British in the making. Fears of popery and arbitrary government were shaped in crucial respects by the public perception of what was going on in Ireland (where there was the threat of popery) and Scotland (where there was evidence of arbitrary government). And by the time of the Exclusion Crisis there did seem a very real prospect of renewed civil violence and perhaps civil war. Ireland seemed inherently unstable, and there was repeated talk that the Irish Catholics might rise in conjunction with the French in an attempt to overthrow English domination. Scotland actually did rise in rebellion in 1679, and thereafter a group of radical Presbyterians (the Cameronians) continued to represent themselves as being in a state of war with the government. In England the Whigs had been able to rally hundreds of thousands of people in support of their cause, mobilizing them in political demonstrations and petitioning campaigns, and there seemed a genuine possibility that the more radical discontented elements might contemplate a rebellion (in alliance with the disaffected north of the border) should they not obtain what they wanted through peaceful means. By 1679–81 the Restoration regime had lost its hold over the hearts and minds of many of the people of Britain and Ireland, and there seemed a fair chance that the monarchy could go the same way that it had done in the 1640s, if appropriate measures were not taken to prevent it.

The immediate trigger for the crisis was the Catholicism of the heir to the throne, the King's brother, the Duke of York. Yet younger brothers, of course, do not normally succeed, so this in itself was an issue only because Charles II was unable to father any legitimate children. It might seem, then, that the crisis was ultimately due to a contingent factor – the barrenness of Charles's queen, Catherine of Braganza. Was it not thus one of those notorious accidents in history? Would things not have been very different if Catherine had been fertile or if Charles had married someone else? Blaming major historical upheavals on contingency has become something of a fad in recent years, and exercises in counterfactual history always make for entertaining parlour games, because ultimately we can never know for sure what might have happened if one small thing had been slightly different. Yet in this instance we can be pretty confident in asserting that the root cause of the problems lay much deeper than the infertility of one particular woman (albeit a rather important woman in the context of an hereditary monarchy). There were major structural problems with the Restoration polities in all three kingdoms, as the previous chapters have made clear. Charles would have found his a difficult inheritance to manage whether or not he had had a legitimate Protestant heir. His inheritance could not stand the strains of being presented with the prospect of a popish successor, it is true. Yet the underlying political and religious tensions bequeathed by the struggles earlier in the century were causing so much bitter division both within and among the three kingdoms that coping with these was already proving a difficult juggling act. Hence when the crisis came, triggered by Oates's revelations of a Popish Plot and centring around fears of a Catholic succeeding to the throne, the issues at stake were about much more than what might happen, in England, one day in the future, should a Catholic become king. They were also about what had been going on in all three kingdoms over the last two decades under the present monarch.

The Whigs were able to exploit the situation to their advantage through the skilful use of propaganda designed to rally public opinion behind their cause, playing on fears of popery and arbitrary government and the potential threat to people's lives, liberties and estates. Their hope was that Charles would eventually bow in the face of considerable public pressure. After all, even the most absolute kings were supposed to rule in accordance with the wishes of their people, otherwise they would be tyrants. Moreover, Charles was known to be determined not to go on his travels again. Hence it seemed reasonable to assume that an appropriate display of what his subjects felt (with the hint that trouble might follow if they were not appeased) was bound to make him yield. Yet, although Whigs harnessed this popular energy in support of their cause, it would be misleading to suggest that they created it, or that they created the crisis through their use of propaganda. The reason why the Whigs were so successful was because they were able to appeal to the lived experiences of ordinary men and women. It did not take a pamphlet to tell an English Protestant (especially one with nonconformist sympathies) or a Scottish Presbyterian (whether in Scotland or Ireland) – or an Irish Catholic, for that matter – that all was not well with the Restoration regime. People were already disaffected as a result of the policies pursued by the Restoration monarchy in (and towards) the three kingdoms. All the Whigs sought to do was to exploit this pre-existing disaffection in such a way as to make it most serviceable to their cause. And in this they were undoubtedly brilliantly successful.

By early 1681 it was clear to Charles II that he could not risk calling another parliament in London. Instead, he would retreat to royalist Oxford. But the Oxford Parliament was to prove a crucial turning point for the fortunes of the Restoration monarchy. When Charles's father had run away from his capital, in 1642, civil war soon followed. When Charles II himself did so, in 1681, it marked the beginning of a period of political revival for the Stuart monarchy. The turnaround in the monarchy's fortunes was impressive. How it was achieved is in itself a fascinating story which tells us much about the nature and realities of political power in this period in England, Scotland and Ireland – about what it was necessary to do, within this particular political culture, to make political rule effective. It is to a consideration of how this royal recovery was made possible, then, that we now turn.

PART TWO

The Royalist Reaction,
c. 1679–1685

Some had ẙ hands stuck off & hanged, others beheaded.   *Some hanged*

Some taken & instantly shot in ẙ Fields.   *Some banished, &*

tered   Some Tortured by boots thumbkins firematches

d in   wrack. women hanged, others drowned at stakes in the sea.

(preceding pages) *A Hind Let Loose*: Woodcut illustrating the types of punishments meted out to Presbyterian dissidents in Scotland during the reign of Charles II.

4

The Remedy for the Disease

*The Ideological Response to the
Exclusionist Challenge*

*'Tis the Press that has made 'um Mad, and the Press must set
'um Right again.*[1]

Both Charles II and the Duke of York survived the Exclusion Crisis. The hereditary succession was kept intact, and York duly became king when his brother eventually died on 6 February 1685, at the age of fifty-four. Yet Charles did not merely survive; instead, as one historian has put it, he emerged 'from the Exclusion Crisis as incontestably the strongest seventeenth-century monarch'.[2] The purpose of Part II of this book is to examine how he achieved this.

It used to be argued that the Whig challenge was defeated from above. When the third Exclusion Parliament, which met at Oxford on 21 March 1681, proved as obstreperous as the last, Charles dissolved it after just eight days; buoyed up by French subsidies and increased revenues from customs and excise, he then simply refused to call another parliament for the rest of his reign. Without parliament, Exclusion effectively became an impossibility, unless it could be brought about through popular insurrection. Yet Charles also launched a ruthless campaign to suppress all forms of political and religious dissent, carrying out a radical purge of local government and the court system to oust the Whigs and dissenters from office and replace them by loyal supporters of the crown, which in turn enabled him to turn the full weight of the law against his opponents. During these years of Tory Reaction, all forms of political opposition to the King and his heir were effectively crushed, and the Whigs and their nonconformist allies were driven underground. The crown also interfered with electoral franchises in parliamentary constituencies, so that, when a parliament eventually was called, a loyal body would be returned. On the ideological front, Charles's Tory and high-Anglican allies vaunted the powers of the crown: they condemned the Whig championship of mixed monarchy and appeal to opinion out-of-doors, and instead insisted that England's was a divine-right, hereditary monarchy, where the succession was indefeasible and sovereignty was vested solely in the king, who was accountable to God alone. Whether or not it was Charles's ambition to establish a French-style royal absolutism in England has always been a source of contention.[3] Nevertheless, Charles's last years have been characterized as a period of personal rule when the King 'at last emerged as an unfettered sovereign'.[4] In this view, the crown defeated Exclusion by suppressing the voice of the people.

In recent years we have come to recognize that the royal response to the Exclusion Crisis was more multidimensional than such an account would suggest. The crown and its Tory allies did not simply ride roughshod over public opinion; rather, they made a deliberate attempt to woo it, through a carefully crafted propaganda campaign. In the process, they sought to address public anxieties about the threat of popery and arbitrary government, insisting that the best way to avoid both was for people to resist the Whig challenge and rally behind the crown in defence of the traditional constitution in Church and state. And their efforts, we have been told, were successful. As the Exclusion Crisis progressed, there was a swing in public opinion to the Tories, which manifested itself in the form of loyal addresses and processions, as people sought to demonstrate their loyalty to the crown and the succession and their opposition to the Whigs and dissenters.[5] One historian has even gone so far as to argue that Tory attempts to seduce the people were so successful that all but a few hardliners abandoned the Whigs and became Tories.[6] By this account, persuasion rather than suppression was the key to the defeat of the Exclusionist challenge. Indeed, rather than riding roughshod over public opinion, Charles II and his government became in tune with it.[7]

There is, however, a danger that this line of interpretation can be pushed too far. A major question it raises is: what happened to the Whigs? Did they really all virtually disappear? If so, why was the Tory Reaction necessary at all? And, since most histories of the Glorious

Revolution attribute a significant role to the Whigs in the making of the Revolution settlement, where did the Whigs suddenly reappear from? Then we have the issue of where Scotland and Ireland fit in. We have seen that the crisis that had engulfed the crown by 1680 was not just an English crisis, but a crisis of the three kingdoms. Was it dealt with in the same way in England, Scotland and Ireland, or was it managed very differently in the respective kingdoms?

In fact, rather than emphasizing suppression or persuasion to the exclusion of the other, we should see the crown's success in meeting the Exclusionist challenge as a combination of the two – though the balance between them, as we shall see, was different in the different kingdoms. The defeat of the Whigs was the result of both policy and police: exploitation of the media to convince moderates, waverers or unsure loyalists to pledge their allegiance to the crown and the succession and to allow themselves to stand up and be counted was backed up by a rigorous campaign to suppress all forms of political and religious opposition, to remove Whigs and nonconformists from positions of power at the central and local levels, and to intimidate the sizeable number of people who still sympathized with the Whig agenda into political silence or acquiescence. Indeed, the truly interesting question is: why did it need a combination of the two? Why was police by itself not enough? The answer tells us much about the importance of public opinion within this polity and about the vitality of the public sphere. It also sets the nature of Charles's success in meeting the Exclusionist challenge in a new light, and helps us to understand better the problems that were to emerge during the reign of his brother, James II.

This chapter will examine the ideological response to the Whig challenge. It will explore why the court and its Tory allies sought to woo public opinion, the types of argument they used to counter the Whig ideological offensive, and the extent to which they were able to deflect people's concerns about popery and arbitrary government while at the same time developing an ideological platform that was distinctively Tory in nature. It will also emphasize the importance of the three-kingdoms perspective in shaping the nature of the Tory response to the Whigs. The focus will be on England, in the sense that this chapter will deal overwhelmingly with works published in

London whose authors (no doubt) would have thought of themselves as writing primarily for an English audience. Having said that, there is a sense in which Tory – i.e. Cavalier-Anglican – ideology was Tory ideology for all three kingdoms. We have to remember that the press in both Scotland and Ireland was relatively underdeveloped and that most printed material that Scottish and Irish people read would probably have originated in England. Moreover, Scottish episcopalians and Church of Ireland Protestants would undoubtedly have identified strongly with the type of Tory ideology that was coming out of England (as subsequent chapters will show). In other words, Scottish and Irish Protestants of the Established Church would not only have been familiar with the types of argument discussed here, but would also probably have encountered many of the specific works upon which this chapter draws. The next chapter will seek to measure the success of the Tory propaganda campaign in England, investigating the rise there in public support for the crown during the final years of Charles II's reign, as well as examining the government's drive against Whiggery and dissent during the years of the Tory Reaction to show how persuasion and suppression went hand in hand in defeating the Exclusionist challenge. Chapters 6 and 7 will then look specifically at Scotland and Ireland in turn.

THE TORY APPEAL TO PUBLIC OPINION

Charles made it clear throughout the Exclusion Crisis that he would not alter the succession. He was prepared, he often said, to offer any other safeguards that could ensure the security of the Protestant religion under a Catholic successor, but tampering with the succession itself was something he would not contemplate. That he should be so unswerving on this issue when he had proved so willing to bend on others astounded many contemporaries. It was certainly not because of any love he might have felt towards his younger brother.[8] Rather, he appears to have felt that the monarchy, so newly restored after a period of republican experimentation, could not survive in any meaningful sense if parliament were allowed to dictate the succession. In his opposition to Exclusion he was backed by a number of prominent individuals, who formed the phalanx of the Tory party: the second Earl of Clarendon (Henry Hyde), treasurer and receiver-general of the Queen's revenues (1680–84); Clarendon's brother, Laurence Hyde (from 1682 the Earl of Rochester), the First Lord of the Treasury (1679–84); Sir Leoline Jenkins, Secretary of State (1680–84); Sir Edward Seymour, treasurer of the navy (1673–81) and Speaker of the Commons (1679); and Sir Francis North (Baron Guilford from 1683), Lord Chief Justice of Common Pleas (1674–82) and Lord Keeper (1682–5). One of the most prominent opponents of Exclusion in the Lords was the mercurial Earl of Halifax (Marquis from 1682), Lord Privy Seal (1682–5), who had allied himself with the country opposition of the mid-1670s and who during the years of the Tory Reaction was to proclaim himself to be the archetypal trimmer, but who during the Exclusion Crisis emerged as Shaftesbury's main opponent in the upper house. In the Lords the Tories could also rely on the support of the episcopal bench, to a man, which helped ensure a Tory ascendancy there. In the Commons, however, the Tories were significantly outnumbered, by at least three to two.

The government's instinct, it needs to be stressed, was not to try to woo public opinion but rather to neutralize or silence critics of the regime. Hence the court initially responded to the Whig challenge (as we have seen) by trying to co-opt key political opponents in parliament within the administration, remodelling the privy council in April 1679 in order to bring in some of its fiercest critics, including Shaftesbury and Essex. It also sought to silence critical voices in the press through the use of the common law of seditious libel (again as discussed in the previous chapter). Neither strategy proved effective. It was only as a result of the failure of this approach that the court and its Tory allies came to appreciate that they would need to beat the Whigs at their own game. They therefore launched a counter-propaganda campaign, with the deliberate aim – as government licenser of the press Roger L'Estrange, put it – of trying to instil 'Dutyfull and Honest Principles into the Common People'. Indeed, L'Estrange came to see this as the only 'Remedy to the Disease'.[9] How, then, did they do this?

Tory propaganda matched the range of that of the Whigs. There were lengthy treatises and legal-historical tracts for those with the requisite literacy skills and intellectual sophistication to grapple with complex constitutional and philosophical issues; pamphlets, broadsides and almanacs for a broader audience; songs, poems, prints and playing cards for those on the margins of literacy; and political periodicals, which appealed to a broad clientele and allowed readers to keep up to date with day-by-day political events. The first Tory newspaper was Nathaniel Thompson's *True Domestick Intelligence*, which ran from June 1679 to May 1680. Tory periodicals picked up with a vengeance, however, from 1681. The two most influential were L'Estrange's *Observator*, which appeared at first twice then three times a week and ran from 13 April 1681 to March 1687, and Thompson's *Loyal Protestant and True Domestick Intelligence*, another bi-turned-tri-weekly which ran to 247 issues between 9 March 1681 and 20 March 1683. There were, however, other periodicals with lesser print runs, such as *Heraclitus Ridens*, which ran from 1 February 1681 to 22 August 1682, and *The Weekly Discovery of the Mystery of Iniquity*, which ran from 5 February to 27 August 1681. The press was backed up by the pulpit, as high-church clergy rushed to defend the government and condemn the Whigs in their sermons, while there were also a number of anti-Whig plays put on in the London playhouses as the stage became another site for the on-going propaganda war between the two parties.[10]

The precise role that the government played in directing this activity is difficult to ascertain. Many loyalist writers and clerics worked on their own initiative, and did not need any government prompting to give expression to their disagreements with the Whigs. Some loyalist works appeared anonymously, leaving us no way of knowing who the author was and what connection, if any, he may have had with the government. Nevertheless, there undoubtedly was direction from the centre. Sir Francis North gave advice on strategy and helped craft royalist propaganda himself. His papers contain detailed notes on how to write a treatise to 'undeceive' the people about the Popish Plot; they urge the need to write 'persuasively' rather than 'authoritatively', and to show that the real enemies of the Church and state were the republicans, Presbyterians and sectarians who had been disaffected ever since the restoration of monarchy and episcopacy – a classic example of turning the charge against one's enemies. According to his brother and biographer, Roger North, Sir

Francis also advised that the King 'should order nothing extraordinary, to make people imagine he was touched to the quick', but should instead 'set up counter writers' who could take to task every libel that came out and answer it. For 'either we are in the wrong, or in the right,' he said; 'if the former, we must do as usurped powers, use force, and crush all our enemies, right or wrong.' But there was 'no need of that, for we are in the right', and nothing was done by the King and his ministers 'but what the law will warrant'. Therefore the Whig scribblers could 'lie and accuse till they are weary'; we will simply 'declare at the same time . . . that all they say is false and unjust'. This was not a straightforward case of letting the truth speak for itself (however much Sir Francis or Roger North may have wanted to believe it was), since the men hired – among them L'Estrange (for his *Observator*) and the authors of *Heraclitus Ridens* – were clearly to offer a distinctively Tory interpretation of 'the truth'. Nevertheless, the government undoubtedly had quite a sophisticated understanding of how to construct a counter-propaganda campaign.[11] The most prolific pro-government publicist was L'Estrange himself, whom Gilbert Burnet described as 'the chief manager of all those angry writings'. L'Estrange produced not only one of the most influential periodicals of the period, but also a host of important pamphlets and broadsides; indeed, some 64,000 copies of L'Estrange's tracts were in circulation in the two years before the launching of his *Observator*. Secretary Jenkins and the Lord Lieutenant of Ireland, Ormonde, also played a role in organizing the government's propaganda efforts, while both Ormonde and L'Estrange established their own clubs to help coordinate their activities.[12] Then there was the official government news organ, the *London Gazette*, which appeared twice a week with a print run of about 15,000 per issue and reported events in a way that was most favourable to the crown.[13] Charles even contributed to the propaganda campaign himself, publishing work in his own name – most famously his declaration of April 1681 justifying his stance against the Whigs. The government also attempted to exploit the medium of the pulpit to its own advantage; Charles ordered all the clergy to read his declaration to their congregations,[14] while officially appointed days of thanksgiving – such as that for the deliverance from the Rye House Plot in 1683 – provided a cue for an outpouring of loyalist sermonizing across the land.[15] Not that high-Anglican zealots among the clergy needed much encouraging; Burnet (in the original draft of his *History*) recalled how during the height of the Exclusion Crisis such clerics would go 'to Taverns and Ale-houses' and rail 'scurrilously against those that differ[ed] from them'.[16] Furthermore, in February 1681 Charles set up a commission on ecclesiastical promotions – expanded in July 1681 to include lay commissioners, and which was staffed by William Sancroft, Archbishop of Canterbury, Bishop Compton of London, Halifax, Lawrence Hyde, Seymour and the Earl of Radnor – to ensure that only those of proven loyalty and sound Tory credentials obtained preferment within the Church.[17]

Some of the Tory media, to be sure, had a narrow target audience, sociologically speaking. The lengthier treatises elaborating upon the finer points of the precise extent of royal power could have been fully understood only by the better educated, and were presumably intended primarily for those who sat in parliament and the leaders of local society. Nevertheless, much Tory propaganda was deliberately crafted to be accessible to a lower-class audience – some of it more successfully than others, no doubt. The Anglican divine William Sherlock claimed that he wrote his 1684 tract about the inadmissibility of resistance because existing books on the topic were 'too learned for ordinary Readers' and he saw the need 'for such a small Treatise as this' that would be 'fittest to the understanding of the meanest men'; yet he was perhaps being overly optimistic, since his tract – by no means a light read – is 221 pages long.[18] On the other hand, L'Estrange most certainly designed his *Observator* 'purely for the People', and for that reason made it 'Course, and Popular' as well as 'Timely, Cheap, and Easy'.[19] Short tracts and periodicals used a prose style designed to resonate with the lower orders: simple words, colourful language, and frequent allusions to activities or functions that were an everyday part of human existence – from drinking, to health-care provision, sexual acts, and going to the toilet. A favourite device was the dialogue, used in a number of tracts and in the periodicals *Heraclitus Ridens* and the *Observator*, which allowed the Whig case to be put first, only to be refuted point by point by the more ingenious and compelling arguments of the spokesman for the other side. Dialogues also mirrored the way that people themselves discussed political issues, capturing in written form an oral exchange of ideas; they were thus ideal texts for reading aloud, to bridge the gap between literate and oral culture, and served to stimulate further political discussion in turn.[20] Sermons were also often delivered in a style designed to be appealing to a social mix of people. For example, the noted Anglican preacher Edward Pelling boasted that he found 'the Delivery of plain Truths after a plain manner (however some may call it Intemperate Zeal) . . . the most Effectual way of Instructing People, especially the ordinary sort of Men, who are most apt to run away with mistakes'.[21]

Yet why should the Tories have wanted to target the lower orders? After all, they are normally seen as an anti-populist party, with some justification. Indeed, they were at times quite scathing in their criticisms of the Whig appeal to opinion out-of-doors, and of the political intelligence 'of the poor unthinking and deluded Multitude'.[22] There were, however, a number of reasons why it was important for the government to be seen to have the people on its side. One was linked to the ideology of self-legitimization in which early modern monarchs cloaked themselves. Even the most outspoken champions of divine-right absolute monarchy would nevertheless have agreed that rulers were supposed to be just and to promote the welfare of their subjects. Yet it was pretty difficult for the government to claim that it was fulfilling its divinely ordained duty of guaranteeing 'the Safety and Happiness of all the People'[23] if the people were always taking to the streets to protest against it. There was also the recognition that government, to be effective, relied on the cooperation of a host of unpaid public servants at the local level – from county JPs and town magistrates down to local jurors, constables, nightwatchmen and other parish officers. If government policy was to be enforced effectively, these people had to be convinced that what the government was doing was right; indeed, as we have seen, it was the fact that so many of these types did not agree that what the government was doing was right which explains why the situation had become so critical for the government by 1679–81. Most worryingly, perhaps, widespread popular disaffection might threaten civic peace. In the 1640s the parliamentary opposition's appeal to opinion out-of-doors had led England into a bitter civil war, resulting ultimately in regicide and the setting-up of a republic, and by 1679 there were already fears that England might be on the road to civil war once more, or that '41 was come again, as contemporaries put it. This helps explain the Tories' somewhat schizophrenic attitude towards 'the multitude'. Because of what had happened in the 1640s, they were quick to condemn any appeal to the masses to put pressure on the crown to change royal policy. At the same time, they knew that they could not afford to allow the masses to remain disaffected, but would need to court opinion out-of-doors if they were to avoid a repeat of the 1640s. L'Estrange made the logic of Tory thinking explicit in his *Observator*. He shared the view that the 'common people' were 'Rude and Illiterate', and that nothing was 'more Dangerous' or 'Ridiculous' than 'a Pretending Multitude'. But he was convinced that the people were 'as Susceptible of Good, as of Bad', if 'Seditious Instruments' did not poison them 'with False Doctrines, and Positions, upon the Subject of Power, and Duty'. Furthermore, L'Estrange remained confident that, 'if the Kings Friends' took but 'Half the Pains, to set them Right' as his enemies did to mislead them, 'the Common People' would be 'as well Dispos'd to Preserve the Government, as they are Otherwise, to Embroil it'. It followed that the government was partly to blame if the people went astray: 'When they do Amiss, 'tis not so much the Malevolence of their Nature, as the Looseness of a Political Discipline . . . Insomuch, that the Government itself is Answerable in a High Measure for the Distempers of the Multitude.'[24] Or, as Pelling put it, it was 'the ordinary sort of Men' who needed 'the most of our Care and Instructions, because they are the Hands and Tools which Politick Male-contents imploy to Disturb the Peace and Establisht Government'.[25]

WERE THE TORIES ABSOLUTISTS?

What sort of arguments, then, did the Tories use to counter the Exclusionist challenge? The Tories are normally thought of as being champions of divine-right royal absolutism, their political ideology epitomized by Sir Robert Filmer's *Patriarcha*, a work written before the Civil War, though published for the first time in 1680.[26] Thus, according to one scholar, the Tories maintained that a king's author-ity was 'absolute, arbitrary and irresistible' and 'put the interests and privileges of the propertied classes at the mercy of an arbitrary and absolute king'.[27] According to another, 'Filmer's patriarchal and con-stitutional theses were central to Tory absolutism'; Filmer may have 'put the case starkly and comprehensively – but he was scarcely a lone voice'. This was 'the decade of Tory absolutism'; Tory ideas were 'remarkably homogeneous', and showed striking continuity with earlier seventeenth-century crescendos of absolutist theorizing.[28]

There is much truth to this view, although it needs qualification. The contours of Tory political ideology can be traced through a wide variety of sources: from rigorously thought-through philosophical tracts (intended to lay down timeless principles), to more low-brow, polemical works (designed very much for the moment), speeches in parliament (made in the heat of public debate) and sermons by high-Anglican clerics (often geared to mark a particular occasion, such as the anniversary of the regicide or deliverance from a Whig plot). Some of these sources may be said to reflect an official Tory line, in the sense that they were the work of people who had close ties to the court or whose views were endorsed by those in power. Others, however, reflect no more than the personal opinions of people writing or speaking on their own initiative. Given this, we should be wary of making too straightforward generalizations. We can detect different emphases within Tory thought, depending on authorship and context; we should not expect (nor do we find) complete consistency between all spokesmen, on all occasions. Having said this, however, it is fair to say that we are dealing with difference only of emphasis; there is a discernible core Tory ideology that most people who sided with the court would have embraced. We also have to recognize that it could never have been a satisfactory response to the Whig ideological chal-lenge simply to say that the King was a divinely ordained absolute ruler, and that, whatever one's anxieties about the succession or polit-ical developments under Charles II, there was nothing one could do about the situation. Rather, the Tories realized that they needed to respond to the concerns that the Whigs had raised about popery and arbitrary government and to try to convince people that there was nothing to fear if one supported the Tory position. In the process, they developed a range of arguments to show that they were committed to the defence of the true Protestant religion, the rule of law, and the protection of people's lives, liberties and estates – arguments which were a more significant dimension to their ideological platform than their pronouncements about divine-right monarchy, and which run the risk of being obscured if we choose simply to represent the Tories as Filmerian absolutists.

It might seem logical, at first glance, to try to make distinctions on the basis of genre. Did tracts intended for the educated elite make somewhat different arguments from more low-brow works? Were defences of divine-right monarchical absolutism, perhaps, more commonly articulated in the former, where the target audience was more likely to be sympathetic to hierarchical notions of government, with arguments which emphasized what the Tories had to offer the lower orders being reserved for the latter? On close analysis, such distinctions prove impossible to sustain. In the first place, there could never have been total separation between genres, because of the way that political ideologies were disseminated in practice. Ideas put forth in a lengthy philosophical treatise might be picked up on by an Anglican clergyman in church, whose sermon might in turn help shape the views of the writer of a witty Tory broadside or a piece of anti-Whig vitriol; the author of the last might never have read the first, but as a churchgoer he could well have been all too familiar with its main line of argument. Second, and following naturally from this, it is by no means clear that populist works did reflect a different style of Toryism from the more philosophical treatises. Some arguments might be more likely to find emphasis in certain contexts rather than others, but high-brow and low-brow Tory works essentially embraced the same core Tory ideology – if there were variants, they were to be found within all genres, not between genres. The way to proceed, then, is to deconstruct this core Tory ideology, with all its varieties and shades of emphasis, using whatever sources best enable us to unpack the Tory worldview.

Let us start by considering whether the Tories were Filmerian absolutists. This is a complex issue, but one which it is important to get right, not just because it affects our understanding of the ideology of the Tory Reaction, and whether there was a potential for royal absolutism in the final years of Charles II's reign, but also because it affects our comprehension of developments under James II. As we shall see in the sequel to this book, Tories and high Anglicans did not stand by as James II set about using his prerogative to promote the interests of his co-religionists in defiance of the laws upholding the Anglican monopoly of office, worship and education; in fact they put up considerable opposition. Why they should have felt able to do this will become clearer once we fully understand the precise nature of the Tory view on the theoretical powers of the crown.

It has been suggested that Filmer was an untypical royalist, because somewhat extreme in his championship of monarchical absolutism.[29] But in fact his views chimed nicely with the theory of Restoration royalism as articulated by high-church divines, and after 1680 many royalist polemicists recognized *Patriarcha* as reflecting the quintessence of their case; indeed, it was published at the behest of Archbishop Sancroft to bolster the Tory cause.[30] The Whigs certainly saw Filmer's work as epitomizing the royalist position, which was why the leading works of Whig political philosophy written at this time, including John Locke's *Two Treatises of Government* and Algernon Sidney's *Discourses*, took Filmer as their main ideological opponent.[31] Filmer's arguments proved serviceable to the anti-Exclusionist cause on a number of levels. He held not only that government was by divine right, but that God, at the Creation, had given the world to Adam and his heirs in succession, exclusive of the rest of posterity. The king's power was equivalent to that enjoyed by Adam, as husband, father, property-owner and king; monarchical power was the same as paternal power and was absolute; and kings enjoyed their power by hereditary descent, not by election or because power was conferred on them by the people. Filmer's researches into medieval history also confirmed that parliaments were subordinate to the crown.

Tories agreed that government originated at the Creation. As Thomas Goddard put it, government 'began with the World, and God, who had the Sovereign Right of Power over the whole Universe, invested Adam with so much as was necessary for the Government of this World', giving him 'the rule over his Wife Eve' and 'a Right of Power over those whom himself begot'. After the Flood, Noah, like

Adam, became father and sovereign to the whole world, and his various sons became fathers of different kingdoms and countries. Thus people had always lived under some form of government; no natural state of liberty had ever existed.[32] The apostle Paul had confirmed there was 'no power but of God' and that 'the powers that be' were 'ordained of God' (Romans 13:1). English kings therefore ruled by divine right; they were 'Gods Ministers, and Vice-Gerents'. It followed that the Whigs were wrong to claim that the people were the fountain and foundation of power, or that princes would forfeit their power if they did not perform their trust.[33] The point was made repeatedly. One pamphleteer attacked the view of the 'Original Sovereign Power of Mr. Multitude'; another condemned those who 'infused into people minds . . . that Power is radically and revokably in them', and that they had the 'Right . . . upon the Maleadministration' of their rulers to 'take all the Power into their own hands again'. God was the author of government, and government was unalterable.[34]

Tories did not try to claim that the kings of England were literally descended from Adam; they knew 'very well, that all the Kingdoms upon the Earth have oftentimes chang'd their Masters and Families'.[35] Rather, Adam's rule was seen as the archetype of all monarchy, and monarchy as the most natural form of government since it was a species of fatherhood and all government began as paternal power. For Matthew Rider, monarchy was not only 'the best and ancientest' but indeed 'the sole justifiable form of Government'; 'Aristocracy and Democracy' were 'rather Usurpations upon Monarchy, than any institution of God or nature'.[36] Sir Philip Warwick took a somewhat different tack in a tract written in 1678, insisting that, although 'God made paternal power the foundation of all civil government,' he allowed people to choose whether to lodge that government in one or more persons; nevertheless 'the whole diffusive body of the governed' was analogous to wives, for, although a woman 'might have chosen, whether she would have disposed her self to such a man to be her husband, yet having done it, she was always under his Subjection'. Warwick also said that he thought that hereditary monarchy was best.[37]

Many Tories and Anglican divines explicitly embraced patriarchalism. As Samuel Crossman maintained in a sermon preached at Bristol Cathedral on 31 January 1681, 'the Sovereign' was 'the common Father of the Country . . . he the Husband, the Kingdom his Spouse'.[38] Filmer did not teach the English to be patriarchalists; his views appealed because they resonated deeply with the way in which the English understood how their society operated. Indeed, the familial analogy had long been used to describe political relationships in the state; as far back as 1399 the Bishop of Carlisle, in a speech condemning the deposition of Richard II (which was printed in 1679 as a contribution to the Exclusion debate), had argued that 'the Prince is *Pater patriae*, the Father of our Countrey: And therefore more sacred and dear unto us, than our Parents by nature, and must not be violated, how imperious, how impious so ever they be.'[39] Once the familial analogy was established, the authority of the monarch seemed to be further reinforced by the fifth commandment, to honour one's father and mother.[40]

It was a concomitant of divine-right theory that the succession was divinely ordained and indefeasible. As Sir Leoline Jenkins claimed in a speech against Exclusion on 4 November 1680, 'the kings of England have their Right from God alone . . . no power on earth can deprive them of it.'[41] 'The Succession to the Crown', one pamphleteer proclaimed, 'is inseparably annexed to proximity of Blood by the Laws of God and Nature', and 'all Statute-Laws contrariant to the Laws of God and Nature' were 'ipso facto null and void'; 'No Human Power can hinder the Descent upon the Right Heir of the Crown,' he continued, since 'The Descent makes the King.'[42] According to the vice-chancellor of Cambridge University, Dr Humfrey Gower, speaking before Charles II at Newmarket in September 1681, kings derived their titles not 'from the People, but from God', and came to be 'Sovereign . . . by a Fundamental Hereditary Right of Succession, which no Religion, no Law, no Fault or Forfeiture can alter or diminish'.[43] Similarly, Rider upheld that 'the Crown descends upon the next Heir of the Blood Royal, by the Law of God and Nature, by inherent Birth-right, and undoubted Succession.' Indeed, 'the Heir and the actual Possessor' had 'the same right to the Crown' and differed 'only in the time of their enjoying the Sovereignty': 'as an inanimate Embryo', Rider went on, 'has the same right to life, as a Child already born', and abortion is 'as much perfect murther in the sight of God' as taking away the life of a living child, so likewise 'what right the Actual Possessour hath to the Crown during his Life, the same hath the Heir Apparent, or next of blood to enjoy it after his Precessor's death.'[44] Yet natural-law arguments in defence of the succession were not by themselves enough if, as Warwick conceded, God had initially allowed people to choose what sort of government they preferred, or if, as even Rider was prepared to concede, some monarchies were elective. Hence Tories also insisted that historically England always had been a hereditary monarchy. As the author of *A Letter on the Subject of the Succession* put it, 'the Law of the Land, and constant Practice of this Kingdom', showed 'that the Imperial Crown of these Nations is Hereditary, and the Succession is universally acknowledged and determined to be vested in the lawful Heir'.[45] 'It hath been often declared in Parliaments', another author insisted, that 'the Monarchy of England [was] hereditary; and that the crown by the Laws of God and Nature doth descend, according to Birth-right and Proximity of blood'.[46] How, therefore, did Tories deal with the historical precedents for breaches in the succession? Simply by maintaining that these were usurpations 'in Factious times'.[47] 'Tho the right Heirs have been excluded and set aside,' the author of *Antidotum Britannicum* proclaimed, 'it doth not follow, that the act was just and warrantable.'[48]

Did it follow, then, that the English monarch was absolute? For Filmer it did, while many Tory writers and Anglican clerics also pronounced that the king was absolute. Care is needed, however, when discussing this issue. Within early modern political discourse, we need to recall, the term 'absolute' possessed a variety of discrete, if overlapping, meanings.[49] It was used most commonly in the sense of 'complete': a ruler was absolute if he had complete power – that is, if he did not share his sovereignty with anyone else. As the Anglican cleric and Tory ideologue John Nalson put it, the 'monarchy of Great Britain' was 'absolutely Independent' (revealingly, his marginal gloss reads 'absolute and Independent').[50] In one sense, English monarchs had been absolute ever since the Henrician Reformation had removed the pope's ecclesiastical jurisdiction from England; they no longer shared their sovereignty with any foreign prince or potentate. Many

Elizabethan and early Stuart Puritans had been happy to endorse the view that English monarchs were absolute in this respect; it could even be argued that the monarch's authority was absolute in the international sphere, but limited on the domestic front.[51] The king was absolute on the domestic front, on the other hand, if he did not share his sovereignty with any domestic body, such as parliament. 'Absolute' also held the connotation of being unaccountable to the law, or, in Latin, *ab legibus solutus*. If a ruler was unaccountable to law, it followed that his subjects had no legitimate grounds to oppose his authority if he failed to rule according to law; he certainly could not be resisted by his subjects. An appeal to absolutist ideology could therefore be a way of deflecting resistance theory.

A ruler with complete and undivided sovereignty, who was unaccountable to the law and could not be resisted, might also possess considerable discretionary powers, and in that sense be an arbitrary monarch, even an unfettered sovereign. Yet he need not be, and it is important not to equate absolute government with tyranny or even arbitrary government. The vast majority of Tories who held that England's monarchy was absolute would have denied that it was arbitrary, or that the king was free to rule in whatever way he wished. Unlike the despotic rulers of the Ottoman Empire or the absolute kings of France, England's monarchs were also, in some respects, limited. Indeed, some Tory authors thought the differences with the absolute sovereigns of the Continent so great that they preferred to deny that England's monarchy was absolute – even though they concurred that the English king was sovereign, unaccountable and irresistible.

Tories repeatedly denounced the theory of coordination – the view that the king was co-equal in power with the two houses of parliament. L'Estrange was typical when he pronounced in 1679 that the king was not a coordinate power, and that the three estates comprised not king, Lords and Commons, but the Lords spiritual, the Lords temporal and the Commons.[52] Tories similarly denied the Whig theory of the ancient constitution; the Norman Conquest of 1066, they insisted, had fundamentally transformed the polity, and parliaments, rather than dating back to Anglo-Saxon times, were in reality a medieval invention, called into being by the crown and initially no more than an extension of the king's council – an argument found in Filmer, but which was to be most fully substantiated by the historical researches of Robert Brady.[53]

Opponents of Exclusion were also quick to pour scorn on the Whig view that parliament derived its power from its position as the representative of the people. As Sir Benjamin Thorogood pointed out in a tract of 1680, 'Parliament as now usually Elected' was 'not at all the Representative of the People', since under the existing franchise no one could vote but 40-shilling freeholders and citizens and burgesses. There were also inequities in the geographical distribution of seats, which meant that even 'the meanest Borough', such as Old Sarum, might return as many MPs 'as the greatest County in England'.[54] If the Whigs were right about parliament being the representative of the people, Rider wondered, why were 'Peasants, Servants, Women and Children', who were 'undoubtedly the major part of the Nation', denied the vote?[55] Likewise George Hickes asked why, if sovereignty was in the people, women were excluded from the franchise: 'Who gave the men authority to deprive them of their birthright, and set them aside as unfit to meddle with Government; when Histories teach us that they have wielded Sceptres, as well as Men, and Experience shews, that there is no natural difference between their understandings and ours, nor any defects in their knowledge of things, but what Education makes?'[56] Such authors were not calling for franchise reform, however; the point they were trying to establish was that parliament did not derive its authority from the people, but was an institution of the king's creation.

A concomitant of the denial of coordination was that it was the king, rather than the two houses of parliament, who made the law. One had to 'distinguish betwixt the Consent, and the Sanction', L'Estrange explained: 'The Two Houses Consent to a Bill,' yet 'the Fiat, that superinduces an Authority, and is Only, and Properly the Act of Legislation, is singly in the King.'[57] Tories also concurred that the king was above the law. As Filmer had maintained, 'To Majestie or Sovereignty belongeth an Absolute Power not to be subject to any law.'[58] Likewise, Lawrence Womock insisted that 'no Sovereign is under the Coercive Power of his own Law.'[59] If the king broke the law, he certainly could not be resisted. As Thomas Pomfret put it in a thanksgiving sermon preached at Ampthill, Bedfordshire, in September 1683, for deliverance from the Rye House Plot, 'the Supreme Power, is both by God's express order, and the consent of all Nations, absolute and unaccountable.'[60] Champions of non-resistance did allow, however, for what they termed passive obedience. If a ruler commanded something that was contrary to the law of God, one had to obey God before man. One should never obey an ungodly command; but one could not actively resist, and one had to accept passively whatever punishments might be meted out for non-compliance.[61]

This did not mean, however, that the king could 'Reign without controul'. Even 'the most Absolute Prince' was 'subject to the Laws of his God, his own Conscience, and the Rules of Common Justice', explained one author; indeed, princes were 'tied and circumscribed in the exercise of their Power by Laws', though they were not 'restrained by the Efficient and Compulsive part of them, but by the Exemplary only'.[62] Indeed, most Tories would have held that a king could be both absolute and limited. Precisely how they struck the balance between the two varied from writer to writer.

All Tories were agreed that the kings of England were supposed to rule according to law, and that they were accountable to God if they did not. As L'Estrange wrote, the king promised 'at his Coronation to Observe All Just Laws', and he was 'Answerable to God for the Performance of That Promise' – though L'Estrange was quick to add that the king himself was 'the Judge of his Own Obligation'.[63] Goddard recognized that there was considerable disagreement over what was meant by 'an absolute Monarch', but felt that the various definitions offered by philosophers over the centuries shared the same fault: that they had failed to exclude tyranny. Goddard wanted 'to destroy the Tyrant, and yet preserve the absolute Monarch', and therefore defined 'an absolute Monarch' as one 'who having receiv'd a just authority, executes the Laws of God and Nature without controul'. This definition not only excluded usurpers, whose authority was not just, but also placed limits on obedience: such a ruler's power was so large, Goddard explained, 'that he who acts beyond it . . . is deservedly esteem'd a Tyrant, and in such case the people are not oblig'd to obey'. Goddard did not fully explore the implications of this remark, though he seems to have been thinking of passive resistance, explaining that 'the Prince never having receiv'd an authority to command that which is unjust, that is, contrary to the Laws of God and Nature, the people are acquitted from their obedience as to that particular command.' Elsewhere he was adamant that the only limitation on the kings of England was that they could not 'by their own Grant sever their Prerogatives from the Crown'; indeed, 'neither the King's Acts, nor any Act of Parliament' could 'give away his Prerogative'.[64] Even the most extreme Tories nevertheless embraced the rhetoric of rule by law. Thus the author of *An Apostrophe from the Loyal Party*, who pleaded with Charles 'to make your self a King' and 'at least for a time' to appear 'as absolute' over his people as the king of France, nevertheless insisted that God had brought about the Restoration so that Charles might govern his people 'in the strict observance of Justice and Equity; and after that perfect Model which he himself hath left . . . in his Sacred and Divine Laws'. Since, this author continued, Charles had given his 'Royal word' that 'our Laws' would be his 'Rule and Measure', by which he was 'resolved to Govern', then a little fear would not come amiss, and he should 'roar like the King of Lions' when he next met parliament, till he made it tremble, like his predecessor Henry VIII.[65]

Many Tory champions of monarchical authority proclaimed that the king was both above the law and also in some ways bound by it. Womock insisted he agreed with Bracton's dictum that 'The King in his Realm hath two Superiours, God and the Law.' He also said that 'The most high and absolute Power of the Realm of England, consisteth in the Parliament,' though he clarified this by stating that parliament comprised the king and the three estates (the Lord spiritual, the Lords temporal and the Commons). Yet Womock subsequently explained that the legislative power was not vested in the two houses of parliament, but rather belonged to the sovereign. Every law was an act of grace in the prince: when a new law was required, the Commons petitioned, the Lords assented to the petition, but it was the king who made the law. It was not 'the people's Law' but 'the Royal-Law, which the Prince prescribes unto Himself'. At the same time, Womock seems to have assumed that the king could enact laws that could limit his own power. Thus he suggested that parliament might redeem its honour by restoring 'what has been clipt off the Crown by surprize or fraud; and return what has been taken from the Prerogative by Duress'.[66] The author of *Antidotum Britannicum* insisted that the king of England was 'an absolute Monarch', whose power came from God, not from the people, and that 'the Two Houses of Parliament' had 'no share in the Legislative Power', which was vested 'solely in the King'. He even saw the king's legislative power as arbitrary. Discussing the fact that the king had the right to veto legislation, he asserted that 'The Supream Power is always Arbitrary; for that is Arbitrary which hath no Superior to controul it.' He further claimed that the king had the power to determine which parts of the law were current and which were not – in other words, that he had a certain discretion over which laws to enforce. At the same time this author could insist that 'the Government of England' was 'a rare and admirable mixture of Monarchy, Aristocracy, and Democracy', which had been 'so excellently tempered by the wisdom of our Ancestors' as to give the kingdom 'the conveniences of all, without the inconveniencies of any one' and to preserve both the king's prerogatives and the subjects' liberty. Thus the king could not 'make use of his high and Supream Power to the prejudice of those for whose good he hath it'; he could not make laws without the consent of the two houses; only the Commons had the right to introduce bills for the levying of taxation, and the Commons could also impeach those who had violated the law; while the Lords were 'trusted with a judiciary Power' to assist both the king and the people 'against the encroachments of the other'.[67]

Indeed, it was not uncommon to claim that the English monarchy was both absolute and mixed. As Warwick put it, 'We all know, that our Government is a mixt Monarchy, and yet by all Foreigners (as Bodin, Grotius, and others) is reputed an absolute Monarchy.' Warwick embraced patriarchalism and non-resistance, denounced coordination, and proclaimed that all persons were 'under the King, and the King under none'. Nevertheless, he recognized that the king could not make laws without the consent of the three estates in parliament (the nobility, clergy and commons), though the need for such consent did not mean that the king was not absolute, simply that he was 'not an arbitrary Monarch'. 'The raising of money or taxes' was 'one of those particulars' wherein the English monarch was 'limited', for he could not 'raise money upon the Subject, but by his Commons, and with the consent of the Lords, or by the concurrence of them both'.[68] Nalson insisted that 'so great and absolute [was] the Property of the English Subjects' that they could not be taxed without the consent of their representatives.[69] William Assheton maintained that the king of England was 'an Absolute Monarch' in the sense that he knew 'no Superior but God', was admitted to his kingdoms without 'any Limitations or Conditions', did not share his power with the three estates, and could not be resisted. Yet, Assheton went on, if

the King's Power, in respect of its Original, is Absolute, i.e. He received it from none but God . . . when we speak of the King's Authority, with respect to the Execution and Administration of it, the Case is very different. For the Kings of England out of their abundant Grace and Favour . . . have suffer'd themselves to be so limited in the Exercise of their Power; That they can neither make Laws, nor raise Taxes but in Parliament; much less can they pretend to take away the Life, or dispose of the Estate of the meanest of their Subjects but by due course of Law: And therefore in this second Consideration of his Authority . . . The King of England is not an Absolute but a limited Monarch.[70]

Opponents of Exclusion recognized that kings of England could dispense with the law, though only under certain specific circumstances. Thus the author of *Plain Dealing is a Jewel* of 1682 agreed that it was 'undoubtedly in the power of the King by His Royal Prerogative to dispence with the penalty of any Statute whatever . . . upon any Emergency of State', though only 'where the matter dispensed with [was] not *malum in se* [wrong in and of itself], but only *malum quia prohibitum* [wrong because prohibited]'. In other words, a king could not give someone a dispensation to commit murder, say, but he could dispense someone from a law which merely prohibited a particular type of activity that had been perfectly legal and morally acceptable before the law prohibiting it had been passed (say, a ban on trading with a particular foreign country). However, he could not, according to this author, suspend the law. For 'to Suspend a Law', the author explained, 'is in the nature of an Obrogation, and he that can obrogate may as well assume the power of making Laws'; a prince who can do that could make 'a Law to raise Mony and Forces' and would 'never need call a Parliament' and 'ergo may govern his

Subjects Arbitrarily at his Royal Pleasure'. The author offered such remarks in the context of discussing Charles's Declaration of Indulgence of 1672 – 'the only thing to my remembrance, done since the King's Restauration', he wrote, 'that had the least tendency to the setting up Arbitrary Power or Popery'. Not, he went on, that either of these was designed by the King, who merely wanted to ease the plight of the dissenters. Instead, those to blame were 'our Premier Minister of State' at that time – those who were also responsible for the Stop of the Exchequer and the anti-Dutch foreign policy in alliance with the French. Though he forbore to name names, it would have been clear to all readers that the principal person he was thinking of was the Earl of Shaftesbury.[71]

Paradoxically, therefore, monarchical absolutism was not an absolute; there could be different degrees of absolute authority. Thus Nalson, discussing Aristotle's assertion that monarchy was apt to degenerate into tyranny, claimed that this was possible only where monarchy was 'absolute, Arbitrary and unbounded'. 'In our English Monarchy', he went on, the case was 'clearly different', for, although the king was 'so absolute, that where he has not precluded himself by his gracious Concessions to his People, his will is his Law, and is not to be limited by any other Power than that of his own Royal pleasure', over the generations English sovereigns had in fact given so many 'gracious concessions' to their subjects as to set 'Bounds and Limits' to their 'absolute Sovereignty'.[72] For some Tories, the logic of this interpretation of the English constitution led them to conclude that English kings were not as absolute as they had once been, or even that they were no longer absolute at all. John Northleigh said that the old Britons, the Saxons, the Danish princes and the Normans for several successions 'were far more absolute than of late our succeeding Sovereigns', since over time kings had given several concessions to their subjects 'and dispens'd with that power and right enjoyed by their Royal Ancestors' – he cited in particular the fact that kings could not now levy taxes on their subjects without the latter giving their consent in parliament. And, although he denounced coordination, Northleigh was nevertheless adamant that the English monarchy should 'be call'd mixt in Opposition to its being Absolute and Tyrannical'.[73] One anonymous champion of divine-right monarchy, writing in 1679, insisted that he was not pleading 'for a Despotical Soveraignty, an absolute Power, such as the great Turk this day exercises over his Subjects'; rather, he maintained, he wanted 'only such Royal, Paternal Soveraignty, as we and our Ancestors have lived long, and happily under. This . . . hath its Royal Prerogatives inherent naturally in the Crown, and inseparably from it,' he continued, 'so it trencheth not upon the liberty of the person, or the propriety of the Goods of the Subjects, but in and by the lawful and just acts of Jurisdiction.'[74] L'Estrange did not like the term 'Mixt Government', because it implied 'Popular Participation of Power with the King', but he was happy to 'call it a Qualifi'd Government, so as to distinguish it from an Absolute and Unlimited Government'.[75]

William Sherlock, in his classic work condemning resistance theory, written in the aftermath of the Rye House Plot, forthrightly proclaimed that the English monarchy was limited and not absolute. 'The difference between an absolute and limited Monarchy', he explained, is 'not, that resistance is unlawful in one case, and lawful in another'; resistance could never be lawful. Rather, the difference was that 'an absolute Monarch is under no Law, but his own will; he can make and repeal laws at his own pleasure, without asking the consent of his Subjects; he can make what Taxes he pleases, and is not tied up to strict Rules and formalities of Laws in the execution of Justice.' It was 'quite contrarie in a Limited Monarchy, where the exercise of Soveraign Power is regulated by known and standing Laws, which the Prince can neither make nor repeal without the consent of the People', where 'no man can lose his Life or Estate without a legal process and Tryal', and no taxes be 'imposed on the Subject, but by the Authority of Parliament'. Sherlock rejoiced that, in the 'long succession of Princes in this Kingdom', no prince had ever 'cast off the Authority of Laws, or usurpt an absolute and arbitrary Power', and that there was 'no prospect' of 'ever our kings attempt[ing] to make themselves absolute'. And although in a limited monarchy 'Subjects must not resist such a Prince, who violates the Laws of his Kingdom', they were 'not bound to obey him in his usurpations' but 'to yield an active obedience onely according to Law'.[76] For Sherlock, the doctrine of passive resistance proved that the English monarchy was not absolute.

Valuable insights into the limits of the Tory belief in royal absolutism can be gleaned by looking at Dr Nathaniel Johnston's *The Excellency of Monarchical Government*, published in 1686. Johnston was an extreme high Tory – a believer in divine-right hereditary monarchy who was later to defend some of the stretches of the royal prerogative that occurred under James II and was to end his life a Jacobite. In several parts of his lengthy treatise he appears to be arguing that the English monarchy is absolute, 'unaccountable to any but God', protesting as he does against those who raise objections 'against the Absoluteness of the King's Power', and citing the great French theorist of absolutism, Jean Bodin, in defence of his position. Yet he is also at pains to show that the English monarchy is not 'Absolute, Arbitrary, and Unbounded'. Although 'Kings of England . . . are not limited by any other Power than their own Royal Pleasure,' Johnston affirms, nevertheless they have given many 'Concessions' to their subjects, which have been formed into laws, and these provide 'Mounds and Boundaries' which prevent English rulers from acting in 'an Arbitrary and Tyrannical way'. In particular, 'we have our Properties so well secured and provided for, by the gracious Grants of our sovereigns in Magna Charta, the Petition of Right, and other Acts.' Johnston further maintains that

The Kings of England may not rule their People by their Will, or by Proclamation . . . or make new Laws, or change any of the old standing Laws, without the mutual Consent of the two Houses of Parliament: He may not oppress the People, or in an Arbitrary way, take from them their Liberties or Estates, under any pretence whatsoever, without due course of Law . . . He cannot do anything against the Law of the Nation, or against common Right.

It is true that Johnston does insist 'That when a King doth not act according to such Laws, he is not thereby Capable of any Punishment for the transgressing of them'. Yet, in a section of his tract where he refutes Hobbes's assertion 'That the Sovereign should be so absolute and so arbitrary, that he should upon Exigents of State, or at his own pleasure, have the disposal of every Subjects fortune', Johnston acknowledges that 'in several Cases Actions may be brought in defence of a Man's right, even against the Crown', and not only admits that 'the Judges have pronounced Sentence against some claims of the King', but says that in such circumstances they 'ought to do so'.[77]

To the modern reader it might seem unclear exactly how English subjects benefited from living under this type of limited monarch if there was no way of bringing the king to account if he chose not to observe the limits. Johnston's mention of judges hints at the answer. Only the king was unaccountable, not his ministers or other public officials. As Sherlock put it, 'Though the Prince himself is unaccountable and irresistible, yet his Ministers may be called to an account, and . . . punish't' if they serve the prince 'contrary to Law'.[78] Likewise Rider stated that, although 'the king be always exempt' from the law, 'yet his officers and Ministers, without whom he can never execute his Will, are . . . still liable to Punishment, whenever they proceed contrary to Law, tho by the Kings command'.[79] A tract of 1680, discussing the dictum that the king could do no wrong, explained that the reason for this was because nothing could

be done in this Commonwealth by the King's grant, or any other Act of his, as to the Subject's Persons, Goods, Lands, or Liberties, but must be according to established Laws, which the Judges are sworn to observe, and deliver between the King and his People impartially, to Rich and Poor, High and Low; and therefore the Justices and the Ministers of Justice are to be questioned and punished if the Laws be violated.[80]

Based on their understanding of the English constitution, opponents of the Whigs concluded that Exclusion was not only unlawful but also unnecessary. It was unlawful because it would violate the divinely ordained succession, and subjects could no more depose the heir than a wife could depose her husband.[81] Secretary Jenkins, speaking in the Commons on 4 November 1680, thought Exclusion was 'contrary, not only to the law of God, but the law of the land too': 'It would change the essence of the monarchy, and make the crown elective.' It was also against the oath of allegiance, which bound 'all persons to the king, his heirs and successors'; moreover, it was not in parliament's power to 'disinherit the heir to the crown', and thus 'if such an Act should pass, it would be invalid in itself.'[82]

Yet Exclusion was also unnecessary, because the law would protect English Protestants under a popish successor. As Rider maintained, 'while our Laws stand firm and unrepealed, we cannot prudently apprehend any danger from a King, that must of necessity rule according to Law,' since 'no old Law [could] be annulled, nor new one enacted without our own consent and approbation in Parliament.'[83] The argument was repeated again and again. Indeed, Charles II had shown himself willing to impose additional limitations on a popish successor, telling MPs that 'the Restraints' with which he offered to bind his successor, 'together with those which are already in place upon Him', would make them 'as safe as Lawes can make you'.[84] Secretary Coventry insisted in the Commons in late April 1679 that he could 'never believe that a Prince' who came to the crown 'so clogged with prejudice against Popery' could 'ever set it up', and urged that it was up to MPs 'to make Tests and Oaths against it'.[85] In fact, even without further limitations, most opponents of Exclusion agreed that the Protestant religion was 'sufficiently guarded by several Acts of Parliament', which a future Catholic king could 'never repeal'.[86] Thus there was 'little danger of Popery prevailing' if a popish successor should happen to inherit the throne, the author of *Plain Dealing* thought, for he would not 'be able to break through the Laws, made for the Defence of our Religion', any more than he could 'Violate those made for Security of our Liberties and Properties': the law could be changed only with the consent of parliament, and the Test Acts ensured that no one could sit in parliament unless he had first renounced popery. Furthermore, no ruler could 'Govern Arbitrarily without a Force', and a Protestant parliament would never give a popish prince 'Revenue sufficient to maintain' a standing army.[87]

THE TORY CASE AGAINST POPERY AND ARBITRARY GOVERNMENT

The Tories did not merely maintain that Exclusion was unlawful and unnecessary; they insisted further that the King's subjects would be worse off if the Whigs were to get their way. They were well aware that the Whigs had aroused popular anxieties over a number of emotive issues in their efforts to bring pressure on the King to bar the

Catholic heir from the succession, and they knew that if they truly were to have any hope of bringing the people to their due allegiance they would need to find some way of alleviating these anxieties. They therefore addressed the same range of concerns as had the Whigs – over the prospect of arbitrary government, rule by a standing army, the threat to lives, liberties and estates, and the threat of popery – but sought to show that if people wanted to avoid all these evils they should rally behind the crown against the Exclusionist challenge. Yet in doing so they did not simply steal the Whigs' ideological clothes; in making their case against popery and arbitrary government, the Tories developed an ideological perspective that was distinct from that of the Whigs, and which was likely to appeal to a somewhat different constituency of support.

The starting point for the Tory case was that civil war was likely to follow if the Whigs were to get their way. In the Commons, York's friends took the line that when the succession had been interrupted in the past it had always led to civil war.[88] During the various Commons debates on Exclusion of May 1679, November 1680 and March 1681, several members even warned that if York were deprived of his inheritance he would descend upon the people of England with an army to recover his rights.[89] Likewise, a pamphlet penned by Halifax insisted that, the minute the Exclusion Bill passed, the Duke would be 'at liberty to recover his Right by secret or open Violence, Foreign or Domestic'.[90] The history of the Wars of the Roses was often recalled to show 'the Deplorable Miseries Which ever attended Doubtful Titles to the Crown', as the subtitle of one treatise on the wars put it.[91] Above all else, however, the Tories were worried about a possible repeat of the events of the 1640s and '50s. There seemed to be a frightening similarity between the tactics adopted by Shaftesbury and the Whigs and those of John Pym and the parliamentary opposition to Charles I in 1641 – both appealed to opinion out-of-doors through pamphleteering and used the specious pretence of the threat of popery to whip up popular opposition to the court.[92] Tory propagandists also pointed to the close alliance between the Whigs and the nonconformists, and suggested that the real aim of the Whigs, as with the parliamentarian Puritans of the 1640s, was to destroy the episcopalian Church establishment. In May 1679 Sir Thomas Clarges argued in the Commons that most of those who were for the Exclusion Bill 'were either presbyterians or their sons'.[93] Furthermore, if one followed through the logic of the Whig position, Tories insisted, it was clear that the Whigs truly aimed at a commonwealth. As one author put it, the Whigs 'under the notion of crying against Popery and Arbitrary Government, would pull down the King and the Bishops, and set up a Common-wealth again'.[94]

As the Exclusion Crisis unfolded – and especially once the Tory Reaction set in and hopes of an eventual parliamentary solution to the succession crisis began to disappear – some more radical Whigs did begin to contemplate more extreme action in order to secure their goals. Thus Shaftesbury's alleged Protestant Association of 1681 and the Rye House Plot of 1683 both seemed to confirm that the Whigs really were seeking to take England back down the path of civil war. As L'Estrange pointed out in his *Observator*, 'the Conspiracy of Eighty Three' was 'a Parallell of Forty One' –

The Method the same; the Positions the Same; the Pretences the Same; and the very Train of Prosecuting it, the very same too. The King, Calumniated; the Church Vilify'd; the Schismatiques, made the Godly Party; Popery suggested; his Majesties Friends made Papists; the King blam'd for not Hearkening to his Parliament; his Prerogative Invaded.[95]

However, this was 1683, and the Rye House Plot involved only a minority of the more extreme Whigs. The majority of Whigs refused to countenance extremist action, and, besides, before 1681 all were committed to achieving a peaceful, parliamentary, solution to the problem of the Catholic succession. Yet opponents of Exclusion were raising fears of civil war from the beginning of 1679. Moreover, Tories repeatedly talked about the threat posed by the Presbyterians, whereas the English Presbyterians were the most conservative of all English nonconformists. How much of a threat did they really pose? Within a purely English perspective, we may wonder how convincing Tory scaremongering about renewed civil war and the Presbyterian threat might have seemed. What we have to recognize, however, is that the Tories were not thinking within a purely English perspective; they were thinking within a multiple-kingdom framework.

As opponents of Exclusion were quick to point out, the English parliament had no right to determine the succession for Scotland or Ireland. If the Whigs excluded York in England, there was no guarantee that the Scots and Irish would accept this; indeed, it seemed inherently unlikely – especially in Scotland, where York had a demonstrable following and the line of the Stuarts was the ancient Scottish dynasty. If an Exclusion Bill were to pass in England, therefore, war between the three kingdoms would inevitably follow. During the Commons debate of 11 May 1679, Sir William Hickman argued that Scotland and Ireland would continue to back York and thus passing the Bill would 'entail a War for ever upon England'.[96] When the second Exclusion Bill was discussed in the Commons on 2 November 1680, Edward Seymour said, 'It cannot be imagined, that such a law will bind all here in England, or any in Scotland; and it is disputed whether it will be binding in Ireland: so that in all probability it will not only divide us amongst ourselves, but the three kingdoms one from the other, and occasion a miserable civil war.'[97] In the debate in the Lords on 15 November, Halifax insisted 'how imprudent it would be to declare the Duke an enemy to the State', when York 'was actually at the head of a powerfull Nation [Scotland], where there was an Army too', and when 'his power was no less considerable' in Ireland, 'where there was 10, or 15 Papists for one Protestant'.[98] York himself was convinced 'that Scotland and Ireland were both firme to his intrest'.[99] It seemed inevitable, as one Tory pamphleteer predicted, that Exclusion would 'imbroyl Three Kingdoms in a Bloody War, and destroy Thousands of Innocent Persons'.[100]

Many predicted that Scotland and Ireland would 'rejoice at another Civil War', in the hopes of freeing 'themselves from the Inconveniences of being Provinces'.[101] During the Exclusion debates of May 1679, York's supporters repeatedly insisted 'that Scotland . . . would never joyn in changing the Succession', but 'would catch at such an occasion to separate again from England'.[102] Independence would also inevitably follow if the English decided to move down the path towards a commonwealth. As Goddard asked, 'what reason hath Scotland to truckle under the Dominion of the English Commonalty', and why should Ireland agree to 'become a Province to an English Parliament'? Yet if the three kingdoms became independent once again, dire consequences would follow. 'Shall these people', Goddard continued to ask, 'notoriously known to have hated one another, whilst formerly they were under different Governours, become the strictest friends, when they shall return unto those circumstances, under which they were the greatest enemies?' And would the French king 'take no advantage . . . of our Divisions'? It was, Goddard thought, difficult to foresee anything 'but most desperate wars'.[103] And what if the Exclusionists were to be defeated in these wars? Halifax thought that York would easily find a party 'in the Three Kingdoms to fight his Quarrel', and if he were to come in 'by Force' he might 'use us like a conquer'd Nation, break our old, and give us what Laws and Religion he pleases'.[104]

The British dimension further helps us to understand why the Tories were so concerned about the Presbyterian threat. They were not simply associating the Whigs with the English Presbyterians; they were associating them with the Scottish Presbyterians. That was, after all, why they called the Exclusionists 'Whigs' in the first place – it was a shortened form of 'whiggamore', a Scottish Presbyterian rebel. As we have seen, in Scotland there did exist a radical strand of Presbyterianism which continued to cause problems for the Restoration regime throughout the 1660s and '70s (even if this radicalism was in part created by the stern measures the authorities took to try to suppress dissent): the field conventiclers of the south-west had risen in armed rebellion in 1666; in 1668 the convenanting minister James Mitchell and some associates had hatched an unsuccessful plot to assassinate the Archbishop of St Andrews, Dr Sharp, a leading advocate of the policy of repression; and in 1679 Sharp actually was murdered by radical covenanters. Then in the spring of 1679 the convenanters rose in rebellion once more, and this seemed to confirm that the crisis of the three kingdoms which had led to civil war in the 1640s was threatening to play itself out again. In his initial revelations of the Popish Plot, Oates had in fact predicted a rerun of the events of 1637–42: Jesuits, disguised as Presbyterians, would first stir up the Scots to rebel as a precursor to rebellions in Ireland and England. The first step had now come true; Ireland seemed far from stable; and Shaftesbury and his associates seemed to be imitating the tactics of the parliamentary opposition of 1641. This was why Tories argued that '41 was come again. And, although the Bothwell Bridge rebellion was put down by the government, the radical covenanting faction the Cameronians continued to pursue their crusade against Charles II and the Duke of York, and in a series of public proclamations proceeded to declare war against the royal brothers and call for them to be overthrown.[105]

The Tory press frequently highlighted the danger posed by the radical Presbyterians north of the border, seeking to taint the English nonconformists by association. In a lengthy tract published in 1678, L'Estrange compared 'the Platform of the Scottish Presbytery' with the position of the English Presbyterians, in order 'to observe the Harmony betwixt Simeon and Levi'.[106] Another pamphleteer, writing shortly after the dissolution of the Oxford Parliament specifically against the tactics of the English Whigs, posed the question whether 'the Phanaticks' were as 'truely zealous' for the preservation of the present government as they claimed. In Charles I's time, he asserted, they had made 'the whole Kingdom a Bloody Theatre', and, after asking what signs they had since given of their repentance for committing 'such hellish Tragedies', he replied, 'No other than that they have drawn the Sword in Scotland.'[107] The tactics pursued by the English Whigs were often interpreted against a Scottish backdrop. Northleigh thought that Shaftesbury's alleged Association to guard against a Catholic succession paralleled the Scottish Covenant of 1643: 'Now there remains nothing to do', he sarcastically remarked, 'but to drive the King out of his Palace, Proclaim all his followers Delinquents; all his adherents Enemies to King and Countrey; send post to Scotland, Messengers to the Field-Conventicles, get another Army from the North, swallow a second Solemn League; and then we shall have exactly a second 43.'[108] The same writer was later to claim that Shaftesbury's March 1679 speech in the Lords, declaiming against the sufferings of the Scots, was responsible for animating Scottish zealots to murder the Archbishop of St Andrews and prompting the Bothwell Bridge rebellion.[109] One loyal balladeer rhymed that

> . . . all that have Eyes,
> Be they foolish, or wise,
> May see the sly Presbyter through his disguise;

> Their Brethren in Scotland have made it well known,
> By murd'ring their Bishop, what sins are their own.[110]

In November 1681 the authors of *Heraclitus Ridens* pointed out that it was 'not so long since the Cargillites in Scotland set themselves up for the only true Protestants there', as the English Whigs had done in England, and thus there was 'no great difference between our rigid Whigs and them, but only that ours are greater masters in the Art of the Cloak'.[111]

The government and the Tory press found there was much mileage simply in reporting the activities of the radical covenanters north of the border, partly in the hope of condemning the English Whigs by association, but also simply to try to frighten the King's English subjects into remaining loyal. In November 1680 the *London Gazette* carried an account of the trial, in Edinburgh, of the Scottish covenanter James Skein, who not only refused to renounce Bothwell Bridge, the murder of the Archbishop of St Andrews, or Cargill's Covenant, but insisted that there was 'a Declared War between those that serve the Lord, and those that serve the King against the Covenant', that it was 'lawful to Kill any of the King's Counsellors and Soldiers in defence of the Gospel', and that it was even lawful to kill the King for being in breach of the covenant.[112] In March 1682 Thompson reported how about twenty fanatics in Lanark 'fell upon' a soldier while his party were away getting provisions: 'having seized him', they 'first cut off his Nose, Ears, and Privities, then pull'd out his Eyes and Tongue; and having cut off every Finger and Toe one after another, left him in that miserable condition, that he might be the longer dying, and then fled'.[113]

The political views of the radical covenanters raised questions about their moral principles. One author complained that the Scots had been 'brought into such a corruption of Morals, as has not been hitherto known among Christians'.[114] A humorous tract of 1682 accused the covenanters in Scotland of all forms of sexual promiscuity and licentiousness: 'Yea Buggery, Bestiality, incest, Adultery'.[115] George Hickes's account of the covenanting preacher James Mitchell, who was eventually executed in January 1678 for his part in the assassination plot against Archbishop Sharp, carried similar accusations, and even referred to the covenanters as 'Filthy, Cruel, Lying Ranters'. Hickes also discussed Mitchell's associate, Major Weir, who was indicted on 9 April 1670 on charges of incest, adultery and bestiality (with a mare and a cow). Weir, who confessed to the charges, was sentenced to be strangled at the stake and his body burned. At his execution, Hickes tells us, 'the Body of this Unclean Beast gave manifest tokens of its impurity, by the erection of his Yard, and emission of Seed, as soon as it began to be heated by the Flames.'[116]

This hints at another important strand of the Tory case against dissenters: ridicule. There was certainly a real threat to take seriously: the radical Presbyterians north of the border had dangerous ideas and threatened civil peace; going down the road of 1637–41 and hence to 1642 was no laughing matter. But of course it has always been a classic tactic for propagandists to make the enemy appear laughable or ridiculous – objects not only of scorn but also of humour. And, if Protestant nonconformists south of the border were tainted, in part, by association with the Scottish Presbyterians, it should not be forgotten that Tory satirists had plenty of material to work with within England and Wales as well. L'Estrange repeatedly ridiculed dissenters. 'There goes a story of some of them', he wrote in one of his tracts, 'that made it a Matter of Religion, to Piss a Bed, and Ride Hobby-Horses, because it is said, Except you become as little Children, you shall not enter into the Kingdom of Heaven.'[117] Jokes circulated satirizing their beliefs, such as the one about 'the Welshmen refusing to pay their debts, because crossing of Books was Popery'.[118] Aphra Behn's play *The Roundheads*, which was put on in the London theatres in 1682, attacked the alleged hypocrisy of the Puritans and accused them of sexual licentiousness.[119] It was a theme that Thompson's *Intelligence* frequently addressed with relish. In September 1681 Thompson published an account of how 'an Anabaptist' from Carlisle 'was Committed to the Gaol for getting his own Natural Mother with Child'. In June 1682 he carried a story of how a Devon man who had stayed away from church for over ten years 'and been a great frequenter of Conventicles, hath (by that means) been a great Proficient in the Art of Bastard-getting'. Apparently, straight after 'the hearing of their Spiritual Exercise' he would exercise 'the Carnal Comforts upon one of the Holy Sisters; by which means (with the help of some

Brothers)', the report alleged, 'there has been in a little time at least a dozen Bastard-children begotten'. Indeed, it was 'feared they will in time erect a common Stews, if they be not suddenly suppressed'.[120]

Not only did the Tories try to scaremonger by suggesting that civil war would probably follow if the Whigs got their way; they also sought to insinuate that the Whigs were the true promoters of popery and arbitrary government. The real threat of arbitrary government, Tories concluded, came from those who pretended to clamour against it.[121] Any alteration in the succession, the author of *Plain Dealing is a Jewel* predicted, could only 'be maintained by a . . . standing Army', for York was 'an Excellent Soldier', and was bound to have help from friends here and allies abroad 'to assist him in recovering his Right'. 'And if such an Army must be raised', this author continued, 'must not the People of England pay them'? And 'what Arbitrary Power' might 'that Prince . . . set up, that hath such an Army at his Devotion'?[122] If civil war were to break out, and the Whigs were to be victorious, arbitrary government would inevitably follow – as it had in mid-century. L'Estrange recalled that during the 1640s and '50s the legal government of England, in both Church and state, had been overturned in the most arbitrary manner and English liberties totally destroyed.[123] Similarly, Nalson alleged that during this time the dissenters had 'governed with the most Arbitrary Injustice imaginable'; they had 'Taxed, Assessed, Decimated, Fined, Imprisoned, Sequestred, Plundred, Banished'. In short, they set up 'their uncontrolled will and pleasure' as 'theirs and our only Law'.[124] In the 1650s, Nalson pointed out in another tract, laws were even passed without the consent of a parliament, and under Cromwell Englishmen were governed essentially by the will of the Protector and his officers, and by a standing army.[125] The author of *A Plea for Succession* argued that Exclusion would lead to civil war, which would in turn lead to 'severe Taxations, Which Payments must be rais'd not according to Laws' but by the pleasures of those who had usurped power; 'our Persons and Estates' would lie 'at the mercy of every Proud and Greedy Committee' – 'the Height, and Perfection, of what is Arbitrary' – and there must necessarily be 'a standing Army'.[126] The frontispiece to Sir Thomas May's 1683 history of England's mid-century experiment with republicanism – revealingly entitled *Arbitrary Government*

Display'd in the Tyrannick Usurpation of the Rump Parliament, and Oliver Cromwell – was an elaborate print which showed the commonwealth as a dragon, with armed troops on its neck, breathing the fiery motto 'A blessed reformation'. At its front end was the food necessary to feed this monster: laws, customs, episcopacy; monarchy, statues; Magna Carta, prerogative, privileges, liberty; church land and tithes; nobility and house of peers; and 'gaine' (i.e. economic prosperity). In its stomach was parliament. At its rear end were 'the Fruits of a Commonwealth', with the dragon being shown excreting taxes, excise, assessments, loan money, and oaths of covenants, engagements and abjuration. Its tail was a chain, labelled 'Liberties', which was rounding up the Anglican clergy, with the caption 'O wonderfull Reformation'.[127]

Tory propagandists often played on elite fears of a potential threat to the political and social hierarchy from the lower orders. The Whigs, a loyal ballad from 1682 proclaimed, wanted to 'teach the Nobles how to bow, / And keep their Gentry down'.[128] In an assize sermon preached at Chester in 1682, John Allen advised 'the Nobility, the Gentry, [and] the Freeholders in general' to 'remember how much they suffered respectively, in their Honours or Estates, in their Liberties and Properties, by Popular fury, and Military insolence'.[129] Yet, although they inveighed against what they saw as the anarchy of popular government and prayed for deliverance from 'the Insolent Rabble',[130] the Tories were nevertheless concerned to show that they, rather than the Whigs, truly had the best interest of the lower orders at heart. 'The Common sort' should consider, one broadside intoned, 'that in all Tumults and Seditions, their Lives are chiefly Sacrificed'.[131] During the Civil War and Interregnum, L'Estrange recalled, heavy taxes had robbed the lower orders of what little property they had. He also pointed out how the Puritan attack on traditional pastimes – 'Comedies, Interludes, Wrastlings, Foot-Ball Play, May-Games, Whitson-Ales, Morrice-Dances, Bear-Batings, etc.' – had made people's lives a misery.[132] The Whigs were not really interested in preserving 'the Lives, Liberties and Properties of the people'; they wanted to 'be disposers thereof' themselves.[133]

Opponents of Exclusion also sought to turn the charge of popery against the Whigs. Again, this was quite easy to do once the Tories had established that the Whigs were at heart political and religious radicals bent on overthrowing the existing establishment in Church and state. The reasoning worked at a number of different levels. One was by analogy. The pope's ultimate aim was to overthrow the Protestant monarchy and the Church of England; yet this was exactly what the parliamentarian Puritans had managed to achieve in the 1640s. As one author put it, 'the Papists would destroy our Church and State; so would the Commonwealthsmen'; but, whereas the Catholics had 'only plotted to do so', the 'Phanatick Protestants' had actually succeeded in overthrowing 'a Protestant Church' and murdering 'a Protestant King'.[134] Similarly L'Estrange asked: was not the 'Devillish Murder' of Charles I and 'the Subversion of the Church of England, a matter of Rejoycing, and Advantage, to the Church of Rome'?[135] A related line of reasoning was that the Whigs and dissenters, by their actions, would unwittingly help promote popery. The Whig demand for religious toleration risked letting the Catholics in at the back door; indeed, a number of schemes that had been tried in the 1660s and '70s to secure liberty of conscience for Protestant dissenters (notably the royal Indulgences of 1662 and 1672) had also extended certain religious freedoms to English Catholics. As the authors of *Heraclitus Ridens* put it, 'Popery could never come into England, unless the Phanatiques let it in at the back door of Toleration.'[136] One Anglican cleric, preaching on 5 November 1682, feared that the dissenters might 'bring us againe into that corrupt religion, by provoking God to take away the light we have so long abused'.[137] Others stressed that the domestic divisions that the Whigs were creating could only serve the interests of France and Rome. Some even suggested that the Whigs and papists were working together in a deliberate alliance, and that the dissenters were papists in masquerade, or French pensioners.[138] The point was perhaps not as far-fetched as it may seem. Shaftesbury and the country opposition to Charles II had worked with the Duke of York in 1675 to try to force Charles II to dissolve the Cavalier Parliament, while some Whigs had accepted payments from the French king during the early stages of the Exclusion Crisis, at a time when Louis XIV saw it as being in France's best interests to neutralize Charles II on the foreign-policy front by keeping him embroiled at home.

The main thrust of Tory reasoning, however, was that the political principles of Whigs and dissenters – especially their views on resistance – were quite literally Catholic in origin. Preaching on the anniversary of the regicide in 1682, Pelling maintained that 'the Principles, upon which those Delicate Protestants . . . acted, when they fought against their King . . . were once the Proper Creed of the Jesuites'; they were taught 'originally', he explained, 'by Mariana, by Bellarmine, by Azorius, and divers Jesuites more'.[139] Likewise Hickes, in his sermon before the London Artillery Company of November 1682, insisted that the Whig view that the people were the fountain of power and that princes forfeited their power if they broke their trust was 'a Popish principle, because the Papists, of all Christians, first taught it, to arm the subjects at their pleasure against their Sovereign, and by that means to revenge themselves upon the Princes that would not submit unto the Pope'.[140] Popery was a religion 'full of rebellious Principles', one author averred; but so too was the religion of Knox, Buchanan and Baxter. Indeed, 'some of the very Reformers of our Religion, have been so little Friends to Monarchy, and so much agreed with the Romanists they dissented from, as to tolerate . . . the dangerous Doctrine of deposing Kings.'[141] If 'a Queen Elizabeth Protestant' coolly surveyed 'the Writings of our Modern Pamphleteers', another proclaimed, 'He must justly conclude, that the Jesuits and some sort of Protestants are of a Clubb.'[142] It was 'a Protestant's Duty', one Wiltshire cleric insisted in May 1682, 'to defend the Birth-right of Kings'; it was 'not lawful to depose or exclude them from their lawful Inheritance, as these two Brethren, the Papist and Presbyterian, maintain by their Doctrine and Practice'.[143]

Most Tories and Anglican divines professed to be as vehemently opposed to popery as they were to Protestant dissent. In a sermon preached on 5 November 1681, Pelling first justified the split with Rome before going on to condemn the various atrocities he believed had been committed by the Catholic Church in Europe and England over the previous century and a half:

witness the continual Diabolical attempts which have been made against This Kingdom in every age since the beginning of the Reformation; as the Troubles under King Henry the 8th, the Insurrections under King Edward the 6th, the huge Sacrifices and Offerings by fire under Q. Mary; the Spanish Invasion; and Domestick Conspiracies under Q. Elizabeth, and . . . the Powder Plot under King James.

And witness the Popish Plot, he even added.[144] Some supporters of the court, however, with an eye to courting the favour of the heir to the throne, claimed that the Protestant dissenters were worse than the Catholics. Goddard, in a tract of 1684 dedicated to York, thought the papists might be more safely tolerated than the dissenters, since the dissenters 'did actually destroy both our lawful King and Governour, as well as government', whereas 'the Papists have ventured both their lives and fortunes to support our present Government, as it is by Law established, even against these very Dissenters.' Goddard went on to argue that most Catholics (with the exception of the Jesuits) no longer supported the pope's deposing power, and thus could be loyal even to a Protestant monarch.[145]

L'Estrange encapsulated the Tory case against the Whigs in brilliant fashion in an illustrated broadside of 1680 called *The Committee; Or, Popery in Masquerade*. The broadside is divided in two, the top half being a print, the bottom an explanatory poem; it is something that could have been 'read' by literates and illiterates alike. The print recalls the turmoils of the 1640s and '50s. It shows a committee seated around a table, presided over by a Presbyterian and representing the different Protestant religious sects that emerged during the Civil War and Interregnum: a Muggletonian, raving; a Ranter, ranting; a Quaker, telling arguments on his fingers; an Anabaptist, holding a dagger; an Independent, arguing with the rest; a Fifth Monarchist; the radical Quaker James Naylor, preaching; and an Adamite, naked. Over their heads is a scroll which reads, 'Behold we are a Covenanting People.' On the table are papers inscribed, 'Church and Crown Lands', 'Sequestrations', 'Remonstrances', 'Petitions', 'Courts of Justice' and 'Humiliation'. Standing before the committee are an 'Elder's Mayd', shouting 'No service book', with her dog barking 'No bishops', and two petitioners (a Quaker and an ass), crying out 'No Popish Lords' and 'No evill Counsellors.' On the left side of the picture is a mob of men carrying a crown, a mitre and banners inscribed 'A Thorough Reformation', 'Liberty', 'Property' and

'Religion', and leading in chains the Earl of Strafford (the chief minister of Charles I's personal rule, attainted for high treason and executed in 1641), Archbishop Laud (the architect of Charles I's religious policy, executed in 1645) and Sir Richard Gurney (the royalist Lord Mayor of London of 1641–2, impeached by the Long Parliament in the summer of 1642). Before their feet are the sceptre, orb and bust of Charles I. On the right are reminders of what this alliance of mob and schismatics had brought: sequestered livings, excise, army accounts, ordinances, widows' tears, and the blood of orphans. Among the things discarded by the committee are the Holy Bible and Magna Carta. In the top left-hand corner we can see through a window a 'close Caball' plotting against Church and state. In the top right we see peering out of a double-framed window Isaac Pennington, the promoter of London's root-and-branch petition against episcopacy of December 1640, and the pope, who is encouraging the committee with the words 'Courage, mes enfants.' Underneath the pair is a banner which reads, 'A Solemn League and Covenant: Come and let us join our Selves unto the Lord in a perpetuall Covenant that shall not be forgotten.'[146]

In many respects, then, Tory propagandists exploited the same fears and anxieties and appealed to the same catchphrases as the Whigs. Thus they claimed to be against popery and arbitrary government, for the Protestant religion and the rule of law, and keen to protect the people's lives, liberties and properties. Yet it would be wrong to suggest that the Tories simply stole the Whigs' ideological clothes. Tories and Whigs may have been for and against the same general things, but they were for and against them in very different ways. The Whigs were pro-dissent, and critical of the Established Church; the Tories anti-dissent and staunch defenders of the existing Church establishment. The Whigs championed the sovereignty of parliament and even claimed that the original foundation of power was in the people; the Tories denied both. Those people whose support for the Whigs had stemmed from a superficial concern about the prospect of popery and arbitrary government might conceivably have been persuaded to return to their 'due allegiance' by Tory arguments that the real threat of popery and arbitrary government came from the Whigs themselves. But those whose identification with the

The father and son who were both to lose their three kingdoms. Charles I was to die with a certain dignity on the scaffold on 30 January 1649; James II (here Duke of York) was to run away in December 1688.

The man whom all the fuss was over: Charles II's younger brother and heir, James, Duke of York, whom the Whigs wanted to exclude from the succession on account of his Catholicism.

The epitome of French Catholic influence at the court of Charles II: the royal mistress Louise de Kéroualle, Duchess of Portsmouth, typically referred to as 'Carwell' (the Anglicized version of her name) in the verse satire of the period.

One of the most shameful moments in English history: the Dutch sail up the Medway to Chatham in June 1667 and destroy four of the navy's largest vessels and capture the English flagship.

The Great Fire of London: 'In sixteen hundred and sixty six, London town was burnt to sticks.' The Monument built to commemorate where the fire started still stands in Pudding Lane; in 1681 it was affixed with the inscription: 'This Pillar was sett up in Perpetual Remembrance of that most Dreadfull Burning of this Protestant City, Begun and Carried on by the Treachery and Malice of the Papists.'

The man who ruled
Ireland for much of
this period: James
Butler, 1st Duke of
Ormonde.

The most influential man in Scottish politics in the 1660s and 1670s, the 'proud,
ambitious, insolent and imperious' John Maitland, Duke of Lauderdale, with his wife,
regarded by contemporaries as beautiful, greedy and ambitious.

Thomas
Sborne
Duke
Leed
ather to
Ann
oke.

Charles II's leading
minister in the mid-
1670s and the effective
founder of the Church
and King party: Thomas
Osborne, Earl of Danby.

Courtier turned
Country politician
and subsequently
one of the leaders
of the first Whigs:
Anthony Ashley
Cooper, 1st Earl
of Shaftesbury.

Whig print from the Exclusion Crisis depicting a Tory layman and a Tory cleric ('Tantivee') galloping off towards Rome; the Pope offers the cleric promotion to a bishopric. Tory publicist Roger L'Estrange appears as the dog Towzer, barking the words 'Forty One'.

Illustration to a Tory broadside celebrating the stance taken by the loyal London apprentices in defence of Church and State against the Whigs.

The man who started it all with his revelations of a Popish Plot: the unsavoury Titus Oates.

The Tory case against the Whigs in a nutshell. Roger L'Estrange, the Tories' most prolific propagandist, said it all in this one print (see pp. 249–50).

A representation of the Whig pope-burning procession in London of 17 November 1680 – for those who missed the event, and for those who did not but who wanted a reminder of what had taken place.

Whigs had stemmed from a more profound understanding of what the Whig platform had been all about, or whose concern about the security of their lives, liberties and estates had arisen from their personal experience of rule under the restored monarchy, were highly unlikely to have been persuaded to abandon their Whiggery by Tory propaganda; indeed, they would only have been further alienated by it. Tory propaganda, in other words, was divisive as much as it was consensus-building. It aimed to turn people who saw themselves as loyal supporters of the Established Church and the Restoration monarchy against those whom the Tories defined as the enemy within.

What of the Duke of York himself? It was not enough simply to insist that it was unnecessary or undesirable to exclude him from the succession. Tory propagandists had also to construct a positive image of the Catholic heir, to show that it was actually desirable to have him as the next king. One way they did this was by stressing York's supposed military prowess and bravery. After all, had he not shown himself to be a successful naval commander, particularly in the wars against the Dutch of 1664–7 and 1672–4: 'a great Hero of loud Fames First Rate', as one poet put it; virtuous and courageous, a good man who would make a good king, in the opinion of another?[147] Thorogood believed that York was 'the most passionate Lover of his Country', a man of 'invincible Courage, of mature Wisdom, and singular Industry and Application to business'; should he become king the country would 'undoubtedly be as happy' under him 'as under any that swayed the English Scepter since the Conquest'.[148]

Opponents of Exclusion also argued that, despite being a Catholic, York would protect the Church of England. The author of *Plain Dealing is a Jewel* insisted that people did not know the Duke if they thought him so irreligious or void of understanding of his own interest 'as to accept the Crown, [and] take the Coronation Oath' if he did not intend 'to keep and observe the same, by Governing according to Law, and securing his Subjects in Peace, by preserving to them their Religion, as well as their Liberties and Properties'.[149] Tories based this opinion not on blind faith in the Duke's integrity, but rather on seeing him in action as head of state – in Scotland. During the Exclusion Crisis, Charles had twice sent his brother into temporary exile in Scotland – from November 1679 to February 1680, and again from October 1680 to March 1682 – and York had to all intents and purposes served as viceroy there. His hatred of the Scottish Presbyterians led him to form a firm alliance with the episcopalian interest north of the border, and this so impressed the Scottish bishops that they wrote a number of letters to their episcopal brethren in England assuring them that the Duke would prove a good friend to the Established Church.[150] The Tory press was quick to hold up York's conduct in Scotland as indicative of what an excellent ruler he would be if he came to the throne of England. One pamphleteer, writing in 1681, told how York's 'noble Acts' for Scotland's well-being had procured him 'a general respect' and tied the hearts of the Scottish people to him 'in Loyalty and Affection'; Scotland had been 'in a most thriving Posture' ever since York had been in charge, 'And now, like the Sun, he begins to shine with greater Splendor.'[151] In March 1682 Thompson reported how the Scottish bishops had informed the Archbishop of Canterbury 'what great Benefit the Church there hath received by the presence of His Royal Highness, who hath been a great Repairer of their Breaches, and put a stop to the growth of Schism . . . And that he did both privately and publickly demonstrate his Zeal to the Church of England'.[152] The author of *A Plea for Succession* insisted that York should be judged by 'His Conduct', pointing out that 'He hath, like a cheering Sun, thaw'd the Northern World, and overcome the Scottish Nation; not with Arms, but with Love, and Wisdom; where He is now become, next His Majesty, the Pride, and Darling of the Age.'[153] Thus Scotland not only explained why Exclusion was impossible (without civil war), it also provided empirical proof of why the English would have nothing to fear from this particular popish successor.

THE DISSOLUTION OF THE OXFORD PARLIAMENT AND THE IDEOLOGY OF THE TORY REACTION

The crucial turning point in the Exclusion Crisis proved to be the dissolution of the Oxford Parliament at the end of March 1681. Even though Charles had opened the meeting on the 21st with a speech re-emphasizing his opposition to Exclusion, the Commons immediately moved to bring in another Exclusion Bill. The Lords and Commons then became at loggerheads over the proposed impeachment of the Irish Plot informer Edward Fitzharris for an alleged libel against the King. It was business as normal – or, as far as the effective running of the country was concerned, no business as usual – and Charles had had enough. On 28 March, just after the lower house had completed its first reading of the Exclusion Bill, Charles summoned the Commons for immediate attendance in the House of Lords, dissolved the parliament, and then made haste to Windsor. His decision not to call another parliament for the rest of his reign destroyed any possibility of an Exclusion Bill passing, while the dissolution was followed by a rigorous drive against the government's political and religious enemies intended to destroy the Whig power base at the local level.

A prerequisite for rule without parliament was royal financial independence. Three days before the meeting of the Oxford Parliament, Charles concluded another secret treaty with the King of France, whereby Louis XIV agreed to pay Charles 5 million livres over the next three years if he did not call a parliament to support Spain against France. In total Charles collected some 4,300,000 livres (c. £322,500) from the French king between March 1681 and February 1685; Louis made good the shortfall to James II. Not that Charles became a complete puppet of the French king – in late 1681, for example, he threatened to call parliament if Louis invaded Flanders or Holland – but the French subsidy certainly afforded him room for manoeuvre at home. Charles was also able to divert funds from Ireland, whose economy was doing rather well in the early 1680s, though the sums involved were modest – a mere £30,000 each year from 1684. The main reason for the King's new-found financial independence, however, was increased revenues from customs and excise, due to improved efficiency in collection (following the government's decision to stop farming out the customs in 1671, ironically one of Shaftesbury's initiatives as Chancellor of the Exchequer), the expansion of English trade following peace with the Dutch in 1674, and then the lifting of the French trade embargo in 1681. By 1681–2 customs and excise were yielding £1.29 million (compared to about

£800,000 in the early years of the Restoration); by 1684–5 the figure was £1.37 million.[154]

On 8 April, Charles followed the dissolution of the Oxford Parliament by issuing a declaration explaining why he had taken the action he had against his previous two parliaments.[155] It was a skilfully crafted document, probably penned by Sir Francis North,[156] designed to turn public opinion decisively against the Whigs and dissenters and to associate the crown firmly with a defence of the true Protestant religion, the traditional English constitution, and the subjects' liberties at law. To ensure that it reached as wide an audience as possible, the government ordered it to be read in all churches and chapels throughout England.[157] The Scottish lawyer Sir John Lauder of Fountainhall was surprised by the initiative, claiming that 'some think a prince at a losse when he is put to give ane accompt of his actions, or to apologize to his subjects.'[158] Modern historians, however, recognize it as brilliant propaganda coup.[159]

Charles opened his declaration by protesting that 'it was with exceeding great trouble' that he was 'brought to the Dissolving of the Two Last Parliaments', but he insisted he had been left with no alternative. Despite telling the last Westminster parliament that he would secure his subjects 'against all their just Fears' and 'concur in any Remedies that could be proposed for the Security of the Protestant Religion, that might consist with preserving the Succession of the Crown, in its due and legal Course of Descent', he had met with 'the most unsuitable Returns from the House of Commons'. And despite warning the Oxford Parliament 'of the Errors of the former', in the hope of preventing 'the like Miscarriages', and promising 'to hearken to any Expedient by which the Religion Establish'd might be preserv'd, and the Monarchy not Destroyed', it had soon become clear that 'no Expedient would be entertain'd, but that of a total Exclusion.' Echoing points made by opponents of Exclusion in parliament and the press, Charles explained that, 'After the sad Experience . . . of the late Civil Wars', he could not consent to a law that would 'establish another most Unnatural War, or at least make it necessary to maintain a Standing Force for the Preserving the Government and the Peace of the Kingdom'. Besides, he had good reason to believe that Exclusion was intended as a prelude to more wide-scale constitutional change. When the Lords and Commons fell out over the impeachment of Fitzharris, it was clear that the two houses were incapable of transacting any business together, so 'We found it necessary to put an end to this Parliament likewise.' Yet, Charles insisted, this did not mean 'that we intend to lay aside the use of Parliaments'. 'No Irregularities in Parliaments', he emphasized, could 'ever make Us out of Love with Parliaments, which we look upon as the best Method for healing the Distempers of the Kingdom, and the onely means to preserve the Monarchy in that due Credit and Respect which it ought to have both at home and abroad'. He was thus resolved 'to have frequent Parliaments', and he would do his utmost 'both in and out of Parliament . . . to extirpate Popery, and to Redress all the Grievances of Our good Subjects, and in all things to Govern according to the Laws of the Kingdom'. Indeed, he hoped that 'a little time' would 'so far open the Eyes of all Our good Subjects, that Our next meeting in Parliament, shall perfect that Settlement and Peace which shall be found wanting either in Church or State'. He ended by recalling that 'Religion, Liberty and Property were all lost and gone, when the Monarchy was shaken off, and could never be restored till that was restored.' The declaration contained no hint of any royal pretension to absolute power; the emphasis was on the King's commitment to parliamentary government and the rule of law.

Charles reaffirmed his determination to stick by the law on a number of occasions. In his opening speech to the Oxford Parliament he had urged MPs to 'make the laws of the land [their] rule', adding that he was 'resolved they shall be mine'.[160] He reiterated his promise to 'stick to that that is law' shortly after the dissolution of the Oxford Parliament, as also to 'maintain the Church as it is now established'.[161] He not only would 'govern by law' but also would use the law to defeat the challenge of the Whigs and their nonconformist allies – points he made time and time again.[162] Tory polemicists repeatedly drove home the point about the King's commitment to the rule of law and the need to use the law to defeat the enemies of Church and state. Dryden, in his famous poem *Absalom and Achitophel*, has Charles II declare, 'The law shall still direct my peaceful sway, / And the same law teaches rebels to obey.' He later adds, 'Law they require, let Law then show her face.'[163] In May 1682

L'Estrange proclaimed in his *Observator*, 'That's the Best Government that has the Best Laws; And those are the Best Governors, that Cause those Laws to be duly Executed.' In a later issue he has his Whig protagonist proclaim, 'The King has promis'd . . . to Govern by Law; And I hope he'l be as good as his Word,' to which the Observator replies, 'Why then, You and I are Agree'd at last; for . . . I hope so too,' adding, 'And then the putting of the Laws in Execution, will do the Kings bus'ness, and the bus'ness of All his Loyall subjects, Both in One.'[164] In particular, supporters of the court urged the need for a strict enforcement of the laws against Protestant nonconformists, and condemned the misguided leniency of the previous few years. 'I grant Moderation to be many times seasonable,' John Northleigh wrote in 1682, 'but not when Transgressors break the Laws most Immoderately . . . The Law certainly is the greatest, and only Pillar to support the Church, and State.'[165] And it was an ideology which undoubtedly had a powerful purchase in the localities. As the Bishop of Norwich wrote to the Earl of Yarmouth in the third week of April 1681, 'If it pleas God to bless the King with a stedfast resolution to keep the Laws and encourage his officers, I do not question but our turbulent men will soon be quieted.'[166]

Anglican clerics repeatedly used their sermons to call for a clampdown on dissent, urging local magistrates and parish constables to do their duty and ensure that the penal laws were enforced. William Allen, vicar of Bridgwater in the notoriously disaffected county of Somerset, preaching in February 1681, implored, 'Would to God that all the Subordinate Magistrates of this Realm . . . would . . . courageously appear for that Righteousness which is established by Law,' for then there would be peace; he then went on to call for the enforcement of the law against papists and nonconformists alike.[167] His namesake John Allen, at the Chester assizes in April 1682, preached a sermon which attacked nonconformists, occasional conformists, and jurors who failed to convict alike. He proclaimed, 'While we have good Laws, for God's sake, let us live and act according to them; and let them have their course upon All those, that do violate, affront, and defie them. Those that pretend to complain of Arbitrary power', he added, 'ought to have Law enough, their belly full, that they may complain for something.'[168] Royal chaplain John

Standish, preaching at the Hertfordshire assizes in the spring of 1683, urged his auditors in their 'several Spheres' to take care to 'Govern according to Law' and ensure 'that our wholesome Laws be vigorously and impartially executed'.[169] A little over a year later, also at the Hertfordshire assizes, Miles Barne insisted upon the need for 'a constant, vigorous and resolute Execution of all the Laws' in force against the nonconformists.[170] And this would not be persecution. As Hickes put it, one could suffer persecution only for doing something which God commanded, whereas the nonconformists were being 'justly prosecuted' for disobeying the law.[171] In urging 'all Consciencious Magistrates' to put the laws against dissenters in execution, Richard Pearson hoped that none would 'be afrighted from doing of their Duty, by the Odious Name of Persecution for Religion'; what dissenters meant by religion was 'nothing else but Violence and Rapine, Murder and Rebellion', and enforcing the law would stop them from persecuting others.[172]

Those who defended the Tory Reaction did not see it as ushering in a new experiment in personal rule. Most Tories remained committed to what they understood to be the traditional role of parliament within the constitution. In late April 1681 both the characters Jest and Earnest in the Tory periodical *Heraclitus Ridens* said they hoped to 'have a Parliament yet will heal all, and take care to secure the foundation of the Government from the attempts both of Popish and Protestant Jesuits'. Earnest added, however, that, since the King had 'been graciously pleased to assure his People that the unwarrantable proceedings of the former Parliaments shall not prevent his meeting his people with all the affection imaginable', he further hoped that the people would 'endeavour to chuse such persons to represent them, as by complying with his Majesty's just commands and the Nations true Interest, may secure our Laws, Liberties and Religion against the arbitrary practices of Papist, and Commonwealth Dissenters'.[173] Nalson claimed that he 'own[ed] the Excellent Constitution of an English Parliament, and honour[ed] it with all the becoming Veneration of a Subject born in England, a Lover of Liberty, a sincere Protestant . . . of the Church of England'; but he hated and abhorred 'all Usurpations', such as the claim that 'not to suffer Parliaments to sit to answer the great ends for which they were Instituted' was 'expressly contrary to Common Law . . . the Law of God, of Nature, and a violence offered to the Government', or that 'the King ought to have no Negative Voice.'[174] Similarly, L'Estrange protested that he was 'for Parliaments', so long as they acted as subjects and did not try to seize powers that did not belong to them; he was 'For a House of Commons that will do the bus'ness they were Call'd for' and 'do their Part toward the Furnishing of Materialls for New Laws where they are Wanting; The Amending of Old Laws where they are Defective; and that will Live, and Act in Conformity to the Laws we have in Being, till we may have Better in their Places'.[175]

CONCLUSION

The challenge of the Whigs, then, was met by an ideological counter-challenge from the Tories. The Tory propaganda counter-offensive was highly sophisticated, designed to target a socially diverse audience, including not just the elite and the middling sort but even the lower orders, and embracing arguments intended to appeal to the political and religious sensibilities of those whom the Tories were trying to reach. There is a sense in which the Tories were absolutists; after all, they frequently said they were, and Tory controversialists often explicitly championed the irresistible nature of divine-right absolute monarchy and the indefeasibility of the hereditary succession. But they did not meet the Whig challenge simply by stating that the King was absolute, the succession could not be changed, and there was nothing anyone could do about it. Instead, they carefully appealed to public fears about popery and arbitrary government, but sought to show that people had most to fear from these if the Whigs were to get their way. They also stressed their own commitment to the rule of law and what they regarded as the true Protestant religion. Thus, to some degree, they turned Whig arguments against their authors; in the process, however, they articulated a distinctively Tory ideology which was in fact the antithesis of what true and committed Whigs stood for. Charles II went along with all this; indeed, he actively portrayed himself in the role of a king who was committed to the rule of law and to protecting the existing establishment in Church and state as by law established. In doing so, of course, he nailed the monarchy's sails very firmly to the Tory ideological mast. For the time being, this seemed a price well worth paying.

5

Keeping the Reins of
Government Straight
The Tory Reaction in England

*Their Choler boils mightily, that His Majesty should conde-
scend to undeceive his people, but much more that a great part
of the people should be undeceived, and give His Majesty
thanks for that gracious condescention.*[1]

*The Vulgar . . . are like unto Fire and Water, good Servants but
bad Masters; if you keep the Reins of Government strait in
your hands . . . good use may be made of these People, but if
you be slack in the exercise of your Authority, they may
become ungovernable, and like a mighty Floud, or dreadful
Flame, they will bear down, or consume all before them.*[2]

The previous chapter has shown not only how the court and its Tory
allies sought to justify their opposition to Exclusion, but also how
they endeavoured to appeal to public opinion in their stance against
the Whigs. We now need to ask if they succeeded. Did they manage
to 'undeceive' the people? If so, what sorts of people, and how did
people's new-found loyalism manifest itself? What was the impact of
Charles II's declaration of April 1681, and to what extent did the
crown remain true to the promises contained therein, or do the policies that the royal administration pursued during the years of the Tory
Reaction that followed make a mockery of the government's claims to
be committed to the rule of law? We also have to address the question
of what happened to the Whigs. Did their support evaporate as the
Tory propaganda campaign grew ever more successful, or were they
crushed by a ruthless campaign of persecution, which had the effect

of intimidating the vast majority into quiescence but of driving a minority of hardliners into political conspiracy against the state?

On the surface, it seems that Tory efforts to appeal to opinion out-of-doors met with considerable success. In the years following the dissolution of the Oxford Parliament there was a dramatic surge of loyalist activity, which took the form of addresses and demonstrations expressing commitment to the King and to the hereditary succession in opposition to the demands and tactics of the Whigs. It is not clear, however, whether we can take these public displays of loyalist sentiment at face value. Were they genuine expressions of public opinion, or were they orchestrated from above, reflecting no more than the opinions of their elite sponsors, as contemporary Whigs and even some modern historians have claimed?[3] If, in recent years, scholars have come to accept that Toryism did have a genuine appeal at the grass-roots level,[4] disagreement still exists concerning the precise significance of this apparent rise in popular Tory sentiment. Were grass-roots opponents of Exclusion becoming more vocal and self-assertive, or more effectively mobilized, perhaps, without necessarily increasing in number? Or was there a genuine swing in public opinion away from the Whigs and in favour of the Tories? And, if so, how large a swing? A small one – perhaps the equivalent of the sorts of swing we see nowadays between general elections? Or a dramatic one, with the result that the pro-Whig consensus of the early years of the Exclusion Crisis became a pro-Tory consensus in 1681–3, as one historian has claimed?[5]

There can be no doubt that there was some swing in public opinion towards the Tories as time progressed – a swing which developed momentum following Charles II's declaration of April 1681 and which became even more pronounced in the aftermath of the revelations of the Rye House Plot of the summer of 1683. We cannot, however, talk about the emergence of a Tory consensus. Whether we look at addresses, crowd activity, the purges of local government, or the drive against dissent, all the evidence points to the continuance of bitter partisan strife during the years of the Tory Reaction; indeed, it was during the years 1681–3 that Whig–Tory rivalries reached their fiercest intensity. The loyal addresses and Tory demonstrations were not all spontaneous outbursts of grass-roots sentiment; there is plenty of evidence to suggest that often they were encouraged and even sponsored from above (normally by local party activists among the elite, though on occasion by the royal government itself). This does not mean that they were therefore insincere expressions of local Tory sentiment, though it does mean that they cannot be taken as a straightforward barometer of public opinion. They are best seen as another form of propaganda. The government and its Tory supporters were trying to claim that they were the true representatives of public opinion. They sought to do this by encouraging their sympathizers to be more active in manifesting their support for the crown, so that this would swamp any public manifestations of support for the Whigs. Making it appear that the people were on the government's side – even if the people as a whole really were not – could have significant advantages. It might make the local agents of law enforcement less reluctant to take action against the Whigs and their nonconformist allies, because they would no longer feel they were acting against public opinion. It might make the implementation of some of the more controversial policies of the Tory Reaction (such as the purges of local government or the attacks on borough corporations) easier to swallow, because they would seem to be in tune with the public's desire to rid the nation of factious troublemakers. It could also defuse the potential for popular unrest, because if the radicals and the discontented could be encouraged to believe that public opinion was deserting them, there would be less likelihood that they would risk their necks engaging in conspiratorial activity that seemed unlikely to attract sufficient support to stand a chance of success. Ultimately, it took a campaign of legal repression to defeat the Whig movement – though it should be stressed that the government did, by and large, act within the law. Yet the government's ability to claim that the people were on its side and that it was in tune with public opinion was crucial to the success of the Tory Reaction – which is why the two need to be examined in conjunction. The King needed to 'undeceive his people', but he also needed to 'keep the Reins of Government strait in [his] hands' if he was to ensure that 'The Vulgar' were not to become ungovernable.

POPULAR TORYISM
Loyalism before the Oxford Parliament

Before considering the extent to which people shifted allegiance following the dissolution of the Oxford Parliament, we need to recognize that the Tories did not start from a position of no support. The high-Anglican platform of commitment to Church and king and hostility towards Protestant nonconformists had long shown itself to have an intrinsic appeal to broad cross-sections of the population; indeed, at the time of the Restoration itself there was a considerable degree of popular antagonism towards not just the sects but also more moderate Puritan groups, and of support for the Established Church of the bishops and the Prayer Book.[6] During the 1670s, fear of popery tended to overtake fear of Puritan dissent, and this – combined with growing public anxiety about the foreign and domestic policies of the court – meant that political agitation out-of-doors took on a decidedly country, and subsequently Whiggish, coloration. Nevertheless, even at the height of the Whigs' popularity there is evidence that significant sections of the population never identified with the Whig cause. Some 38 per cent of those MPs who voted in the division over the first Exclusion Bill in the Commons in May 1679 voted against Exclusion, while it has been estimated that about 40 per cent of the parliaments of 1680 and 1681 supported the court,[7] implying that the opponents of Exclusion had some sort of following in the parliamentary constituencies. It is true that, in general, Whigs tended to do better than court candidates in the larger, more open, constituencies. However, this was not invariably the case. For example, in all three general elections between 1679 and 1681 two Tories were returned for Southwark, where the right of election was vested in the inhabitant householders not receiving alms – approaching 3,500 people – and two more in Norwich, where some 2,800 freemen possessed the vote. Furthermore, we should not assume that, where Whigs were successful at the polls, there was no support for the Tories: in some constituencies, the Whigs won only after a bitterly fought local contest.[8]

Other evidence hints at the existence of public support for the Tories before the dissolution of the Oxford Parliament. When Charles sent his brother to Scotland in the autumn of 1679, York and his wife chose to travel by land and in effect turned the trip into a long royal progress. The *London Gazette* reported every stage of the journey, documenting for its readers the welcome reception York received at the places he visited en route – particularly from persons of quality (the nobility, gentry, town magistrates, principal citizens and various ecclesiastical dignitaries, together with the local militias), in order to highlight the amount of backing that the heir to the throne had from the political elite in the provinces. To be fair, the reality was not always quite what the *Gazette* made it appear: the Yorkshire squire Sir John Reresby noted that the reception for the Duke in Yorkshire was lukewarm, while the city of York itself received him 'very coldly', for which the Lord Mayor and aldermen were later reprimanded by the King. Nevertheless, the *Gazette*'s reports cannot be dismissed totally out of hand. Their royal highnesses received a particularly enthusiastic reception at Durham, where the bishop and most of the county gentry (totalling some 5,000 horse), together with the militia troop, met the royal couple at the bridge on the outskirts of town, while 'the people . . . and the Trained-Bands' lined both sides of the streets from the suburbs to the castle gates as the Duke and Duchess made their entry, to be greeted by the mayor, recorder, aldermen and principal citizens. The day concluded with bells and bonfires, including a huge fire in the shape of a pyramid in the Minster Yard, as 'the Country throng in', as the *Gazette* put it, 'to see their Royal Highnesses'.[9]

When York returned to Whitehall from Scotland on 24 February 1680 there were several bonfires at the west end of town (including at Temple Bar and along the Strand) to celebrate his safe arrival. There was certainly court orchestration. Lauderdale put up £150 to pay for two of the bonfires, while the King ordered the Lord Mayor to forbid any bonfires within the walls of the City of London, clearly fearing that they would be provocative to the Whigs. On the other hand, one manuscript account alleges that 'a great many persones' would have put on bonfires in the City if the Lord Mayor had not prohibited them. There were also similar pro-York displays at Portsmouth, Barsham Downs (Suffolk) and Canterbury.[10] Further loyal demonstrations followed on 8 March, when the King took his brother to a dinner with the Lord Mayor of London. They were received at the mayoral residence 'amidst the shouts of the people'; the bells rang and bonfires were made, and when the royal brothers left they were followed 'by a great multitude of people' exclaiming, 'God bless the King, God bless the Duke.'[11]

Later that month the Whig JP Sir William Waller uncovered a 'conspiracy' by Tory apprentices from the Strand, in Westminster, to burn the Rump and effigies of Oliver Cromwell 'in A Formal procession' on 29 May, after which they planned to pull down nonconformist meeting houses throughout the London area. The design was intended as a counter to the Whig pope-burning procession of the previous 17 November (when the scheme was initially hatched), and was apparently well organized: the apprentices were led by a bell-founder's apprentice named Thomas Alford, who styled himself their captain, with a cobbler's apprentice and an oilman's apprentice serving as lieutenant and ensign respectively; the ringleaders had listed their supporters into rolls totalling some several thousand (estimates vary wildly, from 4–5,000 to over 40,000 apprentices); they had supposedly visited a herald-painter to discuss 'Colours', which were 'to be painted full of Rumps'; and they were said to have had a number of meetings at the house of the Tory printer Nathaniel Thompson, who was suspected of having encouraged the plan. The Whigs believed the proposed Rump-burning was part of a broader Catholic design against the government, and that 'a considerable number of the Popish Party were in the conspiracy'; others thought 'no great matter' would 'be found in it', and that 'the apprentices dear delights of bonfires and ale was at the bottom of it.' Although the authorities initially had the ringleaders imprisoned upon suspicion of high treason, they were eventually released without trial. It seems that what we have here is an attempt by Tory youths (perhaps egged on by Tory publicists) to promote grass-roots Tory activism among the apprentices of the metropolis, to show that they did not all support the Whigs; indeed, one of the ringleaders – probably Alford himself – had at first tried to hatch a similar design among the apprentices of the City of London, but the Lord Mayor had issued a warrant against him, hence he moved his efforts to Westminster, where he met with a more favourable reception.[12]

Charles and his brother were again cheered through the streets of the City at the end of April 1680, as they went to dine at Sheriff Raymond's house following their return from Newmarket.[13] York's presence at court over the spring and summer of 1680 also gave a spark to the moving of loyal addresses to the crown by grand juries and other bodies in various parts of the country, abhorring the tactics of the Whigs. However, many of these 'abhorrences' stemmed from the initiative of a few energetic courtiers, and so perhaps do not tell us that much about public opinion.[14] Following the elections to the Oxford Parliament in early 1681, as some constituencies sent in Whiggish instructions urging their newly elected MPs to promote Exclusion and toleration for Protestant dissenters, others – among them Cambridge, Bristol, Southwark and Cheshire – drew up instructions urging their members to uphold the existing establishment in Church and state as by law established, to defend the King's prerogatives, and to enforce the laws against all dissenters whatsoever: not just papists, but also Protestant sectaries and separatists.[15]

Addresses and Abhorrences, 1681–2

There is no doubt that some individuals changed sides as the Exclusion Crisis unfolded. Most famously, Charles II's Secretary of State the Earl of Sunderland voted for Exclusion in the Lords in November 1680 and was dismissed from office as a result in January; but he insinuated his way back into royal favour, was reinstated in January 1683, and was to become the main architect of Charles's pro-French foreign policy in the King's final years. Sunderland, however, was always a courtier: it was just that he was mistaken in thinking he could see which way the tide was turning in the autumn of 1680 and that Charles would inevitably have to abandon his brother. (It was not to be the last time that Sunderland was to make an ill-timed conversion to a losing cause.) A better example is the Earl of Huntingdon. Once one of Shaftesbury's trusted political associates, he had backed Exclusion in the Lords in November 1680; yet in October 1681 he kissed the King's hand and subsequently became a key figure of the Tory Reaction. In 1682 he justified his about-face by saying that he was convinced there were 'laws sufficient for the

Security of the Monarchy and the property of the Subject' and that 'other laws such as the late parliament aimed tended to undermine the Government both in the Church and State'.[16] Others can be added to the list. Sir Thomas Putt, MP for Honiton, voted for Exclusion in 1679 but subsequently went over to the court – though it should be said that he was always a high churchman. Similarly, Sir William Portman, who sat first for Taunton and then for Somerset in the Exclusion Parliaments, switched from a proponent of Exclusion to a defender of the Duke of York, signed his county's loyal addresses of 1681, and led the East Dorset militia against the Duke of Monmouth at Sedgemoor in 1685.[17] The London merchant John Verney initially leaned towards the Whigs and dissenters, but grew more Tory Anglican in outlook over time.[18] The moderate newspaper publishers John Smith and Thomas Benskin switched from being pro-Whig in 1680 and early 1681 to pro-Tory by the spring of 1681; one suspects that commercial considerations played a part here, but if so this is significant since these would reflect a belief that the political views of readers were changing in the aftermath of the dissolution of the Oxford Parliament and the King's declaration of April 1681.[19] Was this indeed the case?

Initial reactions to the King's declaration were somewhat mixed. The contemporary political diarist Narcissus Luttrell thought 'it was not very well relished,' because it arraigned the proceedings of the Whig parliaments, and when it came to be read from the pulpit throughout the kingdom it proved 'in many places' to be 'not very pleasing'.[20] Edward L'Estrange in Norwich, however, found that the declaration 'put new Life, and Soul, into all His Majesties Loyall Subjects', because the King 'hath therein given such Weighty reasons for His late pro-ceedings, and such great assurances that he will protect all His Dutifull and Loyall Subjects from all Arbitrary Power'.[21] Richard Grahme in Yorkshire informed Reresby that the declaration was read in church and at the sessions 'to the generall applause of all'.[22] Others noted a dis-tinct change of mood in the country. The Earl of Conway, based at the royal court, observed in mid-April how things were 'much more quiet since the late dissolution than they were before', and in the following month how 'His Majesties Affairs' were 'amended beyond all men's expectations'.[23] One London correspondent described how the coffee houses had 'become soe modeste in their discourses, and the Cittie so quiet', because 'the countrie seems to bee influenced by the great example of it [Charles's declaration]'; indeed, 'in several of our Market townes', he continued, the people spoke 'in a much different dialect' than they used to, querying 'what the P[arliament] had done for them' and 'why the P[arliament] did not more complye with his Majestie in some things'.[24]

Over the next few months some 211 loyal addresses were presented to the King from all over England and Wales thanking him for his declaration.[25] Drawn up in the name of grand juries, JPs, militia officers, borough corporations, apprentices and groups of individuals (including such unlikely groups as the company of cooks and chandlers of Salisbury and the tinners of Cornwall), some could claim large numbers of signatories. That from the tiny county of Rutland boasted 1,200, Derbyshire 2,500, Nottinghamshire some 6,000, Northamptonshire supposedly some 10,000, the Cornish tinners reputedly the same, Devon 'above 16,000 Persons', and the loyal apprentices of the City of London some 18,000. If we add the figures for subscribers cited in the contemporary compilation *Vox Angliae* we get a figure of just under 27,500. However, *Vox Angliae* did not always enumerate signatories; often it merely reported that 'many thousands' subscribed to a particular address. It does not mention the purported totals for Devon, Northamptonshire, the Cornish tinners or the apprentices of London, for example. If we add these, the total jumps to 81,500, and this still does not account for everyone who put their name to an address (although, to be fair, some of the totals claimed may have been exaggerations).[26] Fifty-five of the addresses came in from boroughs or counties where two MPs hostile to the court had been elected to serve in the Oxford Parliament, and a further 41 from where one opposition MP had been elected.[27] In some areas – notably London, Bristol and East Anglia – local Tories backed up their thanks to the King for getting rid of the Whig parliaments with attempts to raise voluntary contributions in support of the crown (although the efforts of the Norfolk gentry in this respect failed to gain support, despite rumours that they had subscribed £40,000).[28]

How should we interpret the evidence of these loyal addresses, then? Are they indicative of a massive and spontaneous groundswell of support for the Tories? Do they suggest that the tide of public opinion turned suddenly and decisively against the Whigs in the aftermath of the King's declaration of April 1681? To resolve these questions, we need to address a number of issues: exactly how Tory were these addresses? how sudden and spontaneous were they? whose opinions did they represent? and to what extent did they reflect a newly emerging consensus at the local level?

We must start by recognizing that the addresses do not speak with a uniform voice. Charles's declaration had been a cleverly worded document, intended as much to reassure people about the King's commitment to uphold the law and rule through parliament as to condemn the proceedings of the Whigs. It could thus appeal to people of varying political persuasions for different reasons, as the addresses themselves testify. Burnet divided the addresses into three broad types: some 'were more modestly penned, and only expressed their joy at the assurances they saw in the king's declaration'; 'the greater number . . . declared they would adhere to the unalterable succession of the crown in the lineal and legal descent, and condemned the bill of exclusion'; others 'went higher, and arraigned the late parliaments as guilty of sedition and treason', 'reflected severely on the nonconformists', and greatly magnified 'the king's person and government'. Or, to put it another way, we might characterize the addresses as ambiguous, moderate Tory and high Tory. The Chesterfield address provides an example of the last: it pledged support for the 'Royal Prerogative, in Calling, and Dissolving Parliaments at . . . Pleasure'; condemned 'the late growing Usurpation, of Arbitrary Government . . . by the late House of Commons'; called for the execution of the laws 'against all Dissenters, of what sort soever, from the True Protestant Church of England' (calling 'the Phanaticks, the Nurslings of the Pope'); and vowed to defend the King's 'most Sacred Person' and 'the Lawful Heirs of [the] Imperial Crown', as well as 'the Established Laws of this Nation'. Revealingly, however, Burnet thought the moderate Tory addresses, which formed the majority of the whole, were 'the most acceptable' to the court.[29] Even these, while embracing the language of constitutional moderation, made very clear their opposition to the Whigs. For example, the address of 10 May 1681 from the bailiff and burgesses of Haslemere in Surrey thanked the King for promising that he would 'never use Arbitrary Government' but let 'the known and establish'd Laws of [his] Kingdom . . . be the Rule' of his government, and for not consenting to a law, namely the Exclusion Bill, that would 'establish another Civil War, or make it necessary to maintain a standing Force . . . to Preserve the Peace of [his] Kingdoms'. It concluded by promising in future to return MPs who were 'zealously affected to your Majesty's Person and Family, and also to the Government Ecclesiastical and Civil, as it is now by Law established'.[30]

Some addresses, however, left the subscribers' attitude to the key issue of Exclusion unclear. For example, in the late spring of 1681 the mayor and aldermen of King's Lynn (Norfolk) thanked Charles for his continued affection 'to the Excellent Constitution of the Church of England, and constant care to defend it against the ill designs of Popery, and all other Oppositions whatsoever', and also for his 'firm Resolution, to maintain the Just Rights of the Monarchy, and the Liberty and Property of [his] People'; yet, although promising to support the King's royal authority and wishing Charles a long and prosperous reign, they made no mention of the succession, the Duke of York or the penal laws.[31] Particularly revealing is the address from the city of Winchester, drawn up on 20 May 1681. This thanked Charles for the promises in his declaration to 'suppress Popery, and not use arbitrary government, nor permit it in others', to have 'frequent Parliaments and make the Laws of the Land [his] Rule', and to 'preserve the Church in its Rights, and the true Protestant Religion' as by law established, while the subscribers promised in return to defend the King 'against all Popish and Phanatical persons whatsoever'. Yet perhaps what is most revealing is Charles's reply, in which he stated that he was very well satisfied with the addressors' loyalty, and assured them that he would 'defend the Protestant Religion as by law established and all that are Friends to it against both Papists and Phanaticks', adding that as long as he lived 'the lawes of the land' would 'be the Rule of the government'.[32] The addressors did not mention the issue of the succession, and as far as the King was concerned that did not seem to matter! In some areas, Whigs found they could subscribe to an address without betraying their political principles.

For example, Arthur Onslow, Whig MP for Surrey, was restored to the commission of the peace when he signed the loyal address from the Surrey lieutenancy, but was again removed when he made it clear that he nevertheless still supported Exclusion.[33] Likewise, Sir Henry Oxenden signed the Kent address because he found it contained 'some articles' he could set his hand to, but he remained committed to getting an Exclusionist MP returned to parliament, should another be called.[34]

A further point to note is that the addresses did not all come in at once. The first was drawn up in mid-April 1681, whereas the last domestic one was presented in January 1682. It was not that communities all over the land were suddenly wowed by the King's declaration and rushed to proclaim their loyalty; many dragged their feet and delayed as long as they could. It became difficult to hold out indefinitely, however, as more and more communities rushed to proclaim their loyalty and as it grew clear, by the way the addressing movement was reported in the *Gazette*, that the crown not only welcomed but also expected these addresses. With the passage of time, in other words, the informal pressure to conform became immense. It was because everyone else appeared to be striving to 'out goe each other in Expressions of loyalty' that the mayor, magistrates, militia officers, freemen, freeholders and other loyal subjects of Lyme Regis eventually agreed in November 1681 that they should 'no longer hold from Expressing' theirs. In the end they agreed to an address which was quite high-Tory in tone, expressing abhorrence of all seditious principles and practices that tended to the subversion or alteration 'of this most Excellently constituted Government in Church and State', promising to elect men of known loyalty and integrity to serve in the next parliament, and offering to defend 'with their Lives and Fortunes' the King's 'Royal Person and Prerogatives, Heirs, and lawful Successors, and the Protestant Religion, as now by Law established'.[35]

Then we have the difficulty of determining the extent to which the addresses were in tune with opinion at large. At first glance, 211 addresses from all over the country, with a total of over 80,000 signatories, might seem impressive. Certainly the way in which addresses were reported in the media – individually, over several months, in the

Gazette, and then again in pamphlet compilations – was designed to give the general public an impression of a massive groundswell of loyalist support.[36] Nevertheless, 80,000 was less than 2 per cent of the total population of England and Wales, or less than 8 per cent of the adult male population. The early-eighteenth-century historian of the addressing movements John Oldmixon – admittedly a Whig – who estimated the total number of signatories more conservatively at 40,000 (though his point is the same even if we double that figure), thought that figure no great achievement, especially given the 'Industry' it took to procure the signatures, since in William III's reign we find 'mention made of near 370,000 Hands to several Addresses, without any of those Artifices'.[37] One Whig pamphleteer, writing in 1681, while the addressing movement was still under way, thought the number of subscribers was not 'so considerable, as to bear any proportion to those who are against them'. He observed that many places, including many counties and some of the chiefest cities and towns, had 'declined presenting any' addresses, and 'that even where they have been obtained, not One in Ten, and in some places not One in a Hundred had any hand in, or gave concurrence to them'. If those who either avoided subscribing or refused to subscribe were taken as being against them, he proclaimed, 'then the Tale of the Addressers will make but a very small show and appearance in the muster Roll of the Nation'.[38]

There was, in fact, considerable opposition to the addressing movement in many parts of the country. Nowhere was this more so than in the capital itself. On 13 May the common council of London rejected an address of thanks for the King's declaration and instead opted to draw up a petition for the sitting of parliament (though only after a close vote of 91 to 77), which was presented to the King the next day.[39] Similarly, at about the same time the Middlesex grand jury presented the Lord Chief Justice with a petition desiring the King 'speedily to call a parliament'; it further presented the Norwich loyal address as a seditious libel, and considered taking similar action against the King's declaration itself, though in the end it backed down.[40] This is not to say that the loyalists in the capital had no voice; rather, London and its suburbs were divided along party lines. The very first loyal address presented to the King was from the JPs of

Middlesex on 18 April. At about the same time 'many thousands of the most Eminent Citizens and Inhabitants' of London petitioned the Lord Mayor and aldermen to urge them to present their address of thanks in the corporation's name, although the officials declined. The lieutenancies of London, the Tower, and Middlesex and Westminster, the Artillery Company of London, and the grand jury of the borough of Southwark all presented addresses of thanks.[41] As mentioned above, some 18,000 loyal apprentices of the City allegedly put their hands to a loyal address that was presented at the end of June, while at the end of August some 5,000 apprentices from Westminster presented their own address.[42] In early September the Whig apprentices of the City responded by presenting the Lord Mayor with their own petition, boasting over 20,000 signatories, disowning the recent Tory-apprentice address (which they claimed in reality had only 3,000 subscribers) and expressing unanimous support for the corporation's efforts to petition the King for a new parliament.[43] The lawyers were among the most bitterly divided. The Middle Temple rejected a loyal address presented for its consideration by some of its members in June 1681, and after some riotous proceedings, during which each party attempted to get its own candidate to preside over a poll, the addressors eventually adjourned to the Devil Tavern to sign their address, which they subsequently presented to the King in the name of 'the Loyal Society of the Middle Temple' on 19 June. Similarly, Gray's Inn rejected a loyal address that same month, so the addressors went to a tavern and subscribed an address in the name of the 'Truly Loyal Subjects' of Gray's Inn. There were likewise 'great heats' at the Inner Temple over whether to address or not. In the end, the Templers decided by a majority of just three votes 'against proceeding immediately with it'; the Inner Temple eventually sent in what turned out to be the very last address of thanks for the King's declaration, on 15 January 1682. An address was 'endeavoured' at Lincoln's Inn, 'but to no purpose', though Clifford's Inn did address.[44]

The addresses proved equally contentious in many other parts of the country. John Lambert, a yeoman from Chivelstone in Devon, was convicted at the Devon quarter sessions for having declared in September 1681 that they were 'all knaves or fooles that signed the Addresse'.[45] In July 1681 a Lyme Regis man was bound over to the assizes to answer for 'having spoken very scandalously and unbecomingly of the Addresses in general, and particularly, of that which was Presented to His Majesty by the Gentlemen of' Dorset.[46] The mayor of Richmond, Yorkshire, refused to meddle with the address being promoted there, saying, 'Those that meddle least, had least to answer for!'[47] The latitudinarian clergyman Dr John Tillotson, at the time dean of Canterbury, 'absolutely refused' to sign the address that was being promoted at Canterbury in September.[48] In the West Riding of Yorkshire, Lord Stafford refused to sign an address which thanked the King 'for every part of his declaration', saying that the only parts of the declaration that deserved thanks were those where the King promised to govern according to law and to hold frequent parliaments, and that 'he would never thanke the King for desolveing Parliaments.'[49] At the assizes at Lincoln in July 1681 the grand jury unanimously rejected an address promoted by the Earl of Lindsey.[50] In Hampshire a large minority of the assize grand jury were opposed to the loyal address eventually adopted in that county in the summer of 1681 because 'they apprehended the proceedings of the 2 last Parliaments deserved not an aspersion.'[51] Coventry presented two addresses in the summer: one, returning thanks for His Majesty's declaration, was signed by over 800 loyal persons, according to Thompson; the other, 'of a different nature', was promoted by 'some disaffected persons' in the name of the mayor, bailiff and common council.[52]

The examples could be extended: one scholar has documented further disagreements over addressing at Durham, Great Yarmouth, Kent, Northumberland, Oxford and Winchester, and his account is not exhaustive.[53] Some degree of opposition to addressing can be detected even in staunchly Tory areas. For example, at Derby the grand jury unanimously signed the county's address of July 1681, as did many of the nobles and most of the gentry; indeed, to quote one local correspondent, 'the high Sheriffe and most of the Gentry heer' were 'high Toryes', who had taken to 'wearing little red ribbons in theyr hatts'. The qualifier 'most', however, implied not all; the same correspondent noted that, of the gentry, Sir Thomas Grisley refused to sign.[54] Furthermore, in some places the appearance of consensus behind an address was deceptive, because of a silent majority that were never invited to subscribe. This explains why so many constituencies that had returned Whig MPs to the Oxford Parliament soon thereafter drew up loyal addresses: the people doing the addressing were only a fraction of the people who had recently done the electing. In both Norfolk and Bedfordshire only 10 per cent of the shire electorate signed their respective county's address. The Berkshire, Cheshire, Herefordshire and Surrey addresses came from the counties' grand juries (and in Surrey's case the militia and JPs as well), not from the freeholders. Similarly, in a number of boroughs (among them Bridgwater, Derby, Dover, Nottingham, Reading, Taunton and Windsor) the loyal addresses came from a restricted group among the corporate elite, not the entire borough electorate.[55] Even those addresses which claimed to have a wider subscription base invariably made the qualification that they were signed by the county or borough elite and other 'loyal' inhabitants, begging the question of how many disloyal inhabitants there might have been. It was thus with some justice that one Whig pamphleteer could claim that the 'Mind and Hearts' of the people were 'best known' not 'by the Addresses', but 'By the Parliament'.[56]

One further qualification needs to be made concerning the authenticity of the addresses. Although some may have been the result of a spontaneous local initiative, many were encouraged from above, in the sense of being promoted by local activists with close connections to the court or with axes to grind against the Whigs. The Lord Lieutenants, who were government appointees and the main arm of the executive in the counties, played an active role in organizing the loyal addresses from their respective shires.[57] So too did the high-Anglican clergy. According to one pamphleteer, the clergy were 'as diligent as bees to get such Addresses signed', while another alleged that it was the 'ignorant clergy-men' who 'in divers places set these Addresses at work', especially those which included a clause against the Protestant dissenters.[58] Assiduous politicking by powerful individuals with strong local connections could sometimes produce wondrous results. In September the Duke of Newcastle wrote to Reresby thanking him for a copy of the address from the corporation of cutlers of Hallamshire in Yorkshire, proclaiming that Reresby had worked 'a miracle in making them loyal for they have ever been most factious'.[59] Charles II himself also made it clear that he supported such local initiatives and was strongly opposed to any demands for a new parliament. Thus when the King received the addresses of thanks from the London lieutenancy and the borough of Southwark on 19 May, 'the lord chancellour descanted of the seasonablenesse of them and loyalty of the persons, giveing them his majesties thanks for the same'. However, he gave the Lord Mayor and aldermen who presented the corporation of London's petition for the sitting of parliament a very severe reprimand, telling them 'they had meddled with matters which did not concern them, and bid them go home and mind their own affairs'.[60] Indeed, Charles was not above giving rewards to those who sent in addresses. In September 1681, for example, he sent the loyal inhabitants of Aylesbury in Buckinghamshire a brace of bucks so they could hold a special feast in honour of the addressors.[61]

It is difficult, then, to see the addresses of 1681 as a straightforward measure of how public opinion was changing. Although some addresses were spontaneous and from below, many were promoted by local party activists, and the addresses often divided communities rather than united them behind a loyalist consensus. This does not mean that we cannot see the addresses as in some way indicative of public opinion. There is no reason to doubt that those who signed the loyal addresses embraced the sentiments behind them; indeed, the evidence suggests that people typically were able to oppose or distance themselves from the addresses if they disagreed with them (although we should add that there does seem to have been a considerable amount of both formal and informal pressure to address). It may well have been that – at least in some parts of the country – public opinion was shifting away from the Whigs and in favour of the Tories, though this is extremely difficult to test. Yet, rather than treat the loyal addresses as an index of public opinion, it is better to see them as what the government intended them to be – as propaganda. The government and its Tory allies wanted to be able to show that the Whigs did not have the people on their side. This involved encouraging their supporters in the localities to take an active stance in proclaiming their loyalty. It also involved publicizing such displays of loyalty to the widest possible audience – hence why the addresses were published so fully in the *Gazette* and again in pamphlet compilations. This in itself is a powerful testimony to the important role that public opinion had come to play in Restoration politics. What mattered, however, was not so much whether in reality one had public opinion on one's side, but whether one could convincingly stake a claim that one did.

This interpretation seems to be reinforced by an examination of the abhorrence movement of 1682. According to the *Gazette*, between January and September a further 157 addresses from across England and Wales were presented to the King expressing abhorrence of Shaftesbury's alleged scheme for a Protestant Association, which had come to light following the Whig leader's arrest on suspicion of treason in the summer of 1681.[62] The abhorrences served a somewhat different function from the addresses of the previous year. Most of them came from grand juries, JPs, inns of court, assizes and quarter sessions, and, although they might claim to be backed by 'other inhabitants', they typically did not boast substantial numbers of signatories. They were intended, therefore, not as expressions of popular sentiment, but as official reactions to the London grand jury's decision to throw out the indictment against Shaftesbury in November 1681, to proclaim the view of legal experts, magistrates and juries elsewhere in the kingdom that Shaftesbury's Association was indeed treasonous.[63] The main exceptions were an abhorrence delivered to the King in the name of the loyal young freemen and apprentices of the City of London in July 1682, signed by 12,000 hands, and another by above 1,000 'Loyal Young Men and Apprentices' of Bristol, presented in September.[64] The abhorrences were also more blatantly orchestrated by courtiers than the previous year's addresses had been. In January, Sir John Reresby was responsible for exhorting the Middlesex JPs to draw up an abhorrence, and the King was said to have told Reresby at the beginning of the abhorrence campaign that he 'should be pleased that this intended abhorrancie of the association might proove as generall as the former addresses'. One Whig pamphleteer alleged that L'Estrange was responsible for 'framing the draughts which are remitted into the Countrey', where the Lord Lieutenants, JPs and local clergy were 'commissioned to procure subscriptions to them'.[65] Some of those who sent in abhorrences were appropriately rewarded. In

May, Lord Conway invited 'a crowd of addressers' from Coventry to Windsor to dine with him at court; Coventry was a notoriously factious town, which had divided over the address in 1681, so Conway was presumably trying to nurture this budding loyalist faction.[66] The loyal freemen and apprentices of London were treated to a lavish nine-course feast at Merchant Taylors' Hall on 9 August, presided over by leading members of the court nobility, such as the dukes of Ormonde, Albemarle, Grafton and Richmond, and the earls of Halifax and Sunderland; in total, near twenty bucks were consumed, some of which were donated by the King himself.[67] Again, these abhorrences were afforded due publicity in the press.

As with the addresses of 1681, the abhorrences cannot be taken as indicative of a local consensus. Whether or not a particular local jury chose to deliver an abhorrence depended on who was doing the impanelling, namely the sheriffs. As one Whig pamphleteer pointed out, 'the great care in returning select Men for Grand Juries' and 'the Arts that were us'd to draw many of them into these Abhorrences' were 'well known to All the Nation'. No one doubted, he told his Tory adversary, 'but you have choice of Gentlemen to make Sheriffs fit for your Turn' and 'that Seventeen or Eighteen Men may be found in most Counties, for your turn', though in some 'you could not find above Thirteen', and in several 'you have failed absolutely.'[68] In the spring of 1682 the Earl of Lindsey, the Lord Lieutenant of Lincolnshire, with the 'High Sheriff's assistance and wise conduct', managed to get the Lincolnshire grand jury to draw up an abhorrence. It passed unanimously, but only because the new sheriff, a Lindsey nominee, had packed the body which drew it up. Lindsey had tried to get the grand jury to adopt a loyal address at the assizes the previous summer, but that particular grand jury had rejected it. 'By this you may observe', Lindsey confessed, 'what influence High Sheriffs . . . have in this county.'[69] When the sessions were held for the city of Oxford on 27 April 1682, the two Whig bailiffs were able to defeat an expected abhorrence by 'empanelling a jury they knew to be "true blue".' This Whig jury also went on to throw out bills against Quaker and Baptist meetings.[70] The Whigs were not to remain in control for long, however. By the time the July sessions came around, the magisterial bench had been purged, and a new bailiff was able to return a Tory jury, which then brought in an abhorrence for the court to subscribe. Even though several justices were absent and the recorder and the mayor objected to it, the sergeant declared 'that the Court did concur with what the Jury had done'.[71] The return of two 'very loyal' grand juries for the Yorkshire assizes in March 1682 made it inevitable that they would draw up an abhorrence, which they combined with an address congratulating the Duke of York on his safe return to England from Scotland. It was also signed by the deputy Lieutenants, JPs, 'most of the considerable Gentlemen of the County', and the archbishop and about thirty of the clergy, and was presented to the King at Newmarket by Sir Thomas Slingsby. It proved highly controversial, however, making 'a great noise . . . and such distinguishing of Whegs and Toryes' that they were 'averse to be seen in one anothers company'. Several local gentry and clergy refused to sign it, because they had not been consulted; there were even violent scuffles between rival partisan groups.[72] Sometimes the court failed to influence the composition of local juries. In Nottinghamshire, the Duke of Newcastle told both Halifax and Reresby that he did all he could to get the sheriff and under-sheriff to do 'their parts', but nevertheless the abhorrence still failed. The sheriff returned a jury made up 'of both parties', and then presented them with two arguments against the abhorrence: 'that it would reflect upon my Lord Shaftesbury' and 'that the Grand Jurey was as the Shireiff pleased, soe it could not be thought to be the sense of the County'.[73]

Town magistrates and corporate officials sometimes tried to frustrate abhorrences. The Whig mayor of the otherwise largely loyalist city of Wells, Somerset, suppressed an abhorrence of Shaftesbury's Association subscribed by the local inhabitants, claiming that he feared that if he presented it he might be made to answer for it by the next parliament.[74] At the Chester quarter sessions the magisterial bench refused to endorse the grand jury's abhorrence following an impassioned speech by the recorder condemning the initiative. The recorder protested that 'he had taken the oaths of allegiance and supremacy, which he looked on to be more binding than subscribing that paper,' and that 'that was a new way of expressing their loyalty, and no honour to his Majesty,' as 'it tended to set Thomas against

Richard, and William against Edward.' Besides, he went on, 'it was not proved that any one person was concerned in that Association.'[75] At Dover, the mayor refused to join with the abhorrence being promoted by local loyalists.[76]

Even where corporations sent in abhorrences, the appearance of consensus was often deceptive. At Hereford, only 22 out of 31 members were present when the common council voted unanimously in favour of an abhorrence in February.[77] In April the corporation of Coventry sent in an abhorrence which claimed also to have the backing of the deputy Lieutenants, the grand jury, the gentry, and other inhabitants of the city and county; at the same time it sent the central government a list of names of those who refused or failed to subscribe, warning that they were men 'of dangerous principles'.[78] Lyme Regis delivered an abhorrence in May, but only 67 members subscribed, compared to the 151 who had put their names to the loyal address of the previous year.[79] There was some opposition in Reading to a proposed abhorrence. A draft was first considered in late March, but when it came to be discussed in early April one junior assistant proclaimed 'hee would have nothing to doe with it', another that he 'desired time to consider it', and several members appear to have been absent. It took further discussion and some alterations to the wording before the corporation eventually approved the abhorrence (though not unanimously) in early May.[80]

In London, divisions were particularly marked once again. Most of the gentlemen of Gray's Inn refused its abhorrence of February; 'the promoters thereof' signed it on behalf of themselves and delivered it to the King.[81] The Whig apprentices of the City drafted an alternative to the abhorrence promoted by the Tory youths, protesting their loyalty to the King but proclaiming against the plots of the papists to dethrone the King and set up 'an Arbitrary and Bloody Monarchy in this Kingdome', though the document appears never to have been presented.[82] The Artillery Company and the lieutenancy presented abhorrences, but a plan by the 'honest party' in the common council to promote an abhorrence was quickly nipped in the bud by the royal government, who thought it would provoke the 'opposite party' into promoting a petition for parliament, which would likely draw in 'many moderate men', and thereby 'produce an ill precedent, and ferment that humour again throughout the Kingdom'.[83]

Rhyming Noise to Noise – Tory Street Politics

The years following the dissolution of the Oxford Parliament saw a dramatic upsurge in loyalist demonstrations out-of-doors, as crowds took to the streets to demonstrate their opposition to the Whigs and support for the King and the hereditary succession. The most important day in the Tory calendar was 29 May, which was Charles II's birthday and the anniversary of his restoration. There were also demonstrations on the Queen's birthday (15 November) and even on Gunpowder Treason Day, as Tory groups sought to appropriate this anti-Catholic commemoration for their own ends, as well as whenever Charles or the Duke of York made a royal entry into a major town or city.

In 1681 29 May fell on a Sunday, but on the following day 'severall places', among them Windsor, Portsmouth and King's Lynn, honoured the King's birthday with 'bells, bonfires, fireing of guns, conduits running with wine, etc.'. At Derby there were 'more than ordinary expressions of Joy': among other things, 'some eminent persons' arranged for 'a Puppet to be dressed in the formal Habit of Jack Presbyter, with his short Cloak . . . and Black Cap', and 'delivered [it] to the Common people', who 'carried it about the streets, shouting and crying, Remember Forty One!', before eventually burning the effigy at the market cross to the cries of 'No Papist, No Presbyterian.'[84] There were 'publick demonstrations of joy' at Cambridge when Charles and his wife made a quick visit to the university at the end of September during a stay in Newmarket, and there were bonfires in London to celebrate their royal majesties' eventual return from Newmarket on 12 October. On 29 October the King and Queen were cheered through the City as they went to dine at Guildhall on Lord Mayor's Day – though simply cheering the King and Queen, of course, cannot be interpreted as a distinctively Tory gesture, even if the dinner was to celebrate the election of a Tory Lord Mayor.[85] There was a pointedly anti-Whig demonstration in Westminster on 5 November, however, when, in Dean's Yard, the scholars of Westminster School chose to burn an effigy of Jack Presbyter bearing a pamphlet styled 'Vox Patriae' in his right hand and the Solemn League and Covenant in his left.[86] There were bonfire celebrations in the capital again on 15 November, to commemorate the Queen's birthday.[87]

York's return to England in March 1682, after an eighteen-month 'exile' in Scotland, became the cue for loyalist demonstrations explicitly in support of the Catholic heir. At both Great Yarmouth (where he landed on 10 March) and Norwich (where he proceeded later that day) he was greeted with 'all imaginable demonstrations of joy'. At Great Yarmouth the sailors of the town were so excited by York's arrival 'that several went up to their necks in water and carried him out of the sea on their heads a great way into the land'; at Norwich the streets were 'crowded with People and full of Bonfires'.[88] When York arrived back in London, on 8 April, there were numerous Tory demonstrations throughout the capital. At the Dog-Wonder Tavern in Ludgate a crowd burned an effigy of Jack Presbyter together with the Rump, the Association, and the Bill of Exclusion; in Covent Garden, the Rump, Covenant, Association and green ribbons were ceremoniously burned together; in Drury Lane, Shaftesbury himself was burned in effigy, with the words 'The Association' writ on his right hand, 'Treason' on his left, and 'Anarchy' on his breast; in Cornhill, in the heart of the City, Jack Presbyter, the Association and various Whig newspapers were committed to the flames amid cries of 'No whig, no whig.'[89] The news of York's arrival in the capital triggered celebrations in other parts of the country. On 13 April 1682 the inhabitants of Shaftesbury in Dorset burned 'the hated Rump, and the detested Association', in order 'to shew their detestation of the Practices of some ill men, and their joy for the safe Arrival of His Majesty and Royal Highness'.[90] Similarly there was 'great rejoicing' at Dover, and 'several bonfires at night'.[91]

Demonstrations in support of the Duke continued through the spring. Well-wishers cheered the Catholic heir as he processed through the City of London to attend the Artillery Company's feast on 20 April. The evening concluded with the inevitable bonfires in the evening: at the Dog-Wonder Tavern in Ludgate the crowd shouted, 'God Bless the King and his Royal Highness; No Bill of Exclusion; No

Associators.'[92] On 13 May 1682, when news reached Salisbury that York had survived the storm which had wrecked his ship on his way back to Scotland – he was returning to collect his wife – such was the relief that 'the bells of that place rang, bonfiers were made, and healths drank in the midst of the Market place on their knees.'[93] There were bonfires and loyal healths at Oundle in Northamptonshire a few days later for the same reason, and bonfires in London on the 27th when York returned to the capital.[94]

May 29 that year was the occasion of exuberant loyalist and antiWhig displays in many towns throughout the kingdom. London saw several. At Covent Garden a crowd burned Titus Oates in effigy, together with the Association and the Solemn League and Covenant. In Whitefriars, the Association was first read and then committed to the flames 'by vote of the vast multitude', while in London's legal district the societies of the Middle and Inner Temples staged bonfires where the Covenant and the Association were burned.[95] Similar rituals were repeated in the provinces. At Norwich on 29 May an effigy of Jack Presbyter was reportedly burned at 'a very great Bonfire' in the centre of the city, to the 'lowd acclamations of God Save the King and His Royal House'. Then various 'Seditious and Rebellious Papers' were committed to the flames, with someone reading their titles to the assembled crowd as they were thrown in – 'The Solemn League and Covenant, The Engagement, The Directory, The Long Members Speech in the Long Parliament, The 19 Propositions made by the Long Parliament to King Charles I, The Bill of Comprehension, The Exclusion Bill, The Association' – together with effigies of several Whig publicists, including Henry Care, Langley Curtis, Richard Janeway and Francis Smith.[96] There was an elaborate civic celebration in Durham. In the morning the mayor, the high sheriff, the aldermen, and various other local gentlemen – 'about 100 Persons beside their Servants, with every man a Red Ribband in his Hat', to signify support for York – went to church to hear a sermon by the prebendary of Durham; they then attended a huge feast, where 'Royal Healths were Drunk with Drums beating to Every Glass'; after dinner they returned to church, presumably quite tipsy; and in the evening the mayor invited the company, together with the bishop of Durham, back to the guildhall for more loyal healths. The day concluded with a great bonfire in the town centre, where various Whig tracts were committed to the flames: 'The Solemn League and Covenant; The Late Horrid Association; Care's, Janeway's, and Curtis's Infamous and Seditious Prints', and so on, 'Each Paper being distinctly Named, and follow'd with a Huzza as it was cast into the fire' from the 'Multitudes of Spectators . . . that Joyn'd in the Common Joy and Satisfaction of the day'.[97] There were similar anti-Whig rituals at Derby and Manchester, while at Bristol chairs from a Quaker meeting house were used for a bonfire.[98]

The Duke of York's visit to Cambridge University on his birthday on 14 October prompted 'great rejoicing'. That evening two bonfires were lit in the town, with plenty of wine and drink, and people 'unanimously' drank the healths of the King, York and the university's chancellor, the Duke of Albemarle; the bonfires were 'so great' that people from the surrounding countryside thought the town was on fire.[99] There was a fireworks display at St James's Palace to commemorate the day, and also several bonfires in London (including three along Fleet Street, at Clifford's Inn, Chancery Lane and Temple Bar), where loyal youths drank the King's and York's health.[100] There were some Tory groups out in London on Gunpowder Treason Day – which in 1682 was commemorated on the 6th, since the 5th was a Sunday – shouting 'A York! A York!' as a deliberate act of provocation to the Whigs,[101] and there were bonfires again to commemorate the Queen's birthday on the 15th.[102] The young gentlemen of the Temples planned to burn Cromwell in effigy on the 17th – Elizabeth's accession day – though fear of disorder prompted the King to issue a proclamation forbidding tumultuous assemblies.[103] The government clampdown effectively put a stop to anti-Whig bonfire parades in the capital, although they continued in the provinces. Thus 29 May 1683 saw commemorations at York, Durham and Chichester, and even at the notoriously Whiggish town of Taunton in the West Country, where crowds gathered at a bonfire and drank healths to Charles II, the Duke of York and the bishops.[104]

This list has not been exhaustive. Given the way that contemporaries tended to report provincial celebrations, noting perhaps a couple of towns by name but adding that the like occurred in several other places, it is impossible to document everywhere in England that saw loyalist displays. Loyalists were undoubtedly active in 1681–2 in a way that they had not been before; no longer was the only voice being heard on the streets a Whig one. As with the addresses, however, we have to be careful how we treat the evidence of loyalist demonstrations. They certainly do not point to the conclusion that droves of people were abandoning the Whigs and becoming Tories.

In the first place, many of these loyalist demonstrations were sponsored from above. The pro-York demonstrations in Dover in April 1681 were well orchestrated. When the bonfires were lit, '13 great guns were fired from the Castle and 7 apiece from the two forts,' and 'all the vessels in the harbour that carried guns fired at the same time.'[105] As we have noted, the effigy-burning at Derby on 30 May 1681 was organized by 'some eminent persons of this Town', who provided the puppet of Jack Presbyter.[106] The celebrations in Durham on 29 May 1682 were planned three weeks beforehand by some 'gentlemen of quality', and the evening's bonfire, we are told, was 'prepar'd by the Mayor'.[107] The loyal demonstration at Taunton on 29 May 1683 was sponsored by the Tory mayor, Stephen Timewell, as a counter to the festivities that took place on 11 May to commemorate the parliamentarian victory there over the royalists during the Civil War.[108] The King himself even played a role in planning the enthusiastic reception his brother received in London on 8 April 1682 following York's return from Scotland, instructing the Lord Mayor in advance to give York such a welcome 'as became him', and dropping a strong hint when he added that he 'doubted not but his loyal apprentices in London would make a body for his reception'.[109] The bonfire at the Dog-Wonder Tavern in Ludgate on the 8th was allegedly put on at the behest of 'Several of the Duke's servants',[110] while 'several persons of quality' were present at the pro-York demonstrations in Ludgate on 20 April, pledging the loyal toasts to the assembled crowd as the King's life guards reminded 'the Boys and Mobile . . . of their Duty, to Shout and Hallow'.[111]

A second thing to emphasize is that there was no sudden decline in Whig demonstrations. If anything, they were on the rise in the years after the Oxford Parliament. On 5 November 1681, in addition to the normal pope-burnings throughout London,[112] there were several elaborate affairs in the provinces. At Salisbury an effigy of the pope, 'in his Chair of State, with a Triple Crown on his Head, a Cross in one hand, and a Scepter in the other, very richly gilded', was paraded through the streets of the city, with two men carrying 'the Picture of the Devil by him', accompanied by other pageants representing the Gunpowder Plot and the Popish Plot, and followed by 'Thousands of People'. At five in the evening the pope was burned at 'a great bon-fire, in the great Market-place'. The day's proceedings were put on 'at the Charge of the Young-men of the City', though the civic authori-ties also did their bit, since a great banquet was held at the council house for the mayor, aldermen, common councilmen and their wives, 'with a free Well-come to all other Loyal and Honest Gentlemen who came thither'. The carpenters of the royal shipyard at Chatham 'pre-pared several Carved Images, of the Pope, Jesuits, etc. which they carried in a Solemn Procession, through Chatham to Rochester' and back, accompanied by 'a multitude of joyful spectators', before burn-ing them at a huge bonfire 'at the end of the Town, and after having Sentence of Condemnation read against them, for many horrid Crimes, whereof they were proved Guilty'. At Taunton-Dean in Somerset effigies of the pope and the Devil were paraded through the streets of the town by 'a great number of Loyal Protestants', preceded by 'two persons, representing Fryers in their proper Habits' and 'two Popish Prelates, with Miters on their Heads'; behind the pope was 'the Representation of a Judge, in his Scarlet Gown, riding upon a Horse led by two Boys . . . attended by persons representing the Sheriff and officers, the rear of which Pageantry was brought up by a Country-man, on Horseback'. The effigies were not burned on that occasion, however, being saved for the forthcoming pope-burning on 17 November.[113]

The pope-burning procession in London on 17 November 1681 was the grandest yet. Several new pageants had been devised, 'at the cost of . . . Loyal Citizens and others'. This year 'His Holiness' had on his lap 'a fine fawning Spaniel, called Towzer, with an Observator in his Mouth' – an allusion to Roger L'Estrange. After a long procession through the crowded streets of the capital, beginning at Whitechapel in London's east end, the pope was finally committed to the flames at Smithfield in the west, the site of the heresy burnings under Queen

Mary, where the crowds were also treated to a splendid firework display.[114] On 24 November the news that a London jury had thrown out the treason charge against the Earl of Shaftesbury saw celebratory bonfires throughout the capital – more 'than ever yet was seen on the 29th of May', according to Thompson.[115] There was similar rejoicing in 'severall parts of this kingdome' as the news reached the provinces.[116] At Woodbridge, in Suffolk, local Whigs and dissenters gathered 'more money . . . towards Bonfires', Thompson tells us, 'than ever was known to be contributed by that Party to any Loyal or Charitable use in all their lives'.[117] At Dorchester, a town which had delivered a loyal address in defence of the succession earlier that year, the inhabitants expressed 'their joyfulness' at Shaftesbury's deliverance by bells and bonfires, as reportedly did many towns in the west, including Salisbury, which had recently seen an elaborate anti-Whig Presbyter-burning, and even Bristol, a city with a marked and aggressively active Tory presence.[118]

There also appeared to be no manifest decline in support for the Duke of Monmouth, who by now had emerged as the darling of the Whig crowds and seemed to be actively courting popularity as he staked his claim as the only viable Protestant alternative to the Duke of York.[119] Great crowds of people flocked to see him when he visited the Earl of Sunderland at Althorp in Northamptonshire in April 1681.[120] When the sessions opened at Warminster, Wiltshire, on 13 July 1681, a crowd of about forty persons turned up at the court house, 'with every one a Blew Ribbon in his Hat', to signify allegiance to Monmouth, since 'the men of Salisbury were now wearing red for the duke of York'.[121] Monmouth himself attended the London pope-burning at Smithfield on 17 November, and the assembled crowds drank his and the King's healths 'conjunctively'.[122] When the government banned the Whigs from holding a dinner at Haberdashers' Hall on 21 May 1682 to reward their supporters among the London apprentices, the apprentices responded by holding their own pope-burning outside Lord Colchester's lodgings, where 'many thousand of spectators' gathered, crying out 'No Pope, no Papist, God Bless the King and the Duke of Monmouth.'[123] When Monmouth made a progress through the Midlands to the north-west in September 1682 – ostensibly to attend the races at Wallasey in the Wirral, but in reality to test support for a potential uprising – he was greeted with much popular acclaim in many places he visited. At Chester 'the mobile' welcomed the Duke by making bonfires, around which they shouted, 'Let Monmouth reign, let Monmouth reign.' The arrest of some of the participants caused further disturbances the next day, when a group of about thirty, after having visited their friends in jail, 'came in a body through the streets shouting, A Monmouth, a Monmouth, and threatened to knock down and kill some they met, calling them Tories'. There were more bonfires that evening, and further disorders: an alderman who had come to suppress the crowd was beaten up, one of his assailants saying 'he cared not a f[art] for the King or Parliament, God Save the Duke of Monmouth.'[124] There was trouble at Coventry on 14 September, when 'the Rabble' rang the bells and made bonfires on Monmouth's behalf, and when an alderman tried to persuade the people 'to depart Peaceably . . . they fell upon him'. Later that evening 'The Mobile Muster'd' near the town cross 'with their Clubs; Menacing the Magistrates'.[125]

From surveying the evidence, it appears that many places were divided and at different times witnessed rival Whig and Tory demonstrations. On a number of occasions Whig and Tory groups actually came into direct conflict with each other. In London, on 5 November 1681, Tory youths, as well as staging their own presbyter-burning, tried to disrupt Whig pope-burnings in other parts of the capital. Whig apprentices, shouting 'A Monmouth, a Monmouth, no York, no York', tried to extinguish Tory bonfires celebrating York's return to London on 8 April, and to counter them with their own pope-burning; violent scuffles followed in several parts of the capital. There were similar violent confrontations on 20 April, 27 May and 29 May.[126] By the autumn, tensions were running high. On 14 October, Whig youths tried to extinguish the bonfires in Fleet Street to commemorate York's birthday. The Tory youths drove them away, but 'stood briskly on their guard, for fear of a second Attaque'.[127] There was serious violence on 6 November as groups shouting 'A York, a York' tried to extinguish Whig bonfires commemorating deliverance from the Gunpowder Plot. The Whigs retaliated, beating off the Tory youths, and then went on the rampage through the streets, shouting 'No York, a Monmouth, a Monmouth', attacking the residences of known 'Tory Rogues', and destroying distasteful pub signs, such as those of the Duke of York's Head, the Cardinal's Head, and the Mitre.[128]

Similar conflicts occurred in the provinces. In Derby the presbyter-burning procession on 30 May 1681 was disturbed by some local Whigs, who unsuccessfully attempted to seize the effigy.[129] While Tory supporters were allegedly burning effigies of Jack Presbyter and leading Whig journalists at the market place in Norwich on 29 May 1682, groups of Whigs celebrated the King's birthday and restoration by burning 'the Pope on the other side of the Water'.[130] In Oxford the Monmouth/York split might to some degree have corresponded to town v. gown rivalries. On 11 April 1683 an angry confrontation developed between some townsmen, who had been drinking healths to Monmouth in 'the Magpie' alehouse, and some scholars who responded by toasting York. The Monmouth men drank to York's confusion, and when the scholars left the pub they followed them outside, assaulted a number of them, and ran up and down the High Street crying 'A Monmouth! A Monmouth! No York!'[131]

The irony, of course, is that by appealing to opinion out-of-doors the Tories, who had condemned the rabble-rousing tactics of the Whigs, had in effect become rabble-rousers themselves. By encouraging people to take to the streets to manifest their opposition to the Whigs, the party of order had actually managed to create more disorder. Yet Tory propagandists were well aware that the price of not promoting loyalism among the masses could be greater. Thus, as L'Estrange reminded the readers of his *Observator* in November 1681, the people had been 'Fool'd and Enflam'd into a Rebellion' in 1641 by a group of men claiming to assert 'the Protestant Cause against Popery'; the same pretence was 'now set afoot again', and it was necessary 'to beware that it lead us not into the same Condition'.[132] Or, as he put it in a subsequent issue, 'Noise rhymes to Noise; and Noise . . . must be Oppos'd to Noise.'[133] The evidence of the loyal demonstrations, together with that of the loyal addresses and abhorrences, enabled the Tory media to claim that the Whigs did not have all the people on their side. Thus Thompson could boast in his *Intelligence* in May 1681, 'It doth now appear that those [Whig] Petitions and Addresses published in the Names of several Counties and Corporations were Mis-Representatives, and not Vox Populi; For we now abound with Addresses, Letters and Congratulations of a different nature.'[134] Another author, writing in 1685, could claim that it was clear that the Exclusion Bill was not the people's general desire, because 'the generality have for the most part protested against it.'[135]

It was precisely because the court and its Tory allies were trying to claim that the generality of the people were really on their side that Whig activity out-of-doors in turn intensified over the course of 1681–2. Neither group could let it be seen that the other predominated. This is why Whig apprentices in London were quick to counter the addresses of the Tory apprentices with addresses of their own, and also why there was conflict over rival pope- and presbyter-burning processions. And because we are dealing with propaganda – an attempt to convey the public impression that one side rather than the other monopolized people's sentiments – there was conflict over the way these rival demonstrations were represented in the media. Thus Tory newspapers tended to play up loyalist demonstrations and ignore Whig ones; Whig newspapers countered by questioning the reality of supposed Tory displays and highlighting the continued commitment of the people to the Whigs. Let us take Thompson's detailed coverage of the anti-Whig demonstrations at Norwich on 29 May 1682 as an example. Norwich was England's second city, and had a sizeable nonconformist population. To be able to report that it had now turned loyalist would be a major propaganda coup – much more impressive than the demonstrations on the King's birthday in Derby and Durham that Thompson had reported the previous year. For the same reason, the Whigs could not let Thompson's account of events go uncontested. A week later the Whig *True Protestant Mercury* published a letter from Norwich expressing great surprise 'at those impudent Forgeries of Nat. Thompson, which he says were acted on 29th of May'. 'We did indeed rejoice . . . that day,' this correspondent continued, 'being His Majesties Birth-day and Restauration', but, in fact, 'we burnt the Pope on the other side of the Water.'[136] Thompson did not fabricate his account; indeed, the letter denouncing his 'Forgeries' later concedes that some sort of loyalist display, promoted 'by two or three illiterate persons', did go on. Instead, there appear to have been rival Whig and Tory demonstrations in Norwich on that day, and

Thompson's 'forgery' lay in reporting only part of what went on. So here, in the press, we have a struggle over whose voice was going to be heard, and therefore over how the crowd was going to be read.

Whether the Whigs actually were losing support to the Tories is difficult to tell. The Tories probably were successful in recapturing the soft middle ground – the waverers, the less rabidly partisan, people who had been concerned about popery and arbitrary government but were otherwise not fully committed to the Whig platform – though I suspect we are dealing with a minority of the population rather than a wholesale shift among the general public at large from one side to the other. However, not all contemporaries – not all those who supported the Tories, even – were convinced that Toryism was becoming more popular than Whiggery. When William King, the future archbishop of Dublin, took the waters at Tunbridge in 1683 he noted that those who 'stood for the king', whom he praised as being 'sober men, imbued with a sense of religion', were 'much less popular' than the impious faction, 'for the cause which they were defending was displeasing to the whole English people'.[137] The loyal addresses and demonstrations nevertheless undoubtedly boosted the confidence of loyalists throughout the kingdom, and proved a significant blow to the morale of the Whigs. In August 1681 Reresby could report to Halifax how all was 'very quiet' in the West Riding of Yorkshire, 'for I doe not find a man Altered in the least in principles, except it be for the better, and then the well meaning party must . . . be very numerous in this Quarter'.[138] One London newsletter writer reported in June 1682 how 'the Whig party' were 'quite down in the mouth. They do not open in coffee-houses as formerly and the thinking men every day desert them. Their confidence is broken.'[139] Whatever the reality of the situation, what counted was that more and more people were becoming convinced that the people were turning Tory. As Luttrell noted in his diary in March 1683, 'The tempers of men are much altered to what they were within this twelvemonth, most now seeming tories.'[140]

Yet, if both parties wanted to be able to claim that they had the people on their side, they had to be the right sort of people. Thus Tory writers repeatedly condemned the lowly status of those who comprised the Whig crowds, while claiming the support of the more respectable types. Those who participated in Whig demonstrations or signed Whig addresses in London, for example, they castigated as the 'giddy Multitude', 'Butchers men and other mean fellowes', 'Porters and Broom-men'; the Tory apprentices, by contrast, were 'the greatest, and best bred part of the London Apprentices'.[141] Whig journalists naturally refused to accept such representations, but instead maintained that the opposite was true. Thus Janeway insisted that those London youths who signed Tory addresses were 'Ruffians and Beggerly Vermine, drawn in by Pots of Ale, and not Prentices'; the Whig apprentices, on the other hand, were 'ingenious well bred Youth[s]', who had 'Substantial Parents in the Countrey, and Trades to expect'.[142] More generally, one Whig pamphleteer alleged that 'the greatest part of those who have given thanks for Dissolving Parliaments, are such as either for want of years, or poverty, were never capable of giving a Vote in Election of Members to sit in them' and were 'made up of the scum and refuse of the places where they live'.[143]

In reality, it is difficult to say much about the sociology of support for the different parties. For the most part, the members of the various crowds we have examined retain their anonymity; unless participants were arrested for riotous behaviour (and, although a few degenerated into disorder, most of the demonstrations were relatively peaceful), they do not leave a trace in the historical record. Likewise with petitions; rarely do the actual sheets with subscribers' names survive, and, when they do, all we have to go on are the names, and it is not easy to identify who these people were or what they did for a living. The evidence we do have suggests that, although certain groups may have been more prone to support one side or the other (the weavers the Whigs, for example), on the whole the divisions cut vertically through society, not horizontally. Rich, middling sort and poor alike can be found on both sides of the divide, as can people both from the countryside and from the towns. The most striking predictor of political allegiance was religious affiliation; dissenters were overwhelmingly Whig, hardline Anglicans were Tory, though it has to be remembered that there were many moderate Anglicans who sympathized with dissent and who therefore also tended to side with the Whigs.[144]

THE PURGE OF LOCAL
OFFICE-HOLDERS

The efforts to appeal to opinion out-of-doors and encourage public manifestations of support for the crown were accompanied by a campaign to expel the Whigs and dissenters from local office. The government's first priority was to make sure the militia was in safe hands. In February 1681 the King removed the three remaining Lord Lieutenants who had supported Exclusion (the Earl of Manchester in Huntingdonshire, the Earl of Suffolk in Suffolk and Cambridgeshire, and the Earl of Essex in Hertfordshire) and replaced them with committed loyalists. This was followed by a widespread purge of the deputy Lieutenants and militia officers who had shown that they were disaffected with the government.[145] The government also set about removing suspect JPs. Before the end of August, new commissions had been sealed for every English county except Cambridgeshire, Dorset and Norfolk. This time the government showed no hesitation in taking on men of high social standing; thus those great Whig magnates who had kept their place on the bench in 1680 were now ousted. It also restored some of those displaced for disloyalty in 1680 who had made it clear that they had now mended their ways. Although Burnet exaggerated when he claimed that 'none were left either on the bench, or in the militia, that did not with zeal go into the humour of the court' – there were further adjustments in 1682, and even then a handful of men with Whiggish political sympathies did remain in various commissions in a few localities – the purges ensured that by the end of Charles II's reign county governance was well and truly in the hands of Tory loyalists, committed to defending their particular vision of government in Church and state as by law established.[146]

The purge of county government was accompanied by an even more dramatic purge of the corporations. The problem, from the government's point of view, was not just that the boroughs returned about four-fifths of MPs; it was also that municipal jurisdictions were exempt from the county commissions of the peace and policed themselves with borough magistrates appointed not by the crown but by the townsmen themselves. They were, in effect, little republics within the English monarchy. The drive to rid the towns of the politically and religiously disaffected led to a wholesale onslaught on corporate liberties via the notorious *quo warranto* proceedings, whereby the crown (or those acting in its name) sought to challenge 'by what warrant' a particular corporation claimed to exist. Many corporations were forced either to surrender their charter and request a new one from the crown or to risk facing a challenge to the legality of their charter by a writ of *quo warranto*. The policy, which continued into the early years of James II's reign, resulted in the granting of new charters to some 134 corporations between early 1682 and early 1687. It used to be thought that the crown's main aim was to influence the composition of the Commons by changing the electoral franchise in the corporations; yet over one-third of England's parliamentary boroughs (79 out of 217) were left unscathed, while many corporations which were not parliamentary boroughs came under attack. Although the campaign against the corporations certainly did have some electoral ramifications, its main purpose, it seems, was to limit the independence of the municipal law courts.[147]

As we saw earlier, over the course of the 1660s and '70s dissenters had managed to intrude themselves back into municipal government in many areas, despite the existence of the Corporation Act, and by the time of the Exclusion Crisis many town magistracies had come to be dominated by those who were critical of the government's political and religious policies and who were often prepared to shield the Whigs and nonconformists from efforts by the central government to use the law against dissidents. The greatest problem was in London itself, where in 1681 a number of leading Whigs accused of high treason – including Shaftesbury himself – won reprieves by dint of the fact that packed Whig juries threw out the bills of indictment *ignoramus* (i.e. no case to answer). Charles II himself was alleged to have acknowledged 'that his view in overturning the city-charters, was to take the nominations of the juries from the popular party'.[148]

Not that all the corporations were bastions of Whiggery. There were some loyal corporations, and there were loyalist interests in most. Indeed, many corporations witnessed bitter power struggles between rival Whig and Tory factions as each sought to gain control of town government – something which served only to increase the corporations' reputation for unruliness and to emphasize the need for reform. If anything, it was in the aftermath of the Oxford Parliament that party rivalry in many corporations came to a head. One of the most notorious examples is that of Rye, which became split between two rival corporations following a disputed mayoral election in August 1681, with 'the Whiggish party' setting up its own candidate, John Turney, as mayor in opposition to the conformist Mr Crouch. The King ordered Crouch to be mayor until the case was decided at law, but Turney eventually won his action, and in late May 1682 he broke into the town hall at the head of 'a rabble of near three hundred' and took possession. At the election the following August, rival mayors were once again set up: Turney 'by the Whigs', and Joseph Radford by 'the loyal inhabitants'.[149]

Local studies show that by the early 1680s many town councils had become bitterly divided along party lines, from Norwich and Bristol (England's second and third cities) to lesser population centres such as Leominster in Herefordshire.[150] London itself was far from being in a Whig stranglehold. In September 1681 a moderate Tory, Sir John Moore, was elected Lord Mayor, though his candidacy was helped by the fact that he was the most senior alderman and it was thus his turn to serve. The following year a more extreme Tory, Sir William Pritchard, was chosen as mayor, though only after the votes of religious nonconformists were disqualified. The most significant turning point for the Tories in London was when they recaptured control of the shrievalty in the summer of 1682, after a bitterly disputed election. There were two sheriffs in London, and in theory the Lord Mayor had the right to nominate one, although in recent years common hall, the City's freeman electorate, had elected both. At the poll on Midsummer Day 1682, Sir John Moore tried to impose his own nominee, the Tory Dudley North, as one of the sheriffs, but he was shouted down and jostled out of the court, after which the two outgoing Whig sheriffs, Thomas Pilkington and Samuel Shute, held a poll for two places. The election was violent and farcical. The Whigs claimed that their candidates, Thomas Papillon and John Dubois, had won, but the Tory candidate, Ralph Box, was declared elected to serve alongside North. Box then declined to serve, necessitating a fresh election in September. The Whigs, believing that Papillon and Dubois had been properly elected, refused to participate, and the Tory Sir Peter Rich was elected by a show of a mere 500 hands. Pilkington was soon to suffer a double whammy. In November the Duke of York brought an action against him for *scandalum magnatum*, for having said at a meeting of the court of aldermen shortly after York had returned from Scotland that York 'had burnt the city, and was now come to cut the citizens' throats'. Pilkington gave little defence, and the jury awarded York a staggering £100,000 in damages. With no hope of paying, Pilkington was committed to prison. Then in February 1683 Pilkington, Shute and twelve others were indicted and convicted for the riot at the shrieval election the previous summer: Shute was subsequently fined 1,000 marks (£666 13s. 6d.), and Pilkington a further £500 – a lesser sum by reason of his being already in jail.[151]

In its campaign to destroy the Whig influence in the corporations, the crown found that it could rely on the support of local Tories. Indeed, often the pressure for the purges came from the localities themselves, as excluded local Tories sought government assistance to restore themselves to local office or else an established Tory faction strove for greater control by displacing its Whig opponents.[152] The first *quo warranto* case to go all the way to judgement in the 1680s was that of Worcester; it was initiated by local Tories against the Whig mayor, James Higgins, and twenty-five other members of the corporation, who were accused of usurping 'upon the King' by holding office without subscribing the declaration against the Covenant. Although proceedings had begun as early as the autumn of 1680, the case was not finally resolved until the winter of 1682–3, when the twenty-six were convicted and replaced by more reliable men.[153] It was probably the Worcester example which inspired the government to initiate *quo warranto* proceedings against London in December 1681. The charge against London was that it had violated its charter, and thus ceased to exist as a corporation, by collecting illegal market tolls and by inciting 'the king's subjects to a hatred of the king's person, and government' by printing and dispersing a petition stating that Charles had been wrong to dissolve parliament. The government hoped for a voluntary surrender, but the City Whigs chose to fight to the bitter end. The courts decided on 12 June 1683 that the franchise of the City of London should be seized into the King's hands, and judgement was finally entered against the City on 4 October. The King then put the City government into commission, with all officers to be appointed by the crown and to act at royal pleasure.[154]

Over the course of 1682–3 the crown's legal officers tentatively came to develop a more general policy towards the corporations, using the threat of *quo warranto* proceedings to induce corporations to surrender their charters voluntarily, in return for which each would receive a new charter with extra privileges, though containing provisions requiring royal approbation of the choice of certain key municipal offices. Again, it seems to have been Tory partisans in the towns vying for the crown's support in their power struggles with local Whigs who showed the crown the way forward. The first town to surrender its charter was Thetford, Norfolk, in early 1682, following a disputed mayoral election the previous autumn, after which the outgoing mayor, John Mendham, had refused to swear in the newly elected mayor, Wormley Hethersett, on the grounds of electoral irregularities and the fact that Hethersett had not subscribed the declaration against the Covenant. When King's Bench insisted that Mendham install Hethersett or go to jail, Mendham decided that the only way to defeat his political enemies was to induce the corporation to agree to surrender its charter – although this involved some procedural deception and disqualifying the votes of his opponents. On 6 March the King granted a new charter, whose only new provision was a clause requiring the King's approval for the appointment of the recorder and town clerk. As the drive against the town charters gained momentum, the crown came to demand the right not just to approve but also to nominate corporation members (although the nominations would technically be just suggestions which the corporation had to approve) and also to remove members at will if they acted against royal pleasure (though Charles – unlike his brother, when king – used his power of displacement very sparingly). Some towns were induced to surrender relatively easily; others needed more prodding. Worcester surrendered its charter in 1684, despite its earlier *quo warranto* judgement, to prove its loyalty to the crown. At Berwick it took pressure from the leaders of the garrison to persuade the corporation to surrender rather than contest the *quo warranto*. The most trifling of deviations from the terms of the original charter could be used as the grounds for the threat of forfeiture. For example, St Ives, Huntingdonshire, was accused of having four constables instead of three, and three serjeants at mace instead of two. The complaint most often heard, however, concerned the miscarriage of justice in the borough courts.[155]

Many corporations experienced bitter partisan struggles over whether to surrender, with both local Tories and Whigs often seeking to enlist the support of local nobility and gentry in their efforts either to gain or to hold on to power. In 1682 Norwich saw an intense and drawn-out conflict. Although the Tories, who dominated the assembly, eventually prevailed, they met with stiff opposition from the Whig aldermen and their supporters among the citizenry, who managed to procure some 8–900 signatories to their petition against the surrender.[156] The surrender of Nottingham's charter in 1682 – which, according to Luttrell, 'was done by the mayor and 13 of the burgesses, against the farr greater number of the aldermen and burgesses' – similarly provoked 'great fewds in the Town'. One part of the corporation refused to recognize the new charter, which they said was fraudulently taken from them, and on 29 September the Whig burgesses, led by William Sacheverell, in alliance with the local dissenters, proceeded to elect their own mayor (Alderman Greaves), sheriffs and chamberlains 'by the vertue of the Old Charter'. A tumultuous crowd that gathered at the common hall frustrated the attempts by the outgoing mayor, the Tory Gervase Wild, to swear in the officers nominated under the new charter, and violently seized the mayor's books and the mace of one of the sheriffs. In the end the mayor had to retire to his home and swear in his officers there, but, when he came to the town cross publicly to proclaim the officers, former sheriff and nonconformist John Sherwin, 'with a crew of Dissenters . . . appeared in the street and in a riotous manner' cried, 'No new Charter, a Greaves, a Greaves.'[157] Party tensions remained intense in Coventry even after the surrender of its charter. Lord Brooke, the recorder, had advised against too severe a purge of the Whigs, arguing that less harm would be done by continuing most of them in office and thereby hoping to draw them over to the King's interest than by turning out any with 'great influence upon the poorer sort'. As a result, however, the Tories found that they were often 'not able to doe much against so prevalent a party', and complained that most of those in power under the new charter were 'such as courted the Duke of Monmouth when he passed through this City' in the autumn of 1682.[158]

The effect of the purges was to give greater control over the corporations to the landed class. In a number of corporations, local gentry were installed as honorary burgesses, while local grandees were often able to secure appointment to key corporate offices, such as those of recorder or steward – the Earl of Huntingdon became recorder of Leicester, for example, and the Earl of Yarmouth recorder of Norwich. This has led one historian to characterize the Tory Reaction as marking a political renaissance for the English aristocracy.[159] The purges also served to make the towns bastions of Toryism, and to ensure that the municipal law courts could be relied upon to enforce the law against political and religious dissidents. Yet, despite being motivated by blatant political objectives, the purges were legal in the sense that the crown always followed due legal procedure. Indeed, it was typically the corporation proceeded against that had been guilty of some violation of the law.

In many corporations the triumphant Tories staged public celebrations when they eventually received their new charter. Great Yarmouth celebrated the arrival of its new charter in July 1684 'with great Joye and bone Fyres and shooting of great gunnes in severall places of the Towne'.[160] There was an elaborate civic ceremony at Colchester when the town's recorder, the Duke of Albemarle, brought the new charter on 20 November 1684, the Duke himself being 'welcomed all the way . . . with the lowd acclamations of the people, who testified their joy at night by making bonfires'.[161] Chester's new charter was brought to the city's guildhall on 6 March 1685 'amidst the loud and repeated Acclamations of the People', helped no doubt by the fact that the mayor had ordered the conduit to run with wine.[162] York celebrated the arrival of its new charter in August 1685 with the 'continued Acclamations of the people', loyal toasts and bonfires.[163] The examples could be extended. The granting of a new charter, marking as it often did the victory of a local Tory interest over the Whigs, no doubt was genuinely welcome to certain sections of the population in the localities – further evidence, perhaps, of a shift in public sentiment towards the Tories as the 1680s progressed. Yet these displays also show signs of orchestration from above, while the *Gazette* did its best to give them due publicity, reinforcing our earlier argument about how important it had become to the Tories (and the government) to be seen to have the people on their side.

DESTROYING THEM IN THEIR LIVES, LIBERTIES AND ESTATES – THE DRIVE AGAINST DISSENT

The remodelling of the magisterial benches and the borough corporations paved the way for a ruthless drive against Protestant nonconformists in the final years of Charles's reign. From 1681 onward the government made repeated calls for the enforcement of all laws against Protestant dissent, resulting in the most sustained and most intense period of religious persecution in English history. All the weapons in the government's legal arsenal were brought to bear in an attempt to crush the dissenting schism – not only those laws enacted at the Restoration, such as the Five Mile Act of 1665 and the Conventicle Act of 1670, but also old Elizabethan laws, including the notorious act of 1593 against seditious sectaries (the Act of 35 Elizabeth). The government even used the Elizabethan and Jacobean recusancy laws against Protestant dissenters who failed to come to church, despite repeated complaints from dissenters that these had initially been enacted in order to deal with Catholic recusants. Although the fines for attendance at conventicles were relatively low (5 shillings for the first offence), many conventiclers found themselves being indicted for riot, which carried stiffer penalties; according to the law at the time, a riot was when three or more people gathered to commit an illegal act, and by this definition all nonconformist conventicles, however peaceful, were technically riots. The fine for recusancy was £20 per month, while the 1593 act against seditious sectaries potentially carried the death penalty for repeat offenders. If they suspected dissenters of disloyalty to the government, local officials had the option of imposing the oath of allegiance, which could prove an effective tool against the Quakers (and also some Baptists), who refused on principle to swear oaths. Other weapons were also used to try to intimidate dissenters into conformity, such as excommunication or the withholding of poor relief. Yet, although the government was prepared to use the full weight of the law against nonconformists, Charles himself was careful not to overstep the letter of the law. Indeed, when, in December 1681, the London lieutenancy proposed sending out eleven companies of trained bands to suppress meetings, the King forbade it from doing so, stating that he would always govern by law and that the conventicles should be suppressed by the civil magistrates.[164]

Legal though it may have been, there is no doubting the savageness of the persecution that resulted. Whigs and dissenters frequently complained of the brutality of the law-enforcement officers and informers who came to suppress their meetings. One report from mid-December 1681 describes how officials executing a warrant against an illegal conventicle in Salisbury 'beat many of the Persons Assembled' and dragged 'Men, Women, and Children . . . by the Hair' and threw them 'down the Stairs' as they made their arrests, tearing down the pulpit and seats and throwing all the Bibles they could find into the river.[165] The fines levied could soon mount up. In Bristol in 1683 fines totalling £16,440 were levied on just 191 Quakers for recusancy. In Suffolk in May 1685 exchequer processes against Quakers for failure to attend church amounted to an astonishing £33,300.[166] In Leicestershire, recusancy fines levied on nonconformists in September 1685 came to £31,000.[167] Those who could not pay were liable to have their goods distrained or face imprisonment. According to one Quaker petition, there were some 1,460 Friends in prison at the time of the accession of James II.[168] Such heavy punishments could be devastating: entire families were reduced to poverty, and many were forced to leave their homes and their businesses. Not just the dissenters but also the local economy suffered. In September 1682 Langley Curtis reported how the fines levied on dissenters in Bristol for not coming to church would 'force above 500 Families to relinquish their Houses and leave the Town'; indeed, so many had already left the city that 'the Trade thereof [was] Lessened' and the customs did not yield 'one third so much as . . . before the said Prosecution'.[169] Luttrell noted in December 1682 that the dissenters in London and several other parts of the kingdom had been prosecuted so severely that 'severall tradesmen and others [had] left their callings' and 'gone beyond sea, chusing rather to wander the wide world then undergoe (as they call it) such persecution'.[170] In Devon some 500 serge-makers were laid off work when their employers were imprisoned for nonconformity. In Suffolk some 200 woollen workers suffered when their Quaker employer went to jail.[171] The conditions in Restoration jails were so bad that those who were sent there were lucky if they came out without their health being seriously impaired. In March 1682 Curtis received a report that 86 Quakers and 52 Presbyterians had lately been committed in Bristol, where they were 'almost stifled', being forced 'to lay upon another, being at least 26 or 30 in a small room'.[172]

No one was actually executed for their religious beliefs in the 1680s. However, Quaker merchant Richard Vickris lay under penalty of execution in Bristol jail in 1682 after being convicted under the terms of the Act of 35 Elizabeth and required to abjure the realm; as a Quaker he refused to take the necessary oath and was adjudged a felon without benefit of clergy, although in this instance William Penn was able to use his influence with the Duke of York to get the conviction quashed on the grounds of errors in the original indictment.[173] Then in October 1684 the Presbyterian preacher Thomas Rosewell was found guilty of high treason for preaching a seditious sermon at a conventicle: he had questioned the King's ability to cure scrofula (adding that, in any case, the people should flock not to the King but to the nonconformist divines); had compared Charles to the 'most wicked Jeroboam', the idolatrous Old Testament king; and had promised his auditors that they 'would overcome their enemies'. Jeffreys, the presiding judge, faced with the jury's verdict, chose to suspend judgement, however, and Rosewell was ultimately saved by a royal pardon.[174] Nevertheless, large numbers of dissenters did die in Restoration jails. In 1687 William Penn put the total at some 5,000,[175] although this was undoubtedly an exaggeration. More reliably, the historian of the Quakers has calculated that some 450 Friends died in custody during the reigns of Charles II and James II.[176]

The Quakers were the smallest sect, albeit the best documented one and the one most vulnerable to imprisonment (both because of their poverty and also because their refusal to engage in the practice of occasional conformity left them particularly vulnerable to charges of recusancy). Given that the 1680s saw the most intense religious persecution of the Restoration period, it seems fair to conclude that several hundreds, at the very least, paid the ultimate price for their religious beliefs during the years of the Tory Reaction. As the Baptist Thomas Delaune put it in 1684, persecution was 'destroying them in their Liberties, Estates, yea Lives also'.[177]

As with the campaign against the borough corporations, we should see the persecution of dissenters during the final years of Charles II's reign as the result of a combination of pressure from the centre and from the localities. Indeed, in some areas Anglican zealots were calling for a rigorous enforcement of the laws against Protestant dissenters long before the central government took any action in this regard. For example, on 14 September 1679 Bristol JP Sir Robert Cann disturbed a couple of meetings in the castle precincts, claiming 'that he came thither to execute the Kings Lawes'; one of the conventiclers derisively enquired 'whether he had heard lately from the King or when he had spoken with him', clearly not believing that Charles II was backing such a policy at this stage.[178] For many loyalist Anglicans the close alliance between Exclusionists and the dissenters, which had already become apparent in 1679, reaffirmed that there was an inevitable link between political and religious heterodoxy, and that by striking at the latter one could help prevent the former. Furthermore, the purge of the magisterial bench over the winter and spring of 1679–80 resulted in there being more JPs who were keen to take action against Protestant nonconformists – not simply by displacing those who were soft on dissent with hardline Anglicans, but also by making those who had managed to hold on to their commissions more eager to prove their loyalty to the crown by acting against nonconformists. In Somerset, Dorset and Wiltshire there was a dramatic increase in the number of nonconformists (Presbyterians, Baptists and Quakers) indicted at the Easter sessions in 1680.[179] Persecution appears to have picked up again during the elections to the Oxford Parliament, even though the government was then urging the judges to be 'very tender as to the dissenters'.[180]

The central government's call for a rigorous enforcement of the penal laws from the summer of 1681 onward thus met with an enthusiastic response in some communities. For example, when the mayor of Bristol sent the constables and other local officers to pull down the pulpits, pews and seats of the various meeting houses in the city in December 1681, 'the Common People' were said to have rejoiced, seeing the chance of getting some free lumber.[181] Magistrates in Yorkshire, having read in the *Gazette* that the Middlesex JPs had been ordered to implement the laws against nonconformists, were disappointed not to receive similar instructions themselves when their sessions convened in January 1682; they nevertheless decided that such was the insolence of the nonconformists that it was necessary to humble them.[182] 'Severall freeholders of Middlesex' petitioned the justices at Hicks Hall in October 1682, asking them 'to intercede with' the King 'that the dissenters might be prosecuted all over England'.[183] In January 1683 a grand jury made up of 'the numerous party of Honest Trading men' of Southwark appealed to the Lord Mayor to be more vigorous in suppressing conventicles.[184]

Indeed, the presentments of grand juries up and down the country show that many had internalized Tory propaganda concerning the threat posed by the dissenters. At the Bristol sessions in the spring of 1682 the grand jury presented its opinion 'that the Best Expedient to Secure the Prerogatives of the Crown, and Liberty, and Property of the People' was by 'a Due and Impartiall Execution of the Penall Laws, the Defect of which gave way to the Late Rebellion'.[185] In December 1682 the grand jury for the hundred of Ossulston in Middlesex charged 'That Popery and Phanaticism' were 'equally dangerous to the Government by Law Established', the main difference being that the papists had always failed in their plots, whereas the fanatics had been successful, laying aside the monarchy, destroying the church, and exercising 'for almost Twenty Yeares . . . Arbitrary and Tyrannical Government against Law'.[186] Similarly in March 1683 the grand jury of Kent presented its opinion that 'Popery and Fanaticisme' were 'equally dangerous to the Government' and 'that the best and most effectual way to maintain and preserve His Majesties Sacred Person, the Church and State by Law Established, together with the just Liberties, Priviledges, and Properties of the

Subject' was by 'an Impartial and due Execution of the Laws'.[187]

However, in many places it was a small band of local zealots, even individual activists, who led the war against dissent, sometimes in the face of considerable local opposition. In Taunton, Somerset, Stephen Timewell, who served two terms as mayor from 1682 to 1684, found that his energetic attempts to disperse and dissolve all the conventicles in 'that Rebellious, Factious towne' almost brought about his economic ruin as a tradesman, since people refused to do business with him.[188] In Lincolnshire a clergyman who had 'been very careful to prosecute seditious Conventicles' had a number of vexatious lawsuits brought against him by disgruntled locals, and ended up in prison himself as a result, the local under-sheriff's deputy having decided to ignore an order from the court of King's Bench putting a stop to the actions against him.[189] In London between 1682 and 1686 John Hilton and his younger brother George led a gang of more than forty men and women who roamed the metropolis suppressing meetings in order to claim the portion of the fine due to informers under the provision of the 1670 Conventicle Act.[190] Yet informers in the capital did not have an easy time of it; they were frequently the target of physical abuse by angry crowds of nonconformist sympathizers seeking to rescue their prisoners.[191]

Wherever we look, we find evidence of considerable sympathy for nonconformists. In several areas, attempts to enforce the penal laws met with concerted resistance. When a nonconformist minister preaching in Southwark in May 1682 was arrested by a company of foot guards, the local apprentices 'rose to his rescue', beating off the soldiers and wounding their captain; so proud were they of their victory that they spent the whole night parading the streets, armed with cudgels, in celebration.[192] In Abingdon, Berkshire, in 1682 the Tory mayor enjoyed a brief period of success in prosecuting conventiclers, until his constables were assaulted in the town by a mob of over forty men, armed with swords and staffs, who were determined to protect the meetings; there were no further prosecutions of nonconformists at the Abingdon quarter sessions for several months after that.[193] Local officials were often reluctant to act, either out of sympathy for the Protestant dissenters or from a reluctance to alienate their friends, neighbours and business associates. This was especially true in the towns in the earlier years of the Tory Reaction, before the purges of municipal office-holders had made much progress. One Windsor resident pointed out in December 1681 that 'our magistrates here live by their trades,' and would 'not lose a customer to execute a law'.[194] Yet we also find magisterial opposition to persecution in the countryside, even after the purge of the bench in 1681–2. In September 1683 it was reported that, 'for fear of being thought too active in prosecution', some of the justices in East Sussex had 'totally neglected' to act against conventicles, and had discouraged others from doing so by blackening the credit of informers and by withholding the proportion of the fines due to them upon conviction; indeed, one justice at the summer quarter sessions had 'warned the people of extortion in ecclesiastical offices and of the many errors in their proceedings' against nonconformists.[195] In Dorset that same summer one JP not only discouraged informers but also gave the third of the fine levied on a nonconformist minister which by the provisions of the 1670 Conventicle Act should have gone to the poor of the parish back to the convicted preacher to distribute as he saw fit.[196]

It was the parish constables, however, who as a group proved the most unwilling allies in the war against dissent. As unpaid, part-time and temporary law-enforcement officers, drawn from the middle and lower ranks of the communities they were being asked to police, they were naturally hesitant about being too strict on the sins of their neighbours at the best of times; unless they were motivated by a particular animus against dissent (which some, in some areas, undoubtedly were), they could not easily be induced to take a tough stance on those who were merely worshipping peacefully in their own religious conventicles. The *Conventicle Courant*, the periodical produced by London's grand informer John Hilton between July 1682 and February 1683, abounds with complaints about the negligence of parish constables. At Sheffield in the summer of 1682 the local constables failed to make a return to a warrant issued by the justices of the quarter sessions requiring them to report all conventicles in their precincts; on this occasion their inaction was connived at by a local JP (the leader of the godly party in the area, who had been absent when the initial warrant had been issued), who not only refused to bind the constables over to answer for their omission but also went on to argue that all the proceedings against nonconformists were illegal.[197] At the Coventry sessions in January 1684 an ultra-loyalist grand jury handpicked by the Tory sheriffs presented 'all the constables' who had served over the last year 'for not doeing their duty in suppressing conventicles'.[198] That same month a London grand jury at the Old Bailey blamed the violation of the penal laws on 'the general neglect of Church Wardens and Constables'.[199] In September of that year the Middlesex magistrates brought indictments against the constables of Spitalfields and Bethnal Green 'for not informing and disturbing of conventicles'; some were fined £100, others £50, and some were ordered to stand in the pillory.[200]

The evidence of the drive against dissent, as with the campaign against borough corporations, reveals deep divisions in many communities during the final years of Charles II's reign. The precise balance between the conflicting political and religious interests varied considerably from place to place, of course, and it would require a series of detailed local studies in order to map the configurations of local partisan allegiance with any degree of subtlety. What is clear, however, is that there was no consensus behind the policies of the Tory Reaction. The Whigs of 1678–80 had not become the Tories of 1681–3; rather, in the years after the dissolution of the Oxford Parliament, Tories and Whigs, and anti- and pro-dissenting interests, became locked in a bitter struggle – for supremacy, on the one hand, and for survival (at times, literally life or death) on the other.

High-Anglican and Tory apologists were convinced that the drive against dissent helped reclaim people for the Church, thus putting an end to the schism which, to their minds, had been the source of all the political turmoil in seventeenth-century England. It is certainly true that many dissenters were intimidated into abandoning their conventicles and coming to church. One correspondent wrote from Bristol in November 1681 that 'this putting the Laws in Execution' had already 'brought more to Church . . . than have gone for several years past'.[201] Lord Norreys informed Secretary Jenkins in February 1682 that the only news worth reporting from Wiltshire was 'that the fanatics generally come to church, wherever they are prosecuted'.[202] The following month came a report from Somerset that the churches there were suddenly very full, 'for those who for many years past have been rigid Phanaticks, do frequent their Parish-Churches'.[203] Similar reports came in from all over the country – even of Baptists and Quakers who had supposedly converted to the Church of England.[204] Gloucestershire JP Lord Herbert of Ragland predicted in January 1682 that if the goverment kept 'steady in [its] proceedings against the Dissenters' it would 'have no more trouble with them', and that 'in a short time . . . a Dissenter will scarce be heard of.'[205] Conventicles seemed to have ceased completely in Coventry by the end of 1684, 'executing the law upon the non-conformists', and 'making them pay', having succeeded in bringing 'them all to church'.[206] Local research confirms this picture. In Kent, for example, persecution produced a significant shrinkage in the dissenting congregations.[207]

Most were well aware, however, that it was fear, rather than changed religious conviction, that was bringing the dissenters back to church. Thompson reported in his *Intelligence* in September 1682 that, since the recent appointment of a Baptist as parish constable in a town near Aylesbury, in Buckinghamshire, those nonconformists who had been going to church had started returning to their conventicles – 'By which 'tis apparent', Thompson continued, 'that by a due execution of the Laws, many of them (for Interest, not Conscience) would conform . . . But by the wilful neglect of some in office, these Vipers do daily increase.'[208] Many erstwhile conventiclers opted for partial conformity; they abandoned their meetings and went to church, but salved their consciences by declining to participate in those aspects of the liturgy which they found offensive. In July 1684 the Exeter general sessions concluded that, 'though Almost All our Sectaries do now Resort to their Parish-Churches', it was apparent from 'their Rude and Disorderly Behaviour there' that it was 'not in Conscience of their Duty, but only to Save their Money, and Avoid the Penalty of the Law; They Behaving themselves with All Imaginable Irreverence and Sawcy Demeanour in time of Divine Service'. The court therefore ordered the constables and churchwardens to present 'All such as do not Kneel at the Prayers in the Church; Stand up at the Repeating of the Creed, and in giving Glory to the Blessed Trinity, and at Other Hymns of the Church; and Observe All Other Decent Ceremonies, as they are Enjoyn'd by the Rubrique'.[209] Some dissenters remained recalcitrant, or held out for as long as they could. Others tried to move to where they hoped they might be left in peace. When the persecution began in Norwich in mid-1681, half a dozen or so of the more substantial nonconformist merchants decided to leave town and set up their trades at Ipswich.[210] At Hertford, in February 1682, it was said that the suppression of the meetings had brought some to church but had left others resolved 'never to go the Church of England more'. Some decided to emigrate overseas. Others contemplated suicide; two did, in fact, kill themselves, by jumping into a local lake.[211]

RADICAL CONSPIRACY AND THE RYE HOUSE INTRIGUES OF 1682–1683

In the face of the Tory Reaction, some radical Whigs did contemplate trying to bring down the government by force. Such is the nature of the evidence that it is not always easy to get at the truth behind the various alleged plots of the early 1680s: the government was convinced that the Whigs and dissenters were at heart republicans bent on destroying the monarchy and Church, and thus tended to believe the worst; in return for financial reward, informers were all too willing to exploit the government's anxieties by feeding it information that tended to confirm its worst fears; and, whenever allegations of Whig conspiracy came to the fore, it was in the government's interest to assume they were true and try to bring the alleged conspirators to justice so as to further tarnish the image of the Whigs in the public's mind. The first Whig to be successfully prosecuted for conspiracy was Stephen College, in August 1681, for an alleged plot to seize the King when parliament met at Oxford – although the evidence against him was flimsy, the original indictment against him having been thrown out by a Whig *ignoramus* jury in London, and his conviction was secured only after a second indictment was brought before an ultra-loyalist jury at Oxford.[212] Earlier generations of historians tended to be somewhat sceptical of the truth of the alleged Whig plots of the final years of Charles II's reign. Recent research, however, has shown that there was indeed a radical underground, headed by some

powerful figures from within the Whig elite who, following the failure of the parliamentary Exclusion movement, sought to mobilize discontented elements in all three kingdoms in an effort to effect radical
reform in Church and state by other means.[213]

When the King called parliament to meet at Oxford in March
1681, Shaftesbury and other Whig leaders (including the Earl of
Macclesfield, Lord Ford Grey of Warke and William Lord Russell)
appear to have had discussions with Monmouth about contingency
plans should Charles, as expected, strike out against the Exclusionists. The idea was that Shaftesbury should stay behind in London,
where he could raise his supporters in the City should the Oxford
Parliament be suddenly adjourned; Whig MPs would then quickly
return to London and reassemble at Guildhall. However, the King
took the precaution of stationing a large detachment of royal guards
in London during his absence, to prevent any possibility of trouble,
and Shaftesbury decided to call the plan off.[214] Shaftesbury's subsequent arrest that July, and his detention in the Tower until the end of
November, put a temporary stop to the Earl's intrigues. They were
revived in 1682, after York's return from Scotland in the spring.
When the King suddenly fell ill in May 1682, Shaftesbury, Grey,
Russell, Monmouth, Sir Thomas Armstrong and others met at
Shaftesbury's London residence, Thanet House, and apparently
decided that if Charles should die they would launch a rebellion with
the aim of summoning a parliament to determine the succession.
Charles recovered, but plans for an uprising were revived following
the Tory success at the London shrieval elections that summer. Whigs
and dissenters could now no longer expect to be secured from conviction by *ignoramus* juries, and, for those who had reason to fear for
their lives, the time for desperate measures had come. According to
Grey, Shaftesbury said that 'our friends in London now saw their
necks in danger, and that there was a necessity of having recourse to
arms, if they would save themselves.'[215] Shaftesbury, Grey,
Armstrong, Russell and Monmouth reconvened at Thanet House,
and after a number of follow-up meetings, during which more discontented Whigs were drawn in, the group decided upon coordinated
uprisings in different parts of the country. Shaftesbury would be
responsible for raising London; Russell was to sound out the West

Country; Grey to canvass Essex; while Monmouth was to make a progress to Cheshire, under the guise of attending the horse races at Wallasey, to gauge the level of support in the north-west and discuss options with the Whig peers Macclesfield and Delamere, and their sons Lord Gerard of Brandon and Henry Booth. As we have seen, Monmouth's tour of the north-west in September was very successful, and Shaftesbury was keen for immediate action, but Monmouth declined to act and Russell warned that the west was not ready.

At the same time, another group of conspirators began to discuss a plan to assassinate Charles and York on their return from the races at Newmarket in October (the idea being first suggested by the former Leveller John Wildman). Shaftesbury, growing increasingly disillusioned with Monmouth, warmed to the proposal, though the monarchist Whigs did not like it, fearing it would lead to a republic, and Monmouth refused to support any plot that threatened the life of his father. Robert Ferguson, the Scottish Independent divine and Shaftesbury's chaplain, emerged as the main intermediary between the two groups of conspirators – seemingly working for Monmouth, who hired him as an agent provocateur to find out as much as he could about the plot in order to obstruct it, though he may have been working as a double agent for Shaftesbury as well. The assassination plot fell through at this time, however, and so instead Shafesbury decided to persevere with the plans for joint uprisings. The conspirators set a date for the evening of 19 November, shortly after Gunpowder Treason Day and the anniversary of Elizabeth's accession (the two days of anti-Catholic commemoration in the Whig calendar), and a Sunday, when the shops would be shut and enough people would be on the streets to provide a cover for the comings and goings of the rebels. However, the scuffles that broke out between local Whig and Tory crowds in London on 6 November prompted the government to take extra security measures to prevent any bonfire celebrations on the 17th, and, with the west still not ready, the conspirators decided to postpone their plans. Shaftesbury, losing patience, and fearing for his life, fled England for the Low Countries on 28 November; he was to die in Amsterdam on 21 January 1683.

The idea of an uprising now came to be pursued by a newly formed 'Council of Six', comprising Monmouth, Russell, Essex, Lord

Howard of Escrick, Algernon Sidney and John Hampden. A separate group of conspirators, led by Robert West, proceeded with the assassination plot, now planning to ambush the King and his brother on their return from the spring races at Newmarket at the Rye House in Hoddesdon in Hertfordshire. (So called because the previous owner had been a maltster, the house now belonged to a Baptist and former Cromwellian officer named Richard Rumbold, who had married the maltster's widow.) The Council of Six decided to draw in the disaffected Earl of Argyll and his Scottish supporters, with the idea of launching coordinated rebellions in London, the West Country, Cheshire and Scotland. Some of the Scottish plotters came to London to meet with the English conspirators under the guise of buying lands in Carolina; the English authorities, delighted at the prospect that these relentless troublemakers might finally transport themselves off to the New World, were only too pleased to see them come to London to carry out what they understood to be their business.[216] Again, Ferguson was intimately involved in all these intrigues. The Council of Six was fatally split, however, between those who favoured the establishment of a commonwealth (Essex, Sidney and Hampden) and those who simply wanted to force the King to come to terms. As it turned out, the assassination plot was frustrated by a fire that broke at Newmarket on 22 March, which forced the royal brothers to depart several days earlier than anticipated. The Council of Six nevertheless continued to push ahead with its plans, and by June it had reportedly reached agreement on a draft manifesto, which provided for parliament's control of the militia, the right of counties to elect sheriffs, annual parliamentary elections, liberty of conscience, and the degrading of those nobles who had acted contrary to the interest of the people.[217] It is to this period that the two classic works of Whig resistance theory belong – John Locke's *Two Treatises of Government* and Algernon Sidney's *Discourses upon Government*, neither of which was published at the time, but which were clearly written as justification of the resistance that the radical Whigs were planning in 1682–3.[218]

The Rye House intrigues came to nothing, however. A Baptist oilman by the name of Josiah Keeling betrayed the conspiracy to the government on 12 June, and the authorities quickly made a series of arrests. The trials of the accused plotters began in the second week of July. On the 12th and 13th the government tried five men – Thomas Walcott, William Hone, Lord Russell, John Rouse and William Blague, of whom the first four were found guilty of treason and executed. For the first generation of Whigs and those earlier historians who doubted the reality of the plot, the trials were a travesty of justice and therefore indicative of the tyranny of the government. Modern scholars, however, have adopted a more balanced view. With regard to the trials of these particular individuals, at least, the government acted reasonably fairly by the standards of the time; there was certainly no universal presumption of guilt, as Blague's acquittal suggests, while there is strong evidence for the guilt of the other four. Lord Chief Justice Jeffreys certainly gave a blatantly partisan summing up in Russell's trial, and used the news (which reached the court while the trial was under way) that one of the other accused conspirators, the Earl of Essex, had allegedly committed suicide in the Tower to affirm the reality of the plot. This undoubtedly had some influence on the jury, and today would most likely result in a mistrial. Yet Russell was not the innocent of Whig legend; he himself subsequently admitted that he was guilty of at least misprision of treason, an offence which might well have cost him his life in any case. Russell's counsel tried to claim that the government had violated the law by not impanelling a jury of freeholders, but in fact the law was not clear on this point and seemed to apply only to felony trials at the county assizes, not treason trials or trials in corporations (where a local jury was highly unlikely to comprise landed freeholders).[219] .

The death of Essex on 13 July was controversial at the time, and has been the subject of speculation ever since. From the wounds inflicted, it seems highly unlikely that he could have slit his own throat with a razor, as was alleged. Indeed, one scholar has made a strong case that York and Sunderland commissioned the assassination of Essex in order to bolster public belief in the reality of the plot and help secure the conviction of Russell and other conspirators.[220] If true, this would perhaps be enough by itself to indict the regime in the eyes of posterity, although the evidence is such that no firm conclusions can be reached. The Whig lawyer, and erstwhile member of the Green Ribbon Club, Laurence Braddon was convinced that Essex had been murdered, and began collecting evidence to prove it. The government was understandably nervous; even if it had had nothing to do with Essex's death, whatever Braddon chose to represent as the truth could have been extremely damaging politically. In September 1683 it therefore had him arrested upon suspicion of suborning a witness and set bail at a staggering £12,000 for his appearance before King's Bench; if he were to meet bail, he was then to give sureties of £6,000 for his good behaviour. Upon petition, bail was eventually reduced at the end of October to £2,000, and Braddon was released. He was eventually tried the following February, found guilty, fined £2,000 and bound to his good behaviour for life, and remanded in prison until he paid. He was not to be released until after the Glorious Revolution.[221]

On 12 July, the day before Essex's death, the government also brought indictments against a number of conspirators who had already fled, among them Monmouth, Armstrong, Grey, Ferguson, and some more minor figures including Nathaniel Wade and James Holloway. Monmouth had gone into not so secret hiding at his mistress's house at Toddington in Bedfordshire.[222] With the government needing whatever information Monmouth might be able to provide to help secure the convictions of the other members of the Council of Six now in custody – Sidney and Hampden – Halifax managed to effect a reconciliation between the King and his son in the autumn, and to induce Monmouth to surrender himself on 24 November, acknowledge his guilt before the King and the Duke of York, and reveal all he knew of the conspiracy on the understanding that his confession would be kept secret. The next day Charles announced that Monmouth had submitted and that he had decided to stop all further proceedings against him. In the meantime, the government had decided to try Sidney using the unpublished drafts of his *Discourses* as the second witness against him; the plotter turned informer Lord Howard of Escrick was the first. Although at his trial on 14 November Sidney did a good job of attacking Howard's credibility and denied (much less convincingly) writing the papers that had been seized in his study, the jury took less than thirty minutes to find him guilty and he was sentenced to be hanged, drawn and quartered on 26 November. On the same day that Sidney was executed,

Monmouth received his formal pardon and a gift of £4,000 from his father. Monmouth was furious, however, when the news that he had submitted was published in the *Gazette*, and he publicly denied knowing of any plot.[223] His denial, coupled with the lenient treatment he received, lent credibility to suspicions that the government had concocted the plot in order to strike at leading Whigs. On 6 December Charles managed to get him to sign a vaguely worded document affirming that he had 'owned the late Conspiracy' and lamenting his role in it (though protesting his ignorance of any design against the King's life),[224] but Monmouth retracted it the next day – fearing it would be used to secure the conviction of his friend Hampden – and Charles was left with no option but to banish his son from court. When the government issued subpoenas for Monmouth to give evidence at Hampden's trial on 25 January 1684, Monmouth fled to the Continent. By April he was in Brussels.

Hampden was brought to trial on 6 February, but, without a second witness to prove an act of treason, he was convicted only of disturbing the peace and spreading sedition – a misdemeanour. The court nevertheless fined him a staggering £40,000, and ordered him to remain in custody until the fine was paid, which effectively condemned him to life imprisonment. The government did manage to capture two alleged conspirators who had fled overseas: James Holloway was arrested in the Caribbean in January 1684, and Sir Thomas Armstrong was seized in the Low Countries in May. Since both had been attainted as outlaws after they had fled justice following their indictments for high treason, the court had the power to sentence them to death without a trial. However, the government chose to give Holloway a King's Bench trial, indicting him for illegal flight, and offered to waive the judgement already given against him so he might defend himself against the treason charge, even though he had confessed shortly after his arrest; the logic was 'to make more public what he has confessed of that damnable conspiracy'.[225] Rather than plead his case, Holloway decided to throw himself on the mercy of the court, but he was sent to the gallows on 30 April. By contrast, the government denied Armstrong's request for a trial, and on 14 June King's Bench sentenced him to death on a charge of outlawry for treason. In a paper delivered to the sheriff on the scaffold, Armstrong claimed he could have produced witnesses to prove his innocence, cited the precedent of Holloway, and claimed that an act of Edward VI's reign gave a fugitive a right to a trial if he turned himself in within a year. Armstrong had hardly surrendered himself, however, and in having him condemned without a trial the government was not violating due legal process.[226]

One further victim of the Rye House Plot investigations was Sir Samuel Barnardiston, the foreman of Shaftesbury's *ignoramus* jury of November 1681. In February 1684 he was indicted for having written four scandalous letters the previous summer about how the investigations into the plot were going. The letters were privately addressed and not particularly scandalous – although they did contain sentences in favour of Russell and Sidney, and a reflection on Lord Chief Justice Jeffreys – but Jeffreys, as presiding judge, instructed the jury to convict and imposed a fine of £10,000. Barnardiston remained in prison until June 1688, when he was released upon payment of £6,000 and giving bond for the rest.[227]

The government was also determined to make an example of Titus Oates, the man who in its view had started all this mess with his phoney revelations of a Popish Plot. On 18 June 1684 York brought an action against him for *scandalum magnatum*, alleging that Oates had circulated false news and lies about him – specifically in a coffee house in December 1682, when he had publicly proclaimed York to be a traitor. Jeffreys gave another scathing summing-up, and the jury inevitably convicted, assessing the damages at an incredible £100,000 and ordering Oates to pay an additional 20 shillings in costs. Such steep fines were arguably contrary to Magna Carta, 'which provided that no man should be fined to his utter ruin'.[228] Indeed, excessive fines and the setting of excessive bail were to emerge as major grievances against the Stuart regime at the time of the Glorious Revolution, and were condemned by the Declaration of Rights in one of the document's few clauses that addressed abuses of government under Charles II as well as under James II. Charles II's regime was arguably guilty of abusing at least the spirit, if not the letter, of the law in this regard, since the tactic was deployed to keep in prison men whom the government regarded as dangerously disaffected but whom the law would otherwise not have been able to detain.

The revelations of the Rye House Plot brought a further reaction in the country at large against the Whigs and dissenters. To ensure that no one could fail to know who was to blame, the King published a declaration – again apparently penned by Lord Keeper North[229] – which he ordered to be read in all churches and chapels throughout the kingdom, detailing the conspiracy of radical Whigs and noncon-formists against his and his brother's life. Revealingly, it began by observing the recent rise in loyalist sentiment out-of-doors. Boasting of his own 'Zeal for the Maintenance of the Protestant Religion, and . . . Resolutions to Govern according to Law', Charles observed how of late 'Our good Subjects' had already begun to see 'what Troubles' the tactics of the Whigs would produce, and had thus 'upon all Occasions' taken the opportunity to 'Manifest their Resolution and Readiness in Defence of our Person, and Support of Our Government, and the Religion Established'. 'By these means', Charles claimed, 'the Factious Party lost ground daily,' so that in the end they became des-perate, 'and Resolved . . . to betake themselves to Arms'.[230] The dec-laration concluded by announcing that 9 September would be a day of thanksgiving for deliverance from the plot. The occasion provided the cue for a round of loyal sermonizing, as clerics up and down the country preached in vindication of the principles of loyalty and passive obedience and lashed out against the dissenters, the proceed-ings of 'the whig party' and the 'late houses of commons' – although a few preachers, it should be said, 'inveighed both against this plott and the late popish plott, taking notice that there was no thanksgiving day for our deliverance from that'.[231] As part of this Tory ideological offensive, on 21 July 1683 the University of Oxford issued a decree condemning 'certain pernicious books and damnable principles' which it took to be destructive to royal government – among them the views that authority was derived originally from the people, that tyrants forfeited their right to rule, that the king shared his sovereignty with the two houses of parliament, that subjects were not obliged to a passive obedience when a ruler commanded something against the law, and that Charles I was lawfully put to death.[232]

The revelations of the plot became the cue for a third bout of loyal addresses. Between early July and the end of the year some 283 addresses came in from all over England and Wales expressing abhorrence of the plot and pledging loyalty to the crown.[233] Most of them came from the same types of body as the abhorrences of 1682 – town corporations, grand juries, lawyers – though there were also addresses from independent groups who had no official responsibility for law enforcement, such as the Merchant Adventurers of England, the Thames watermen, and a group who styled themselves 'the Gentlemen of the Loyall Clubb at Newport in the County of Essex'.[234] The address of the mayor, aldermen, assistants and grand jury of Reading of 13 July 1683 typified the tone of many. It began by congratulating the King on his delivery 'from the dreadfull effect of the most horrid and traiterous Conspiracy that hath been hatched in any age, contrived and fomented by persons of Phanaticke and Anti-monarchicall Principles', and went on to offer the addressors' lives and fortunes in defence of the King's person, 'the Government both in Church and State and the Succession in the right Lyne against all traiterous Conspirators and factious Sectaryes'.[235]

Not only were there more loyal addresses in 1683 than there had been in either 1681 or 1682, but they came in more rapidly – sometimes too rapidly for the government's liking. On 27 July the Earl of Derby, the Lord Lieutenant of Cheshire, wrote to Ormonde at court stating that he had been waiting over a fortnight for 'some model of an address', but having not received one he had decided to delay no longer. He had therefore drawn up his own address, signed by the 'principal gentlemen' who were officers in the county militia, and stated that he was 'desirous to be as early as possible in appearing to be very zealous in abhorring those wretches who were for destroying so good a King, and subverting so good a government'. Ormonde replied that he wanted 'more hands to it', and suggested waiting until the assizes met towards the end of August so that an address could be delivered in the name of the whole county.[236] Indeed, there was little need for much prodding from the government to produce loyal addresses this time around; local rulers in both town and countryside had good reason to distance themselves from such radical conspiracy – especially, one might add, if they came from areas whose loyalty had long been suspect. It is revealing that the first address against the Rye House Plot came from the Lord Mayor, aldermen and common council of the City of London; recent elections had given the Tories control of the mayoralty and a narrow majority on the common council, while the *quo warranto* proceedings against the City's charter had made those who now headed the City government anxious to offer their congratulations to the King and his brother for their safe deliverance and to pledge their own 'Lives and Fortunes' in defence of the King's person, his 'Heirs and Successors' and the 'Government Established in Church and State'.[237] In Lyme Regis at the end of August 182 people signed an address in the name of the corporation, freeholders and other loyal subjects of the borough, expressing joy at the King's safe deliverance from the Rye House Plot and abhorrence of all plots and associations against the King's person, 'his heirs and Lawfull Successors, and the Government as now by Law Established in Church and State'. This was 31 more than had signed the address of 1681, and 115 more than had signed the abhorrence of 1682. Lyme Regis, it is worth noting here, would be the place where the Monmouth Rebellion would start in June 1685.[238] It is important to emphasize that most Whigs had steered clear of conspiratorial activity, and even those who could never have been induced to thank Charles for his declaration of April 1681 or to express abhorrence of Shaftesbury's supposed Association were likely to have been horrified by the revelations of a conspiracy to assassinate the King and his brother. The addresses do, however, reflect a variety of political outlooks. Some were ultra-loyalist, and not only condemned the Rye House Plot but also inveighed against the proceedings of the last two Houses of Commons. Some of the addresses from borough corporations came with an offer of a surrender of the town charter.[239] The address of the mayor and common council of the city of Oxford, by contrast, started by condemning the conspiracy, but then proceeded to attack the *quo warranto* proceedings, urging the crown not to judge the addressors by the faults of some factious persons, protesting their own loyalty, and imploring the King to show clemency and confirm their ancient liberties and franchises.[240]

In addition to the addresses, there were a number of bonfire displays on 9 September to celebrate deliverance from the Rye House Plot.[241] Portsmouth, Plymouth and Wells all staged noteworthy commemorations; at the last, we are told, 'The Loyall Gentlemen in the towne' made an effigy of Jack Presbyter, which they affixed with papers marked 'Association', 'Anarchy', 'Ignoramus' and 'No Bishops' and paraded around the streets in a solemn procession before finally burning it at a huge bonfire at the market cross.[242] At Oxford there were many bonfires in the city and the university. The city sponsored musical entertainment and paid for a barrel of ale and a bonfire, while on the pump in front of the Star Inn someone had set a tub containing an effigy of Jack Presbyter. 'The smart lads of the city', we are told, 'march'd downe the streets with cudgells in their hands, crying for the King and the duke of York', though 'all people', it was said, 'had York in their mouths', and the Duke's health was drunk publicly in most college halls at dinner.[243] At Coventry, which reserved its festivities for Monday the 10th, loyalists carried effigies of Shaftesbury and Ferguson together with 'The Damn'd Association', 'The Scotch Covenant' and 'Liberty of Conscience' from house to house through the town, with one of their number reading and expounding upon them 'all the way they went'. They processed to the town jail, and from there to the market cross, 'where they Hung them up, upon a Gibbet', with a bonfire underneath. One thousand people allegedly witnessed the mock execution, shouting 'God save the King and the Duke of York,' to the accompaniment of 'Vollies of Shot, and Ringing of Bells'.[244]

As the above accounts imply, these were not spontaneous rituals; they clearly had some degree of official sponsorship. In Reading the municipal authorities decided in advance that after the appropriate solemnities on 9 September the church bells should ring, 'a Bonfire be made in the markett place, and a Barrell of Beere, foure bottells of Sack and twelve of Clarett' be provided to help celebrate 'his Majesties happy deliverance'.[245] Taunton – 'lately esteemed one of the most disloyal and factious places in England' our source correctly informs us – saw 'great outward expressions of joy' on both Sunday the 9th and Monday the 10th, the latter being marked 'by ringing of bells, beating of drums, bonfires, feasting, etc. as was never known there'. This was partly a reflection of the fact that some of the 'great Whigs' of the town were eager to give 'public testimony of their returning to their allegiance', but mainly owing to the energies of the Tory mayor, Stephen Timewell, and his fellow magistrates, who were the 'great encouragers of the solemnity, treating the people very liberally with liquors and beginning healths to the King and the rest of the royal family'.[246] On 12 September the Tories of Cheshire held a hunt, followed by a feast, in Delamere Forest, to celebrate 'the Kings, Dukes, and Kingdomes Deliverance from the Rage, and Malice of a Phanaticall Conspiracy'; they toasted both Charles's and the Duke of York's healths to the accompaniment of 'Huzzas, Musick, Trumpets, and Hunters Horns', before going off to the races at Wallasey. Even 'the very Mobile', we are told, 'were Converted by the Example, and struck-in with their Acclamations too'.[247]

Yet, although loyalists may have made all the noise, and in some of the more notoriously disaffected areas Whigs may have been keen to be seen to be loyal, we should not assume that partisan tensions were now dead or that most people had at last turned Tory. At Keighley, in Yorkshire, at the beginning of July, 'the King's arms were . . . pulled down and defaced' in what was unmistakably an anti-Stuart – if not an antimonarchical – public gesture.[248] 'A poor mechanical man' from Elham in Kent commemorated 9 September by toasting Monmouth's health in a local tavern, though he was severely rebuked by someone else in the pub, who subsequently reported him to the authorities.[249] The loyalist display at Coventry on the 10th was in part a reaction to a 'contemptuous piece of Pageantry' on the previous day, when a group had tried to hold up the town's vicar to public ridicule by setting up a malkin at his door, dressed in the canonical habit.[250] At Reading, the day after the town's loyalist display on the 9th, Lord Lovelace and a group of local Whigs aroused suspicion by holding a private dinner at the Three Ton Tavern; someone even arranged for the bells of St Grace's church to be rung, 'for joy of these gentlemen meeting', though one of the town's Tory magistrates quickly ordered the ringers to stop. There appear to have been some in the community, at least, who were taking heart at the news that the area's Whigs were still active, and that their cause might therefore not be totally lost.[251] In some parts of the country the Rye House revelations became an excuse for Tory and Anglican zealots to lash out at their Whig and nonconformist neighbours. For example at Wigan on 9 September one couple, Richard and Martha Anice, both 'much in drinke' after the day's festivities, led a crowd of somewhere between thirty and sixty people through the middle-class area of the town, abusing residents known for their sympathy for Whiggery or dissent 'in many foule and abusive words, Calling them Rogues and presbiterian Rascalls and papists doges and sinners and whores'.[252]

The Rye House revelations led to an intensification of the drive against dissent.[253] With the link between religious nonconformity and political disaffection now firmly established in the public mind, many communities adopted a policy of zero tolerance. As a Cheshire grand jury explained in October, when justifying its decision that 'all Persons not Frequenting the Church according to Law' should be presented as recusants, it was 'Impossible to know the Hearts of Men, for what Cause they refuse to come to Church', and any 'Connivance and Indulgence in that Case' was 'the ready Road to Rebellion, Popery, and Arbitrary Power'.[254] The plot also gave the local Tory grand juries an excuse to strike at their Whig opponents among the local gentry. In July 1683 a Northamptonshire grand jury presented fifty-one 'ill-affected' gentlemen to be bound over to keep the peace, claiming they were members of 'a dissaffected party in this County' who had presented 'a Seditious Address' in support of Exclusion to their members for the Oxford Parliament, and had 'held severall Meetings, Clubbs, or Caballs' to carry on various 'Dangerous Designs against the Government', 'their Discourses being notoriously bold, and their Party generally furnished with a Proportion of Arms rather for some Dangerous Designs, then for the use of private Persons'.[255] This resulted in one Mr Butler being brought to trial at King's Bench for presenting the supposedly seditious address; he was convicted and fined 500 marks (£333 6s. 8d.).[256] On 17 September a specially selected Cheshire grand jury presented some twenty-eight leading magnates 'from a Dissatisfy'd Party in the County' (or 'the whigg party', as Luttrell called them) – including the Earl of Macclesfield, Lord Brandon, Henry Booth and Sir Robert Cotton – to be bound over for good behaviour, on bonds of £500 apiece, for various 'Dangerous and Seditious' activities. The particular causes of concern were that they had promoted an address in favour of Exclusion at the election of Booth and Cotton to the Oxford Parliament; had held 'Severall Meetings and Caballs' in the county since, which had caused great suspicion 'by the Store of Arms, many of them were Provided with'; and in September 1682 had assembled with 'Schismatiques and

Dissaffected Persons, in the Publick Reception of James Duke of Monmouth', a man who was 'a Prime Confederate in the Late Treasonable Conspiracy'.[257] On 1 October the Sussex grand jury for the general quarter sessions at Midhurst presented thirty gentlemen, one baronet, and several esquires – 'all men of estates in the county' – because they had 'either Associated with some of the Ring-Leaders' of the Rye House Plot 'or declared their dislike of this present Government, or have countenanced Non-conforming Preachers, either by frequenting their Meetings, or Protecting them in their houses'.[258] Likewise the grand jury for the Isle of Ely at the general assizes which was held in September requested that the 'Many Seditious, and Ill-Affected Persons' in that isle be bound over for good behaviour.[259] In the spring of 1684 at the assizes at Taunton a grand jury presented three prominent West Country Whigs – George Speke, William Strode and Edward Clarke – as disaffected and dangerous persons, and bound them over to good behaviour.[260]

CONCLUSION (AND A NOTE ON TRIMMERS)

The years following the dissolution of the Oxford Parliament saw a dramatic rise in public manifestations of support for the King in his stance against the Whigs, which undoubtedly reflected some degree of shift in public opinion from the Whigs to the Tories. But we do not see the emergence of a Tory consensus. In fact England became bitterly divided along partisan lines, as Whigs and Tories confronted each other in the courts, in the corporations, and in the streets. If anything, it was in the years after the dissolution of the Oxford Parliament that partisan tensions reached their highest intensity. This is reflected in linguistic usage: the terms 'Whig' and 'Tory', which had first been employed in an English political context in 1680, became everyday currency to describe the competing factions that existed in both the metropolis and in the localities during the years of the Tory Reaction, having been popularized by L'Estrange's *Observator*, which started as a dialogue between Whig and Tory in April 1681.[261] The labels began as terms of abuse, and they were thus often used negatively. One manuscript newsletter records how in December 1681 two students of Lincoln's Inn got into a quarrel over 'reproaching each other with those popular names of distinction of Tory and Whig' and decided to have a duel, in which one was killed.[262] In the autumn of 1684 the deputy recorder of Northampton gave a speech to the mayor-elect in which he claimed that 'this Town' was 'the Nation in little', with two groups of men 'branding one another with the ignominious Name of Whig and Tory', both of which he thought were 'vile'.[263] Increasingly, however, the labels were used purely descriptively – as in an account referring to political disputes in Wigan in November 1682, which concluded with the remark 'and so the question lies between Whig and Tory'.[264] Indeed, political partisans also began to be apply the terms to themselves, wearing them as badges of honour. Thus in March 1682 Richard Ferrar, writing from London to his cousin John in Little Gidding, could complain about being 'now shammed with such abominable Tory & Tantivy mens fables, that an honest Whigg can scarce distinguish Truth'.[265] In early September 1682 five drunken Tories marched through Whitechapel forcing 'all they met with to say God Bless the Tories', and when taken before a JP to account for their actions they swore 'damn 'em . . . they were true Tories and no Whiggs.'[266] Shortly after the hotly contested London shrieval elections of the summer of 1682, a scholar from Newington School asked a bookbinder's apprentice in Little Britain whether his master was 'a Whig or a Tory'. The apprentice replied, 'A Tory.' The scholar later told the bookbinder himself that he wished he could do business with one of his own judgement – implying that he clearly thought of himself as a Whig.[267] The same willingness to adopt party labels is noticeable in the provinces. In response to a feast held by 'some of the most eminent Whigs' of the area, the mayor of Reading in the autumn of 1681 decided to hold what he termed, quite straightforwardly, a 'Tory-Feast'.[268]

It would be too simplistic, however, to argue that England polarized neatly into two camps of Whig and Tory. Just as there were radical and moderate Whigs, so too there were hardline and moderate Tories. Revealingly, the deputy recorder of Northampton who castigated both Whigs and Tories in 1684 recognized the existence of another sort in the town, whom he styled 'Loyal Men' – those who 'always have, and ever will endeavour to support the established Government in Church and State' – but who sound to us rather like Tories (albeit of a more moderate kind). An account of political divisions in Norwich from February 1682 spoke of three parties in the town – 'the violent Tories' and 'the violent Whigs', as they were called, but also a third group of moderates, who were 'for the present government both in church and state, but go soberly to work'.[269]

We have also to recognize the emergence of a group of self-styled 'trimmers' in this period – people who saw themselves as trimming between the two extremes. Famously, in 1684 the Marquis of Halifax published his *Character of a Trimmer* – in part a defence of his own career and shifting political alliances – which argued for a politics of moderation and compromise.[270] Yet L'Estrange had recognized trimmers as a force in politics much earlier, and in November 1682 had changed his *Observator* from being a dialogue between Whig and Tory to one between Trimmer and Observator.[271] There were also trimming divines in the Church. During the height of the Tory Reaction, a group of latitudinarian clergymen in London – including John Sharp, John Tillotson, Thomas Tenison, Simon Patrick and Edward Fowler – published a series of tracts urging the necessity of unity between Anglicans and dissenters in the face of the popish threat, their professed aim being to save the nonconformists from persecution by persuading them back into communion with the Church of England.[272]

The subject of trimmers is an important one, and deserves fuller treatment than can be afforded here. There certainly were people who saw themselves as occupying a middle position between the two extremes, who espoused an ideological position which they saw as being distinct from that of either party, and who often applied the label 'trimmer' to themselves. What is less clear is whether we can we talk about the trimmers as a distinctive and coherent third force in politics at this time. The term 'trimmer' was used in a variety of different ways. L'Estrange, who was no friend to trimming, maintained there were 'severall sorts of Trimmers; as Your State-Trimmer, Your Law-Trimmer; Your Church-Trimmer, Your Trading-Trimmer'.[273] There were trimmers who belonged to the court, city and country too.[274] The main point of L'Estrange's attack on trimmers was to convince those inclined to moderation of the necessity of taking stern measures against Protestant dissenters. Neutrality was not an option; one could not claim to be of no party and be both for the King and soft on those who had 'gone astray'. 'Neuters' were 'a Faction as well as Enemies', having 'Cast-off the Duty of a Subject' in their 'Bare Neutrality'.[275] When Sir Edward Herbert was made Lord Chief Justice of King's Bench in 1685, Chancellor Jeffreys advised him not only to let the law wreak its vengeance on the Whigs, but 'likewise to remember the snivelling trimmers; for you know what our Saviour Jesus Christ says in the Gospell, that "they that are not for us are against us."'[276] To some, then, trimmers were those who betrayed what the Tories stood for. Yet not all trimmers fitted this categorization. Francis North, Lord Guilford, said that he came to be regarded as a trimmer in 1684 because he was critical of the way that Jeffreys was accelerating the drive against corporate charters and kept emphasizing the need to adhere strictly to the rule of law. Yet Guilford was the man who had penned that masterpiece of Tory propaganda, Charles II's declaration of April 1681. Indeed, he claimed that the term 'trimmer' was taken up to divide the Tory party, following the rise to prominence in the King's counsels of Sunderland and Jeffreys and the restoration to full political power of the Duke of York in the final year of the King's reign, alleging that 'all (however loyal, and of the established church professed) that did not go into all the lengths of the new high-flown party at court' were styled trimmers.[277] For others, trimmers were simply nonconformists who went to church: 'A Church-Trimmer is the Beelzebub or Prince of Trimmers . . . a Conforming Non-conformist, a Spiritual Jugler.'[278] According to an account written after the Glorious Revolution, trimmers were those 'who join'd with the Dissenters in . . . desiring moderation both in Church and State'.[279] For the radical Whig lawyer Thomas Hunt, trimmers were 'the more moderate sort of Tories'; for Dryden, they were 'secret Whigs'.[280] It is difficult to see any coherence here.

What is apparent, however, is how difficult it was to avoid taking sides over most of the divisive issues of the final years of Charles II's reign, because when it came down to it there were basic either/or choices that had to be made. Should the succession be changed or not? Should the laws against dissenters be enforced or not? Was one going to rejoice at the deliverance from the Rye House Plot or not? 'There are no Neuters in Treason,' as one Anglican preacher reminded his congregation.[281] It was, L'Estrange insisted, 'Ridiculous to talk of Moderation in a Case that Admits of no Excess. Did you ever hear of any man that was too Just, too Wise, too Temperate, too Brave, too Loyall, too Pious, too Continent, too Charitable?'[282] There was 'a great Difference', he told his trimmer adversary on another occasion, 'betwixt a Tenderness for the Person, and a Plea for the Malefactor'.[283] Thus a Southwark grand jury could proclaim in January 1683 that 'all who do less than their utmost towards the Suppressing all Conventicles prohibited by Law, and yet stile themselves his Majesties Loyal Subjects', were 'meer Usurpers of that Title'. Likewise, those 'who plead for the Relaxation of the Penal Laws against either Popish, or Protestant Dissenters, at this time, under what specious Pretext soever', were 'Enemies to the King'. What was needed was 'a thorow and impartial Execution of the Penal Laws against all Dissenters what-soever'.[284] Those latitudinarian clergymen who argued for the need to try to win back the dissenters by persuasion nevertheless agreed that, in the context of the times, enforcing the penal laws was necessary.[285] Even then, they often found themselves reproached by hardliners among their parishioners who thought they were being too soft on dis-sent. Fowler's 'Impartiality in Preaching' thus created a number of 'Bitter Enemies' for him in his parish of St Giles Cripplegate – a parish with a large concentration of nonconformists. Some, he said, 'took such offence as to declare they would never hear' him preach again. Others took legal action, prosecuting him in the Court of Arches for alleged uncanonical practices: admitting excommunicated persons without absolution, backing Whigs and dissenters at the elections for common councilmen, and discouraging the presenting of dissenters. As a result, he was suspended from his clerical functions on 9 December 1685.[286]

This discussion of trimmers further serves to emphasize why the government and its Tory allies felt that winning back public opinion was so important. In order to defeat the Whig and nonconformist challenge, local agents of law enforcement had to be willing to take action against the political and religious enemies of the crown. Constables had to make arrests; magistrates had to bring charges;

juries had to convict. The government could not have these types of people effectively determining policy for themselves and saying that things would be all right if people were not too strict about dissent. Hence the court and its Tory allies had to persuade people that it *was* necessary to take action against Whigs and nonconformists (the purpose of their propaganda campaign); and they had to give people the courage to do so, and to assure them that by supporting a legal campaign of repression they would not be acting in the face of public opinion. Thus it became important for the government to be able to show that it had public opinion on its side – and the support of the right sort of people – and to encourage its supporters to be more proactive in expressing their loyalty. It was a policy of legal repression that defeated the Whig challenge rather than one of political conversion through the gentle arts of persuasion. We must not lose sight of the brutality of the persecution that England witnessed in the final years of Charles II's reign. Yet the success of that legal repression was predicated upon the success of the Tory counter-propaganda campaign. Policy and police went hand in hand, and as a result the Whigs were destroyed as an effective political force and the dissenting schism was seriously weakened.

6

From Bothwell Bridge to Wigtown

Scotland and the Stewart Reaction

The Scottish Whigs were of as Rank a Tincture . . . as any of our English Ones; their Meetings; their Numbers; and their Resolutions, much more Considerable (in proportion) then they were here in England . . . And yet you see now, the Power of Good Laws; and a Steady Administration of them, in the Instance of that Kingdom. The Meetings are not only Suppress'd; but the Venome it self of that Virulent Faction Corrected and Aswag'd.[1]

Since Pentland Engagement till this Period . . . there was some kind of shadow from the present iniquous Laws, to countenance what was done this Way: But in the Period we are now entring upon, besides the new barbarous Laws made, the Execution of them was very bloody and very extensive; and the blood-thirsty Executioners, in many Cases, gave not themselves the Trouble to keep by their own Laws, but harassed and murdered in the publick Roads, open Fields, and almost every where upon the South-side of Tay.[2]

We have seen how in England, through a combination of policy and police, Charles II was able to extricate himself from the crisis that developed in the late 1670s and early 1680s and steadily rebuild the position of the monarchy during the final years of his reign. In the process, the crown set itself in firm alliance with the Tory-Anglican interest, representing itself as acting in accordance with the rule of law and in defence of the present establishment in Church and state as by law established. Yet the crisis that had faced Charles in the late 1670s and early 1680s was not purely English in nature. Those who feared the threat of popery and arbitrary government had pointed to developments in Ireland and Scotland to suggest what the royal brothers had in store for England, while the royal administration remained concerned, as it had been throughout much of the Restoration period, about the possible threat to political stability posed by the disaffected in Charles II's two other kingdoms. Of the three kingdoms, Scotland appeared to pose the greatest danger to the security of the Restoration regime. On 3 May 1679 a group of radical Presbyterians had murdered the Archbishop of St Andrews, James Sharp, while shortly thereafter some 8,000 covenanters in the southwest had risen in arms against the government. Even after the defeat of the rebel forces at Bothwell Bridge on 22 June, there remained a threat from the radical Cameronian faction, who in various public declarations proceeded to excommunicate Charles Stuart and declare war on a man they regarded as both a tyrant and a usurper.

We need to consider, then, how the government responded to the crisis in Scotland, and how this response differed from its actions in England. Do we likewise see an attempt to build up public support for the government's position and a similar concern to be seen to be acting in accordance with the rule of law? What sort of measures did those in authority pursue in order to deal with the challenge of political and religious dissent, and what were their consequences? We also have to recognize that what was done in Scotland was not simply a solution to a Scottish problem; it was also part of a British solution to a larger British problem. Charles II sent his brother, the Duke of York (or Duke of Albany, to give him his Scottish title), to Scotland for two periods during the Exclusion Crisis: the first from November 1679 to February 1680, and the second from October 1680 to March 1682. York played an active role at the head of the government north of the border, and served as high commissioner to the parliament which Charles II summoned to assemble in Edinburgh during the summer of 1681. We must assess what York was able to achieve in Scotland, why Charles held a parliament there when he had already given up on parliaments in England, and what impact such initiatives north of the border had on political developments and informed opinion within England.

THE AFTERMATH OF BOTHWELL BRIDGE AND YORK'S FIRST SPELL IN SCOTLAND, 1679–1680

Although Scotland had proved to be a more rebellious country than England, we should be careful not exaggerate the extent of disaffection north of the border. Their inherent political and religious conservatism meant that the ruling elite in Restoration Scotland were never likely to join forces with popular discontented elements to cause the types of problem for Charles II as had faced his father in the late 1630s. As one historian has put it, in 1679, in contrast to 1637, 'popular anger was not fused with aristocratic dissent.'[3] Yet there was also opposition to the covenanters from those below the level of the elite. The Duke of Monmouth, captain-general of the English army and the man Charles dispatched to put down the Bothwell Bridge rebellion, was cheered by 'all his Majesties good subjects' when he arrived in Edinburgh on 18 June, we are told.[4] Similarly, 'Great Multitudes' lined both sides of the street for 2 miles out of town when the captured rebels were brought to the Scottish capital on 24 June, maliciously 'jesting and reproaching the Prisoners as they went by', while there were 'publick Rejoycings' in Edinburgh on 14 August following the execution of John King and John Kid, two field preachers taken for alleged involvement in the uprising (although on this occasion the Scottish privy council had given orders for the lighting of bonfires).[5]

The covenanters were no match for Monmouth's professionals when they met at Bothwell Bridge on the outskirts of Glasgow on 22 June. Several hundreds were killed as they fled the battle – estimates vary between 200 and 400, although the actual total was probably nearer the lower end, since Monmouth himself was opposed to slaughtering men in cold blood.[6] Some 1,200 surrendered in the field and were taken prisoner, with subsequent arrests swelling this total to about 1,400. Troops dispatched to the south-west under the command of John Graham of Claverhouse in search of rebels who had fled committed a number of severities, exacting free quarter, rifling the houses of suspects, and imposing excessive fines of dubious legality. The brutality was fuelled by Charles's having authorized the use of torture on those who refused to inform. Soldiers strung up one boy by his thumbs when he refused to declare which of his neighbours had been at Bothwell Bridge. They tied a cord around the head of another 'harmless youth', secured it to the butt of one of their pistols, and then twisted it 'about the upper Part of his Head . . . so hard, that the Flesh was cut round in to the Skull'. The cries of pain could be heard for miles around, and the unfortunate youth subsequently died of his wounds.[7]

Monmouth, however, urged moderation in the treatment of the arrested rebels. Most were released under the terms of the indemnity issued at Windsor on 27 July and proclaimed in Scotland on 14 August, after the executions of King and Kid; this offered a general pardon to all field or house conventiclers and those engaged in the rebellions of 1666 and 1679 – with certain exceptions – provided they took out a bond never to carry arms against the King or his royal authority. The exceptions were heritors and ministers involved in the Bothwell Bridge uprising, and those who had refused to obey the summons to join the government host to put down the rebels, threatened or abused any of the orthodox clergy, or denied that the uprising was a rebellion or that the killing of Archbishop Sharp was murder.[8] Of the presumed ringleaders and recalcitrant rebels, only seven were sentenced to death. In addition to Kid and King, thirty men were tried on charges of treason or denying Sharp's killing to have been murder, but all were given the opportunity to save themselves by taking the bond. Twenty-four did so, and one was acquitted; the remaining five were executed. Some 3–400 were slated for transportation to the colonies; tragically, more than 220 of these died when the overladen ship carrying them to Barbados was wrecked off the Orkney coast on 10 December.[9] Some thirty-five heritors excluded from the indemnity were dispossessed: Claverhouse was duly rewarded with one of the forfeited estates; some of the other land seized, it was said, was given to Catholics. Heavy fines were also imposed on those heritors who had failed to attend the militia muster – Lord Duddingstoun, for example, was fined £1,000 Scots for not sending out men.[10]

By the summer of 1679 it was again apparent that the policy of repression had not worked. Not only had it provoked another rebellion in Scotland, but it had also created a storm in England, encouraging the complaint that the royal administration was bent on establishing arbitrary government.[11] Charles therefore decided to try once more to reach an accommodation with the more moderate Presbyterians. On 29 June, just three days after he had learned of the defeat of the rebels at Bothwell Bridge, he issued a third Indulgence, which, while still calling for the suppression of field conventicles, suspended all laws against house conventicles south of the Tay, except those held within 2 miles of Edinburgh or 1 mile of St Andrews, Glasgow and Stirling. Although the royal suspending power was to emerge as a major issue at the time of the Revolution in both Scotland and England, on this occasion Charles could claim he was acting in accordance with a provision in the Scottish Conventicle Act of 1670, which had left it to the King's discretion whether or not to continue the act after three years had lapsed. The historian of the Presbyterian sufferings Robert Wodrow, although he certainly had his own politico-religious agenda, was probably correct when he said that 'this Indulgence was no Exercise of a dispensing Power, but agreeable to the Laws then in being.'[12] The orthodox clergy, however, were upset by the Indulgence, and urged the council to extend the exclusion zone around Edinburgh to 6 miles, though to no avail.[13]

Bothwell Bridge marked the effective end of Lauderdale's dominance of Scottish affairs. Although he did not formally resign as Secretary of State until October 1680, and Charles continued in the meantime to seek his advice, his influence was already gone. Some in Scotland would have liked to have seen Monmouth fill Lauderdale's role, but Monmouth was to lose favour at court in the autumn of 1679. Instead, it was the Duke of York who was to emerge as the dominant figure in Scottish affairs.

Charles allowed his brother to go to Scotland in the autumn of 1679 as an alternative to York's remaining in exile in the Low Countries. He gave his brother no clear brief, though he did decide that James should sit on the Scottish privy council, which provoked some controversy, since as a Catholic York would need to be dispensed from the oath of allegiance and supremacy required of all office-holders by an act of 1661. The Lord Advocate, Sir George Mackenzie of Rosehaugh, who was to emerge as one of the staunchest defenders of absolute monarchy in Scotland during the final years of Charles II's reign, protested to Lauderdale that the King could not dispense with this act, any more than he could 'dispens with all other statutes conceaved principallie in favours of the people', since it amounted to 'a parliamentarie contract betuixt King and people for the securitie of the kingdome'. Mackenzie also warned that, at a time when the court was advocating limitations on a popish successor as an alternative to Exclusion, a dispensation would hurt York's cause in England, since 'his Majestie's subjects . . . would never think themselfs secure by any Limitation to be put upon the successor whilst they saw that none could bind the subject.'[14] Lauderdale likewise did his best to persuade York to take the oath, urging that refusal would 'give too great advantage' to his enemies in England and 'to that pitifull Caball in Scotland' who preferred Monmouth. York nevertheless refused, and in the end Charles II authorized his brother to serve on the Scottish council without taking the oath, claiming that the wording of the act of 1661 did not comprehend the 'lawful sons and brothers' of the king.[15]

York and his duchess arrived at the Scottish border on 21 November, to be met by Chancellor Rothes, thirty-eight privy counsellors, and most of the nobility and gentry from the southern shires, and escorted in grand style to the Scottish capital. They entered Edinburgh on 24 November, the streets from Leith (2 miles away) being lined with 'many thousands of people' shouting 'Long life and Prosperity to the King' and 'Health and Wellcome to the Duke and Duchess.' At the Watergate, the town magistrates presented York with the keys to the city, with the Lord Provost making a speech expressing the city's 'great joy at his Royal Highnesses arrival there', and giving 'fresh assurances of their constant Loyalty to His Majesty', 'their firm adherence and affection to the Royal Line' and 'their particular respect and affection for his Royal Highness'. That evening the streets were filled with so many bonfires 'that the whole Town seemed one fire', and all night the conduits at the market cross ran with wine. The reception had been well planned, and the celebrations were obviously staged – though perhaps no less sincere for that, since undoubtedly many Scots were genuinely pleased 'to see a Prince so nearly related to His Majesty and the Crown among them'. York himself was delighted, writing a few days later that he had 'had as handsome a reception' as he could desire, of which he had 'great reason to be satisfyed'. Yet the extravagant displays of loyalty were also intended to send a message to the English. Shortly after the adverse parliamentary election results in England of August and September, and just a few days after the first great London pope-burning procession of the Exclusion Crisis, the *London Gazette* was able to report that there remained considerable support for the King and his heir, among both the political elite and those out-of-doors, in the Stuarts' ancient kingdom. It was the first public indication that the continued pursuit of Exclusion would probably cause a severe breach between the two realms of England and Scotland.[16]

Recognizing the need to establish as wide a base of support in Scotland as possible, York initially pursued a policy of accommodation. Many of those who had been excluded from power by Lauderdale, or had become alienated as a result of his policies, resumed their seats on the council – including Atholl, Queensberry and the Earl of Perth – all of whom were to become key players in the royal administration of the 1680s. Only Hamilton continued to remain aloof. Hardliners – and especially the bishops – complained about the concessions granted to Presbyterians, yet York recognized that he could not afford to alienate those who had welcomed Monmouth's initiatives, and so decided that the policy of indulgence should continue for the time being. As he put it in a letter of 14 December, he was determined not to become prisoner of 'either party here', but would endeavour 'to give offence to none, and to have no partialitys'. York admitted that he did not like the Indulgence, saying he feared it would encourage another rebellion; nevertheless, he thought it not 'proper to take it from them till they forfitt it againe'.[17] Even the Whiggish Burnet conceded that 'upon his first going to Scotland' the Duke behaved himself in a very obliging manner, and carried things 'so gently . . . that there was no cause of complaint'.[18]

As a result, York did much to build up a loyalist following among the political elite in Scotland. When he left for England in February 1680, the Scottish nobility and gentry present at court presented him with 'the view of the Crown, Sceptre and Sword of Scotland' and unanimously declared 'that they would all as one man venture their lives and fortunes in defence of his Majesty and his right successors against any opposition whatsoever'.[19] The Scottish council likewise wrote to Charles praising York's 'moderation of spirit and equalitie of justice' – observing how he had 'much encouraged the orthodox clergy without being greivous to such other protestants as differ from them' – and assuring the King that they would do all they could to 'mantaine your sacred Majestie and your royall successours in the ordinary degrees of succession, according to their unalterable right of blood, which you and they derive only from God Almighty'.[20] York himself was pleased with how things had gone during his stay in Scotland; as he told the council after learning he was being recalled to England, he would inform the King 'that he had in Scotland both a loyal nobility and gentry, and a Councill and his other judicatures filled with able and loyall persons'. Revealingly, in reporting this speech for readers in England, the *London Gazette* claimed that York then added 'that he had observed those restless People, who used to give them some trouble, were nothing so considerable as their Friends the Republican Party in England' represented them to be, and that the Scottish ruling elite 'were not only able and ready to keep those unquiet People in Order', but were 'so firmly united to the Royal Interest as he doubted not but the good Condition of this Kingdom, would have a very good Influence upon His Majesties Affairs in His other Dominions'.[21]

Only the Cameronians, the radical covenanting wing of Scottish Presbyterianism, remained 'restless' and 'unquiet'. The vast majority of the Presbyterians appeared willing to work within the terms of the Indulgence. However, shortly after York's departure the policy of moderation came to be abandoned. The Scottish bishops, worried about the threat to their position posed by the Indulgence, sent Bishop John Paterson of Edinburgh to London to complain to Lauderdale and Archbishop Sancroft about the plight of the Scottish Church. At the same time, the English bishops were keen for a drive against dissent in both kingdoms, while York himself, now more confident of his support among the Scots, saw an opportunity to strike at his rival Monmouth, who had been a leading advocate of concessions. Between them, these various interests convinced Charles that the Indulgence was not working, that its provisions were frequently being violated, and that field conventicles were still being held. In May 1680, Charles therefore placed a series of restrictions on the Indulgence: henceforth, no house conventicles were to be allowed within a mile of any parish church where a regular incumbent served; no nonconformist minister who had preached at field conventicles was to be licensed; none was to be licensed in a parish where he had formerly served as minister, or where the generality of people were conformist; and the exclusion zone around Edinburgh for house conventicles was extended from 2 to 12 miles. Meeting houses were shut down or demolished, conventiclers began to be prosecuted in increasing numbers, and licences were steadily recalled.[22]

The antics of the Cameronians in the summer of 1680 – the denunciations of Charles II and the Established Church in the Queensferry paper and Sanquhar declaration of June, and the subsequent excommunication of the King and the Duke of York at the Torwood conventicle in September[23] – provoked a further reaction. The government issued a proclamation offering financial rewards to any who should help bring in – 'dead or alive' – Richard Cameron, Donald Cargill or any of the other traitors involved in publishing the Sanquhar declaration.[24] In July 1680 Cameron and his brother were slain by dragoons at Airds Moss in Ayrshire, along with two dozen of their followers. David Hackston, one of Archbishop Sharp's murderers, was arrested, and brutally executed at the end of the month, having first his right hand cut off, 'and after some time his left hand', before being 'hanged up and cut down alive', disembowelled, and quartered. At least thirteen others taken either at Airds Moss or the Torwood conventicle were executed, including two women, Isobel Alison and Marian Harvey. A number of those arrested were tortured in an attempt to secure confessions. Four or five were 'so tortured with the boots', one anti-covenanter account tells us, 'that their legs, from their kness or their heels' were 'broke as flat and thin as a fingers breadth, so that the bloud and marrow coms out of their toes'.[25]

The government took a variety of other measures to clamp down on the expression of dissident opinion. On 6 January 1680 the council ordered that any gazettes or newsletters deposited in the coffee houses for public consumption should be first presented to the Bishop of Edinburgh or another privy counsellor for approval, so as to prevent the spread of 'false and seditious news and slanders'.[26] The discovery that some 'scandalous and seditious' news-sheets were still getting through prompted the authorities early in 1681 to require that all masters of coffee houses, or 'houses of intelligence', take out a bond for 5,000 merks not to 'vent any newes or papers nor suffer the same to be read in their houses' except such as were allowed by the officers of state.[27] Seditious utterances were also to be treated severely. In mid-July 1680, John Niven (or Nevin), the captain of a London-based ship and an Englishman, was convicted of treason and sentenced to death for saying that York was 'in a plot to take the king's life, and had combined with the French king to invade England', and further 'that the duke had come into Scotland to make a party for introducing popery, but our good old English hearts would not suffer that'. The judgement was a harsh one; the jury, in fact, split fifty-fifty, and the chancellor of the assize gave the deciding vote in favour of conviction. The contemporary Scottish lawyer Sir John Lauder of Fountainhall thought that 'in England such a process would be laughed at', believing that at most Niven's words amounted to *scandalum magnatum* and that the law could not 'stretch it to death', although the verdict was in fact based upon an act of 1587 which had made maliciously accusing an innocent person of treason treasonous itself. It appears, however, that 'this was done to fright England,' as Fountainhall put it, the judges knowing that Charles II, following York's intervention, intended to remit the sentence.[28]

YORK'S SECOND VISIT, 1680–1682

Charles sent his brother to Scotland again in October 1680, shortly before the second Exclusion Parliament convened, ostensibly (as the King informed his Scottish council) to oversee the reorganization of the militia and procure 'the generall settlement of the peace and quiet' of that kingdom.[29] More generally, however, Charles hoped that James's presence in Scotland would help secure the allegiance of the Scottish ruling elite, and thus guarantee that his northern kingdom remained loyal while he was facing the challenge from parliament and discontented elements out-of-doors in England.

At Charles's prompting, the Scottish council saw that there were suitable 'publick Demonstrations of Joy' when York arrived, the details of which were reported in a broadside published simultaneously in Edinburgh, London and Dublin. Large numbers of the nobility and gentry, plus 'a multitude of People', came to greet York and his wife (who were this time travelling by sea) at Kirkcaldy, on the north side of the Firth of Forth, on 25 October. After staying with Chancellor Rothes for a few nights, the royal couple made their way to the Scottish capital on the 29th. At Burntisland, just across the Forth from Edinburgh, they were received with guns, bells and the cheers of the people, and they crossed to Leith accompanied by the firing of 'the great Guns' of Edinburgh Castle. At Leith the shore was allegedly 'so throng with Persons of all Ranks, that the noise of the Cannon, Trumpets, Kettle-drums, and Drums, were almost drowned with the lowd and reiterated Acclamations of the People'. Thence they proceeded to Holyroodhouse, saluted all the way by the guns from the castle and 'the whole body of the People universally shouting with great joy and chearfulness, "Lord preserve His Majesty, and their Royal Highnesses, the Duke and Dutchess of Albany."' Throughout the Scottish capital, the bells continued ringing most of the night, and 'all the streets of the City', the published account tells us, 'were filled with great Bonefires, whither many of the Citizens repaired to drink their majesties and Royal Highnesses Health.'[30]

The joy at York's arrival was not as 'universal' as this account suggests; as we saw in Chapter 3, the students of the university, with the assistance of the local apprentices and tradesmen, were to orchestrate a pope-burning procession in the capital on Christmas Day 1680 to testify their concern about the prospect of a popish successor.[31] Nevertheless, York's return to Scotland was undoubtedly welcome to certain interest groups. Those who were most enthusiastic were the episcopalian clergy. On 30 October the Bishop of Edinburgh and other clergy in town waited upon the Duke, to express their 'general Satisfaction . . . at his Arrival'.[32] A week later the Scottish bishops wrote to their English brethren expressing how 'exceedinglie releeved and comforted' they were by His Royal Highness's return, anticipating that he would again come to their assistance in their continuing struggles against 'incendiarie shismatiques'.[33] The Scottish council likewise wrote to the King to thank him for sending his brother to reside among them and confirming their commitment to the lawful succession, 'the least invasion' of which, they alleged, 'could not but procure us a civill war' – 'a boast', Fountainhall thought, made 'to hector the House of Commons, and generality of the English nation', who wanted to exclude York on account of his religion.[34]

The Scottish authorities saw the value in trying to exploit this loyalist sentiment to the full by promoting public displays in support of the King and his heir. Rothes wanted to lay on bonfires in Edinburgh to celebrate the news that the House of Lords in England had thrown out the second Exclusion Bill on 15 November 1680, though on this occasion York advised that any celebrating would be premature, since he feared there was a chance he might be impeached.[35] In February 1681 York made a royal progress to Linlithgow and Stirling, attended by the nobility and the gentry, in a deliberate attempt, Wodrow tells us, to 'affect somewhat of the State of our old Kings, before he came to the Throne, and render himself a little more popular'. To judge from the official printed account, the progress was a great success: York found 'the Kindness and Affection of the People, in all the Towns and Villages' he visited, 'very remarkable'; large numbers came out to greet him 'with great shouts and Acclamations of Joy'; at Stirling there was apparently 'a Bon-fire before every House'; and on his return to Edinburgh 'great multitudes' formed 'one continual Crowd of people' from the west port to Holyroodhouse, 'all Blessing and Praying for the King and Duke'.[36] York also lent his presence to the celebration of the King's birthday in Edinburgh at the end of May 1681. The 29th, which was a Sunday, saw 'Sermons Preached in all the Churches Suitable to the occasion', although the festivities themselves were put off until the following day. The 30th proved a spectacular affair. The city authorities laid on a 'most Noble Banquet' for their royal highnesses at the market cross, where, amid the noise of guns, trumpets, drums and bells, and 'the Acclamations of the People' (intoxicated by wine flowing from the town conduits), the Duke and the town magistrates drank a health to the King. In the evening, York and his wife attended a huge bonfire at Palace Gate, where all the nobility and gentry in town, together with the city magistrates, 'Pledged upon their Kness . . . Health and Prosperity to their

Majesties, their Royal Highnesses, and all the Royal Family'. The celebrations continued throughout the night, 'with Ringing of Bells, discharging the great Guns, Bonfires, and all other publick expressions of Joy'. Nothing had been left to chance. The city constables had arranged in advance for bonfires to be built at 40-foot intervals along the High Street, and an informal tax was levied on the local inhabitants to defray the expenses. Yet, despite being orchestrated from above, the festivities seemed to offer reassuring confirmation of the depth of support for the royal family in the Scottish capital. Moreover, the news of the celebrations, which quickly reached England, helped to bolster the impression of revived public support for the royal brothers that Charles II was actively trying to encourage in the aftermath of the Oxford Parliament.[37]

The Parliament of 1681

Having rebuffed the English Whigs by his speedy dissolution of the Oxford Parliament, Charles decided to call a parliament to assemble in Edinburgh on 28 July. The idea appears to have come from within Scotland itself, with many of the 'chief men' of that kingdom having convinced both York and Charles that 'the loyal disposition of the greatest part of the nobilitie and Gentrie, together with the Duke's presence and winning behaviour, which had gain'd such an influence over that Kingdom', would undoubtedly 'make a Parliament not only contribute to the quiet and advantage of Scotland, but by running counter to that of England, be a check and bar to such violent proceedings as hitherto distracted that Nation'.[38] In other words, as one Edinburgh newswriter put it, a parliament was 'to be called in Scotland, by their good example to mother the English to a better compliance with the counsel'.[39]

There is little evidence that the government tried to influence the complexion of the parliament by interfering with elections. Some gentry from the Merse (in the Scottish south-east) did complain to the council that their sheriff, the Earl of Home, had tried to surprise them by giving only one day's notice of the intended election, but the council responded by instructing the sheriff to give at least six days' warning, so that voters might have the chance to make it to the poll.

'The Fanatick Party', on the other hand (according to Lord Advocate Mackenzie), tried their utmost to secure the election of 'as many of those infected with their principles . . . as the little Power and Interest they had in the Nation could procure'. As a result, the parliament was not the overwhelmingly loyalist body that some hoped for. York believed there were 'some turbulent people amongst them', while Mackenzie even claimed 'he saw seditious Bothwel Bridge faces sitting as members', although he later retracted this remark. Nevertheless, supporters of the court were clearly in the majority – Mackenzie in fact claimed that 'Loyal Members . . . were Ten to One of the disaffected' – and carried most divisions by 30 to 40 votes.[40]

Charles decided to appoint his brother as high commissioner, York having insisted that no one else should be allowed to represent the King while he himself was present in the kingdom. Some forty members objected, claiming that two acts of 1567 and 1609 prohibited anyone but Protestants from holding office under the crown, and tried to persuade Hamilton to introduce a motion to this effect. Hamilton backed down, however, when his lawyers explained that a commission to represent the king's person did not fall under the notion of an office.[41] The Marquis of Atholl was appointed president of the parliament, as a last-minute replacement for Chancellor Rothes, who had died shortly before the session opened. The 'great champions and Hectors' of York's interest in this parliament, according to Fountainhall, were Lord Advocate Mackenzie, Treasurer-Depute Charles Maitland (Lauderdale's younger brother), Sir George Gordon of Haddo, and the Lord Advocate's namesake George Mackenzie of Tarbat. York could also count on the unswerving support of the bishops.[42]

Before the meeting of parliament, the government initiated a further clampdown on field conventicles. In April the council issued a proclamation making heritors responsible for reporting any such conventicles held on their lands, empowering landlords to examine upon oath any person they suspected could give information about such offences and imposing fines of a quarter of a year's rent on those who failed to act.[43] The authorities finally caught up with Donald Cargill, now the leader of the Cameronian faction, at Covington, Lanarkshire, on 12 July 1681. Cargill, two of his associates and two

Bothwell rebels were convicted and sentenced to death on the 26th; the five men were executed in Edinburgh on the 27th, the day before the parliament met.[44]

Charles hoped to use the Scottish parliament to bolster the powers of the crown in Scotland and strengthen the position of the Stuart monarchy within the three kingdoms as a whole. In his letter to the assembly, read on the opening day of the session (28 July), he insisted that the crown's and his subjects' interests were inseparable, and that any invasion or diminution 'of the Rights and Prerogatives of Our Crown' would 'prove fatal, and destructive to the Security and Property of Our People'. He therefore urged parliament to pursue suitable remedies against rebellious principles, schism, and separation in the Church, as the best way of ensuring that 'our Government in Church and State as by law presently established . . . receive its due reverence and obedience'. Expanding upon the royal agenda, York explained that the King was determined to maintain the Protestant religion 'as now Established by Law' under the government of the bishops, and wanted effective action taken to suppress 'Seditious and Rebellious Conventicles'. Charles further wanted it understood, York continued, that he would ensure 'that Law should have its due Course, for the Security of His Subjects Properties and Rights'; in return, however, he expected parliament to be vigorous in asserting 'His Royal Prerogative' and 'in declaring the Rights of His Crown in its Natural and Legal course of Descent', and 'to settle and provide such seasonable and necessary Supplies, which the Support and Interest of His Government call for and require'. Parliament showed itself duly sympathetic to the crown's desires. In their formal response to the King's letter on 1 August, members said they wanted to let Charles's 'other Kingdoms and all the world sie that we esteem Our lyves and fortunes to be best imployed in manteining of the just rights and Prerogatives of your Majesties Croune and Monarchie, The Native succession whereof', they added, could not 'be invaded without utter Subversion of the Fundamental Laws of this your Majesties antient Kingdome'. The Scots were well aware, it seems, that they had been assembled in order to make a political point to the English. Moreover, to ensure the English got the message, Charles's letter, York's speech and parliament's answer were all published in London.[45]

The government made every effort to manage the parliamentary session so that the desired legislation might go through smoothly. Charles gave his brother explicit instructions not to allow anything to be transacted that had not passed through the Lords of the Articles, and to suppress any unusual or extraordinary meetings, cabals and conventions during the session, to prevent the emergence of the type of party discipline that had been seen in England during the Exclusion Crisis.[46] This did not prevent opposition, however.

The Lords of the Articles began by establishing a number of committees to prepare acts for securing the Protestant religion, upholding the succession, and voting a supply for the crown.[47] The committee for religion immediately proved troublesome. At the instigation of Sir James Dalrymple of Stair and the Earl of Argyll, it proposed an act for the 'securitie of the protestant religion against poperie and a popish King'. This would have confirmed the Confession of Faith of 1567; prevented any alteration to the public worship of the Church except by a national synod; required all office-holders to subscribe to the Confession of Faith on oath; made it a capital offence for any Jesuit, priest or person in monastic orders to celebrate mass; ratified and approved all those laws enacted since the accession of James VI against popery and imposed fines on magistrates who did not enforce them; and required all future monarchs, at both their accession and their coronation, to take the coronation oath of 1567 and a further oath not to 'endeavour to nor consent to any alteration or change of the said protestant religion' nor to give office to non-Protestants. Various other clauses were suggested to strengthen the act even further. One was that it should be high treason, pardonable only by the king and parliament acting jointly, for any to hold office without subscribing to the Confession of Faith. It was also proposed that, if no parliament were sitting at Charles II's death, the members of the former parliament should reassemble and sit for six months so they could settle all ecclesiastical, civil and military offices in Protestant hands, along the lines of the scheme of limitations on a popish successor that Charles had proposed to the English parliament in April 1679. Such a measure, if passed, would have significantly eroded the royal supremacy established in 1669, considerably enhanced the power of the Scottish parliament at the expense of the crown, and effectively tied the hands of a popish successor. As such, it was obviously unacceptable to York, who dismissed the committee.[48]

As a compromise, parliament agreed to defer the question of additional safeguards to protect the Protestant religion (such as a religious test for office-holders), and on 13 August it passed a very short act ratifying all the laws passed since the reign of James VI 'for settling and secureing the Liberty and Freedome of the true Kirk of God, and the Protestant Religion presently professed within this Realme, and all acts made against Popery'.[49] In giving the royal assent, York declared 'That he did heartily go along with them in providing for the security of the Protestant Religion' – a remark that received due publicity in England through the agency of the *London Gazette*. For Burnet, York's motive was purely cynical, thinking 'it would give a good grace to all that should be done afterwards, to begin with such a general and cold confirmation of all the former laws.'[50]

That same day parliament passed an act guaranteeing the succession. Asserting that the kings of Scotland derived 'their Royall power from God almightie alone', it proclaimed that upon the death of the monarch the 'right and administration' of the government devolved immediately upon 'the nixt Immediat and laufull heir, either male or female', that 'no difference in Religion . . . nor act of Parliament' could 'alter or divert the Right of Succession and lineal descent of the Croun', and that it was high treason for any subject to endeavour to alter the succession or debar 'the nixt laufull Successor from the Immediat, Actual, full and free Administration of the Government, conform to the laws of the Kingdom'. The measure was intended not only to ensure York's succession to the Scottish crown, but also to make it impossible to contemplate excluding him in England, unless the King's subjects wanted to expose themselves, as the act put it, 'to all the fatall and dreadfull consequences of a Civil warr'. To make sure the English got the point, a copy of the act was duly published in London (by Nathaniel Thompson), and its passage was reported in the *Gazette*.[51] By establishing that the next heir succeeded immediately, the Succession Act appeared to rescind the Coronation Act of 1567, which required that all monarchs take an oath promising to protect the true religion 'at the tyme of their coronatioun, and ressait [receipt] of thair princely authoritie';[52] it was thus at variance with the act just passed ratifying all laws passed since the accession of James VI for the security of the Protestant religion, of which the Coronation Act was one. Some members pressed for a formal repeal of the Coronation Act; others, convinced that a repeal had in effect been achieved, argued the need for a new measure that would oblige the king to take the coronation oath.[53] Neither suggestion came to anything. There was one potential loophole in the Succession Act, however: Fountainhall read the clause making it treason to attempt to debar the heir from the administration of the government, 'conform to the laws of the Kingdom', as implying that allegiance ceased 'if the next heir administrate contrary to the standing laws for the Protestant Religion' or sought 'to introduce Popery'.[54]

Parliament passed a variety of measures designed to strengthen the position of the Stuart dynasty in Scotland. On 20 August it voted an additional five years' supply to pay for the armed forces needed to protect the realm from possible 'rebellious commotions'; this was to follow on from the subsidy granted by the Convention of Estates in 1678, not due to lapse until 1683.[55] On 6 September followed an act authorizing the continued collection of the excise for five years after the death of the King, so that 'the Royal Government of the Kingdom should not be then destitute of a due and suteable support for defraying the exigences thereof'.[56] Opponents of the measure argued that it was impolitic for the present king to advance his heir to such heights, and worried that this supply might 'be made use of to introduce and establish poperie'. Supporters replied that it was 'too probable factious spirits' would stir in opposition to York's accession on the death of Charles, and therefore it was essential he have the means 'to pay ane army for suppressing such rebells'.[57] The generosity of the Scottish parliament provides a strong contrast with the English parliaments of 1680–81, which had actually withheld supply in an attempt to force Charles to agree to Exclusion. Some in Scotland even suggested that the excise should be perpetually annexed to the crown 'in all time coming', and that the king and his privy council should be empowered, upon emergency, to raise taxes without parliament, although neither of these proposals came to anything.[58]

There were a number of legislative initiatives designed to deal with the threat posed by religious radicals. On 29 August parliament passed an act which, after first ratifying and approving all laws in favour of episcopacy, made landlords and masters responsible for collecting the fines incurred by their tenants or servants for attending field conventicles or for sheltering preachers who had been declared fugitives; if their tenants or servants did not have the means to pay, the landlords and masters were to turn them off their land or dismiss them from their service. Almost as an after-thought, it announced that the fines imposed by former laws on field conventicles were to be doubled.[59] On 13 September an Act against Assassination made it treason not only to carry out an assassination, but even to maintain or assert that it was 'lawfull to kill any man upon difference in opinion' or because he had been employed in the service of the king or Church.[60] Perhaps the most remarkable act, however, was that passed on 16 September, which recognized that 'all Government and Jurisdiction' within Scotland resided 'in his sacred Majesty, his Laufull Heirs and Successours', and that therefore the king could 'by himself, or any commissionated by him, take cognizance and decision of any Cases or causes he pleases'.[61] The measure was designed to bring the independent noble jurisdictions in the Highlands under the control of the crown, but was rushed through at such a speed and was so carelessly worded as to subject all courts of justice 'to the King's pleasure'.[62] In effect, it allowed Charles to bypass the judges and magistrates and give authority to any he designated – such as members of the armed forces – to try and to punish political and religious dissidents. It was a discretionary power that Charles was to use with a vengeance in Scotland during the final years of his reign.

The Scottish Test

The most controversial measure passed by the parliament of 1681 was the Act anent the Test, which received the royal assent on 31 August. The idea of a Test to ensure the commitment to the Protestant faith of all office-holders under the crown had been mooted earlier in the session, and the court managers had promised that it would be possible to introduce further legislation to provide for the security of the Protestant religion as soon as the act for guaranteeing the succession had passed. The episcopalian interest was keen for a measure that would protect the existing establishment not just from the threat of popery but also from Presbyterianism. York was prepared to agree to such an act in order to appease those who remained concerned about the prospect of a popish successor, but he also saw the value in a measure that might allow him to strike further at the Presbyterians and at the same time bind his Protestant subjects more firmly to the crown and the Catholic succession by incorporating an oath of non-resistance. There was considerable debate in parliament over the Test. Hamilton and Argyll tried to frustrate its passage by moving that those parts which concerned Protestants should be separated from those which dealt with Catholics; Mackenzie and Bishop Paterson of Edinburgh retorted that this would defeat the design of the act, and a proposal that there should be two tests, one for Catholics and another for Presbyterians (the latter with milder censures), was scornfully rejected, some suggesting 'that they were in more danger from the presbyterians than from the papists'. In the end, the Test Act passed by the narrow margin of just seven votes.[63]

The act began by requiring that all the laws against Catholic worship, Protestant separatists, and house and field conventicles be put in 'full and vigorous execution'.[64] To prevent the employment of 'Papists and Phanaticks . . . in offices and places of publict trust', it required all members of parliament, those who had the right to vote in parliamentary elections, privy counsellors, judicial officers, clergymen, local officials (such as sheriffs and justices of the peace), town magistrates, teachers in universities and schools, and officers and soldiers in the armed forces to swear an oath pledging their commitment to the Protestant religion and loyalty to the crown. (This list was further extended by an additional act of 17 September 1681 to include the admiralty, officers in the trained bands, and any who had a voice in electing deacons of trades.)[65] However, the act did exempt 'the Kings lawfull Brothers and Sons' – much to the dismay of Argyll, who protested that any exception made should be solely for the Duke of York, warning that it would be unwise to 'open a Gap for the Royal Family to differ in Religion'.[66]

The second half of the oath was loaded with propositions designed to ensure the unconditional loyalty of all public officials to the king, the royal supremacy and the hereditary succession. Thus office-holders were asked to 'affirm and Swear . . . that the Kings Majesty is the only Supream Governour of this Realme . . . in all Causes as weill Ecclesiastical as Civill'; to promise 'faith and true allegiance to the Kings Majestie, his heirs and laufull successors'; to 'assist and defend' the king in all his rights and prerogatives; to swear the unlawfulness of taking up arms 'against the King or those Commissionated by him', or of holding meetings 'to treat, consult or determine in any mater of State, Civil or Ecclesiastick' without leave from the king; and to swear that they lay under 'no obligation . . . from the National Covenant or the solemn League and Covenant . . . to endeavour any Change or alteration in the Government, either in Church or state as it is now established by the Laws of this Kingdom'. All this served York's, the court's and the episcopalian interest's agenda very well. Fountainhall thought that this part of the oath subverted the fundamental constitution of the kingdom, and went a long way to making the Scottish monarchy 'absolute, arbitrarie and uncontrollable'.[67] However, it was not much different, it should be said, from the oaths of allegiance and non-resistance that had been imposed on office-holders in England and Ireland since the early years of the Restoration.

The internal consistency of the Test oath, however, was seriously undermined by the wording of the first part, designed to ensure that office-holders adhered to the Protestant religion. The Lords of the Articles were unclear as to how to define the general term 'the Protestant Religion'. Stair therefore moved that they should take as their standard the Confession of Faith of 1567, which technically was still law, even though it had long since fallen into disuse.[68] The problem was that the Confession of Faith held that Jesus Christ, and not the king, was the supreme head of the Church, and that non-resistance was conditional upon the supreme magistrate performing his duty to maintain the true religion and suppress idolatry and superstition.[69] Stair's aim was to sabotage the Test, but, since virtually no one in parliament was familiar with the Confession, his motion was able to succeed. Office-holders were thus required to swear never to consent 'to any change nor alteration' to the 'true protestant Religion contained in the Confession of Faith' and to renounce all principles that were 'inconsistent with the said Protestant Religion and Confession of Faith'. Moreover, the act required that the oath be taken 'in the plain genuine sense and meaning of the words without any Equivocation, mental Reservation, or any manner of evasion whatsoever'. Given the oath's inherent contradictions, this was something that the more scrupulous would find it difficult to do.

The act required all office-holders to take the Test by 1 January 1682. Most of the privy counsellors took it on 22 September 1681, at the first meeting of the council following the prorogation of parliament on the 17th. Queensberry, however, a staunch episcopalian, waited to see what his colleagues would do, and then took it only after first protesting that he did 'not understand himself to be against Alterations, in case it should seem good to his Majesty to make them in Church of State'. No one took exception to Queensberry's equivocation. The same day the council determined that none of those absent should be allowed to resume their seats until they had taken the Test.[70] A few refused to subscribe, and were dismissed from office. Sir Thomas Murray lost his position as clerk register. Stair, the Lord President of the Court of Session, although happy with the securities provided for the Protestant religion, objected to the second half of the oath, relating to unconditional loyalty, and as a result not only had to step down from the council but also found his name omitted from the new commission for the Lords of Session issued later that year. Shortly thereafter he withdrew to Holland. Stair was to claim after the Revolution that his dismissal had been illegal, since an act of James VI's reign had provided against the arbitrary dismissal of judges by establishing that they should be appointed for life. Whether he was correct is open to question: the Test Act did explicitly require Lords of Session to take the oath. Under the terms of the new commission, however, judges were appointed at royal pleasure, making it possible for the king in the future to dismiss them at will.[71] The council demanded that the Duke of Monmouth be administered the Test, since he was a privy counsellor and held a number of offices in Scotland, even though Monmouth claimed that since he was out of the country he could not be forced to take it. The demand was designed as much to make a public statement about Monmouth's illegitimacy as anything else, since the act had provided that only the king's 'lawful sons' should be exempt. Monmouth refused to subscribe and was stripped of his offices. Hamilton initially had qualms, and agreed to let the council nominate deputies to the jurisdictions in his possession; he eventually took the oath in March 1682. The earls of Cassillis, Haddington, Nithsdale and Sutherland all refused the Test, and forfeited their heritable jurisdictions as a result.[72] The most notorious refuser, however, was the Earl of Argyll.

Argyll had shown himself to be 'a valiant assertor of the Protestant interest' in the 1681 parliament, but he was not, at this stage, an irreconcilable opponent of the Duke of York. Indeed, he had signed the letter from the Scottish council to Charles II of February 1680 praising York's achievements during his first spell in Scotland, and had even supported the Succession Act of 1681.[73] However, given his extensive power base in the West Highlands, the government was worried about the threat he might pose if he sought to set himself up as head of a Protestant interest in opposition to the court. He had not endeared himself to the conservative faction that dominated the government by the fact that he had gone around trying to incite the clergy and laity, both in Edinburgh and in his own territorial base in Argyllshire and Tarbet, against the Test.[74] Argyll therefore had to be broken, and he had many political enemies and personal rivals who were willing to pounce when the opportunity presented itself. After delaying for several weeks, the Earl eventually took the Test before the council on 3 November, mumbling some words of explanation which no one appears to have taken much notice of at the time, and was allowed to take his seat. Some of Argyll's enemies, however, informed York that his explanation had been seditious, and so Argyll was asked to take the Test again the next day without any qualifications. Argyll refused, saying he would take the Test only in the sense and with the meaning that he had taken it the day before, presenting a written paper outlining the explanation he had offered. This stated that he was sure that 'Parliament never intended to impose contradictory oathes', and that therefore he took it in so far as it was 'consistent with itself and the Protestant religion', adding that he was not prepared to bind himself not to endeavour any alteration which he thought might be 'to the advantage of church or state' and 'not repugnant to the Protestant religion and [his] loyaltie' – a qualification, one might suggest, similar to that voiced earlier by Queensberry. The council determined not only that Argyll had not taken the Test according to the terms required by the act, but also that his paper was 'of dangerous consequence, reflecting upon his Majesties authority and government'; it dispatched him to Edinburgh Castle, and instructed the Lord Advocate to initiate proceedings for treason. The trial took place on 12 and 13 December, and Argyll was duly found guilty. The blatant bending of the law caused concern even among the supporters of the government. In England, Halifax told Charles II 'that he knew not the Scots law, but by the law of England that Explanation could not hang his dog'. Even the Scottish bishops were concerned, protesting to the Lord Advocate that they wanted to see Argyll cleared, for they thought his death would 'ruin their interest'. In fact neither Charles nor York desired to see Argyll executed; they merely wanted him to forfeit some of his jurisdictions. Charles therefore ordered sentencing to be deferred until he had decided what course of action to take. In the meantime, on the evening of 20 December, Argyll managed to escape from the castle, making his way to London, and subsequently to the Low Countries. On 22 December the sentence of death was pronounced on him in his absence, and his estates were forfeited. Again, the justness of the sentence was questionable; according to both Fountainhall and the Earl of Longford, Scottish law allowed for forfeitures in absence only in cases of rising in arms against the king.[75]

Both the Test and the treatment of Argyll became the subject of derision. The boys of Heriot's Hospital, Edinburgh, decided that their guard dog had a public office and should therefore take the Test, but when they offered him a paper containing the oath the animal 'absolutely refused it'. The youths tried to make it more palatable by smothering it with butter – 'which they called ane Explication of the Test in imitation of Argile' – but the dog simply licked the butter and spat out the rest. They therefore proceeded to try the dog for treason, and, finding him guilty, condemned him to be hanged like a dog. When a passing curate rebuked the youths for 'such presumptuous mockery', they replied 'that he and his Brethren deserved better to be hanged . . . since they had swallowed that which the Tyke had refused'. On the day after Christmas, the students of the university demonstrated their contempt of the Test by burning an effigy of the pope, clasping the Test oath in one hand, at the market cross in Edinburgh.[76]

The wording of the Test proved a stumbling block to many of the orthodox clergy. The Bishop of Aberdeen and his diocesan clergy refused to take it, wondering how they could swear that the king was the only supreme governor when the Confession of Faith held that Jesus Christ was the only head of the church. The Confession, they insisted, contained a number of obscure and questionable passages, and among other things implied that obedience and non-resistance were due to magistrates only if they executed their office properly; on the other hand, by asking subscribers to acknowledge the royal supremacy (and, with it, the king's power to alter the present establishment in the Church at will), the oath seemed to run counter to a belief in divine-right episcopacy and the apostolic succession.[77] Some of the conformist ministers who had qualms about the Test outlined their views in a tract which circulated in manuscript. Since the Test was designed to strike at popery and fanaticism, it was ridiculous, they claimed, to impose it on the orthodox clergy, who could not rationally be thought to be inclined to either. Yet because of the way the Test was framed, they went on, it would divide sober Protestants among themselves. The renunciation of the Covenant would alienate moderate Presbyterians who were willing to conform, while others would find it difficult to swear to the Confession of Faith without limitation because of its position on resistance. Furthermore, those who believed in divine-right episcopacy would not be able to subscribe an oath that required them to recognize the royal supremacy, while those who held episcopal government to be indifferent would not be able to swear never to alter something which they judged to be, by definition, alterable. The Test bound people to maintain the monarchy and laws and the present line of kings even if they were popish, but this was contradictory to the Coronation Act of 1567, which (the authors insisted) had been ratified by the present parliament when it confirmed all acts made in favour of the Protestant religion. Yet, alarmingly, the powers given by the present laws to any king that should happen to be Catholic would be 'very prejudicial to the Protestant interest', since by the terms of the Supremacy Act the king might 'not only dispose of the external policy of the church, but may emit such acts concerning the persons employed therein, in all ecclesiastical meetings and matters to be treated upon therein', as he thought fit, effectively meaning that the enemies of the Protestant religion would be able to overturn all.[78]

To alleviate such concerns, in November 1681 the Scottish government issued an 'Explanation of the Sense in which the Test is to be interpreted'. This established that those who took the Test did not swear 'to every proposition or clause' contained in the Confession of Faith, 'but only to the true protestant religion . . . as it is opposit to popery and phanatisisme'. Further, it asserted that no clause in the Test was intended as an 'invasion or encroachment . . . upon the intrinsick spirituall power of the church' or should be construed as prejudicial 'to the episcopall government of this nationall church'.[79] Eventually, most of the episcopal clergy did subscribe, many of those who had initially had doubts being won over by the Explanation.[80] Some who remained obstinate finally relented when the full implications of refusing to subscribe began to hit home.[81] Andrew Lumsden, the minister of Duddinston, near Edinburgh, not only refused the Test, but publicly condemned it from the pulpit as unlawful and contradictory. He was duly deprived, but subsequently found he was able to satisfy his scruples, offered to take the Test, and was restored to his living.[82] The ministers of Aberdeen held out the longest. At the beginning of January 1682, with the final deadline for ministers to subscribe having passed, the Archbishop of St Andrews and the Scottish council informed the magistrates of Aberdeen that, since the ministers had refused to subscribe, their churches were now vacant, and that they should find replacements within twenty days. Several of the deprived clergy subsequently caved in, took the Test, and were restored by special order of the council on 23 February.[83]

Estimates of the total number deprived vary, but the final count was probably at least fifty, and may have been as high as eighty. They included the noted Edinburgh minister George Meldrum, and Laurence Charteris, professor of divinity at Edinburgh University. About twenty went to England, where they were settled in parishes; those who stayed were forced into nonconformity.[84] The legacy of the Test was therefore further divisions within the Church. Parishioners often resented having their ministers taken from them. There was a nasty incident at Prestonpans, to the east of Edinburgh, in February 1682, when the man appointed to preach in the place of the deprived minister was attacked by 'a great rable of men, women and boyes' throwing stones and dirt; they subsequently dragged the intruded cleric from the church and would have trodden him to death had not some passers-by come to his rescue.[85] At Dron, just south of Perth, on 21 May, some 300 armed men and women violently assaulted George Drummond as he tried to serve an edict appointing a new minister to replace the former incumbent, an indulged Presbyterian who had refused to take the Test, thwacking Drummond on the legs and arms with staves, and dragging him along the ground to a nearby swamp, where they tried to drown him.[86]

The Test enabled the central authorities to conduct a purge of local government. A number of heritable local jurisdictions – regalities, stewartries and shrievalties – reverted to the crown as a result of their possessors' failure to subscribe, and were passed on to men of known loyalty. The anti-Presbyterian zealot John Graham of Claverhouse, for example, was commissioned as sheriff of Wigtown.[87] Catholics, of course, also lost their positions in the process, although sometimes care was taken to ensure that their power base was not really undermined. The Laird of Stonehouse, 'a violent papist and persecutor' according to Wodrow, was replaced as sheriff of Nithsdale (Dumfriesshire) by one of his own clients, James Mitchel, a small heritor. The campaign against conventiclers continued, and Stonehouse was still able to collect most of the sheriff's share of the fines himself, with Mitchel receiving only a very small cut.[88] The militia was purged, as those officers who refused the Test lost their positions.[89] The Test also provided the government with the means to secure control over the composition of local town councils. A number of royal boroughs and towns – among them Ayr, Cupar, Dunfermline, Inverkeithing, Irvine and Queensferry – decided to postpone the annual magisterial elections scheduled for the autumn of 1681 until after the 1 January deadline for taking the Test had passed. Others proceeded with elections as normal, but did not immediately require their magistrates to take the Test. The Scottish council was quick to react, ordering all towns that had not held elections to proceed to do so or else be denounced as rebels, and to remove those officials who had been elected but had not yet subscribed the Test. Those towns which persisted in their refusal to hold elections – such as Cupar and

Irvine – forfeited the privilege, and the King and the Scottish council were able to appoint the magistrates directly themselves.[90]

Despite the trouble with the conformist clergy over the Test, the parliamentary session was a remarkable success for the crown: the succession of the Duke of York had been guaranteed by law; attempting to divert the succession had been made a treasonable offence; generous grants of supply had freed both the King and his heir from the need to call parliament for some time; and additional powers had been given to the King to enable him to resist the challenge of political and religious dissidents, including the remarkable act recognizing the Scottish king's cumulative power of jurisdiction. In short, the parliament of 1681 had done much to establish the basis of royal absolutism in Scotland and to provide legal sanction for the ruthless pursuit of conventiclers during the final years of Charles II's reign. Even the Test Act was on the whole beneficial, since it assured the government of the loyalty of all who held office under the crown, and guaranteed that, whenever it needed to be convened in the future, parliament would be dominated by ultra-royalists and episcopalians. The Scottish council was not exaggerating when it wrote to Charles II in January 1682, after most of the initial furore over the clergy's taking the Test had died down, that the Test had proved 'a most happie expedient for filling all offices with persons who are well affected to the Protestant religion and your Majesties government, and from whom your Majestie and your people may expect the unanimous and firme prosecutions of your laws against all manner of irregularities'.[91] Moreover, everything the Scottish parliament of 1681 had done was reported in the English press, thereby making a powerful ideological and political statement to discontented elements in England, demonstrating both how loyal subjects were supposed to behave and also the impossibility of continuing to pursue Exclusion any longer without embroiling Charles II's kingdoms in civil war. In the spring of 1682, following his brother's return from Scotland, Charles wrote to his Scottish council to express his delight at 'the extraordinary zeal' that parliament and the council had demonstrated in his service, 'whereof we have already seen very good effects', he said, 'both there and here', in England.[92]

'The Darling of the Age'

During the remainder of his stay in Scotland, York continued his efforts to build up loyalist support. At the beginning of October 1681 he and his wife visited Glasgow and Dumbarton. At Glasgow the archbishop, nobility, gentry and magistrates entertained him 'in the best manner the Country could afford' and presented him with the freedom of the city in a large gold box; multitudes 'of all sorts of People' lined the streets, cheering in support; while at night there were bonfires in all the streets. Similarly, at Dumbarton the Duke was greeted 'with all imaginable expressions of joy' and given the freedom of the town. A minor incident marred the visit to Glasgow, when someone slipped a paper into the Duke's hand as he was processing through the streets. Thinking it to be a petition for charity, York accepted it, only to discover it to be a lengthy Cameronian diatribe, protesting against 'the King in all his Tyranny', his oppression of the people of God, the sending of a papist to Scotland to execute his pol- icy, and the imposition of the Test renouncing the covenants.[93] York's birthday, on 14 October, was celebrated in style in the Scottish capi- tal, with bells, guns, fireworks and 'more bonfires' than one normally saw on the King's birthday,[94] while the Queen's birthday on 15 November was likewise kept by the court at Holyrood 'with great solemnitie', including bonfires and the firing of cannons.[95] When the Duke set off for England, on 7 March 1682, he was attended all the way from Holyrood to Leith by his privy counsellors, most of the nobility of the kingdom, and several thousand people crying out 'God Bless His Royal Highness.'[96] A brief return visit to Edinburgh in May to collect his wife led to him once again being 'very joyfully received'.[97]

Loyalist displays continued after York's departure. Thus the King's birthday on 29 May 1682 was celebrated in a grandiose manner in the Scottish capital. After first going to church, the Lord Provost and the magistrates of the city processed through the streets to the market place, where they held a great feast, to which they had invited the newly appointed Lord Treasurer of Scotland, the Marquis of Queens- berry, and many other persons of quality. When the meal was over, a huge bonfire was erected, around which gathered 'innumerable

Spectators, crying God bless the King, and the Royal Family; which were seconded with their Healths, a Gun going off at every one of them'.[98]

Nor was it just in the Lowlands that York was successful in building up support. In fulfilling his brief for curbing the disorders of the Highlands, he took a more conciliatory approach than had typified Lauderdale's regime, actively cultivating the goodwill of a wider circle of clan chiefs (a task undoubtedly helped by the forfeiture of Argyll). His efforts saw fulfilment with the setting-up of a commission for securing the peace of the Highlands, through which he made the gentry and lesser clan chiefs, rather than the great magnates, responsible for keeping peace. The commissioners were soon feeding the council with fulsome reports of their success (doubtless exaggerated, though the results were real enough); more significantly, perhaps, James's initiatives help explain why many Highland clans continued to remain loyal to the house of Stuart, long after its fortunes had taken a turn for the worse.[99]

The Scottish ruling elite were delighted with York's spell in charge. On 9 March the Archbishop of St Andrews and six of his brethren wrote to Archbishop Sancroft in England to report that the Duke had done much to rescue and relieve 'our Church and order' and stop the growth of schism, adding that 'he looks on the Enemies of the Church, as Adversaries to the monarchy it self'. The letter was not only published but also reported by the Tory press in England, to ensure the widest possible publicity.[100] In May the Scottish council wrote to Charles II praising 'the kindnes, justice, moderation and examplary loyalty' the Duke had demonstrated, and his success in composing 'all our disorders' and 'sustaining the orthodox clergy'.[101]

York's support for the episcopalian establishment in Scotland did much to reassure the English bishops that they had no cause to fear for their Church when the Duke eventually succeeded to the throne. As we saw in Chapter 4, it also enabled Tory propagandists to put the case to the English public that there was no reason to fear the succession of the Catholic heir, since he had proved himself to be such a good ruler when head of the government in Scotland, and had become to the Scots the 'Darling of the Age'.[102] Not that everyone agreed. The English Whigs were horrified by developments in Scotland under

York, and especially by the passage of the Test Act and the subsequent action against Argyll, which merely heightened their anxiety that York would 'prove a terrible master when all should come into his hands'; indeed, Burnet claimed that, following the Scottish parliament of 1681, York was 'more hated than ever'.[103] The point is, however, that what was going on in Scotland became central to the ideological debate in England over the succession, and that both Charles and York managed the situation in Scotland not simply to improve their position north of the border, but also to appeal to the constituency of support they were managing to generate in England, namely the Anglican-royalist interest. In both these respects, York's mission to Scotland had been an unquestionable success.

PERSECUTION AND THE LAW, 1682–1685

York's departure from Scotland was followed by a reconstruction of the Scottish ministry. The Marquis of Atholl, the president of the parliament, was expected to succeed the deceased Rothes as chancellor, but instead York appointed Sir George Gordon of Haddo, an ardent royalist and key champion of the Duke's cause, but nevertheless a mere gentlemen. Haddo was soon to receive the title Earl of Aberdeen, but York's slight to the existing nobility was a clear indication that he was determined to have his own creature in the top position. Queensberry, as mentioned above, became Lord Treasurer and was raised to the rank of marquis, being replaced in his old position of justice-general by the Earl of Perth, who had opposed Lauderdale back in 1678. The Earl of Middleton was added to the Scottish council and made one of the Secretaries of State, along with the Earl of Moray. The new men in charge set out to destroy Lauderdale's remaining influence. They combined to bring down Lauderdale's brother, Charles Maitland, who was replaced as treasurer-depute by Perth's brother, John Drummond of Lundin, and when Lauderdale eventually died, in August 1682, his posts were shared out between Perth, Queensberry and Middleton. Hamilton and the Earl of Tweeddale were restored to the privy council, with the former being given Lauderdale's place in the Order of the Garter in an attempt to reconcile him to the new regime.[104]

The government in Scotland nevertheless continued to be bedevilled by a tendency towards factional infighting. The traditional ruling elite were upset by the rapid rise of Aberdeen and were soon conspiring to bring him down. In late 1683 they convinced the King to let all policy be proposed by a 'secret committee' of the Scottish council, which was to include Aberdeen, Atholl, Queensberry, Perth, Lundin and two others, as a way of ensuring they could control the new chancellor. They finally secured Aberdeen's downfall in late June 1684, with the chancellorship passing to Perth, while Lundin was made Secretary of State for Scotland and Queensberry was promoted to duke.[105] As a result of the Test, however, there was at least a considerable degree of ideological consistency among those left in charge of Scotland following York's departure. The majority of the council were implacably hostile to all forms of political and religious dissent, and the position of the hardline episcopalians was strengthened with the addition of John Graham of Claverhouse 1683.[106] Hamilton – the only erstwhile voice of moderation to remain – was too isolated to take any stance, even if he had so desired. The change in governors, as Fountainhall pointed out, brought 'no change in the arbitrary government'; indeed, when it came to 'putting the military and ecclesiastick laws to strict and vigorous execution', these new statesmen surpassed even Lauderdale's 'arbitrarie way'.[107]

The last years of the reign saw the ruthless persecution of the political and religious enemies of the crown. Again, it was the actions of the Cameronians that first provoked the government's wrath. The 'Remnant', as they came to be known after losing their leaders Cameron and Cargill, were now no more than a group of praying societies, but at the end of 1681 they began to reorganize themselves, and they established a union or general correspondence between the societies, making arrangement for the distribution of circular letters every fortnight and the holding of quarterly meetings.[108] On 15 December they held their first meeting, at Lesmahagow in Lanarkshire, where they drew up their 'Apologeticke Declaratione of the trew Presbyterians of the Church of Scotland'. This condemned Charles II for 'tyrannically obtruding his Will as Law, both in matters civill and ecclesiasticall' and denounced the proceedings of the 1681 parliament, particularly the passing of the Test Act. The authors then proclaimed their desire 'to extricat our selves from under a tyrants yocke, and to reduce our state and church, to what they were in the years 1648 and 1649', and concluded by ratifying both the Rutherglen and the Sanquhar declarations, which they said rescinded everything done by Charles II and his parliaments since the Restoration.[109]

On 12 January the Society People dispatched a quasi-military delegation of forty horse and twenty foot, all well armed, to Lanark to publish their declaration. After first posting their paper in the market place and elsewhere, and distributing copies to some of the local inhabitants, they built a bonfire where they burned copies of the Test Act and Succession Act of 1681, which they had seized from the local bailiff's house. The Scottish council, alarmed that the local magistrates and townspeople had not done more to stop this Cameronian troop – only one man, a local weaver named William Harvey, was arrested (he was subsequently executed) – fined the burgh 6,000 merks, to be paid by a tax on the local inhabitants, and sent an army under Major Andrew White to Lanarkshire to disperse conventicles and bring to justice those responsible for the Lanark manifesto and any Bothwell rebels and fugitive ministers.[110] It also dispatched Claverhouse to Wigtown, Dumfries and Kirkcudbright with the power to fine recusants, conventiclers and harbourers of rebels, and to hold courts 'as a Justice in that part' to prosecute any one below the rank of heritor who might be apprehended for being in the late rebellion, and by the end of March the shires of Fife, Haddington, Kinross, Perth and Linlithgow were also under military occupation.[111] The troops were often brutal in their treatment of the local populations. In June 1682 the Whig press in London carried a story of how dragoons in Clydesdale, Lanarkshire, tortured six men, arrested on suspicion of harbouring rebels, in an attempt to obtain a confession. 'Fired Matches', we are told, were 'put betwixt their fingers', and they were 'kept in that crewel torment near to the space of an hour'. So bad were their wounds that it was thought that two of them would 'at least lose their hands, if not their arms to the elbow'. None of them confessed; it is not clear that they had anything to confess.[112]

The government made some attempts to discipline the traditional law-enforcing agencies in the localities. Thus in early May 1682 the council passed an act obliging sheriffs and other magistrates, on hearing of any field conventicles, to take immediate action to dissipate them or else to alert the council or some other officer of state.[113] Increasingly, however, the government saw the advantage of simply bypassing the civil authorities and relying on the military. On 3 August 1682 the council, having received complaints about the remissness of various sheriffs, stewarts and magistrates in punishing rebels and nonconformists, granted a special commission of justiciary to Major White, for Ayrshire, and to the Laird of Meldrum (a captain of a troop of horse), for the counties of Haddington, Selkirk, Berwick and Peebles, enabling them to act with the sheriffs and magistrates in those areas in examining all suspects brought before them, and even giving them the authority to act by themselves if the civil authorities proved negligent. In November the council granted a commission to the Earl of Linlithgow for enforcing the law in the shire of Linlithgow, because of the 'remissness' of 'some of the magistrates ... in discharge of their duties'. That same month it vested jurisdiction over the burgh of Linlithgow in the hands of the Earl of Livingston, to combat the problem caused by the 'negligence of the provost and the rest of the magistrates', while in December 1683 the council simply appointed Livingston provost of Linlithgow. Wodrow was later to complain that the council's members had taken it upon themselves 'materially to vacate and make null the executive Powers lodged by the parliament in the Hands of inferior Magistrates, and fix them in Creatures of their own making', and saw the attack on Linlithgow as a direct violation of the privileges of the royal burghs. The authority for such actions, however, came from the statute of 1681 acknowledging the cumulative jurisdiction of the king.[114] On 1 March 1683 the council ordered Claverhouse, Meldrum and White to scrutinize the records of rural magisterial courts for evidence of collusion or illegal mitigation of fines.[115] The following month Charles authorized his Scottish council to issue a proclamation calling for the rigorous execution of all laws against the covenanters and setting up six circuit courts for the western and south-western shires, to last for three years, for dealing with recusants and suspected rebels. Those who were found guilty merely of harbouring or conversing with rebels were also to be prosecuted as traitors. An indemnity was, however, to be given to anyone who swore the Test on their knees before 1 August – a deadline that was subsequently extended till 1 March 1684. The oath of the Test, originally intended only for office-holders, now came to be used as a general test of loyalty. Burnet thought the world had not seen such a proclamation 'since the days of the Duke of Alva' and the notorious Spanish persecutions of Protestants in the Low Countries in the late 1560s.[116]

Only a handful of people were pursued to death during the years 1682–3 – for suspected involvement in Archbishop Sharp's murder, the Bothwell Bridge rebellion or the burning of the Test at Lanark, or for refusing to acknowledge the King's authority – resulting in a total of seven executions for each of the two years. A few convicted rebels received reprieves or had their sentences commuted to banishment. Many of those convicted of attending field conventicles were transported, to either Carolina or New Jersey.[117] Exorbitant fines were imposed on those found guilty of lesser offences. In June 1682 two nonconformist preachers were fined 5,000 merks each for illegally baptizing children.[118] Many suffered periods of imprisonment if they could not pay, or if they refused to take the bond or Test. At the beginning of January 1683 'a great many' Edinburgh merchants were imprisoned for failing to pay fines ranging as high as 1,000 merks for not coming to church or for having their children baptized by nonconformist ministers.[119] The areas subject to military occupation were the hardest hit. The troops committed a number of brutalities, exacting free quarter, pillaging houses, even beating and torturing suspects or those who they felt were withholding information.[120] Many of the military commanders simply assumed that everyone who lived in the area they were asked to police was guilty; Claverhouse, for example, on one occasion remarked that 'there were as many Elephants and Crocodiles in Galloway, as loyal or regular persons'.[121]

Occasionally it proved possible to obtain legal redress for abuses committed by the soldiers. In April 1682 John Chiesly of Dalry brought a process before the Lord Advocate against two soldiers in the king's life guard, claiming that they had assaulted both him and his servants, taken possession of his stables, and thrust out his horses.

The jury found the soldiers guilty of invasion and oppression, and Mackenzie sentenced one to be banished and the other to be dismissed from the army and to find sureties for his good behaviour.[122] Powerful local landlords were sometimes able to offer some protection to their tenants. In October 1683 Hamilton complained to Meldrum about his posting six dragoons at the house of James Wilson, one of Hamilton's vassals, without showing cause, demanding that they be removed. He further protested against Meldrum's citing a number of his tenants and feuars in his regality of Lesmahagow to appear at Lanark for some unknown cause, stating that since he had a jurisdiction of his own he had discharged those people from appearing before Meldrum.[123] On occasion the local inhabitants tried to resist the exactions of the troops, or even to prevent them from collecting corn or straw for their horses (which they were legally entitled to do), although they normally fell foul of the law for their efforts.[124] As usual, it was the Cameronians who were the most extreme in their resistance. At Lanark, in early March 1682, about twenty attacked a dragoon who had been left on guard while the rest of his party had gone off to get provisions; they cruelly mutilated him, leaving him to bleed slowly to death.[125] In June 1683 a group of seven fanatics ambushed a detachment of five of the King's guards as they were escorting a conventicler from Stirling to Glasgow, killing one and wounding another as they carried out their rescue.[126]

From 1684 the government's policy of repression came to be characterized by a greater degree of brutality and an increasing straining of the law. This was in part a reaction to the revelations of the Rye House Plot in the summer of 1683: informers alleged not only that there were thousands of Scots in England, many of them former Bothwell Bridge rebels, who were ready to join an insurrection there, but also that plans had been laid for an uprising in Scotland, to be led by the Earl of Argyll. The English authorities interrogated large numbers of Scottish suspects, many of whom clearly had not engaged in any plotting, and identified a core group of Scots, in addition to Argyll himself, who appeared to have been involved in some sort of conspiracy. Some they were unable to reach. Sir John Cochrane, Cochrane's son (John), Lord Melville and the Earl of Loudon had all fled to the Continent; in April 1684 legal proceedings were initiated in Scotland against all four *in absentia*, whereupon they were found guilty and had their estates forfeited.[127] Argyll was in the Low Countries, and already lay under sentence of death. However, by the end of July 1683 the crown did have a number of Scots in custody in England for alleged involvement in the Rye House Plot, among them Sir Hugh Campbell of Cessnock, William Spence, William Carstares, Alexander Monro and Robert Baillie of Jerviswood. Finding it difficult to fix anything on any of them, in violation of the English Habeas Corpus Act in October 1683 the government decided to deport them to Scotland, where the authorities had the option of using torture to extort confessions.[128] Moreover, since there was no habeas corpus in Scotland, the suspects could be kept in prison, without being charged or brought to trial, until the government had managed to accumulate enough evidence against them.[129]

Sir Hugh Campbell of Cessnock was brought to trial at the end of March 1684. Unable to construct a case for his involvement in the Rye House Plot, the government charged him with being in the rebellion at Bothwell Bridge. The jury acquitted him, but he was nevertheless detained in prison, the court arguing that, since he was the King's prisoner, they would need to know His Majesty's mind before he could be set free. Cessnock was eventually to plead guilty to treason in June 1685, following the confessions of Carstares and Monro, and suffered forfeiture of his estate.[130] In order to ensure better success with the other alleged Scottish conspirators, on 14 June 1684 Charles II wrote to his Scottish council to authorize the use of torture.[131] The rules concerning the use of torture were somewhat vague; there was no positive law or act of parliament in Scotland regulating its use, instead only custom and common law.[132] Nevertheless, there seemed a general agreement in legal circles that certain principles had to be adhered to. Torture was to be applied only against someone accused of a capital offence, and enduring the torture purged one of all suspicion of the crime – in other words, the accused was not to be tortured again if he failed to confess the first time around. Moreover, the torture could not be excessive; if death resulted, those who carried out the torture would be guilty of murder. There was also supposed to be one witness against the accused – the so-called *semiplena probatio*, or half-proof (the law requiring there to be two witnesses for full proof) – and a solid presumption of guilt before torture could be used.

The first to be subjected to torture were Spence and Carstares, and in neither case were the above principles respected. Both were being held on suspicion only, there being no half-proof in either case. Both were asked to swear an oath to answer all questions put to them; both refused on the grounds that it was illegal to force them to incriminate themselves, which it most certainly was in capital cases. The council's position, however, was that it had promised Spence and Carstares that, in return for their information upon oath, they would not be charged with a capital crime; by refusing to take the oath under these conditions, the council claimed, the accused had implicated themselves, providing sufficient grounds for the use of torture.[133] Spence was a target of the government investigation because he had been Argyll's secretary and was believed to know how to decipher some of his master's coded correspondence.[134] The council subjected him to three different types of torture in order to get him to reveal the cipher. His interrogation began on 25 July 1684, when he was put to the boot, with the wedge against his shins being given eighteen knocks of the mallet instead of the usual six or seven. They then tried sleep-deprivation, a procedure used against witches, keeping Spence awake for several days and nights by dressing him in a hair shirt and pinching him or prodding him with hot pokers whenever he seemed about to collapse from exhaustion. On 7 August they moved on to the thumbscrews. At last Spence broke down, agreed to help decipher the correspondence, and confirmed that Argyll, Stair and other Scots had formed a design to raise an army in Scotland.[135]

In September the council moved on to Carstares, who, after being subjected to the thumbscrews and threatened with the boot, confessed to the plot. He named many, and those whom the authorities were able to apprehend were likewise threatened with torture to reveal what they knew. Hamilton vigorously protested against the council's blatant abuse of due process, alleging that 'at this rate, they might, without accusers or witnesses, take any person off the street, and torture him', and refused to be present for any of the interrogations.[136] His fellow privy counsellors remained unperturbed. In December they moved against Robert Baillie of Jerviswood. Baillie was now very ill, having languished in prison in Scotland for well over a year, with no formal charge against him, and the council decided it would be better to establish his guilt before he died in custody. Two of those who had been arrested and interrogated on the basis of Carstares's confession, Walter Scott, Earl of Tarras, and James Murray, Laird of Philiphaugh, were brought forward as witnesses to prove that Baillie had been involved in the Rye House conspiracy. Baillie's trial began on 23 December, but the council, fearing that Tarras's and Philiphaugh's testimonies would not amount to enough to convince a jury beyond reasonable doubt, ordered Carstares's confession to be read in court, even though, in criminal proceedings, depositions by absent witnesses were not admissible as evidence and, in return for his confession, the council had promised Carstares that anything he might say would not be used as king's evidence. The council claimed, however, that the confession was to be read not as evidence but merely to satisfy the jury that the witnesses could be believed. It did the trick. Baillie was found guilty on the 24th, and was executed the same day.[137]

Increasing governmental severity was also a reaction to a revival of the Cameronians. The Rye House investigations had produced reports that the Society People kept in touch with discontented elements on the Continent, and the council's concerns intensified from September 1683 when James Renwick returned from his studies in the Low Countries as ordained minister to lead the Remnant and field conventicles began to start up again. Reports of continued disturbances by conventiclers, including the stabbing of horses belonging to the dragoons in Carstairs and Lesmahagow, prompted the council to take a series of new initiatives. In January and February 1684 it issued new commissions for several counties in the south-west, granting full justiciary powers to certain named local magistrates, sheriffs and army officers to hold courts and execute justice on malicious rebels and those who disowned the King's authority. A further act of April targeted those who harboured or otherwise conversed with rebels.[138] Nevertheless, the south-west was still proving remarkably difficult to police. Near the beginning of June, Renwick preached in the fields at Blackloch in Lanarkshire before about a hundred armed followers (eighty men and twenty women); although troops were immediately dispatched in pursuit, they were unable to make any arrests, and for several days this small armed band marched freely through the countryside, allegedly threatening the orthodox clergy and murdering some of the King's soldiers. On 22 July Charles responded with a proclamation complaining about the remissness of the local officials and the heritors, and commanding the sheriffs, stewarts, heritors and commoners to apprehend and bring to justice the rebels, and all who intercommuned with them – in effect, raising the hue and cry for the entire south-west.[139] At the beginning of August, following the rescue of a group of prisoners at Enterkin in Dumfriesshire, on the road from Dumfries to Edinburgh, involving a violent struggle with soldiers resulting in deaths on both sides, the council placed the south-western shires under military rule, empowering army officers to search for rebels and field conventiclers and any who aided or abetted them.[140] Towards the end of the month Charles authorized the council to hold courts in the districts of Glasgow, Ayr, Dumfries and Dunse (in the Scottish south-west); with just three privy counsellors serving on each court, they were to try Bothwell rebels and those who disobeyed the laws against conventicles or refused to come to church, and they had the power to fine, imprison, banish and even inflict capital punishment on those who remained obstinate. The enormous discretionary powers this gave the counsellors convinced Wodrow that Scotland was now under 'an arbitrary and absolute Government Scotland', with 'Life, Liberty, and every Thing, left in the managers Hands'.[141]

The High Court of Justiciary, Scotland's supreme criminal court, became more ruthless in dealing with prisoners who refused to acknowledge the King's authority, leading to twelve executions in the first six months of 1684 alone. There were a further five executions in August: three for assisting in the rescue of the party of prisoners at Enterkin; a fourth for boldly disclaiming the King and owning the Covenant after the accused had managed to get himself arrested at the above three's execution for calling the hangman 'a dog and villain'; and a fifth 'for owning Bothwel-bridge, the Lanerk declaration, [and] the excommunication of the King'.[142] It was not just those with dangerous political opinions who were targeted; all Presbyterians came to feel the lash of the law. Those who refused to come to church suffered heavy fines – for instance, a document from August 1684 records fines totalling £274,737 levied on the heritors of

Roxburghshire alone.[143] In February 1684, by a questionable extension of the law, husbands began to be fined for the recusancy of their wives. It is true that a number of statutes passed since the Reformation, including the Conventicle Act of 1670, had explicitly stated that husbands should be liable for the offences of their wives. The original Act against Separation of 1663, however, had included no such provision. What it did say was that 'all and every such person or persons' who withdrew from church should be fined, and Perth maintained that this implied that husbands were to pay their wives' fines, since married women held no property of their own. Even Aberdeen, who at the time was still chancellor, found this reasoning dubious, but he was now falling from favour, and the King gave a ruling backing Perth's reading of the law.[144] In April 1684 Charles authorized the transportation to Carolina of those prisoners who refused to take the Test but who in other respects appeared penitent.[145] The heavy reliance on the military to keep the peace made it difficult to ensure that due process was always followed. During the summer of 1684 one man was murdered in the fields by troops as he was returning home from a conventicle; a party of soldiers came across the unfortunate victim when he was taking a rest, and 'without any probation or process, shot him'.[146]

It should not be assumed that the campaign against dissent was directed solely from above. Episcopalian clergymen, especially those intruded into areas which had previously been Presbyterian strongholds, were often active in informing against nonconformist activity and in exhorting their parishioners to help bring to justice those who failed to come to church or who attended conventicles. The government's policy of repression also appears to have attracted a certain amount of support from local landowners in some of the most troubled areas. On 9 October the heritors of Kirkcudbrightshire presented an address to the King offering to make an additional voluntary contribution of twenty months' cess, spread over four years, to help maintain the standing forces in the area, and pledging themselves for the good behaviour of their tenants and cottars. Similar pledges came in from the heritors of Wigtown, the shire of Dumfries and the stewartry of Annandale, the districts of Clydesdale and Ayr, and the shire of Stirling.[147] It seems to have been the case, however, that it was the privy counsellors sent out as circuit judges who were responsible for encouraging such addresses; Queensberry received a letter from the council in late 1684 thanking him for the Dumfries and Annandale address and telling him he had 'answered in this the just expectation of the King and his Royal Highness'.[148]

On 8 November 1684 the Society People responded to the intensification of persecution by issuing an *Apologetical Declaration and Admonitory Vindication of the True Presbyterians of the Church of Scotland*, which they affixed to market crosses and church doors throughout much of the south-west. After first stating that they remained committed to their earlier declarations disowning Charles Stuart and declaring war against him and his accomplices, they proceeded to condemn all who stretched forth their hands against them – judges, army officers, militia men, soldiers, the 'viperous and malicious Bishops and Curates', and the gentry and commons who served as informers – and warned that such people would be punished as 'enemies to God and the covenanted work of reformation . . . according to our power and the degree of offence'.[149] The first victims of their retaliatory justice were two soldiers in the king's life guards, by the names of Kennoway and Stuart, both notorious persecutors, who were murdered 'in a most barbarous manner' while sleeping in Swine Abbey, near Blackburn in Linlithgow, on the night of 19 November.[150] The Cameronians were said to hold 'mock-courts of justice', before which they cited 'any they judge their inveterate enemies', whom they subjected to the ritual of a trial before condemning them to death. In early December the council learned that 'the wild fanatics' (as Fountainhall termed them) had murdered the minister of Carsphairn in Kirkcudbrightshire, a Mr Peirson, 'a great delater of them, and zealous in rebuking them in his sermons'.[151]

The council responded to this declaration of war with a series of savage measures. It had the three men who were brought before it for posting the *Apologetical Declaration* brutally tortured by the now favoured method of the thumbscrews and then executed.[152] On 22 November it passed a resolution that anyone who refused to disown the *Apologetical Declaration* upon oath should be immediately put to death by persons commissioned by the council, provided there were two witnesses present, and it followed this up three days later with an abjuration oath that could be tendered to anyone thought suspect.[153] Most of the west and south-west was put under martial law. At the beginning of December the council issued a commission to Lieutenant-General Drummond to hold courts of justiciary in the south-western shires to execute justice on suspected rebels and their adherents, and with the forces under his command 'to persew, take, apprehend and kill the forsaids rebells and ther resetters'; a few days later it authorized the Laird of Orbistoun to raise a volunteer force of 200 Highlanders to march to any parts of Dunbartonshire and Renfrewshire with authority to 'kill, wound or destroy' any they found in arms resisting.[154] On 30 December Charles issued a proclamation imposing the abjuration oath on everyone over the age of sixteen; no one was to travel without a certificate testifying to their having taken the oath, and any who refused the oath or failed to produce a certificate of loyalty when required were to be reputed supporters of the *Apologetical Declaration* and proceeded against accordingly.[155] By an order of council of 13 January 1685, this meant that men were to be hanged and women drowned.[156]

Perhaps as many as 100 people were executed in total during what have become known as 'the Killing Times', most of them in the fields.[157] Some of those who refused the oath were summarily shot on the spot; others were given time to reconsider or were afforded some form of trial before eventually being hanged.[158] In April 1685 a justiciary commission at Wigtown sentenced sexagenarian Margaret Maclauchlan and eighteen-year-old Margaret Wilson to death by drowning, without any legal trial. Upon appeal by friends and relatives of the convicted, the council ordered a stay of execution, but for reasons that remain unclear the magistrates at Wigtown never received notification, and the two women were tied to stakes on the seafront and had their heads thrust beneath the waves of the oncoming tide by the town officers.[159]

The persecutions in Scotland during the years of the Stuart reaction were much more severe than anything seen in England. One London Whig newspaper commented in the autumn of 1682 upon the 'Unparallelled Severity Exercised upon the Non-conformists' north of the border, while Wodrow, writing of the year 1683, observed that the 'Sufferings in England for Conscience sake' could scarce be called 'suffering' compared to what was going on in Scotland.[160] Moreover, whereas in England the government had to work within laws that were already on the statute book before the crisis over the succession erupted, in Scotland we see a process of continual innovation, as new acts of parliament or council were passed and fresh initiatives were taken for dealing with political and religious subversives. In 1687 the covenanter apologist Alexander Shields complained how the Scottish authorities, in their 'ambition to outdo all the Nero's, Domitians, Dioclesians, Duke of Alva's, or Lewis de Grands' in tyranny, 'scorned all formes as wel as Justice of Law', especially after the *Apologetical Declaration*, when 'they acted with an unheard of Arbitrariness.'[161] Presbyterian controversialists, writing after the Revolution, similarly condemned the years of the Stuart reaction in Scotland as a period of tyranny, when the authorities, through a host of arbitrary and illegal proceedings, ruthlessly oppressed and condemned multitudes of innocent people, male and female, without 'due course of Law'.[162]

Those in the government felt that the policies pursued in Scotland were a wholly appropriate – and legally justifiable – way of dealing with the threat of malicious malcontents who were bent on destroying the peace of the nation. As Mackenzie of Rosehaugh, Charles II's Lord Advocate, was to write after the Revolution, Charles II's penal laws were justified because the dissenters had 'overturned the Government and Laws', and 'this Cause was much more just in Scotland, than even in England, because the Dissenters in Scotland were more bigoted to the Covenant, which is a constant Fond for Rebellion.' The subsequent laws against field conventicles, Mackenzie continued, were but 'the necessary product of new accessional degrees of Rebellion; and were not Punishments design'd against Opinion in Religion, but merely against Treasonable Combinations'; indeed, he could boldly say 'That no Man in Scotland ever suffer'd for his Religion'.[163] Similarly, in July 1683 the Lord Lieutenant of Ireland, Ormonde, observed that the 'Dissenters in Scotland' were 'possessed with the spirit of contradiction and rebellion and that no mild nor moderate exercise [could] cast out that devil'.[164] The answer lay in a rigorous enforcement of the law. The Scottish bishops repeatedly maintained that the fanatics had become a problem only because of the misguided policies pursued by ministers of state in the 1670s (especially the various experiments with Indulgences), and insisted that a steady and effective application of the laws would keep all quiet.[165] Likewise, Mackenzie of Tarbat, in a letter to Hamilton in November 1683 concerning the alleged neglect of some local authorities in suppressing conventicles, pointed out, 'Theer is a course prescribed by law and if it be prosecute all places will be too warm for conventicles.'[166] An unnamed correspondent wrote to Queensberry in late 1682 that 'wee must doe things legallie,' although he was also confident that 'wee have always law enough if wee follow it right.'[167] Government apologists in England pointed to the effectiveness of a strict application of the laws in Scotland as a way of suggesting that the same needed to done in England to deal with the problem of dissent south of the border. Thus in January 1683 L'Estrange commented in his *Observator* how 'Good Laws and Resolution have done the work in Scotland,' with the result that meetings were suppressed and the churches 'fill'd with the Persons of the Reclaim'd'.[168] A little over a month later he observed 'how Easily . . . that Stubborn and Headstrong Faction' in Scotland had been mastered, and 'how willingly . . . the Generality of that Perswasion deliver'd themselves up to be Reclaim'd' as a result of the steadiness and vigour of the authorities in enforcing the law.[169] As in England, adherence to the rule of law became the main self-justificatory trope of the advocates of stern measures against political and religious dissenters in Scotland. It is only from the second half of 1684, when the Scottish authorities came to think of themselves as being at war with the radical Presbyterians, that we see the emergence of a more violent discourse. Thus in August 1684 Lord Advocate Mackenzie compared the Cameronians to 'the Anabaptistical boors of Germany' who 'in a levelling fury . . . rose up both against the Nobility and Gentry to murder them'; he pointed out that Luther and other Protestant divines 'were clear that these sectaries were to be hunted and killed as wolves, and other ravenous beasts of prey'.[170]

As far as the supporters of the government were concerned, the campaign against dissent in Scotland was a success. One author, writing after the Revolution, claimed that Charles, at his death, 'left this Church of Scotland in more peaceful condition, then it had been of a long time before; it was united to a very desirable degree:

Generally all Scotchmen were of one Communion', for there were very few Catholics, fewer Quakers, and the Presbyterians, with the exception of the small sect of Cameronians, 'had for the most part returned to the Churches Unity; their Preachers were generally become our Hearers, attended duely our Public Assemblies, and many participated of the same Sacraments with us'.[171] Local officials on the front line reported stories of their success. In March 1683 the sheriff-depute of Lanarkshire, one of Scotland's most troubled shires, could boast that his regular holding of courts over the last couple of months 'in every parish in the upper ward' had resulted in the churches there being 'better filled than they had been for many years past'.[172] Critics of the government agreed that nonconformists were now going to church, but pointed out that they were doing so out of fear, not conviction. Thus Fountainhall concluded that the persecution was 'fruitlesse', for, although 'it drove many . . . to the church, yet compelled prayers' had no worth, 'force making but hypocrites, and the church like a prison house to them'.[173] Some fled to Ulster, others to the new world (particularly New Jersey and Carolina).[174]

What we have here, of course, is a polemical debate between two sides locked in mutual antagonism; it is understandable that the critics of the regime of the 1680s should want to accuse it of tyranny, and that its defenders should seek legitimacy by appealing to the rule of law. Yet the point that needs to be made is that in Scotland the law gave the king, and those who served under him, far greater discretionary power than in England. The law not only provided stiffer penalties for dealing with dissent (including capital punishment), and harsher weapons in bringing people to justice (such as the use of torture), it also enabled the king to set himself up above the law, to sidestep the traditional civil authorities, to use the armed forces to execute his policy, and even to sanction summary execution. In that respect we can talk about the exercise of arbitrary government in Scotland in the final years of Charles II's reign; there were extra-legal proceedings, many people suffered without due legal process, and numerous instances might be cited where justice can scarcely said to have been done. Whether the King, or those commissioned by him, ever exceeded his legal powers, however, is more of a moot point. Nevertheless, by the end of Charles II's reign Scotland had gone a long way to becoming an absolute monarchy – not just in theory, but also in practice.

The theoretical foundations of Scottish absolutism were spelled out in full by Lord Advocate Mackenzie in a lengthy treatise published in 1684. Mackenzie boldly proclaimed 'that our Monarchs derive not their Right from the People, but are absolute Monarchs, deriving their Royal Authority immediately from God Almighty', and set out to support this contention by reference to positive law, fundamental law, divine law, and the principles of reason. For Mackenzie, the king was supreme, limited 'in nothing'; parliaments were 'not co-ordinate with our kings in the Legislative Power', which resided 'solely . . . in the King'; indeed, the king not only was 'above Law', but could 'break Laws justly' – that is, when justice required – 'for a strict and rigid Law is a greater Tyrant, than absolute Monarchy'.[175] There were some limitations on the king's authority, however: 'this Title of absolute Monarch', Mackenzie admitted, did not 'empower him to dispose of our Estates'. That was why the Militia Act declared that the people should not be subject to free quarter. But all the land of Scotland had once been the king's, and so he was presumed proprietor of all. The king therefore had 'a Paramount and Transcendant Right over even Private Estates, in case of necessity, when the common Interest cannot be otherwise maintained'; thus, for example, in time of war he might quarter freely.[176] Furthermore, kings could not 'be punished by their own Subjects'; a king was 'lyable to the Directive Force of the Law, that is to say, He ought to be Governed by it as his Director', but he was 'not liable to the Coercive Force of the Law'. 'Free Monarchs' could not be judged 'save by God alone'. Resistance, even in the name of self-defence, could never be justified. 'As it is not lawful for Subjects to punish their Kings, so neither is it to rise in Arms against them, upon what pretext soever, no not to defend their Liberty nor Religion.'[177]

Mackenzie went to equal lengths to prove that 'neither the People, nor Parliaments of this Kingdom, could exclude the Lineal Successor, or could raise to the Throne any other of the same Royal Line.' Indeed, not even an absolute monarch could alter the succession. He refuted the notion that the coronation oath ensured that only a Protestant could become king. In Scottish (as in English) law 'The king never dies,' which meant that at the moment the last king dies the successor is king. The Coronation Act related only to the crowning of the king, not to the succession; a coronation was not absolutely necessary, since a king was still a king without being crowned; and there was no clause in the Coronation Act 'debarring the Successor, or declaring the Succession Null, in case his Successor gave not this oath'. Besides, the Succession Act, by stipulating that the government devolved to the next lawful heir, regardless of his religion, immediately upon the death of the monarch, abrogated the Coronation Act 'as to this Point; for how can the administration be devolv'd immediately upon the Successor, if he cannot administer till he be Crown'd, and have sworn this Oath?' It seems, then, that Mackenzie was telling his readers not only that their present king was absolute and irresistible, but also that they would soon have a Catholic one who was absolute and irresistible and limited in nothing. Mackenzie did however say that 'The Lawful Successor, though he were of a different Religion from his People, (as God forbid he should be) may easily swear, That he will maintain the Laws now standing.' Indeed, he conceded that 'any Parliament' might 'legally secure the Successor from overturning their Religion or Laws, though they cannot debar him'. For, even if the successor did not swear to maintain the laws, Scottish Protestants would nevertheless be 'in little danger by his Succession; since all Acts of Parliament stand in force till they be repeal'd by subsequent Parliaments, and the King cannot repeal an Act without the consent of Parliament', Mackenzie explained.[178] It was an important qualification – one that was to be put to the test in the reign of the Catholic successor.

7

Malcontents and Loyalists

The Troubles and Disquiets in Ireland from the
Popish Plot to the Royalist Reaction

While our neighbour nations have been haunted by conspira-
cies and confusions, we . . . suffered nothing under the force
of such enchantments . . . All here was peace and quietness.
And what is further observable, all things prospered in our
land. Merchandise increased, trades thrived, artificers were
encouraged; the King's revenue . . . considerably augmented
and the whole country improved to a very sensible advantage;
and all this at the same time when others were preparing for a
state of war and when we ourselves in this kingdom were
represented to our friends abroad as a desperate, miserable,
forlorn people, and exposed as a prey to the common enemy.[1]

On the surface, Ireland appears to have been where the restored polity
was most vulnerable. The Protestants of the Established Church were
a small minority, outnumbered even by the Protestant dissenters, let
alone by the Catholic majority who made up three-quarters of the
total population. The Restoration settlement had left an uneasy political, religious and economic situation. Both Catholics and Protestant
dissenters were unhappy about their exclusion from political power
and trading privileges and the formal restrictions on their religious
freedoms, while the land settlement had left a deep well of bitterness
and resentment, with not only dispossessed Catholics feeling cheated
at not being allowed to regain what they believed was rightfully theirs
but also many Protestants either feeling angry at having to return land
that they had recently purchased or else nervous about whether they
would be allowed to keep what they had. There were repeated alarms

in the 1660s and '70s both that Protestant dissenters in Ireland were conspiring with radical discontented elements elsewhere in the British Isles to bring down the restored monarchy and that Irish papists were in league with the Catholic superpowers of Europe to extirpate Protestantism in this north-west corner of the continent. Those who ruled Ireland had to be careful how they trod; enforcing the strict letter of the law against Catholics and dissenters would only build up further resentment in the vast majority of the population, whereas being too lenient would create fears in both Ireland and England about the security of the Protestant ascendancy.

Having said this, in the 1670s there were signs that Ireland was beginning to recover from the devastations of the 1640s and '50s and, despite the tensions that lay not far beneath the surface, to enjoy a relative degree of stability. It took the revelations of the Popish Plot in England and the subsequent Exclusion Crisis to destabilize the situation in Ireland. Oates's initial revelations had alleged that the Catholics in Ireland were planning another uprising, which was seemingly confirmed in the spring of 1680 when Shaftesbury claimed to have uncovered an Irish plot involving a French-backed conspiracy to massacre Protestants in Ireland. In addition, the covenanters' rebellion in Scotland in May–June 1679 prompted fears that the Scottish Presbyterians in Ulster might rise in support. And it was undoubtedly the case (as we have seen) that the perception of what was going on in Ireland had a vital impact on public opinion in England during the Exclusion Crisis.

The purpose of this chapter, therefore, is to examine exactly what was going on in Ireland. We will assess what impact the revelations of the Popish Plot had there and how those who lived in Ireland reacted, in order to determine the extent to which Ireland did become destabilized at this time. We will also explore how the government of Charles II responded to the Irish situation. The royal administration in Dublin – headed for most of this time by the Duke of Ormonde, who served his second spell as Lord Lieutenant from 1677 to 1685, with his son the Earl of Arran serving as his deputy between 1682 and 1684 – pursued a cautious policy of damage limitation. Thus it took appropriate security measures to prevent any possibility of insurrection, and made some effort to shore up the Protestant establishment, but it remained careful not to overreact against Catholics and Protestant nonconformists (most of whom were peaceful and loyal) for fear of provoking more genuine discontent. The revelations of the Rye House Plot, with its supposed Irish dimension, made it necessary to clamp down more rigorously on public meetings of dissenters and Catholics and to conduct a purge of local office-holders to ensure loyalty to the existing regime. Nevertheless, throughout this period Ormonde and Arran remained careful to adhere strictly to the rule of law. Although there was some disaffection in Ireland at this time, it was in fact limited, and much less of a threat than that which existed in Scotland or even in England. Yet Ireland did mimic England in the sense that it witnessed a marked loyalist reaction in the final years of Charles II's reign, as conformist Protestants across the kingdom sought to demonstrate their backing for the crown in its struggle against the English Whigs through a campaign of loyal addresses. Thus in Ireland, as in England, the years of the Tory Reaction saw a dramatic groundswell of support for the King and his brother – at least among Protestants of the Established Church.

THE AFTERMATH OF THE POPISH PLOT

Despite the intrinsic fragility of the situation in Restoration Ireland, it would be misleading to paint too bleak a picture. The Protestant ascendancy may have felt nervous about the potential threat from both popery and dissent, and resented interference by the English parliament in its own economic affairs, but basically it had no alternative but to look to England for support, and in reality it was doing quite well from the imperial relationship. Moreover, in practice the Restoration regime afforded a considerable degree of toleration to Protestant dissenters and Catholics, which meant that religious tensions in Ireland were not fuelled by government-backed persecution, as they were in England and Scotland. The vast majority of Protestant nonconformists – including the Scottish Presbyterians of Ulster – made their peace with the Restoration regime, and even seemed to thrive under it. Many Catholic merchants managed to achieve a certain degree of prosperity despite the legal impediments under which they operated; indeed, in some towns they were able to become freemen and even gain access to corporate office. The land settlement remained the major grievance for Catholics, but for the time being they appeared willing to put their trust in the Restoration regime in the hope that Charles II might open up the land question again – as, in fact, he seemed prepared to do in 1672, before pressure from the English parliament forced him to back down, and again in 1678. In addition, York's public acknowledgement of his conversion to Rome, following his non-compliance with the Test Act in 1673, gave the Catholic majority in Ireland the prospect of one day having a king of their own faith. All they had to do was to bide their time; launching a challenge to the Protestant ascendancy at this juncture would have served only to fuel English anxieties over the Catholic succession, and more likely than not would have rebounded to their disadvantage.

Furthermore, following the devastations and depopulation wrought by the wars of the 1640s and a somewhat shaky start in the early years of the Restoration, the Irish economy was showing signs of recovery. As the land settlement began to acquire an air of stability, the longer it remained unchallenged, the more willing the new owners were to invest in their property and make improvements. Likewise trade picked up, despite temporary setbacks caused by the Dutch Wars of 1664–7 and 1672–4 and the restrictions placed on the Irish economy by the English. The Navigation Act of 1671, which stipulated that all colonial imports should be landed first in England, nevertheless left Ireland free to export directly to the colonies and in any case proved fairly easy to evade, while the Cattle Acts of 1663 and 1667, despite destroying a profitable export trade to England, stimulated a diversification of the Irish agricultural economy into salt beef, butter and sheep, and helped promote an expansion of trade with the Continent and the colonies. Growing economic prosperity was reflected in a dramatic rise in receipts from customs and excise, which more than doubled between 1665 and 1683. The population also began to grow, at a time when that of England and Wales was stagnating or even in decline. The most dramatic increase was in Dublin, which at least doubled and may even have tripled in size between 1660 and 1685; by the latter date, with a population of between 50,000 and 60,000, it was the second largest city of the Stuart kingdoms – exceeded only by London. Not that this prosperity was evenly distributed among Ireland's inhabitants; the lion's share of the wealth remained in Protestant hands. Nevertheless, this was not a kingdom that was struggling to keep itself together, or that seemed on the verge of imminent political or economic collapse.[2] In the mid-1670s, then, on the eve of the Exclusion Crisis, neither the ascendant Protestant interest, the Protestant dissenters nor the Catholics in Ireland appeared to have anything to gain from rocking the boat.

It took external factors to threaten the relative stability of Ireland at this time. The revelations of the Popish Plot in England in the late summer and autumn of 1678 made it necessary for the authorities in Ireland to be seen to be taking tougher measures against Catholics. On 16 October 1678 the Dublin administration issued a proclamation requiring all Catholic bishops, Jesuits and regular clergy to leave Ireland, and all convents to be closed.[3] This was followed two weeks later by an order prohibiting all Catholics from carrying or possessing arms, unless licensed by the Lord Lieutenant, and enjoining them to surrender whatever weapons they had. On 20 November the government issued proclamations prohibiting Catholics from entering Dublin Castle or any fort in the kingdom, or even from living in garrison towns unless they had dwelt there for twelve months, and excluding converts to the Roman faith from the guards.[4] The orders were not that strictly enforced, and additional proclamations had to be issued over the next two years to urge the disarming of Catholics and the apprehension of popish clergy not permitted to stay in the country.[5] Shaftesbury and the English Whigs complained bitterly in the English parliament that Ormonde was being too soft on the Catholics, but the Lord Lieutenant refused to be pressured into taking panic measures that might serve only to provoke the majority Catholic population and thus do more harm than good.[6]

The revelations of the Popish Plot in England nevertheless caused panic in Ireland. One correspondent, writing from Ireland to England in early February 1679, claimed that even 'before wee became acquainted with the horrid Plott, the Irish who had perfect knowledge of it, told many of their English friends, that most woefull bloody times were at hand.' In paranoid fashion, he then went on to allege that

Ormonde was in collusion with the Catholics and had ordered their weapons to be returned and allowed arrested clerics to be released. Indeed, this correspondent protested, both Ormonde and Arran continued to employ Catholics in those parts of the country where they held influence, while the revenue-farmers even appointed Catholics as hearth-tax or excise officials, thereby providing them with the 'opportunity to search our houses and cut our throats'. Despite the proclamation forbidding papists from keeping houses in Dublin, he went on, prominent Catholics remained in the capital: most of the constables were Catholics; 'Popish postmasters' had been 'put in the Country'; popish schools had been set up in Ormonde or Arran territory; and masses were publicly held 'and more frequented than our churches'. This author even claimed that Ormonde's elder son, the Earl of Ossory, who came to Ireland briefly in early 1679 to deputize while his father was away in England, had in reality come over to enlist his own private forces and gauge how ready the papists were to assist their brethren in England – though 'whether our throats or yours' were 'first to be Cutt', or 'whether the meeting of the Parliament be the time to doe both', the author conceded he did not yet know.[7] Exhibiting a similar degree of paranoia, the Earl of Orrery, governor of Clare in the west of Ireland, warned in February 1679 of an impending French invasion, predicting the likelihood of French success if something were not done quickly to put the kingdom in a better defensive posture. All the major sea ports in his part of the country, he claimed, had within their walls many more Irish Catholics – 'and that of the loosest sort apt for any mischiefe' – than soldiers or Protestant inhabitants, with the exception of Cork, whose suburbs were nevertheless filled with 'dangerous people'. Moreover, not only was the countryside filled with Catholics, but their clan chiefs continued to live among them (despite having forfeited their estates for the last rebellion), as did 'the romish Clergy' (despite the proclamations ordering them to leave the kingdom). 'When the Bulke of the Common people are influenc'd by their lay Cheifes, and by their spiritual guides, how ready will they bee for rebellion,' Orrery forecast – especially if to those two powerful groups 'there bee the accession of a French invasion accompanied with Declarations of restoring them to their forfeited estates, and their Clergy to their honors, dignityes and revenues'.[8]

Such fears may have been unfounded, but they were certainly genuinely felt. Sir William Talbot, the Duke of York's agent in Ireland, observed how the Popish Plot awakened the Protestants 'from a lethargy of security' and made them 'fly to their armes'. The papists, by contrast, 'confounded with the blacknesse of the designe of which they protest[ed] their ignorance', feared a backlash which would lead to 'their inviolable ruine'. Talbot himself believed the plot was 'bloune up . . . by the clandestine and secret instigation of malcontents to bring all to confusion', but felt that 'only the hands of providence' could 'put a stay to the incensed minds of the multitude'.[9] Orrery's suspicions seemed confirmed when an Irish Catholic named Murphy deposed before the Dublin authorities in the spring of 1679 'that several Irish Papists were Privatly Inlisted men', though Dublin subsequently informed Orrery that Murphy was 'a man of a Craved Braine' and his testimony unreliable. Orrery found that he had to defer an intended trip to London while fears remained of a possible French attack, the Protestants telling him they 'would be the more disanimated' were he to leave the country.[10] Then in September one David Fitzgerald, a Protestant sea captain, informed him about a long-standing French design to invade Ireland with an army and some 5–6,000 firearms, to land somewhere between Waterford and Dungarvan. Orrery took 'the alarm warmly'; Ormonde thought an invasion highly unlikely, given that there was no corroborating intelligence, but nevertheless launched an appropriate investigation. (When the French ship supposed to be carrying the arms arrived at Waterford and was searched, it was found to be laden only with salt.)[11] A Protestant minister preaching at Youghall on 29 December 1679, speaking of 'the troubles and disquiets that are amongst us', warned his congregation that this could be their last communion, since they did not know when their liberty might 'be snatcht away' from them.[12] Fears generated mutual suspicions and increasing tensions between Protestants and Catholics. For instance, trouble erupted when one John Totty, an officer of the mace in Dublin, was sent to shut down a mass house on the Merchant's Key on 1 April 1679: Totty 'pulled away the priest by the shoulders'; the priest cried out 'that he wou'd be revenged for it', and later that night two men caught up with Totty at the Tholsell and left him for dead.[13]

Protestants in Ireland who harboured fears of Catholic conspiracy realized that their fate depended on how those in England chose to respond to the Popish Plot. They therefore came to put their faith in the English parliament as the only body that seemed determined to get to the root of the plot, and grew frustrated with Charles II's attempts to foil the English Whigs through recourse to his powers of prorogation and dissolution. There was, in other words, some kind of Irish counterpart to the English Whig movement, albeit modest in scope, committed to securing the regular sitting of the English parliament so that it could deal with the challenge facing Protestants on both sides of the Irish Sea. On 1 March 1681 Viscount Clare and the JPs and grand jury of Country Clare drew up a petition to Ormonde at the Ennis assizes in which they alleged that the recent dissolution of the parliament in England had encouraged the papists in Ireland to great insolence: while there was no parliament, they explained, nothing was done to investigate the plot, and the Catholics formed the opinion that they were favoured. The petitioners therefore implored Ormonde to persuade the King to let parliament sit on 21 March and continue sitting until an effective course had been taken to secure the Protestants of Ireland from popish designs. Whether Clare's initiative was coordinated with the Whig petitioning campaign in England is unclear; Thompson in his *Intelligence*, perhaps not the most reliable source, claimed that Clare's petition 'was first draw'd here in England, and sent over by two Persons of Honour'. It nevertheless does seem to have been part of a broader campaign at least within this part of Ireland: there was an attempt to promote a similar petition from County Limerick, although this failed to get off the ground when the grand jury there refused to have anything to do with it. Charles II was furious with Clare, proclaiming that the inhabitants of Ireland were 'out of their sphere whenever they pretend to give counsel to his Majesty touching his affairs in England', and had him removed from the commission of the peace, the militia, and all other employments. Under pressure, the grand jury and two of the JPs retracted the petition in late April, early May; Clare himself claimed that his intention had been misunderstood and that he was by no means disloyal, although it was not until December 1683, in the aftermath of the Rye House Plot, that he offered to make a formal retraction too.[14]

It was not only the revelations of the Popish Plot in England that destabilized Ireland; so too did the outbreak of Presbyterian unrest in Scotland. Protestants of the Established Church in Ireland had long been uneasy about the sizeable nonconformist presence in their own country, and especially that of the Scottish Presbyterians in Ulster, who were more geographically concentrated than the English dissenters and also more highly organized. Many, among them Archbishop of Armagh Michael Boyle himself, were unhappy with the *de facto* toleration afforded Protestant nonconformists and would have liked to have seen the laws penalizing dissent more strictly enforced. Ormonde, although he recognized the need for a policy of pragmatic toleration, nevertheless thought Presbyterians were as bad as Catholics. Churchmen's fears were made worse by the heavy influx of Scottish Presbyterians fleeing persecution in 1678 and of Scottish rebels seeking asylum in 1679.[15] In September 1678 the English government instructed Ormonde to maintain a close surveillance over the North Channel to stop militant covenanters from the Scottish southwest escaping into Ireland.[16] Such efforts were renewed in June 1679, following the outbreak of the covenanter rebellion in Scotland, lest the Ulster Presbyterians should rise in sympathy.[17] Such fears were not totally without foundation. Following the murder of the Archbishop of St Andrews by Scottish fanatics in May 1679, a Derry Presbyterian named Henry Osborne was heard to say in public that he was pleased that the Archbishop was killed, while the following year copies of Cargill's Sanquhar declaration were found circulating in the province.[18]

Nevertheless, the Ulster Presbyterians remained quiet, with most of their ministers at pains to dissociate themselves from the activities of extremists across the North Channel and to affirm their loyalty to the government. At the end of June 1679 the presbytery of Down drew up an address to Ormonde protesting its loyalty to the king and declaring that it had had no prior knowledge of the rebellion in Scotland and had taken no part in it. In September, eight Presbyterian ministers from Londonderry and adjacent counties drew up a further address, declaring they would 'remain steadfast' in their loyalty, continue 'to pray for his majesty's person and government' and 'obey his lawful commandments', and even when they could not 'in conscience actively obey his majesty's laws' they would 'yet peaceably . . . submit to his majesty's undoubted authority'. Likewise in July 1680 four leading Presbyterian ministers from County Armagh sent a petition to Ormonde disowning the Sanquhar declaration and protesting that 'the ministers and people of our profession in this county' knew nothing 'but principles of loyalty and due obedience to his Majesty'.[19]

'THIS KINGDOM IMPROVES VISIBLY' – THE BEGINNINGS OF THE ROYALIST REACTION

With the passage of time, doubts began to increase in Ireland about the reality of the popish threat. To many on the ground, it soon became apparent that the rumours of Catholic conspiracy were baseless. For example, at the end of July 1680 a Protestant clergyman, writing from Cashel in County Tipperary about the difficulties he was having in trying to convert the local Catholics, could nevertheless reassure his correspondent in England that all was quiet and 'the reports of troubles found fals'.[20] In the third week of March 1681 William Molyneux wrote from Dublin that, although it was conceivable that 'Our Plots in Ireland' were 'begotten short', he was convinced they were 'brought forth in England, for we hear nothing off [sic] them but from thence'.[21] What plots were 'brought forth' in Ireland were shown to be fabrications. For example, when two Catholic converts to Protestantism accused two Catholics of being involved in 'a designe to Introduce the French, Subdue the Kingdome, alter the Religion Established, and Introduce Popery' at the assizes for County Mayo in August 1681, a Protestant jury found that the prosecution 'was altogether malitious and groundles' and returned a verdict of not guilty.[22] In February 1682 three individuals were sentenced to stand in the pillory – two were also to have an ear cut off – for making false accusations about the supposed Irish Plot.[23] At the Cork assizes in August 1682 the principal witness against the titular Bishop of Cork for alleged involvement in the Irish Plot retracted his evidence and declared 'that what he had before sworn, was all false, and that he was stirred up to do what formerly he did'.[24] Of course it would be wrong to convey the impression that all Protestants were suddenly convinced that their worst fears of the Catholics were groundless. Nevertheless, it is clear that many Protestants of the Established Church in Ireland were becoming less credulous of stories of Irish conspiracies they were hearing out of England and increasingly suspicious of how the alleged Irish Plot was being used to try to discredit those in charge in Ireland. Illustrative of this trend is the fact that in May 1681 the Dublin assembly issued a formal condemnation of a pamphlet called *Ireland's Sad Lamentation*, which had accused Ormonde, Arran and Archbishop Boyle of acting under Roman Catholic influences, in opposition to the true interests of the English in Ireland.[25]

The Tory press in England did its best to convey the impression that all was well in Ireland, as part of the strategy to calm English anxieties about the alleged popish threat and rally support behind the crown. Thus on 9 March 1681, in the very first issue of his *Intelligence*, Thompson reported how letters from Dublin showed that Ireland was quiet, contrary to the lies of factious scribblers – in particular he insisted that there was no truth to recent rumours of great meetings of Catholic clergy or of a secret stash of Catholic arms being found near Cork.[26] Likewise, in April 1682 Thompson assured his readers that Ireland was 'in a very quiet and peaceable Condition'.[27] Ormonde agreed. Writing to the King in July 1681 from his family seat at Kilkenny, he reported how 'this kingdom improves visibly, and is improved beyond what could have been reasonably hoped for in the space of twenty years.' It was true that there was no faction in any of Charles's other kingdoms that did not have 'some abettors and well wishers in this', but the King's 'late conduct in [his] Court, councils and magistracy' – that is, the way he had responded to the Exclusionist challenge in England – had 'evidently and advantageously influenced [his] affairs here'.[28]

In fact we see the same type of royalist reaction in Ireland following the dissolution of the Oxford Parliament in March 1681 as we do in England. This manifested itself in two ways: a desire to uphold and protect the existing Protestant establishment against potential challenges from either Protestant dissenters or Catholics, and a sudden rise in public professions of support for the crown and the hereditary succession in the form of loyal demonstrations and addresses. Not that the trends were identical in the two kingdoms. Indeed, the term 'reaction' is somewhat less appropriate in the Irish context; in England there was a marked reaction against the Whigs and their nonconformist allies and a definite swing in public opinion in favour of Charles II and the Duke of York, whereas in Ireland the loyalty of those Protestants of the Established Church who rallied in support of the crown's position had never been in doubt. For this reason it proved unnecessary for the crown to conduct the same sort of purges of local office-holders as in England. Moreover, given that Protestants of the Established Church in Ireland were such a small minority of the total population, they had to be careful not to over-react against those outside the existing establishment. Thus we do not see the same drive against dissent and the strict enforcement of the penal laws which were such central features of the Tory Reaction in England. Nevertheless, we can detect the same type of process at work in Ireland, namely a cementing of the ties between the Protestant establishment and the crown, centred around a commitment to the hereditary succession, the rule of law, and the ascendancy of the Established Church.

A number of towns took measures to ensure that they remained bulwarks of the Protestant establishment. On 28 May 1681 the Trim assembly ordered all those not free of the corporation to leave by 10 June, and required all freemen to take the oaths of allegiance and supremacy.[29] Similarly in July of that year the corporation of Dublin affirmed that no one would 'hereafter be admitted to the freedom of this cittie without takeing the oaths of allegiance and supremacy'.[30] Ormonde, as Lord Lieutenant, took steps to ensure that those responsible for keeping law and order in Ireland were loyal to the Established Church, issuing a proclamation in November 1681 requiring all officers in the army to produce certificates proving that they had taken the Anglican sacrament, and another the following April requiring the same of all JPs.[31]

The religious complexion of Ireland made it impossible to contemplate a strict enforcement of the laws against those who worshipped outside the Protestant establishment. Yet, as the governments in Scotland and England began to take an increasingly harsh line against

Protestant dissent, so the authorities in Ireland found it necessary to make some gestures against nonconformist activity, especially if it seemed to threaten existing authority structures within the kingdom. The first hint of a hardening attitude came towards the beginning of 1681, in response to the decision by the Lagan Presbyterian meeting in Ulster to call a fast for 17 February to avert the judgement of God at a time when, so the meeting believed, 'Popery was making great Advances.' Although meetings had often called fasts in the past, technically only the king could do so, and so this amounted to a usurpation of royal authority. The ministers responsible were summoned before the Lord Lieutenant and council in Dublin, prosecuted for violating the Act of Uniformity, fined £20 each, and imprisoned for the best part of the year for failure to pay, being released only when the Exchequer reduced the fines to 20 shillings.[32] During the years 1681–2 Dublin Quakers found themselves being pursued for unpaid tithes, and occasionally soldiers were sent to disperse Quaker meetings in private houses.[33] However, the authorities in Ireland seemed somewhat unsure of the legal powers they had to act against nonconformist conventicles. In July 1682 Ormonde, in response to an enquiry from Archbishop Boyle about whether the King might do anything to 'give more force to those Acts of Parliament that we have in Ireland for the suppression of conventicles', warned, 'We must goe no further then Law will carry Us.' 'Our lawyers in Ireland', he explained, were unsure whether any of the laws of England could be used against anyone but the papists, though all agreed that 'the Law against riots and unlawfull Assemblyes' might possibly be interpreted to reach Protestant dissenters.[34] For the time being, however, the Irish government chose to tread cautiously.

As with England and Scotland, there were loyalist demonstrations in Ireland. Whether these were on the increase is difficult to say, because ever since the Restoration there had been a strong tradition among Church of Ireland Protestants of celebrating royal anniversaries, especially Restoration Day itself.[35] Nevertheless, the continued commemoration of royal anniversaries undoubtedly took on a new significance in the altered political context of the Exclusion Crisis, and in particular during the years of the Tory Reaction in England, when the Tory press in England was keen to point to examples of loyalist commitment throughout the three Stuart kingdoms in order to substantiate its claim that the majority of people did not support the Whigs. Thus in June 1682 Thompson's *Intelligence* carried a detailed report of how Dubliners had celebrated 29 May 'with all the expressions of Joy imaginable', there being innumerable bonfires throughout the city, including three huge ones constructed at the Lord Mayor's orders at the town hall, the gates of the college, and in Castle Street, 'where great numbers of People' drank loyal toasts 'upon their Knees', amidst acclamations of 'God bless the King, and all the Royal Family.'[36] At Lifford, County Donegal, on that day, those described by our hostile source as 'the drunken gentry and justices of the peace' burned effigies of the Earl of Shaftesbury and a local Presbyterian minister – the latter only recently released from jail after having been imprisoned by the same magistrates for holding an illegal fast.[37] There were no royal entries or progresses in Ireland – as in Scotland and England – to provide occasion for loyalist displays, but in the absence of the King or the Duke of York the viceroy could serve just as well. Thus when Ormonde returned to Dublin in the autumn of 1681, after a stay at his country home in Kilkenny, he 'was received with great signs of Joy, not only by the Inhabitants making Bonefires, but also by the Militia, who were drawn out in order for his Reception'.[38]

Ireland also followed England in presenting a number of loyal addresses to the crown. Charles II's declaration of April 1681, explaining why he had dissolved his two previous parliaments in England, related as it was predominantly to the English context, did not suggest the obvious need for a response from Ireland. Nevertheless, 'the loyal and well affected citizens' of Dublin did draw up an address in May, thanking the King for removing 'the causeless Fears and Jealousies of Popery and Arbitrary Power'.[39] Forty-three further addresses came in from corporations and counties all over Ireland in the spring and summer of 1682, pledging commitment to the King, the succession and the Protestant religion. The first was that of the grand jury for County Cork on 22 March. Claiming to have been 'animated' by the loyal addresses in England, the authors acknowledged they had lived in peace and prosperity under Charles II and promised to do their utmost to maintain the King's 'rights, the lawful Succession and the Protestant religion now by law established'.[40]

That the royal administration in England did not orchestrate this initiative seems confirmed by the fact that the Earl of Barrymore later felt compelled to write to Ormonde (who was then in London) to apologize that the address 'was not soe full as it might and ought to have been', since it did not specifically condemn Shaftesbury's Association (as the English addresses of 1682 did), and offering to promote another address at the next quarter sessions 'in Expresse tearmes against that Late Rebellious association'.[41]

The Cork address was soon followed by others that were more 'full'. That from County Limerick claimed that Charles II's government was 'famous through the neighbouring World for the Unbyassed and Uncorrupted Justice wherewith the Lawes of the Land' had been administered 'and an uninterrupted trade and commerce caryed on beyond what hath been known in any former times'. However, certain malcontents were stirring up trouble, spreading 'Volumes of libellous Pamphlets against your Majesties happy Government' in an attempt 'to alienate the hearts of your Majesties good Subjects', and thereby threatening to engage them in another civil war. The addressors concluded by promising to defend the King in his 'regall rights and Prerogatives' against foreign and domestic force and the evil practices of any who might endeavour to weaken the government under either Charles II or his 'legall Successors'.[42] The address from the corporation of Dublin thanked the King for 'the great happinesse, peace, security, and tranquility' now enjoyed under his 'most gracious government', expressed a 'detestation of all those wicked practices and contrivances . . . by some factious and ill minded men to alienate from your majestie the affections of your subjects, and to seduce them from the duty and obedience that they owe', and concluded with a promise 'to defend and preserve' the King's 'royall person and Protestant religion and the government, as it is now by law established in church and state, against all confederacies, attempts and associations whatever . . . by either Papists or fanaticks, or other disturbers of the publick peace'.[43]

Most of the subsequent addresses followed a similar pattern. The corporation of Waterford, claiming inspiration from the Dublin address, thanked Charles II for the way he and Ormonde had governed them, expressed their 'utter detestacion of all those malevolent practices and seditious machinations which have been of late drawn into practice by some mutinous and ill designing persons', and pledged to defend and preserve the King's royal person and prerogative', 'the lawful descent of the imperial crowne of these realms in the lineall and lawful course of it', 'the true Protestant religion' and 'the government as it is now established by law, both in church and state, against all combinacions and confedracyes and associations whatsoever', whether by 'papists or sectaries'.[44] The address from the grand jurors of County Meath offered Charles II thanks for his 'repeated assurances' that he would defend 'the Protestant Religion as it is now established by Law in this . . . Kingdom' and govern 'according to the Laws', expressed an abhorrence of associations, and made professions of duty not just to the King but also to 'your Majesties heires and lawful Successors'. The grand jurors of County Wicklow said they would 'defend and preserve your Majesties most Royal person and prerogative, the lawful discent and Succession of your Imperial Crowne, and the true Protestant Religion as it is now Established by Law'. The town and borough of Wexford expressed an abhorrence of the Association and promised to defend the King, his prerogative and heirs, and 'the Religion and government in church and state as now by Law Established against all associations, Covenanters and confederates Whither Papists, fanaticks or Other disturbers of the Peace of Whatsoever Principle or perswasion'.[45]

Initially the royal administration did not seem to know what to make of the addresses from Ireland. Ormonde, for one, was troubled by the Dublin address of May 1681. 'Such applications out of Ireland' were new, he observed, or 'at least never practised . . . in good times'; besides, there was bound to be some opposition, and he worried that 'the number of the disaffected' might be found to be greater than anyone thought. Similarly Charles, though 'very glad' that Dubliners were 'generally so well inclined', feared that the promotion of addresses might 'make them factious there', as had already proved to be the case in the City of London.[46] When the addresses from Cork and Dublin of 1682 were read to the King at Windsor they were laughed at, the Earl of Conway tells us. Secretary Jenkins apparently made 'a pleasant mistake . . . in the reading' – whether a mere slip of the tongue or a deliberate attempt at humour is unclear, though

Conway concluded that the Irish addresses were regarded as 'of little valew', because they were 'out of the Rode', and thought that Ormonde would be instructed to suppress them.[47] Yet, whatever the court at Windsor thought of these addresses, the administration in Ireland believed it was important, once the ball had started rolling, to keep them coming. Thus on 9 May 1682 Thomas Parnell in Dublin sent a chastizing letter to Sir George Rawdon in Lisburn, County Antrim, complaining of 'the Backwardness of [his] county in making an Addresse to his Majesty' and urging that it 'should do one speedily', so as not to be the last.[48]

What do these addresses allow us to conclude about the climate of public opinion in Ireland? Clearly we are dealing with a small segment of the population. The addresses were issued in the names of the ruling elites of the towns or counties; unlike in England, there were no addresses from humble groups such as apprentices, cooks or tinners. The addressors were also overwhelmingly Protestants of the Established Church, although occasionally Irish names can be detected among the signatories: for example, two Magennises signed the Down address of April 1682, though this nevertheless expressed a commitment to the 'Religion as now Established by law amongst us'.[49] Furthermore, not every county or corporation sent in an address (if they had, there would have been four times as many), while some of those that did dragged their feet or showed a distinct lack of enthusiasm. The Dublin administration was concerned about the slowness of certain parts of Ulster to address. Neither the county of Antrim nor the corporation of Belfast ever did, though County Londonderry drew up an address on 25 April. The corporation of Carrickfergus was one of the last, not drawing up its address until 10 July.[50] There was also a pocket of disaffection in County Tipperary, which Ormonde thought 'the worst affected [shire] in the Kingdom'. Although the county did deliver a loyal address at the beginning of May, Arran found that the majority of the grand jury, egged on by the disaffected mayor of Clonmel, Stephen Moore, had refused to sign it. Arran therefore decided to hold it back until he had had the chance to remove Moore from the commission of the peace, and the address from County Tipperary was not to be finally agreed to until 18 July.[51] The very last address was County Kerry's of 9 August, though Kerry's slowness may have had more to do with its remoteness from Dublin than with the level of disaffection in the county.[52] Some places obviously felt they had to follow the trend and send in loyal addresses lest they be suspected of disaffection. Thus the address from the corporation of Irish Town of 26 April expressed a concern that by 'pretenses of Slavery and Arbitrary Government' the enemies of the crown were seeking to destroy the 'antient monarchy' and threatening a return to the 'late fatall confusions and Unparaleled tyranny', and the addressors wanted to let the world know that they were not tainted 'with any of those Republican and Seditious Principles'.[53]

However, there is no doubting that in many areas Protestants were more than willing to make a public profession of their loyalty to the crown. The town of Kilkenny, for example, in the heart of Ormonde territory, despite not getting around to drawing up an address until 19 May, was nevertheless 'unanimous in it', as Arran cheerfully reported to his father back in England.[54] Indeed, taken as a whole the Irish addresses point to a genuine desire among the Protestant ascendancy in Ireland to be associated with their Tory-Anglican brethren in England in a publicly stated commitment of support for the King and the succession during the years of the Tory Reaction. Like their English counterparts, the Irish addressors appreciated that their own security was inextricably bound up with the security of the Stuart regime in England. The Irish addresses, however, represent the threat to stability as external – as coming essentially from England, not Ireland. Most of them stress that Ireland had experienced peace and prosperity under Charles II; the sources of concern were libellous pamphleteers, the supporters of Shaftesbury's alleged Association, and those who wanted to challenge the King's prerogatives or subvert the succession. There was, of course, a recognition that the evil contrivances of such malcontents might prompt disaffection among the King's subjects in Ireland (hence the desire of the addressors to show that they were not disloyal), and there was also a concern about the possible threat to the present establishment in Church and state posed by both papists and fanatics, which might reflect the concerns and anxieties of the ruling Protestant minority in an overwhelmingly Catholic country. Yet on the whole these Irish addresses were reactions to developments within England, and their possible destabilizing effects in Ireland, rather than reactions to developments within Ireland itself. They are, in other words, addresses against the activities of the English Whigs, and thus are essentially Tory (in the English sense) in nature. Moreover, like the Tory addresses in England, the Irish ones expressed a firm commitment to 'our Religion as it is now Established by Law' and the 'Impartial Administration of the wholesome Laws enacted' to secure the King's subjects 'in their Religion and property'.[55]

There is some evidence of Protestant disaffection in Ireland in the early 1680s, beyond the lukewarm enthusiasm for the loyal addresses we have detected in parts of Ulster and County Tipperary. Significantly, however, it took an external stimulus to bring it into the open. Huguenot refugees fleeing persecution in France had been encouraged by Charles II to settle in Ireland. Some went to Cork, but most settled in Dublin, where there was a colony of several hundred French Protestants by the end of the reign. The authorities even allowed them to set up a church in the chapel of St Patrick's Cathedral, where they conducted their own prayer-book services in French.[56] The Protestant artisans and apprentices in Dublin, however, regarded the immigrants as a threat to their livelihood, while the fact that they were French and held their services in a foreign tongue made people suspect that they were really Catholics. On arriving in Dublin at the end of April 1682, to assume his responsibilities as Lord Deputy, Arran received intelligence 'that the Apprentices were to rise the next day, to turn out the French Protestants'. Although Arran ordered the constables to keep a strict watch and tradesmen to keep their apprentices at home, some 300 apprentices – mainly from the outliberties rather than the city itself – assembled the next morning near the new hospital at Kilmainham, on the outskirts of town, armed with staves and a few swords, protesting 'that the masse and Popish priests should not be tolerated as they ware', and offering to prove that several of the French refugees 'ware truely Papists, and seen at Messe, and who could have no other designe but of another massacre'. The guards managed to disperse the crowd, taking some ten or twelve prisoner, and this seems to have settled the matter. A London newsletter writer reported that it had been alleged that the apprentices 'were to have made two parties, one for the Duke of York and the other for the Duke of Monmouth, the latter of which was to have seized on the Guards', but admitted that this had not been confirmed. Sir John Lauder of Fountainhall in Edinburgh heard that the Dublin apprentices had 'also declared against a Popish successor to the Croun', but he may simply have been repeating what he had read in the London newsletters. There is no hint in Arran's correspondence out of Ireland that the apprentices were trying to make a political statement about the succession.[57]

An alleged Catholic plot again threatened to disturb the relative tranquillity of Ireland in the second half of 1682 and the early months of 1683. In August 1682 a Catholic Irish mercenary, variously described in the sources as Tilly or Tool, made revelations before Viscount Preston in Paris of a design by Louis XIV 'to possess himself of Ireland, by which he should curb England and make it subservient to his ends'. The plan, supposedly, was to land 40,000 men in Ireland, whereupon 'great numbers of the natives were to rise and seize Cork, Limerick, and Galway' and join with the French forces. According to Tilly, the Irish end of the conspiracy was being coordinated by Colonel Justin MacCarthy, MacCarthy's kinsman the Earl of Clanrickard, and Viscount Clare, who had fallen into disfavour over his promotion of the County Clare petition of 1681. Preston was sufficiently concerned to send Tilly for questioning by the privy council in England, where in the early months of the new year further details of the plot were brought to light: the people of Ireland were to recognize Louis XIV as king, the French were to be given special trading privileges with the Irish, and Roman Catholicism was to be re-established. A man by the name of Peter Stepkins came forward and swore that he had seen an address, in Tilly's handwriting, from the nobles and people of Ireland to the French king, bemoaning their 'wretched condition from the loss of their property and from being every day hindred in practising their religion'. He also affirmed that the design was to be executed 'on a Sunday in service time in all the most considerable towns in Ireland by surprising the people at the church doors, giving no quarter' – thereby hinting at the possibility of a massacre of Protestants. For a while the plot threatened to make some noise in England, but Tilly overstepped himself by claiming that he had already imported thousands of weapons into Ireland; when the

English council demanded he reveal where they were or they would lock him up and deny him a pardon, he made himself scarce. In Ireland, Arran had been sceptical from the start, believing the informer to be a cheat. A broadside appeared shortly afterwards exposing the plot as a sham and the informer as a man pursuing a personal vendetta against Colonel MacCarthy.[58]

Revealing insights into the climate of opinion in Ireland in late 1682 are provided by Archbishop Boyle in a letter to Ormonde dated 10 October, in which he discusses the prospect of calling another parliament in Ireland. 'It is without doubt', the primate confidently proclaimed, 'that this kingdom never enjoyed such peace, plenty, liberty and ease as they have done under your Grace's government', and 'the generality of the people' seemed to be 'in such a quiet temper at present' that Boyle felt he could confidently predict the return of a parliament, 'if carefully elected', that would do for the King whatever he wanted. Yet Boyle was well aware that this happy state of affairs was dependent upon things in England continuing 'in as good a posture as now they are', and that it would not take much to unsettle the situation. For 'if there should happen to be a recidivation into the late disorders and disturbances in England', he warned, 'I doubt we have some, perhaps many, ill-affected spirits amongst us who would take the boldness to be very instant and troublesome to the Government who would not dare to show themselves or appear in such a juncture as this seems to be.'[59]

THE IMPACT OF THE RYE HOUSE PLOT

There was, of course, to be 'a recidivation into the late disorders' in England with the revelations in the late spring and summer of 1683 of the Rye House Plot. Arran was under no doubt that 'those villains had some of their accomplices here in this kingdom . . . chiefly in the North, and in Munster'.[60] In his examination before the King and council on 8 July, Thomas Walcott reported that plans had been laid to raise disaffected elements in England, Scotland and Ireland, and that Robert Ferguson had claimed that he expected 20–30,000 Ulster Scots to rebel. Other informants implicated the West Country Whig

Sir William Courtenay, who sat in the three Exclusion Parliaments as MP for Devon, in a design to engage discontented Protestants from Waterford in a plot to put Monmouth on the throne. However, the government believed Courtenay when he produced a written dis-avowal of any knowledge of such plotting, and chose not to take any action against him.[61]

Indeed, the government failed to uncover any firm evidence of an Irish dimension to the Rye House Plot; the nearest it came was dis-covering fragments of a treasonable Scottish declaration in the pos-session of a Taunton man who was arrested in the English West Country as he was en route to Ireland.[62] The Presbyterians in Ulster, fearful that the clampdown on conventicles that had already begun in England would be extended to Ireland, started, it was said, to engage in 'mutinous and petulant discourses, and plain menaces of resisting it unto blood'; one informer even claimed that they were raising money to ship arms into the country, though he was discred-ited as someone who framed 'his intelligence for profit'. Yet, while the 'Dissenting party' in the north may have been 'generally discon-tented' – speaking of 'persecuting times just coming' – there is no firm evidence to suggest any genuine conspiracy.[63] There is, however, one tantalizing snippet of evidence which could possibly hint at more than appears on the surface. In mid-August 1683 Viscount Mountjoy wrote to Ormonde from Newtownstewart in County Tyrone to report that, despite 'all the great noise' the Ulster nonconformists had made 'of going in great numbers to Carolina', and the fact that they had kept 'a great ship at Derry to transport them', now the time had come 'not one man goes', and the ship had been forced to alter her voyage.[64] Bizarre, no doubt, but seemingly irrelevant, until one recalls that in 1683 the Scottish Rye House plotters had come to London to meet with their English conspirators under the guise of buying lands in Carolina.[65] Could the Scottish Presbyterians in Ulster similarly have been using a scheme to emigrate to Carolina as a cover for their involvement in the Rye House conspiracy? It is not incon-ceivable, and it would explain why the boat was no longer needed after the government had got wind of the conspiracy. However, clearly one ship would not have been enough to transport a very size-able contingent of Ulster Scots to join in an uprising in England and

Scotland, and we have to concede that we have no corroborating evidence.

The assize records for Clonmel point to some disaffection in the south of Ireland at this time. For example, at the September assizes John and Barbara Lane were indicted for having said the previous April 'that it was base and unlawfull for his Majestie that he did not exile the Duke of York out of his Dominions for feare he shold breede any Disturbance among the Nation'; John Pryor was charged with saying 'that he hoped his Royall Highness should never be King whilst his Majestie and the Duke of Monmouth Live'; and Henry Shrimpton was indicted for predicting 'That the Duke of Monmouth should succeed after his Majesties death and Reigne as King, or else noe King at all', and for further asserting 'that his Majestie was as unjust a King as ever was and that he never perform'd any promise that he gave, and . . . if Cromwell had lived he was as powerfull and as just a King as ever was'. However, since Shrimpton and the Lanes were found not guilty, while Pryor was discharged by proclamation without being brought to trial, one has to wonder how much truth there was behind such accusations.[66]

The revelations of the Rye House Plot nevertheless prompted a new series of security initiatives. To deal with the potential threat of insurrection, the Dublin administration commanded all officers to their quarters, dispatched additional troops to the north, and issued orders to examine passengers entering Ireland.[67] In mid-July Ormonde instructed Arran 'to disarme all frequenters or keepers of Conventicles . . . forthwith', using the laws for disarming Catholics as a guide, though he insisted that the Catholics themselves should be left alone, since only those granted special licences had been able to retain their weapons and there was no reason to revoke these.[68]

Concern that the Scottish Presbyterians in Ulster were meeting in greater numbers than before prompted Arran towards the end of July to instruct local magistrates to suppress unlawful nonconformist meetings and arrest the preachers. Although in some parts of the north local militias had to be deployed to put a stop to conventicling – the local constables proved wholly unreliable, since many were dissenters themselves – most nonconformist ministers throughout Ireland (including Ulster) chose to cooperate with the government, voluntarily shut down their public meetings, and took out bonds for their good behaviour. On 8 August Arran could confidently report to Secretary Jenkins in England that he had 'without disturbance suppressed the Fanatic meetings here and in great measure those in the North', while a few days later Mountjoy informed Ormonde that the northern Presbyterians had proven 'more complaisant than he expected', and that he could not 'hear of one meeting, neither public nor private'. Ormonde remained suspicious of the 'sudden change of temper and submission' of the Ulster Presbyterians and thought 'their acquiescence ought no less to be apprehended and provided against than their stiffness and obstinacy', while Arran admitted that the methods taken would not 'convert many of the Dissenters'. Nevertheless, the immediate results must have been satisfying. Dissenters began to return to church, and for a while, at least, most conventicles in Ireland, even in Ulster, were suppressed. Only the Quakers continued to meet, but the Dublin administration did not 'look upon them as a dangerous sect'.[69]

The government had to be careful not to be seen to be singling out Protestant nonconformists for punishment and turning a blind eye to the activities of the Catholics. The Archbishop of Dublin persuaded the Catholics in Dublin to close their chapels, which had never been legally authorized, even though they had hitherto 'been overlooked and neglected by the government', while the Earl of Longford convinced the authorities in Limerick that they would need to put down public mass houses as well as conventicles.[70] Although Catholics were allowed to exercise their religion in their own homes, they had to be discreet. When the authorities learned in August 1683 of the setting-up of a public nunnery and four public mass houses near the west-coast port of Galway, and a friary in Burrishoole, near Newport, County Mayo, they were swift to take action, lest people insinuate that the government was soft on 'that sorte of People'. The nunnery and priory were quickly dispersed, and several of the priests, friars and nuns were proceeded against at the assizes for violating the laws prohibiting the saying of mass.[71] In October, Ormonde was outraged to learn that some friars were planning to set up four chapels in his own home town of Kilkenny, and warned his son that the government would need 'to use severities to bring them into their wits' and let them see how impossible it was, 'whilst Protestant Dissenters are pro-ceeded against, to suffer the other to assume greater liberty than they have heretofore been allowed'.[72] The clampdown against Catholics, however, seems to have eased off before the end of the reign. It was clear that, although for some time after the proclamations ordering the titular bishops and the Catholic regular clergy out of the country the Catholic clergy 'kept themselves quiet', many had in fact remained in Ireland, and by late 1684 they were becoming increasingly active. In January 1685 Ormonde could tell Sunderland that there were 'now in this kingdom at least as many bishops of the Roman com-munication as of the Protestant', while 'friars and other regulars do abound in all the parts of the kingdom.' Ormonde thought the regu-lars 'an intolerable surcharge upon the poor people of the Romish religion', because, 'besides what these regulars get off them, and besides what they pay to the legal incumbents [i.e. Church of Ireland ministers], they maintain the bishops and a priest in every parish.' Be that as it may, Charles was happy that the Catholics in Ireland should be able to worship as they saw fit. Indeed, towards the end of that month Sunderland could inform Ormonde that the King had learned that the Archbishop of Dublin had shut down Catholic chapels in the Irish capital and wanted to know why.[73]

The revelations of the Rye House Plot prompted a certain cleans-ing of the personnel of local government, though there was not to be a dramatic purge of local offices as took place in England. At the beginning of July 1683 Ormonde informed Arran that it was being 'insinuated' in England that Ireland was 'very ill governed', and that many of the army officers, JPs and town magistrates were disaffected. It was certainly true, as Archbishop Boyle admitted, that many who had served under Cromwell, or the children of those who had, were in the commission of the peace for want of suitable alternatives, though he insisted that there were very few – if any – JPs who would not take the oaths of allegiance and supremacy or conform to the Established Church. The problem was that the Dublin administration was not quite sure of this, since few JPs, commissioners of array or militia officers had sent in certificates proving they had taken the sacrament, as required by the proclamations of November 1681 and April 1682. Arran did proceed to remove several JPs from the commission, though not for nonconformity – only one JP who was a dissenter could be found, and his appointment had been sanctioned by Ormonde – but because they were negligent or incompetent. By dint of the powers vested in him by Essex's rules of 1672, Arran refused to approve Clonmel's decision to re-elect Stephen Moore as mayor, though beyond this there is little evidence of the Lord Deputy actively interfering to ensure that the corporations chose well-affected men. Nevertheless, Arran felt confident he had loyal men in charge even in the more suspect areas. Thus towards the end of September he could report that the sovereign of Belfast was 'a very honest man', even though the town was 'as fanatic a one as any in Ireland'.[74]

As the government was policing potential disaffection, the Church of Ireland clergy were busy trying to cement loyalty to the existing regime. In a sermon delivered at Christ Church Cathedral in Dublin on 29 July 1683, Bishop Anthony Dopping of Meath held forth on the Pauline doctrine of non-resistance, before affirming that the doctrine of non-resistance had always been the 'constant opinion' of the Church of England and was enshrined in the Irish Act of Uniformity. Dopping's conclusion was in accord with the standard line taken by Tory propagandists and Anglican clergy in England: those who justified resistance to oppose a supposed inundation of popery were not sons of the Church, but borrowed their principles from Rome, or Scotland, or Geneva, and were 'either acted by the Jesuit or the fanatick'.[75] As in England, 9 September was set aside in Ireland as a day of thanksgiving for deliverance from the Rye House Plot.[76] Although no printed versions of their sermons have come to light, given that they were instructed to follow the same form of prayer as prescribed in England the Church of Ireland clergy presumably used the occasion to focus on the themes of passive obedience and non-resistance. This was certainly true when John Vesey, minister of Abbeyleix in Queen's County (Laois) – not to be confused with the Archbishop of Tuam of the same name – delivered a sermon the following week at the opening of the Clonmel assizes. Vesey urged the need for obedience to one's superiors, and quoted St Peter's teaching on non-resistance: 'Submit yourselves to every ordinance of man for the Lord's sake' (1 Peter 2:13). Rebellion was 'a most grievous Sin', he intoned, and 'the pretences of Defending Liberty and Property, of Destroying Popery and Arbitrary Government', could not make it not a sin. 'We must not do evil, that good may come thereof,' he continued; 'when we find our selves oppressed, let us examine our Lives, and try whether our own Wickedness is not the Cause of Gods punishing us with such Rulers' – prophetic remarks, as they turned out, since under James II Protestants in Ireland were to find themselves oppressed and did have to consider whether they might do evil so that good might come of it or disobey their superiors in the defence of liberty and property. Yet Vesey's sermon is also revealing for the picture of a vibrant popular political culture it paints for Ireland at this time. 'There is no person so inconsiderable', Vesey thought, 'but may contribute to the general Good of a Nation, either by his Endeavours or Prayers: nay, we commonly find, that Insurrections and Civil Wars are often begun, but always carried on by the Common people.' People should study to be quiet and mind their own business. 'If every single person' would follow St Peter's advice 'and imploy his thoughts about his own Concerns, and not meddle with State affairs, we should be much happier than we are'. But the problem was that people *were* meddling with state affairs. 'How usual is it for men', Vesey observed, 'upon a story in a Gazzet, or a News Letter, to descant upon the Government, and censure, if not reproach the Higher Powers.' 'Trust the Modelling of the Government to your Superiors, whose business it is to govern,' he exhorted, and 'Let us not speak evil of the Ruler of the people.'[77]

There is no evidence of any loyal demonstrations in Ireland on 9 September to celebrate deliverance from the Rye House Plot. Nevertheless, counties and towns throughout the kingdom were quick to testify their loyalty by drawing up addresses in abhorrence of the conspiracy. Some fifty-two such addresses were presented to the crown in the summer and autumn of 1683.[78] That from the city of Waterford of 29 July gave thanks to God for preserving Charles II and the Duke of York 'from the seditious and horred designes of rebellious and profligate wretches', and declared an abhorrence 'of all traiterous and wicked conspiracies' against the King's 'person or government'. The addressers went on to 'acknowledge the blessings of peace, prosperity, and happiness and the exercise of the true Protestant religion established by law' that they enjoyed under Charles II's government, 'according to the fundamental lawes of these kingdomes'; expressed the hope that the 'seasonable and impartial' execution of the laws would deter anyone who might be so 'wicked as to stretch forth his hand against the Lords anointed'; and concluded with a promise to maintain the King's 'roiall person, the lawes, government, prerogatives, and the established religion . . . against all traiterous oppositions whatsoever'.[79] As with the 1682 addresses, the early ones, at least, appear to have been spontaneous testimonies of loyalty, although as time went on other places clearly felt under some informal pressure to conform to the trend. Thus Trim's address to the King of 22 August began by admitting that 'the late horrid plotts and conspiracyes' against the King and his brother had 'made it necessary for all dutifull and loyall subjects to express their abhorrence of them, and to give . . . summ publicke assurance of theyr loyalty and allegiance'. The addressors then went on to assure Charles that they were prepared to lay down their lives and fortunes 'for the preservation of your Majesties sacred person, your heires and lawfull successors against all opposers whatsoever, and for the maintenance of the Protestant religion as now by Law established, in opposition to Popery and Fanaticizme'.[80] This time the county of Antrim did send in an address, as did the town of Clonmel (belatedly); Belfast, however, again did not.

The addresses of 1683, like those of 1682, represented in the main the voice of the Protestant ruling elite of town and countryside. Again, most of the addresses professed a commitment not just to the crown, the succession and the royal prerogative, but also to the rule of law and the existing establishment in the Church. Some Catholics – either in their capacity as freeholders or grand jurors or even perhaps as members of corporations – found themselves able to sign some of the addresses, doubtless keen to demonstrate their own loyalty to the King and his Catholic heir and hostility to the alleged antics of the Protestant dissenters, even if this meant pledging not to challenge the existing legal settlement in Church and state. Ormonde found 'many of their names in addresses that come out of Ireland', but, although no one doubted 'their aversion to the other sort of Dissenters', he warned Arran that he questioned 'whether they would make a distinction betwixt Protestants, if both were in their power'.[81] The address of 4 October from the grand jury, deputy Lieutenants,

JPs, clergy and gentlemen of the county of Dublin created something of a stir because it omitted any reference to the Protestant religion established by law. Catholics outnumbered Protestants on the grand jury that drew up the address by eight to six, and, although the judges tried to have the address amended to include a reference to the Established Church, the foreman refused, saying 'so they had made it and so it should goe.'[82]

In the absence of addresses from humbler types or of loyalist demonstrations, it is difficult to get a sense of the social depth of the royalist reaction after Rye House. The overall impression the evidence leaves is that the Protestants of the Established Church rallied behind the crown and succession in very much the same way as their Tory-Anglican counterparts in England; that Catholics were often keen, given the opportunity, to profess their loyalty to the crown and antipathy to the supposed plots of Protestant dissenters, and were undoubtedly sincere in their commitment to the hereditary succession; and that the majority of Protestant nonconformists were innocent of any conspiracy against the government and were prepared to cooperate with the authorities as the Dublin administration took the necessary precautionary measures in the wake of conspiratorial activity in Scotland and England. This is not to suggest that there was no disaffection in Ireland at all towards the end of Charles II's reign. Some Protestants, especially in Ulster but also elsewhere, had their grievances with the existing regime and were worried about the Catholic succession, while it would clearly be naive to assume that the Catholic majority were happy with their lot. Nevertheless, it is difficult to avoid the conclusion that, despite all the tensions that existed in Ireland, it essentially took external factors to destabilize the situation in this kingdom. Developments in England and Scotland, rather than within Ireland itself, were what were responsible for creating an Irish problem at this time.

There was little to disturb the peace of the government for the rest of the reign. In the spring of 1684 Arran received information about 'a new plot', but thought there was 'no truth in it', since it came 'from a soil very fertile of sham plots'.[83] There were signs that the Ulster Presbyterians were again growing restless towards the very end of the reign. In August 1684 Charles expressed his nervousness to Ormonde about the Scottish rebels who had fled to Ireland, and ordered that they be sent back to Scotland.[84] In mid-November magistrates found a letter in Belfast, subscribed by twenty hands, enjoining Presbyterians not to attend the services either of clerics of the Established Church or of those dissenters who prayed for the King, and promising assistance to Scottish covenanters fleeing to Ireland to escape persecution in their homeland. Although Ormonde – by this time back in Dublin – at first did not think the discovery significant enough to warrant informing the King, his subsequent investigations revealed an alleged design by the Ulster Presbyterians 'of rising up in arms', with certain individuals employed in listing men and others assigned the job of riding 'up and down the country . . . to give notice of the time'. Once more, the truth behind the matter is difficult to discern; one historian has dismissed the alleged conspiracy as 'probably nothing more than the musings of irate malcontents'.[85] Nevertheless, the story reveals that the north of Ireland continued to remain a security concern for the Dublin administration right up to the end of Charles II's reign – something that was to condition the way the government was to respond at the beginning of James II's reign when faced with rebellions from Scotland and England under Argyll and Monmouth.

Conclusion

Despite having suffered short bouts of illness in 1679, in 1680 and again in 1682, as he approached his mid-fifties Charles II was generally thought to be in excellent health; the most he had was a touch of gout. The illness which struck on the morning of Monday 2 February 1685 therefore took everyone by surprise. The King rose early, having not slept well the night before (he was normally a heavy sleeper), and at about seven o'clock, 'coming from his private Devotions, out of his Closet', he suddenly collapsed in what contemporaries described as 'a Fit of an Apoplexy'. He was immediately bled, but it was clear that he was desperately ill. Over the next few days various doctors applied all the latest treatments in a frantic attempt to save his life: he was purged, bled, blistered and cauterized; red-hot irons were applied to his shaved skull; and he was administered in total some fifty-eight drugs. For a while he seemed to revive, but by Thursday he had again taken a turn for the worse. Later that day Father John Huddleston, the Catholic priest who had assisted Charles in his escape from Worcester back in 1651, was smuggled into the royal bedchamber to receive the King into the Roman Catholic Church and to administer the last rites. Charles was to die at about a quarter to twelve the following morning, Friday 6 February. He was not yet fifty-five. Despite the contemporary diagnosis of apoplexy, Charles had not had a stroke. Instead, he was suffering from chronic glandular kidney disease (a form of Bright's disease) with uraemic convulsions. Unconvincing allegations were later to be made that his brother had poisoned him. It is more conceivable that Charles had poisoned himself. The King was a keen amateur chemist, and had spent much time in recent years experimenting with mercury; his kidney failure and uraemia thus could well have been induced by mercury poisoning, although this remains pure speculation. What seems clear, however, is that, for all the torture Charles's doctors inflicted upon their patient, they did not kill him; the King would have died of the disease in any case.[1]

The story of Charles II's death has often been told. Perhaps the most remarkable thing about this scene, however, but something that is rarely commented upon, is where it took place: the King's bedchamber in the royal palace of Whitehall. Charles II's father had had his head severed from his body on a specially erected scaffold outside his own Banqueting House. Charles II's brother and successor was forced to flee his realms after less than four years on the throne and was to end his days ignominiously in exile – albeit in his bed, but not as king. Charles II had faced similar problems to his father: a rebellion in Scotland, a destabilized Ireland, and an alliance of opposition politicians and discontented elements throughout England protesting against an alleged threat of popery and arbitrary government. By 1679–80 it had seemed to many contemporaries that '41 was come again. And, of course, Charles II faced the self-same problems that his brother was to find unmanageable and which were to cost him the thrones of his three kingdoms. For the Merry Monarch to have died in his bed, still as reigning king of England, Scotland and Ireland, was no mean achievement.

It is clear that by 1685 the crown had escaped the crisis that had confronted it in 1679–81. By the time of James II's accession the position of the monarchy had been considerably strengthened and the Whig challenge effectively defeated. When James called his first parliament that spring, a mere 57 Whigs were returned to a House of Commons of some 513 members. This was not merely the result of the royal interference in electoral franchises that had taken place in the final years of Charles II's reign, since those years had also seen a swing in public opinion towards the crown; in the 1685 general election the Tories also did well at the polls in the more open constituencies with large electorates, which were least susceptible to court management. In fact it is undoubtedly the case that James was popular at the time of his accession. There was widespread rejoicing throughout the three kingdoms when he was proclaimed king in February, and over the next several months some 439 congratulatory addresses came in from various places and groups across England, Wales, Scotland, Ireland and the crown's foreign dominions, pledging allegiance to the new king, acknowledging his just and rightful succession, and rejoicing at the failure of Exclusion.[2] Not that James's accession was all plain sailing. There was a rebellion in 1685 – or rather two (since they were not, in the end, the coordinated efforts they were intended to be): one led by the Earl of Argyll in Scotland, the other by the Duke of Monmouth in England. Yet neither proved to be much of a threat; between them, in fact, they were able to muster fewer supporters than had joined the Bothwell Bridge rebellion of 1679, and both were fairly easily put down. During the Exclusion Crisis, many people had genuinely feared the possibility of renewed civil war and had doubted whether a Catholic successor could succeed peacefully – after all, there was talk of Protestants associating themselves to ensure that he did not. James's accession in 1685 could have triggered a real bloodbath. It did not. The crisis had passed. The threat had not been entirely eradicated, but it had been effectively contained.

It is the story of how Charles II's regime first fell into crisis and then got itself out of it that this book has sought to tell. Why, when the restoration of monarchy had appeared so welcome to all groups across the British Isles in 1660, did the Restoration polity appear on the verge of collapse within less than two decades? Undoubtedly, things would have gone easier for Charles II if he had been able to father a legitimate son (assuming that son was brought up a Protestant) or had had a Protestant heir. But to blame the crisis on some contingent factor – an accident of the succession – it has been shown here, is misguided. There were fundamental structural problems with the Restoration polity in each of the three kingdoms – problems that made Charles II's inheritance extremely difficult to manage. Although most people welcomed the return of monarchy in 1660, they expected different things from the restored monarch – and not just different things, one must add, but mutually incompatible things. This was true within each kingdom. In England, there were those who wanted the monarchy to be more accountable to parliament; there were others who thought the monarchy had already become too accountable to parliament. There were separatists who wanted liberty of conscience, Presbyterians who wanted to be comprehended within a reformed Church of England (and who initially would have agreed with the Anglicans that the last thing one could do was to allow the separatists liberty of conscience), and hardline Anglicans who were as much against comprehending Presbyterians as they were against tolerating the sects. In Scotland, there was the bitterly divisive conflict between Presbyterians and episcopalians. And in both kingdoms religious conflict was to be further inflamed by bouts of intense religious persecution. In Ireland, there were tensions between Catholics, Church of Ireland Protestants and Protestant nonconformists, partly over religion (although here persecution was less of an issue), but also over the questions of economic and political rights, access to legal justice, and – the most controversial issue of all – the land settlement. Charles could not please all groups. If he gave the Catholics in Ireland back their land, he would upset the Protestants from whom he took that land. If he did not enforce the laws designed to prop up episcopacy in Scotland and keep the Scottish Presbyterians in their place, he would upset the Scottish episcopalians. If he did not enforce the penal laws designed to meet the challenge of dissent in England, he would alienate the high-Anglican interest, the group most supportive of his attempts to consolidate and strengthen royal power after years of civil war and republican experiment in government. Yet if he did not give the Catholics in Ireland justice, or if he allowed the full weight of the law to be used against Scottish and English nonconformists, he ran the risk of driving significant numbers of his subjects in each of his kingdoms into rebellion.

However, the problems were not simply within each kingdom; they were also between the kingdoms. Charles II could not devise a strategy that he thought might work in one of his realms without having to think about the knock-on effects it could have on one of his others. For example, he could not easily work to appease discontented Catholic elements in Ireland without running the risk of being accused in England of being soft on popery. He could not easily deal with the very real and subversive threat posed by the radical Presbyterians in Scotland – a country that by dint of the nature of its terrain was not particularly easy to police at the best of times (particularly by an absentee monarch) – without having recourse to measures that could make him vulnerable in England to charges of promoting arbitrary government in his northern kingdom. The crisis that had emerged by the end of the 1670s, in other words, was genuinely a three-kingdoms crisis. It was a crisis that stemmed from the problems of managing a troubled multiple-kingdom inheritance where the political and religious tensions that existed within each kingdom cut deep into society, and where any initiatives taken to try to deal with the problems that these tensions generated were likely to cause further difficulties. Thus when the crisis came in 1679–81 – triggered, it is true, by fear of an imminent Catholic succession in the aftermath of the supposed Popish Plot – it was about much more than what might happen, in the future, should the Catholic Duke of York inherit his brother's crowns. It was about the failings of the Restoration polity; it was about Charles II's style of government in all three of his kingdoms; it was about the threat of popery and arbitrary government in the present.

In the event, '41 did not come again. Charles II never lost control of the situation in the way that his father had done. A number of factors were important here. Although Charles II faced a rebellion in Scotland in 1679, this time the Scottish rebels were not to be victorious as they had been on the eve of the Civil War. The Scots were thus not able to hold the English to ransom as they had in 1640–41, when they had occupied the north of England and demanded that the English parliament pay them off before they went home. This had made it impossible for Charles I to dissolve his English parliament when faced with demands for reform in England; with his hands thus tied, the English parliament was even able to induce Charles to assent to an act preventing its dissolution without its own consent.[3] Charles II never became trapped in that way. He retained his freedom to determine when, and for how long, parliament should sit, and this gave him considerably more room for manoeuvre than had been available to his father. He was able to use his prerogative to prorogue and dissolve parliament to forestall the Whig challenge – and, having forestalled it, to devise mechanisms whereby he could then go on and defeat it. Part of the reason why '41 did not come again must therefore relate to why the Scots were unable to launch a successful rebellion in 1679. The simple explanation is that the Scots were much less united in 1679 than they had been in 1637–41 (itself a legacy of the Civil War and Interregnum) and therefore were unable to mount such a significant challenge to the Stuart regime as they had done earlier. In 1637–41 it was the Scottish nation that rose up against Charles I; in 1679 it was just one faction within that nation. Although there was considerable disaffection in Scotland by the late 1670s, there were too many Scots who were willing to remain loyal to Charles II. And, perhaps most importantly, Charles never lost the affection of the Scottish ruling elite, as his father had done. Moreover, with regard to Ireland, although the situation did not always look that healthy and there were repeated reports of a potential Irish rebellion during Charles II's reign, there was in fact to be no repeat of the Irish Rebellion of 1641. The British crisis of 1637–41, although it threatened to, did not duplicate itself in 1679–81.

Yet this is not the sole reason. James II did not face a rebellion in Ireland either – nor really in Scotland, if we discount Argyll's paltry affair. He also held on to his prerogative power of proroguing and dissolving parliaments, and was not trapped into meeting with an assembly he would rather have got rid of in the way that Charles I had been. Indeed, because of the improved financial circumstances of the crown in the 1680s, James was to be more independent of parliament than his brother. And yet James II was unable to hold on to his kingdoms. Besides, Charles II did not merely escape a crisis; he rebuilt the power and authority of the monarchy in the face of a crisis.

Charles's success here was due in large part to his ability to win over public opinion. The court and its Tory allies sought to persuade the King's subjects that the greater threat to English liberties and the Protestant religion was posed by the Whigs and their nonconformist allies rather than the Catholic successor, and that if they wanted to prevent popery and arbitrary government they needed to stick by the existing government in Church and state as by law established and rally in support of the crown and the heir to the throne. What impresses is the very scope of Tory propaganda at this time: the Tories sought to reach not just the ruling classes and the educated elite, but also the middling and lower sorts. The opinions of ordinary people mattered; it was important to have these people on one's side, and to be seen to have them on one's side, especially in England. The reasons for this relate to the way that governance worked in early modern England. To make its rule effective, the crown depended on the co-operation and unpaid assistance of a wide range of people at the local level – not just the Lord Lieutenants, and their deputies, and the gentry JPs who ran the counties, and the merchants and businessmen who ran the corporations, but also the more humble types who played a crucial role in governance and law enforcement in their capacities as trial jurors, parish constables, nightwatchmen, militiamen and even informers. By the late 1670s it was the fact that Charles II had lost the support of many of these types of people, across the social spectrum, that explains why he was finding it difficult to govern the country in the way he would have wanted. It was his ability to win enough of these people back in the early 1680s which helps explain the success of his final years. Appealing to public opinion was not by itself enough, admittedly; the government also embarked on a policy of repression (to remove the Whigs and their nonconformist supporters from positions of power and to make sure they bore the full brunt of the law for any transgressions that they might have committed), in order to make sure that the Whig threat was neutralized. It took both policy and police to defeat the Whig challenge, and we must never lose sight of the importance of the policing part of this formula. Nevertheless, the Tory Reaction would not have been as successful as it was without being predicated upon a swing in public opinion towards the crown and its Tory allies which had already begun to take place.

Charles II also recognized that his multiple-kingdom inheritance, although problem-ridden, need not necessarily be a problem for the crown. Indeed, he realized that he could make it work to his advantage. Hence Charles quite self-consciously developed a British solution to defeat the challenge posed by the Whigs in England. Thus after dissolving the Oxford Parliament in March 1681 he called a parliament in Scotland, where he knew he would meet with greater success in getting his legislative agenda accepted, and was rewarded with a Succession Act which affirmed that parliament could not exclude the heir to the throne in Scotland. This in turn made Exclusion in England non-viable, unless people wanted to risk embroiling the three kingdoms once more in civil war. Moreover, Scottish MPs in 1681 were well aware that they had been called to make a political point to their English counterparts; they, too, understood the nature of the British game they were being invited to play. Indeed, we have seen time and time again how important the three-kingdoms factor was in the defeat of the English Whig movement. Tory propagandists raised public anxieties about the alleged threat of the English Whigs and their nonconformist allies by pointing to what the radical Presbyterians were still up to north of the border. Tory polemicists were further able to point to the Duke of York's success during his two stints as head of the government in Scotland between 1679 and 1682, and also to his keen support for the episcopalian establishment north of the border, as showing that the English had nothing to fear from York's succession. Yet York's popularity in Scotland, as evidenced by the enthusiastic receptions he received when he visited that kingdom or went on a royal progress there – together with the lack of support for Exclusion in Ireland – showed the English why they should have everything to fear from those who pressed to exclude York from his rightful inheritance. It was two kingdoms against one; if the English were to act unilaterally, war with the other two would inevitably follow.

This book, then, has testified to the importance of public opinion in later-Stuart England, Scotland and Ireland. Yet we face the question of how genuine were the manifestations of public opinion we have encountered. The court and its Tory allies made a deliberate effort not only to appeal to public opinion but also to encourage people to demonstrate their loyalism, by subscribing to a loyalist address, say, or by celebrating at a bonfire; indeed, courtiers and local Tory leaders actively promoted such addresses and bonfires. The same could also be said of the Whigs, since they too orchestrated petitioning campaigns and public demonstrations in support of their cause, although for some reason it has always been easier for historians to believe that 'the people' (whoever they were) were against the government of Charles II than in favour of it. Moreover, once we have evidence of mass opposition to the government by 1679–81, it seems difficult to understand how so many people could have changed their minds so quickly in such a short space of time. Could the Tory position really have been popular?

What hampers our understanding here is the fact that the historiography of popular political agitation in the early modern period has for so long been fixated on the question of authenticity.[4] Instead, we should recognize that the real issue at stake is that of mobilization. When we ask whether a particular movement was authentically popular we typically elide two different issues: whether the people who participated in it genuinely agreed with the principles that the movement stood for, and whether the movement was actually organized by the people. There is plenty of evidence to suggest that those below the elite, whether they opposed or supported the government, could orchestrate their own petitions, addresses or demonstrations; yet often they did not. Frequently, as we have seen, local political leaders led the way, and encouraged people to join in through appropriate incentives (such as free alcohol or firework displays, to encourage the masses to come out and cheer at a bonfire, for example). Indeed, we can find examples of the privy council or even the King himself ordering local political leaders to see that bonfires were put on or that there were appropriate public displays of loyalist affection. This does not necessarily mean, however, that those who joined in such loyalist displays were not giving expression to their authentic opinions. To suggest that the chance of a free drink would make people who really supported the other side come out and cheer for their enemies strains credibility – especially when the choices they faced were so stark (do we exclude the Duke of York or not? do we persecute the dissenters or not?), and especially when there was plenty of opportunity to join in counter-demonstrations (which again might be promoted by local political leaders with liberal supplies of free food and alcohol). This is why, in order to understand the political leanings of the mass of the population in early modern England, Scotland and Ireland, the place to start is not with the appeal to 'the people' from 'above' (by politicians, propagandists or whoever they might be) but with the lived experiences of the people themselves. We must first explore the extent to which people had or had not become alienated as a result of the policies pursued by those in power – recognizing all along, of course, that we are dealing with a multiplicity of interest groups and that different groups of people were therefore likely to respond to government policies in different ways. This in turn helps us to recognize that the apparent fickleness of the people – the apparent dramatic swing from opposition to loyalism from 1679 to 1683 – is precisely that: no more than an appearance. There was undoubtedly some swing in public opinion away from the Whigs and in favour of the Tories in those years – and probably an even greater swing following the revelations of the Rye House Plot in the summer of 1683, as many of those who would have regarded themselves as decently minded, middle-of-the road, respectable Protestants would have become sickened by the extremes to which some, at least, of the Whigs had sunk. Nevertheless, when we take a closer look at what was going on at the ground level, it is clear that for the most part those who were critical of the government's agenda in 1679–81 and those who actively supported it in 1681–3 were different people.

The crucial issue at stake here, to reiterate, is mobilization. As should be apparent to readers of this book, it is not clear that the spectrum of opinions across England, Scotland and Ireland in, say, 1681–5 was any different from what it had been in 1674–81, or even in the early years of the Restoration. The same various interest groups that we see in the different kingdoms at the beginning of the period were still there at the end; if anything, the sources of tension and the causes of division had become intensified by the end of Charles II's reign, as a result of the policies of the Tory Reaction. What changed over time was the degree to which the various interest groups had been mobilized to give public articulation to where they stood on the crucial political issues of the day. In the late 1670s the Whigs were very successful in mobilizing the masses against the government of Charles II and the Catholic succession by playing on people's fears of popery and arbitrary government in both the future and the present, but in doing so they were able to exploit genuine disaffection that already existed at the grass-roots level in many places across the three kingdoms. The fact that so many people were willing to take to the streets or sign petitions to demonstrate their opposition to the government made many others, who perhaps did not instinctively see themselves as opponents of the later Stuart regime, sit up and wonder whether perhaps something quite serious might be wrong and feel that something needed to be done about it. It also left those who did not support the Whigs feeling isolated and out of tune with public

416

sentiment; so they remained quiet, and did not say or do anything to reveal their own political proclivities. The task that the court and its Tory allies set themselves in the early 1680s was to mobilize this last group – those natural Tories who had been intimidated into silence by the success of the Whig appeal to opinion out-of-doors – in the hope that, by encouraging loyalist activism among them, these might in turn be able to rally those who were not natural Whigs but who had temporarily become convinced that something must be wrong because of all the noise that the Whigs were generating. Now the Tories were making a lot of noise themselves – they were rhyming noise with noise, as L'Estrange put it in his own inimitable way.[5] It was by no means clear to the casual observer that public opinion was behind the Whigs. Whether local magistrates or humble parish constables, those in positions of authority who had not liked the Whigs or the nonconformists in the first place now began to gain the confidence to act against enemies of the crown who violated the law. Those who might have wondered whether the Whigs had a point increasingly came to doubt that they did. Those who feared trouble should York succeed increasingly came to see that, given the number of outspoken loyalists, there was likely to be even more trouble if the Duke were not allowed to succeed. And, as the Whigs became more and more desperate as they lost the political momentum, some of the more extreme of their number began to engage in the sort of radical conspiratorial politics that seemed only to confirm what the Tories had been saying of the Whigs all along.

This is why the mobilization of public opinion was so important. What mattered was whether one could be seen to have public opinion – and the opinions of the right sort of people – on one's side. This was not totally divorced from what the political opinions of the people actually were, of course; the more real Tories there were out there, the more it helped the government's cause. Yet there might not necessarily be a close correlation between the representation of public opinion and what public opinion actually was, as the case of Ireland illustrates. In Ireland, as we have seen, there was a movement of loyalist addresses in 1682–3, similar to that in England. There was no such counterpart in Scotland at this time. Certainly there is evidence of popular loyalism in Scotland, but the sorts of public loyalist display we see north of the border were so blatantly encouraged, even orchestrated, by the government that some may have reason to doubt their authenticity. Ireland, as the reader will surely have noticed, seems much more like England than does Scotland. But that is in large part because Ireland was a dependent colony (albeit theoretically a kingdom in its own right), which was governed by a narrow ruling elite belonging to the Established Church who saw themselves both as the English interest and as Anglicans, and who governed through an administrative system of counties, quarter sessions and assizes based on the English model. The loyal addresses that came out of Ireland represent the opinions almost exclusively of Protestants of the Established Church in Ireland, who formed less than 10 per cent of the entire population, and then only the social and political elite within this group. Clearly the addresses do not say much about opinion in the kingdom as a whole. No doubt the loyal addresses that came out of England and Wales say more about public opinion there, but they still represent the opinions of only the anti-Whig Anglican interest. Nevertheless, having these pledges of support from so many different groups and places across England and Wales proved a major propaganda coup for the government – one that greatly facilitated its task in taking on the Whigs and their nonconformist allies.

There was an irony here, of course. At the same time as the court and its Tory allies were trying to mobilize public opinion in support of the crown and the hereditary succession, they were embarked upon policies designed to strengthen the position of the crown and to make the monarchy less vulnerable to public criticism or to any institutional checks on its authority. For all his readiness to appeal to the public sphere, Charles II was hardly a monarch who was committed to the flourishing of that sphere. The government's preferred strategy was to prevent ordinary people debating politics – in other words, to shut down the public sphere. When it found that that did not work, and that the Whigs had managed to excite the public against the government and the succession, the government recognized the need to beat the Whigs at their own game and appeal to public opinion. But its basic intent was to use all the media available to get its own message across to the people while at the same time doing its best to silence dissenting voices – by using the law of seditious libel against Whig polemicists who overstepped the mark, by using the authority of England's oldest university to censure certain offensive doctrines, by using the laws against nonconformity to strike at dissenting preachers, by making sure that the Anglican pulpits were filled with men loyal to the government's cause, and by issuing orders to stop bonfire commemorations on Whig anniversaries on the grounds of preserving public order. Significantly, once the tide of public opinion had seemingly begun to turn in favour of the Tories by the end of 1682, the government tried to reimpose a clampdown on the press by urging the Stationers' Company of London to enforce its own by-laws regulating the publishing trade. As a result, not only were the Whig newspapers stopped, but most of the Tory ones too – with the notable exceptions of L'Estrange's *Observator* and the government organ the *London Gazette*.[6] What we see, in other words, is a government which realized that it had been unable to contain the public sphere, which recognized that it temporarily needed to engage with it, and which, after having successfully done so, then sought to contain it once again.

Indeed, some would see the final years of Charles II's reign as witnessing a drift towards royal absolutism. On the surface there seem to be compelling reasons to conclude that they did. Defenders of the crown certainly embraced absolutist rhetoric, openly professing that the king was absolute, that he shared his sovereignty with no one, and that he was irresistible. After 1681 Charles did not call another parliament in any of his three kingdoms; in England, this left him in violation of the 1664 Triennial Act, which required parliaments to be called every three years. It is true that Charles could not tax without parliamentary consent, but with subsidies from Louis XIV and improvements in the customs and excise he did not need a parliamentary subsidy in England, while the Scottish parliament had already been sufficiently generous in the taxes it had voted the crown that the monarchy was well covered for several years to come. Nor did parliament seem likely to cause much of a threat in any of the kingdoms in the near future. The Scottish parliament was fairly easy to control because it was a single-chamber assembly where legislative initiatives were managed by the Lords of the Articles, the composition of which was controlled by the crown. The Irish parliament was subject to Poynings' Law, which meant that all legislation had to be approved by the privy council in England. Only the English parliament could really pose a threat to the king's autonomy, but the measures taken in England during the years of the Tory Reaction ensured that when a parliament eventually was called, at the start of James II's reign, it proved to be an overwhelmingly loyalist body. Furthermore, during his final years Charles made sure that the crown had effective control over various other bodies or institutions that might serve as independent checks on the crown's authority: the borough corporations, the judicial and magisterial benches, local juries, and so forth. Indeed, by 1684 Charles was able to maintain formidable standing armies in both England and Ireland (8,865 and 7,500 men respectively) without recourse to parliamentary taxation.[7] Was this not, in effect, royal absolutism in practice, as well as in theory? Charles may well have had considerable numbers of the traditional ruling elite and a significant cross-section of the (Protestant) population on his side in all three of his kingdoms (and the acquiescence and perhaps even active support of many Catholics in Ireland), but the establishment of royal absolutism in France in the seventeenth century (so at least some would argue) was also achieved by coopting the traditional ruling elites in the localities, and even by a careful marketing campaign designed to persuade people to see the merits of this system of government.[8]

If we are not careful, the debate over whether or not Charles emerged as an absolute monarch runs the risk of becoming somewhat sterile, caught up in endless discussions over the definition of terms and what would truly meet the criteria of an absolutist regime. The crux of the historical enterprise is understanding the reality of a given situation in the past, not haggling over whether a particular label or 'ism' is appropriate or not. It is therefore the realities of the political power that the monarchy enjoyed in the final years of Charles II's reign that we need to comprehend, and which Part II of this book has sought to describe in detail. As we have seen, there were ways in which the monarchy of Charles II was both absolute and limited, as contemporary champions of royal authority themselves were prepared to acknowledge. Moreover, the nature of Charles's powers was different in his three kingdoms. For instance, as mentioned above, he was beholden to his respective parliaments in England, Scotland and Ireland in different ways. He seems to have had greater arbitrary power in Scotland in the 1680s than in England, to judge by the respective ways he was able to deal with the challenge posed by Protestant dissent in these two realms. Yet, if the king was in theory and in practice above the law in all three of his kingdoms, he was nevertheless supposed to rule according to law. Indeed, Charles II was quick to insist throughout his final years that he was determined to rule by law – and by and large he did do so (the main exception being his violation of the Triennial Act, although there was undoubtedly also some bending of the law in other respects). This in itself should come as no surprise. Some of the worst tyrants in history have sought to manipulate or exploit the law in order to justify their actions. Moreover, in monarchical regimes the law tends to be set up in such a way as to give greatest advantage to the monarchy. The law in England, Scotland and Ireland recognized that the monarch possessed considerable discretionary powers, while numerous laws had been passed since the Restoration that were designed to protect the crown from the challenge of political and religious dissidents. It was in Charles's best interest to do things 'by colour of law', but to make sure that he put men in charge who could give him the most favourable reading of the law possible.[9] There is nevertheless an interesting contrast here between the three kingdoms. In England and Ireland during the final years of his reign Charles used existing law to defeat his political and religious enemies; in Scotland, by comparison, the regime self-consciously innovated, passing new laws in 1681 designed to give the crown even greater power in its efforts to crush all forms of dissent. Since contemporaries themselves recognized that there could be different degrees of royal absolutism, we might say that Charles II was more absolute in his northern kingdom in his final years than he was in either Ireland or England, but that that greater degree of absolutism had been conferred upon Charles by parliamentary statute.

Yet, if Charles had established royal absolutism, we are entitled to ask 'to what end?' In France, absolutism had been constructed not only to secure internal peace, but also to enable France's divinely ordained monarchy to pursue an aggressive and ambitious foreign policy in pursuit of 'la gloire'. Charles's aim had been purely defensive: to defeat his political enemies and avoid possible civil strife. He was unable to pursue any positive policy to promote the greatness of his newly created absolutist state. In fact, given the way that Charles had sought to strengthen the position of the monarchy in his final years, it is difficult to see how he left the crown in a position to pursue an ambitious, independent policy of its own. We can see this most clearly with regard to England. Here the King and his Tory allies had tapped into anti-nonconformist and anti-Catholic prejudices and sentiments in support of the existing constitution in Church and state as by law established that were deeply held by large sections of the population. Indeed, in many areas of policy – such as in the drive against corporations or against dissent – we can see the crown following the lead of Tory and Anglican zealots in the localities. For all his theoretical absolutism, Charles had effectively made the crown the prisoner of a party; he had made the crown strong because he was at last doing what the Tories and Anglicans wanted him to do, and they were therefore willing to give the crown their wholehearted support. The real test of the extent to which royal absolutism had effectively been established in England would surely come if and when the crown found it necessary or desirable to break free from its Tory-Anglican allies and pursue a policy in Church and state not to their liking. That day would come under James II. James was convinced he was an absolute monarch and therefore would face no difficulties as he sought to undermine the Tory-Anglican ascendancy in an effort to help his co-religionists. History was to prove him wrong.

The situation in both Scotland and Ireland was in this regard quite similar to that in England. In these two kingdoms Charles had likewise been able to gain the enthusiastic support of Protestants of the Established Church because he had shown himself willing to back their interest. Royal strength in Scotland and Ireland, as in England, depended upon picking the right allies and then making sure that they got sufficient of what they wanted that they would remain loyal servants of the royal interest and use the power they enjoyed or were given in order to eradicate any forms of dissent that might prove a threat to the position of the crown. James II was also to run into problems in his other two kingdoms when he failed to nurture these loyalist interests in the way that they expected.

Charles's genius was to recognize the realities of where royal power lay. After a highly inauspicious first couple of decades, by the last years of his reign he had at last learned how to play the game effectively. He and his advisers had come to appreciate the value of propaganda, the importance of pronouncements about the theoretical powers of the monarchy, and the value of winning over the hearts and minds of the people. They had come to realize that in order to destroy one's political opponents one needed first to strip them of public support, to make their cause appear illegitimate in the eyes of the nation, before using all the repressive forces available to the state to eradicate the threat they posed. They had further come to appreciate that possessing a multiple-kingdom inheritance could be a boon and not just a burden: that, with skill, the different kingdoms could be played off against each other in order to obtain an outcome favourable to the interests of the crown. And they had come to recognize that by doing all this in a skilful enough way they could actually set about undermining those very institutions that had imposed any check on the authority of the crown, thus greatly strengthening the crown's power in the process. Charles II did all this because he wanted to avoid civil war, not because he harboured any pretensions to cut a figure in Europe as a budding absolutist monarch; his strategy was defensive, rather than aggressive. But then one might say that the construction of French absolutism likewise started as a defensive measure to avoid civil war.

The political analyst can admire Charles's achievement, and might even congratulate him on the skilful way in which he managed to extricate himself from a major crisis of the sort that could well have brought the monarchy down – a crisis of the sort that did indeed bring down the monarchy under Charles I and under James II. The historian, however, cannot end on such a positive note. There was an enormous human cost to Charles's success. We recalled in Chapter 1 how the popular image of Restoration England is that of a country reacting against the austerities of Puritan rule, presided over by a merry monarch eager to have a good time while he could and determined never to go on his travels again if he could avoid it. Granted, Charles's sexual exploits would have shocked the Victorians. Yet they are much less offensive to present-day sensibilities, and at least people were having fun again: after all, people got Christmas, the theatre and their maypoles back. Put like that, the image seems rather cosy (if perhaps overly hedonistic), and Charles eminently benign. This is to give a seriously distorted impression. Charles was, in the words of one biographer, 'the most savage persecutor' ever to wear the English crown.[10] It is true that fewer people were executed for their religious beliefs in Restoration England than under Mary I, who burned nearly 300 Protestants at the stake between 1555 and her death in 1558. Nevertheless, Charles's reign saw tens of thousands of English nonconformists suffer heavy fines and imprisonment for their religious beliefs; many of them lost their jobs and had their lives ruined, while several hundreds – maybe many more – were to die in Restoration jails. Whole communities were torn apart as loved ones were lost, employers were thrown in prison or fined out of business and forced to lay off workers, and neighbours were encouraged to inform against neighbours. People were stripped of their basic rights and privileges, as judicial and magisterial benches were purged and juries were packed to ensure that justice was administered in the way the King saw fit, and as corporations were forced to surrender their charters and thereby lose their much-cherished political autonomy. And this was just in England. Things were much worse in Scotland, where not only did thousands suffer brutal persecution for failure to conform to an episcopalian Church that had been restored by royal fiat, but many were brutally tortured and others shot in the fields or drowned on beaches for their political and religious principles. Ireland may not have faced the degree of religious persecution that either Scotland or England experienced. Nevertheless, three-quarters of the population – the Irish Catholics – were denied basic political, economic, religious and legal rights (whatever benefits they enjoyed were by connivance or dispensation rather than by law), while many from the Catholic landowning classes failed even to get a hearing to stake their claim to regain the land that had been wrongfully taken from them in the 1640s and '50s. On top of this, the Protestant dissenters in Ireland were likewise treated as second-class subjects.

Restoration history is the story of human tragedy. People were exploited, brutalized, persecuted, hounded to death by a regime that felt desperately insecure after two decades of civil war and republican rule. The tragedy – the suffering – reached its height during the years of the Tory Reaction. Charles II and his supporters would have justified their actions by claiming that they were merely defending the monarchy and the existing establishment in Church and state against those who wanted to bring both down again. After what had transpired in the 1640s and '50s, we can understand where they were coming from. To put it in modern-day parlance, they saw themselves as engaged in a war on terrorism. They would also have claimed that the terrorists were a small minority, and that the vast majority of the populations in all three kingdoms supported this war on terror. And in making such claims the government had a point: this *was* the reality of the situation, as far as the government saw it. Indeed, as this book has been at pains to emphasize, the islands of Great Britain and Ireland were bitterly divided places, where political and religious tensions ran deep. It would be overly melodramatic to proclaim that they contained societies at war with themselves, though on occasions they did: literally so in parts of Scotland, across the entire period; somewhat more than metaphorically so in England during the years of the Tory Reaction; while there were unresolved problems and tensions that cut deep into Irish society which made whatever equilibrium that was achieved seem inherently fragile and which from time to time were to erupt in open sectarian violence. For all Charles's skill in escaping from the political crisis that the monarchy faced by 1679–81, the royal physician had done little to heal the wounds which had been kept bleeding for so long, as he had promised he would do in his Declaration of Breda issued on the eve of his Restoration. If anything, the policies he pursued during his last years had made the wounds even deeper.

Yet Charles had devised a workable solution. He had made the monarchy strong – stronger than at any other time in the seventeenth century – and he had also successfully built up a considerable degree of goodwill towards the crown, in all three of his kingdoms, among those of his subjects who belonged to the Established Church. The quid pro quo for this was that Charles had had to promise that the monarchy would protect the existing government in Church and state as by law established – but for the time being this seemed a minor price to play. He had seemingly placed the Stuart monarchy in a situation where it could even survive the succession of his Catholic brother and heir. At first it looked as if it would. Arguably it should have done. It did not. Within less than four years James II was gone. How and why this came about is the subject of the sequel to this book.

Notes

N.B. All works cited were published in London, unless otherwise stated.

ABBREVIATIONS

APS	*The Acts of the Parliaments of Scotland*, ed. Thomas Thomson and Cosmo Innes (12 vols., Edinburgh, 1814–75)
BL	British Library
Bodl.	Bodleian Library, Oxford
Burnet, *HOT*	Gilbert Burnet, *History of His Own Time: From the Restoration of King Charles the Second to the Treaty of Peace at Utrecht, in the Reign of Queen Anne* (1850)
Cal. Anc. Rec. Dub.	*Calendar of the Ancient Records of Dublin, in the Possession of the Municipal Corporation of that City*, ed. John T. Gilbert (16 vols., Dublin, 1889–1913)
CJ	*Journals of the House of Commons*
CSPD	*Calendar of State Papers Domestic*
DNB	*Dictionary of National Biography*
Dom. Int. Imp.	*The Domestick Intelligence; Or, News both from City and Country Impartially Related*
FSL	Folger Shakespeare Library, Washington, DC
HJ	*Historical Journal*
HMC	Historical Manuscripts Commission
Hunt. Lib.	Huntington Library, San Marino, Cal.
Imp. Prot. Merc.	*The Impartial Protestant Mercury*
LC	Library of Congress, Washington, DC
LJ	*Journals of the House of Lords*
LMA	London Metropolitan Archives (formerly Greater London Record Office)
Lond. Gaz.	*London Gazette*
Loy. Prot. Int.	*Loyal Protestant and True Domestick Intelligence*

427

Luttrell	Narcissus Luttrell, *A Brief Historical Relation of State Affairs from September, 1678, to April, 1714* (6 vols., Oxford, 1857)
Morrice	Dr Williams's Library, London: Roger Morrice, Entr'ing Book, vols. P, Q, R
NA	National Archives (formerly Public Record Office)
NAS	National Archives of Scotland (formerly Scottish Record Office)
NLI	National Library of Ireland
NLS	National Library of Scotland
Parl. Hist.	*The Parliamentary History of England from the earliest Period to the Year 1803*, ed. William Cobbett (36 vols., 1806–20)
POAS	*Poems on Affairs of State*, ed. Geoffrey de Forest Lord et al. (7 vols., New Haven, 1963–75)
RO	Record Office
RPCS	*The Register of the Privy Council of Scotland. Third Series, 1661–1691*, ed. P. H. Brown, et al. (16 vols., Edinburgh, 1908–70)
SR	*The Statutes of the Realm*, ed. A. Luders, T. E. Tomlins and J. France (12 vols., 1810–28)
ST	*State Trials*, ed. T. B. Howell (33 vols., 1809–26)
Steele	Robert Steele, *A Bibliography of Royal Proclamations of the Tudor and Stuart Sovereigns and of others Published under Authority 1485–1714* (3 vols. in 2, New York, 1967)
TCD	Trinity College, Dublin
True Prot. Merc.	*True Protestant Mercury*
WYAS	West Yorkshire Archives Service, Sheepscar, Leeds

Introduction

1. *HMC, 5th Report*, p. 167; *The Diary of John Evelyn*, ed. E. S. De Beer (6 vols., Oxford, 1955) III, 246; *The Diurnal of Thomas Rugg, 1659–1661*, ed. William L. Sachse, Camden Society, 3rd series, 91 (1961), pp. 88–91.
2. BL, Add. MSS 32,095, fols. 303–4, 308–9. See also John Miller, *James II: A Study in Kingship* (1978), pp. 206–7.
3. Conrad Russell, *The Causes of the English Civil War* (Oxford, 1990), p. 209.
4. Steven Pincus, 'The Making of a Great Power? Universal Monarchy, Political Economy, and the Transformation of English Political Culture', *The European Legacy*, 5 (2000), 541. For a discussion of how the transforma-

tions of the later seventeenth century in England led to the birth of modern statecraft, see Alan Houston and Steven Pincus, 'Introduction. Modernity and Late-Seventeenth-Century England', and Steven Pincus, 'From Holy Cause to Economic Interest: The Study of Population and the Invention of the State', in Alan Houston and Steven Pincus, eds., *A Nation Transformed: England after the Restoration* (Cambridge, 2001), pp. 1–19, 272–98.

5. House of Lords, *Parliamentary Debates* (Hansard), 5th series, vol. 472 (17 Mar. 1986), p. 796.

6. Lois G. Schwoerer, 'Celebrating the Glorious Revolution, 1689–1989', *Albion*, 22 (1990), 1–20; Eveline Cruickshanks, *The Glorious Revolution* (Basingstoke, 2000), pp. 1–2.

7. W. A. Maguire, ed., *Kings in Conflict: The Revolutionary War in Ireland and its Aftermath 1689–1750* (Belfast, 1990), p. 3.

8. Edmund Burke, *Reflections on the Revolution in France: A Critical Edition*, ed. J. C. D. Clark (Stanford, 2001), pp. 39, 30, 181.

9. Thomas Babington Macaulay, *The History of England from the Accession of James the Second*, ed. Sir Charles Firth (6 vols., 1913–15), III, 1306, 1310, 1311–12.

10. George Macaulay Trevelyan, *The English Revolution 1688–1689* (1938), pp. 7, 11; John Morrill, 'The Sensible Revolution', in Jonathan I. Israel, ed., *The Anglo-Dutch Moment: Essays on the Glorious Revolution and its World Impact* (Cambridge, 1991), pp. 73–104.

11. Christopher Hill, *The English Revolution, 1640* (1940); *The Century of Revolution 1603–1714* (1961); and 'A Bourgeois Revolution?', in J. G. A. Pocock, ed., *Three British Revolutions: 1641, 1688, 1776* (Princeton, 1980), pp. 109–39.

12. Lawrence Stone, *The Causes of the English Revolution 1529–1642* (New York, 1972), p. 147; Lawrence Stone, 'The Results of the English Revolutions of the Seventeenth Century', in Pocock, ed., *Three British Revolutions*, p. 24.

13. John Morrill, *The Nature of the English Revolution* (Harlow, 1993), pp. 1, 17; Mark Kishlansky, *Parliamentary Selection* (Cambridge, 1986).

14. Derek Hirst, *England in Conflict, 1603–1660* (1999), p. 255.

15. Stone, 'Results of the English Revolutions', p. 24.

16. An important exception is Pincus, 'Making of a Great Power?', which offers a foretaste of some of the arguments to be developed in his forthcoming *The First Modern Revolution* (Cambridge).

17. Lois G. Schwoerer, *The Declaration of Rights, 1689* (Baltimore, 1981); W. A. Speck, *Reluctant Revolutionaries: Englishmen and the Revolution of 1688* (Oxford, 1988).

18. An important exception is Schwoerer, *Declaration of Rights*, which does attempt to integrate high and low politics and to examine the machinations

of the political elite with propaganda aimed at swaying opinion out-of-doors, though chronologically the focus of the book is very narrow.

19. Tim Harris, 'Introduction: Revising the Restoration', in Tim Harris, Paul Seaward and Mark Goldie, eds., *The Politics of Religion in Restoration England* (Oxford, 1990), p. 23.

20. Ronald Hutton's biography of *Charles II, King of England, Scotland and Ireland* (Oxford, 1989) does look at all three kingdoms, but is naturally a top-centred history and does not take the story beyond 1685.

21. Since this introduction was written, we now have Clare Jackson's important *Restoration Scotland, 1660–1690: Royalist Politics, Religion and Ideas* (Woodbridge, 2003).

22. For a fuller discussion, see Tim Harris, 'Understanding Popular Politics in Restoration Britain', in Houston and Pincus, eds., *Nation Transformed*, pp. 125–53.

23. John Miller, 'Public Opinion in Charles II's England', *History*, 80 (1995), 375.

24. Steven C. A. Pincus, '"Coffee Politicians Does Create": Coffeehouses and Restoration Political Culture', *Journal of Modern History*, 67 (1995), 812–14; Jackson, *Restoration Scotland*, p. 41; Raymond Gillespie, 'The Circulation of Print in Seventeenth-Century Ireland', *Studia Hibernica*, 29 (1995–7), 53; Bodl., MS Carte 39, fol. 592.

25. Adam Fox, *Oral and Literate Culture in England 1500–1700* (Oxford, 2000), pp. 370–5 (quote on p. 375). See also Harold Love, *Scribal Publication in Seventeenth-Century England* (Oxford, 1993).

26. NLS, Wod. Qu. XXX.

27. Toby Barnard, 'Learning, the Learned and Literacy in Ireland, c. 1660–1760', in Toby Barnard, Dáibhí Ó Cróinín and Katharine Simms, eds., *'A Miracle of Learning': Studies in Manuscript and Irish Learning* (Aldershot, 1998), pp. 218–19.

28. David Cressy, *Literacy and the Social Order: Reading and Writing in Tudor and Stuart England* (Cambridge, 1980), pp. 72–5, 176–7; Keith Thomas, 'The Meaning of Literacy in Early Modern England', in Gerd Baumann, ed., *The Written Word: Literacy in Transition* (Oxford, 1986), pp. 100–103; Jonathan Barry, 'Literacy and Literature in Popular Culture: Reading and Writing in Historical Perspective', in Tim Harris, ed., *Popular Culture in Early Modern England, c. 1500–1850* (Basingstoke, 1995), pp. 69–94; Barry Reay, 'The Context and Meaning of Popular Literacy: Some Evidence from Nineteenth-Century Rural England', *Past and Present*, 131 (1991), 112–14.

29. Rab Houston, 'The Literacy Myth? Illiteracy in Scotland 1630–1760', *Past and Present*, 96 (1982), 81–102 (esp. pp. 89–91, 96); R. A. Houston, *Scottish Literacy and the Scottish Identity: Illiteracy and Society in Scotland*

and Northern England 1600–1800 (Cambridge, 1985), esp. pp. 33, 72.

30. Gillespie, 'Circulation of Print', pp. 32–3; Barnard, 'Learning, the Learned and Literacy in Ireland', pp. 220–21

31. *CSPD, 1682*, pp. 303, 456, 587; Guildford Muniment Room, MS 111/10/14/1–14.

32. Ethan H. Shagan, 'Rumours and Popular Politics in the Reign of Henry VIII', in Tim Harris, ed., *The Politics of the Excluded, c. 1500–1850* (2001), pp. 30–66; Fox, *Oral and Literate Culture*, ch. 7.

33. R. R. Davies, 'In Praise of British History', in R. R. Davies, ed., *The British Isles 1100–1500: Comparisons, Contrasts and Connections* (Edinburgh, 1988), p. 17.

34. The disparities between the two kingdoms are well drawn out in Mark Goldie, 'Divergence and Union: Scotland and England, 1660–1707', in Brendan Bradshaw and John Morrill, eds., *The British Problem c. 1534–1707* (Basingstoke, 1996), pp. 220–45.

35. These figures are taken from Basil Duke Henning, ed., *The House of Commons, 1660–1690* (3 vols., 1983).

36. Geoffrey Holmes, *The Electorate and the National Will in the First Age of Party* (Lancaster, 1976); J. H. Plumb, 'The Growth of the Electorate in England from 1600–1715', *Past and Present*, 45 (1969), 90–116.

37. Kathleen Colquhoun, '"Issue of the Late Civil Wars": James, Duke of York and the Government of Scotland 1679–1689', unpub. Ph.D. dissertation, University of Illinois, Urbana–Champaign (1993), p. 117; *APS*, VIII, 231–3; D. W. Hayton, ed., *The House of Commons 1690–1715* (5 vols., Cambridge, 2002), I, 141–5; Robert S. Rait, *The Parliaments of Scotland* (Glasgow, 1924), esp. pp. 6–7, 11–15, 165–6, 210–13, 232–3, 265–8, 272, 275; William Ferguson, 'The Electoral System in the Scottish Counties before 1832', *Miscellany II*, ed. David Sellar, Stair Society, 35 (1984), pp. 261–94.

38. Rait, *Parliaments of Scotland*, pp. 8, 364, 368, 370–71, 380–84; *An Account of the Affairs of Scotland, In Relation to their Religious and Civil Rights* (1690), pp. 4–6; John R. Young, 'The Scottish Parliament and the Covenanting Heritage of Constitutional Reform', in Allan I. MacInnes and Jane Ohlmeyer, eds., *The Stuart Kingdoms in the Seventeenth Century: Awkward Neighbours* (Dublin, 2002), p. 227.

39. *English Historical Documents 1042–1189*, ed. David C. Douglas and George W. Greenaway (2nd edn, 1981), pp. 828–30; Sir Richard Cox, *Hibernia Anglicana: Or, The History of Ireland from the Conquest thereof by the English to this Present Time . . . In Two Parts* (2nd edn, 1692), I, 2–4.

40. *The Statutes at Large, Passed in the Parliaments held in Ireland . . . A.D. 1310 to . . . A.D. 1800* (21 vols., Dublin, 1786–1804), I, 176.

41. John Morrill, 'The British Problem, c. 1534–1707', in Bradshaw and Morrill, eds., *British Problem*, pp. 12–13.

42. *Statutes at Large*, I, 44, 246–7; D. B. Quinn, 'The Early Interpretation of Poynings' Law', *Irish Historical Studies*, 2 (1941), 241–54; R. D. Edwards and T. W. Morley, 'The History of Poynings' Law: Part I, 1494–1615', *Irish Historical Studies*, 2 (1941), 415–24.

43. J. G. Swift MacNeill, *The Constitutional and Parliamentary History of Ireland till the Union* (1917), pp. 30–36; T. W. Moody, F. X. Martin, F. J. Byrne and Art Cosgrove, eds., *A New History of Ireland* (9 vols., Oxford, 1976–84), IX, map 50.

44. J. L. McCracken, 'The Political Structure, 1714–60', Moody et al., eds., *New History of Ireland*, IV, 72–4.

45. Swift MacNeill, *Constitutional and Parliamentary History*, pp. 1–14 (quotes on pp. 3–4, 8); *The Correspondence of Henry Hyde, Earl of Clarendon, and of His Brother Laurence Hyde; With the Diary of Lord Clarendon from 1687 to 1690*, ed. Samuel Weller Singer (2 vols., 1828), I, 183–5.

46. *Clarendon Correspondence*, I, 185.

47. Charles O'Kelly, *Macariae Excidium, Or, The Destruction of Cypress; Being a Secret History of the War of the Revolution in Ireland*, ed. John Cornelius O'Callaghan (Dublin, 1850), p. 8; Cox, *Hibernia Anglicana*, II, 1.

48. Breandán Ó Buachalla, 'James our True King: The Ideology of Irish Royalism in the Seventeenth Century', in D. George Boyce, Robert Eccleshall and Vincent Geoghegan, eds., *Political Thought of Ireland since the Seventeenth Century* (1993), pp. 36–72; Brendan Fitzpatrick, *Seventeenth-Century Ireland: The War of Religions* (Dublin, 1988).

49. R. A. Houston, *The Population History of Britain and Ireland, 1500–1750* (Cambridge, 1995), p. 16. Revised techniques of historical demography have revised upward the figures presented in E. A. Wrigley and R. S. Schofield, *The Population History of England, 1541–1871: A Reconstruction* (1981). See Jim Oeppen, 'Back Projection and Inverse Projection: Members of a Wider Class of Constrained Projection Models', *Population Studies*, 47 (1993), 245–67.

50. Geraint H. Jenkins, *The Foundations of Modern Wales: Wales 1642–1780* (Oxford, 1987), p. 88.

51. John Miller, *Popery and Politics in England, 1660–1688* (Cambridge, 1973), pp. 11–13, 23–4; Tim Harris, *Politics under the Later Stuarts* (1993), pp. 12–13.

52. Anne Whiteman, ed., *The Compton Census of 1676* (1986); Harris, *Politics under the Later Stuarts*, pp. 9–12 (and references cited therein).

53. Houston, *Population History*, p. 17.

54. Bob Harris, '"A Great Palladium of our Liberties": The British Press and the 'Forty-Five', *Historical Research*, 165 (1995), 76; Edinburgh University

Library, La. III. 350, no. 134; [Alexander Monro], *The History of Scotch-Presbytery* (1692), p. 30; Linda Colley, *Britons: Forging the Nation 1707–1837* (New Haven, 1992), p. 15; David Stevenson, 'The English Devil of Keeping State: Elite Manners and the Downfall of Charles I in Scotland', in Roger Mason and Norman Macdougall, eds., *People and Power in Scotland* (Edinburgh, 1992), pp. 141–2.

55. Robert Wodrow, *History of the Sufferings of the Church of Scotland, from the Restauration to the Revolution* (2 vols., Edinburgh, 1721–2), I, 498.

56. Allan Macinnes, 'Catholic Recusancy and the Penal Laws, 1603–1707', *Records of the Scottish Church History Society*, 23 (1987), p. 35; Donald Maclean, 'Roman Catholicism in Scotland in the Reign of Charles II', ibid., 3 (1929), 47. J. Darragh, 'The Catholic Population of Scotland since the year 1680', *Innes Review*, 4 (1953), pp. 52, 58, suggests the figure was nearer 5 per cent if we include covert Catholics, church papists and Catholic converts under James II, although his data are far from convincing.

57. I. B. Cowan, *The Scottish Covenanters 1660–88* (1976), ch. 3; Elizabeth Hyman, 'A Church Militant: Scotland, 1661–1690', *Sixteenth Century Journal*, 26 (1995), 49–74.

58. Categories are adapted from Michael Perceval-Maxwell, *The Outbreak of the Irish Rebellion of 1641* (Montreal, 1994), pp. 8–9, incorporating the dramatic rise in Protestant dissent since the 1640s, for which see Phil Kilroy, *Protestant Dissent and Controversy in Ireland, 1660–1714* (Cork, 1994); Richard L. Greaves, *God's Other Children: Protestant Nonconformists and the Emergence of Denominational Churches in Ireland, 1660–1700* (Stanford, 1997).

59. T. C. Barnard, 'Conclusion. Settling and Unsettling Ireland: The Cromwellian and Williamite Revolutions', in Jane H. Ohlmeyer, ed., *Ireland from Independence to Occupation 1641–1660* (Cambridge, 1995), p. 282.

60. L. M. Cullen, 'Economic Trends, 1660–91', in Moody et al., eds., *New History of Ireland*, III, 389; R. Gillespie, 'Explorers, Exploiters and Entrepreneurs: Early Modern Ireland and its Context, 1500–1700', in B. J. Graham and L. J. Proudfoot, eds., *An Historical Geography of Ireland* (1993), pp. 142–3; Raymond Gillespie, 'The Presbyterian Revolution in Ulster, 1660–1690', in W. J. Sheils and Dianne Wood, eds., *The Churches, Ireland and the Irish*, Studies in Church History, 25 (Oxford, 1989), pp. 159–70. In 1672 William Petty estimated that the population of Ireland was about 1.1 million, 800,000 of whom were Roman Catholics, 100,000 Protestants of the Established Church, 100,000 Scottish Presbyterians, and 100,000 other Protestant dissenters. Although he underestimated the size of the population, his figures give an approximate idea of the balance between the religious groups: William Petty, 'Political Anatomy', in Charles Henry Hull, ed., *The*

Economic Writings of Sir William Petty (2 vols., Cambridge, 1899), I, 149.

61. Richard L. Greaves, '"That's No Good Religion that Disturbs Government": The Church of Ireland and the Nonconformist Challenge', in Alan Ford, James McGuire and Kenneth Milne, eds., *As By Law Established: The Church of Ireland since the Reformation* (Dublin, 1995), p. 120.

62. John Gillingham, 'Images of Ireland 1170–1600: The Origins of English Imperialism', *History Today*, 37 (Feb. 1987), 16–22.

63. *The Rawdon Papers*, ed. Rev. Edward Berwick (1819), p. 220; Bodl., MS Clarendon 89, fols. 169, 173.

64. *Clarendon Correspondence*, I, 373.

65. Cox, *Hibernia Anglicana* I, quotes on sigs. b2v, f, l, l2v, p. 1. Cf. Liam de Paor, *The Peoples of Ireland: From Prehistory to Modern Times* (1986), ch. 2.

66. O'Kelly, *Macariae Excidium*, pp. 8, 28, 173 (n. 10).

67. *A Jacobite Narrative of the War in Ireland*, ed. J. T. Gilbert (Dublin, 1892; rev. edn with an introduction by J. G. Simms, Shannon, 1971), p. viii.

68. BL, Evelyn Papers, JE A2, fol. 52; *Diary and Correspondence of Samuel Pepys, F.R.S.*, ed. Richard Lord Braybrooke (6th edn, 4 vols., 1858), IV, 244.

69. Luttrell, I, 550.

70. BL, Harleian MS 7315, fol. 167.

71. *The History of the Late Great Revolution in England and Scotland* (1690), preface.

72. Edward Hyde, Earl of Clarendon, *The History of the Rebellion and Civil Wars in England*, ed. W. Dunn Macray (6 vols., Oxford, 1888, 1969), VI, 220; George Hickes, *A Sermon Preached at the Cathedral Church of Worcester, On the 29th of May, 1684* (1684), p. 17; Cox, *Hibernia Anglicana*, II, 'Letter Containing a Brief Account of the Transactions in the Kingdom, since 1653', pp. 2, 3; *The Life of James II*, ed. J. S. Clarke (2 vols., 1816), I, 381.

73. J. R. Western, *Monarchy and Revolution: The English State in the 1680s* (1972), p. 1; V. F. Snow, 'The Concept of Revolution in Seventeenth-Century England', *HJ*, 5 (1962), 167–74.

74. BL, MS Stowe 304, fol. 6.

75. John Locke, *Two Treatises of Government* (1690), ed. Peter Laslett (Cambridge, 1960, 1988), *Second Treatise*, para. 223.

76. Sir George Mackenzie, *Memoirs of the Affairs of Scotland from the Restoration* (Edinburgh, 1821), pp. 5, 113.

77. R[obert] L[awrie], *God Save the King* (Edinburgh, 1660), p. 10.

78. Burnet, *HOT*, p. 44.

79. HMC, *Egmont*, II, 148.

80. Roger L'Estrange, *The Observator in Dialogue* (3 vols., 1684–7), III, 'To Posterity', p. 3.

81. NA, SP 8/1, pt 2, fol. 75.

82. John Paterson, *Post Nubila Phoebus; Or, A Sermon of Thanksgiving for the Safe and Happy Returne of our Gracious Soveraign* (Aberdeen, 1660), p. 6.

83. *Lond. Gaz.*, no. 1713 (17–20 Apr. 1682).

84. *Clarendon Correspondence*, I, 185.

85. L'Estrange, *Observator*, III, no. 205, (1 Sep. 1686).

86. *Life of James II*, I, 515.

87. NLS, Wod. Qu. XXXVIII, fols. 2, 112v, 115.

88. Hunt. Lib., HA 7, [Sir Edward Abney] to the Earl of Huntingdon, 18 Dec. 1688.

89. *An Apology for the Protestants of Ireland* (1689), p. 30; H. B., *Mephiboseth and Ziba* (1689), p. 41; *The Melvilles Earls of Melville and the Leslies Earls of Leven*, ed. Sir William Fraser (3 vols., Edinburgh, 1890), III, 194; Andrew Hamilton, *A True Relation of the Actions of the Inniskilling-Men* (1690), p. i.

90. Cox, *Hibernia Anglicana*, II, sig. e2, 'Transactions since 1653', p. 1.

91. *The State Prodigall His Returne, Containing a True State of the Nation. In a Letter to a Friend* [1689], pp. 1, 3.

92. *The Present Conjuncture in a Dialogue between a Church-Man and a Dissenter* (1689), p. 3.

93. Leicestershire RO, DG7, Scot. 3.

94. Jonathan Scott, *Algernon Sidney and the Restoration Crisis, 1677–1683* (Cambridge, 1991).

95. Jonathan Scott, *England's Troubles: Seventeenth-Century English Political Stability in European Context* (Cambridge, 2000).

1 The Nation Would Not Stand Long

1. *Mercurius Reformatus*, 2, no. 23, (14 May 1690).

2. *Diurnal of Thomas Rugg*, p. 84.

3. Centre for Kentish Studies, U275/A3, p. 14.

4. *Jacobite Narrative*, p. 1.

5. *LJ*, XI, 7.

6. All Souls College Library, Oxford, MS 169, pp. 236–7; *CSPD, 1677–8*, p. 279.

7. Anne Wentworth, *The Revelation of Jesus Christ* (1679), p. 5.

8. Anne Wentworth, *A Vindication* (1677), p. 2.

9. NA, SP 8/1, pt 2, fol. 75.

10. Burnet, *HOT*, p. 61.

11. For the view that Charles I was unfit to be king, see Russell, *Causes*, p. 207.

12. *SR*, V, 179.

13. Ibid., pp. 226–34.

14. *CSPD, 1660–61*, pp. 408, 506.

15. Useful general accounts of the Restoration settlement are Ronald Hutton, *The Restoration: A Political and Religious History of England and Wales, 1658–1667* (Oxford, 1985); Paul Seaward, *The Cavalier Parliament and the Reconstruction of the Old Regime, 1661–1667* (Cambridge, 1989); N. H. Keeble, *The Restoration: England in the 1660s* (Oxford, 2002).

16. *CSPD, 1660–61*, p. 109.

17. Ibid., p. 59.

18. Ibid., pp. 37, 39.

19. *Middlesex County Records*, ed. J. C. Jeaffreson (4 vols., 1888–92), III, 303, 304, 306.

20. *Depositions from the Castle of York*, ed. James Raine, Jr, Surtees Society, 40 (Durham, 1861), pp. 83–4.

21. See, for example, *CSPD, 1660–61*, p. 5; Henry Townshend, *Diary*, ed. J. W. Willis Bund (2 vols., 1920), I, 40; *Records of the Borough of Leicester . . . 1603–88*, ed. Helen Stocks (Cambridge, 1923), p. 465.

22. For the survival of radicalism after the Restoration, see Christopher Hill, *The Experience of Defeat: Milton and Some Contemporaries* (1984), and Richard L. Greaves's *Deliver Us from Evil: The Radical Underground in Britain, 1660–1663* (Oxford, 1986), *Enemies under His Feet: Radicals and Nonconformists in Britain, 1664–1677* (Stanford, 1990), and *Secrets of the Kingdom: British Radicals from the Popish Plot to the Revolution of 1688–89* (Stanford, 1992).

23. Alan Marshall, *Intelligence and Espionage in the Reign of Charles II, 1660–1685* (Cambridge, 1994); Tim Harris, 'The Bawdy House Riots of 1668', *HJ*, 29 (1986), 537–56.

24. Particularly illuminating in this respect is the work of Gary S. De Krey: 'London Radicals and Revolutionary Politics, 1675–1683', in Harris et al., eds., *The Politics of Religion*, pp. 133–62; 'The London Whigs and the Exclusion Crisis Reconsidered', in Lee Beier, David Cannadine and James Rosenheim, eds., *The First Modern Society: Essays in English History in Honour of Lawrence Stone* (Cambridge, 1989), pp. 457–82; 'The First Restoration Crisis: Conscience and Coercion in London, 1667–73', *Albion*, 25 (fall 1993), 565–80; 'Rethinking the Restoration: Dissenting Cases for Conscience, 1667–1672', *HJ*, 38 (1995), 53–83; 'Reformation in the Restoration Crisis, 1679–82', in Donna B. Hamilton and Richard Strier, eds., *Religion, Literature and Politics in Post-Reformation England, 1540–1688* (Cambridge, 1996), pp. 231–52; 'Radicals, Reformers, and Republicans: Academic Language and Political Discourse in Restoration London', in Houston and Pincus, eds., *Nation Transformed*, pp. 71–99.

25. Harris, *Politics under the Later Stuarts*, pp. 35–6.

26. *SR*, V, 237.

27. *Diurnal of Thomas Rugg*, p. 41; H[enry] J[essey], *The Lord's Loud Call to England* (1660), pp. 4, 15–16; Michael R. Watts, *The Dissenters: From the Restoration to the French Revolution* (Oxford, 1978), p. 215; Barry Reay, 'The Quakers, 1659, and the Restoration of Monarchy', *History*, 63 (1978), 193–213; Tim Harris, *London Crowds in the Reign of Charles II* (Cambridge, 1987), pp. 52–5.

28. BL, Add. MSS 10, 116, fols. 208v, 224, 247–9; Steele, I, no. 3306; Harris, *Politics under the Later Stuarts*, pp. 42–4 (and references cited therein).

29. *The Remonstrance of the Apprentices in and about London* (1659).

30. *SR*, V, 321–3, 364–70, 350–51, 516–20, 575, 648–51.

31. Ibid., IV, 841–3.

32. Ibid., V, 782–5, 894–6.

33. I. M. Green, *The Re-establishment of the Church of England, 1660–1663* (Oxford, 1978).

34. Seaward, *Cavalier Parliament*, p. 193.

35. See above, pp. 28–9.

36. *SR*, V, 648–51.

37. Cited in Paul Seaward, *The Restoration 1660–1688* (1991), p. 14.

38. [Earl of Shaftesbury and John Locke], *A Letter from a Person of Quality to his Friend in the Country* (1675), pp. 1–2; Andrew Marvell, *An Account of the Growth of Popery and Arbitrary Government in England* (Amsterdam, 1677).

39. A useful survey is James Daly, 'The Idea of Absolute Monarchy in Seventeenth-Century England', *HJ*, 21 (1978), 227–50.

40. Sir Philip Warwick, *A Discourse of Government . . . Written in the Year 1678* (1694), pp. 50, 65.

41. Ibid., p. 41.

42. [Marchamont Needham], *A Pacquet of Advices and Animadversions, Sent from London to the Men of Shaftesbury* (1676), p. 43.

43. Sir John Dalrymple, *Memoirs of Great Britain and Ireland; From the Dissolution of the Last Parliament of Charles II till the Capture of the French and Spanish Fleets at Vigo. A New Edition, in Three Volumes; With the Appendices Complete* (1790), I, 'Review', pp. 190, 193.

44. SR, V, 308–9, 358–64.

45. Ibid., pp. 321–3, 364–70.

46. Ibid., p. 308.

47. Ibid., pp. 428–33.

48. Francis Gregory, *David's Returne from His Banishment* (Oxford, 1660), p. 12; Harris, *Politics under the Later Stuarts*, pp. 36, 58; Mark Goldie, 'John Locke and Anglican Royalism', *Political Studies*, 31 (1983), 61–85.

49. *ST*, V, 989, 1030.

50. C. D. Chandaman, *The English Public Revenue 1660–1688* (Oxford, 1975); Lionel K. J. Glassey, 'Politics, Finance and Government', in Lionel K. J. Glassey, ed., *Reigns of Charles II and James VII and II* (Basingstoke, 1997), pp. 36–70.

51. Kishlansky, *Parliamentary Selection*.

52. *SR*, V, 306.

53. Andrew Swatland, *The House of Lords in the Reign of Charles II* (Cambridge, 1996), p. 29.

54. Ibid., ch. 6.

55. *LJ*, XI, 248; Harris, *Politics under the Later Stuarts*, pp. 36–7; Seaward, *Cavalier Parliament*, pp. 17–18; David L. Smith, *Constitutional Royalism and the Search for Settlement, c. 1640–1649* (Cambridge, 1994), ch. 9.

56. Kenyon, *The Stuart Constitution* (2nd edn, 1986), pp. 391–2; A. F. Havighurst, 'The Judiciary and Politics in the Reign of Charles II', *Law Quarterly Review*, 66 (1950), 62–78, 229–52.

57. *ST*, VI, 999–1026.

58. Sir William Searle Holdsworth, *A History of English Law* (17 vols., 1922–72), VI, 217–23; Paul Birdsall, '"Non Obstante": A Study of the Dispensing Power of English Kings', in Carl Frederick Wittke, ed., *Essays in History and Political Theory in Honor of Charles Howard McIlwain* (Cambridge, Mass., 1936), pp. 37–76; Carolyn A. Edie, 'Tactics and Strategies: Parliament's Attack on the Royal Dispensing Power, 1597–1689', *American Journal of Legal History*, 29 (1985), 197–234; Alan Cromartie, *Sir Matthew Hale, 1609–1676: Law, Religion, and Natural Philosophy* (Cambridge, 1995), pp. 126–31.

59. Speck, *Reluctant Revolutionaries*, pp. 150–51.

60. *Parl. Hist.*, IV, 262.

61. [Shaftesbury and Locke], *Letter from a Person of Quality*, p. 4. See also NA, SP 30/24/30, no. 49, for a paper reflecting Shaftesbury's views on the royal supremacy and the dispensing power.

62. *CJ*, IX, 251; *Parl. Hist.*, IV, 526.

63. *LJ*, XII, 540, 549.

64. *Parl. Hist.*, IV, 665; John Childs, *The Army of Charles II* (1976).

65. See below, pp. 174–5. For the anti-standing-army controversy, see Lois G. Schwoerer, *'No Standing Armies!': The Anti-Army Ideology in Seventeenth-Century England* (Baltimore, 1974), esp. ch. 6.

66. Childs, *Army of Charles II*, p. 70.

67. Harris, 'Bawdy House Riots'.

68. Richard M. Dunn, 'The London Weavers' Riot of 1675', *Guildhall Studies in London History*, 1, no. 1 (Oct. 1973), 13–23; Harris, *London Crowds*, pp. 191–204.

69. Victor Stater, *Noble Government: The Stuart Lord Lieutenancy and*

the Transformation of English Politics (Athens, Ga., 1994), ch. 3.

70. Anthony Fletcher, *Reform in the Provinces: The Government of Stuart England* (New Haven, 1986), pp. 21–2; Lionel K. J. Glassey, *Politics and the Appointment of Justices of the Peace 1675–1720* (Oxford, 1979), pp. 32–8.

71. Paul D. Halliday, *Dismembering the Body Politic: Partisan Politics in England's Towns, 1650–1730* (Cambridge, 1998), pp. 85–124.

72. Michael J. Braddick, 'State Formation and Social Change in Early Modern England', *Social History*, 16 (1991), 1–17. See also Michael J. Braddick, *State Formation in Early Modern England, c. 1550–1700* (Cambridge, 2000), esp. pt 1.

73. Thomas P. Slaughter, ed., *Ideology and Politics on the Eve of Restoration: Newcastle's Advice to Charles II* (Philadelphia, 1984), p. 45. See also Conal Condren, 'Casuistry to Newcastle: *The Prince* in the World of the Book', in Nicholas Phillipson and Quentin Skinner, eds., *Political Discourse in Early Modern Britain* (Cambridge, 1993), pp. 164–86.

74. Evelyn, *Diary*, III, 246; *The Diary of Samuel Pepys*, ed. R. C. Latham and W. Mathews (11 vols., 1970–83), I, 163; *Mercurius Publicus*, no. 22 (24–31 May 1660); *HMC, 5th Report*, pp. 167–8, 184, 199; *Diurnal of Thomas Rugg*, pp. 88–91.

75. *SR*, V, 237; *Kingdomes Intelligencer*, nos. 22 (27 May–3 Jun. 1661), p. 351, and 23 (3–10 Jun. 1661), pp. 353–5; BL, Add. MSS 10, 116, fol. 204; Ronald Hutton, *The Rise and Fall of Merry England* (Oxford, 1994), pp. 249–51.

76. *Rawdon Papers*, p. 201; Pepys, *Diary*, ed. Latham and Matthews, II, 81–8; John Ogilby, *The Entertainment of His Most Excellent Majestie Charles II, in His Passage through the City of London to His Coronation* (1662); Eric Halfpenny, '"The Citie's Loyalty Display'd": A Literary and Documentary Causerie of Charles II's Coronation "Entertainment"', *Guildhall Miscellany*, 1, no. 10 (Sep. 1959), 19–35; Gerard Reedy, 'Mystical Politics: The Imagery of Charles II's Coronation', in P. J. Korshin, ed., *Studies in Change and Revolution: Aspects of English Intellectual History, 1640–1800* (Menston, 1972), pp. 20–42; Paula Backscheider, *Spectacular Politics: Theatrical Power and Mass Culture in Early Modern England* (Baltimore, 1993), ch. 1.

77. G. E. Aylmer, *The Crown's Servants: Government and Civil Service under Charles II, 1660–1685* (Oxford, 2002), pp. 247–8

78. *Loy. Prot. Int.*, no. 141 (13 Apr. 1682).

79. Burnet, *HOT*, p. 207.

80. Maureen Bell and John Barnard, 'Provisional Count of *Wing* Titles 1641–1700', *Publishing History*, 44 (1998), 90–91; *The Cambridge History of the Book in Britain*, vol. 4: *1557–1695*, ed. John Barnard and D. F. McKenzie (Cambridge, 2002), p. 783; Joad Raymond, *Pamphlets and*

Pamphleteering in Early Modern Britain (Cambridge, 2003), pp. 163–5, 184.

81. John Spurr, *England in the 1670s: 'This Masquerading Age'* (Oxford, 2000), ch. 6.

82. Steele, I, nos. 3622, 3625.

83. Steven C. A. Pincus, *Protestantism and Patriotism: Ideologies and the Making of English Foreign Policy, 1650–1668* (Cambridge, 1996); J. R. Jones, *The Anglo-Dutch Wars of the Seventeenth Century* (1996).

84. Ronald Hutton, 'The Making of the Secret Treaty of Dover, 1668–70', *HJ*, 29 (1986), 297–318; K. H. D. Haley, *William of Orange and the English Opposition, 1672–1674* (Oxford, 1953); Steven C. A. Pincus, 'From Butterboxes to Wooden Shoes: The Shift in English Popular Sentiment from Anti-Dutch to Anti-French in the 1670s', *HJ*, 38 (1995), 333–61; Steven C. A. Pincus, 'Republicanism, Absolutism and Universal Monarchy: English Popular Sentiment during the Third Dutch War', in Gerald MacLean, ed., *Culture and Society in the Stuart Restoration* (Cambridge, 1995), pp. 241–66; Steven C. A. Pincus, 'The English Debate over Universal Monarchy', in John Robertson, ed., *A Union for Empire: Political Thought and the British Union of 1707* (Cambridge, 1995), pp. 37–62.

85. BL, Harleian MS 7317, fol. 68; *POAS*, I, 424, where the wording is slightly different.

86. Catharine MacLeod and Julia Marciari Alexander, eds., *Painted Ladies: Women at the Court of Charles II* (New Haven, 2001), pp. 94–6, 98.

87. Ibid., p. 136.

88. Ibid., pp. 166–8.

89. BL, Harleian MS 7317, fol. 68; *POAS*, I, 424.

90. Spurr, *England in the 1670s*, p. 204.

91. Bodl., Douce MS 375, fol. 124.

92. BL, Add. MSS 27, 407, fol. 120.

93. Spurr, *England in the 1670s*, p. 209.

94. BL, Harleian MS 7317, fols. 91–6; *Lyme Letters, 1660–1760*, ed. Lady Newton (1925), pp. 85–90.

95. John Ayloffe, 'Britannia and Raleigh', in *POAS*, I, 230, 233, ll. 25, 117–20.

96. Miller, *Popery and Politics*, pp. 55–6, 101, 105–6, 139, 145–8, 163–4; *SR*, V, 782–5, 894–6.

97. W. A. Speck, *James II* (2002), pp. 24–5, contains a useful brief discussion of the dating of York's conversion.

98. K. H. D. Haley, *The First Earl of Shaftesbury* (Oxford, 1968), p. 331.

99. *Calendar of State Papers Venetian, 1673–5*, p. 168. The shoe had been placed there by the republican lawyer and poet John Ayloffe: Haley, *Shaftesbury*, p. 626.

100. Haley, *Shaftesbury*, pp. 357–8, 360; *LJ*, XII, 618.

101. Mark Goldie, 'Danby, the Bishops and the Whigs', in Harris et al., eds., *Politics of Religion*, pp. 82–7.

102. Ellis Hookes, *For the King and . . . Parliament. Being A Brief and General Account of the Late and Present Sufferings of Many of the Peaceable Subjects called Quakers* (1675), p. 5.

103. Norman Penney, ed., *The First Publishers of Truth*, with an introduction by Thomas Hodgkin (1907), p. 313.

104. W. C. Braithwaite, *The Second Period of Quakerism* (Cambridge, 1961), pp. 107–8.

105. BL, Add. MSS 10,117, fol. 50v.

106. Hookes, *Brief and General Account*, p. 17.

107. T. W. Davids, *Annals of Evangelical Nonconformity in the County of Essex* (1863), p. 334.

108. Tim Harris, '"Lives, Liberties and Estates": Rhetorics of Liberty in the Reign of Chartes II', in Harris et al., eds., *Politics of Religion*, pp. 223–9.

109. *The Englishman* (1670), p. 9.

110. W. D. Christie, *A Life of Anthony Ashley Cooper, First Earl of Shaftesbury. 1621–1683* (2 vols., 1871), II, app. 6, lxxvii–lxxx.

111. [Shaftesbury and Locke], *Letter from a Person of Quality*, p. 1.

112. Keeble, *Restoration*, pp. 159–60.

113. Thomas Vincent, *God's Terrible Voice in the City* (5th edn, 1667), pp. 30–31.

114. Keeble, *Restoration*, pp. 162–4; J. Bedford, *London's Burning* (1966), pp. 149–76; Harris, *London Crowds*, p. 79.

115. Richard Kingston, *Pillulae Pestilentiales* (1665), pp. 37–8, 40.

116. Robert Elborough, *London's Calamity by Fire* (1666), pp. 10–11.

117. Burnet, *HOT*, p. 151.

118. Vincent, *God's Terrible Voice*.

119. 'The History of Insipids' (1674), in *POAS*, I, 243–51 (esp. stanzas 1 and 23).

120. Ayloffe, 'Britannia and Raleigh', p. 235, ll. 156–7.

121. Ibid., p. 234, ll. 141–2, 153.

122. 'A Dialogue between the Two Horses', in *POAS*, I, 281, ll. 135–6, 138–40.

123. BL, Harleian MS 7317, fols. 41, 42v.

124. Haley, *Shaftesbury*, chs. 17–20, *passim*.

125. Evelyn, *Diary*, IV, 26; *Correspondence of the Hatton Family, 1601–1704*, ed. E. M. Thompson (2 vols., 1873), I, 119; *Calendar of State Papers Venetian, 1673–5*, pp. 85–6; *The Burning of the Whore of Babylon* (1673).

126. CSPD, *1673–5*, pp. 40, 44.

127. *The Pope Burnt to Ashes* (1676), pp. 2–6; *Hatton Correspondence*, I,

157; *CSPD, 1677–8*, p. 446; Miller, *Popery and Politics*, p. 184; J. R. Jones, 'The Green Ribbon Club', *Durham University Journal*, 49 (1956), 17–20.

128. De Krey, 'London Radicals', pp. 138–9; Haley, *Shaftesbury*, pp. 409–10; *CSPD, 1676–7*, pp. 184, 253–6; *ST*, VI, 1189–1208 (quote in col. 1190).

129. Samuel Parker, *History of His Own Time*, trans. Thomas Newlin (1727), pp. 403–4.

130. Marvell, *Account*, p. 3.

2 Popery and Arbitrary Government

1. [Nicholas French], *A Narrative of the Settlement and Sale of Ireland* (1668), p. 1.

2. Scottish countryman's saying, time of Charles II, cited in Wodrow, *Sufferings*, I, 102.

3. This and the following paragraph are based on J. C. Beckett, *The Making of Modern Ireland 1603–1923* (1966), ch. 5; R. F. Foster, *Modern Ireland, 1600–1972* (1988), ch. 5; Patrick J. Corish, 'The Cromwellian Regime, 1650–60', in Moody et al., eds., *New History of Ireland*, III, 353–86; Aidan Clarke, *Prelude to Restoration in Ireland: The End of the Commonwealth, 1659–1660* (Cambridge, 1999), ch. 1.

4. Steele, II, no. 605a.

5. J. I. McGuire, 'The Dublin Convention, the Protestant Community and the Emergence of an Ecclesiastical Settlement in 1660', in Art Cosgrove and J. I. McGuire, eds., *Parliament and Community* (Belfast, 1983), pp. 121–46; Godfrey Davies, *The Restoration of Charles II, 1658–60* (San Marino, Cal., 1955), ch. 13; Clarke, *Prelude to Restoration*.

6. BL, Add. MSS 28,085, fol. 217.

7. Christie, *Life of . . . Shaftesbury*, I, 210.

8. Cambridge University Library, Add. MS 1, fol. 2; *Parliamentary Intelligencer*, no. 22 (21–8 May 1660), 337–40; *Cal. Anc. Rec. Dub.*, IV, 188–9, 572–3; Steele, II, no. 615.

9. Cox, *Hibernia Anglicana*, II, 'Transactions since 1653', p. 3.

10. NLI, MS 2992/8; Clarke, *Prelude to Restoration*, pp. 293–4.

11. TCD, MS 808, fol. 156; McGuire, 'Dublin Convention'; Clarke, *Prelude to Restoration*, chs. 7, 8; *Cal. Anc. Rec. Dub.*, IV, 185–6.

12. *Kingdomes Intelligencer*, no. 7 (11–18 Feb. 1660[/61]), pp. 97–101; James McGuire, 'Policy and Patronage: The Appointment of Bishops 1660–61', in Ford et al., eds., *As by Law Established*, pp. 112–19.

13. Steele, II, nos. 628, 644, 646a.

14. Patrick Adair, *A True Narrative of the Rise and Progress of the Presbyterian Church in Ireland (1623–1670)*, with an introduction and notes

by W. D. Killen (Belfast, 1866), pp. 255, 262–3; McGuire, 'Dublin Convention', p. 138; Kilroy, *Protestant Dissent*, pp. 39–40, 226–8; James Seaton Reid, *History of the Presbyterian Church in Ireland* (3 vols., Belfast, 1867), II, 255–6.

15. TCD, MS 1038, fol. 73.

16. *Statutes at Large*, III, 139–50 (quote on p. 142); [Edward Wetenhall], *The Case of the Irish Protestants* (1691), pp. 2–3.

17. *Statutes at Large*, I, 275–90.

18. *Cal. Anc. Rec. Dub.*, IV, xxiii, 400, 425, 527–8; *Council Books of the Corporation of Waterford 1662–1700*, ed. Seamus Pender (Dublin, 1964), pp. 2–3, 7, 8, 13–14, 16–18, 34–5, 41; Leicestershire RO, DG7, Ire 10, fol. 1; J. Hill, *From Patriots to Unionists* (Dublin, 1997), pp. 33–4.

19. Steele, II, no. 620; Cox, *Hibernia Anglicana*, II, 'Transactions since 1653', p. 3.

20. *Jacobite Narrative*, pp. 4, 9; [French], *Settlement and Sale*, pp. 2–4; [Nicholas French], *The Unkinde Desertor* (1676), pp. 421–2.

21. *Statutes at Large*, II, 245–63.

22. [French], *Settlement and Sale*, pp. 6–7.

23. *Jacobite Narrative*, pp. 57–8; [French], *Settlement and Sale*, p. 7; *Kingdomes Intelligencer*, no. 21 (20–27 May 1661), p. 326; BL, Add. MSS 72,885, fol. 62; J. G. Simms, 'The Restoration, 1660–85', in Moody et al., eds., *New History of Ireland*, p. 423.

24. *Statutes at Large*, II, 239–348.

25. Edward Hyde, Earl of Clarendon, *Continuation of His Life* (Oxford, 1759), pp. 123–4; NLI, MS 1453.

26. *Statutes at Large*, III, 2–137; O'Kelly *Macariae Excidium*, p. 191, n. 27; Simms, 'The Restoration', pp. 422–9; Beckett, *Making*, pp. 118–21; S. J. Connolly, *Religion, Law and Power: The Making of Protestant Ireland, 1660–1760* (Oxford, 1992), pp. 13–15; Karl S. Bottigheimer, 'The Restoration Land Settlement in Ireland: A Structural View', *Irish Historical Studies*, 18 (1972), 1–21; BL, Egerton MS 917, fols. 85–7; L. J. Arnold, 'The Irish Court of Claims of 1663', *Irish Historical Studies*, 24 (1984–5), 417–30.

27. *Jacobite Narrative*, p. 35.

28. [French], *Settlement and Sale*, pp. 18, 24. French repeated his attack on the land settlement in the mid-1670s: *The Bleeding Iphigenia* (1675); *Unkinde Desertor* (1676). Cf. *Jacobite Narrative*, pp. 19–21, 25–8.

29. *The Poems of David Ó Bruadair*, ed. and trans. Rev. John C. MacErlean (3 vols., 1910–17), III, 17, 23.

30. *Kingdomes Intelligencer*, no. 18 (29 Apr.–6 May 1661), p. 268; *Cal. Anc. Rec. Dub.*, IV, 208–9; *The Council Book of the Corporation of Kinsale, from 1652 to 1800*, ed. Richard Caulfield (Guildford, 1879), p. 62.

31. *Statutes at Large*, II, 237–8.

32. See, for example: *Cal. Anc. Rec. Dub.*, IV, 419; ibid., V, 25, 139; *Council Books of Waterford*, pp. 42, 46; *The Council Book of the Corporation of Youghall, from 1610 . . . to 1800*, ed. Richard Caulfield (Guildford, 1878), pp. 326, 334–5, 338, 346.

33. *Statutes at Large*, II, 526–28; T. C. Barnard, 'The Uses of 23 October and Irish Protestant Celebrations', *English Historical Review*, 106 (1991), 889–920. For examples of the commemoration, see *Council Book of Youghall*, pp. 352, 355; T. C. Barnard, 'Athlone, 1685; Limerick, 1710: Religious Riots or Charivaris?', *Studia Hibernica*, 27 (1993), 61–75.

34. *SR*, V, 410.

35. C. A. Edie. 'The Irish Cattle Bills: A Study in Restoration Politics', *Transactions of the American Philosophical Society*, NS, 60, pt 2 (1970); *SR*, V, 451, 597, 641–2.

36. Cambridge University Library, Add. MS 1, fol. 1.

37. TCD, MS 1180, p. 17.

38. BL, Add. MSS 21,135, fol. 37.

39. Beckett, *Making*, pp. 128–9, 131; Simms, 'The Restoration', pp. 443–4.

40. *A Letter from a Gentleman in Ireland To his Brother in England, Relating to the Concerns of Ireland in Matter of Trade* (1677), pp. 8, 21.

41. TCD, MS 844, fols. 223–4; Greaves, *Deliver Us from Evil*, pp. 140–50.

42. *CSPD, 1664–5*, pp. 149, 544.

43. Greaves, 'That's No Good Religion', pp. 125–6; Greaves, *Enemies*, pp. 24–31.

44. TCD, MS 844, fol. 223.

45. NLI, MS 4908, fols. 3v, 4, 7, 14, 31v.

46. Cambridge University Library, Add. MS 4, fol. 42; Add. MS 1, fol. 1.

47. Clement E. Pike, 'The Origin of the Regium Donum', *Transactions of the Royal Historical Society*, 3rd series, 3 (1909), 255–69; Greaves, 'That's No Good Religion'; Kilroy, *Protestant Dissent*, esp. chs. 1, 8; Raymond Gillespie, 'Dissenters and Nonconformists, 1661–1700', in K. Herlihy, ed., *The Irish Dissenting Tradition 1650–1750* (Dublin, c. 1995), pp. 11–28; Simms, 'The Restoration', p. 437.

48. [Luke Plunkett, Earl of Fingall], *To the King's Most Excellent Majesty, The Faithful Protestation and Humble Remonstrance of the Roman Catholic Nobility and Gentry of Ireland* [1662?]; Peter Walsh, *The History and Vindication of the Loyal Formulary, or Irish Remonstrance* (1674), p. ii; Clarendon, *Continuation of His Life*, pp. 200–203; Jane Ohlmeyer, 'Introduction: For God, King, or Country? Political Thought and Culture in Seventeenth-Century Ireland', in Jane Ohlmeyer, ed., *Political Thought in Seventeenth-Century Ireland: Kingdom or Colony* (Cambridge, 2000), p. 26; Simms, 'The Restoration', pp. 429–30; Connolly, *Religion*, pp. 19–21.

49. [French], *Settlement and Sale*, pp. 25–7.

50. Steele, II, nos. 821, 828–31a; *CSPD, 1671–2*, p. 185; *Essex Papers*, ed. Osmund Airy, vol. 1: *1672–1679*, Camden Society, NS, 47 (1890), 30–31; *Statutes at Large*, III, 205–39; *Cal. Anc. Rec. Dub.*, I, 56–67, and V, v–xii, 548–54, 562–5; *Council Book of Kinsale*, p. 126; Leicestershire RO, DG7, Ire 10, fol. 6; Hill, *From Patriots to Unionists*, pp. 49–55.

51. TCD, MS 844, fols. 229, 231; Cox, *Hibernia Anglicana*, II, 'Transactions since 1653', pp. 11–12; BL, Add. MSS 28,085, fols. 17–19.

52. BL, Add. MSS 28,053, fols. 49v–51.

53. *LJ*, XII, 451; *Parl. Hist.*, IV, 477–8.

54. *Parl. Hist.*, IV, 579–81.

55. *Cal. Anc. Rec. Dub.*, V, 164; *Council Books of Waterford*, pp. 174–7; *Council Book of Kinsale*, p. 157.

56. Leicestershire RO, DG7, Ire 13, Earl of Conway to Lord Finch, 7 Sep. 1678; BL MS Stowe 746, fols. 1–2; NLI, MS 8171.

57. Cox, *Hibernia Anglicana*, II, 'Transactions since 1653', pp. 7–8; *Council Book of Kinsale*, p. li; NLI, MS 4908, fol. 6ov.

58. Christie, *Life of . . . Shaftesbury*, II, 192.

59. Hunt. Lib., HA 15394, information of John Moyre, 27 Dec. 1676.

60. *An Apology for the Protestants of Ireland* (1689), pp. 2–3.

61. Julia Buckroyd, *Church and State in Scotland, 1660–1681* (Edinburgh, 1980), ch. 2.

62. Earl of Balcarres, *An Account of the Affairs of Scotland* (1714), p. 7. Cf. Jackson, *Restoration Scotland*, pp. 14–15.

63. *Diurnal of Thomas Rugg*, pp. 95–6; Steele, III, no. 2171; *The Diary of Sir Archibald Johnston of Wariston*, vol. 3: *1655–1660*, ed. James D. Ogilvie (Edinburgh, 1940), p. 182; Wodrow, *Sufferings*, I, 5–6; John Nicoll, *A Diary of Public Transactions . . . from January 1650 to June 1667* (Edinburgh, 1836), pp. 283–4, 292–4.

64. J[ames] R[amsey], *Moses Returned from Midion* (Edinburgh, 1660), pp. 10–11. See also L[awrie], *God Save the King*; Matthias Symson, *Mephiboseth: Or, The Lively Picture of a Loyal Subject* (Edinburgh, 1660).

65. Michael Lynch, *Scotland: A New History* (1991), p. 287.

66. *APS*, VII, 8–9; *Kingdomes Intelligencer*, no. 4 (21–28 Jan. 1661), p. 55. Each estate was able to choose twelve representatives. For the act of 1640, see *APS*, V, 290–91.

67. For the Restoration settlement in Scotland, see in particular Buckroyd, *Church and State*, chs. 3, 4; Julia Buckroyd, 'Bridging the Gap: Scotland, 1659–1660', *Scottish Historical Review*, 66 (1987), 1–25; Buckroyd, 'Anti-clericalism in Scotland during the Restoration', in Norman MacDougall, ed., *Church, Politics and Society: Scotland 1408–1929* (Edinburgh, 1983), pp. 167–85; Cowan, *Covenanters*, ch. 2; Jackson, *Restoration Scotland*, ch. 5.

68. *APS*, VII, 7; Wodrow, *Sufferings*, I, 22–3 and app. 1, no. 10, p. 11; Mackenzie, *Memoirs*, p. 23; Buckroyd, *Church and State*, p. 29.

69. *APS*, VII, 10–11.

70. Ibid., pp. 12–13.

71. Ibid., p. 16.

72. Ibid., p. 86–8.

73. Mackenzie, *Memoirs*, pp. 27–9. Cf. Jackson, *Restoration Scotland*, pp. 77–8.

74. Rev. James Kirkton, *The Secret and True History of the Church of Scotland from the Restoration to the Year 1678* (Edinburgh, 1817), p. 94.

75. [Alexander Shields], *The Hind Let Loose* (Edinburgh, 1687), p. 107. Cf. [Sir James Stewart and John Stirling], *Naphtali, Or the Wrestlings of the Church of Scotland for the Kingdom of Christ* ([Edinburgh], 1667, rev. edn 1680), p. 175; [Gilbert Rule], *A Vindication of the Presbyterians in Scotland* (1692), p. 6; Wodrow, *Sufferings*, I, 21.

76. *Diurnal of Thomas Rugg*, pp. 179–80; *Kingdomes Intelligencer*, no. 18 (29 Apr.–6 May 1661), pp. 270–71; Nicoll, *Diary*, p. 327; Wodrow, *Sufferings*, I, 106.

77. *APS*, VII, 199–200; *Kingdomes Intelligencer*, no. 21 (20–27 May 1661), pp. 327, 333–5, and no. 24 (10–17 Jun. 1661), 364–5; BL, Add. MSS 10,116, fol. 213; [Stewart and Stirling], *Naphtali*, p. 154; Kirkton, *Secret and True History*, pp. 105–8; Nicoll, *Diary*, pp. 332–3, 335; Wodrow, *Sufferings*, I, 106; C. A. Whatley, 'Royal Day, People's Day: The Monarch's Birthday in Scotland c. 1660–1860', in Mason and Macdougall, eds., *People and Power*, pp. 173, 176.

78. Nicoll, *Diary*, pp. 306, 374–5, 449, 451; Wodrow, *Sufferings*, I, 17, 107; BL, Add. MSS 10,117, fol. 41v; R. A. Houston, *Social Change in the Age of Enlightenment: Edinburgh, 1660–1760* (Oxford, 1994), p. 48; *RPCS, 1661–4*, pp. 15, 62–3.

79. *ST*, V, 1370–1516; Wodrow, *Sufferings*, I, 42–71, 77–8, 172–5 and app. 1, nos. 21–2, pp. 30–47; NLS, MS 14,493, fol. 4; Kirkton, *Secret and True History*, pp. 69–70.

80. *APS*, VII, 415–16, 420–29; Wodrow, *Sufferings*, I, 121–2; Cowan, *Covenanters*, p. 55; Keith M. Brown, *Kingdom or Province? Scotland and the Regal Union, 1603–1715* (1992), pp. 145–6.

81. *APS*, VII, 78, 88–95.

82. Ibid., pp. 503–4.

83. All Souls College Library, Oxford, MS 255, fol. 104; Gordon Donaldson, *Scotland: James V to James VII* (Edinburgh, 1965), pp. 287–8.

84. *SR*, V, 246–50.

85. Nicoll, *Diary*, p. 430; Wodrow, *Sufferings*, I, 220; William Ferguson,

Scotland's Relations with England: A Survey to 1707 (Edinburgh, 1977), pp. 153–4.

86. *APS*, VII, 78, 88–95, 503–4, 529–35, 540–47.

87. Childs, *Army of Charles II*, pp. 196–7.

88. *APS*, VII, 480–81; Nicoll, *Diary*, p. 399.

89. Brown, *Kingdom or Province?*, p. 145; Allan Macinnes, 'Repression and Conciliation: The Highland Dimension 1660–1688', *Scottish Historical Review*, 65 (1986), 167–95.

90. Kirkton, *Secret and True History*, pp. 118–20; NLS, Wod. Oct. XXIX, fol. 20; *Kingdomes Intelligencer*, no. 19 (6–13 May 1661), pp. 298–301; Wodrow, *Sufferings*, I, 37–41 and app. 1, nos. 15A and 15B, pp. 15–22; Mackenzie, *Memoirs*, pp. 53–6; Buckroyd, *Church and State*, p. 44.

91. *RPCS*, 1661–4, pp. 28–9, 30–32; Wodrow, *Sufferings*, I, 96–8, 115; Steele, III, no. 2210.

92. Buckroyd, *Church and State*, pp. 41–5.

93. *APS*, VII, 370–71, 372–4, 376–9, 405–6, 449.

94. Cowan, *Covenanters*, pp. 53–4; Hyman, 'Church Militant', p. 55.

95. [John Sage], *The Case of the Present Afflicted Clergy of Scotland Truly Represented* (1690), preface; BL, Add. MSS 4106, fol. 257.

96. Hunt. Lib., HA 14960, John Hartstonge to Sir James Graham, 7 Nov. 1675.

97. Mackenzie, *Memoirs*, p. 53; Wariston, *Diary*, III, 180–81.

98. *A Dismal Account of the Burning of Our Solemn League and National Covenant . . . at Linlithgow, May 29* (1662, reprinted Edinburgh, 1832), reproduced in Wodrow, *Sufferings*, I, 151–2; BL, Add. MSS 10,117, fols. 31–2; Kirkton, *Secret and True History*, pp. 126–7; Robert Chambers, *Domestic Annals of Scotland*, vol. 2: *From the Reformation to the Revolution* (2nd edn, Edinburgh, 1859), pp. 291–2; James King Hewison, *The Covenanters: A History of the Church of Scotland from the Reformation to the Revolution* (2 vols., 1908), II, 105.

99. Kirkton, *Secret and True History*, pp. 161–3; Wodrow, *Sufferings*, I, 177–82; Cowan, *Covenanters*, pp. 56–7.

100. Kirkton, *Secret and True History*, pp. 180–91; *Lauderdale Papers*, ed. Osmund Airy, Camden Society, NS, 34, 63, 38 (3 vols., 1884–5), II, 207; Burnet, *HOT*, p. 166; Wodrow, *Sufferings*, I, 157; [Stewart and Stirling], *Naphtali*, p. 181.

101. [Sage], *Case of the Present Afflicted Clergy*, p. 17.

102. Wodrow, *Sufferings*, I, 156.

103. Burnet, *HOT*, p. 70; Clarendon, *History*, IV, 320.

104. *APS*, VII, 455–6.

105. Nicoll, *Diary*, pp. 408–11; Wodrow, *Sufferings*, I, 191–9; [Stewart and

Stirling], *Naphtali*, pp. 176–7, 184–90; Kirkton, *Secret and True History*, p. 201; *HMC, Laing*, I, 360; Buckroyd, *Church and State*, pp. 55, 58–61, 63–4; Cowan, *Covenanters*, p. 59. For the act of 1584, see *APS*, III, 293.

106. Kirkton, *Secret and True History*, pp. 199–200, 221–5; [Stewart and Stirling], *Naphtali*, p. 195; Hewison, *Covenanters*, II, 187–8; [Rule], *Vindication of the Presbyterians*, pp. 10–11.

107. *A Brief and True Account of the Sufferings of the Church of Scotland* (1690), p. 2.

108. [John Brown], *An Apologeticall Relation of the Sufferings of the Faithfull Ministers of the Church of Scotland since August 1660* (n.p., 1665); BL, Add. MSS 35,125, fol. 130.

109. *RPCS, 1665–9*, p. 231; BL, Add. MSS 35,125, fol. 145; BL, Add. MSS 10,117, fol. 183; [Shields], *Hind Let Loose*, p. 109.

110. Kirkton, *Secret and True History*, pp. 225–6.

111. Wodrow, *Sufferings*, I, 265; [Stewart and Stirling], *Naphtali*, p. 226.

112. Hewison, *Covenanters*, II, 212–13; Cowan, *Covenanters*, ch. 4; Greaves, *Enemies*, pp. 64–84.

113. *HMC, Laing*, I, 359.

114. [Stewart and Stirling], *Naphtali*; [James Stewart], *Jus Populi Vindicatum, Or, The People's Right to Defend Themselves and their Covenanted Religion* ([Edinburgh], 1669); Ian Michael Smart, 'The Political Ideas of the Scottish Covenanters, 1638–88', *History of Political Thought*, I (1980), 183–7; Robert von Friedeburg, 'From Collective Representation to the Rights of Individual Defence: James Steuart's *Ius Populi Vindicatum* and the use of Johannes Althusius' *Politica* in Restoration Scotland', *History of European Ideas*, 24 (1998), 19–42; Jackson, *Restoration Scotland*, pp. 70–71, 125.

115. *RPCS, 1669–72*, pp. 38–40.

116. *APS*, VII, 372; *HMC, Laing*, I, 372–3; Wodrow, *Sufferings*, I, 304–5, 307, 313–15; Hewison, *Covenanters*, II, 227; *Lauderdale Papers*, II, lxiv–lxvii; Julia Buckroyd, 'The Dismissal of Archbishop Alexander Burnet, 1669', *Records of the Scottish Church History Society*, 18 (1973), 149–55.

117. *APS*, VII, 554–5; NLS, Wod. Qu. XXXVIII, fol. 2; Burnet, *HOT*, p. 192; *Lauderdale Papers*, II, 164.

118. *RPCS, 1669–72*, pp. 61–2; Steele, III, no. 2331.

119. Mackenzie, *Memoirs*, p. 163; *APS*, VII, 556–7.

120. *APS*, VIII, 8–9.

121. *APS*, VIII, 9–10; [George Rule], *A Vindication of the Church of Scotland. Being an Answer to a Paper, Intituled, Some Questions Concerning Episcopal and Presbyterial Government in Scotland* (1691), pp. 25–6.

122. *APS*, VIII, 11–12.

123. *RPCS, 1669–72*, pp. 586–9; Hyman, 'Church Militant', pp. 58–9.

124. *APS*, VII, 89.

125. *HMC, Hamilton*, pp. 142, 143, 148 (quote on p. 148).

126. *HMC*, Laing, I, 400–401.

127. Steele, III, no. 2389; *RPCS, 1673–6*, pp. 197–200.

128. Wodrow, *Sufferings*, I, 362.

129. *RPCS, 1673–6*, pp. 425–6, 447; Wodrow, *Sufferings*, I, 391.

130. *RPCS, 1676–8*, pp. 206–9; Steele, III, no. 2421; Wodrow, *Sufferings*, I, 449–51; *HMC*, Hamilton, p. 156; Mackenzie, *Memoirs*, pp. 329–30.

131. *RPCS, 1676–8*, pp. 300–301; Longleat House, Coventry MSS, XVI, fols. 197, 205; Wodrow, *Sufferings*, I, 454–8 and app. 2, no. 80, pp. 174–5; Hewison, *Covenanters*, II, 265–6; Sir George Mackenzie, *A Vindication of the Government in Scotland, during the Reign of King Charles II* (1691), p. 12.

132. Wodrow, *Sufferings*, I, 467; *CSPD, 1677–8*, p. 593; Lynch, *Scotland*, p. 294; Paul Hopkins, *Glencoe and the End of the Highland War* (Edinburgh, 1986), pp. 62–3.

133. Wodrow, *Sufferings*, I, 462–3, 467–9, 471; Hewison, *Covenanters*, II, 267–8; Ruth Richens, 'The Stewarts in Underbank: Two Decades in the Life of a Covenanting Family', *Scottish Historical Review*, 178 (1985), 108–9.

134. Wodrow, *Sufferings*, I, 478–80, 487–93; Longleat House, Coventry MSS, XVI, fol. 205; Lynch, *Scotland*, p. 294.

135. NAS, GD 224/171/1, p. 57.

136. NLS, Adv. 31.6.5, fol. 167.

137. *RPCS, 1676–8*, pp. 347–9; Wodrow, *Sufferings*, I, 472–3.

138. Wodrow, *Sufferings*, I, 499–500.

139. NLS, Wod. Oct. XXIX, fol. 105; Wodrow, *Sufferings*, I, 469, 508, 509 and app. 2, nos. 82–3, pp. 176–8. Cf. *HMC, Laing*, I, 415.

140. Wodrow, *Sufferings*, I, 508; NLS, Wod. Qu. XXX, fol. 50.

141. *RPCS, 1676–8*, pp. 413–14.

142. BL, Add. MSS 28,053, fol. 120; *RPCS, 1676–8*, p. 467.

143. *RPCS, 1676–8*, pp. 425–9. For the fifteenth-century legislation, see *APS*, II, 19, 35.

144. BL, Add. MSS 32,095, fol. 176. See *APS*, II, 332, for the 1529 act.

145. *HMC, Hamilton*, p. 162; Wodrow, *Sufferings*, I, 518, 520–21, 523–6.

146. Sir John Lauder of Fountainhall, *The Decisions of the Lords of Council and Session from June 6th, 1678, to July 30th, 1713* (2 vols., Edinburgh, 1759–61), I, 13–14; Wodrow, *Sufferings*, I, 521–2; *Brief and True Account of the Sufferings of the Church of Scotland*, p. 11.

147. *CSPD, 1678*, pp. 353, 365, 370.

148. *APS*, III, 36; ibid., VII, 26

149. Wodrow, *Sufferings*, I, 342, 447.

150. *CSPD, 1678*, p. 232.

151. *RPCS*, *1676–8*, pp. 233–4; Mackenzie, *Memoirs*, p. 325; Buckroyd, *Church and State*, p. 127.

152. *Parl. Hist.*, IV, 625–30, 683–8, 699 (quote in col. 684); *HMC, Laing*, I, 393.

153. NA, SP 30/24/5/291, fols. 276–89 (quote on fol. 276); BL, Add. MSS 4106, fols. 255–64.

154. Longleat House, Coventry MSS, XVI, fol. 201.

155. Buckroyd, *Church and State*, pp. 72, 112, 117–18.

156. *CSPD, 1673–5*, p. 289; Leicestershire RO, DG7, Ire 13, Earl of Conway to Lord Finch, 30 Nov. 1674; Hunt. Lib., HA 14528, [Earl of Conway] to Sir George Rawdon, 10 Jul. 1674; Hunt. Lib., HA 14151, Duncan Campbell to Sir James Graham, 14 Jan. 1677[8]; Longleat House, Coventry MSS, XVI, fol. 195.

157. Ferguson, *Scotland's Relations with England*, pp. 152–7; Jackson, *Restoration Scotland*, pp. 89–90.

158. Kirkton, *Secret and True History*, pp. 299–300; Wodrow, *Sufferings*, I, 309.

159. Mackenzie, *Memoirs*, pp. 138–9.

3 Fearing for the Safety of the People

1. *Life of James II*, I, 515.

2. Alan Marshall, *The Strange Death of Edmund Godfrey: Plots and Politics in Restoration London* (Stroud, 1999), pp. 57–73.

3. *The Discovery of the Popish Plot, Being the Several Examinations of Titus Oates* (1679); Titus Oates, *A True Narrative of the Horrid Plot and Conspiracy of the Popish Party against the Life of His Sacred Majesty* (1679). For the plot in general, see J. P. Kenyon, *Popish Plot* (1972).

4. Marshall, *Strange Death*.

5. Hutton, *Charles II*, p. 357

6. Scott, *Restoration Crisis*, pp. 9–21; Jonathan Scott, 'Radicalism and Restoration', *HJ*, 31 (1988), 459–60; Mark Knights, *Politics and Opinion in Crisis, 1678–81* (Cambridge, 1994), esp. pp. 4–5, 350.

7. Miller, *Popery and Politics*, pp. 154, 170, 188; J. R. Jones, *The First Whigs: The Politics of the Exclusion Crisis, 1678–83* (Oxford, 1861), pp. 18, 214.

8. Kenyon, *Popish Plot*, jacket.

9. Scott, *Restoration Crisis*; Jones, *First Whigs*, pp. 13–14.

10. Knights, *Politics and Opinion, passim*; Scott, *Restoration Crisis*, pt 1; Haley, *Shaftesbury*, chs. 21–30.

11. Anthony Wood, *Life and Times, 1632–1695*, ed. A. Clark (5 vols., Oxford, 1891–1900), III, 42; David Allen, 'Political Clubs in Restoration London', *HJ*, 19 (1976), 561–80; Grant Tapsell, 'Parliament and Political

Division in the Last Years of Charles II, 1681–5', *Parliamentary History*, 22 (2003), 259; Harris, *London Crowds*, p. 100.

12. M. Dorothy George, 'Elections and Electioneering, 1678–81', *English Historical Review*, 45 (1930), 552–78; Douglas R. Lacey, *Dissent and Parliamentary Politics in England, 1661–1689* (New Brunswick, 1969), ch. 6.

13. Bell and Barnard, 'Provisional Count of *Wing* Titles', p. 91.

14. Knights, *Politics and Opinion*, p. 168.

15. For a full publishing history of Exclusion Crisis newspapers, see R. S. Crane and F. B. Kaye, *A Census of British Newspapers and Periodicals, 1620–1820* (1927). For general discussions, see James Sutherland, *The Restoration Newspaper and its Development* (Cambridge, 1986); C. John Sommerville, *The News Revolution in England: Cultural Dynamics of Daily Information* (Oxford, 1996). For newsletters, see Love, *Scribal Publication*; Fox, *Oral and Literate Culture*, pp. 370–79. Care has been the subject of an important recent biography: Lois G. Schwoerer, *The Ingenious Mr Henry Care, Restoration Publicist* (Baltimore, 2001).

16. *ST*, VII, 926–60, 1111–30; Timothy J. Crist, 'Francis Smith and the Opposition Press in England, 1660–1688', unpub. Ph.D. thesis, Cambridge University (1977) pp. 107–41.

17. Luttrell, I, 34; Bodl., MS Carte 228, fol. 145; *CSPD, 1679–80*, p. 397.

18. *The Snotty Nose Gazette*, no. 1 (24 Nov. 1679), cited in Knights, *Politics and Opinion*, p. 172.

19. Titus Oates, *A Sermon Preached at St. Michael's, Wood Street* (1679); LC, MS 18,124, VII, fol. 98; *Memoirs of the Verney Family*, Lady Frances Parthenope Verney, compiler (4 vols., 1892–9), II, 329; *Protestant (Domestick) Intelligence*, nos. 59 (27 Jan. 1679[/80]), 66 (17 Feb. 1679[/80]), 67 (24 Feb. 1679[/80]); Guildhall Library, MS 5026/1; *Loy. Prot. Int.*, nos. 38 (19 Jul. 1681), 41 (26 Jul. 1681).

20. Susan J. Owen, *Restoration Theatre and Crisis* (Oxford, 1996); Odai Johnson, *Rehearsing the Revolution: Radical Performance, Radical Politics in the English Revolution* (Newark, Del., 2000); J. D., *The Coronation of Queen Elizabeth* (1680).

21. O. W. Furley, 'The Pope-Burning Processions of the Late Seventeenth Century', *History*, 44 (1959), 16–23; Sheila Williams, 'The Pope-Burning Processions of 1679–81', *Journal of the Warburg and Courtauld Institutes*, 21 (1958), 104–18; Johnson, *Rehearsing the Revolution*, ch. 2.

22. Haley, *Shaftesbury*, pp. 499, 553; O. W. Furley, 'The Whig Exclusionists: Pamphlet Literature in the Exclusion Campaign, 1679–81', *Cambridge HJ*, 13 (1957), 20–21; Knights, *Politics and Opinion*, pp. 162–3; Harris, *London Crowds*, p. 101.

23. Pepysian Library, Magdalene College, Cambridge, Pepys Miscellanies,

VII, pp. 474, 475, 478, 484–5; David Cressy, *Bonfires and Bells: National Memory and the Protestant Calendar in Elizabethan and Stuart England* (Berkeley, 1989), p. 180.

24. Dalrymple, *Memoirs*, I, 'Review', p. 390.
25. All Souls College Library, Oxford, MS 257, no. 98.
26. Longleat House, Coventry MSS, VI, fol. 210.
27. Ibid., fol. 189.
28. *CSPD, 1682*, p. 456.
29. Ibid., p. 303.
30. *Loy. Prot. Int.*, no. 228 (2 Nov. 1682).
31. See, for example, *True Prot. Merc.*, no. 11 (29 Jan.–1 Feb. 1680[/81]), and above, p. 17.
32. See above, pp. 75–6.
33. *HMC, Stuart*, VI, 1; Dalrymple, *Memoirs*, I, 'Review', p. 257.
34. Haley, *Shaftesbury*, 472; Anchitell Grey, *Debates of the House of Commons from the Year 1667 to the Year 1694* (10 vols., 1763), VI, 148.
35. *Parl. Hist.*, IV, 1035; *CJ*, IX, 536; FSL, Newdigate Newsletters, Lc. 704 (11 Nov. 1678), 705 (14 Nov. 1678); *HMC, Ormonde*, NS, IV, 470; LC, MS 18, 124, VII, fol. 138.
36. *CJ*, IX, 605; Grey, *Debates*, VII, 137–51; FSL, Newdigate Newsletters, Lc. 779 (1 May 1679), 784 (15 May 1679).
37. *Reasons for the Indictment of the D. of York* [1680]; Morrice, P, 280; *Life of James II*, I, 666–7; Knights, *Politics and Opinion*, pp. 72, 89, 95 (n. 102), 279, 307; Haley, *Shaftesbury*, p. 580; Roger North, *Examen* (1740), p. 564; Luttrell, I, 49, 69; *Original Papers Containing the Secret History of Great Britain from the Restoration to the Accession of the House of Hannover*, ed. James MacPherson (2 vols., 1775), I, 114.
38. *Life of James II*, I, 620, 622–3, 636–7. For the parliamentary debate over Tangier, and how members linked it with the issue of Exclusion, see Grey, *Debates*, VIII, 4–21.
39. BL, Add. MSS 4,236, fols. 225, 276.
40. Spurr, *England in the 1670s*, p. 298.
41. Caroline Robbins, ed., *Two English Republican Tracts* (Cambridge, 1969), pp. 61–200.
42. Burnet, *HOT*, p. 303.
43. Bodl. MS Clarendon 87, fol. 334. Cf. *Life of James II*, I, 635, 670–71.
44. Dalrymple, *Memoirs*, I, 'Review' pp. 371, 374–5.
45. Centre for Kentish Studies, U275/A3, p. 42. See also Grey, *Debates*, VII, 169; William Cavendish, Duke of Devonshire, *Reasons for His Majesty Passing the Bill of Exclusion* (1681), p. 5; [Sir William Jones and Algernon Sidney], *A Just and Modest Vindication of the Proceedings of the Two Last Parliaments* (1681), pp. 30–33.

46. Sir John Lauder of Fountainhall, *Historical Observes of Memorable Occurents in Church and State from October 1680 to April 1686*, ed. David Laing and A. Urquhart (Edinburgh, 1840), p. 100; Lois G. Schwoerer, *Lady Rachel Russell: 'One of the Best of Women'* (Baltimore, 1988), p. 37.

47. *A Most Serious Expostulation with Several of my Fellow-Citizens* [1679], p. 3.

48. [Elkanah Settle], *The Character of a Popish Successour* (1681), pp. 8, 9, 14. See also Harris, 'Lives, Liberties and Estates'.

49. J. S., *Popery Display'd in its Proper Colours* (1681), p. 4.

50. Grey, *Debates*, VII, 401, 413.

51. Corporation of London RO, Journal 49, fol. 224; ibid., Rep. 86, fols. 151, 162.

52. *England's Calamity, Foreshewn in Germanie's Misery* (1680).

53. Sir John Temple, *The Irish Rebellion* (1646, 2nd edn 1679), p. 5.

54. *A Collection of Certain Horrid Murthers in Several Counties of Ireland. Committed since the 23. of Octobr. 1641* (1679), sig. A6.

55. [Edmund Borlase], *The History of the Execrable Irish Rebellion* (1680), app. pp. 109–25.

56. BL, Sloane MS 1008, fol. 216.

57. [Borlase], *History*, pp. 311–12.

58. Grey, *Debates*, VII, 411.

59. NLI, MS 803, fol. 39; HMC, *Ormonde*, NS, VI, 251.

60. E[dmund] E[verard], *The Great Pressure and Grievances of the Protestants in France* (1681); *The Humble Petition of the Protestants of France to the French-King, To Recall His Declaration for taking their Children from them at the Age of Seven Years* (1681); *A True and Perfect Relation of the New Invented Way of Persecuting the Protestants in France* [1682]; *Popery and Tyranny; Or, the Present State of France* (1679), pp. 5–6; *The Horrible Persecution of the French Protestants in the Province of Poitou* (1681), pp. 1–2; *The Humble Petition of Protestants of France Lately Presented to His Most Christian Majesty* [1681]; Robin Gwynn, *Huguenot Heritage: The History and Contribution of the Huguenots in Britain* (2nd edn, Brighton, 2001), pp. 26–8, 44; Robin Gwynn, 'The Arrival of Huguenot Refugees in England 1680–1705', *Proceedings of the Huguenot Society of Great Britain and Ireland*, 21 (1965–70), 366–73.

61. *Popery and Tyranny*, pp. 1, 2, 4, 6, 7.

62. J. S., *Popery Display'd*, p. 4.

63. *Parl. Hist.*, IV, 1116.

64. [Charles Blount], *An Appeal from the Country to the City* (1679), p. 2.

65. Knights, *Politics and Opinion*, p. 211.

66. Isaac Barrow, *A Sermon Preached on the Fifth of November, MDCLXXIII* [1679], p. 36. Cf. Gilbert Burnet, *A Sermon Preached at the*

Chappel of the Rolls, on the Fifth of November 1684 (1684), pp. 13, 15, 16.

67. FSL, MS V. a. 403, pp. 137–9.

68. Grey, *Debates*, VII, 144, 147, 148, 151, 252, 255, 259. Similar arguments were developed in the debate on the second Exclusion Bill in November 1680: ibid., pp. 412, 452–3, 458–9. For the relevant clause of the Treason Act of 1571, see *SR*, IV, 527.

69. [Henry Care], *English Liberties; Or, The Free-born Subject's Inheritance* [1681], pp. 83–4.

70. John Somers, *A Brief History of the Succession* (1680), p. 13.

71. *Parl. Hist.*, IV, 1189.

72. W. G., *The Case of Succession to the Crown* (1679), pp. 7, 8.

73. *An Impartial Account of the Nature and Tendency of the Late Addresses* (1681), p. 20.

74. J. G. A. Pocock, *The Ancient Constitution and the Feudal Law* (Cambridge, 1957), ch. 8; C. C. Weston and J. R. Greenberg, *Subjects and Sovereigns: The Grand Controversy over Legal Sovereignty in Stuart England* (Cambridge, 1081), ch. 7; Mark Goldie, 'Restoration Political Thought', in Glassey, ed., *Reigns of Charles II and James VII and II*, pp. 29–35.

75. [Thomas Hunt], *The Great and Weighty Consideration . . . Considered* (1680), pp. 5, 15, 20 (Wing H3751 edn).

76. *A Dialogue at Oxford Between a Tutor and a Gentleman* (1681), pp. 5, 6.

77. *Heraclitus Ridens*, no. 18 (31 May 1681).

78. See, for example, [Settle], *Character*, p. 13; *A Letter from a Person of Quality to his Friend, Concerning his Majesty's Late Declaration* [1681], p. 8.

79. HMC, *Hastings*, IV, 303.

80. Julian H. Franklin, *John Locke and the Theory of Sovereignty* (Cambridge, 1978), pp. 39–49; Mark Goldie, 'Introduction', in Mark Goldie, Tim Harris, Mark Knights, John Spurr, Stephen Taylor and Jason McElligott, eds., *The Entring Book of Roger Morrice* (6 vols., Woodbridge, forthcoming), I.

81. *Vox Populi: Or, the People's Claim to their Parliament's Sitting* (1681), pp. 2, 13.

82. *Impartial Account of . . . the Late Addresses*, pp. 13–15.

83. [Jones and Sidney], *Just and Modest Vindication*, pp. 2, 29–30, 43–4.

84. [Edmund Hickeringill], *Second Part of the History of Whiggism* (1682), pp. 36–8, 46.

85. [Samuel Johnson], *Julian the Apostate* (1682), pp. vii–viii, 73, 78, 83–6, 89.

86. W. G., *Case of Succession*, p. 13.

87. [Settle], *Character*, pp. 20, 21–2.

88. *A Copy of the Bill Concerning the Duke of York* (1679).

89. Grey, *Debates*, VII, 431–3; *CJ*, IX, 648; NA 31/3/147 ('Baschet Transcripts'), fol. 19; Robin Clifton, *The Last Popular Rebellion: The Western Rising of 1685* (1984), pp. 131–2; Haley, *Shaftesbury*, pp. 597–8, 634.

90. K.H.D. Haley, 'Shaftesbury's Lists of the Lay Peers and Members of the Commons 1677–8', *Bulletin of the Institute of Historical Research*, 43 (1970), 88; J. R. Jones, 'Shaftesbury's "Worthy" Men', ibid., 30 (1957), 234.

91. Clifton, *Last Popular Rebellion*, pp. 121–3.

92. This paragraph draws on Clifton, *Last Popular Rebellion*, ch. 4, and my article on Monmouth in the *Oxford DNB*.

93. Miller, *Popery and Politics*, p. 160.

94. WYAS, MX/R/12/112, Thomas Yarburgh to Sir John Reresby, 9 Nov. 1678.

95. Philip Jenkins, 'Anti-Popery on the Welsh Marches in the Seventeenth Century', *HJ*, 23 (1980), 275–93; Todd Galitz, 'The Challenge of Stability: Religion, Politics, and Social Order in Worcestershire, 1660 to 1720', unpub. Ph.D. dissertation, Brown University (1997), ch. 4; Newton Key, 'Comprehension and the Breakdown of Consensus in Restoration Herefordshire', in Harris et al., eds., *Politics of Religion*, pp. 191–215; Dan Beaver, 'Conscience and Context: The Popish Plot and the Politics of Ritual, 1678–1682', *HJ*, 34 (1991), 297–327.

96. All Souls College Library, Oxford, MS 169, p. 306.

97. *LJ*, XIII, 513–15; HMC, *Ormonde*, NS, V, 69; Harris, *London Crowds*, p. 111.

98. *Reliquiae Baxterianae*, ed. Matthew Sylvester (1696), III, 184–5.

99. Berkshire RO, T/F41, fol. 237; East Sussex RO, Rye 1/17, pp. 37–8; Miller, *Popery and Politics*, pp. 162–9; Galitz, 'Worcestershire', pp. 124–7.

100. *The Diary of William Lawrence. Covering the Periods between 1662 and 1681*, ed. G. E. Aylmer (Beaminster, 1961), p. 37.

101. Jonathan Scott, 'England's Troubles: Exhuming the Popish Plot', in Harris et al., eds., *Politics of Religion*, pp. 115–16; Scott, *England's Troubles*, esp. pt 1; Pincus, 'Butterboxes to Wooden Shoes'; Pincus, 'The English Debate over Universal Monarchy', pp. 37–62.

102. Lawrence, *Diary*, pp. 37–9.

103. Centre for Kentish Studies, U275/A3, p. 98.

104. Luttrell, I, 5.

105. Hunt. Lib., HM 30315, no. 199.

106. Somerset RO, DD/SF/3074, Aldred Seaman to Edward Clarke, 21 Dec. 1678.

107. Lawrence, *Diary*, p. 36; *Life of James II*, I, 546–7; Somerset RO, DD/SF/3074, Aldred Seaman to Edward Clarke, 5 Apr. 1679.

108. Grey, *Debates*, VII, 107–8.

109. Johannes Philanglus, *England's Alarm* (1679), p. 5. For concerns about the economic threat posed by French immigrants, see Harris, *London Crowds*, pp. 200–204; Daniel Statt, *Foreigners and Englishmen: The Controversy over Immigration and Population, 1660–1760* (Newark, Del., 1995), ch. 3.

110. Scott, 'England's Troubles', p. 117.

111. All Souls College Library, Oxford, MS 169, p. 311.

112. Hunt. Lib., HA 5967, Earl of Huntingdon to John Gery, 13 Nov. 1679.

113. Longleat House, Coventry MSS, VI, fol. 199.

114. Grey, *Debates*, VII, 109.

115. Pedro Ronquillo, *The Last Memorial of the Spanish Ambassador* (1681).

116. Grey, *Debates*, VII, 258.

117. C. B., *An Address to the Honourable City of London, And All Other Cities, Shires and Corporations, Concerning their Choice of a New Parliament* (1681), epistle dedicatory.

118. *True Prot. Merc.*, no. 16 (16–19 Feb. 1680[/81]).

119. *Parl. Hist.*, IV, 1116–18.

120. Ibid., 1166–7.

121. Grey, *Debates*, VII, 188, 194–5, 199; *Parl. Hist.*, IV, 1130; *CJ*, IX, 614.

122. *Some Particular Matter of Fact, relating to the Administration of Affairs in Scotland under the Duke of Lauderdale* [1679], pp. 1–4; [William, Duke of Hamilton], *Some Farther Matter of Fact Relating to the Administration of Affairs in Scotland Under the Duke of Lauderdale* [1679], pp. 1–4; BL, Add. MSS 28,938, fols. 12–13; Wodrow, *Sufferings*, II, 101–5; Burnet, *HOT*, p. 312.

123. *CSPD, 1682*, p. 505.

124. [Earl of Shaftesbury], *A Speech Lately Made by a Noble Peer of the Realm* (1681), p. 5.

125. [Jones and Sidney], *Just and Modest Vindication*, p. 23.

126. FSL, MSX. d. 195, 'Quem Natura Negat, Facit Indignatio Versum, Qualum Cunque Potest'.

127. *LJ*, XIII, 478.

128. Ibid., pp. 488–91. For the proclamations, see Steele, II, nos. 889, 891, 895, 897, 898, 903, 913, 917; *HMC, Ormonde*, II, 350–59, *passim*.

129. *LJ*, XIII, 491, 493, 499, 527–8, 532.

130. Bodl., MS Carte 228, fol. 161.

131. Haley, *Shaftesbury*, pp. 569–99 *passim*, 617–18, 643–61 *passim*.

132. Fitzpatrick, *Seventeenth-Century Ireland*, pp. 236–45.

133. [French], *Narrative of the Settlement*, p. 27; Connolly, *Religion*, p. 28; Hunt. Lib., HA 15394, info. of John Moyre, 27 Dec. 1676.

134. Bodl., MS Carte 39, fol. 107; TCD, MS 844, fol. 233.

135. BL., Sloane MS 1008, fol. 197; F. L., *Ireland's Sad lamentation* (1680[/81]).

136. *Parl. Hist.*, IV, 1166–7; *Life of James II*, I, 602. See above, pp. 168–9.

137. *LJ*, XIII, 733; Grey, *Debates*, VIII, 251–2.

138. *True Prot. Merc.*, no. 7 (15–18 Jan. 1680[/81]); ibid., no. 12 (1–5 Feb., 1680[/81]).

139. Ibid., no. 11 (29 Jan.–1 Feb. 1680[/81]).

140. C. B., *Address to the City*, epistle dedicatory.

141. [Sir William Petty], *The Politician Discovered* (1681), 'The First Discourse', p. 9.

142. David Ogg, *England in the Reign of Charles II* (Oxford, 1934), pp. 553–4, 574.

143. Berkshire RO, R/AC1/1/15, p. 181.

144. Grey, *Debates*, VII, 64–5.

145. Ibid., 67–73; FSL, Newdigate Newsletters, Lc. 767 (3 Apr. 1679).

146. *SR*, V, 934; Joyce Lee Malcolm, *To Keep and Bear Arms: The Origins of an Anglo-American Right* (Cambridge, Mass., 1994), p. 107.

147. Ogg, *Charles II*, p. 578.

148. Grey, *Debates*, VII, 19; *LJ*, XIII, 466, 471; *Parl. Hist.*, IV, 1113–15.

149. Grey, *Debates*, VII, 25–9; Andrew Browning, *Thomas Osborne, Earl of Danby and Duke of Leeds, 1632–1712* (3 vols., Glasgow, 1944–51), I, 300–329.

150. Hunt. Lib., Hastings Parliamentary Box 4, no. 21, 'Grounds on which a royal pardon may be disputed'.

151. E.g. Grey, *Debates*, VII, 28, 58, 151–4, 175–6, 183.

152. Grey, *Debates*, VII, 30.

153. Ibid., p. 57.

154. Ibid., pp. 153–4.

155. Ibid., p. 176.

156. Ibid., p. 183.

157. Ibid., p. 181.

158. *CJ*, IX, 633.

159. Bodl., MS Rawlinson D 924, fol. 248; FSL, Newdigate Newsletters, Lc. 766 (31 Mar. 1679), 767 (3 Apr. 1679); BL, Add. MSS 61,903, fols. 47–9; Hunt. Lib., EL 8425; Morrice, P, 152. Grey's account of Winnington's speech is in his *Debates*, VII, 25–9.

160. J. P., *A Letter to a Friend in the Country* (1679), p. 2–3.

161. *LJ*, XIII, 475–521, 537–40, 553; *Parl. Hist.*, IV, 1116–21, 1129; Ogg, *Charles II*, p. 588; Browning, *Danby*, I, 333–41, 436; Goldie, 'Danby, the Bishops and the Whigs'.

162. Knights, *Politics and Opinion*, pp. 25–8.

163. *Impartial Account of . . . the late Addresses*, p. 31.

164. Henry Horwitz, 'Protestant Reconciliation in the Exclusion Crisis',

Journal of Ecclesiastical History, 15 (1964), 201–17; Lacey, *Dissent*, pp. 144–5.

165. Lawrence, *Diary*, p. 43.

166. *The Contents (Hats for Caps) Contented* (1680); *The Time-Servers; Or, A Touch of the Times* (1681).

167. Guildhall Library, Print Room, Playing Cards 238, 'Knave of Clubs'; BL, Add. MSS 34,362, fol. 107, 'On the Prorogation'.

168. *The Weekly Discoverer Strip'd Naked*, no. 2 (23 Feb. 1680[/81]).

169. *Omnia Comensta à Bello; Or, An Answer out of the West to a Question out of the North* (1679), p. 3.

170. Hunt. Lib., EL 8764, 'The Magpye, Or the Song against the Bishops'.

171. Bodl., MS Don b. 8, p. 696, 'The Antiphone to the Late Protestant Petition'.

172. *HMC, Montagu*, pp. 174–5; Henning, ed., *House of Commons*, I, 199.

173. *Essex's Excellency* (1679), p. 4; *A Faithfull and Impartial Account of the Behaviour of a Party of the Essex Freeholders* (1679), p. 6; Wood, *Life and Times*, II, 516; *CSPD, 1680–81*, p. 232; Henning, ed., *House of Commons*, I, 229, 360.

174. *CSPD, 1680–81*, p. 31.

175. Somerset RO, Q/SR/148/24–6.

176. Centre for Kentish Studies, U275/A3, pp. 97–9.

177. *CJ*, IX, 683.

178. *Parl. Hist.*, IV, 1294.

179. Luttrell, I, 63.

180. BL, Add. MSS 28,938, fol. 54; Morrice, P, 276; Corporation of London RO, Journal 49, fols. 156–7.

181. [Jones and Sidney], *Just and Modest Vindication*, p. 1.

182. *Vox Populi*, p. 6. Cf. *Impartial Account of . . . the Late Addresses*, pp. 18–20; *A Modest Account of the Present Posture of Affairs* (1682), pp. 7–8; [Hickeringill], *Second Part of the History of Whiggism*, pp. 65, 70–75; Care, *English Liberties*, pp. 75–7, 95; *Dialogue at Oxford*, p. 10.

183. *CSPD, 1682*, pp. 72, 82.

184. Henning, ed., *House of Commons*, I, 106; BL, Add. MSS 4236, fol. 227.

185. This section draws on Knights, *Politics and Opinion*, chs. 8, 9.

186. Mark Knights, 'London's "Monster" Petition of 1680', *HJ*, 36 (1993), 39–67.

187. Steele, I, no. 3703.

188. Petitions were started, without being seen through to fruition, in Buckinghamshire, Cumberland, Derbyshire, Dorset, Kent, Lancashire, Monmouthshire, Norfolk, Suffolk, Yorkshire, Bridgwater, Oxford, Wells, and the London Inns of Court.

189. FSL, Newdigate Newsletters, Lc. 881 (30 Dec. 1679); *CSPD, 1679–80*, p. 377; LC, MS 18,124, VII, fol. 1.

190. North, *Examen*, pp. 563–4; *CJ*, IX, 691; 'Thomas Dare', in *Oxford DNB*; Morrice, P, 286–8.

191. FSL, Newdigate Newsletters, Lc. 1032 (20 Jan. 1681).

192. Luttrell, I, 63.

193. *A True Narrative of the Proceedings at Guild-Hall* (1681).

194. BL, MS Stowe 746, fol. 16.

195. *CSPD, 1680–81*, p. 203.

196. *Domestick Intelligence*, no. 40 (21 Nov. 1679).

197. *The Pope's Down-fall at Abergaveny* (1679); *Domestick Intelligence*, no. 39 (18 Nov. 1679); Philip Jenkins, 'Anti-Popery on the Welsh Marches in the Seventeenth Century', *HJ*, 23 (1980), 285.

198. *True Prot. Merc.*, nos. 89 (9–12 Nov. 1681), 90 (12–16 Nov. 1681); Cressy, *Bonfires and Bells*, p. 179.

199. Bodl., MS Carte 228, fol. 169; *The Scots Demonstration of their Abhorrence of Popery* (Edinburgh?, 1681); N. M., *A Modest Apology for the Students of Edinburgh Burning a Pope December 25. 1680* (1681); L. L., *The History of the Late Proceedings of the Students of the Colledge at Edenborough* (1681); *True Prot. Merc.*, nos. 3 (1–3 Jan. 1680[/81]), 8 (18–22 Jan. 1680[/81]), 11 (29 Jan.–1 Feb. 1680[/81]), 12 (1–5 Feb. 1680[/81]); [Alexander Monro], *The Spirit of Calumny and Slander, Examin'd, Chastis'd, and Expos'd, in a Letter to a Malicious Libeller* (1693), p. 64; *RPCS, 1681–2*, pp. 1, 4, 13–14, 23–4; *ST*, IX, 1007–1008. For a modern account, see Johnson, *Rehearsing the Revolution*, pp. 1–3.

200. Harris, *London Crowds*, p. 160; *CSPD, 1679–80*, p. 296.

201. *Protestant (Domestick) Intelligence*, no. 65 (17 Feb. 1679[/80]).

202. WYAS, MX/R/15/33, newsletter, 1 Jul. 1680.

203. *Protestant (Domestick) Intelligence*, no. 87 (11 Jan. 1680[/81]).

204. *CSPD, 1680–81*, p. 31.

205. Ibid., p. 170.

206. *True Prot. Merc.*, no. 19 (26 Feb.–2 Mar. 1680[/81]).

207. Luttrell, I, 19–20; Ogg, *Charles II*, p. 591.

208. BL, Add. MSS 25,358, fol. 139; Wood, *Life and Times*, II, 466–7.

209. Hutton, *Charles II*, p. 357.

210. E. S. De Beer, 'The House of Lords in the Parliament of 1680', *Bulletin of the Institute of Historical Research*, 20 (1943–5), 27–8, 37.

211. Miller, 'Public Opinion', p. 377.

212. Hutton, *Charles II*, p. 371.

213. Guildford Muniment Room, LM 1331/69; Grey, *Debates*, VIII, 284.

214. *CJ*, IX, 640; Grey, *Debates*, VII, 370–72.

215. *CJ*, IX, 642–3, 653, 656–7, 662; Grey, *Debates*, VII, 372–4, 378–9, 385–93, 460–71; ibid., VIII, 52–3, 67–71.

216. *CJ*, IX, 661, 688–92, 697–9; Grey, *Debates*, VIII, 53–60, 205–9, 285–9; North, *Examen*, pp. 563–4; 'Thomas Dare', in *Oxford* DNB; Morrice, P, 286–8.

217. Grey, *Debates*, VII, 456.

218. *CJ*, IX, 683, 688–92.

219. *CJ*, IX, 655, 660, 663, 664, 682; Grey, *Debates*, VIII, 21–31, 38–51, 73–97, 175–81.

220. North, *Examen*, pp. 550–51.

221. Glassey, *Politics*, pp. 45–52; Norma Landau, *The Justices of the Peace, 1679–1760* (Berkeley, 1984), p. 74; Stater, *Noble Government*, p. 141.

222. David F. Allen, 'The Crown and the Corporation of London in the Exclusion Crisis, 1678–1681', unpub. Ph.D. thesis, Cambridge University (1977).

223. John T. Evans, *Seventeenth-Century Norwich: Politics, Religion, and Government, 1620–1690* (Oxford, 1979), p. 251.

224. J. J. Hurwich, 'A Fanatick Town: Political Influence of Dissenters in Coventry, 1660–1720', *Midland History*, 4 (1977), pp. 31–3.

225. David Underdown, *Fire from Heaven: Life in an English Town in the Seventeenth Century* (New Haven, 1992), p. 241.

226. Wood, *Life and Times*, II, 463, 490; *Letters of Humphrey Prideaux, Sometime Dean of Norwich, to John Ellis, Sometime Secretary of State, 1674–1722*, ed. Edward Maunde Thompson, Camden Society, NS, 15, (1875), p. 80; *Victoria County History, Oxford*, IV, 123.

227. *Lond. Gaz.*, no. 1455 (27–30 Oct. 1679).

228. Halliday, *Dismembering*, pp. 124–31.

229. Longleat House, Coventry MSS, VI, fol. 117.

230. *HMC, Montagu*, p. 174; Henning, ed., *House of Commons*, I, 199, and II, 398–9.

231. WYAS, MX/R/18/124, Sir Thomas Fairfax to Sir John Reresby, 16 Jan. 1681[/2]; ibid., MX/R/20/14, same to the same, 8 Apr. 1682.

232. Haley, *Shaftesbury*, ch. 28.

233. *HMC, Ormonde*, NS, VI, 193. Cf. Thomas Sprat, *A True Account and Declaration of the Horrid Conspiracy* (1685), p. 5.

234. Harris, *London Crowds*, pp. 71–2.

235. LC, MS 18, 124, VII, fol. 304.

236. *A True Account of the Horrid Murder committed upon His Grace, the late Lord Archbishop of Saint Andrews* (1679).

237. Wodrow, *Sufferings*, II, 44; *The Martyrs and Wrestlers: Their Testimonies and Declarations at Rutherglen, Sanquhar and Lanark* (Glasgow, 1770); 'The Testimony published at Rutherglen, May 29th, 1679',

www.truecovenanter.com/Rutherglen.html (accessed 22 Jun. 2004); *RPCS, 1678–80*, pp. 208, 210.

238. *The Declaration of the Rebels now in Arms in the West of Scotland* (1679); Greaves, *Secrets*, pp. 58–69.
239. Longleat House, Coventry MSS, VI, fol. 73.
240. *Depositions from the Castle of York*, p. 239
241. Fountainhall, *Observes*, p. 19.
242. [Donald Cargill], *A True and Exact Copy of a Treasonable and Bloody Paper, Called, The Fanaticks New-Covenant . . . together with the Execrable Declaration Published at the Cross at Sanquhair* (1680), pp. 4, 6, 9, 10; *RPCS, 1678–80*, pp. 481–3.
243. [Shields], *Hind Let Loose*, pp. 138–9; Hewison, *Covenanters*, II, 337–8.
244. Dalrymple, *Memoirs*, I, 'Review', p. 299.
245. Grey, *Debates*, VII, 151.
246. *Parl. Hist.*, IV, 1236–50.
247. *Parl. Hist.*, IV, 1257; Fountainhall, *Observes*, p. 20.
248. *ST*, VIII, 786.
249. *Records of the Borough of Leicester*, p. 549.
250. *Depositions from the Castle of York*, p. 238.
251. LMA, MJ/SR/1596, recs. 17 (to prosecute), 95, *ignoramus* indictment 1; *Middlesex County Records*, IV, 153.
252. *CSPD, 1682*, p. 217.
253. WYAS, MX/R/18/12.
254. *HMC, Ormonde*, NS, VI, 117.
255. *CSPD, 1682*, p. 504.
256. Luttrell, I, 233.
257. *Depositions from the Castle of York*, pp. 265–7.

4 The Remedy for the Disease

1. L'Estrange, *Observator*, I, no. 1 (13 Apr. 1681).
2. J. R. Jones, *Country and Court: England 1658–1714* (1978), p. 216.
3. John Miller, 'The Potential for "Absolutism" in Later Stuart England', *History*, 69 (1984), 187–207.
4. J. R. Jones, *Charles II, Royal Politician* (1987), p. 162.
5. Harris, *London Crowds*, chs. 5, 6; Tim Harris 'The Parties and the People: The Press, the Crowd and Politics "Out-of-doors" in Restoration England', in Glassey, ed., *Reigns of Charles II and James VII and II*, pp. 125–51; Knights, *Politics and Opinion*, pp. 329–45; Phillip Harth, *Pen for a Party: Dryden's Tory Propaganda in its Contexts* (Princeton, 1993), pp. 80–84, 149–53, 213–14.
6. Scott, *Restoration Crisis*, pp. 47–8.
7. Speck, *Reluctant Revolutionaries*, p. 135.

8. Sir John Reresby, *Memoirs*, ed. Andrew Browning (Glasgow, 1936; 2nd edn, with a new preface and notes by Mary K. Geiter and W. A. Speck, London, 1991), p. 120; F. C. Turner, *James II* (1948), pp. 91–5.

9. L'Estrange, *Observator*, I, 'To the Reader'; ibid., no. 1 (13 Apr. 1681).

10. Harris, *London Crowds*, ch. 6; Harth, *Pen for a Party, passim* (esp. pp. 78–80, 159–61); Knights, *Politics and Opinion*, pp. 166–8; Owen, *Restoration Theatre*; Johnson, *Rehearsing the Revolution*, ch. 1.

11. BL, Add. MSS 32,518, fols. 144–52; Roger North, *Lives of the Norths* (3 vols., 1826), I, 320–21.

12. Burnet, *HOT*, p. 307; Violet Jordan, ed., *Sir Roger L'Estrange: Selections from the Observator (1681–1687)*, Augustan Reprint Society, 141 (1970), introd., p. 1; Harris, *London Crowds*, p. 132; Knights, *Politics and Opinion*, pp. 164–5, 316–25. Our only book-length study of L'Estrange is George Kitchin, *Sir Roger L'Estrange: A Contribution to the History of the Press in the Seventeenth Century* (1913).

13. Thomas O'Malley, 'Religion and the Newspaper Press 1660–1685: A Study of the *London Gazette*', in Michael Harris and Alan Lee, eds., *The Press in English Society from the Seventeenth to the Nineteenth Centuries* (1986), pp. 25–46.

14. All Souls College Library, Oxford, MS 257, no. 96.

15. Harth, *Pen for a Party*, pp. 224–8.

16. BL, Add. MSS 63,057B, fol. 50.

17. Robert Beddard, 'The Commission for Ecclesiastical Promotions, 1681–84: An Instrument of Tory Reaction', *HJ*, 10 (1967), 11–40.

18. William Sherlock, *The Case of Resistance* (1684), sig. A2v.

19. L'Estrange, *Observator*, I, no. 470 (9 Jan. 1683[/4]).

20. Dagmar Freist, *Governed by Opinion: Politics, Religion and the Dynamics of Communication in Stuart London 1637–1645* (1997), pp. 248–52.

21. Edward Pelling, *A Sermon Preached before the Lord Mayor and Court of Aldermen, at St Mary le Bow, on November 5 1683* (1683), epistle dedicatory.

22. *Protestant Loyalty Fairly Drawn* (1681), p. 8.

23. Thomas Willis, *God's Court . . . a Sermon Preached at the Assizes Held at Kingston Upon Thames, July 26 1683* (1683), p. 22.

24. L'Estrange, *Observator*, III, nos. 151 (6 Mar. 1685[/6]), 153 (10 Mar. 1685[/6]), 206 (4 Sep. 1686).

25. Pelling, *Sermon . . . Nov. 5 1683*, epistle dedicatory.

26. Sir Robert Filmer, *Patriarcha and other Writings*, ed. Johann P. Sommerville (Cambridge, 1991).

27. H. T. Dickinson, *Liberty and Property: Political Ideology in Eighteenth-Century Britain* (1977), p. 26.

28. Goldie, 'Restoration Political Thought', p. 19.

29. James Daly, *Sir Robert Filmer and English Political Thought* (Toronto, 1979), esp. ch. 6.

30. Goldie, 'Restoration Political Thought', p. 19.

31. Goldie, 'Locke and Anglican Royalism'; Scott, *Restoration Crisis*; Alan Craig Houston, *Algernon Sidney and the Republican Heritage in England and America* (Princeton, 1991), ch. 2.

32. Thomas Goddard, *Plato's Demon* (1684), pp. 76–89 (quote on pp. 76–7).

33. George Hickes, *A Discourse of the Soveraign Power* (1682), pp. 4, 19–20.

34. *A Letter to a Friend. Shewing . . . How False that State-Maxim is, Royal Authority is Originally and Radically in the People* (1679), p. 4; T[homas] L[ambert], *The True Notion of Government* (1680), pp. 8, 12, 18.

35. Goddard, *Plato's Demon*, p. 105.

36. [Matthew Rider], *The Power of Parliaments in the Case of Succession* (1680), p. 19.

37. Warwick, *Discourse of Government*, pp. 13–17.

38. Samuel Crossman, *Two Sermons* (1681), p. 24.

39. Thomas Merke, *The Bishop of Carlile's Speech in Parliament, Concerning the Deposing of Princes* (1679).

40. William Allen, *A Sermon Preacht in Bridgewater* (1681), p. 4.

41. *Parl. Hist.*, IV, 1190.

42. E. F., *A Letter from a Gentleman of Quality in the Country to His Friend* (1679), pp. 2, 4.

43. *The Speech of Doctor Gower, Vice-Chancellor of the University of Cambridge, to his Sacred Majesty* (Edinburgh, 1681).

44. Rider, *Power of Parliaments*, pp. 21–2, 35.

45. *A Letter on the Subject of the Succession* (1679), p. 2.

46. W. W., *Antidotum Britannicum* (1681), p. 14.

47. Rider, *Power of Parliaments*, pp. 27–33.

48. W.W., *Antidotum Britannicum*, p. 23.

49. See above pp. 57–8.

50. John Nalson, *The Common Interest of the King and People* (1677), p. 139.

51. Glenn Burgess, *The Politics of the Ancient Constitution: An Introduction to English Political Thought, 1603–1642* (University Park, Pa., 1992); Glenn Burgess, *Absolute Monarchy and the Stuart Constitution* (New Haven, 1996); William M. Lamont, *Godly Rule: Politics and Religion, 1603–60* (1969); Paul Christianson, *Reformers and Babylon: English Apocalyptic Visions from the Reformation to the Eve of the Civil War* (Toronto, 1981).

52. [Roger L'Estrange], *The Free-born Subject; Or, The Englishman's Birthright* (1679), p. 5.

53. Goldie, 'Restoration Political Thought', pp. 23–4; Pocock, *Ancient Constitution*, ch. 8. Brady's works are *Full and Clear Answer* (1681) and *Introduction to the Old English History* (1684). Cf. *The Arraignment of Co-Ordinate Power* (1683).

54. [Sir Benjamin Thorogood], *Captain Thorogood His Opinion of the Point of Succession* (1680), pp. 3–4.

55. [Rider], *Power of Parliaments*, p. 4.

56. Hickes, *Discourse of the Soveraign Power*, p. 22.

57. Roger L'Estrange, *Citt and Bumpkin* (1680), p. 36.

58. Robert Filmer, *The Power of Kings* (1680), p. 1.

59. [Laurence Womock], *A Short Way to a Lasting Settlement* (1683), p. 26.

60. Thomas Pomfret, *Passive Obedience, Stated and Asserted* (1683), p. 2.

61. John Okes, *A Sermon Preached at the Assizes held at Reading* (1681), pp. 13–14; Sherlock, *Case of Resistance*, esp. pp. 192–3, 199; Erasmus Warren, *Religion Loyalty* (1685), pp. 24–5; Pomfret, *Passive Obedience*, p. 10.

62. L[ambert], *True Notion*, pp. 26–7 (misnumbered pp. 18–19).

63. L'Estrange, *Observator*, I, no. 464 (29 Dec. 1683).

64. Goddard, *Plato's Demon*, pp. 196–8, 306.

65. *An Apostrophe From the Loyal Party* (1681), pp. 2–3. Luttrell, I, 93, described the work as seditious, alleging it aimed 'to overthrow the ancient constitution of this government by parliaments'.

66. [Womock], *Short Way*, pp. 3–4, 25–6, 28–9.

67. W.W., *Antidotum Britannicum*, quotes on pp. 6–7, 34, 75, 86, 94, 104, 162–3.

68. Warwick, *Discourse of Government*, quotes on pp. 41, 42, 44.

69. Nalson, *Common Interest*, p. 153.

70. [William Assheton], *The Royal Apology* (1684), quotes on pp. 38, 43–4.

71. *Plain Dealing is a Jewel* (1682), pp. 5–7. The examples of the crimes are mine.

72. Nalson, *Common Interest*, p. 116.

73. John Northleigh, *The Triumph of Our Monarchy* (1685), pp. 180, 250–51, 256–7.

74. *Letter to a Friend. Shewing . . . How False*, p. 8.

75. L'Estrange, *Citt and Bumpkin*, p. 36.

76. Sherlock, *Case of Resistance*, pp. 208–9, 211–13.

77. Nathaniel Johnston, *The Excellency of Monarchical Government* (1686), pp. 29, 31–2, 33, 71, 128, 131, 135, 154.

78. Sherlock, *Case of Resistance*, pp. 211–12.

79. [Rider], *Power of Parliaments*, p. 42.

80. [David Jenkins], *The King's Prerogative* (1680), pp. 4–5.

81. [Rider], *Power of Parliaments*, pp. 9, 15.

82. *Parl. Hist.*, IV, 1190–91. In the Ship Money ruling of 1637, Lord Chief

Justice Finch had asserted that 'Acts of parliament . . . cannot bar a succession', since 'No act of parliament' could 'bar a king of his regality', and thus any such acts of parliament were void: *ST*, III, 1235.

83. [Rider], *Power of Parliaments*, p. 42.

84. Leicestershire RO, DG7, P.P. 73 [iii].

85. Grey, *Debates*, VII, 163.

86. [Thorogood], *His Opinion*, p. 9. Cf. *Fiat Justitia* (1679), p. 2.

87. *Plain Dealing is a Jewel*, pp. 3, 15, 17, 19.

88. *Life of James II*, I, 549–50.

89. Grey, *Debates*, VII, 243, 246–8, 257, 313, 402–3, 407–9, 450–51; ibid., VIII, 318.

90. [Earl of Halifax], *A Seasonable Address to Both Houses of Parliament Concerning the Succession* (1681), p. 14.

91. *England's Happiness In a Lineal Succession* (1685).

92. *A Letter to a Friend in the Country, Touching the Present Fears and Jealousies of the Nation* (1680), p. 1.

93. Dalrymple, *Memoirs*, I, 'Review', p. 301.

94. *Plain Dealing; Or, A Second Dialogue between Humphrey and Roger* (1681).

95. L'Estrange, *Observator*, I, no. 379 (23 Jul. 1683).

96. Grey, *Debates*, VII, 248.

97. *Parl. Hist.*, IV, 1185–6; Grey, *Debates*, VII, 408.

98. *Life of James II*, I, 621.

99. Ibid., p. 614.

100. *A Plea for Succession in Opposition to Popular Exclusion* (1682), p. 2.

101. *England's Concern in the Case of His R. H.* (1680), p. 10.

102. *Life of James II*, I, 550.

103. Goddard, *Plato's Demon*, pp. 363–4. Cf. *Misleading the Common People* (1685), p. 17.

104. [Halifax], *Seasonable Address*, p. 15.

105. See above, pp. 198–9.

106. Roger L'Estrange, *Tyranny and Popery Lording it Over the Consciences, Lives, Liberties and Estates both of King and People* (1678), quote on p. 4.

107. *A Vindication of Addresses in General, And of the Middle-Temple Address and Proceedings in Particular* (1681), p. 7.

108. [John Northleigh], *The Parallel; Or, The New Specious Association* (1682), p. 13. See also *The Two Associations* (1681); *Remarques upon the New Project of Association* [1682].

109. Northleigh, *Triumph of our Monarchy*, pp. 735–6.

110. 'The Plot is Vanish'd', in Nathaniel Thompson, ed., *A Collection of One Hundred and Eighty Loyal Songs* (1685), p. 172.

111. *Heraclitus Ridens*, no. 41 (8 Nov. 81).

112. *Lond. Gaz.*, no. 1566 (18–22 Nov. 1680). For the trial, see *ST*, VIII, 123–4. Skein was executed in December.

113. *Loy. Prot. Int.*, no. 128 (14 Mar. 1681[/2]). See also *CSPD, 1682*, pp. 118–19.

114. [James Crauford], *A Serious Expostulation With that Party in Scotland, Commonly Known by the Name of Whigs* (1682), p. 4.

115. *A Letter from Scotland, with Observations upon the Anti-Erastian, Anti-Praelatical, and Phanatical Presbyterian Party There* (1682), p. 2.

116. [George Hickes], *Ravillac Redivivus* (1678; 2nd edn, 1682), pp. 35, 43.

117. L'Estrange, *Tyranny and Popery*, p. 93.

118. BL, Sloane MS 1008, fol. 313.

119. Susan J. Owen, '"Suspect My Loyalty when I Lose my Virtue": Sexual Politics and Party in Aphra Behn's Plays of the Exclusion Crisis, 1678–83', *Restoration*, 18 (1994), 37–47.

120. *Loy. Prot. Int.*, nos. 55 (13 Sep. 1681), 164 (6 Jun. 1682).

121. John Nalson, *Complaint of Liberty and Property against Arbitrary Government* (1681), p. 5.

122. *Plain Dealing is a Jewel*, pp. 14, 17.

123. Sir Roger L'Estrange, *The Character of a Papist in Masquerade* (1681), p. 10.

124. [John Nalson], *The Character of a Rebellion* (1681), pp. 4–5.

125. Nalson, *Complaint of Liberty*, pp. 2–3.

126. *Plea for Succession*, pp. 3–4.

127. 'The Commonwealth Ruling with a Standing Army', frontispiece to [Sir Thomas May], *Arbitrary Government Display'd in the Tyrannick Usurpation of the Rump Parliament, and Oliver Cromwell* (1683).

128. *Whig's Exaltation* [1682], in Thompson, ed., *Songs*, p. 6.

129. John Allen, *Of Perjury* (1682), p. 29.

130. *A Litany from Geneva* (1682). Cf. *The Cavalier's Litany* (1682); L'Estrange, *Observator*, I, no. 38 (10 Jul. 1681); *The Convert Scot, and Apostate English* (1681), p. 52.

131. *Jack the Cobler's Caution to His Country-Men* (1682).

132. [L'Estrange], *Tyranny and Popery*, pp. 82–3, 93.

133. *A Vindication of Addresses*, p. 1.

134. *Advice to the Men of Shaftesbury* [1681], pp. 1–2.

135. L'Estrange, *Observator*, I, no. 318 (12 Apr. 1683).

136. *Heraclitus Ridens*, no. 7 (15 Mar. 1681). Cf. [John Nalson], *Foxes and Fire-Brands* (1680), preface; *Plea for Succession*, p. 10.

137. Evelyn, *Diary*, IV, 295.

138. *Heraclitus Ridens*, nos. 2 (8 Feb. 1681), 4 (22 Feb. 1681); [John Andrewes], *A Gentle Reflection on the Modest Account* (1682), p. 11; *Plain*

Dealing is a Jewel, pp. 10–11; *Mad-Men's Hospital* (1681), in Nathaniel Thompson, ed., *A Collection of Eighty-Six Loyal Poems* (1685), p. 59.

139. Edward Pelling, *A Sermon Preached On the Anniversary of that Most Execrable Murder of K. Charles The First Royal Martyr* (1682), pp. 13–14.

140. Hickes, *Discourse of the Soveraign Power*, pp. 20–21. For a modern scholarly examination of the extent to which Calvinist resistance theory derived from Catholic thought, see Quentin Skinner, *The Foundations of Modern Political Thought* (2 vols., Cambridge, 1978).

141. [Andrewes], *Gentle Reflection*, p. 12.

142. *Protestant Loyalty*, preface.

143. Nicholas Adee, *A Plot for a Crown, In a Visitation-Sermon, At Cricklade, May the Fifteenth, 1682* (1683), p. 16.

144. Edward Pelling, *The True Mark of the Beast* (1681), pp. 29–30.

145. Goddard, *Plato's Demon*, pp. 340–61 (quotes on pp. 347–8).

146. Roger L'Estrange, *The Committee; Or, Popery in Masquerade* (1680).

147. *The Charter* (1682), in Thompson, ed., *Poems*, p. 150; 'To His Royal Highness the Duke' [1679?], in Thompson, ed., *Poems*, pp. 247–9.

148. [Thorogood], *His Opinion*, p. 10.

149. *Plain Dealing is a Jewel*, p. 17.

150. See below, pp. 335–6, 338–9.

151. [J. S.], *A New Letter from Leghorn* (1681), p. 1.

152. *Loy. Prot. Int.*, no. 132 (23 Mar. 1681[/2]).

153. *Plea for Succession*, p. 2.

154. Chandaman, *English Public Revenue*, pp. 185, 332; Geoffrey S. Holmes, *The Making of a Great Power: Late Stuart and Early Georgian Britain 1660–1722* (1993), pp. 88–92; Toby Barnard, 'Scotland and Ireland in the later Stewart Monarchy', in Steven G. Ellis and Sarah Barber, eds., *Conquest and Union: Fashioning a British State, 1485–1725* (1995), p. 269; Hutton, *Charles II*, pp. 401, 410.

155. Charles II, *His Majesties Declaration To all His Loving Subjects, Touching The Causes and Reasons That Moved Him to Dissolve The Two last Parliaments* (1681).

156. North, *Lives*, I, 381.

157. All Souls College Library, Oxford, MS 257, no. 96.

158. Fountainhall, *Observes*, I, 34.

159. Knights, *Politics and Opinion*, ch. 10; Harth, *Pen for a Party*, pp. 68–72.

160. *Parl. Hist.*, IV, 1306.

161. Cited in Keith Feiling, *A History of the Tory Party, 1640–1714* (Oxford, 1924), p. 186.

162. *True Prot. Merc.*, no. 159 (12–15 Jul. 1682); HMC, *Ormonde*, NS, VI, 155; LC, MS 18,124, VII, fol. 309; ibid., IX, fol. 326.

163. John Dryden, *Absalom and Achitophel* (1681), in *POAS*, II, 491–2.
164. L'Estrange, *Observator*, I, nos. 142 (24 May 1682), 222 (23 Oct. 1682).
165. [Northleigh], *Parallel*, p. 29.
166. BL, Add. MSS 27,448, fol. 18.
167. Allen, *A Sermon Preacht in Bridgewater*, pp. 6, 14.
168. Allen, *Of Perjury*, p. 28.
169. John Standish, *A Sermon Preached at the Assizes at Hertford* (1683), p. 28.
170. Miles Barne, *A Sermon Preach'd at the Assizes at Hertford* (1684), p. 20.
171. George Hickes, *The True Notion of Persecution Stated* (1681), pp. 5–6; Mark Goldie, 'The Huguenot Experience and the Problem of Toleration in Restoration England', in C. E. J. Caldicott, H. Gough and J.-P. Pittion, eds., *The Huguenots and Ireland: Anatomy of an Emigration* (Dublin, 1987), pp. 175–203.
172. Richard Pearson, *Providence Bringing Good out of Evil* (1684), pp. 34–5.
173. *Heraclitus Ridens*, no. 13 (26 Apr. 1681).
174. John Nalson, *Vox Populi, Fax Populi* (1681), pp. 4–5.
175. L'Estrange, *Observator*, I, no. 135 (10 May 1682).

5 Keeping the Reins of Government Straight

1. *Vindication of Addresses*, p. 1.
2. *The Speech of Robert Clerk, Esq, Deputy-Recorder of Northampton to the Mayor-Elect for the Year Ensuing* (1684).
3. John Oldmixon, *The History of Addresses* (2 vols., 1709–11), I, 53; *Impartial Account of ... the Late Addresses*, p. 9; *Imp. Prot. Merc.*, no. 104 (18–21 Apr. 1682); Haley, *Shaftesbury*, pp. 640, 687; Arthur G. Smith, 'London and the Crown, 1681–1685', unpub. Ph.D. dissertation, University of Wisconsin (1967), p. 150.
4. Harris, *London Crowds*, ch. 6; Harris, 'The Parties and the People'; Knights, *Politics and Opinion*, pp. 329–45; Harth, *Pen for a Party*, pp. 80–84, 149–53, 213–14.
5. Scott, 'England's Troubles', p. 126; Scott, *Restoration Crisis*, pp. 45, 47, 48. Scott has toned down his views somewhat in his latest work, *England's Troubles*.
6. Harris, *London Crowds*, ch. 3; Harris, *Politics under the Later Stuarts*, ch. 2; David Underdown, *Revel, Riot and Rebellion: Popular Politics and Culture in England, 1603–1660* (Oxford, 1985), ch. 10.
7. Andrew Browning and D. J. Milne, 'An Exclusion Bill Division List',

Bulletin of the Institute of Historical Research, 23 (1950), 205–25; Henning, ed., *House of Commons*, I, 65.

8. Henning, ed., *House of Commons*, I, 329–31, 414–16 (and *passim* for the electoral contests of 1679–81); Victor L. Stater, 'Continuity and Change in English Provincial Politics: Robert Paston in Norfolk, 1675–1683', *Albion*, 25 (1993), 212–13.

9. *Lond. Gaz.*, nos. 1455 (27–30 Oct. 1679) to 1465 (1–4 Dec. 1679) (the account of the Durham festivities is in no. 1460 (13–17 Nov. 1679)); Reresby, *Memoirs*, pp. 190–91; *HMC, Ormonde*, NS, V, 234–5; *CSPD, 1679–80*, p. 278.

10. *HMC, Ormonde*, NS, IV, 580; *Protestant (Domestick) Intelligence*, no. 68 (27 Feb. 1680); LC, MS 18,124, VII, fol. 23; Bodl. MS Carte 39, fol. 111; Corporation of London RO, Rep. 85, fol. 88; FSL, Newdigate Newsletters, Lc. 905 (24 Feb. 1679[/80]); *Current Intelligence*, no. 7 (28 Feb.–6 Mar. 1679[/80]); Knights, *Politics and Opinion*, p. 264.

11. *Lond. Gaz.*, no. 1493 (8–11 Mar. 1679[/80]); LC, MS 18, 124, VII, fol. 28; Luttrell, I, 37–8; *Some Historical Memoires of the Life and Actions of . . . James Duke of York* (1683), p. 117.

12. *HMC, Ormonde*, NS, V, 293, 296; *Mercurius Civicus*, 24 Mar. 1679[/80]; FSL, Newdigate Newsletters Lc. 916–21 (23 Mar. – 3 Apr. 1680); BL, Althorp Papers C2, Sir William Hickman to the Earl of Halifax, 23 Mar. 1679[/80] and 27 Mar. 1680; NLS, MS 14,407, fol. 65; *CSPD, 1679–80*, pp. 422, 423; LC, MS 18,124, VII, fols. 34, 35; *Protestant (Domestick) Intelligence*, nos. 77 (30 Mar. 1680), 78 (2 Apr. 1680), 79 (6 Apr. 1680), 81 (13 Apr. 1680); *A Protestant Prentice's Loyal Advice* (1680); Harris, *London Crowds*, pp. 164–8.

13. BL, Althorp Papers C4, Sir William Coventry to the Earl of Halifax, 1 May 1680.

14. Jones, *First Whigs*, pp. 119, 167–73; Evans, *Seventeenth-Century Norwich*, p. 272; Knights, *Politics and Opinion*, pp. 266–8.

15. *Loy. Prot. Int.*, nos. 4 (19 Mar. 1680[/81]), 5 (22 Mar. 1680[/81]); *True Prot. Merc.*, nos. 21 (5–9 Mar. 1680[/81]), 24 (16–19 Mar. 1680[/81]) (which claims that the Bristol Tory address was a forgery); *The Southwark Address* (1681).

16. Hunt. Lib., HA 6014, draft letter, Earl of Huntingdon to [blank], n.d. (1682 or later).

17. Henning, ed., *House of Commons*, I, 201, and III, 266, 305.

18. Susan E. Whyman, *Sociability and Power in Late-Stuart England: The Cultural World of the Verneys, 1660–1720* (Oxford, 1999), pp. 65–7.

19. Harth, *Pen for a Party*, p. 78.

20. Luttrell, I, 73, 77.

21. BL, Add. MSS 27,488, fol. 16.

22. WYAS, MX/R/19/15, Richard Grahme to Sir John Reresby, 6 May 1681.

23. BL, Add. MSS 35,104, fols. 11v, 13v. Cf. *Rawdon Papers*, p. 265.

24. WYAS, MX/R/19/27, John Wentworth to Sir John Reresby, 25 Apr. 1681.

25. *Vox Angliae* (1682), which lists 212 addresses, including one from Barbados.

26. Knights, *Politics and Opinion*, pp. 335–6; HMC, *Ormonde*, NS, VI, 91.

27. Knights, *Politics and Opinion*, p. 338.

28. *Loy. Prot. Int.*, nos. 20 (14 May 1681), 22 (21 May 1681), 46 (13 Aug. 1681); Luttrell, I, 84; Tapsell, 'Parliament and Political Division', p. 247.

29. Burnet, *HOT*, p. 329; *Vox Angliae*, I, 25.

30. *Vox Angliae*, I, 5–6.

31. Ibid., p. 4.

32. Hampshire RO, W/B1/6, fols. 132v–133; *Vox Angliae*, I, 8.

33. Henning, ed., *House of Commons*, III, 176.

34. BL, MS Stowe 746, fol. 48.

35. Dorset RO, DC/LR/A3/1, 'Addresses Book', pp. 1–2; *Vox Angliae*, II, 15.

36. The compilations are *A Collection of Addresses from All Counties* (1681); *Vox Angliae*.

37. Oldmixon, *History of Addresses*, I, 53.

38. *Impartial Account of . . . the Late Addresses*, pp. 9–10.

39. HMC, *Ormonde*, NS, VI, 62; Luttrell, I, 84.

40. Luttrell, I, 85, 91; Morrice, P, 305, 306.

41. *Vox Angliae*, I, 1–2, 4–5, 18, 41, 44.

42. HMC, *Ormonde*, NS, VI, 91; *Loy. Prot. Int.*, no. 51 (30 Aug. 1681); *Vox Angliae*, I, 24; *Lond. Gaz.*, no. 1647 (29 Aug.–1 Sep. 1681).

43. *The Address of above 20,000 of the Loyal Protestant Apprentices of London* (1681); *Just and Modest Vindication of the Many Thousand Loyal Apprentices* (1681); NA, SP 29/416, nos. 136–8; *Imp. Prot. Merc.*, nos. 33 (12–16 Aug. 1681), 39 (2–6 Sep. 1681).

44. Luttrell, I, 94, 99–101; Oldmixon, *History of Addresses*, I, 53; *Lawyer's Demurrer* (1681); *Vindication of Addresses*, p. 4; *Vox Angliae*, I, 14, 18, 21, and II, 19.

45. Devon RO, QS/B, Epiphany 1681[/2], indictment of John Lambert and informations of Christopher Gillard and John Jarring.

46. *Lond. Gaz.*, no. 1636 (21–25 Jul. 1681).

47. *True Prot. Merc.*, no. 48 (18–22 Jun. 1681).

48. Luttrell, I, 128.

49. WYAS, MX/R/17/44–46a, Christopher Tanckred to Sir John Reresby, 27 Jun. 1681; WYAS, MX/R/18/9, Sir Thomas Fairfax to Sir John Reresby, 27 Jun. 1681.

50. BL, Althorp Papers C2, John Wilmington to the Earl of Halifax, 27 Jul. 1681; Luttrell, I, 113.
51. Andrew Coleby, *Central Government and the Localities: Hampshire 1649–1689* (Cambridge, 1987), p. 213.
52. *Loy. Prot. Int.*, no. 36 (9 Jul. 1681).
53. Knights, *Politics and Opinion*, pp. 334–5.
54. BL, Althorp Papers C2, John Wilmington to the Earl of Halifax, 27 Jul. 1681.
55. Knights, *Politics and Opinion*, p. 342.
56. [Edmund Hickeringill], *The History of Whiggism; Or, The Whiggish-Plots, Principles, and Practices* (1682), p. 12.
57. Stater, *Noble Government*, pp. 147–9.
58. [Robert Ferguson] *The Second Part of the Growth of Popery* (1682), p. 297; *Impartial Account of . . . the Late Addresses*, p. 32.
59. WYAS, MX/R/18/51, Duke of Newcastle to Sir John Reresby, 23 Sep. 1681; *Vox Angliae*, II, 5–6.
60. Luttrell, I, 87; *HMC, Ormonde*, NS, VI, 67.
61. *Loy. Prot. Int.*, no. 56 (17 Sep. 1681).
62. *Lond. Gaz.*, nos. 1686 (12–16 Jan. 1681[/2]) to 1759 (25–28 Sep. 1682). The total excludes those from Ireland, hence is lower than that cited by Harth in the note below.
63. Harth, *Pen for a Party*, pp. 150–53.
64. *Lond. Gaz.*, nos. 1738 (13–17 Jul. 1682), 1756 (14–18 Sep. 1682); *Loy. Prot. Int.*, no. 181 (15 Jul. 1682); *Loyal Impartial Mercury*, no. 29 (15–19 Sep. 1682).
65. Reresby, *Memoirs*, p. 246; *The Addresses Importing an Abhorrence* [1682], p. 3; Harth, *Pen for a Party*, p. 150.
66. *CSPD, 1682*, p. 203.
67. Luttrell, I, 212; WYAS, MX/R/22/16, William Russell to Sir John Reresby, 10 Aug. 1682; *Dom. Int. Imp.* no. 126 (3–7 Aug. 1682), 127 (7–10 Aug. 1682); *Loyal London Mercury*, nos. 17 (5–9 Aug. 1682), 18 (9–12 Aug. 1682); LC, MS 18, 124, VIII, fol. 220.
68. *Modest Account of the Present Posture*, p. 6.
69. *CSPD, 1682*, pp. 137–8; Clive Holmes, *Seventeenth-Century Lincolnshire* (Lincoln, 1980), pp. 245–6; Glassey, *Politics*, pp. 53–4; Landau, *Justices of the Peace*, p. 75.
70. *Loy. Prot. Int.*, no. 149 (2 May 1682); *CSPD, 1682*, p. 279.
71. *True Prot. Merc.*, no. 160 (15–19 Jul. 1682); Luttrell, I, 209.
72. WYAS, MX/R/18/20, Thomas Fairfax to Sir John Reresby, 28 Feb. 1681[/2]; WYAS, MX/R/18/65, Thomas Yarburgh to Sir John Reresby, 22 Mar. 1681/2; WYAS, MX/R/20/15, H. Marwood to Sir John Reresby, 23 Mar. 1682[/3]; *Lond. Gaz.*, no. 1707 (27–30 Mar. 1682).

73. WYAS, MX/R/20/19, Duke of Newcastle to Sir John Reresby, 1 Apr. 1682.

74. *CSPD, 1682*, p. 168; P. J. Norrey, 'The Relationship between Central Government and Local Government in Dorset, Somerset and Wiltshire, 1660–1688', unpub. Ph.D. thesis, University of Bristol (1988), p. 276.

75. *CSPD, 1682*, pp. 157–8; *Lond. Gaz.*, no. 1717 (1–4 May 1682).

76. *CSPD, 1682*, p. 102.

77. *Proceedings of the Citizens of Hereford* (1682), p. 1.

78. *CSPD, 1682*, p. 212; Coventry City Archives, BA/H/C/17/2, fol. 281; *Lond. Gaz.*, no. 1720 (11–15 May 1682).

79. Dorset RO, DC/LR/A3/1, 'Addresses Book', pp. 1–4.

80. Berkshire RO, R/AC1/1/15, pp. 264–8.

81. Luttrell, I, 165.

82. LC, MS 18,124, VIII, fol. 64.

83. *HMC, Ormonde*, NS, VI, 335–6.

84. *Loy. Prot. Int.*, no. 30 (14 Jun. 1681); Luttrell, I, 92.

85. Luttrell, I, 130, 134; *Imp. Prot. Merc.*, no. 50 (11–14 Oct. 1681); *Current Intelligence*, no. 55 (29 Oct.–1 Nov. 1681).

86. LC, MS 18,124, VII, fol. 264; *Loy. Prot. Int.*, no. 74 (8 Nov. 1681); Luttrell, I, 142; Fountainhall, *Observer*, I, 51–2; *A Dialogue upon the Burning of the Pope and Presbyter* (1681).

87. Luttrell, I, 144; *Imp. Prot. Merc.*, no. 60 (15–18 Nov. 1681); *Loy. Prot. Int.*, no. 78 (17 Nov. 1681); *CSPD, 1680–81*, p. 571; *HMC, 10th Report*, app. 4, p. 173.

88. *CSPD, 1682*, pp. 119, 124; *Lond. Gaz.*, no. 1703 (13–16 Mar. 1681[/2]); Luttrell, I, 171; *True Prot. Merc.*, no. 125 (15–18 Mar. 1681[/2]).

89. *Imp. Prot. Merc.*, no. 101 (7–11 Apr. 1682); *Loy. Prot. Int.*, no. 140 (11 Apr. 1682).

90. *Loy. Prot. Int.*, no. 143 (18 Apr. 1682).

91. *CSPD, 1682*, p. 165.

92. *Loy. Prot. Int.*, no. 145 (22 Apr. 1680).

93. *True Prot. Merc.*, no. 142 (13–17 May 1682).

94. *Loy. Prot. Int.*, no. 159 (25 May 1682); LC, MS 18,124, VIII, fol. 63; *True Prot. Merc.*, no. 147 (31 May–2 Jun. 1681); *Heraclitus Ridens*, no. 70 (30 May 1682); Luttrell, I, 189.

95. *Loy. Prot. Int.*, no. 162 (1 Jun. 1682); LC, MS 18, 124, VIII, fol. 63.

96. *Loy. Prot. Int.*, no. 165 (8 Jun. 1682); *Dom. Int. Imp.*, no. 108 (1–5 Jun. 1682).

97. L'Estrange, *Observator*, I, no. 151 (8 Jun. 1682).

98. Luttrell, I, 193; *HMC, Kenyon*, p. 142; *A Farther Account from Several Letters of the Continuation of the Cruel Persecution of the People Called Quakers in Bristol* (1682), p. 3.

99. *Loy. Prot. Int.*, no. 222 (19 Oct. 1682).

100. *Dom. Int. Imp.*, no. 146 (12–16 Oct. 1682); *Loyal Impartial Mercury*, no. 37 (13–17 Oct. 1682); *Loy. Prot. Int.*, no. 221 (17 Oct. 1682).

101. *Loy. Prot. Int.*, no. 231 (9 Nov. 1682).

102. Ibid., no. 234 (16 Nov. 1682).

103. Ibid., no. 232 (11 Nov. 1682); *Loyal London Mercury*, no. 24 (8–11 Nov. 1682); *Dom. Int. Imp.*, no. 155 (13–16 Nov. 1682); LC, MS 18, 124, VIII, fols. 259, 260, 262.

104. *CSPD, Jan.–Jun. 1683*, pp. 286–7; Reresby, *Memoirs*, p. 303; L'Estrange, *Observator*, I, no. 357 (14 Jun. 1683).

105. *CSPD, 1682*, p. 165.

106. *Loy. Prot. Int.*, no. 30 (18 Jun. 1681).

107. L'Estrange, *Observator*, I, no. 151 (8 Jun. 1682).

108. *CSPD, 1683*, pp. 286–7; Norrey, 'Relationship', p. 271.

109. LC, MS 18, 124, VIII, fol. 27.

110. Ibid., fol. 40.

111. *Loy. Prot. Int.*, no. 145, (22 Apr. 1682); *Imp. Prot. Merc.*, no. 104 (18–24 Apr. 1682).

112. Luttrell, I, 142; *Imp. Prot. Merc.*, no. 57 (4–8 Nov. 1681); *True Prot. Merc.*, nos. 88 (5–9 Nov. 1681), 89 (9–12 Nov. 1681); *Loy. Prot. Int.*, no. 75 (10 Nov. 1681).

113. *True Prot. Merc.*, nos. 89 (9–12 Nov. 1681), 90 (12–16 Nov. 1681).

114. *HMC, 10th report*, app. 4, p. 174; *CSPD, 1680–81*, p. 571; *True Prot. Merc.*, no. 91 (16–19 Nov. 1681); *The Procession* (1681); Luttrell, I, 144; *Dom. Int. Imp.*, no. 51 (14–17 Nov. 1681); *Imp. Prot. Merc.*, no. 60 (15–18 Nov. 1681).

115. *Loy. Prot. Int.*, no. 82 (26 Nov. 1681); NA, SP 29/417, no. 115; BL, Add. MSS 25,363, fol. 125; *True Prot. Merc.*, no. 93 (23–26 Nov. 1681); *Heraclitus Ridens*, no. 64 (18 Apr. 1681); *HMC, Ormonde*, NS, VI, 237.

116. Luttrell, I, 148.

117. *Loy. Prot. Int.*, no. 85 (3 Dec. 1681).

118. *True Prot. Merc.*, no. 95 (30 Nov.–3 Dec. 1681). For Dorchester's loyal address, see *Vox Angliae . . . The Second Part* (1682), p. 8; Underdown, *Fire from Heaven*, p. 255.

119. For evidence of support for Monmouth in London through to the end of 1682, see Harris, *London Crowds*, ch. 7.

120. *Loy. Prot. Int.*, no. 12 (16 Apr. 1681).

121. *Loy. Prot. Int.*, no. 39 (19 July. 1681); Wiltshire RO, A1/110 T. 1681; Norrey, 'Relationship', p. 195.

122. *HMC, 10th report*, app. 4, p. 174.

123. LC, MS 18,124, VIII, fols. 46–7; Fountainhall, *Observes*, I, 65–6.

124. *CSPD, 1682*, pp. 381–409, *passim* (quote on p. 406); *Loy. Prot. Int.*, no. 212 (26 Sep. 1682); *HMC, Ormonde*, NS, VI, 444; G. W. Keeton, *Lord*

Chancellor Jeffreys and the Stuart Cause (1965), pp. 163–9; H. Montgomery Hyde, *Judge Jeffreys* (1940), pp. 126–8; Clifton, *Last Popular Rebellion*, pp. 135–7; Greaves, *Secrets*, pp. 109–11.

125. L'Estrange, *Observator*, I, no. 205 (14 Sep. 1682); *CSPD, 1682*, pp. 405–6; Luttrell, I, 222.

126. *True Prot. Merc.*, nos. 88 (5–9 Nov. 1681), 89 (9–12 Nov. 1681), 147 (31 May–2 Jun. 1681); *Imp. Prot. Merc.*, nos. 57 (4–8 Nov. 1681), 101 (7–11 Apr. 1681), 105 (21–25 Apr. 1681); *Loy. Prot. Int.*, nos. 75 (10 Nov. 1681), 140 (11 Apr. 1682), 162 (1 Jun. 1682); LC, MS 18,124, VIII, fols. 40, 63.

127. *Loy. Prot. Int.*, no. 221 (17 Oct. 1682).

128. LC, MS 18,124, IX, fol. 331; NA, SP 29/421, no. 67; *Loy. Prot. Int.*, no. 231 (9 Nov. 1682); *Dom. Int. Imp.*, no. 153 (6–9 Nov. 1682); HMC, *12th* Report, VII, 190; WYAS, MX/R/22/27, Ben Rokeby to Sir John Reresby, 7 Nov. 1682; FSL, Newdigate Newsletters, Lc. 1297 (7 Nov. 1682); Morrice, P, 343.

129. *Loy. Prot. Int.*, no. 30 (18 Jun. 1681).

130. *True Prot. Merc.*, no. 151 (14–17 Jun. 1682).

131. Wood, *Life and Times*, III, 42–3; Greaves, *Secrets*, p. 51.

132. L'Estrange, *Observator*, I, no. 68 (5 Nov. 1681).

133. Ibid., no. 411 (27 Sep. 1683).

134. *Loy. Prot. Int.*, no. 19 (10 May 1681).

135. Northleigh, *Triumph of Our Monarchy*, p. 393.

136. *Loy. Prot. Int.*, no. 165 (8 Jun. 1682); *True Prot. Merc.*, no. 151 (14–17 Jun. 1682).

137. William King, *A Great Archbishop of Dublin. William King D.D., 1650–1719*, ed. Sir Charles Simeon King (1906), p. 19.

138. BL, Althorp Papers C2, Sir John Reresby to the Earl of Halifax, 20 Aug. 1681.

139. *CSPD, 1682*, p. 243.

140. Luttrell, I, 252.

141. LC, MS 18,124, VIII, fol. 257; *Vox Juvenilis* (1681), pp. 1, 3; *A Letter of Advice to the Petitioning Apprentices* (1681), p. 1.

142. *Imp. Prot. Merc.*, nos. 15 (10–14 Aug. 1681), 34 (16–19 Jun. 1681). For an extended discussion of this issue, see Tim Harris, 'Perceptions of the Crowd in Later Stuart London', in J. F. Merritt, ed., *Imagining Early Modern London: Perceptions and Portrayals of the City from Stow to Strype 1598–1720* (Cambridge, 2001), pp. 250–72.

143. *Impartial Account of . . . the Late Addresses*, p. 11.

144. Harris, *London Crowds*, ch. 8; Gary S. De Krey, 'Revolution *Redivivus*: 1688–1689 and the Radical Tradition in Seventeenth-Century London Politics', in Lois G. Schwoerer, ed., *The Revolution of 1688–1689: Changing*

Perspectives (Cambridge, 1992), pp. 205–6; Mark Knights, 'London Petitions and Parliamentary Politics in 1679', *Parliamentary History*, 12 (1993), 41; Knights, 'London's "Monster" Petition', pp. 59–64.

145. Stater, *Noble Government*, pp. 142–3; Luttrell, I, 75, 89; Norrey, 'Relationship', p. 190.

146. Glassey, *Politics*, pp. 53–62; Burnet, *HOT*, p. 330.

147. The best modern study is Halliday, *Dismembering*, ch. 6, on which the following account draws. See also his app. A, pp. 351–2.

148. Dalrymple, *Memoirs*, I, 'Part I', p. 22. Cf. Sprat, *True Account*, pp. 7–8.

149. *An Astrological Diary of the Seventeenth Century: Samuel Jeake of Rye 1652–1699*, eds. Michael Hunter and Annabel Gregory (Oxford, 1988), pp. 156–7; Henning, ed., *House of Commons*, II, 500; Morrice, P, 339; NA, PC 2/69, p. 514; *CSPD, 1680–81*, pp. 422, 439, 444, 583; *CSPD, 1682*, pp. 225–6, 229, 234, 366–8; LC, MS 18, 124, VII, fol. 238.

150. Evans, *Seventeenth-Century Norwich*; Jonathan Barry, 'The Politics of Religion in Restoration Bristol', in Harris et al., eds, *Politics of Religion*, pp. 163–89; Newton E. Key, 'Politics beyond Parliament: Unity and Party in the Herefordshire Region during the Restoration Period', unpub. Ph.D. dissertation, Cornell University (1989), p. 523.

151. *ST*, IX, 187–299; Morrice, P, 346; Harris, *London Crowds*, pp. 184–6.

152. R. G. Pickavance, 'The English Boroughs and the King's Government: A Study of the Tory Reaction of 1681–1685', unpub. Ph.D. thesis, Oxford University (1976), pp. 217, 222.

153. Halliday, *Dismembering*, pp. 201–3.

154. *ST*, VIII, 1039–1358 (quote on p. 1069); Jennifer Levin, *The Charter Controversy in the City of London* (1969).

155. Halliday, *Dismembering*, pp. 203, 212–14, 228; Galitz 'Challenge of Stability', pp. 157–8; Dalrymple, *Memoirs*, I, 'Part I', p. 22; Pickavance, 'English Boroughs', pp. 178–9.

156. Evans, *Seventeenth-Century Norwich*, pp. 252, 280–96.

157. *True Prot. Merc.*, no. 183 (4–7 Oct. 1682); *The Case of the Burgesses of Nottingham* (1682); BL, Althorp Papers C2, Sir John Reresby to the Earl of Halifax, 19 Jul. 1682; Luttrell, I, 222–3, 227; *CSPD, 1682*, pp. 437–8; Pickavance, 'English Boroughs', p. 102. For Sherwin's nonconformity, see *CSPD, 1682*, pp. 192–3.

158. BL, Add. MSS 41,803, fols. 45, 53. See also Coventry City Archives, BA/H/C/17/2, fols. 294–5, 303–4.

159. Pickavance, 'English Boroughs', ch. 6.

160. Hunt. Lib., STT 1514, John Nicholls to Sir Richard Temple, 1 Aug. 1684.

161. LC, MS 18,124, IX, fol. 133.

162. *Lond. Gaz.*, no. 2015 (9–12 Mar. 1684/[5]).

163. Ibid., no. 2060 (13–17 Aug. 1685).

164. *Loy. Prot. Int.*, no. 92 (16 Dec. 1681).

165. *True Prot. Merc.*, no. 101 (21–24 Dec. 1681).

166. Joseph Besse, *A Collection of the Sufferings of the People Called Quakers* (2 vols., 1753), I, 68–70, 687; Braithwaite, *Second Period*, pp. 104–5.

167. Morrice, P, 480.

168. Craig W. Horle, *The Quakers and the English Legal System 1660–1688* (Philadelphia, 1988), p. 102.

169. *True Prot. Merc.*, no. 175 (6–9 Sep. 1682).

170. Luttrell, I, 245–6.

171. Braithwaite, *Second Period*, p. 109.

172. *True Prot. Merc.*, no. 125 (15–18 Mar. 1681[/2]).

173. *CSPD, 1682*, p. 601; Braithwaite, *Second Period*, pp. 106–8.

174. *ST*, X, 147–308 (quotes on pp. 150–51).

175. William Penn, *Good Advice to the Church of England* (1687), p. 57.

176. Braithwaite, *Second Period*, p. 115.

177. Thomas Delaune, *A Plea for the Non-Conformists* (1684), p. 11.

178. Longleat House, Coventry MSS, VI, fol. 129.

179. Norrey, 'Relationship', p. 182

180. Knights, *Politics and Opinion*, p. 290; Morrice, P, 300.

181. LC, MS 18,124, VII, fol. 280; *Current Intelligence*, no. 68 (13–17 Dec. 1681); Luttrell, I, 152 (who also alludes to similar scenes at Salisbury).

182. WYAS, MX/R/18/96, John Kaye to Sir John Reresby, 31 Jan. 1681[/2].

183. Luttrell, I, 231.

184. NA, SP 29/422, no. 22; David J. Johnson, *Southwark and the City* (Oxford, 1969), p. 254.

185. L'Estrange, *Observator*, I, no. 153 (12 Jun. 1682).

186. *The Presentments of the Grand Juries from the Counties of Middlesex* (1682).

187. *The Presentment of the Grand Jury of Kent* (1683).

188. BL, Add. MSS 41,803, fol. 71.

189. LC, MS 18,124, IX, fol. 125.

190. Mark Goldie, 'The Hilton Gang and the Purge of London in the 1680s', in Howard Nenner, ed., *Politics and the Imagination in Later Stuart Britain* (Rochester, NY, 1997).

191. Harris, *London Crowds*, pp. 182–3.

192. LC, MS 18,124, VIII, fol. 56.

193. Pickavance, 'English Boroughs', p. 102.

194. Greaves, *Secrets*, p. 91.

195. *CSPD, Jul.–Sep. 1683*, p. 362.

196. Bodl., MS Tanner 34, fol. 75.

197. BL, Althorp Papers C2, Sir John Reresby to the Earl of Halifax, 19 Jul. 1682.

198. LC, MS 18, 124, IX, fol. 8.

199. Ibid., fol. 10.

200. Luttrell, I, 316; LMA, MJ/SBB/417, pp. 59–63.

201. *Current Intelligence*, no. 60 (15–19 Nov. 1681).

202. *CSPD, 1682*, p. 72.

203. *Loy. Prot. Int.*, no. 126 (9 Mar. 1681/[2]).

204. *Loyal Impartial Mercury*, no. 9 (4–7 Jul. 1682); *Loy. Prot. Int.*, no. 223 (21 Oct. 1682); *True Prot. Merc.*, no. 99 (14–17 Dec. 1681).

205. *CSPD, 1682*, p. 25.

206. *Clarendon Correspondence*, I, 192.

207. Jeremy Gregory, *Restoration, Reformation and Reform, 1660–1828: Archbishops of Canterbury and their Diocese* (Oxford, 2000), p. 201.

208. *Loy. Prot. Int.*, no. 208 (16 Sep. 1682).

209. L'Estrange, *Observator*, II, no. 122 (27 Aug. 1684).

210. *Loy. Prot. Int.*, no. 42 (30 Jul. 1681).

211. Ibid., no. 115 (11 Feb. 1681[/2]).

212. Corporation of London RO, Sessions File, Jul. 1681, indictment of Stephen College; *ST*, VIII, 549–724.

213. For the radical conspiracies of the 1680s, see: Greaves, *Secrets*, ch. 6; Richard Ashcraft, *Revolutionary Politics and Locke's 'Two Treatises of Government'* (Princeton, 1986), ch. 8. Unless otherwise stated, my account draws from these two works.

214. Lord Ford Grey, *The Secret History of the Rye House Plot and of Monmouth's Rebellion* (1685), pp. 16–17.

215. Ibid., p. 23.

216. P. Karsten, 'Plotters and Proprietors, 1682–3', *The Historian*, 38 (1976), 474–84.

217. *ST*, IX, 416.

218. John Marshall, 'Resistance and the Second Treatise', in his *John Locke: Resistance, Religion and Responsibility* (Cambridge, 1994), pp. 205–91; Scott, *Restoration Crisis*, pt 3.

219. *ST*, IX, 585–94.

220. Greaves, *Secrets*, pp. 219–29.

221. 'Laurence Braddon', in *DNB*; *CSPD, Jul.–Sep. 1683*, pp. 174, 215, 341–3, 367, 372, 425; *CSPD, 1683–4*, p. 24; Morrice, P, 385, 432; *ST*, IX, 1127–1352 (see p. 1230 for the bail). Braddon's bail was a personal bond of £6,000 plus two sureties at £3,000 each. Braddon himself claimed that the sureties he had to give for his good behaviour upon his release in fact also totalled £12,000.

222. This account of Monmouth is based on my article in the *Oxford DNB*.

223. Morrice, P, 392.

224. Morrice, P, 406; *ST*, XI, 1099.

225. Dalrymple, *Memoirs*, I, 'Part I', p. 110.

226. *ST*, X, 106–24; Luttrell, I, 310–13. See Sprat, *True Account*, pp. 140–44.

227. *ST*, IX, 1333–72; Morrice, P, 400, 421, 431.

228. *ST*, X, 126–48; Dalrymple, *Memoirs*, I, 'Part I', p. 60.

229. North, *Lives*, I, 332.

230. Charles II, *His Majesties Declaration . . . Concerning the Treasonable Conspiracy* (1683), pp. 4–6.

231. Luttrell, I, 278–9.

232. *The Judgment and Decree of the University of Oxford* (1683).

233. As listed in *Lond. Gaz.*, nos. 1839 (2–5 Jul. 1683) to 1894 (10–14 Jan. 1683[/4]).

234. Centre for Kentish Studies, U275/A4; Luttrell, I, 271; *Lond. Gaz.*, nos. 1844 (19–23 Jul. 1683), 1860 (13–17 Sep. 1683), 1866 (4–8 Oct. 1683).

235. Berkshire RO, R/AC1/1/16, p. 16.

236. *HMC, Ormonde*, NS, VII, 87, 95, 102.

237. Luttrell, I, 264; *Lond. Gaz.*, no. 1839 (2–5 Jul. 1683).

238. Dorset RO, DC/LR/A3/1, pp. 5–6.

239. Luttrell, I, 276–7,

240. BL, MS Stowe 746, fols. 71–2; *Lond. Gaz.*, no. 1863 (24–27 Sep. 1683).

241. Luttrell, I, 279.

242. LC, MS 18,124, VIII, fol. 385; *CSPD, Jul.–Sep. 1683*, p. 395.

243. Wood, *Life and Times*, III, 72.

244. L'Estrange, *Observator*, I, no. 406 (19 Sep. 1683).

245. Berkshire RO, R/AC1/1/16, p. 19.

246. *CSPD, Jul.–Sep. 1683*, p. 398.

247. L'Estrange, *Observator*, I, no. 411 (27 Sep. 1683).

248. *CSPD*, Jul.–Sep. 1683, p. 29.

249. Ibid., p. 392.

250. L'Estrange, *Observator*, no. 406 (19 Sep. 1683).

251. *CSPD, Jul.–Sep. 1683*, p. 389.

252. Michael Mullett, 'Popular Culture and Popular Politics: Some Regional Case Studies', in Clyve Jones, ed., *Britain in the First Age of Party, 1680–1750: Essays Presented to Geoffrey Holmes* (1987), pp. 140–41.

253. Luttrell, I, 279.

254. L'Estrange, *Observator*, I, no. 420 (13 Oct. 1683).

255. *A True Account of the Presentment of the Grand Jury for the Last General Assizes held for the County of Northampton* (1683); L'Estrange, *Observator*, I, no. 385 (11 Aug. 1683); Morrice, P, 378; *CSPD, Jul.–Sep. 1683*, p. 307 (which lists the total as 52).

256. Luttrell, I, 322.

257. L'Estrange, *Observator*, I, no. 420 (13 Oct. 1683); Morrice, P, 378; Keeton, *Jeffreys*, p. 170; Luttrell, I, 284.

258. L'Estrange, *Observator*, I, no. 420 (13 Oct. 1683); Luttrell, I, 283–4.

259. L'Estrange, *Observator*, I, no. 444 (26 Nov. 1683).

260. Somerset RO, DD/SF/1697.

261. Robert Willman, 'The Origins of "Whig" and "Tory" in English Political Language', *HJ*, 17 (1974), 247–64.

262. Hunt. Lib., HA 9614, newsletter, 13 Dec. 1681.

263. *Speech of Robert Clerk*.

264. *CSPD, 1682*, p. 525.

265. Magdalene College Library, Cambridge, Ferrar Papers 615, 23 Mar. 1682.

266. *True Prot. Merc.*, no. 176 (9–13 Sep. 1682).

267. *CSPD, 1682*, pp. 381–2.

268. *Loy. Prot. Int.*, no. 75 (10 Nov. 1681).

269. *CSPD, 1682*, p. 54.

270. *The Works of George Savile, Marquis of Halifax*, ed. Mark N. Brown (3 vols., Oxford, 1989), I, 178–249.

271. L'Estrange, *Observator*, I, no. 240 (13 Nov. 1682).

272. *A Collection of Cases and other Discourses lately written to Recover the Dissenters to the Communion of the Church of England, by some Divine of the City of London* (2 vols., 1685).

273. L'Estrange, *Observator*, I, no. 242 (16 Nov. 1682).

274. Ibid., no. 240 (13 Nov. 1682).

275. Ibid., no. 264 (27 Dec. 1682).

276. Holdsworth, *English Law*, VI, 509.

277. North, *Lives*, II, 101–2.

278. *Character of a Church-Trimmer* (1683).

279. *An Account of the Design of the Late Narrative, Entituled, The Dissenters New Plot* [1690].

280. Thomas Hunt, *A Defence of the Charter* [1683], p. 26; John Dryden, *The Vindication; Or, The Parallel of the French Holy-League and the English League and Covenant* (1683), p. 26.

281. Nicholas Adee, *A Plot for the Crown, In a Visitation-Sermon, At Cricklade, May the Fifteenth, 1682* (1685), p. 16.

282. L'Estrange, *Observator*, I, no. 247 (25 Nov. 1682).

283. Ibid., no. 264 (27 Dec. 1682).

284. *Presentments of the Grand-Jury for the Town and Borough of Southwark* (1683).

285. Tim Harris, 'Was the Tory Reaction Popular?: Attitudes of Londoners towards the Persecution of Dissent, 1681–6', *London Journal*, 13 (1988),

106–20; Mark Goldie and John Spurr, 'Politics and the Restoration Parish: Edward Fowler and the Struggle for St. Giles Cripplegate', *English Historical Review*, 109 (1994), 572–96; John Spurr, '"Latitudinarianism" and the Restoration Church', *HJ*, 31 (1988), 61–82.
286. Edward Fowler, *The Great Wickedness, And Mischievous Effects of Slandering* (1685), preface; Edward Fowler, *A Discourse of Offences. Delivered in Two Sermons* (1683), epistle dedicatory; 'Edward Fowler', in *DNB*.

6 From Bothwell Bridge to Wigtown

1. L'Estrange, *Observator*, I, no. 273 (17 Jan. 1683).
2. Wodrow, *Sufferings*, II, 1.
3. Brown, *Kingdom or Province?*, p. 158.
4. *A Further Account of the Proceedings against the Rebels in Scotland* (1679), p. 1.
5. Wodrow, *Sufferings*, II, 74, 77–8; Hewison, *Covenanters*, II, 317; Houston, *Social Change*, p. 52.
6. BL, Add. MSS 63,057B, fol. 53.
7. Wodrow, *Sufferings*, II, 75–6 and app. 31, p. 27.
8. Wodrow, *Sufferings*, II, 81 and apps. 31–3, pp. 27–9; Steele, III, no. 2470.
9. *Lond. Gaz.*, nos. 1463 (24–27 Nov. 1679), 1467 (8–11 Dec. 1679); Greaves, *Secrets*, pp. 66–7.
10. NLS, Wod. Oct. XXIX, fol. 190; Wodrow, *Sufferings*, II, 73, 112–16. For a general account of the sufferings of the Presbyterians for the period 1679–85, see Cowan, *Covenanters*, chs. 7–8.
11. See above, pp. 198–9.
12. *RPCS, 1678–80*, pp. 264–5; Steele, III, no. 2467; Wodrow, *Sufferings*, II, 96. For the 1670 Conventicle Act, see *APS*, VIII, 9–10.
13. NLS, Wod. Qu. XXX, fol. 63.
14. *Lauderdale Papers*, III, 181–2. For the act of 1661, see *APS*, VII, 44–6.
15. *Lauderdale Papers*, III, 182–5; *CSPD, 1679–80*, p. 296; *Life of James II*, I, 576–8; Wodrow, *Sufferings*, II, 111.
16. *Lond. Gaz.*, nos. 1464 (21 Nov.–1 Dec. 1679), 1465 (1–4 Dec. 1679); HMC, *Dartmouth*, I, 38; *Life of James II*, I, 576; Wodrow, *Sufferings*, II, 110.
17. HMC, *Dartmouth*, I, 41; Dalrymple, *Memoirs*, I, 'Review', p. 332; Buckroyd, *Church and State*, pp. 132–3; Hutton, *Charles II*, p. 387.
18. Burnet, *HOT*, p. 337.
19. *CSPD, 1679–80*, p. 399.
20. *RPCS, 1678–80*, pp. 399–400; *Lond. Gaz.*, no. 1489 (23–26 Feb. 1679[/80]).

21. *RPCS, 1678–80*, pp. 381–2; *Lond. Gaz.*, no. 1485 (9–12 Feb. 1679[/80]).

22. *RPCS, 1678–80*, pp. 459–62; Wodrow, *Sufferings*, II, 119–22; *A Collection of Letters Addressed by Prelates and Individuals of High Rank in Scotland and by Two Bishops of Soder and Man to Sancroft Archbishop of Canterbury*, ed. William Nelson Clarke (Edinburgh, 1848), pp. 8–9, 13–15; Cowan, *Covenanters*, p. 107.

23. See above, pp. 198–9.

24. Steele, III, no. 2488; *RPCS, 1678–80*, pp. 482–5.

25. *RPCS, 1678–80*, pp. 511, 573–5, 583; Bodl., MS Carte 228, fol. 159; NLS, Wod. Qu. XXX, fol. 80v; Fountainhall, *Decisions*, I, 111, 117; Fountainhall, *Observes*, pp. 7–8, 26–7; NLS, MS 7009, fols. 68, 70; [Shields], *Hind Let Loose*, pp. 195–6; *Edinburgh Gazette*, no. 2 (7–14 Dec. 1680); Burnet, *HOT*, pp. 337–8; Wodrow, *Sufferings*, II, 180–83; Cowan, *Covenanters*, pp. 105–6; Greaves, *Secrets*, pp. 69–75.

26. Fountainhall, *Decisions*, I, 73.

27. *RPCS, 1681–2*, pp. 1, 21.

28. *ST*, VIII, 125–8 (quote on p. 126); Fountainhall, *Decisions*, I, 108; Wodrow, *Sufferings*, II, 152; *RPCS, 1678–80*, pp. 439–40, 520–21, 535–6; BL, Add. MSS 32,095, fol. 206; *CSPD, 1679–80*, p. 577. For the act of 1587, see *APS*, III, 450.

29. *RPCS, 1678–80*, p. 565.

30. *A True Narrative of the Reception of their Royal Highnesses at their Arrival in Scotland* [Edinburgh, London and Dublin, 1680]; *RPCS, 1678–80*, pp. 565–7; Wodrow, *Sufferings*, II, 153; *Lond. Gaz.*, no. 1561 (1–4 Nov. 1680).

31. See above, pp. 187–8.

32. Wodrow, *Sufferings*, II, 153.

33. *Letters to Sancroft*, pp. 21–4.

34. *RPCS, 1678–80*, pp. 567–8; Fountainhall, *Decisions*, I, 114.

35. NLS, Wod. Qu. XXX, fol. 81; Wodrow, *Sufferings*, II, 154.

36. *A True and Exact Relation of His Royal Highness, James Duke of York and Albany, his Progress from Edinburgh to Linlithgow, from thence to Strivling [sic]* (Edinburgh, 1681), pp. 2, 3; Wodrow, *Sufferings*, II, 219; *HMC, Dartmouth*, I, 56.

37. *Lond. Gaz.*, no. 1623 (6–9 Jun. 1681); Fountainhall, *Observes*, p. 40; Marguerite Wood and Helen Armet, *Extracts from the Records of the Burgh of Edinburgh 1681 to 1689* (Edinburgh, 1984), pp. 15–16; Luttrell, I, 94; Houston, *Social Change*, p. 49.

38. *Life of James II*, I, 683.

39. NLS, Wod. Qu. XXX, fol. 94.

40. Fountainhall, *Decisions*, I, 146, 150–51, 157; *HMC, Dartmouth*, I, 66;

Sir George Mackenzie, *A True and Plain Account of the Discoveries made in Scotland, of the Late Conspiracies against His Majesty and the Government* (1685, London edn), pp. 1, 3.

41. Fountainhall, *Observes*, pp. 41–2, 46–7; Burnet, *HOT*, p. 338; *Life of James II*, I, 683–4. Some of York's supporters suggested that he should be given the title of viceroy, as more suitable to his station than that of commissioner, but it was objected that viceroys were only ever sent to conquered kingdoms, never to independent crowns. For the acts of 1567 and 1609, see *APS*, III, 24, and IV, 429–30.

42. Fountainhall, *Decisions*, I, 157; *Lond. Gaz.*, no. 1640 (4–8 Aug. 1681).

43. Steele, III, no. 2502; *RPCS, 1681–2*, pp. 93–4.

44. Fountainhall, *Decisions*, I, 148; Wodrow, *Sufferings*, II, 183–7; *ST*, X, 791–920; Greaves, *Secrets*, p. 75.

45. *APS*, VIII, 236; *His Majesties Gracious Letter to His Parliament of Scotland: With the Speech of His Royal Highness the Duke . . . Together with the Parliaments most Loyal and Dutiful Answer* (1681).

46. BL, Add. MSS 11,252, fol. 8.

47. WYAS, MX/R/19/3: 'Account of the Proceedings of the Scottish Parliament', 10–13 Aug. 1681.

48. NLS, Adv. MS 31.6.15, fols. 206–9; NAS, PA 7/11, pp. 299–300, 305; Wodrow, *Sufferings*, II, 190; [Sir James Stewart], *The Case of the Earl of Argyle* ([Edinburgh?], 1683), pp. 1–2; *ST*, VIII, 846–51; Mackenzie, *True and Plain Account*, p. 2.

49. NAS, PA 7/11, pp. 29, 307; *APS*, VIII, 238.

50. *Lond. Gaz.*, no. 1643 (15–18 Aug. 1681); Burnet, *HOT*, p. 338; Wodrow, *Sufferings*, II, 190–91.

51. *APS*, VIII, 238; *An Act Acknowledging and Asserting the Right of Succession to the Imperial Crown of Scotland* (1681); *Lond. Gaz.*, no. 1644 (18–22 Aug. 1681).

52. *APS*, III, 23.

53. Fountainhall, *Decisions*, I, 157; Colquhoun, 'Issue', pp. 157–60. For the act of 1567, see *APS*, III, 23.

54. Fountainhall, *Decisions*, I, 149.

55. *APS*, VIII, 240–41.

56. Ibid., p. 247.

57. NLS, Adv. 31.6.15, fol. 242v.

58. Fountainhall, *Decisions*, I, 152.

59. *APS*, VIII, 242.

60. Ibid., pp. 350–51.

61. Ibid., p. 352.

62. BL, Add. MSS 63,057B, fol. 61v.

63. NAS, PA 7/11, pp. 32–3, 282; Burnet, *HOT*, p. 340; *Life of James II*, I, 696.

64. All quotes from the Test Act are from *APS*, VIII, 243–5.

65. *APS*, VIII, 355.

66. [Stewart], *Case of . . . Argyle*, p. 3; *ST*, VIII, 857–9; Wodrow, *Sufferings*, II, 195; Burnet, *HOT*, 340.

67. NLS, Adv. 31.6.15, fol. 242.

68. Sir James Dalrymple of Stair, *An Apology . . . for Himself* (Edinburgh, 1690), sig. Av.

69. For the 1560 Confession of Faith and the ratification of 1567, see *APS*, II, 526–34, and III, 14–22.

70. *RPCS, 1681–2*, p. 198; Wodrow, *Sufferings*, II, 196; [Stewart], *Case of . . . Argyle*, p. 38; *Lond. Gaz.*, no. 1656 (29 Sep.–3 Oct. 1681).

71. Stair, *Apology*, sigs. A2–A3; *ST*, X, 967–8.

72. *RPCS, 1681–2*; pp. 202, 229, 233–4, 238, 306; Morrice, P, 315, 325; Fountainhall, *Decisions*, I, 158; Wodrow, *Sufferings*, II, 196–7, 224–5; Greaves, *Secrets*, p. 80.

73. *Lauderdale Papers*, III, 192–4; [Stewart], *Case of . . . Argyle*, p. 1; *ST*, VIII, 844–6; Burnet, *HOT*, 338.

74. Mackenzie, *True and Plain Account*, p. 3; Sprat, *True Account*, p. 12.

75. *RPCS, 1681–2*, pp. 242–5; Fountainhall, *Observes*, pp. 53–5; Fountainhall, *Decisions*, I, 160, 166–7; BL, Add. MSS 32,095, fol. 205v; Hunt. Lib. HA 9614, newsletter, 13 Dec.1681; *ST*, VIII, 843–990; [Stewart], *Case of . . . Argyle*; HMC, *Ormonde*, NS, VI, 244–5, 281–2; Burnet, *HOT*, pp. 342–3; Wodrow, *Sufferings*, II, 205–17 and apps. 69–71, pp. 63–79; *Life of James II*, I, 708–10; Andrew Lang, *Sir George Mackenzie, King's Advocate, of Rosehaugh, His Life and Times 1636(?)–1691* (1909), ch. 14; John Willcock, *A Scots Earl in Covenanting Times: Being the Life and Times of Archibald, 9th Earl of Argyll (1629–1685)* (Edinburgh, 1907), chs. 12–14.

76. *An Account of the Arraignment, Tryal, Escape, and Condemnation, of the Dog of Heriot's Hospital in Scotland* (1682); Fountainhall, *Observes*, p. 55 and app. 4, pp. 303–10 (quote on p. 306); *Lond. Gaz.*, no. 1688 (19–23 Jan. 1681[/2]). Cf. [Northleigh], *Parallel*, p. 5.

77. Wodrow, *Sufferings*, II, 199–201, 'Ministers of Aberdeen their Objections against the Test'; *RPCS, 1681–2*, pp. 254–5.

78. *ST*, VIII, 894–6. See also 'A Paraphrase of the Test emitted by one of the conformed Clergy', in [Stewart], *Case of . . . Argyle*, pp. 28–35.

79. *RPCS, 1681–2*, p. 239.

80. *True Prot. Merc.*, no. 96 (3–7 Dec. 1681); *Letters to Sancroft*, p. 54.

81. Wodrow, *Sufferings*, II, 203; Burnet, *HOT*, pp. 341–2; Fountainhall, *Observes*, p. 53.

82. *RPCS, 1681–2*, pp. 253, 262, 274–5.

83. Ibid., pp. 301, 343.

84. Wodrow, *Sufferings*, II, 203; Burnet, *HOT*, pp. 341–2; Cowan, *Covenanters*, p. 109; Colquhoun, 'Issue', pp. 213–14.

85. *RPCS, 1681–2*, pp. 398–400, 422–3; Fountainhall, *Decisions*, I, 176–7, 182–3.

86. *RPCS, 1681–2*, pp. 449, 459–61, 588; Fountainhall, *Decisions*, I, 185; Wodrow, *Sufferings*, II, 234–5; *True Prot. Merc.*, no. 152 (17–21 Jun. 1682).

87. *RPCS, 1681–2*, p. 306.

88. Wodrow, *Sufferings*, II, 224.

89. *CSPD, 1682*, p. 27.

90. *RPCS, 1681–2*, pp. 220, 235, 249, 255–7, 263, 265, 273–4, 421, 504, 548, 597; Fountainhall, *Decisions*, I, 161, 164.

91. *RPCS, 1681–2*, p. 304.

92. *CSPD, 1682*, p. 185.

93. *Lond. Gaz.*, no. 1661 (17–20 Oct. 1681); Luttrell, I, 138; Wodrow, *Sufferings*, II, 219.

94. *Loy. Prot. Int.*, no. 69 (27 Oct. 1681); Fountainhall, *Observes*, pp. 49–50.

95. Fountainhall, *Observes*, p. 51; *Current Intelligence*, no. 61 (19–22 Nov. 1681).

96. *Loy. Prot. Int.*, no. 129 (16 Mar. 1681[/2]); *CSPD, 1682*, p. 124.

97. Luttrell, I, 185.

98. *Loy. Prot. Int.*, no. 165 (8 Jun. 1682).

99. Brown, *Kingdom or Province?*, p. 165; Macinnes, 'Repression and Conciliation'; John L. Roberts, *Clan, King and Covenant: History of the Highland Clans from the Civil War to the Glencoe Massacre* (Edinburgh, 2000), pp. 161–3. Both John Callow, *The Making of King James II* (Stroud, 2000), pp. 288–90, and *RPCS, 1681–2*, pp. xviii–xx, present less optimistic views.

100. *The Copy of a Letter Sent from Scotland, To His Grace The Lord Archbishop of Canterbury* (Edinburgh, 1682); *Loy. Prot. Int.*, no. 132 (23 Mar. 1681[/2]). Cf. *Letters to Sancroft*, pp. 56–7.

101. *RPCS, 1681–2*, p. 432.

102. *Plea for Succession*, p. 2. See above, pp. 251–2.

103. Burnet, *HOT*, p. 343; [Andrewes], *Gentle Reflection*, p. 7; *Modest Account of the Present Posture*, pp. 5, 9.

104. Morrice, P, 334, 427, 437, 441; *HMC, Ormonde*, NS, VI, 192; Hutton, *Charles II*, pp. 413–14; Cowan, *Covenanters*, p. 114.

105. Fountainhall, *Observes*, pp. 127–35; Morrice, P, 441; Burnet, *HOT*, pp. 377–8; Hutton, *Charles II*, pp. 430–31.

106. *CSPD, Jan.–Jun. 1683*, p. 243.

107. Fountainhall, *Observes*, p. 87.

108. Wodrow, *Sufferings*, II, 222; Greaves, *Secrets*, p. 81.

109. NLS, Wod. Qu. XXXVIII, fols. 5v–6; Edinburgh University Library, La. II. 89, fols. 137–8; Wodrow, Sufferings, II, 222; [Shields], *Hind Let Loose*, p. 143. For the Rutherglen and Sanquhar declarations, see above, pp. 196, 198.

110. *RPCS, 1681–2*, pp. 310–13, 329–30, 333–4, 342; Wodrow, *Sufferings*, II, 227; *CSPD, 1682*, pp. 39, 43; Fountainhall, *Decisions*, I, 169–71; Fountainhall, *Observes*, p. 58; *Letters to Sancroft*, p. 54; Morrice, P, 324; Luttrell, I, 162; *True Prot. Merc.*, nos. 115 (8–11 Feb. 1681[/2]), 124 (11–15 Mar. 1681[/2]); *Loy. Prot. Int.*, no. 116 (11 Feb. 1681[/2]); HMC, *Dartmouth*, I, 45; [Shields], *Hind Let Loose*, pp. 143, 197; [Monro], *History*, p. 42.

111. *RPCS, 1681–2*, pp. 326–7, 358, 362, 368–9, 373.

112. *True Prot. Merc.*, no. 153 (21–24 Jun. 1682).

113. Fountainhall, *Decisions*, I, 185.

114. Wodrow, *Sufferings*, II, 236–7, 279; [Rule], *Vindication . . . Being an Answer to a Paper*, p. 27; *RPCS, 1681–2*, pp. 572–4; *RPCS, 1683–4*, pp. 244, 302–3.

115. *RPCS, 1683–4*, p. 70; HMC, *Hamilton*, p. 166.

116. *RPCS, 1683–4*, pp. 133–8; Burnet, *HOT*, pp. 93–5.

117. *CSPD, 1682*, p. 485.

118. *Loy. Prot. Int.*, no. 170 (20 Jun. 1682).

119. Fountainhall, *Observes*, p. 87.

120. Wodrow, *Sufferings*, II, chs. 6–7, *passim*; Cowan, *Covenanters*, pp. 112–17; Greaves, *Secrets*, pp. 82–4.

121. Fountainhall, *Decisions*, I, 201.

122. Ibid., pp. 183–4, 187. Fountainhall, however, thought the soldiers were guilty of hamesucken – 'the felonious seeking and invasion of a person in his own dwelling house' – the penalty for which was death.

123. HMC, *Hamilton*, p. 167. Cf. NLS, MS 7009, fol. 121, for the Marquis of Tweeddale's tenants in Peebles bringing depositions against Meldrum for quartering of troops.

124. See, for example *RPCS, 1681–2*, pp. 327–9, 372, 392, 487; *True Prot. Merc.*, no. 133 (12–15 Apr. 1682).

125. *Loy. Prot. Int.*, no. 128 (14 Mar. 1681[/2]; *CSPD, 1682*, p. 118. See above, p. 243.

126. Fountainhall, *Observes*, p. 96.

127. ST, X, 990–1046; Wodrow, *Sufferings*, II, 385–6; NAS, PA7/12, pp. 7–9, 14–23; *Melvilles and Leslies*, I, 199–201.

128. *CSPD, 1683–4*, pp. 65–7.

129. For the trials of the Scottish Rye House plotters, see Greaves, *Secrets*, pp. 241–6.

130. *ST*, X, 919–88; Wodrow, *Sufferings*, II, 379–85; Burnet, *HOT*, pp. 376–7; NAS, PA7/12, p. 6.

131. *CSPD, 1684–5*, p. 55.

132. Wodrow, *Sufferings*, II, 167.

133. *RPCS, 1684*, pp. 68–9, 73, 94, 98–9; [Sir George Mackenzie], *The Laws and Customes of Scotland* (2nd edn, Edinburgh, 1699), pp. 261–2, 272–3; Sir James Dalrymple of Stair, *The Institutions of the Law of Scotland* (1693), p. 699; Wodrow, *Sufferings*, II, 386; Burnet, *HOT*, p. 378; John Langbein, *Torture and the Law of Proof* (Chicago, 1977), esp. pp. 12–16. Both Mackenzie and Stair concurred that defendants could not be required to swear against themselves when life and limb was at stake.

134. For further details concerning Spence, see *Oxford DNB*.

135. Fountainhall, *Decisions*, I, 299–301; Fountainhall, *Observes*, p. 136; Morrice, P, 441–2; Burnet, *HOT*, pp. 378–9; Wodrow, *Sufferings*, II, 386–7; *HMC, Ormonde*, NS, VII, 271–2.

136. *RPCS, 1684*, pp. 142–4, 159–60; Fountainhall, *Decisions*, I, 302–3; *State Papers and Letters addressed to William Carstares*, ed. Joseph Maccormick (Edinburgh, 1774), pp. 18–20; Mackenzie, *Plain and True Account*, p. 28; Wodrow, *Sufferings*, II, 387–94; *ST*, X, 683–96; Burnet, *HOT*, p. 379.

137. *ST*, X, 647–724; NAS, RH13/20, pp. 332–8; Wodrow, *Sufferings, II*, 394–400; Burnet, *HOT*, pp. 379–80; Luttrell, I, 324; *Carstares State Papers*, pp. 20, 793. For Baillie, see *Oxford DNB*.

138. *RPCS, 1683–4*, pp. 272–3, 318–19, 504; *HMC, Hamilton*, p. 165.

139. *RPCS, 1684*, pp. 55–6; Wodrow, *Sufferings*, II, 343–4.

140. Wodrow, *Sufferings*, II, 347–8.

141. Ibid., pp. 400–403; BL, Add. MSS 37,951, fols. 67–8; Fountainhall, *Decisions*, I, 301–3; Fountainhall, *Observes*, p. 138.

142. Wodrow, *Sufferings*, II, 376–8; Fountainhall, *Decisions*, I, 299, 301; Fountainhall, *Observes*, p. 136; *HMC, Ormonde*, NS, VII, 263; Hewison, *Covenanters*, II, 434–5; Cowan, *Covenanters*, pp. 118–19; *RPCS, 1684*, pp. xii–xiv and *passim*.

143. Wodrow, *Sufferings*, II, 363–4.

144. Burnet, *HOT*, pp. 377–8; Wodrow, *Sufferings*, II, 336–7. For the 1663 Recusancy Act, see *APS*, VII, 455.

145. Wodrow, *Sufferings*, II, 339.

146. Ibid., p. 445.

147. Ibid., pp. 406–7, 416–17.

148. NAS, GD 224/171/1, p. 117.

149. Wodrow, *Sufferings*, II, 430–31 and app. 99, pp. 137–8; [Monro], *History*, p. 43.

150. Fountainhall, *Observes*, p. 141; Fountainhall, *Decisions*, I, 311; Luttrell, I, 322; Wodrow, *Sufferings*, II, 431–2; BL, Add. MSS 28,875, fol. 411.

151. Wodrow, *Sufferings*, II, 449, 467–8; Fountainhall, *Decisions*, I, 320; *RPCS, 1684–5*, p. 109. Wodrow's account of the murder of Peirson is that a contingent of Society People knocked on the minister's door simply to invite him to come and talk with some of their friends about his persecuting them; Peirson attacked them with arms, so they shot him in self-defence.

152. Fountainhall, *Decisions*, I, 309; Wodrow, *Sufferings*, II, 431; *RPCS, 1684–5*, p. 25.

153. *RPCS, 1684–5*, pp. 32–3, 35–6.

154. Ibid., pp. 48–50, 51–2.

155. Ibid., pp. 84–6.

156. Ibid., p. 107.

157. Rosalind Mitchison, *Lordship to Patronage; Scotland, 1603–1745* (1983), p. 78.

158. NLS, Wod. Qu. XXXVIII, fol. 49.

159. Wodrow, *Sufferings*, II, 505–7; [Gilbert Rule], *A Vindication of the Church of Scotland; Being an Answer to Five Pamphlets* (1691), II, 38–9; Cowan, *Covenanters*, pp. 126–7.

160. *True Prot. Merc.*, no. 182 (30 Sep.–4 Oct. 1682); Wodrow, *Sufferings*, II, 289.

161. [Shields], *Hind Let Loose*, pp. 198–9.

162. *The Scottish Inquisition* (1689); *Brief Account of the Sufferings of the Church of Scotland* (1690), esp. pp. 9, 15; [Rule], *Vindication . . . Being an Answer to a Paper*, p. 27.

163. Mackenzie, *Vindication*, p. 8.

164. HMC, *Ormonde*, NS, VII, 82.

165. Fountainhall, *Observes*, p. 88; *Letters to Sancroft*, pp. 34, 57.

166. HMC, *Hamilton*, p. 166.

167. NAS, GD 224/171/1, p. 115.

168. L'Estrange, *Observator*, I, no. 273 (17 Jan. 1682[/3]).

169. Ibid., no. 293 (21 Feb. 1682[/3]).

170. Fountainhall, *Decisions*, I, 301.

171. [Thomas Morer], *An Account of the Present Persecution of the Church in Scotland* (1690), pp. 7–8.

172. HMC, *Hamilton*, p. 166.

173. Fountainhall, *Observes*, p. 87. Cf. Burnet, *HOT*, p. 345.

174. Jackson, *Restoration Scotland*, pp. 154–5. For the Scottish settlement in North America, see Ned Landsman, *Scotland and its First American Colony 1683–1785* (Princeton, 1985); Ned Landsman, 'Nation, Migration and the Province in the First British Empire: Scotland and the Americas 1600–1800', *American Historical Review*, 104 (1999), 463–75.

175. Sir George Mackenzie, *Jus Regium* (2nd edn, 1684), pp. 13, 41, 47, 67.

176. Ibid., pp. 50–51, 54.

177. Ibid., pp. 80–81, 86.
178. Ibid., pp. 141, 154, 162, 184–6.

7 Malcontents and Loyalists

1. Speech of Archbishop Boyle to the Earl of Arran, Dublin, 3 May 1682: *HMC, Ormonde*, NS, VI, 360–61.
2. *English Historical Documents*, vol. 18: *1660–1714*, ed. Andrew Browning (Oxford, 1953), pp. 744–5; Cullen, 'Economic Trends'; Simms, 'The Restoration', pp. 443–5, 448; J. G. Simms, *War and Politics in Ireland, 1649–1730*, ed. D.W. Hayton and Gerard O'Brien (1986), pp. 49–63; Foster, *Modern Ireland*, pp. 126–37.
3. Steele, II, no. 889; *HMC, Ormonde*, II, 350.
4. Steele, II, nos. 891, 895, 897; *HMC, Ormonde*, II, 352, 356.
5. Steele, II, nos. 898, 903, 913, 917; *HMC, Ormonde*, II, 357, 359.
6. Beckett, *Making*, pp. 133–4; Connolly, *Religion*, p. 32; Hutton, *Charles II*, pp. 362, 370.
7. TCD, 1995–2008/1b; BL, Sloane MS 1008, fol. 197; *CSPD, 1679–80*, pp. 71–3.
8. BL, Add. MSS 21,135, fols. 62–3.
9. TCD, 1995–2008/3a.
10. BL, Add. MSS 32,095, fol. 186.
11. *HMC, Ormonde*, II, 291–2; David Fitzgerald, *A Narrative of the Irish Plot, for the Betraying that Kingdom into the Hands of the French* (1680).
12. NLI, MS 4201, p. 257.
13. Steele, II, no. 904.
14. *Loy. Prot. Int.*, no. 40 (23 Jul. 1681); *True Prot. Merc.*, no. 27 (26–30 Mar. 1681); *HMC, Ormonde*, NS, VI, 1, 38–9, 42, 43, 45, 57, 380, and VII, 174, 181.
15. Gillespie, 'Presbyterian Revolution', p. 165; Greaves, *God's Other Children*, pp. 115–17.
16. *CSPD*, 1678, pp. 428–9; *HMC, Ormonde*, NS, IV, 206.
17. *CSPD, 1679–80*, pp. 173, 179; Steele, II, no. 906.
18. Kilroy, *Protestant Dissent*, pp. 236–8.
19. Reid, *History of the Presbyterian Church*, II, app. 10, pp. 571–3; *CSPD, 1679–80*, pp. 193–4, 254–5, 576–7; Greaves, *Secrets*, p. 374, n. 57; Greaves, *God's Other Children*, p. 118; Kilroy, *Protestant Dissent*, p. 237.
20. BL, MS Sloane 1008, fol. 275.
21. Ibid., fol. 301.
22. Bodl., MS Carte 39, fols. 363–4.
23. *Loy. Prot. Int.*, no. 125 (7 Mar. 1681[/2]).
24. *True Prot. Merc.*, no. 174 (2–6 Sep. 1682).

25. *Cal. Anc. Rec. Dub.*, V, xxvii, 216–17; *HMC, Ormonde*, NS, VI, 64.
26. *Loy. Prot. Int.*, no. 1 (9 Mar. 1680[/81]).
27. *Loy. Prot. Int.*, no. 143 (18 Apr. 1682).
28. *HMC, Ormonde*, NS, VI, 104.
29. NLI, MS 2993, pp. 19–21.
30. *Cal. Anc. Rec. Dub.*, V, 219.
31. Steele, II, nos. 921, 922; *HMC, Ormonde*, II, 361.
32. Wodrow, *Sufferings*, II, 171; *True Prot. Merc.*, no. 50 (25–29 Jun. 1681); Kilroy, *Protestant Dissent*, pp. 23–4, 238–9; Reid, *History of the Presbyterian Church*, II, app. 11, pp. 574–89.
33. *Cal. Anc. Rec. Dub.*, V, xxx.
34. *HMC, Ormonde*, NS, VI, 388; Bodl., MS Carte 50, fol. 287; Kilroy, *Protestant Dissent*, pp. 239–41.
35. *Cal. Anc. Rec. Dub.*, IV, 244, 419, and V, 139, 192; *Council Book of Youghall*, pp. 326, 334–5, 338, 346.
36. *Loy. Prot. Int.*, no. 166 (10 Jun. 1682).
37. Reid, *History of the Presbyterian Church*, II, 339–41, 589.
38. *Loy. Prot. Int.*, no. 76 (12 Nov. 1681).
39. *HMC, Ormonde*, NS, VI, 57; *Loy. Prot. Int.*, no. 23 (24 May 1681).
40. NLI, MS 11,960, pp. 85–7. Ibid., pp. 85–170, lists 34 addresses for 1682, but does not include those from the corporation of Dublin, County Cavan, Monaghan, Strabane, County Armagh, New Ross, County Tyrone, Maryborough, and County Antrim found in *Lond. Gaz.*, nos. 1714 (2–24 Apr. 1682) to 1751 (28–31 Aug. 1682).
41. Bodl., MS Carte 39, fol. 359.
42. NLI, MS 11,960, pp. 88–92.
43. *Cal. Anc. Rec. Dub.*, V, 232–4.
44. *Council Books of Waterford*, p. 220; NLI, MS 11,960, pp. 112–14.
45. NLI, MS 11,960, pp. 94, 97, 99.
46. *HMC, Ormonde*, NS, VI, 57, 62.
47. Hunt. Lib., HA 14570, [Earl of Conway] to Sir George Rawdon, 6 May 1682.
48. Ibid., HA 15511, Thomas Parnell to Sir George Rawdon, 9 May 1682.
49. Ibid., HA 15010, County Down, Address to the King, 27 Apr. 1682.
50. NLI, MS 11,960, pp. 166–8.
51. Bodl., MS Carte 168, fol. 4; Bodl., MS Carte 219, fol. 332; *HMC, Ormonde*, NS, VI, 365; NLI, MS 11,960, p. 170.
52. NLI, MS 11,960, pp. 169–70.
53. Ibid., pp. 122–3.
54. Bodl., MS Carte 168, fol. 4; NLI, MS 11,960, pp. 139–40.
55. The quotes are taken from the addresses of the town of Kildare and the corporation of Waterford: NLI, MS 11,960, pp. 114–15.

56. *Cal. Anc. Rec. Dub.*, V, 228–31, 243; *Council Books of Waterford*, p. 222; Bodl., MS Carte 39, fol. 564; Simms, 'The Restoration', p. 438.

57. Bodl., MS Carte 168, pp. 1–4; *HMC, Ormonde*, NS, VI, 359; *CSPD, 1682*, pp. 196, 198; Fountainhall, *Observes*, I, 69–70.

58. *CSPD, 1682*, pp. 325, 345–7, 384–6; *CSPD, Jan.–Jul. 1683*, pp. 13–14, 17–18, 27–9, 34, 62–4, 92, 98; *HMC, Ormonde*, NS, VI, 540–42, 545–6; ibid., NS, VII, 7; *A True Narrative of the Late Plot in Ireland* (1683).

59. *HMC, Ormonde*, NS, VI, 464. Cf. ibid., 539. In the end no Irish parliament was called, because it was thought that indirect taxes in Ireland were already so high that the kingdom would not be able to support the burden of a parliamentary subsidy: *HMC, Ormonde*, NS, VII, 98–9.

60. Ibid., NS, VII, 63, 65.

61. Greaves, *Secrets*, pp. 191–2, 194.

62. Ibid., p. 191.

63. *HMC, Ormonde*, NS, VI, 500–501, 504, 505, 507, 509, 513, 519–20, 525, 526 (quotes on pp. 509, 513, 520).

64. Ibid., NS, VII, 107.

65. Karsten, 'Plotters and Proprietors'.

66. NLI, MS 4909, fols. 31, 34v.

67. Hunt. Lib., HA 360, Robert Ayleway to the Earl of Huntingdon, 30 Jun. 1683; *CSPD, Jul.–Sep. 1683*, p. 17.

68. Bodl., MS Carte 219, fol. 488; *HMC, Ormonde*, NS, VII, 76.

69. *CSPD, Jul.–Sep. 1683*, pp. 202, 268; *HMC, Ormonde*, NS, VII, 76, 89, 95, 96, 102, 107, 108, 121, 124, 200–201, 314–15 (quotes on pp. 95, 107, 108, 124); Hunt. Lib., HA 15690, Sir George Rawdon et al. to Captain Ralph Smith, 30 Jul. 1683.

70. *HMC, Ormonde*, NS, VII, 121, 314–15.

71. Bodl., MS Carte 219, fols. 522–3; *HMC, Ormonde*, NS, VII, 115, 119, 124.

72. *HMC, Ormonde*, NS, VII, 139, 152–4 (quote on p. 152).

73. Ibid., pp. 311–13; BL, Lansdowne MS 1152A, fol. 152.

74. *HMC, Ormonde*, NS, VII, 61–2, 67, 68, 74, 96, 99, 132 (quote on p. 132); *CSPD, Jul.–Sep. 1683*, p. 268.

75. TCD, MS 1688/1, pp. 61–93 (quotes on pp. 70, 77).

76. Steele, II, no. 928; *CSPD, Jul.–Sep. 1683*, pp. 225, 229, 267–8.

77. John Vesey, *A Sermon Preached at Clonmel, on Sunday the Sixteenth of September, 1683. At the Assizes Held for the County Palatine of Tipperary* (Dublin, 1683), quotes on pp. 12–13, 15, 20.

78. NLI, MS 11,960, pp. 171–223, lists 47 addresses but does not mention those from the corporation of Dublin, Tralee (Co. Kerry), Youghall, and Counties Carlow and Wexford: *Cal. Anc. Rec. Dub.*, V, 283; *HMC,*

Ormonde, NS, VII, 86–7, 110; *Council Book of Youghall*, p. 361; *Lond. Gaz.*, no. 1867 (8–11 Oct. 1683).
79. *Council Books of Waterford*, pp. 237–8.
80. NLI, MS 2993, p. 45.
81. *HMC, Ormonde*, NS, VII, 152.
82. Morrice, P, 382.
83. *HMC, Ormonde*, NS, VII, 209.
84. *CSPD, 1684–5*, pp. 114–15; BL, Lansdowne MS 1152A, fols. 182–3.
85. Hunt. Lib., HA 14593, John Corbett to Sir Arthur Rawdon, 18 Nov. 1684; *HMC, Ormonde*, NS, VII, 293–4; Greaves, *Secrets*, pp. 265–6.

Conclusion

1. *A True Relation of the Late King's Death* (1685); Richard Hudleston, *A Short and Plain Way to the Faith and Church* (1688), pp. 35–8; Morrice, P, 455–6; Evelyn, *Diary*, IV, 405–9; M. L. Wolbarsht and D. S. Sax, 'Charles II, A Royal Martyr', *Notes and Records of the Royal Society of London*, 16, no. 2 (Nov. 1961), 154–7; Hutton, *Charles II*, 443–5; Antonia Fraser, *Royal Charles: Charles II and the Restoration* (New York, 1979), pp. 442–57. The classic account is R. H. P. Crawfurd, *The Last Days of Charles II* (1909).
2. The figure is for the number of addresses printed in the *Lond. Gaz.*, 1685–6.
3. Russell, *Causes*, pp. 16–17.
4. See, for example, J. J. Scarisbrick, *Henry VIII* (1968), and G. R. Elton, 'Politics and the Pilgrimage of Grace', in his *Studies in Tudor and Stuart Politics and Government* (3 vols., 1974–83), III, 183–215, on whether the Pilgrimage of Grace was an authentic uprising of the commons.
5. L'Estrange, *Observator*, I, no. 411 (27 Sep. 1683).
6. Harris, *London Crowds*, pp. 154–5.
7. Hutton, *Charles II*, p. 441; Childs, *Army of James II*, pp. 1–2.
8. William Beik, *Absolutism and Society in Seventeenth-Century France* (Cambridge, 1985); Roger Mettam, *Power and Faction in Louis XIV's France* (Oxford, 1988); Nicholas Henshaw, *The Myth of Absolutism* (1992); Peter Burke, *The Fabrication of Louis XIV* (New Haven, 1992); Guy Rowlands, *The Dynastic State and the Army under Louis XIV* (Cambridge, 2002).
9. Howard Nenner, *By Color of Law: Legal Culture and Constitutional Politics in England, 1660–1689* (Chicago, 1977).
10. Hutton, *Charles II*, p. 457.

Index